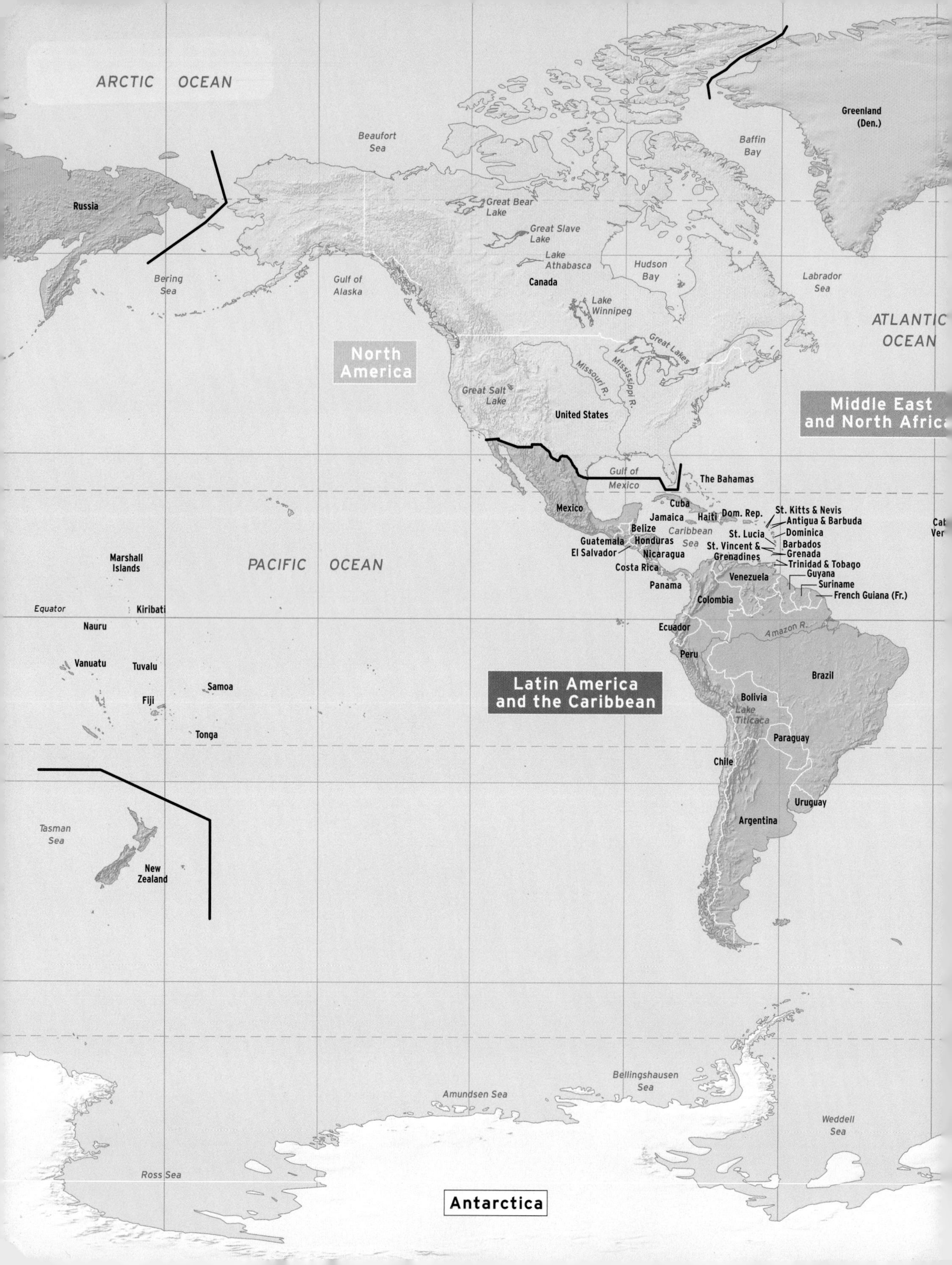

ARCTIC OCEAN
Beaufort Sea
Greenland (Den.)
Baffin Bay
Russia
Great Bear Lake
Great Slave Lake
Lake Athabasca
Hudson Bay
Bering Sea
Gulf of Alaska
Canada
Labrador Sea
Lake Winnipeg
ATLANTIC OCEAN
North America
Great Lakes
Missouri R.
Mississippi R.
Great Salt Lake
United States
Middle East and North Africa
Gulf of Mexico
The Bahamas
Cuba
Mexico
Jamaica
Haiti
Dom. Rep.
St. Kitts & Nevis
Antigua & Barbuda
Belize
Caribbean Sea
St. Lucia
Dominica
Guatemala
Honduras
St. Vincent & Grenadines
Barbados
Grenada
El Salvador
Nicaragua
Trinidad & Tobago
Marshall Islands
PACIFIC OCEAN
Costa Rica
Guyana
Venezuela
Suriname
Panama
French Guiana (Fr.)
Colombia
Equator
Kiribati
Nauru
Ecuador
Amazon R.
Peru
Vanuatu
Tuvalu
Brazil
Samoa
Latin America and the Caribbean
Fiji
Bolivia
Lake Titicaca
Tonga
Paraguay
Chile
Uruguay
Tasman Sea
Argentina
New Zealand
Bellingshausen Sea
Amundsen Sea
Weddell Sea
Ross Sea
Antarctica

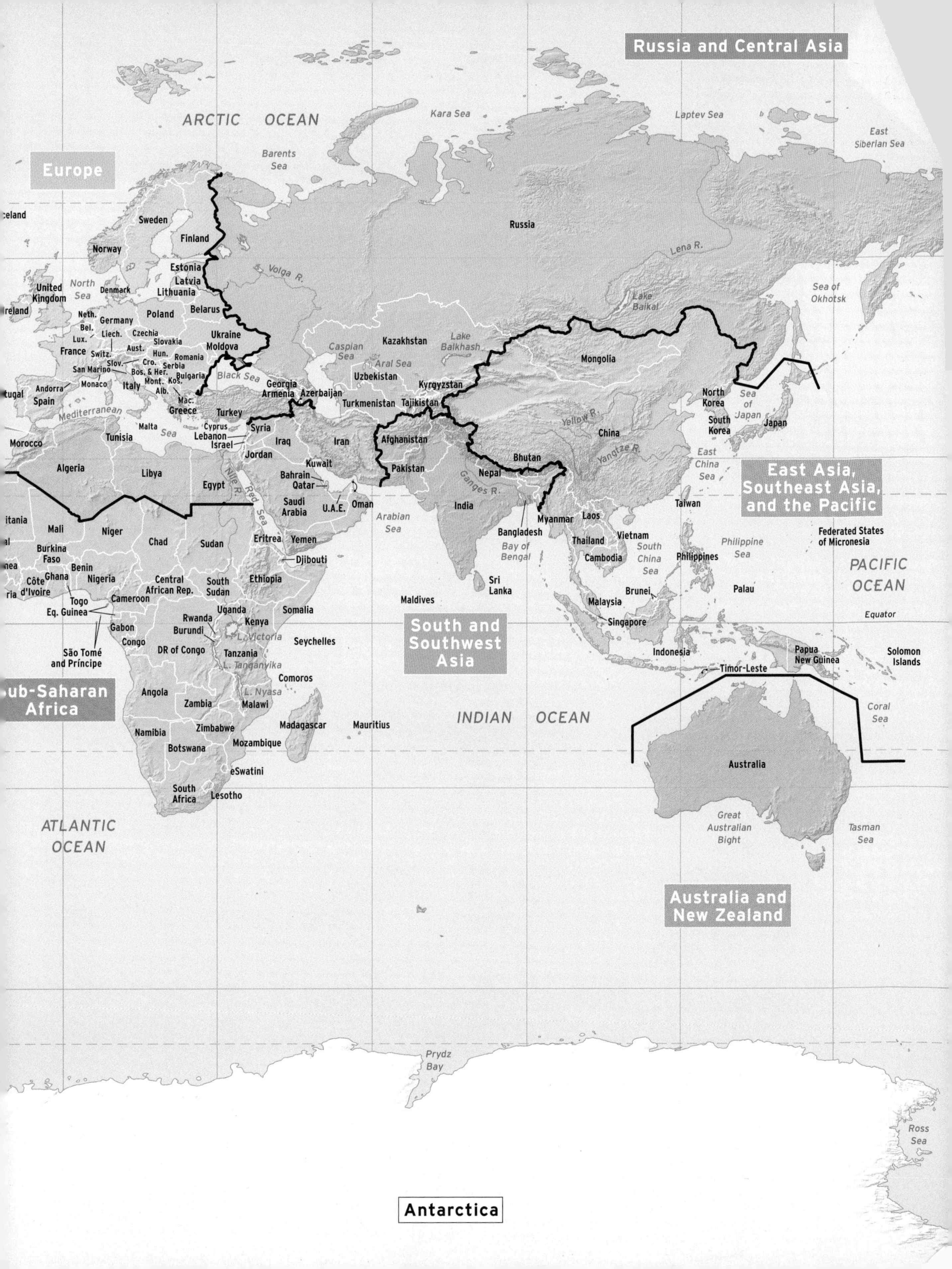

Russia and Central Asia
Europe
East Asia, Southeast Asia, and the Pacific
South and Southwest Asia
Sub-Saharan Africa
Australia and New Zealand
Antarctica
ARCTIC OCEAN
INDIAN OCEAN
PACIFIC OCEAN
ATLANTIC OCEAN
Kara Sea
Laptev Sea
East Siberian Sea
Barents Sea
Sea of Okhotsk
North Sea
Black Sea
Caspian Sea
Aral Sea
Lake Balkhash
Lake Baikal
Mediterranean Sea
Red Sea
Arabian Sea
Bay of Bengal
South China Sea
East China Sea
Sea of Japan
Philippine Sea
Coral Sea
Tasman Sea
Great Australian Bight
Prydz Bay
Ross Sea
Equator
Volga R.
Lena R.
Nile R.
Yellow R.
Yangtze R.
Ganges R.
L. Victoria
L. Tanganyika
L. Nyasa
Russia
Iceland
Sweden
Finland
Norway
Estonia
Latvia
Lithuania
United Kingdom
Denmark
Ireland
Belarus
Poland
Neth.
Germany
Bel.
Lux.
Liech.
Czechia
Slovakia
Ukraine
Moldova
France
Switz.
Aust.
Hun.
Romania
Slov.
Cro.
Serbia
San Marino
Bos. & Her.
Bulgaria
Monaco
Mont.
Kos.
Andorra
Italy
Alb.
Mac.
Portugal
Spain
Greece
Turkey
Malta
Cyprus
Lebanon
Israel
Syria
Georgia
Armenia
Azerbaijan
Kazakhstan
Uzbekistan
Turkmenistan
Kyrgyzstan
Tajikistan
Mongolia
North Korea
South Korea
Japan
China
Iraq
Iran
Afghanistan
Pakistan
Jordan
Kuwait
Bahrain
Qatar
Saudi Arabia
U.A.E.
Oman
Yemen
Nepal
Bhutan
India
Bangladesh
Myanmar
Laos
Thailand
Vietnam
Cambodia
Taiwan
Philippines
Sri Lanka
Maldives
Brunei
Malaysia
Singapore
Indonesia
Timor-Leste
Papua New Guinea
Palau
Federated States of Micronesia
Solomon Islands
Australia
Morocco
Algeria
Tunisia
Libya
Egypt
Mauritania
Mali
Niger
Chad
Sudan
Eritrea
Djibouti
Burkina Faso
Benin
Ghana
Côte d'Ivoire
Togo
Nigeria
Central African Rep.
South Sudan
Ethiopia
Somalia
Cameroon
Eq. Guinea
Gabon
Congo
São Tomé and Príncipe
Uganda
Kenya
Rwanda
Burundi
DR of Congo
Tanzania
Seychelles
Comoros
Angola
Zambia
Malawi
Madagascar
Mauritius
Namibia
Zimbabwe
Mozambique
Botswana
eSwatini
South Africa
Lesotho

Introducing Comparative Politics

The Essentials

SECOND EDITION

Sara Miller McCune founded SAGE Publishing in 1965 to support the dissemination of usable knowledge and educate a global community. SAGE publishes more than 1000 journals and over 600 new books each year, spanning a wide range of subject areas. Our growing selection of library products includes archives, data, case studies and video. SAGE remains majority owned by our founder and after her lifetime will become owned by a charitable trust that secures the company's continued independence.

Los Angeles | London | New Delhi | Singapore | Washington DC | Melbourne

Introducing Comparative Politics

The Essentials

Second Edition

Stephen Orvis

Hamilton College

Carol Ann Drogus

FOR INFORMATION:

CQ Press
An Imprint of SAGE Publications, Inc.
2455 Teller Road
Thousand Oaks, California 91320
E-mail: order@sagepub.com

SAGE Publications Ltd.
1 Oliver's Yard
55 City Road
London EC1Y 1SP
United Kingdom

SAGE Publications India Pvt. Ltd.
B 1/I 1 Mohan Cooperative Industrial Area
Mathura Road, New Delhi 110 044
India

SAGE Publications Asia-Pacific Pte. Ltd.
18 Cross Street #10-10/11/12
China Square Central
Singapore 048423

Printed in Canada

ISBN 9781544379043

This book is printed on acid-free paper.

20 21 22 23 24 10 9 8 7 6 5 4 3 2 1

Acquisitions Editor: Anna Villarruel
Content Development Editor: Jennifer Jovin-Bernstein
Editorial Assistant: Lauren Younker
Production Editor: Kelle Clarke
Copy Editor: Karin Rathert
Typesetter: C&M Digitals (P) Ltd.
Proofreader: Christine Dahlin
Cover Designer: Gail Buschman
Marketing Manager: Jennifer Jones

BRIEF CONTENTS

DETAILED CONTENTS

AP Photo/Sunday Alamba

Billy Mutai/ Nation Media/Gallo Images/Getty Images

Photo by Subhendu Ghosh/Hindustan Times via Getty Images

PART II POLITICAL SYSTEMS AND HOW THEY WORK

Albin Lohr-Jones/Pacific Press/LightRocket via Getty Images

Youssef Karwashan/AFP/Getty Images

John Thys/AFP/Getty Images

Zhao Yuhong/VCG via Getty Images

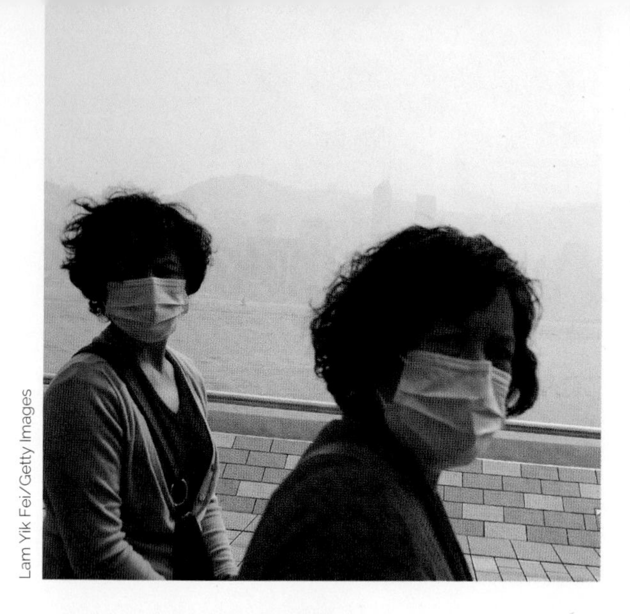
Lam Yik Fei/Getty Images

Tommy Lindholm/Pacific Press/LightRocket via Getty Images

PREFACE

A Concise Guide to Comparative Politics

Essentials of Comparative Politics gives students a holistic, concise overview of the key conceptual debates and arguments in comparative politics. Rather than using any one theoretical or methodological approach, we introduce students to the broad debates in the field to show how comparativists have used various theories and methodologies to understand political phenomena. We do not generally offer definitive conclusions about which approach is best for understanding a particular issue, preferring instead to show students the strengths and weaknesses of each. Occasionally, we make clear that one approach has become the "conventional wisdom" in the field or that we believe it is the most accurate way to analyze a particular phenomenon, but we do this in the context of a broader debate.

The first chapter teaches students the major approaches in the field, and subsequent chapters bring in specific theoretical debates relevant to the areas addressed in the chapter, frequently referring back to how they are part of the broad approaches introduced earlier. Throughout, the driving force is understanding concepts, not individual countries or political systems, for which much information is readily available elsewhere. We do, however, reference numerous countries as brief examples (of a paragraph or two) throughout the text to illustrate how the concepts work in practice. Most of these are classic examples in the literature, such as the Japanese developmental state, the Swedish social welfare system, and the South African transition to democracy.

We believe this thorough, distilled, and pluralistic approach will allow faculty to generate debates among students over key approaches and methodologies. By focusing on the key conceptual debates and illustrating them in the real world, the book enables instructors to move their introductory students beyond the memorization of basic information and toward an ability to assess and debate the real issues in our discipline.

The book also moves firmly away from the traditional Cold War division of the world into first-, second-, and third-world countries. Although many textbooks claim to do this, we have found that they typically suffer from a "Cold War hangover," with the old division lurking just beneath the surface. We consciously set out to show that many theoretical concepts in the discipline are useful in a wide array of settings, that political phenomena are not fundamentally different in one part of the world than they are in another. Throughout, we try to show how long-standing concepts and debates in the discipline illuminate current "hot topics."

Organization of the Book

This book is divided into three main parts. It first examines the theories and concepts that inform and drive research as a way to frame our investigation, then moves to a survey of political institutions and institutional change and, finally, to an examination of political economy and policy debates. **Part I** introduces the major theoretical approaches to the discipline and focuses on the modern state and its relationship to citizens and civil society, regimes, and identity groups. It provides an introduction to the discipline and its key concepts in the modern world. **Chapter 1** provides a broad overview of key conceptual debates and divides the field into three broad questions to help students organize these debates: What explains political behavior? Who rules? and Where and why? These orient students by grouping the many debates in the field into broad categories tied to clear and compelling questions. "What Explains Political Behavior?" gets at the heart of the discipline's major disputes, which we divide among interests (rational choice and its critics), beliefs (political culture and ideology), and structures (Marxism and institutionalism). "Who Rules?" addresses the dispersion of political power, focusing mainly on the debate between pluralist and elite theorists. Although that debate is typically subsumed under the study of American politics, we think it helps illuminate important areas of comparative politics as well. "Where and Why?" introduces students to the importance of and approaches to comparison.

The rest of Part I focuses on the modern state and its relationship to other key areas of modern politics. **Chapter 2** defines and provides an overview of the modern state, its historical evolution around the world, and the concept of state strength/weakness. **Chapter 3** examines modern states in relation to citizens, civil society, and political regimes, arguing that the latter are based first and foremost on political ideologies that define the relationship between state and citizen. **Chapter 4** looks at the debate over political identity and the state's relationship to identities based on nationality, ethnicity, religion, race, class, and gender and sexual orientation.

Part II examines political institutions and participation in both democratic and authoritarian regimes as well as regime transitions. It is the "nuts-and-bolts" section of the book, providing what traditionally has been a core feature of the course. Chapters 5 and 6 examine political institutions in democratic regimes. **Chapter 5** focuses on governing institutions: executive/legislative systems, the judiciary, the bureaucracy, and federalism. The theme throughout is the question of accountability in democracies. **Chapter 6** looks at institutions of participation and representation: electoral systems, parties and party systems, and interest groups. It focuses primarily on how to achieve different kinds of representation and the potential trade-off between active participation and effective governance. **Chapter 7** examines contentious politics, taking up social movements as a follow-on to the prior chapter and then moving on to political violence (civil war and terrorism) and revolution (as contentious political episodes). **Chapter 8** looks at institutions and participation in authoritarian regimes, drawing on the previous three chapters to show how similar institutions function quite differently in nondemocratic regimes, as well as presenting the active debate over authoritarianism over the past decade. **Chapter 9**, on regime transition, focuses not only on democratic transitions but also on transitions to authoritarian rule: authoritarianization, military coups, and revolutions (as regime change).

Part III examines political economy and some key current policy issues that have been foreshadowed earlier in the book. The conceptual and empirical knowledge that students have gained in Parts I and II are used to address important current issues. **Chapter 10** examines the theoretical and historical relationship between the state and the market economy, including key concepts in political economy, economic theories, and globalization, applying those to wealthy countries, including the debate over convergence versus the varieties of capitalism approach. The chapter includes a discussion of the global financial crisis and its implications. **Chapter 11** looks at the political economy of development, using many of the concepts developed in the prior chapter. The theme of **chapter 12** is market failure, examining social policy, health policy, and environmental policy in turn. It draws on chapters 10 and 11 as well as material from Part II to look at different approaches to current hot topics such as universal health care and climate change.

Key Features

A number of pedagogical features reappear throughout. Each chapter begins with **learning objectives** and **key questions** that help students focus on the key issues as they read the chapter and perhaps debate in class. The chapters sometimes provide conclusive answers to some of the key questions, but more often they show students different ways the questions can be answered or approached. Some chapters include one or more **In Context** features that present basic data. These allow students to set an idea into a comparative (and sometimes provocative) context. In most chapters, we include a **Critical Inquiry** box, in which we ask students to think actively about a particular question. Many of these provide students a limited set of data and ask them, simply by visually examining the data, to develop their own hypotheses about key relationships or evaluate competing hypotheses they've studied in the book. Chapter 6, for instance, includes a Critical Inquiry box on the question of what explains women's share of legislative seats around the world. It provides data on the number of women in lower houses broken down by region, electoral system, and length of regime, and it asks students to use these data to informally "test" alternative hypotheses about why women gain better representation. A few Critical Inquiry boxes direct students toward more normative questions, using the concepts in the chapter to address them.

In addition to these themed features, readers will find many original tables, figures, and maps throughout the book that illustrate key relationships or variables around the world. Students will find end-of-chapter lists of **key concepts** with page references to help their study and review, as well as a list of **works cited** and important print and electronic **references for further research**. We hope the design of the book strikes a balance as well: colorful and well-illustrated to help engage student attention but without adding significantly to cost.

New to This Edition

We're grateful to the many users who have graciously and enthusiastically provided us with feedback on the first edition. We've done our best to address their suggestions and comments. The most significant changes are thorough reorganizations of chapters 8 (authoritarian rule) and 9 (regime transition). The recent debates in the field on authoritarianism and the demise of democracy informed these changes. Chapter 4 includes a new section on social class as an identity category. In chapter 6, we reorganized the section on political parties to emphasize different ways in which parties mobilize support, including an extended section on the global rise of populism. Chapter 9 includes extended examples from Turkey and Hungary to illustrate authoritarianization, and we focus on the civil war in Syria in chapter 7 that has led to the global refugee crisis and the debates it has raised in many countries.

This second edition includes a new pedagogical feature, chapter-opening learning objectives that will help guide students' reading of the chapters and help them focus on the important points.

Digital Resources

Because we know from experience that making the leap into a new textbook is no small chore, CQ Press offers a full suite of high-quality instructor and student ancillary materials.

SAGE coursepacks for instructors makes it easy to import our quality content into your school's learning management system (LMS).* Intuitive and simple to use, it allows you to

Say NO to . . .

- required access codes
- learning a new system

Say YES to . . .

- using only the content you want and need
- high-quality assessment and multimedia exercise

***For:** Blackboard, Canvas, Brightspace by Desire2Learn (D2L), and Moodle

Don't use an LMS platform? No problem, you can still access many of the online resources for your text via SAGE Edge.

With SAGE coursepacks, you get

- quality textbook content delivered **directly into your LMS**;
- an **intuitive, simple format** that makes it easy to integrate the material into your course with minimal effort;
- **assessment tools** that foster review, practice, and critical thinking, including
    - diagnostic chapter **quizzes** that identify opportunities for improvement, track student progress, and ensure mastery of key learning objectives,
    - **test banks** built on Bloom's Taxonomy that provide a diverse range of test items with ExamView test generation,
    - **activity and quiz options** that allow you to choose only the assignments and tests you want,
    - **instructions** on how to use and integrate the comprehensive assessments and resources provided;

- an **instructor manual** with chapter-specific discussion questions to help launch engaging classroom interaction while reinforcing important content, chapter objectives, and suggested class activities that align with the concept of the chapters;
- editable, chapter-specific **PowerPoint® slides** that offer flexibility when creating multimedia lectures so you don't have to start from scratch;
- **lecture notes** that summarize key concepts on a chapter-by-chapter basis to help you with preparation for lectures and class discussions
- a **TA Guide** that provides guidance for graduate students and newer instructors who will benefit from a set of goals, points for review, and discussion questions for each chapter; and
- **all tables and figures** from the textbook.

SAGE Edge for Students at **https://edge.sagepub.com/orvisessentials2e** provides a personalized approach to help students accomplish their coursework goals in an easy-to-use learning environment.

- Mobile-friendly **eFlashcards** strengthen understanding of key terms and concepts.
- Mobile-friendly practice **quizzes** allow for independent assessment by students of their mastery of course material.
- **Video and multimedia content** that facilitate student use of Internet resources, further exploration of topics, and visual depictions of key concepts.

Acknowledgments

We have developed numerous debts in the process of writing this book. Perhaps the longest standing is to our students over twenty-five years of teaching introduction to comparative politics at Hamilton College. Figuring out how to teach the course in a way that is interesting, relevant, and clear to them led us to develop the approach taken in this book. We kept them in mind as we wrote the book: Will it be clear to them? Will it interest them? Will it help them see the important concepts and how they matter in the real world?

We owe a substantial thank you to the office of the Dean of Faculty at Hamilton College as well. It has provided support for research assistants for throughout this project, primarily from the Steven Sands Fund for Faculty Innovation. The office also provided sabbatical support for Steve Orvis on Hamilton's program at Pembroke College, Oxford University. The first and second editions also benefited from tremendous research assistance from Carolyn Morgan, PhD, Ohio State University. All were invaluable help for two faculty members taking on a project of this magnitude.

The staff at CQ Press have been pleasant, professional, and efficient throughout this process. Charisse Kiino, now Vice President of College Editorial for SAGE Publishing, patiently walked us through the process of developing the initial ideas with constant good cheer and support. Elise Frasier, our development editor through several editions of the "parent" book, *Introducing Comparative Politics: Concepts and Cases in Context,* was invaluable, putting forth tremendous ideas for pedagogical elements of the book that we would have never thought of on our own, doing much of the research to develop these elements, and being herself an insightful reader and critic of the text. Of all the people we mention in this preface, her valuable input and content for the parent book made the greatest contribution to the creation of *Essentials*. Thanks also to Kathryn Abbott for her excellent support as development editor on this new edition.

Finally, our production editor Kelle Clarke and copy editor Karin Rathert have been fabulous in the final stages of this second edition, improving the prose in innumerable places, pointing out inconsistencies, and working with us in an open, honest, and professional way that has made a tedious process as easy as it could be. We deeply appreciate the work of all at CQ Press who have made the process of writing this book as painless as we could imagine it being.

We wish also to thank the numerous reviewers who read chapters of the book at various stages. Their comments led us to revise a number of elements, drop others, and further develop still others. They have collectively made it a much better book that we hope will serve students well. They are the following:

Joseph Autilio, Northeastern University

William Avilés, University of Nebraska–Kearney

Dinorah Azpuru, Wichita State University

Jody Baumgartner, East Carolina University

Dilchoda Berdieva, Miami University

Michael Bernhard, University of Florida

Anthony R. Brunello, Eckerd College

Gitika Commuri, California State University–Bakersfield

Jeffrey Conroy-Krutz, Michigan State University

Carolyn Craig, University of Oregon

Brian Cramer, Rutgers University

Nicholas B. Creel, Texas A&M University San Antonio

William Crowther, University of North Carolina–Greensboro

Andrea Duwel, Santa Clara University

Gigi Gokcek, Dominican University of California

Glenn Harden, University of Kentucky

Clement M. Henry, University of Texas–Austin

Eric H. Hines, University of Montana

Jennifer Horan, University of North Carolina–Wilmington

Laci Hubbard-Mattix, Washington State University

John Hulsey, James Madison University

Christian B. Jensen, University of Iowa

Neal G. Jesse, Bowling Green State University

Alana Jeydel, American River College

Amie Kreppel, University of Florida
Thomas D. Lancaster, Emory University
Eric Langenbacher, Georgetown University
Ricardo René Larémont, Binghamton University, SUNY
Patrick F. Larue, University of Texas at Dallas
Carol S. Leff, University of Illinois at Urbana-Champaign
Paul Lenze, Northern Arizona University
M. Casey Kane Love, Tulane University
Mona Lyne, University of Missouri–Kansas City
Rahsaan Maxwell, University of Massachusetts
Mary McCarthy, Drake University
Scott Morgenstern, University of Pittsburgh
Stephen Mumme, Colorado State University
Sharmini Nair, Colorado State University
Ali Nizamuddin, University of Illinois Springfield
Piotr Plewa, University of Delaware
Stephanie McNulty, Franklin and Marshall College
Armando Razo, Indiana University Bloomington
Nils Ringe, University of Wisconsin–Madison
Sharon Rivera, Hamilton College
David Sacko, U.S. Air Force Academy
Hootan Shambayati, Florida Gulf Coast University
Edward Schwerin, Florida Atlantic University
Brian Shoup, Mississippi State University
Tony Spanakos, Montclair State University
Boyka Stefanova, University of Texas–San Antonio
Sarah Tenney, The Citadel
Markus Thiel, Florida International University
Erica Townsend-Bell, University of Iowa
Kellee Tsai, Johns Hopkins University
Anca Turcu, University of Central Florida
Dwayne Woods, Purdue University
Michael Wuthrich, University of Kansas
Eleanor E. Zeff, Drake University
Darren Zook, University of California, Berkeley

Last, but far from least, we have to extend thanks to our children, Nick and Will. They didn't contribute ideas or critique the book, but they showed real enthusiasm for understanding things like who the prime minister of Britain is and why there is a Monster Raving Loony Party, and they endured and even participated in occasional dinner table debates on things like the relative merits of parliamentary systems and different concepts of citizenship. Most of all, they gave of themselves in the form of great patience. This project became more of an obsession, at least at key points, than our work usually is. The first two editions of *Introducing Comparative Politics* took us away from them more than we like and made our family life rather hectic. They bore it well, going on with their lives in their typically independent way. Now they're older and off on their own and have become active citizens of whom we are very proud. As with the earlier book, we dedicate *Introducing Comparative Politics: The Essentials* to them and their generation, who give us great hope.

ABOUT THE AUTHORS

Stephen Orvis is Professor of Government at Hamilton College. He is a specialist on sub-Saharan Africa (Kenya in particular), identity politics, democratic transitions, and the political economy of development. He has been teaching introduction to comparative politics for more than twenty-five years, as well as courses on African politics, nationalism and the politics of identity, political economy of development, and weak states. He has written a book and articles on agricultural development in Kenya, as well as several articles on civil society in Africa and Kenya and is currently doing research on political institutions in Africa.

Carol Ann Drogus is a retired Professor of Government at Hamilton College. She is a specialist on Brazil, religion, and women's political participation. She taught introduction to comparative politics for more than fifteen years, as well as courses on Latin American politics, gender and politics, and women in Latin America. She has written two books and numerous articles on the political participation of women in religious movements in Brazil.

PART I

A Framework for Understanding Comparative Politics

1 Introduction

In an increasingly globalized world, civil war in one country can have impacts around the world. Here, migrants arrive on the island of Lesbos in Greece. In 2015 the Syrian civil war produced a massive refugee crisis that flooded Europe with requests for asylum. The political and economic effects of this movement of people were huge, burdening the weak Greek economy, leading to greater support for anti-immigrant parties in many European countries and influencing the successful British vote to leave the European Union.
AP Photo/Petros Giannakouris

Key Questions

- What is comparative politics and how do we study it?
- Do self-interest, beliefs, or underlying structural forces best explain how people act in the political realm?
- What kinds of evidence can help us explain political behavior?
- What can be learned from comparing political behavior and outcomes across countries?

Learning Objectives

After reading chapter 1, you should be able to do the following:

1.1 Explain the theories and methods of comparative politics

1.2 Articulate in detail the three key questions in comparative politics

Understanding political developments and disputes around the world has never seemed more important than it does today. Many people now see the world as more complicated and less comprehensible than it was during the late twentieth century. During the Cold War (1944–1989), the divide between communist and democratic countries seemed stark, and the main question facing newly minted countries in the "Third World" was how they would be governed internally and navigate the Cold War divide externally. The post–Cold War era (1989–2001) seemed to spread democracy, economic growth, and prosperity.

In the first two decades of the twenty-first century, however, political questions that seemed settled and ideas and problems that seemed passé have re-emerged as relevant and vital. In 2008 and 2009, the economic crisis that emerged in the United States and then hit Europe harder revived debates about economic policies and what kinds of political institutions could best enact them. Greece, the hardest hit European country, took an unexpected turn to the left and threatened to leave the European Union (EU). In the Middle East, an unprecedented wave of protests known as the Arab Spring in 2011 overturned several authoritarian regimes, producing one new democracy in Tunisia, new authoritarian regimes elsewhere, and a civil war in Syria. As a result, over a million people fled Syria for the relative safety of Europe. Their arrival has raised questions about Europeans' identity and immigration policies. In response to both immigration and economic crises, populist and nationalist movements that question long-held political and policy assumptions have arisen throughout the Western world, most dramatically in the British vote to leave the EU in 2016 and the electoral victory of Donald Trump as U.S. president a few months later. On the other hand, since the end of the Cold War many countries have established democratic governments, particularly in Eastern Europe and sub-Saharan Africa. East Asia, led by China, has achieved unprecedented economic growth that has lifted more people out of poverty more quickly than ever before in history. The UN admitted 31 new members in the 1990s and six more so far this century, as new nations proclaimed their place in the world. And while still struggling, much of the world has recovered from the Great Recession of a decade ago, in part due to various governments' economic policies.

These current "hot-button" political issues around the world are just the latest manifestations of a set of enduring issues that students of comparative politics have been studying for the last half century: Why do governments form? Why does a group of people come to see itself as a nation? Why do nations sometimes fall apart? How can a government convince people that it has the right to rule? Do some forms of government last longer than others? Do some forms of government serve their people's interests better than others? How do democracies form, and how do they fall apart? Can democracy work anywhere, or only in particular countries and at particular times? Are certain political institutions more democratic than others? Can government policy reduce poverty and improve economic well-being? This book introduces you to the many and often conflicting answers to these questions by examining them comparatively. It will also help you start to assess which answers are the most convincing and why.

Comparative Politics: What Is It? Why Study It? How to Study It?

Politics can be defined as the process by which human communities make collective decisions. These communities can be of any size, from small villages or neighborhoods to nations and international organizations. **Comparative politics** is one of the major subfields of **political science**, the systematic study of politics. Politics always involves elements of power, the first concept we need to examine closely.

Individuals or groups can have power over others in a variety of ways. If someone holds a gun to your head and demands your wallet, you comply because he has great power over you at that moment. If your boss tells you to do something, you do it because she is paying you and could fire you. But if someone has control over a resource you need—say, admission into a college—she also may have power over you. Political theorist Steven Lukes (1974) usefully categorized power into three dimensions. The **first dimension of power** is the ability of one person or group to get another person or group to do something it otherwise would not do, as in the first example above. The focus here is on behavior and active decisions: making someone do something. A **second dimension of power**, first articulated by Peter Bachrach and Morton Baratz (1962), sees power as the ability not only to make people do something but to keep them from doing something. Bachrach and Baratz argued that a key element of political power is the ability to keep certain groups and issues out of the political arena by controlling the political agenda and institutions to allow certain groups to participate and voice their concerns, while preventing or at least discouraging others from doing so: if it takes large amounts of money to run for office, poor people are likely not to try. A **third dimension of power**, which Lukes contributed, is the ability to shape or determine individual or group political demands by causing people to think about political issues in ways that may be contrary to their own interests. The ability to influence how people think produces the power to prevent certain political demands from ever being articulated: if workers making the minimum wage believe that raising it will result in fewer jobs, they won't demand a higher wage in the first place. We examine the role of all three of these dimensions of power in this chapter and in the rest of the book.

politics: The process by which human communities make collective decisions

comparative politics: One of the major subfields of political science, in which the primary focus is on comparing power and decision making across countries

political science: The systematic study of politics and power

first dimension of power: The ability of one person or group to get another person or group to do something it otherwise would not do

second dimension of power: The ability not only to make people do something but to keep them from doing something

third dimension of power: The ability to shape or determine individual or group political demands by causing people to think about political issues in ways that are contrary to their own interests

What Is Comparative Politics?

Comparative politics focuses primarily on power and decision making within national boundaries, from local groups and communities to entire countries. Politics among national governments and beyond national boundaries is generally the purview of the field of international relations, and although comparativists certainly take into account the domestic effects of international events, we do not try to explain the international events themselves. Perhaps it is self-evident, but comparativists also compare; we systematically examine political phenomena in more than one place and during more than one period, and we try to develop a generalized understanding of and explanations for political activity that seem to apply to many different situations.

Why Study Comparative Politics?

Studying comparative politics has multiple benefits. First, comparativists are interested in understanding political events and developments in various countries. Why did peaceful regime change happen in Tunisia in 2011 but civil war break out in Syria? Why did the Socialist Party win back the presidency in France in 2012 after seventeen years of conservative presidents? Also, as the Middle East example shows, understanding political events in other countries can be very important to foreign policy. If the U.S. government had better understood the internal dynamics of Syrian politics, it might have been able to respond more effectively to the outbreak of civil war there.

Second, systematic comparison of different political systems and events around the world can generate important lessons from one place that can apply in another. Americans have long seen their system of government, with a directly elected president, as a very successful and stable model of democracy. Much evidence suggests, though, that in a situation of intense political conflict, such as an ethnically divided country after a civil war, a system with a single and powerful elected president might not be the best option. Only one candidate from one side can win this coveted post, and the sides that lose the election might choose to restart the war rather than live with the results. A democratic system that gives all major groups some share of political power at the national level might work better in this situation. That conclusion is not obvious when examining the United States alone. A systematic comparison of a number of different countries, however, reveals this possibility.

Third, examining politics comparatively helps us develop broad theories about how politics works. A **theory** is an abstract argument that provides a systematic explanation of some phenomenon. The theory of evolution, for instance, explains how species change in response to their environments. The social sciences, including political science, use two different kinds of theories. An **empirical theory** is an argument that explains what actually occurs. Empirical theorists first describe a pattern and then attempt to explain what causes it. The theory of evolution is an empirical theory in that evolutionary biologists do not argue whether evolution is inherently good or bad; they simply describe evolutionary patterns and explain their causes. A good empirical theory should also allow theorists to predict what will happen as well. For example, a comparison of democratic systems in post–civil war situations would lead us to predict that presidential systems are more likely to lead to renewed conflict.

On the other hand, a **normative theory** is an argument that explains what ought to occur. For instance, socialists support a normative theory that the government and economy ought to be structured in a way that produces a relatively equal distribution of wealth. Although comparativists certainly hold various normative theories, most of the discipline of comparative politics focuses on empirical theory. We attempt to explain the political world around us, and we do this by looking across multiple cases to come up with generalizations about politics.

theory: An abstract argument that provides a systematic explanation of some phenomenon

empirical theory: An argument explaining what actually occurs; empirical theorists first notice and describe a pattern and then attempt to explain what causes it

normative theory: An argument explaining what ought to occur rather than what does occur; contrast with empirical theory

How Do Comparativists Study Politics?

Clearly, political scientists do not have perfect scientific conditions in which to do research. We do not have a controlled laboratory, because we certainly cannot control the real world of politics. While physicists can use a laboratory to control all elements of an experiment, and they can repeat that same experiment to achieve identical results because molecules do not notice what the scientists are doing, think about the situation, and change their behavior. In political science, however, political actors think about the changes going on around them and modify their behavior accordingly.

Despite these limitations, comparativists use the scientific method (as explained in the "Scientific Method in Comparative Politics" box) to try to gain as systematic evidence as possible. We use several research methods to try to overcome the difficulties our complex field of study presents. **Research methods** are systematic processes used to ensure that the study of some phenomena is as objective and unbiased as possible.

One common research method we use is the **single-case study**, which examines a particular political phenomenon in just one country or community. A case study can generate ideas for new theories, or it can test existing theories developed from different cases. A single case can never be definitive proof of anything beyond that case itself, but it can be suggestive of further research and can be of interest to people researching that particular country. Deviant case studies that do not fit a widely held pattern can be particularly helpful in highlighting the limits of even widely supported theories. Case studies also deepen our knowledge about particular countries, useful in and of itself. Scholars engaging in case study research search for common patterns within the case or use a method known as process tracing, which involves careful examination of the historical linkages between potential causes and effects, to demonstrate what caused what in the particular case. Case studies serve as important sources of information and ideas for researchers using more comparative methods.

Scholars use the **comparative method** to examine the same phenomenon in several cases, and they try to mimic laboratory conditions by selecting cases carefully. Two approaches are common. The most-similar-systems design selects cases that are alike in a number of ways but differ on the key question under examination. For instance, Michael Bratton and Nicholas van de Walle (1997) looked at transitions to democracy in Africa, arguing that all African countries share certain similarities in patterns of political behavior that are distinct from patterns in Latin America, where the main theories of democratization were developed. On the other hand, the most different-systems design looks at countries that differ in many ways but are similar in terms of the particular political process or outcome in which the research is interested. For instance, scholars of revolution look at the major cases of revolution around the world—a list of seemingly very different countries like France, Russia, China, Vietnam, Cuba, Nicaragua, and Iran—and ask what common elements can be found that explain why these countries had revolutions. Both comparative methods have their strengths and weaknesses, but their common goal is to use careful case selection and systematic examination of key variables to mimic laboratory methods as closely as possible.

With about two hundred countries in the world, however, no one can systematically examine every case in depth. For large-scale studies, political scientists rely on a third method: **quantitative statistical techniques**. When evidence can be reduced to sets of numbers, statistical methods can be used to systematically compare a huge number of cases. Recent quantitative research on the causes of civil

research methods: Systematic processes used to ensure that the study of some phenomena is as objective and unbiased as possible

single-case study: Research method that examines a particular political phenomenon in just one country or community and can generate ideas for theories or test theories developed from different cases

comparative method: The means by which scholars try to mimic laboratory conditions by careful selection of cases

quantitative statistical techniques: Research method used for large-scale studies that reduces evidence to sets of numbers so that statistical analysis can systematically compare a huge number of cases

war, for instance, looked at all identifiable civil wars over several decades, literally hundreds of cases. The results indicated that ethnic divisions, which often seem to be the cause of civil war, are not as important as had been assumed. Although they may play a role, civil war is much more likely when groups are fighting over control of a valuable resource such as diamonds. Where no such resource exists, ethnic divisions are far less likely to result in war (Collier and Hoeffler 2001).

Each of these methods has its advantages and disadvantages. A single-case study allows a political scientist to look at a phenomenon in great depth and come to a more thorough understanding of a particular case (usually a country). The comparative method retains some, but not all, of this depth and gains the

Scientific Method in Comparative Politics

Political science can never be a pure science because of imperfect laboratory conditions: in the real world, we have very little control over social and political phenomena. Political scientists, like other social scientists, nonetheless think in scientific terms. Most use key scientific concepts, including the following:

- Theory: An abstract argument explaining a phenomenon
- Hypothesis: A claim that certain things cause other things to happen or change
- Variable: A measurable phenomenon that changes across time or space
- Dependent variable: The phenomenon a scientist is trying to explain
- Independent variable: The thing that explains the dependent variable
- Control: Holding variables constant so that the effects of one independent variable at a time can be examined

In using the scientific method in political science, the first challenge we face is to define clearly the variables we need to include and measure them accurately. For instance, one recent study of civil wars by Paul Collier and Anke Hoeffler (2001) included, among other variables, measurements of when a civil war was taking place, poverty, ethnic fragmentation, and dependence on natural resources. They had to ask themselves, What constitutes a "civil war"? How much violence must occur and for how long before a particular country is considered to be having a civil war? What many saw as a civil war erupted in Ukraine in 2014, though accompanied by a Russian military invasion supporting one side. Fighting and cease-fires have been off and on ever since, with the situation by 2017 still a stalemate. So should the Ukraine be classified as having a civil war or not, and exactly when?

A second challenge we face is figuring out how to control for all the potentially relevant variables in our research. Unlike scientists in a laboratory, political scientists cannot hold variables constant to examine the effects of one independent variable at a time. A common alternative is to measure the simultaneous effects of all the independent variables through quantitative studies, such as Collier and Hoeffler's study of civil wars. Single-case studies and the comparative method attempt to control variables via careful selection of cases. For instance, a comparative case study examining the same questions Collier and Hoeffler studied might select as cases only poor countries, hypothesizing that the presence of natural resources only causes civil wars in poor countries. The question becomes, In the context of poverty, is ethnic fragmentation or the presence of natural resources more important in causing civil war? If, on the other hand, we think poverty itself affects the likelihood of civil war, we might select several cases from poor countries and several others from rich countries to see if the presence of natural resources has a different effect in the different contexts. None of this provides the perfect control that a laboratory can achieve; rather, it attempts to mimic those conditions as closely as possible to arrive at scientifically defensible conclusions.

advantage of systematic comparison from which more generalizable conclusions can be drawn. Quantitative techniques can show broad patterns, but only for questions involving evidence that can be presented numerically, and they provide little depth on any particular case. Case studies are best at generating new ideas and insights that can lead to new theories. Quantitative techniques are best at showing the tendency of two or more phenomena to vary together, such as civil war and the presence of valuable resources. Understanding how phenomena are connected, and what causes what, often requires case studies that can provide greater depth to see the direct connections involved. Much of the best scholarship in recent years combines methods, using quantitative techniques to uncover broad patterns and comparative case studies to examine causal connections more closely.

No matter how much political scientists attempt to mimic laboratory sciences, the subject matter will not allow the kinds of scientific conclusions that exist in chemistry or biology. As the world changes, ideas and theories have to adapt. That does not mean that old theories are not useful; they often are. It does mean, however, that no theory will ever become a universal and unchanging law, like the law of gravity. The political world simply isn't that certain.

Comparative politics will also never become a true science because political scientists have their own human passions and positions regarding the various debates they study. A biologist might become determined to gain fame or fortune by proving a particular theory, even if laboratory tests don't support it (for instance, scientist Woo Suk Hwang of South Korea went so far as to fabricate stem cell research results). Biologists, however, neither become normatively committed to finding particular research results nor ask particular questions because of their normative beliefs. Political scientists, however, do act on their normative concerns, and that is entirely justifiable. Normative theories affect political science because our field is the study of people. Our normative positions often influence the very questions we ask. Those

Young men look for diamonds in Sierra Leone. Recent statistical research has supported the theory that conflicts such as the civil war in Sierra Leone in the 1990s are not caused primarily by ethnic differences, as is often assumed, but by competition over control of mineral resources.
AP Photo/Adam Butler

who ask questions about the level of "cheating" in the welfare system, for instance, are typically critics of the system who tend to think the government is wasting money on welfare. Those who ask questions about the effects of budget cuts on the poor, on the other hand, probably believe the government should be involved in alleviating poverty. These normative positions do not mean that the evidence can or should be ignored. For example, empirical research suggested that the 1996 welfare reform in the United States neither reduced the income of the poor as much as critics initially feared nor helped the poor get jobs and rise out of poverty as much as its proponents predicted (Jacobson 2001). Good political scientists can approach a subject like this with a set of moral concerns but recognize the results of careful empirical research nonetheless and change their arguments and conclusions in light of the new evidence.

Normative questions can be important and legitimate purposes for research projects. This book includes extensive discussions of different kinds of democratic political institutions. One of the potential trade-offs, we argue, is between greater levels of representation and participation on the one hand and efficient policymaking on the other. But this analysis is only interesting if we care about this trade-off. We have to hold a normative position on which of the two—representation and participation or efficient policymaking—is more important and why. Only then can we use the lessons learned from our empirical examination to make recommendations about which institutions a country ought to adopt.

Where does this leave the field of comparative politics? The best comparativists are aware of their own biases but still use various methods to generate the most systematic evidence possible to come to logical conclusions. We approach the subject with our normative concerns, our own ideas about what a "good society" should be, and what role government should have in it. We try to do research on interesting questions as scientifically and systematically as possible to develop the best evidence we can to provide a solid basis for government policy. Because we care passionately about the issues, we ought to study them as rigorously as possible, and we should be ready to change our normative positions and empirical conclusions based on the evidence we find.

Three Key Questions in Comparative Politics

Comparative politics is a huge field. The questions we can ask are virtually limitless. Spanning this huge range, however, are three major questions. The first two are fundamental to the field of political science, of which comparative politics is a part. The third is comparativists' particular contribution to the broader field of political science.

Probably the most common question political scientists ask is, What explains political behavior? The heart of political science is trying to understand why people do what they do in the world of politics. We can ask, Why do voters vote the way they do? Why do interest groups champion particular causes so passionately? Why does the U.S. Supreme Court make the decisions it does? Why has Ghana been able to create an apparently stable democracy, whereas neighboring Mali had its democracy overthrown by the military? By asking these questions, we seek to discover why individuals, groups, institutions, or countries take particular political actions. Political scientists have developed many theories to explain various kinds of political actions. We discuss them in terms of three broad approaches that focus on interests, beliefs, and structures.

The second large question animating political science is, Who rules? Who has power in a particular country, political institution, or political situation and

CRITICAL INQUIRY

An Orientation to Comparative Politics

Although you are only starting your study of comparative politics, it is never too early to start developing the ability to understand and ultimately conduct systematic research in the field. Throughout this book, you'll see boxes labeled "Critical Inquiry." Most of these will present you with some key evidence, such as data on several variables for a select number of countries. We will ask you to use these data to test or challenge other findings, or to develop hypotheses of your own that attempt to answer some of the key questions we address in that particular chapter. We may invite you to use online and other resources for additional research as well, so you can start to formulate conclusions about whether the hypotheses are true. In some chapters, we also present normative questions for consideration, for these are also essential to the study of comparative politics. Although you won't be able to come to definitive conclusions, these exercises will give you a taste of how comparative politics is done. They will also allow you to think about the limits of the research you've done or encountered, the role of normative questions in the field, and what could be done to answer the questions more definitively. ●

why? Formal power is often clear in modern states; particular officials have prescribed functions and roles that give them certain powers. For example, the U.S. Congress passes legislation, which the president has the power to sign or veto and the Supreme Court can rule as constitutional or not. But does the legislation Congress passes reflect the will of the citizens? Are citizens really ruling through their elected representatives (as the U.S. Constitution implies), or are powerful lobbyists calling the shots, or can members of Congress do whatever they want once in office? The Constitution and laws can't fully answer these broader questions of who really has a voice, is able to participate, and therefore has power.

Virtually all questions in political science derive from these two fundamental questions, and virtually all empirical theories are involved in the debate these two questions raise. Comparativists add a third particular focus by asking, Where and why do particular types of political behavior occur? If we can explain why Americans on the left side of the political spectrum vote for Democrats, can we use the same explanation for the voting patterns of left-leaning Germans and Brazilians? If special interests have the real power over economic policy in the U.S. presidential system, is this the case in Britain's parliamentary democracy as well? Why have military coups d'état happened rather frequently in Latin America and Africa but very rarely in Europe and North America? Comparativists start with the same basic theories used by other political scientists to try to explain political behavior and understand who really has power; we then add a comparative dimension to develop explanations that work in different times and places. In addition to helping develop more scientific theories, comparing different cases and contexts can help us determine which lessons from one situation are applicable to another.

What Explains Political Behavior?

The core activity in all political science is explaining political behavior: Why do people, groups, and governments act as they do in the political arena? It's easy enough to observe and describe behavior, but what explains it? In daily discussions we tend to attribute the best of motives to those with whom we agree—they are "acting in the best interests" of the community or nation. We tend to see those with whom we disagree, on the other hand, as acting selfishly or even with evil intent. You can see this tendency in the way Americans use the phrase *special interest*. We perceive groups whose causes or ideological leanings we agree with as benevolent and general; those we disagree with are "special interests." Logically, however, any **political actor**, meaning any person or group engaged in political behavior, can be motivated by a variety of factors. Political scientists have developed three broad answers to the question of what explains political behavior: interests, beliefs, and structures. Each answer includes within it several theoretical approaches.

Interests

We commonly assume that most people involved in politics are in it for their own good. Even when political actors claim to be working for the greater good or for some specific principle, many people suspect they are just hiding their own self-interested motives. The assumption of self-interest (broadly defined) is also a major element in political science theories about political behavior.

Rational choice theory assumes that individuals are rational and that they bring a set of self-defined preferences into the political arena. This does not mean that all people are greedy or selfish but rather that they rationally pursue their preferences, whatever those may be. The theory borrows heavily from the field of economics, which makes the same assumptions in analyzing behavior in the market. Political scientists use this theory to explain political behavior and its results by making assumptions about political actors' preferences, modeling the political context in which they pursue those preferences, and demonstrating how political outcomes can be explained as the result of the interactions of those actors in that context. For instance, the allocation of money for building new roads is the result of an agreement among members of a congressional committee. All of the members of the committee have certain interests or preferences, based mainly on their desire for reelection and their constituents' demands. The committee members pursue those interests rationally, and the final bill is a negotiated settlement reflecting the relative power of the various committee members, as well as their interests within the context of the committee and Congress more broadly.

Rational choice theorists start their analyses at the level of the individual, but they often seek to explain group behavior. They model group behavior from their assumptions about the preferences of individual members of groups. Group behavior is considered a result of the collective actions of rational individual actors in the group in a particular context. Racial or ethnic minority groups, women's groups, or environmental and religious groups can all be analyzed in this way. Rational choice theorists would argue, for instance, that environmentalists are just as rational and self-interested as oil companies but simply have different preferences. Environmentalists gain benefits from breathing clean air and walking through unpolluted forests; they pursue those preferences in the same way that the oil industry pursues its opposition to environmental regulations. Although self-defined preferences may be easier to see when analyzing battles over material goods and money, they exist throughout the political arena. Rational choice theorists thus are not interested in the second or third dimensions of power we mentioned earlier; they examine behavior, not institutions that prevent behavior, and they do not ask how and why people have certain preferences. They instead accept people's preferences and actions as given and then ask how they can be explained via rationality.

political actor: Any person or group engaged in political behavior

rational choice theory: An explanation for political behavior that assumes that individuals are rational beings who bring to the political arena a set of self-defined preferences and adequate knowledge and ability to pursue those preferences

Secretary of Agriculture Tom Vilsack (under President Barack Obama) and Senator Jeanne Shaheen, D-NH, address reporters at a press conference in 2014 announcing $25 million for the nation's farmers to turn agricultural commodities into value-added products. Agricultural subsidies such as this represent the type of political issue based on material interests that lends itself to rational choice theoretical explanations.
Bill Clark/CQ Roll Call

This raises one of the major criticisms of rational choice theories: they can't explain preferences in advance so can't predict political behavior in advance. Group theorists, such as Christopher Achen and Larry Bartels (2016), argue that rational choice theorists have it exactly backward: individual preferences don't define group behavior; rather, group membership creates individual preferences. When a new political issue arises, political groups have to figure out their preferences and how they will pursue them; individual group members almost always follow leaders of groups with whom they strongly identify.

In economics, it's a pretty safe assumption that people engage in economic activity to make money: businesses seek to maximize profits, and workers look for the highest wage. Knowing preferences in advance is much more difficult in political science. For instance, how can a rational choice theorist explain the electoral choice of a voter who is both a devout Catholic and a union member if the two available candidates are (a) a Democrat who favors raising the minimum wage and other workers' benefits but also favors legalized abortion, and (b) a Republican with the opposite views? Will that person vote as a Catholic or as a union member? Achens and Bartel argue that we have to understand the strength of group membership to answer this question; the simple assumption of individual rationality can't answer how a person faced with such a conflict will vote.

Many comparativists also ask whether rational choice theories can explain the different political behaviors seen around the world. For most of the twentieth century, for example, the most important French labor unions were closely affiliated with the Communist Party and pursued many objectives tied to party beliefs, beyond the basic "shop floor" issues of wages and working conditions. In the United States, by contrast, no major unions were tied to communist or socialist parties, and unions focused much more on improving wages and working conditions, with less concern for broader social changes. In Britain, labor unions were not communists, but they created their own party—the Labour Party—to represent their interests in government. Rational choice theorists might be able to explain political outcomes involving these unions after correctly understanding the preferences of each, but they have a hard time explaining why unions in different countries developed strikingly different sets of preferences. Did something about the working conditions of these three countries produce different definitions of *self-interest*, or do different workers define their interests differently based on factors other than rational calculation?

Psychological theories also focus on individual interests but question the assumption of rational action and are particularly interested in how political preferences are formed. They explain political behavior on the basis of individuals' psychological experiences or dispositions. Psychological theories look for nonrational explanations for political behavior. Comparativists who study individual leaders have long used this approach, trying to explain leaders' choices and actions by understanding personal backgrounds and psychological states. More recently, political scientists have examined the role of emotions in explaining political behavior. Roger Petersen (2002) and Andrew Ross (2013) look at emotions like fear to explain violent ethnic and religious conflict, whereas Marc Hetherington and Jonathan Weiler (2018) show how white Americans' answers to four simple questions about child rearing define personality types and worldviews that explain everything from who they vote for to what cars they drive. In sharp contrast to rational choice theory, psychological theories are often interested in the third dimension of power: influences on the formation of individual political demands. Critics of the psychological approach argue that the inherent focus on the individual that is fundamental to psychological theories makes them irrelevant to explaining group behavior. If so, their utility in political science is limited. Explanations beyond the level of individual motivation, however, might help explain these situations.

Beliefs

Beliefs are probably second only to self-interest in popular ideas about political behavior. If people think a political actor is not simply self-interested, they usually assume she is motivated by a value or belief. Environmentalists care about the environment; regardless of their own personal interests, they think everyone ought to have clean air to breathe and forests to explore. People who are against abortion believe that life begins at conception and therefore abortion is murder; self-interest has nothing to do with it. Political scientists have developed various formal theories that relate to this common sense notion that values and beliefs matter. The main approaches focus on either political culture or political ideology.

A **political culture** is a set of widely held attitudes, values, beliefs, and symbols about politics. It provides people with ways to understand the political arena, justifications for a particular set of political institutions and practices, and definitions of appropriate political behaviors. Political cultures emerge from various historical processes and can change over time, although they usually change rather slowly because they are often deeply embedded in a society. They tend to endure, in part, because of **political socialization**, the process through which people, especially young people, learn about politics and are taught a society's common political values and beliefs. Theories of political culture argue that the attitudes, values, beliefs, and symbols that constitute a given country's political culture are crucial explanations for political behavior in that country. Widely accepted cultural values, they argue, can influence all three dimensions of power: getting people to do something, excluding them from the political arena, and influencing their political demands.

psychological theories: Explanations for political behavior based on psychological analysis of political actors' motives

political culture: A set of widely held attitudes, values, beliefs, and symbols about politics

political socialization: The process through which people, especially young people, learn about politics and are taught a society's common political values and beliefs

Two broad schools of thought within political culture theory exist: modernist and postmodernist. **Modernists** believe that clear attitudes, values, and beliefs can be identified within any particular political culture. The best-known example of this is Gabriel Almond and Sidney Verba's 1963 book *The Civic Culture*. Based on a broad survey of citizens of five countries in North America and Europe, the authors developed a typology—a list of different types—of political cultures. They saw each country as dominated primarily by one particular type of political culture and argued that more stable and democratic countries, such as the United States and Great Britain, had a **civic culture**. This meant that their citizens held democratic values and beliefs that supported their democracies; these attitudes led citizens to participate actively in politics but also to defer enough to the leadership to let it govern effectively. On the other hand, the authors described Mexico as an authoritarian culture in which citizens viewed themselves primarily as subjects with no right to control their government, suggesting that these attitudes helped to produce the electoral authoritarian regime that ruled the country until 2000.

Critics of the modernist approach question the assumption that any country has a clearly defined political culture that is relatively fixed and unchanging, and they contest the argument that cultural values cause political outcomes rather than the other way around. They note that **subcultures**—distinct political cultures of particular groups—exist in all societies. Racial or religious minorities, for instance, may not fully share the political attitudes and values of the majority. The assumption that we can identify a single, unified political culture that is key to understanding a particular country can mask some of the most important political conflicts within the country. Furthermore, political attitudes themselves may be symptoms rather than causes of political activity or a governmental system. For example, Mexican citizens in the 1960s may not have viewed themselves as active participants in government for a very rational reason: they had lived for forty years under one party that had effectively suppressed all meaningful opposition and participation. They really did not have any effective voice in government or any chance for effective participation. According to this view, the political institutions in Mexico created the political attitudes of Mexicans, rather than vice versa.

modernists: Theorists of political culture who believe that clear sets of attitudes, values, and beliefs can be identified in each country that change very rarely and explain much about politics there

civic culture: A political culture in which citizens hold values and beliefs that support democracy, including active participation in politics but also enough deference to the leadership to let it govern effectively

subcultures: Groups that hold partially different beliefs and values from the main political culture of a country

postmaterialist: A set of values in a society in which most citizens are economically secure enough to move beyond immediate economic (materialist) concerns to "quality of life" issues like human rights, civil rights, women's rights, environmentalism, and moral values

Some political scientists also accuse modernists of ethnocentrism, in that many modernist approaches argue that Anglo-American values are superior to others for establishing stable democracies. Still other critics suggest that political culture is more malleable than *The Civic Culture* assumed. The attitudes that surveys identified in the 1960s were just that—attitudes of the 1960s. Over time, as societies change and new political ideas arise, attitudes and values change accordingly, sometimes with breath-taking speed (Almond and Verba 1989). Many cultural theorists, for instance, have argued that both Arab and Islamic cultures tend to have nondemocratic values that support authoritarian regimes in the Middle East. The revolts of the Arab Spring in 2011 suggest that those theorists either misunderstood the cultures or the cultures changed rapidly, and the differential outcomes of those revolts—democracy in Tunisia but a return to electoral authoritarian rule in Egypt—suggest that "Islamic" or "Arab" culture is far from monolithic.

Some modernist approaches examine change in political culture. Ronald Inglehart (1971) coined the term **postmaterialist** in the 1970s to describe what he saw as a new predominant element in political culture in wealthy democracies. He argued that as a result of the post–World War II economic expansion, by the 1960s and 1970s most citizens in wealthy societies were less concerned about economic (materialist) issues and more concerned about "quality of life" issues. They had become "postmaterialist." Economic growth had allowed most citizens to attain a level of material comfort that led to a change in attitudes and values. Individuals

Police confront protesters in Mexico City in 1968. Political culture theory argues that countries like Mexico were not democratic because they did not have a democratic political culture. Critics contend that culture can change quickly, so it isn't a very good explanation of regime type. Mexico transitioned to an electoral democracy in 2000.
Bettmann/Getty Images

had become more concerned with ideas like human rights, civil rights, women's rights, environmentalism, and moral values.

This postmaterialist shift in political culture led to a sea change in the issues that politicians came to care about and the outcomes of elections. It explained, for instance, why many self-identified Catholic voters in the United States shifted from voting Democratic in the middle of the twentieth century to voting Republican by the end of the century. In the 1950s they voted their mostly working-class economic interests, supporting the party that created what they saw as "pro-worker" policies. Later, as they achieved greater economic security as part of an expanding middle class, they came to care more about postmaterialist moral values, such as their religious opposition to abortion, and they shifted their party allegiance accordingly. As the bulk of American voters went through this shift in political culture, political battles focused less on economic issues and more on debates over moral and cultural values. More recently, Russell Dalton, Christian Welzel, and their colleagues have argued that postmaterialist and more participatory values have come to characterize not only Western societies but many societies around the world, and that those more participatory values result in stronger democracy and ability to govern, in contrast to *The Civic Culture*'s thesis that too much participation threatens democracy (Dalton and Welzel 2014).

The postmaterialist thesis shows how political culture can change over time as a result of other changes in society. Nonetheless, these theorists continued to argue that it was useful to think about societies as having identifiable political cultures that explain much political behavior. The **postmodernist** approach, on the other hand, pushes the criticism of modernism further, questioning the assumption that one clear set of values can be identified that has a clear meaning to all members of a society. Postmodernists, influenced primarily by French philosophers such as Michel Foucault, see cultures not as sets of fixed and clearly defined values but rather as sets of symbols subject to interpretation. When examining political culture, post-modernists focus primarily on **political discourse**, meaning the ways in

postmodernist: An approach that sees cultures not as sets of fixed and clearly defined values but rather as sets of symbols subject to interpretation

political discourse: The ways in which people speak and write about politics; postmodern theorists argue that political discourse influences political attitudes, identity, and actions

which a society speaks and writes about politics. They argue that a culture has a set of symbols that, through a particular historical process, has come to be highly valued but is always subject to varying interpretations. These symbols do not have fixed values upon which all members of a society agree; instead, political actors interpret them through political discourse. Influencing discourse can be a means to gain power in its third dimension: influencing how people think about politics.

One example of a symbol that American political actors use in political discourse is "family values." No American politician would dare oppose family values. In the 1980s Republicans under President Ronald Reagan used this concept in their campaign discourse very effectively to paint themselves as supporters of the core concerns of middle-class families. As a result, Democrats and their policies came to be seen at times as threatening to the ideal of the nuclear family. In the 1990s under President Bill Clinton, Democrats were able to gain back some political advantage by reinterpreting family values to mean what they argued was support for "real" American families: single mothers trying to raise kids on their own or two-income families in which the parents worried about the quality of after-school programs and the cost of a college education. Democrats created a new discourse about family values that allowed them to connect that powerful symbol to the kinds of government programs they supported. Family values, the postmodernists would argue, are not a fixed set of values on which all agree but rather a symbol through which political leaders build support by developing a particular discourse at a particular time. Such symbols are always subject to reinterpretation.

Critics of the postmodern approach argue that it really cannot explain anything. If everything is subject to interpretation, then how can one explain or predict anything other than "things will change as new interpretations arise"? Postmodernists respond that the discourses themselves matter by setting symbolic boundaries within which political actors must engage to mobilize political support. The ability of political leaders to interpret these symbols to develop support for themselves and their policies is a central element to understanding political activity in any country.

Advocates of political culture, whether modernist or postmodernist, argue that explaining political behavior requires understanding the effects of political culture at the broadest level. A related but distinct way to examine the effect of beliefs is the study of **political ideology**, a systematic set of beliefs about how a political system ought to be structured. Political ideologies typically are quite powerful, overarching worldviews that incorporate both normative and empirical theories that explicitly state an understanding of how the political world does operate and how it ought to operate. Political ideology is distinct from political culture in that it is much more consciously elaborated. In chapter 3 we examine the predominant political ideologies of the last century: liberalism, communism, fascism, modernizing authoritarianism, and theocracy.

Advocates of a particular political ideology attempt to mobilize support for their position by proclaiming their vision of a just and good society. The most articulate proponents of an ideology can expound on its points, define its key terms, and argue for why it is right. Communists, for instance, envision a society in which all people are equal and virtually all serious conflicts disappear, meaning government itself can disappear. They appeal to people's sense of injustice by pointing out the inequality that is inherent in a capitalist society, and they encourage people to work with them through various means to achieve a better society in the future.

political ideology: A systematic set of beliefs about how a political system ought to be structured

A political ideology may be related to a particular political culture, but political ideologies are conscious and well-developed sets of beliefs rather than vague sets of values or attitudes. Some scholars take political ideology at face value, at least implicitly accepting the idea that political leaders, and perhaps their followers as well, should be taken at their word. These scholars believe that political actors have thought about politics and adopted a particular set of beliefs that they use as a basis for their own political actions and for judging the actions of others. Comparativists Evelyne Huber and John Stephens (2001), for instance, argued that the strength of social democratic ideology in several northern European governments partly explains why those states have exceptionally generous welfare policies.

Critics of this approach point to what they see as the underlying motives of ideology as the real explanation for political behavior. Italian Marxist Antonio Gramsci (1971) argued ideology is a means by which the ruling class convinces the population that its rule is natural, justified, or both (see the "Who Rules?" section on page 19 for a discussion of the ruling class). Clearly, this ties directly to the third dimension of power. Advocates of rational choice models might argue that a particular leader or group adopts a particular ideology because it is in its own self-interest; for example, business owners support an ideology of free markets because it maximizes opportunities to make profits. Similarly, advocates of a political culture approach see cultural values as lying behind ideology. In the United States, for instance, vague but deep-seated American values of individualism and individual freedom may explain why Americans are far less willing to support socialist ideologies than are Europeans.

Structures

The third broad approach to explaining political behavior is **structuralism**. Structuralists argue that broader structures in a society at the very least influence and limit, and perhaps even determine, political behavior. These structures can be socioeconomic or political. An early and particularly influential structuralist argument was **Marxism**, which argues that economic structures largely determine political behavior. Karl Marx contended that the production process of any society creates discrete social classes—groups of people with distinct relationships to the means of production. He argued that in modern capitalist society the key classes are the **bourgeoisie**, which owns and controls capital, and the **proletariat**, which owns no capital and must sell its labor to survive. According to Marx, this economic structure explains political behavior: the bourgeoisie uses its economic advantage to control the state in its interest, and the proletariat will eventually recognize and act on its own, opposing interests. These groups are acting on their interests, but those interests are determined by the underlying economic structure.

A more recent structuralist theory is **institutionalism**. Institutionalists argue that political institutions are crucial to understanding political behavior. A **political institution** is most commonly defined as a set of rules, norms, or standard operating procedures that is widely recognized and accepted and that structures and constrains political actions. Major political institutions often serve as the basis for key political organizations such as legislatures or political parties. In short, institutions are the "rules of the game" within which political actors must operate. These rules are often quite formal and widely recognized, such as in the U.S. Constitution.

Other institutions can be informal or even outside government but nonetheless be very important in influencing political behavior. In the United States, George Washington established a long-standing informal institution, the two-term limit on the presidency. After he stepped down at the end of his second term, no other president, no matter how popular, attempted to run for a third term until Franklin Roosevelt in 1940. Voters supported his decision and reelected him, but after his death the country quickly passed a constitutional amendment that created

structuralism: Approach to explaining politics that argues that political behavior is at least influenced and limited, and perhaps even determined, by broader structures in a society such as class divisions or enduring institutions

Marxism: Structuralist argument that says that economic structures largely determine political behavior; the philosophical underpinning of communism

bourgeoisie: The class that owns capital; according to Marxism, the ruling elite in all capitalist societies

proletariat: A term in Marxist theory for the class of free-wage laborers who own no capital and must sell their labor to survive; communist parties claim to work on the proletariat's behalf

institutionalism: An approach to explaining politics that argues that political institutions are crucial to understanding political behavior

political institution: A set of rules, norms, or standard operating procedures that is widely recognized and accepted by the society, structures and constrains political actions, and often serves as the basis for key political organizations

a formal rule limiting a president to two consecutive terms. Informal institutions can be enduring, as the two-term presidency tradition shows. It held for more than 150 years simply because the vast majority of political leaders and citizens believed it should; in that context, no president dared go against it.

Broadly speaking, two schools of thought exist among institutionalists. **Rational choice institutionalists** follow the assumptions of rational choice theory outlined earlier. They argue that institutions are the products of the interaction and bargaining of rational actors and, once created, constitute the rules of the game within which rational actors operate, at least until their interests diverge too far from those rules. Barry Weingast (1997), for instance, claimed that for democracies to succeed, major political forces must come to a rational compromise on key political institutions that give all important political players incentives to support the system. Institutions that create such incentives will be self-enforcing, thereby creating a stable democratic political system. Weingast argued that political stability in early U.S. history was due to the Constitution's provisions of federalism, a particular separation of powers, and the equal representation of each of the states in the Senate. These gave both North and South effective veto power over major legislation, which enforced compromise and, therefore, stability. The Civil War broke out, in part, because by the 1850s the creation of new nonslave states threatened the South's veto power. This changed context meant that southern leaders no longer saw the Constitution as serving their interests, so they were willing to secede. Rational choice institutionalists argue that political actors will abide by a particular institution only as long as it continues to serve their interests. Therefore, a changed context requires institutions to change accordingly or face dissolution. By looking at institutions and their effects, however, they often include the second dimension of power in their analyses, in contrast to the rational choice theorists mentioned earlier who focus solely on the first dimension of power.

Historical institutionalists believe that institutions play an even bigger role in explaining political behavior. They argue that institutions not only limit self-interested political behavior but also influence who is involved in politics and shape individual political preferences, thus working in all three dimensions of power. By limiting who is allowed to participate, institutions can determine what a government is capable of accomplishing. Stephan Haggard and Robert Kaufman (1995), for example, argued that two key institutions—a strong executive and a coherent party system—shaped political participation in ways that allowed certain countries in Latin America and East Asia to respond positively to economic crises in the 1980s and 1990s, improving their economies and creating stable democracies. Beyond limiting who can participate and what can be accomplished, institutions can create political preferences. Because societies value long-standing political institutions, their preservation is part of political socialization: citizens come to accept and value existing institutions and define their own interests partly in terms of preserving those institutions. Historical institutionalists thus argue that institutions profoundly shape political behavior independent of people's self-interests, and can even help create political values and beliefs, operating on all three dimensions of power.

Critics of institutionalism argue that institutions are rarely the actual explanation for political behavior. Skeptics who follow rational choice theory argue that institutions are simply based on rational actions and compromises among elites who will continue to be "constrained" by these only as long as doing so serves their interests. Scholars who focus on beliefs suggest that institutions are derived from a society's underlying values and beliefs or a more self-conscious ideology, which both shape institutions and explain political behavior.

rational choice institutionalists: Institutionalist theorists who follow the assumptions of rational choice theory and argue that institutions are the products of the interaction and bargaining of rational actors

historical institutionalists: Theorists who believe that institutions explain political behavior and shape individuals' political preferences and their perceptions of their self-interests and that institutions evolve historically in particular countries and change relatively slowly

Political scientists look to three sources as explanations for political behavior: interests, beliefs, and structures. Scholars can use each of these approaches to analyze the same political event. For instance, Chile made one of the most successful transitions to democracy in the 1990s. A rational choice institutionalist might argue that this resulted from the strategic interaction of the major political actors, regardless of what they personally believed about democracy. They came to a compromise with the former military regime and with one another around a set of constitutional rules that, given the political context, they thought was better for them than the available nondemocratic alternatives. Therefore, they agreed to act within the democratic "game." A political culture theorist would point to values in Chilean society that favored democracy, values that perhaps derived in part from the European origins of much of the population, as well as the country's past history with democracy. A historical institutionalist, on the other hand, would argue that Chile's prior stable democratic institutions were easy to resurrect because of their past success and that these institutions represented a legacy that many other Latin American countries did not have. So the question becomes, Which of these theories is most convincing and why, and what evidence can we find to support one or another explanation? This is the primary work of much of political science and the kind of question to which we return frequently in this book. The theories we use are summarized in Table 1.1.

Who Rules?

The second great question in comparative politics is, Who rules? Which individual, group, or groups control power, and how much do they control? At first glance, the answer may seem obvious. In a democracy, legislators are elected for a set term to make the laws. They rule, after the voters choose them, until the next election. Because of elections, it is the voters who really rule. In a dictatorship, on the other hand, one individual, one ruling party, or one small group (such as a military junta) rules. A dictatorship can have all the power and keep it as long as it pleases, or at least as long as it is able.

Political scientists, however, question this superficial view. Even in democracies, many argue that the voters don't really hold the power and that a small group at the top controls things. Conversely, many argue that dictatorships may not be the monoliths they appear to be, in that those officially in charge may unofficially have to share power in one way or another. Political scientists, in trying to dig beneath the surface of the question, have developed many theories that can be grouped into two broad categories: pluralist theories and elite theories.

Pluralist Theories: Each Group Has Its Voice

Pluralist theories contend that society is divided into various political groups and that power is dispersed among them so that no group has complete or permanent power. This is most obvious in democracies in which different parties capture power via elections. When pluralists look at political groups, however, they look at far more than just parties. They argue that politically organized groups exist in all societies, sometimes formally and legally but at other times informally or illegally. These groups compete for access to and influence over power. Policy is almost always the result of a compromise among groups, and no single group is able to dominate continuously. Furthermore, over time and on different issues, the power and influence of groups vary. A group that is particularly successful at gaining power or influencing government on one particular issue will not be as successful

pluralist theories: Explanations of who has power that argue that society is divided into various political groups and that power is dispersed among these groups so that no group has complete or permanent power; contrast to elite theory

TABLE 1.1

What Explains Political Behavior?

TYPE	INTERESTS UNDERSTANDING WHAT INTERNAL FACTORS EXPLAIN POLITICAL ACTIONS		BELIEFS UNDERSTANDING THE EFFECT OF VALUES OR BELIEFS		STRUCTURES UNDERSTANDING HOW BROAD STRUCTURES OR FORCES SHAPE OR DETERMINE BEHAVIOR	
Theory or framework	Rational choice	Psychological theory	Political culture	Political ideology	Marxism	Institutionalism
Assumptions	Political actors bring a set of self-defined preferences, adequate knowledge, and ability to pursue those interests and rationality to the political arena.	Nonrational influences explain political behavior.	A set of widely held attitudes, values, beliefs, and symbols about politics shapes what actors do.	Systematic set of beliefs about how the political system ought to be structured—motivates political action.	Economic structures determine political behavior. Production process creates distinct social classes—groups of people with the same relationship to the means of production.	Political institutions are widely recognized and accepted rules, norms, or standard operating procedures that structure and constrain individuals' political actions—the "rules of the game."
Unit of analysis	Individual actors	Group and individual identity and behavior	Individual actors and groups, political institutions, discourses, and practices	Individual actors and groups	Groups and social classes in particular	Interaction of both formal and informal institutions with groups and individuals
Methods	Observe outcome of political process; identify actors involved, relative power, and preferences; demonstrate how outcome was result of actors' self-interested interactions.	Explain actors' choices and actions by understanding their personal backgrounds and psychological states.	Modernist approach identifies clear attitudes, values, and beliefs within any particular political culture—for example, civic culture or postmaterialist culture. Postmodernist approach holds that cultures do not have fixed and clearly defined values but rather a set of symbols subject to interpretation; focuses primarily on political discourse.	Analyze written and verbal statements of political actors and correlate them with observed behavior.	Conduct historical analysis of economic systems.	institutionalists follow rational choice theory; institutions are products of the interactions and bargaining of rational actors. Historical institutionalists examine the historical evolution of institutions to demonstrate how these institutions limit self-interested political behavior and shape individuals' political preferences.
Critiques	Some difficulty predicting future behavior; hard to explain variation across cases.	Difficult to verify connections between internal state and actions, particularly for groups.	Political culture is not a monolithic, unchanging entity within a given country. Cultural values are not necessarily the cause of political outcomes; the causal relationship may be the other way around. If everything is subject to interpretation, then how can anything be explained or predicted?	Focus on ideology obscures what may be underlying motives, or the real explanation, for political behavior.	Ignores non-economic motives and ignores groups other than social classes.	Difficult to determine if institutions, rather than self-interest or culture, limit behavior.

on another. No group will ever win all battles. Pluralists clearly tend to think about power in its first dimension; they do not believe that any one group has the ability to exclude other groups from the political arena or to influence how another group thinks to the extent necessary to gain permanent power over them.

This pluralist process is less obvious in countries that do not have electoral democracies, but many pluralists argue that their ideas are valid in these cases as well. Even in the Soviet Union under Communist rule, some analysts saw elements of pluralism. They believed that for most of the Soviet period, at least after the death of Joseph Stalin in 1953, the ruling Communist Party had numerous internal factions that were essentially informal political groups. These were based on positions in the party, bureaucracy, economy, or region, as well as personal loyalty to a key leader. For instance, people in the KGB (the secret police) and the military were each a political group, quietly lobbying to expand the influence and power of their organizations. Leaders of particular industries, such as the oil industry, were a group seeking the ruling party's support for greater resources and prestige for their area of the economy. Pluralist politics were hidden behind a facade of ironclad party rule in which the Communist Party elite made all decisions and all others simply obeyed.

Dictatorships in postcolonial countries can also be analyzed via pluralism. On the surface, a military government in Africa looks like one individual or small group holding all power. Pluralists argue, however, that many of these governments have very limited central control. They rule through patron–client relationships in which the top leaders, the patrons, mobilize political support by providing resources to their followers, the clients. The internal politics of this type of rule revolves around the competition among group leaders for access to resources they can pass on to their clients. The top clients are themselves patrons of clients further down the chain. Midlevel clients might decide to shift their loyalty from one patron to another if they don't receive adequate resources, meaning those at the top must continuously work to maintain the support of their clients. In many cases, patrons use resources to mobilize support from others in their own ethnic group, so the main informal groups competing for power are ethnically defined (see chapter 4). Various factions compete for power and access to resources, again behind a facade of unitary and centralized power.

elite theories: Theories arguing that societies are ruled by an economic, gender, racial, or other small group that has effective control over virtually all power; contrast to pluralist theory

Elite Theories

Whereas pluralists see competing groups, even in countries that appear to be ruled by dictators, proponents of **elite theories** argue that all societies are ruled by one or more sets of elites that

President of Chile Michelle Bachelet greets attendees prior to delivering the annual presidential address to the nation at Congress Honor Hall in 2015. Feminist theorists often argue that women are kept out of political power because of the association of political leadership with military experience and prowess. Women heads of state throughout the world, though still small in number, have begun to challenge that norm.
Marcelo Benitez/LatinContent/Getty Images

have effective control over virtually all power. Elite theories usually focus on the second and third dimensions of power to argue that certain elites have perpetual power over ordinary citizens. The longest tradition within elite theory is Marxism, mentioned earlier. Marx argued that in any society, political power reflects control of the economy. In feudal Europe, for instance, the feudal lord, by virtue of his ownership of land, had power over the peasants, who were dependent on the lord for access to land and thus their survival. Similarly, Marx contended that in modern capitalist society, the bourgeoisie, by virtue of their ownership of capital, are the **ruling class**, as the feudal lords were centuries ago. The general population, or proletariat, is forced to sell its labor by working in the bourgeoisie's businesses in order to survive and must generally serve the desires of the bourgeoisie. Thus, in *The Communist Manifesto* Marx famously called the modern state "the executive committee of the whole bourgeoisie."

The Marxist tradition is only one type of elite theory. C. Wright Mills (1956), in *The Power Elite*, argued that the United States was ruled by a set of interlocking elites sitting at the top of economic, political, and military hierarchies. Mills shared with the Marxist tradition an emphasis on a small group controlling all real power, but he did not see the economy as the sole source of this power. He believed that the economic, political, and military spheres, while interlocking, are distinct and that all serve as key elements in the ruling elite.

Recently, Jeffrey Winters (2011) agreed with Weber that elite power can derive from various sources but argued that "material power" in the form of extreme wealth is the basis for the power of a particularly powerful elite—oligarchs—who use that power primarily to protect their own wealth. In modern democracies, including the United States, he argues, oligarchs no longer need to hire their own security forces for protection (because the government protects property rights) but instead hire tax lawyers and lobbyists to protect their income from government redistribution.

Feminist scholars have also developed elite theories of rule based on the concept of **patriarchy**, or rule by men. They argue that throughout history men have controlled virtually all power. Even though women have gained the right to vote in most countries, men remain the key rulers in most places. Today, social mores and political discourse are often the chief sources of patriarchy rather than actual law, but men remain in power nonetheless, and the political realm, especially its military aspects, continues to be linked to masculinity. A leader needs to be able to command a military, "take charge," and "act boldly and aggressively"—all activities most societies associate with masculinity. The second and third dimensions of power help preserve male control despite women now having the same formal political rights as men. Men also continue to enjoy greater income and wealth than women and can translate economic status into political power. According to feminist theorists, men thus constitute an elite that continues to enjoy a near monopoly on political power in many societies.

Similarly, some analysts argue that a racial elite exists in some societies in which one race has been able to maintain a hold on power. Historically, this was done via laws that prevented other races from participating in the political process, such as under apartheid in South Africa or the Jim Crow laws of the southern United States. But, as with feminists, analysts of race often argue that one race can maintain dominance through a disproportionate share of wealth or through the preservation of a particular political discourse that often implicitly places different races in different positions in a hierarchy. Michelle Alexander (2010) argued that laws and discourse around crime, drugs, and "colorblindness"

ruling class: An elite who possess adequate resources to control a regime; in Marxist theory, the class that controls key sources of wealth in a given epoch

patriarchy: Rule by men

constitute a "new Jim Crow" in the United States; they systemically disempower and disenfranchise black men, in particular, by disproportionately putting a large number of them in the criminal justice system. More generally, race theorists contend that in the United States, cultural attributes associated with being white, such as personal mannerisms and accent and dialect of English, are assumed to be not only "normal" but implicitly superior and are thus expected of those in leadership positions. This gives an inherent advantage to white aspirants for political positions.

Determining whether pluralist or elite theories best answer the question of who rules requires answering these questions: Who is in formal positions of power? Who has influence on government decision making? Who benefits from the decisions made? If the answer to all these questions seems to be one or a select few small groups, then the evidence points to elite theory as more accurate. If various groups seem to have access to power or influence over decision making, or both, then pluralism would seem more accurate. Table 1.2 summarizes these theories, which we investigate throughout this book.

TABLE 1.2

Who Rules?

	PLURALIST THEORY	ELITE THEORY
KEY ARGUMENTS	Society is divided into political groups.	All societies are ruled by an elite with control over virtually all power.
	Power is dispersed among groups.	Marxism: political power reflects control of the economy; it is based on the economic power of the bourgeoisie, who owns and controls capital and is the ruling elite in capitalist societies.
	No group has complete or permanent power.	The power elite: elite consists of military and political elite as well as economic elite.
	Even authoritarian regimes have important pluralist elements.	Patriarchy: the ruling elite is male; social mores and political discourse keep men in power. The political realm, especially the military, is linked to masculinity.
		Critical race theorists: the ruling elite is white; assumed superiority of white cultural characteristics keeps whites in power.

Where and Why?

"What explains political behavior?" and "Who rules?" are central questions to all political scientists. The particular focus of comparative politics is to ask these questions across countries in an attempt to develop a common understanding of political phenomena in all places and times. The third major question that orients this book is "Where and why?" Where do particular political phenomena occur, and why do they occur where they do and how they do?

For instance, Sweden is famous for its extensive and expensive welfare state, whereas the U.S. government spends much less money and attention on providing for people's needs directly via "welfare." Why are these two wealthy democracies so different? Can their differences be explained on the basis of competing rational choices? Did business interests overpower the interests of workers and poor people in the United States, while a large and well-organized labor movement in Sweden overcame a small, weaker business class to produce a more extensive welfare state? Or has the Swedish Socialist Party, which has been dominant over most of the last century, simply been successful at convincing the bulk of the population that its social democratic ideology produces a better society, whereas Americans' cultural belief in "making it on your own" leads them to reject any form of socialism? Or are the differences because a strong nongovernmental institution, the Landsorganisationen I Sverige (LO), arose in Sweden, uniting virtually all labor unions and becoming a central part of the policymaking process, whereas in the United States the country's more decentralized labor unions were weaker institutions and therefore not as capable of gaining the government's ear on welfare policy? Comparative politics attempts to resolve this kind of puzzle by examining the various theories of political behavior in light of the evidence found.

We engage in similar comparative efforts when seeking to understand who rules. A case study of the United States, for instance, might argue (as many have) that a corporate elite holds great power in American democracy, perhaps so great that it raises questions of how democratic the system actually is. A Marxist might argue that this is due to the unusually centralized and unequal control of wealth in the United States. A political culture theorist would point instead to American culture's belief in individualism, which leads few to question the leaders of major businesses, who are often depicted as "self-made" individuals whom many citizens admire. An institutionalist, on the other hand, would argue that American political institutions allow corporations to have great influence by funding expensive political campaigns and that members of Congress have little incentive to vote in support of their parties and so are more open to pressure from individual lobbyists. A comparativist might compare the United States and several European countries, examining the relative level of corporate influence, the level of wealth concentration, cultural values, and the ability of lobbyists to influence legislators in each country. This study might reveal comparative patterns that suggest, for instance, that corporate influence is highest in countries where wealth is most concentrated, regardless of the type of political system or cultural values. We examine this kind of question throughout the book.

We proceed in this first part of the book by looking at the biggest questions involving the state: (1) what is it, how does it work, what makes it strong or weak; (2) the state's relationship to citizens and regimes; and (3) the state's relationship with nations and other identity groups. Part II looks at how governments and political systems work, including institutions in democracies and authoritarian regimes, participation outside institutional bounds, and regime change. Part III turns our attention to political economy questions and related policy issues. Every chapter includes key questions at the outset that you should be able to develop answers to, and features that help you understand the ideas in the chapter. "In Context" boxes put particular examples into a larger context, and

A speaker uses a bullhorn during a Black Lives Matter demonstration in Sacramento, California in 2018. Over 100 met to protest the killing of Stephon Clark, an unarmed black man shot by police. Michelle Alexander (2010) called the systematic exclusion of a large percentage of black men from full citizenship via imprisonment for minor crimes the "new Jim Crow." The Black Lives Matter movement exploded in 2014 and was aimed at ending police brutality and excessively harsh sentencing of drug crimes, to undo the "new Jim Crow."
Justin Sullivan/Getty Images

"Critical Inquiry" boxes ask you to develop and informally test hypotheses about key political questions. Throughout, tables of data, maps, and illustrations help illuminate the subjects in each chapter. So let's get going. ●

Sharpen your skills with SAGE Edge at **edge.sagepub.com/orvisessentials2e. SAGE Edge for students** provides a personalized approach to help you accomplish your coursework goals in an easy-to-use learning environment.

KEY CONCEPTS

bourgeoisie (p. 17)

civic culture (p. 14)

comparative method (p. 6)

comparative politics (p. 4)

elite theories (p. 21)

empirical theory (p. 5)

first dimension of power (p. 4)

historical institutionalists (p. 18)

institutionalism (p. 17)

Marxism (p. 17)

modernists (p. 14)

normative theory (p. 5)

patriarchy (p. 22)

pluralist theories (p. 19)

political actor (p. 11)

political culture (p. 13)

political discourse (p. 15)

political ideology (p. 16)

political institution (p. 17)

political science (p. 4)

political socialization (p. 13)

politics (p. 4)

postmaterialist (p. 14)

postmodernist (p. 15)

proletariat (p. 17)

psychological theories (p. 13)

quantitative statistical techniques (p. 6)

rational choice institutionalists (p. 18)

rational choice theory (p. 11)

research methods (p. 6)

ruling class (p. 22)

second dimension of power (p. 4)

single-case study (p. 6)

structuralism (p. 17)

subcultures (p. 14)

theory (p. 5)

third dimension of power (p. 4)

WORKS CITED

Achens, Christopher H. and Larry M. Bartels. 2016. *Democracy for Realists: Why Elections Do Not Produce Responsive Government.* Princeton, NJ: Princeton University Press.

Alexander, Michelle. 2010. *The New Jim Crow: Mass Incarceration in the Age of Colorblindness.* New York: The New Press.

Almond, Gabriel A., and Sidney Verba. 1963. *The Civic Culture: Political Attitudes and Democracy in Five Nations.* Princeton, NJ: Princeton University Press.

———. 1989. *The Civic Culture Revisited.* Newbury Park, CA: Sage.

Bachrach, Peter, and Morton S. Baratz. 1962. "Two Faces of Power." *American Political Science Review* 56 (4): 947–952.

Bratton, Michael, and Nicholas van de Walle. 1997. *Democratic Experiments in Africa: Regime Transitions in Comparative Perspective.* Cambridge, UK: Cambridge University Press.

Collier, Paul, and Anke Hoeffler. 2001. *Greed and Grievance in Civil War.* Washington, DC: World Bank.

Dalton, Russell, and Christian Welzel, eds. 2014. *The Civic Culture Transformed: From Allegiant to Assertive Citizens.* Cambridge, UK: Cambridge University Press.

Gramsci, Antonio. 1971. *Selections From the Prison Notebooks of Antonio Gramsci*, edited and translated by Quintin Hoare and Geoffrey Nowell Smith. New York: International.

Haggard, Stephan, and Robert R. Kaufman. 1995. *The Political Economy of Democratic Transitions.* Princeton, NJ: Princeton University Press.

Hetherington, Marc, and Jonathan Weiler. 2018. *Prius or Pickup? How the Answers to Four Simple Questions Explain America's Great Divide.* New York: Houghton Mifflin Harcourt.

Huber, Evelyne, and John D. Stephens. 2001. *Development and Crisis of the Welfare State: Parties and Policies in Global Markets.* Chicago: University of Chicago Press.

Inglehart, Ronald. 1971. "The Silent Revolution in Europe: Intergenerational Change in Post-Industrial Societies." *American Political Science Review* 65 (4): 991–1017.

Jacobson, Linda. 2001. "Experts Debate Welfare Reform's Impact on Children." *Education Week* 21 (September 19): 1–8.

Lukes, Steven. 1974. *Power: A Radical View.* London: Macmillan.

Mills, C. Wright. 1956. *The Power Elite.* New York: Oxford University Press.

Petersen, Roger. 2002. *Understanding Ethnic Violence: Fear, Hatred, and Resentment in Twentieth-Century Eastern Europe.* New York: Cambridge University Press.

Ross, Andrew A. G. 2013. *Mixed Emotions: Beyond Fear and Hatred in International Conflict.* Chicago: University of Chicago Press.

Weingast, Barry R. 1997. "The Political Foundations of Democracy and the Rule of Law." *American Political Science Review* 91 (2): 245–263.

Winters, Jeffrey A. (2011). *Oligarchy.* Cambridge, UK: Cambridge University Press.

RESOURCES FOR FURTHER STUDY

Blank, Rebecca. 2001. "Declining Caseloads/Increased Work: What Can We Conclude About the Effects of Welfare Reform?" *Economic Policy Review* 7 (2): 25–36.

Dahl, Robert Alan. 1961. *Who Governs? Democracy and Power in an American City.* Yale Studies in Political Science No. 4. New Haven, CT: Yale University Press.

Gaventa, John. 1980. *Power and Powerlessness: Quiescence and Rebellion in an Appalachian Valley.* Urbana: University of Illinois Press.

Katznelson, Ira, and Helen V. Milner, eds. 2002. *Political Science: State of the Discipline.* New York: Norton.

King, Gary, Robert O. Keohane, and Sidney Verba. 1994. *Designing Social Inquiry: Scientific Inference in Qualitative Research.* Princeton, NJ: Princeton University Press.

Landman, Todd. 2003. *Issues and Methods in Comparative Politics: An Introduction.* 2nd ed. New York: Routledge.

Marx, Karl, and Friedrich Engels. 1978. *The Marx-Engels Reader.* Edited by Robert C. Tucker. 2nd ed. New York: Norton.

WEB RESOURCES

CIA, World Factbook

(https://www.cia.gov/library/publications/the-world-factbook)

Organisation for Economic Co-operation and Development (OECD), Data Lab

(http://www.oecd.org/statistics)

Pew Research Center, Global Attitudes & Trends

(www.pewglobal.org)

The World Bank, Data

(http://data.worldbank.org)

2 The Modern State

South Sudanese parade their new flag shortly before the referendum in January 2011 that granted them independence from neighboring Sudan at the conclusion of a long civil war. The world's newest state fell into civil war in December 2013 when the president accused the vice president, his chief political rival, of trying to overthrow the government. A cease-fire was declared and the vice president returned to the government in April 2016, though tensions remained high. New states are almost always quite fragile, as South Sudan demonstrates.
REUTERS/Benedicte Desrus

Key Questions

- What are the common characteristics of all modern states, and how do these characteristics give their rulers power?
- In what ways do the characteristics of modern states limit power?
- Why are some states stronger than others? Why do some states fail completely?

Learning Objectives

After reading chapter 2, you should be able to do the following:

2.1 Discuss the roles of sovereignty, territory, legitimacy, and bureaucracy in modern states

2.2 Detail the historical origins of modern states

2.3 Explain the different characteristics of strong, weak, and failed states

Political development—the origin and development of the modern state—is the starting point for the study of comparative politics. What do we mean by "the modern state"? In everyday language, *state* is often used interchangeably with both *country* and *nation*, but political scientists use the term in a more specific way. *Country,* the most common term in daily discourse, is not used in political science because its meaning is too vague. *Nation,* which we discuss in depth in chapter 4, refers to a group of people who perceive themselves as sharing a sense of belonging and who often have a common language, culture, and set of traditions. *State,* on the other hand, does not refer directly to a group of people or their sense of who they are, though most states are closely related to particular nations. One way to think about the state is to ask how and when we "see" or contact the state. Capitols, courts of law, police headquarters, and social service agencies are all part of the state. If you have attended a public school, gotten a driver's license, received a traffic ticket, or paid taxes, you've come into contact with the state, which provides public goods such as roads and schools, enforces laws, and raises revenue via taxes. These observations lead to a useful, basic definition of the **state** as an ongoing administrative apparatus that develops and administers laws and generates and implements public policies in a specific territory.

The *ongoing* nature of the state sets it apart from both a *regime* and a *government.* Regimes are types of government such as a liberal democracy or fascism (see chapter 3). Americans use *government* and *state* interchangeably, but "governments" are transient. They occupy and utilize the ongoing apparatus of the state temporarily, from one election to the next in a democracy. Americans often refer to governments as *administrations* (e.g., the Trump administration), but the rest of the world uses the word *government* in this context (e.g., the Johnson government of Great Britain).

Modern states have come to be an exceptionally powerful and ubiquitous means of ruling over people. Any number of groups or individuals, such as dictators, elites, or democratically elected politicians, can rule through the state's institutions. Identifying and understanding the key features of the state help us analyze how governments rule and how much power they have. Looking at how much institutional apparatus a particular country has developed and how effectively that apparatus can be deployed (Are people really paying taxes? Are neighborhoods run by drug lords or the police?) can help identify the effective limits

state: An ongoing administrative apparatus that develops and administers laws and generates and implements public policies in a specific territory of official rule. States with stronger institutions are stronger states and give their rulers greater power.

In addition to understanding what the state is and how it operates, comparativists study its origins and evolution: Why did modern states become so universal? Where did they first emerge, and why did strong states develop sooner in some places and later or not at all in others? Though they vary widely, all modern states share some basic characteristics that set them apart from earlier forms of political organization.

Characteristics of the Modern State

Modern states are complex entities with many facets. Some are huge, some are tiny, some are powerful, and some are quite weak. They all share four key characteristics, though, that we can use to identify modern states and distinguish them from other types of political entities: a claim over territory, external and internal sovereignty, a claim to legitimacy, and bureaucracy.

Territory

The first characteristic of the modern state is so obvious that you might overlook it. A state must have **territory**, an area with clearly defined borders to which it lays claim. In fact, borders are one of the places where the state is "seen" most clearly via the signs that welcome visitors and the immigration officers who enforce border regulations.

The size of modern states varies enormously, from Russia, the geographically largest at 6,520,800 square miles, to the seventeen states with territories of less than 200 square miles each. The differences between vast Russia and tiny Tuvalu are significant, but territories and borders help both claim the status of state.

A glance at any map of the world shows no territories not enclosed by state borders, except Antarctica. Many states have inhabited their present borders for so long that we may think of them as being relatively fixed. In truth, the numbers of states and their borders continue to change frequently. The most recent examples are Kosovo's independence from Serbia in 2008 and South Sudan's independence from Sudan in 2011. Border changes and the creation of new states, as both these examples attest, are often attempts to make states coincide more closely with nations, groups with a shared identity that often seek to share a distinct territory and government (that is, a state).

External and Internal Sovereignty

territory: An area with clearly defined borders to which a state lays claim

external sovereignty: Sovereignty relative to outside powers that is legally recognized in international law

internal sovereignty: The sole authority within a territory capable of making and enforcing laws and policies

To have real, effective **external sovereignty**, that is, sovereignty relative to outside powers, a state must be able to defend its territory and not be overly dependent on another power. Governments that lack sovereignty are not truly modern states. Examples include the Japanese-backed and controlled state Manchukuo (Manchuria) from 1932 to 1945, the collaborationist Vichy government in France during World War II, and all colonial states; although they had a local government and clearly defined territory, they were not sovereign states because their most crucial decisions were subject to external authority.

Modern states also strive for **internal sovereignty**—that is, to be the sole authority within a territory capable of making and enforcing laws and policies.

IN CONTEXT

New States and the United Nations

Since 1959, the vast majority of new member states in the United Nations (UN) have been admitted after declaring independence. In the 1960s and 1970s, most newly admitted states were former colonies. In the 1990s, most newly admitted states were the result of the breakup of the Soviet Union and other Eastern-Bloc countries. New UN members continue to be added in the twenty-first century:

- 1945–1959: Eighty-one member states admitted.
- 1960–1969: Forty-two member states admitted.
- 1970–1979: Twenty-five member states admitted.
- 1980–1989: Six member states admitted.
- 1990–1999: Thirty-one member states admitted.
- 2000–2009: Five member states admitted.
- 2010– : One member state admitted.

The example of Kosovo reminds us of another important aspect of territoriality: states exist within an international system of other states (see Table 2.1 on level of state recognition). It is not enough for a state to claim a defined territory; other states must also recognize that claim, even if they dispute a particular border. Political scientists call internationally recognized states sovereign. Essentially, a state achieves **sovereignty** when it is legally recognized by the family of states as the sole legitimate governing authority within its territory and as the legal equal of other states. This legal recognition is the minimal standard for external sovereignty. Legal external sovereignty, which entails being given the same vote in world affairs as all other states, is vital for sovereignty. ●

They must defend their internal sovereignty against domestic groups that challenge it, just as they must defend it externally. Internal challenges typically take the form of a declaration of independence from some part of the state's territory and perhaps even civil war. States rarely are willing to accept such an act of defiance. From the American Civil War in the 1860s to Ukraine in the face of a Russian-supported secession movement, most states use all the means in their power to preserve their sovereignty over their recognized territories.

States try to enforce their sovereignty by claiming, in the words of German sociologist Max Weber, a "monopoly on the legitimate use of physical force" (1970). Put simply, the state claims to be the only entity within its territory that has the right to hold a gun to your head and tell you what to do. Some governments claim a virtually unlimited right to use force when and as they choose. At least in theory, liberal democracies observe strict guidelines under which the use of force is permissible. For example, law enforcement can be called in when a citizen runs a red light or fails to pay taxes but not when she criticizes government policy. All states, though, insist on the right to use force to ensure their internal as well as external sovereignty. As one political philosopher reportedly said in response to students who complained about the university calling in police during a demonstration, "The difference between fascism and democracy is not whether the police are called, but when."

sovereignty: Quality of a state in which it is legally recognized by the family of states as the sole legitimate governing authority within its territory and as the legal equal of other states

Sovereignty does not mean, however, that a state is all-powerful. Real internal and external sovereignty vary greatly and depend on many factors. Because the United States is wealthy and controls much territory, its sovereignty results

TABLE 2.1

The Shifting Borders of Modern States: Not Recognized, Limited Recognition, and Majority Recognition States

NOT RECOGNIZED		
STATE	**DISPUTED SINCE**	**STATUS**
Nagorno-Karabakh	1991	Claimed by Azerbaijan.
Somaliland	1991	Claimed by Somalia.
Transnistria	1990	Claimed by Moldova.
LIMITED RECOGNITION		
STATE	**DISPUTED SINCE**	**STATUS**
Abkhazia	2008	Recognized only by 5 countries: Russian Federation, Nicaragua, Nauru, Syria, Venezuela.
Kosovo	2008	Recognized by 113 countries.
South Ossetia	2008	Recognized only by 4 countries: Russian Federation, Nicaragua, Nauru, Venezuela.
Palestine	1988	Recognized as a proposed state by 137 UN member states.
Turkish Republic of Northern Cyprus (TRNC)	1983	Recognized only by Turkey.
Sahrawi Arab Democratic Republic (SADR)	1976	Recognized by 84 UN member states.
Republic of China (Taiwan) (ROC)	1949	Recognized by 20 countries.
MAJORITY RECOGNITION		
STATE	**DISPUTED SINCE**	**STATUS**
Cyprus	1974	Recognized by all countries except Turkey.
People's Republic of China (PRC)	1949	Not recognized by the Republic of China (Taiwan); the PRC does not accept diplomatic relations with the 19 other UN member states that recognize the ROC.
Israel	1948	Not recognized by 25 countries; no diplomatic relationship with 8 countries.
North Korea	1948	Not recognized by France, South Korea, and Japan.
South Korea	1948	Not recognized by North Korea.

in much greater power than does the sovereignty of Vanuatu, even though both are recognized as legitimate sovereigns over a clear territory. Wealthier states can defend their territories from attack better than poorer and weaker ones, and they can also more effectively ensure that their citizens comply with their laws. Even the United States, though, cannot completely control its borders, as the undocumented immigrants and illegal narcotics crossing its long border with Mexico attest.

The United States Military and Border Patrol agents secure the United States-Mexico border on November 25, 2018, near San Diego, California after hundreds of migrants tried to breach a border fence from the Mexican city of Tijuana. Migration raises issues of territoriality and external sovereignty, but modern states have also committed themselves to recognizing the human rights of migrants and refugees. Where and how to draw the line in controlling who can enter the country and how has become a hot political debate in the United States as well as Europe.
Sandy Huffaker/AFP/Getty Images

Legitimacy

The ability to enforce sovereignty more fully comes not only from wealth but also from legitimacy. Weber argued that a state claims a "monopoly on the *legitimate* use of physical force" [emphasis added]. **Legitimacy** is the recognized right to rule. This right has at least two sides: the claims that states and others make about why they have a right to rule, and the empirical fact of whether their populations accept or at least tolerate this claimed right. Virtually all modern states argue at length for particular normative bases for their legitimacy, and these claims are the basis for the various kinds of regimes in the world today (a subject explored in chapter 3).

Weber described three types of legitimate authority: traditional, charismatic, and rational-legal. **Traditional legitimacy** is the right to rule based on a society's long-standing patterns and practices. The European "divine right of kings" and the blessing of ancestors over the king in many precolonial African societies are examples of this. **Charismatic legitimacy** is the right to rule based on personal virtue, heroism, sanctity, or other extraordinary characteristics. Wildly popular leaders of revolutions, such as Mao Zedong in his early years in power, have charismatic legitimacy; people recognize their authority to rule because they trust and believe these individuals to be exceptional. **Rational-legal legitimacy** is the right to rule of leaders who are selected according to an accepted set of laws. Leaders who come to power via electoral processes and rule according to a set of laws, such as a constitution, are the chief examples of this. Weber argued that rational-legal legitimacy distinguishes modern rule from its predecessors, but he recognized that in practice most legitimate authority is a combination of the three types. For example, modern democratically elected leaders may achieve office and rule on the basis of rational-legal processes, but a traditional status or personal charisma may help them win elections and may enhance their legitimacy in office.

Legitimacy enhances a state's sovereignty. Modern states often control an overwhelming amount of coercive power, but its use is expensive and difficult. States cannot maintain effective internal sovereignty in a large, modern society

legitimacy: The recognized right to rule

traditional legitimacy: The right to rule based on a society's long-standing patterns and practices

charismatic legitimacy: The right to rule based on personal virtue, heroism, sanctity, or other extraordinary characteristics

rational-legal legitimacy: The right of leaders to rule based on their selection according to an accepted set of laws, standards, or procedures

solely through the constant use of force. Legitimacy, whatever its basis, enhances sovereignty at a much lower cost. If most citizens obey the government because they believe it has a right to rule, then little force will be necessary to maintain order. This is an example of the third dimension of power we discussed in chapter 1. For this reason, regimes proclaim their legitimacy and spend a great deal of effort trying to convince their citizens of it, especially when their legitimacy is brought into serious question. As Paul Collier (2017) noted, "Where power is seen as legitimate, the cost of citizen compliance with government is reduced. In the absence of legitimacy, three outcomes are possible. In repression, the state incurs the high costs necessary to enforce its decisions on citizens. In conflict, the state attempts this process but is not strong enough to prevent violent opposition. In theater, the state abandons the attempt to impose its well, merely mimicking the actions of a functional government."

Where modern states overlap with nations, national identity can be a powerful source of legitimacy. This is not always the case, however, and most modern states must find additional ways to cultivate the allegiance of their inhabitants. They usually attempt to gain legitimacy based on some claim of representation or service to their citizens. The relationship between states and citizens is central to modern politics, and chapter 3 addresses it at length. We explore the contentious relationship among states, nations, and other identity groups more fully in chapter 4.

Bureaucracy

Modern **bureaucracy**, meaning a large set of appointed officials whose function is to implement laws, is the final important characteristic of the state. In contemporary societies, the state plays many complicated roles. It must collect revenue and use it to maintain a military, pave roads, build schools, and provide retirement pensions, all of which require a bureaucracy. Weber saw bureaucracy as a central part of modern, rational-legal legitimacy, since in theory individuals obtain official positions in a modern bureaucracy via a rational-legal process of appointment and are restricted to certain tasks by a set of laws. Like legitimacy, effective bureaucracy strengthens sovereignty. A bureaucracy that efficiently carries out laws, collects taxes, and expends revenues as directed by the central authorities enhances the state's power. As we discuss further below, weak legitimacy and weak bureaucracy are two key causes of state weakness in the contemporary world.

In summary, the modern state is an ongoing administrative apparatus that develops and administers laws and generates and implements public policies in a specific territory. It has effective external and internal sovereignty, a basis of legitimacy, and a capable bureaucracy. As we argue below, no state has all of these characteristics perfectly; the extent to which particular states have these characteristics determines how strong or weak they are.

Historical Origins of Modern States

Now that we have clarified what a state is, we need to understand the diverse historical origins of modern states, which greatly influence how strong they are as well as their relationships to their citizens and nations. A world of modern states controlling virtually every square inch of territory and every person on the globe may seem natural today, but it is a fairly recent development. The modern state arose first in Europe between the fifteenth and eighteenth centuries. The concept spread via conquest, colonialism, and then decolonization, becoming truly universal only with the independence of most African states in the 1960s.

bureaucracy: A large set of appointed officials whose function is to implement the laws of the state, as directed by the executive

FIGURE 2.1

The Anatomy of a State

States

A state is an administrative entity that endures over time, develops laws, creates public policies for its citizens, and implements those policies and laws.

A state must have a legitimate and recognized claim to a defined territory that forms its borders and legitimate and recognized authority to govern within its territory.

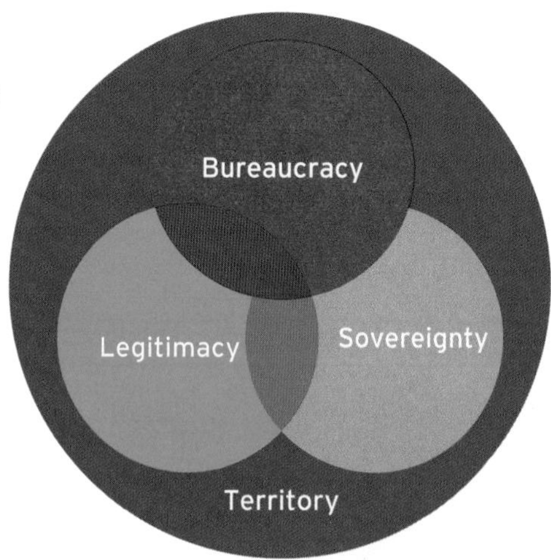

It also must have the institutions needed to administer the state's laws and policies.

Nations

Sometimes the people of a nation may identify as belonging to a particular state and thereby enhance the legitimacy of the state.

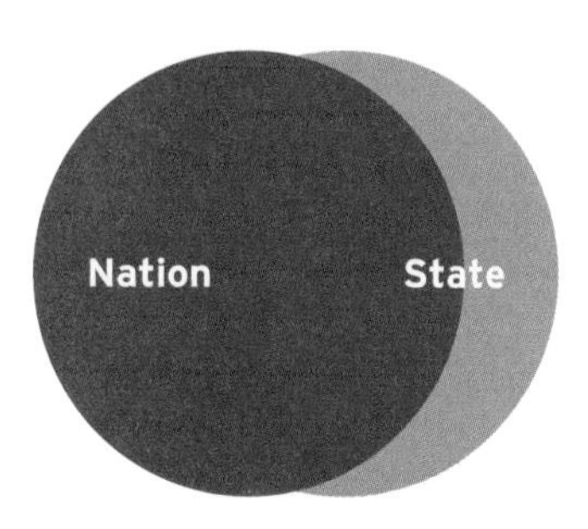

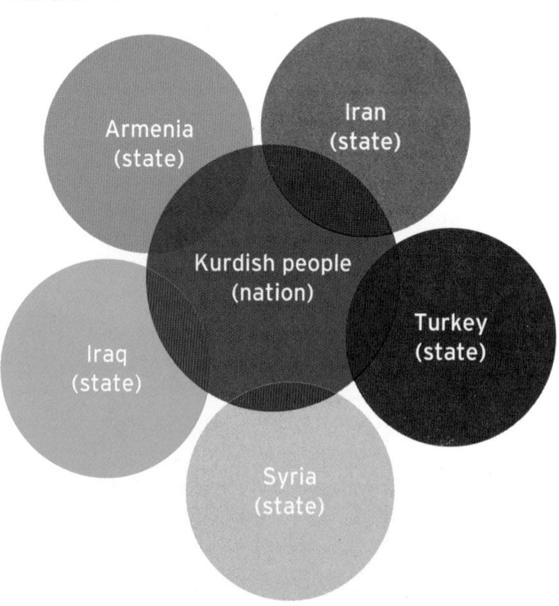

Some nations strongly overlap with states.

But states may contain one or more nation, or a national movement or a group within a state might contest the state's legitimacy. Some nations exist across a number of state borders or may take up only part of a state.

For instance, the Kurdish people live across the borders of at least five states: Armenia, Iran, Iraq, Turkey, and Syria.

Somaliland: Internal Versus External Sovereignty

Somaliland is an interesting recent case of disputed sovereignty. It is a state that has achieved almost unquestioned internal sovereignty, a stable (albeit uncertain) constitutional democracy, and a growing economy. No other state recognizes it, however, so it has no international, legal external sovereignty. This unusual outcome is a result of the collapse of the larger state of Somalia and the international efforts to resolve that country's civil war. Somaliland, the northernmost region of Somalia, originally was a separate colony from the rest of what is now Somalia; it fell under British control while the rest of the country was an Italian colony. In 1960 the former British colony gained independence for a few days but then quickly agreed to become part of the larger state of Somalia, which had also just gained independence.

When Somali dictator Siad Barre was deposed in 1991, the rebel movement in Somaliland declared

MAP 2.1

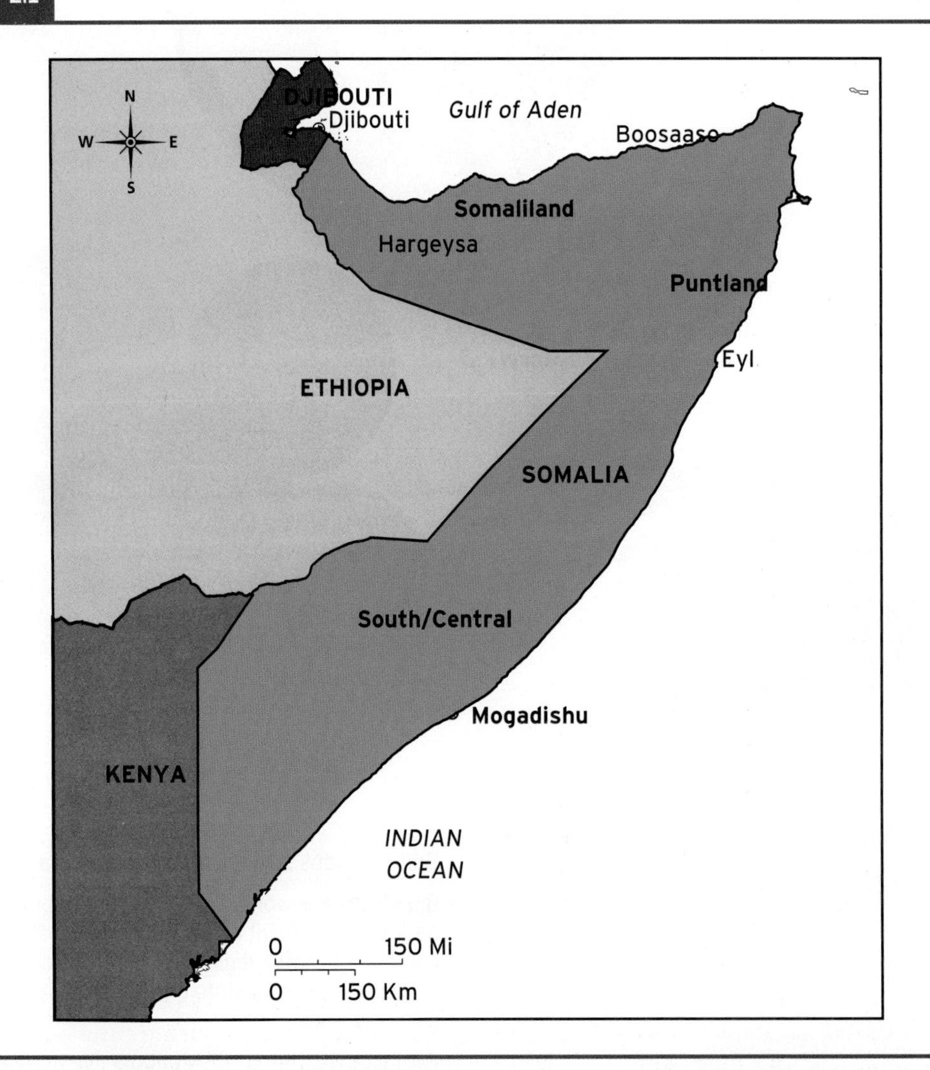

Source: William Clark, Matt Golder, and Sona Nadenichek Golder, Map 4.1, *Principles of Comparative Politics*, 2e, p. 92.

the region independent within a few months, restoring its colonial borders. A conference of the elders of all the major clans of Somaliland in 1993 produced a new government with a parliament modeled after traditional Somali institutions, with representation based on clan membership. In 2001 a referendum approved a new constitution that was fully democratic, with a bicameral legislature: one house is filled by directly elected representatives and the other by clan elders. The country held successful democratic elections for president, parliament, and local governments in 2005 and 2010. A subsequent presidential election, originally scheduled for 2015, was belatedly but successfully held in fall 2017, although parliamentary elections are now a decade overdue.

Despite growing concerns about its democracy, Somaliland's economy has grown substantially, based mainly on exports of livestock to the Middle East and money sent home by Somalis living and working around the world. The government has established much better social services and greater security than exist in the rest of war-wracked Somalia. Recently, oil has been discovered in its territory, which could provide much needed revenue to strengthen the state but could also create what political scientists call a "resource curse" (see p. 47), which would weaken the state by fueling corruption.

Because it has no official recognition from other governments, Somaliland receives very limited foreign aid, has only one embassy in its capital (that of neighboring Ethiopia), and sends no ambassadors abroad. Most of the world fears that officially recognizing Somaliland's external sovereignty will encourage other regions of Somalia to attempt to break away as well, so recognition of the de facto state, expected eventually by many, awaits resolution of the larger civil war in Somalia. Ironically, it looks far more like a modern state than the official government of the larger Somalia, which is internationally recognized as a sovereign state but only partially controls a modest portion of its territory. Indeed, some observers argue that Somaliland's lack of recognition has forced it to create a stronger state than it might have otherwise in order to survive militarily and financially, and the search for international recognition has become a strong basis for a growing sense of nationalism (Richards and Smith 2015).

Modern States in Europe

Prior to approximately 1500, Europe consisted of **feudal states**, which were distinct from modern states in several ways. Most important, they neither claimed nor had undisputed sovereignty. Feudal rule involved multiple and overlapping sovereignties. At the heart of it was the relationship between lord and vassal in which the lord gave a vassal the right to rule a piece of land known as a fief and tax the people living on it, in exchange for political and military loyalty. The system often involved several layers of these relationships, from the highest and most powerful king in a region to the local lord. The loyalty of the peasants—the bulk of the population who had virtually no rights—followed that of their lord. At any given time, all individuals were subject to the sovereignty of not only their immediate lord but also at least one higher lord and often others, and that loyalty could and did change. In addition, the Catholic Church claimed a separate and universal religious sovereignty over all and gave religious legitimacy to the kings and lords who recognized church authority.

By the fifteenth century, feudalism was giving way to **absolutism**, rule by a single monarch who claimed complete, exclusive sovereignty over a territory and its people. Absolutist rulers won battles for power among feudal lords by using superior economic and military resources to vanquish their rivals. Scholars debate the extent to which the absolutist state was a truly modern state, but it certainly introduced a number of the modern state's key elements. Perry Anderson (1974)

feudal states: Premodern states in Europe in which power in a territory was divided among multiple and overlapping lords claiming sovereignty

absolutism: Rule by a single monarch who claims complete, exclusive power and sovereignty over a territory and its people

argued that the absolutist state included at least rudimentary forms of a standing army and diplomatic service, both of which are crucial for external sovereignty; centralized bureaucracy; systematic taxation; and policies to encourage economic development. It took centuries for these to develop into fully modern forms, however. Legitimacy remained based largely on tradition and heredity, and most people remained subjects with few legal rights. Perhaps of greatest importance, the state was not conceived of as a set of ongoing institutions separate from the monarch. Rather, as Louis XIV of France famously declared, *"L'état, c'est moi"* (The state, it is me).

The competition among absolutist states to preserve external sovereignty reduced their number from about five hundred sovereign entities in Europe in 1500 to around fifty modern states today. The states that survived were those that had developed more effective systems of taxation, more efficient bureaucracies, and stronger militaries. Along the way, political leaders realized that their subjects' loyalty (legitimacy) was of great benefit, so they began the process of expanding public education and shifting from the use of Latin or French in official circles to the local vernacular so that rulers and ruled could communicate directly, thus adding a new dimension to the rulers' legitimacy. This long process ultimately helped create modern nations, most of which had emerged by the mid-nineteenth century.

The truly modern state emerged as the state came to be seen as separate from an individual ruler. The state retained its claim to absolute sovereignty, but the powers of individual officials, ultimately including the supreme ruler, were increasingly limited. A political philosophy that came to be known as liberalism, which we discuss in greater depth in chapter 3, provided the theoretical justification and argument for limiting the power of officials to ensure the rights of individuals. The common people were ultimately transformed from subjects into citizens of the state. Bellwether events in this history included the Glorious Revolution in Great Britain in 1688, the French Revolution of 1789, and a series of revolutions that established new democratic republics in 1848.

The relationship between lord and vassal was the heart of the feudal political order. This fifteenth-century work shows peasants paying taxes in the form of money and livestock to their lord. Peasants were born with duties to their lord, and their legal ties to their land gave them no choice but to obey him.
The Granger Collection, NYC

Premodern States Outside Europe

Outside Europe, a wide variety of premodern states existed, but none took a fully modern form. The Chinese Empire ruled a vast territory for centuries and was perhaps the closest thing to a modern state anywhere in the premodern world (including in Europe). African precolonial kingdoms sometimes ruled large areas as well, but their rule was typically conceived of as extending over people rather than a precisely defined territory, having greater sovereignty closer to the capital and less sovereignty farther away. Virtually all premodern empires included multiple or overlapping layers of sovereignty and did not include a modern sense of citizenship.

The Export of the Modern State

Europe exported the modern state to the rest of the world through colonial conquest, beginning with the Americas in the sixteenth century. The earliest colonies in the Americas were ruled by European absolutist states that were not fully modern themselves. Over time, European settlers in the colonies began to identify their interests as distinct from the monarch's and to question the legitimacy of rule by distant sovereigns. The first rebellion against colonial rule produced the United States. The second major rebellion came at the hands of black slaves in Haiti in 1793, which led to the first abolition of slavery in the world and to Haitian independence in 1804. By the 1820s and 1830s, most of the settler populations of Central and South America had rebelled as well. As in the United States, the leaders of these rebellions were mostly wealthy, landholding elites. This landed elite often relied on state force to keep peasant and slave labor working on its behalf, so while some early efforts at democracy emerged after independence, most Central and South American states ultimately went through many decades of strongman rule over relatively weak states. Independence nonetheless began the process of developing modern states.

The colonial origins of early modern states in the Americas created distinct challenges from those faced by early European states. European states went through several centuries of developing a sense of national identity. In the Americas, the racial divisions produced by colonization, European settlement, and slavery meant that none of the newly independent states had a widely shared sense of national identity. Where slavery continued to exist, as in the United States, citizenship was restricted to the "free" and therefore primarily white (and exclusively male) population. Where significant Native American populations had survived, as in Peru and Guatemala, they continued to be politically excluded and economically marginalized by the primarily white, landholding elite. This historical context would make the ability of the new states to establish strong national identities difficult and would produce ongoing racial and ethnic problems, explored further in chapter 4.

After most of the American colonies achieved independence, growing economic and military rivalry among Britain, France, and Germany spurred a new round of colonization, first in Asia and then in Africa. This time, far fewer European settlers were involved. The vast majority of the populations of these new colonies remained indigenous; they were ruled over by a thin layer of European officials. Colonizers effectively destroyed the political power of precolonial indigenous states but did not exterminate the population en masse. Challenges to this new wave of colonialism were quick and numerous. The independence of the first-wave colonies and the end of slavery raised questions about European subjugation of African and Asian peoples. Colonization in this context had to be justified as

A British colonial official arrives with his camel carriage and entourage at an office in the Punjab, India, in 1865. European colonial states in Africa and Asia consisted of a small number of European officials, with military force behind them, ruling over the local population. To rule, they had to rely on local leaders and staff, who collaborated with colonial rule.
SSPL/Getty Images

bringing "advanced" European civilization and Christianity to "backward" peoples. Education was seen as a key part of this "civilizing" mission. It had a more practical aspect as well: with limited European settlement, colonial rulers needed indigenous subjects to serve in the bureaucracies of the colonial states. These chosen few were educated in colonial languages and customs and became local elites, although European officials remained at the top of the colonial hierarchy and exercised nearly unlimited power. In time, the indigenous elites began to see themselves as equal to the ruling Europeans and chafed at colonial limits on their political position and economic advancement. They became the key leaders of the movements for independence, which finally succeeded after World War II. By the 1960s, modern states covered virtually every square inch of the globe.

Postcolonial countries faced huge obstacles to consolidating modern states. Although they enjoyed legal external sovereignty and had inherited at least minimal infrastructure from colonial bureaucracies, legitimacy and internal sovereignty remained problematic for most. The colonial powers established borders with little regard for precolonial political boundaries, and political institutions that had no relationship to precolonial norms or institutions. The movements for independence created genuine enthusiasm for the new nations, but the colonizers had previously tried to inhibit a strong sense of national unity, and typically grouped many religious and linguistic groups together under one colonial state. Political loyalty was often divided among numerous groups, including the remnants of precolonial states. Finally, huge disparities in wealth, education, and access to power between the elite and the majority of the population reduced popular support for the state. All of this meant the new states were mostly very weak versions of the modern state.

Was ISIS a State?

MAP 2.2

ISIS Territory at Its Height, 2015

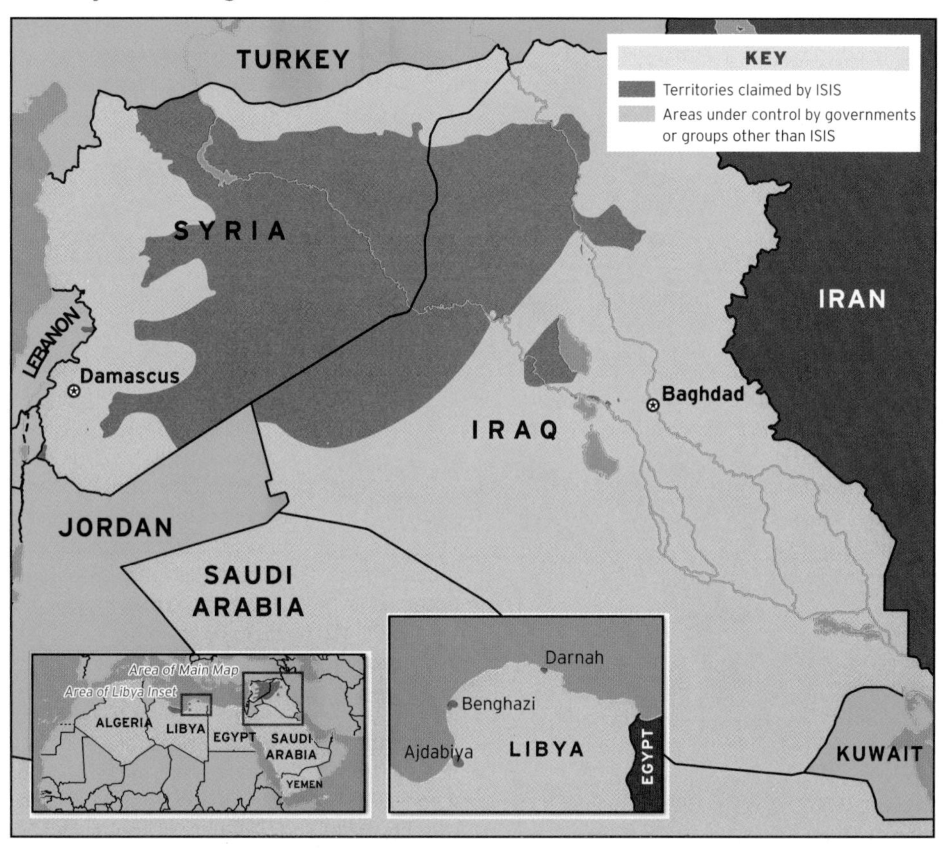

On June 29, 2014, Abu Bakr al-Baghdadi, the head of the Islamic State in Iraq and al-Sham (ISIS), declared the creation of a new caliphate, an Islamic state carved by force out of parts of Syria and Iraq. At its height in late 2015, it had effective control over as many as six million people in a territory the size of Belgium, as Map 2.2 shows. By July 2017, it had lost almost all of its territory, including all major cities, militarily defeated by a combination of U.S., Russian, Syrian, Kurdish, and Iraqi forces. Nonetheless, the three-year caliphate that controlled substantial territory raised an interesting question: ISIS is clearly a terrorist organization, but from 2014 to 2017, was it also a state?

Charles Tilly, one of the foremost scholars of the rise of modern states in Europe, famously declared that "war made the state, and the state made war" (1975, 42). War or the threat of war forced leaders of early modern, European states to develop taxation and conscription, which in turn required functioning bureaucracies and some sense of legitimacy. More recently, Rosa Brooks (2015) noted that "[s]tate formation . . . has always been a bloody business." ISIS is infamously brutal, but brutality alone cannot rule it out as a state. So at its height, how did it fare in terms of our core components of statehood: territory, sovereignty, legitimacy, and bureaucracy?

(Continued)

(Continued)

The proclamation of the caliphate came after ISIS had gained control over significant amounts of territory in Syria and Iraq. Much of ISIS's territory, however, was only nominally under its control. It actually administered policies in only a handful of significant cities along key roadways, while having loose control and free range of movement over the mostly uninhabited spaces in between. It also had eight affiliates around the world, but only the affiliate in Libya controlled significant territory of its own, which it lost in December 2016.

Within its territory, at least in the key cities, ISIS did exercise internal sovereignty. It was divided into twenty provinces (twelve in Syria and Iraq plus the eight affiliates elsewhere), each with its recognized leadership. In its heartland, it gained revenue via taxing the local population in various ways; a report after ISIS's fall said, "Ledgers, receipt books and monthly budgets describe how the militants monetized every inch of territory they conquered, taxing every bushel of wheat, every liter of sheep's milk and every watermelon sold at markets they controlled" (Callimachi 2018). It also confiscated land from its political and religious enemies to rent to its supporters, both to maintain their support and gain revenue from the rental.

External sovereignty is much less clear. ISIS waged war in both Iraq and Syria and was attacked on multiple fronts. No UN member recognized it and, in fact, ISIS itself was uninterested in such recognition. Its ideology rejects the modern state system, proclaiming that all Muslims should be united in one caliphate under ISIS leadership, a re-creation of the medieval, Islamic caliphate. Like some regimes before it (Nazi Germany comes to mind), it is inherently expansionist. ISIS's failure to recognize the international state system suggests the system's members would never recognize it.

ISIS did, however, establish an extensive, efficient administrative bureaucracy beyond just military and tax collection: "It ran a marriage office that oversaw medical examinations to ensure that couples could have children. It issued birth certificates—printed on Islamic State stationery—to babies born under the caliphate's black flag. It even ran its own D.M.V." (Callimachi 2018). After it gained control of an area, it demanded that local officials of the Iraqi bureaucracy get back to work, using them to implement new policies but relying on their bureaucratic knowledge to do so. After the caliphate collapsed, those who lived under the brutal regime were glad it was gone, but some noted that ISIS picked up the garbage more efficiently than the Iraqi government had.

ISIS based its legitimacy on its religious claims. The last Islamic caliphate was the Ottoman Empire, dismantled by Western powers at the end of World War I. ISIS's proclamation of the new caliphate inspired thousands of Islamist fighters from around the world to join its ranks. The brutality with which it treated both its external enemies and any of its "citizens" who dared question it or try to flee was justified in the name of establishing the caliphate. Its leader and other ideologues cite Muslim scripture frequently, claiming they were re-creating the original, medieval Muslim government and spurning any connection to modernity. While most of the population under its control shared ISIS's Sunni Muslim tradition, there is no indication they shared its specific ideology or accepted its brutality any more than they would brutality visited on them by any other "state." ISIS has aspects of effective administration of key state tasks, but legitimacy can rarely be based on that alone.

So was the Islamic State really a "state" in political science terms? The answer has to be "only partially." It consciously established and tried to expand aspects of statehood: territorial control and internal sovereignty, a functioning bureaucracy, and a claim to legitimacy. Indeed, its claim to the caliphate—an Islamic form of statehood—is central to its legitimacy and popularity among radical Islamists. While it provided some political goods such as services, security—individual and territorial—is the most universal political good any state must provide, and ISIS failed on that. Its rejection of the international system and its brutality mean it was a state of constant war, lasting only about three years.

Nigeria illustrates these trends well. Like most African states, it is literally a product of colonialism: prior to colonial conquest, its territory was home to numerous and varied societies. The northern half was primarily Muslim and ruled by Islamic emirs (religious rulers) based in twelve separate city-states. The southern half consisted of many societies, the two biggest of which were the Yoruba and Igbo. The Yoruba lived in a series of kingdoms, sometimes politically united and sometimes not, whereas the Igbo were governed only at the most local level by councils of elders; they had no kings or chiefs. The British conquest began around 1870. The colonial state required educated natives to help staff its bureaucracy. In the south, Christianity and Western education expanded rapidly; southerners filled most of the positions in the colonial state. The northern emirs, on the other hand, convinced colonial authorities to keep Christian education out in order to preserve Islam, on which their legitimacy was based. This meant that northerners received far less Western education and therefore fewer positions in the colonial bureaucracy. Because military service required less education, northerners tended to fill the ranks of the colonial (and therefore postcolonial) army.

The educated elite became the leadership of the nationalist movement after World War II. Given the history of divisions in the country, it is no surprise that the nationalist movement was split from the start. The British ultimately negotiated a new government for an independent Nigeria that would be federal, with three regions corresponding to the three major ethnic groups and political parties formed mainly along regional and ethnic lines. As in virtually all African countries, the new government was quite fragile. Nigerians had no prior experience with the British-style electoral democracy they were handed and little reason to believe it would be a superior system for them. In response to fraudulent elections, a section of the army, led primarily by Igbo officers, overthrew the elected government in January 1966 in the first of six military coups. A countercoup six months later brought a new, northern-dominated government to power, but the Igbo military leadership refused to accept it. In January 1967, they declared their region the independent state of Biafra. A three-year civil war ensued that cost the lives of a million people. The central government defeated the separatists in Biafra and reestablished a single state in 1970. Interrupted by only four years of elected rule, the military governed the reunited Nigeria until 1999. Although all military leaders pledged to reduce corruption and improve development, the discovery and expansion of oil production overwhelmed all other economic activity and fueled both corruption and the desire of those in power to stay there. A weak state grew ever weaker and more corrupt.

In 1999 the military finally bowed to popular and international pressure and carried out the country's first free and fair election in twenty years. Democracy has become the basis of legitimacy since then, but that democracy in practice is very imperfect. The state remains one of the weakest and most corrupt in the world.

Strong, Weak, and Failed States

The modern state as we have defined it is what Weber called an **ideal type**, a model of what the purest version of something might be. Nothing in reality perfectly matches an ideal type; no state indisputably enjoys complete external or internal sovereignty, absolute legitimacy, a monopoly on the use of force, and a completely effective and efficient bureaucracy. Some states, however, are clearly much closer to this ideal than others. States use their sovereignty, territory, legitimacy, and bureaucracy to provide what political scientist Robert Rotberg (2004) called "political goods" to their population. Political goods include security; the rule of law; a functioning legal system; and infrastructure such as roads, public education, and health care. Citizens also expect modern states to pursue economic policies that will enhance their well-being, though exactly what those policies ought

ideal type: A model of what the purest version of something might be

to be is quite controversial. While some political goods, such as basic security, are universally recognized, others, such as specific economic policies, are the core of many contemporary political debates around the world, which we will investigate in subsequent chapters.

A **strong state** is generally capable of providing political goods to its citizens, while a **weak state** can only do so partially. State strength, however, exists on a continuum, with no state being perfectly strong in all conceivable categories. Changes in state strength can also go in both directions. Francis Fukuyama (2014), for instance, argues that the U.S. state has weakened in the last several decades due mainly to what he calls "gift exchange" between legislators, lobbyists, and campaign donors that weakens the state's ability to make independent decisions based on some sense of the public interest. As Table 2.2 shows, stronger states tend to be wealthier and consume a larger share of economic resources; they are simply economically bigger than weak states. They also are less corrupt, indicating the presence of stronger bureaucracies, and tend to be more legitimate. Weak states, on the other hand, are often characterized by what Thomas Risse (2015) termed "limited statehood": they provide some political goods widely but others only in certain areas of the country. Other actors—local strongmen, religious institutions,

strong state: A state that is generally capable of providing political goods to its citizens

weak state: A state that only partially provides political goods to its citizen

TABLE 2.2

The Modern State

COUNTRY	APPROXIMATE YEAR MODERN STATE ESTABLISHED	FRAGILE STATES INDEX, 2019		GDP PER CAPITA (PPP)	GOVERNMENT EXPENDITURE AS % OF GDP	CORRUPTION PERCEPTION INDEX, 2018 (0 = HIGHLY CORRUPT, 100 = HIGHLY CLEAN)	LEGITIMACY (0 = LEAST LEGITIMATE, 10 = MOST LEGITIMATE)
		RANK AMONG 178 COUNTRIES (1 = MOST FRAGILE, 178 = LEAST FRAGILE)	SCORE (12 = LOWEST RISK OF STATE FAILURE, 120 = HIGHEST RISK OF STATE FAILURE)				
Brazil	1889	83	71.8	$15,600	38.6%	35	4.68
China	1949	88	71.1	$16,700	31.6%	39	5.36
Germany	1871	167	24.7	$50,800	43.9%	80	5.84
India	1947	74	74.4	$7,200	27.5%	41	5.21
Iran	1925	52	83	$20,100	18.5%	28	2.04
Japan	1867	157	34.3	$42,900	38.7%	73	6.13
Mexico	1924	98	69.7	$19,900	26.9%	28	3.50
Nigeria	1960	14	98.5	$5,900	10.8%	27	data unavailable
Russia	1917	73	74.7	$27,900	35.4%	28	3.18
United Kingdom	1707	155	36.7	$44,300	41.6%	80	6.21
United States	1787	153	38	$59,800	37.8%	71	5.83

Sources: Fragile state data are from the Fund for Peace, 2019. Data on GDP per capita are from the *CIA World Factbook* (https://www.cia.gov/library/publications/resources/the-world-factbook/index.html). Data on government expenditure as percentage of GDP are from the Heritage Foundation's 2019 Index of Economic Freedom (http://www.heritage.org/index/ranking). Data on corruption are from Transparency International, 2015. Data on state legitimacy are from Bruce Gilley, "State Legitimacy: An Updated Dataset for 52 Countries," *European Journal of Political Research* 51 (2012): 693–699 (doi:10.1111/j.1475-6765.2012.02059.x).

or nongovernmental organizations (NGOs)—may substitute for a weak state in some regions, providing political goods the state cannot or will not.

A state that is so weak that it loses sovereignty over part or all of its territory is a **failed state**. Failed states make headlines—for example, Syria, the Democratic Republic of the Congo, South Sudan, and Afghanistan. Syria collapsed into civil war in 2011, though by 2019 the incumbent ruler had mostly reestablished sovereign control of the state's territory, suggesting that a (probably still weak) Syrian state would re-emerge.

Virtually all elements of state strength are interconnected. If a state lacks the resources to provide basic infrastructure and security, its legitimacy most likely will decline. Lack of resources also may mean civil servants are paid very little, which may lead to corruption and an even further decline in the quality of state services. Corruption in some bureaucracies, such as the military and border patrol, can cause a loss of security and territorial integrity. If the state cannot provide basic services, such as education, citizens will likely find alternative routes to success that may well involve illegal activity (e.g., smuggling), undermining sovereignty that much further. If the state does not apply the rule of law impartially, citizens will turn to private means to settle their disputes (mafias are a prime example of this phenomenon), threatening the state's monopoly on the legitimate use of force. Continuing patterns of lawless behavior create and reinforce the public perception that the state is weak, so weak states can become caught in a vicious cycle that is difficult to break.

Mexico demonstrates some of these problems, even though it is a middle-income country with a state far stronger than the weakest ones. Although it gained independence in 1821, a modern state was not really established until a century later, after a revolution brought the Partido Revolucionario Institucional (Institutional Revolutionary Party, or PRI) to power. It established an electoral-authoritarian regime and maintained power through systemic corruption, bribery, and intimidation. It did, however, create a functioning state that, though corrupt, made important strides in furthering literacy, access to health care, and overall

failed state: A state that is so weak that it loses effective sovereignty over part or all of its territory

Failed states make headlines around the world and have implications far beyond their borders. In Raqa, the former capital of the Islamic State in Syria, a girl walks through the rubble in 2019, two years after Kurdish-led forces overran the city, taking it back from a regime residents described as brutal. The Syrian civil war gave ISIS the opportunity to create a proto-state within its and Iraq's territory, and it produced a massive refugee crisis that has had profound effects in the European Union.
DELIL SOULEIMAN/AFP/Getty Images

economic development. It also used oil wealth and trade with the United States to achieve significant industrialization, transforming Mexico into a middle-income country, though with sharp income and regional inequality. All of this expanded the size, scope, and capability of Mexico's state.

After seventy years in power, the PRI was forced to allow real electoral competition, and in 2000, when the PRI lost the presidential election, the country became a democracy. Despite its democratization, questions over the strength of the state continue. The most critical challenge is a war among rival drug cartels that has killed an estimated 75,000 to 100,000 people in the last decade. Endemic police corruption, lack of alternative economic opportunities, and a supply of small arms from north of the border have all led to the degradation of government authority in the northern region. Various governments have alternated between military-type crackdowns that killed hundreds of people and negotiations with drug cartels to rein in the violence, none of which has worked fully. Drug cartels often bribe local officials to gain their acquiescence, undermining the state's attempts to regain control, most famously when the biggest drug kingpin escaped from prison via an elaborate tunnel dug with the obvious collaboration of prison officials. This has called into question the state's ability to keep a monopoly on the legitimate use of force for the first time since the end of the Mexican Revolution.

Why some states are strong while others are weak has long been a major question in the study of political development. Economists Douglass North and John Wallis and political scientist Barry Weingast used a rational choice institutionalist argument to address this question (2009). They argued that the earliest states were based on elite coalitions created to limit violence among themselves. Power remained very personal, as the earliest states were really just temporary agreements among competing elites, each of whom had control over the means of violence. Elites abided by these agreements in order to gain economic advantages from the absence of warfare and the ability to extract resources. Eventually, some elites negotiated agreements that recognized impersonal organizations and institutions that were separate from the individual leaders. As these developed and functioned credibly, greater specialization was possible, and distinct elites who controlled military, political, economic, and religious power emerged. This required the rule of law among elites. Together with ongoing, impersonal organizations, the rule of law allowed the possibility of a true monopoly over the use of force as individual elites gave up their control of military power. Once established among elites, such impersonal institutions and organizations could expand eventually to the rest of society.

Fukuyama (2014) argued that the continuation of this story—the development of modern states in nineteenth-century Europe—took several different paths. Some, like Prussia (which became Germany), first developed a strong bureaucracy and military in the face of external military threat and only later developed the rule of law and democratic control over the state. Others, such as the United States, saw the rule of law and relatively widespread democratic accountability develop first, resulting in political parties that became corrupt "machine politics"; a modern bureaucracy arose only after industrialization produced a middle class and business interests that demanded reforms to create a more effective government. Following Samuel Huntington (1968), Fukuyama argued that states such as Italy and Greece, which did not develop as strong states early enough, faced the problem of a politically mobilized populace without adequate economic opportunity. This led to corruption as political leaders used the state's resources to provide for their political followers rather than creating a bureaucracy based on merit and equity.

Comparativists have developed several other arguments to explain why states are weak. A common one for non-European countries is the effects of colonialism.

In most of Africa and Asia, postcolonial states were created not by negotiations among local elites but between them and the departing colonial power, and political institutions were hastily copied from the departing colonizers; the kind of elite accommodation to which North, Wallis, and Weingast (2009) pointed did not occur. Not having participated seriously in the creation of the new institutions, elites often did not see themselves as benefiting from them and therefore changed or ignored them. In Africa, postcolonial rulers, lacking functioning impersonal institutions, maintained power by distributing the state's revenue to their supporters and therefore created authoritarian regimes to narrow the number of claimants on those resources. Economic decline beginning in the late 1970s and pressure for democratization a decade later meant those leaders had to try to extract more and more resources from their citizens, leading to a period of widespread state failure and civil war in the 1990s (Bates 2008). In Latin America, the weakest states developed where the earliest Spanish conquest occurred—around the capitals of precolonial kingdoms such as in Mexico and Peru. Stronger states emerged at locations of less population density and therefore greater European settlement and later colonization, whether Spanish (Argentina) or British (the United States and Canada) (Kelly and Mahoney 2015).

Others have looked to the nature of the economy or the modern international system to explain state weakness. Wealth certainly plays a role: states need resources to provide political goods. The type of economic activity within a state, however, may make a significant difference. Countries with tremendous mineral wealth, such as oil or diamonds, face a situation known as the **resource curse**. A government that can gain enough revenue from mineral extraction alone does not need to worry about the strength of the rest of the economy or the well-being of the rest of the population. If the asset exists in one particular area, such as the site of a key mine, the government simply has to control that area and export the resources to gain revenue in order to survive. Rebel groups likewise recognize that if they can overpower the government, they can seize the country's mineral wealth, a clear incentive to start a war rather than strive for a compromise with those in power. Once again, in this situation, elite compromise to create stronger institutions seems unlikely. The resource curse is not inevitable. In countries that already have relatively strong states, like Norway when it discovered oil in the North Sea, abundant resources may simply provide greater wealth and strengthen the state further, but in weak states, greater wealth may do little to strengthen the state and even weaken it, given the incentives it provides to various political actors.

The neighboring states of Sierra Leone and Liberia in West Africa are a classic case of the worst effects of the resource curse. Ironically, both countries began as beacons of hope. Britain founded Sierra Leone to provide a refuge for liberated slaves captured from slaving vessels, and the United States founded Liberia as a home for former American slaves. Descendants of these slaves became the ruling elite in both countries. Both countries, however, also became heavily dependent on key natural resources. The bulk of government revenue came from diamond mining in Sierra Leone and from iron-mining and rubber plantations owned by the Firestone Tire Company in Liberia. The ruling elites kept firm control of these resources until rebellion began with a military coup in Liberia in 1980. The new regime was just as brutal and corrupt as its predecessor, leading to a guerrilla war led by the man who became West Africa's most notorious warlord: Charles Taylor. After taking control of a good portion of Liberia, Taylor helped finance a guerrilla uprising in neighboring Sierra Leone. Once the guerrilla forces gained control of Sierra Leone's lucrative diamond mines, Taylor

resource curse: Occurs when a state relies on a key resource for almost all of its revenue, allowing it to ignore its citizens and resulting in a weak state

smuggled the diamonds onto the international market to finance the rebellions in both countries. The wars were not fully resolved until 2003, when international sanctions against West African diamonds finally reduced Taylor's cash flow and forced him out of power. Both countries are now at peace and have fragile, elected governments, but they still rely too heavily on key natural resources, so the resource curse could cause further problems.

The contemporary international legal system, like resources, can prolong the life of otherwise weak states. Prior to the twentieth century, the weakest states simply didn't last very long; they faced invasions from stronger rivals and disappeared from the map. The twentieth-century international system fundamentally changed this

CRITICAL INQUIRY

Measuring State Strength

In response to growing international concern about state failure, the Fund for Peace (2019) developed a Fragile States Index to highlight countries of imminent concern. In 2019, the twelfth annual index ranked 178 countries on twelve factors in four categories considered essential to state strength:

- Social indicators
  - demographic pressures,
  - refugees or internally displaced persons, and
  - intervention by external political actors
- Economic indicators
  - uneven economic development,
  - poverty/severe economic decline, and
  - sustained human flight and brain drain
- Political indicators
  - legitimacy,
  - deterioration of public services, and
  - rule of law/human rights abuses
- Cohesion indicators
  - security apparatus,
  - factionalized elites, and
  - vengeance-seeking group grievances

Map 2.3 shows the least and most stable countries.

We can use the Fragile States Index to ask a couple of interesting questions. First, what kind of argument can we make about why states are weak or stable based on the index? Look at which countries are most threatened, most sustainable, and in between on the index. Based on what you know about the countries (and it never hurts to do a little research to learn more!), what hypotheses can you generate about why states are weak or strong? Do some of these relate to the arguments we outlined above about why states are weak or strong? Can you come up with other arguments that we haven't discussed in this chapter? If so, on what kinds of theories (from chapter 1) are your hypotheses based?

A second interesting question is, How can we really measure state strength? Take a look at the indicators page of the index: https://fragilestatesindex.org/indicators/. The index measures those twelve indicators and then adds them up, weighting them all equally, to arrive at an overall score for each country. Do the indicators each measure an important element of state strength? Is it feasible to think we can measure the indicators and arrive at a number to represent each of them in each country? Does it make sense to weight all the indicators equally, or are some more important than others? If you think some are more important, which ones and why? Does your answer connect to any of the theories of state strength and weakness we discussed earlier?

Comparativists don't all agree on the answers to these questions, but we look at evidence and try to generate testable hypotheses for state strength, weakness, and failure in an effort to help states develop stronger institutions. We do this because the human consequences of state weakness—civil conflict, refugees, and human rights violations—and the consequences for the international system are severe. ●

MAP 2.3

Fragile States, 2019

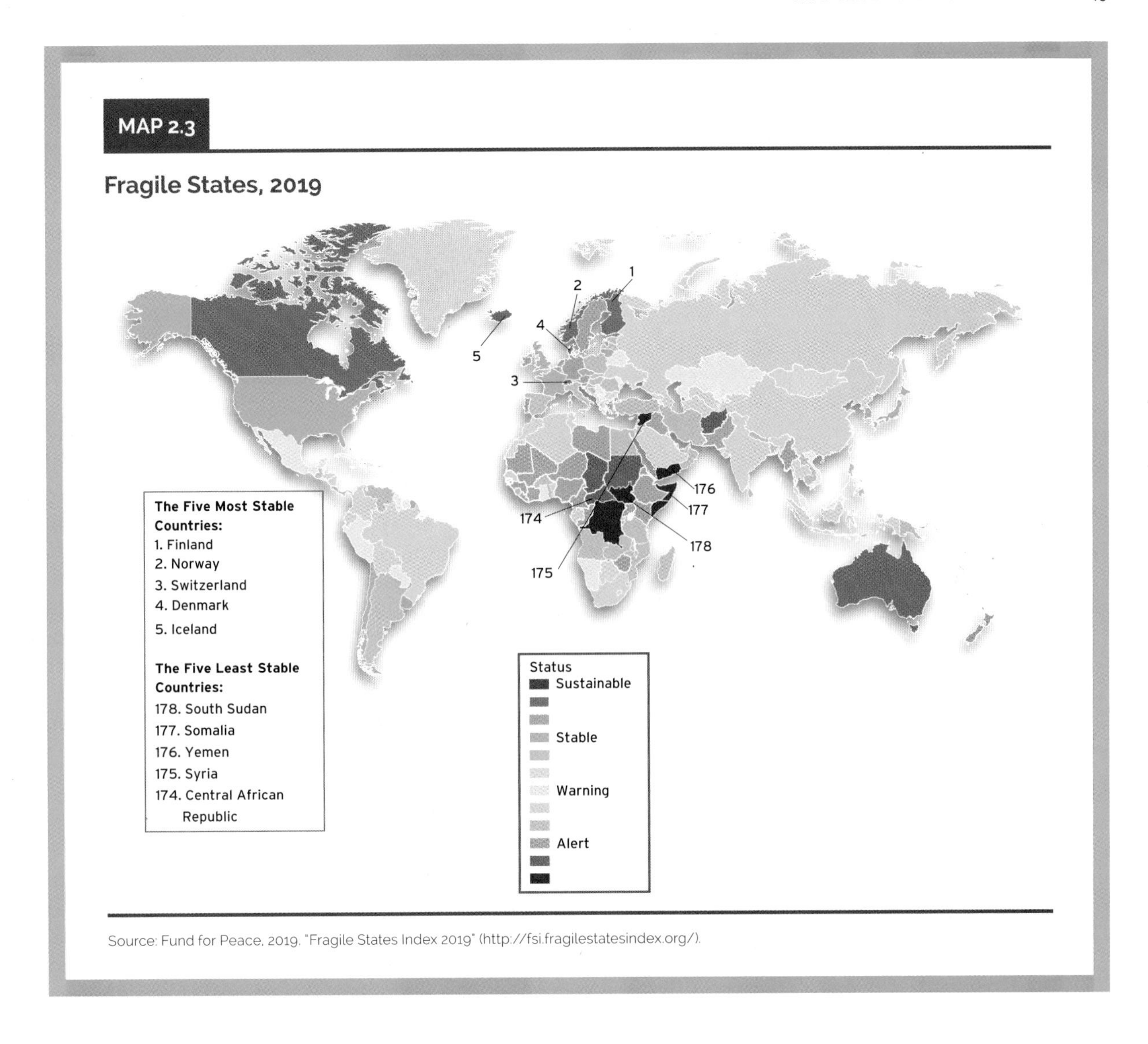

Source: Fund for Peace, 2019, "Fragile States Index 2019" (http://fsi.fragilestatesindex.org/).

dynamic, establishing the norm that the hostile takeover of other states was unacceptable. Exceptions notwithstanding, outright invasion and conquest have become rare, so weak states are more likely to survive. The result can be what Robert Jackson (1990) called **quasi-states**: states that have legal sovereignty and international recognition but lack most domestic attributes of a modern state. Jackson argued that many postcolonial states, especially in Africa, are quasi-states. Ruling elites in these states often come to rely on external resources, including foreign aid, for their survival. Once again, they have little reason to compromise with their domestic rivals, and their rivals, being cut out of all benefits, often take up arms. During the Cold War, the rivalry between the United States and the Soviet Union led each of the superpowers to back dictators who would support their respective sides in global politics. Both sides provided generous aid to dictators who ruled with little interest in providing political goods to their people. Many of these states failed a few years after the end of the Cold War because the elimination of the U.S.–Soviet global rivalry meant that neither side was interested in continuing to support the dictators.

In the post–Cold War era, the international system and major powers have come to see weak and failed states as a significant problem. Weak states produce corruption

quasi-states: States that have legal sovereignty and international recognition but lack almost all the domestic attributes of a functioning state

and illegal activity. They have porous borders through which illegal arms, contagious diseases, terrorists, and illegal drugs might pass. They undermine economic growth and political stability, and democracy is difficult or impossible to foster when a state is unable to provide at least the basic political goods citizens expect. For all these reasons, "state-building" (or "nation-building"—the terms are often used interchangeably, even though comparativists draw a sharp distinction between a state and a nation) has become a common element of the international political system. Wealthy countries and international organizations, including the UN, implement programs to try to rebuild states after conflicts. They try to build or rebuild political institutions, train bureaucrats in proper procedures, hold democratic elections, and restore basic services. Much of the comparative research outlined above suggests that state-building is a very long and complicated process, while official state-building programs often focus on a five- to ten-year program and only certain elements of the state.

The United States and its allies faced these issues as they attempted to extricate themselves militarily from Afghanistan in 2019. While Afghanistan has held several elections, it remains an extremely weak state, dependent on external military support as well as internal support from former warlords who continue to command the personal loyalty of their security forces, some within the national army. The Taliban, against whom the government and external allies have been fighting since 2001, continue to control significant resources, including much of the lucrative poppy trade (poppies are used to make heroin). The United States and Taliban attempted to negotiate an end to the war in 2019, but even if that were to succeed, it is far from clear that a viable Afghan state would emerge. Not just the Taliban but internal divisions among key, armed leaders from various regions could result in a very weak state or, worse, a renewed war.

Conclusion

The modern state is a political form that has been singularly successful. Its characteristics—territory, sovereignty, legitimacy, and bureaucracy—combine to produce an exceptionally powerful ruling apparatus. Arising nearly five hundred years ago, it has spread to every corner of the globe. In fact, the modern world demands that we all live in states. Although state strength can be used to oppress the citizenry, many political scientists argue that long-term strength must come from legitimacy and the effective provision of political goods. In strong states, rulers command military force to prevent foreign attack and domestic rebellion, and they control a set of state organizations that can effectively influence society in myriad ways. When this all works well, it can give ruling elites legitimacy and therefore greater power. Weak states, on the other hand, lack the capacity and often the will to provide political goods. This threatens their legitimacy and often leaves them dependent on international support or key resources for their survival. While they may appear strong because they use a great deal of force against their own people, this is in fact often a sign of weakness: they have no other means of maintaining their rule. The weakest states are prone to collapse; they become failed states, as violent opponents can challenge the state's monopoly on the use of force with relative ease.

This raises a long-standing question: How can weak states become stronger? The answer usually involves the creation of impersonal institutions and the rule of law. This can lead citizens to trust the state, giving it greater legitimacy and strength that it can use to provide political goods. The strongest modern states are virtually all democracies, which are based on such notions as treating all citizens equally and limiting what the state can do, though electoral democracy certainly is no guarantee of state strength.

The strongest states in Europe and elsewhere resulted from centuries of evolution in most cases, as ruling elites ultimately compromised to create more impersonal and powerful institutions that would allow greater economic growth and protect them from attack. These states often began their modern era with strength in one or two particular areas, such as the bureaucracy and military, and developed strength in other areas decades or even centuries later. Postcolonial states had very different historical origins, based on colonial conquest rather than agreements among domestic elites. With independence, these states took the modern form but not necessarily all of the modern content. They often lacked a strong sense of national unity based on a shared history. The international system, however, demands that they act like states, at least internationally. Their rulers therefore act accordingly, often gaining significant power in the process, even in relatively weak states. Lack of wealth, or wealth in the form of a resource curse, also produces very weak states, often in combination with a problematic colonial legacy.

Political scientists have used various theoretical approaches to understand the modern state. Both Marxist and political culture theorists have long made arguments about how and why states develop. Marxists see them as reflecting the power of the ruling class of a particular epoch. Under capitalism, that ruling class is the bourgeoisie, and the liberal state in particular represents the bourgeoisie's interests. In postcolonial countries, weaker states reflect the weak, dependent nature of the ruling elite there. Cultural theorists argue that underlying values, in particular a strong sense of nationalism, are crucial to maintaining a strong state, which must be based on some shared sense of legitimacy. Without this, effective sovereignty will always be limited.

In recent years, rational choice and institutionalist theories have become more prominent. The modern state, these theorists argue, emerged in response to the rational incentives of the emerging international state system, rewarding rulers who developed effective sovereignty, military force, and taxation. Once established, strong state institutions tend to reinforce themselves as long as they continue to function for the benefit of the elites for whom they were created to serve and provide adequate political goods to the citizenry. Weaker states develop where colonial rule did not provide the same set of incentives, and variation in colonial rule often led to variation in postcolonial state strength. As modern states demand more from citizens, they develop a rational interest in establishing some type of popular legitimacy, a subject we look at in much greater depth in the next chapter. ●

KEY CONCEPTS

absolutism (p. 37)
bureaucracy (p. 34)
charismatic legitimacy (p. 33)
external sovereignty (p. 30)
failed state (p. 45)
feudal states (p. 37)
ideal type (p. 43)
internal sovereignty (p. 30)
legitimacy (p. 33)
quasi-states (p. 49)
rational-legal legitimacy (p. 33)
resource curse (p. 47)
sovereignty (p. 31)
state (p. 29)
strong state (p. 44)
territory (p. 30)
traditional legitimacy (p. 33)
weak state (p. 44)

WORKS CITED

Anderson, Perry. 1974. *Lineages of the Absolutist State.* London: New Left Books.

Bates, Robert H. 2008. *When Things Fell Apart: State Failure in Late-Century Africa.* Cambridge, UK: Cambridge University Press.

Brooks, Rosa. 2015. "Making a State by Iron and Blood." *Foreign Policy,* August 19, 2015. https://foreignpolicy.com/2015/08/19/making-a-state-by-iron-and-blood-isis-iraq-syria/.

Callimachi, Rukmini. 2018. "The ISIS Files," *New York Times.* April 4, 2018. https://www.nytimes.com/interactive/2018/04/04/world/middleeast/isis-documents-mosul-iraq.html.

Collier, Paul. 2017. "Culture, Politics, and Economic Development." *Annual Review of Political Science* 20: 11–25.

Fukuyama, Francis. 2014. *Political Order and Political Decay: From the Industrial Revolution to the Globalization of Democracy.* New York: Farrar, Straus, and Giroux.

Fund for Peace. 2019. "Fragile States Index 2019." https://fragilestatesindex.org/.

Huntington, Samuel. 1968. *Political Order in Changing Societies.* New Haven, CT: Yale University Press.

Jackson, Robert H. 1990. *Quasi-States: Sovereignty, International Relations, and the Third World.* Cambridge Studies in International Relations, No. 12. New York: Cambridge University Press.

Kelly, Andrew S., and James Mahoney. 2015. "The Emergence of the New World States." In *The Oxford Handbook of Transformations of the State,* edited by Stephan Leibfried, Evelyne Huber, Matthew Lange, Jonah D. Levy, Frank Nullmeier, and John D. Stephens, 99–115. Oxford, UK: Oxford University Press.

North, Douglass Cecil, John Joseph Wallis, and Barry R. Weingast. 2009. *Violence and Social Orders: A Conceptual Framework for Interpreting Recorded Human History.* Cambridge, UK: Cambridge University Press.

Richards, Rebecca, and Robert Smith. 2015. "Playing in the Sandbox: State Building in the Space of Non-Recognition." *Third World Quarterly,* 36 (9): 1717–1735. doi:10.1080/01436597.2015.1058149.

Risse, Thomas. 2015. "Limited Statehood: A Critical Perspective." In *The Oxford Handbook of Transformations of the State,* edited by Stephan Leibfried, Evelyne Huber, Matthew Lange, Jonah D. Levy, Frank Nullmeier, and John D. Stephens, 152–168. Oxford, UK: Oxford University Press.

Rotberg, Robert I., ed. 2004. *When States Fail: Causes and Consequences.* Princeton, NJ: Princeton University Press.

Tilly, Charles, ed. 1975. *The Formation of National States in Western Europe.* Studies in Political Development No. 8. Princeton, NJ: Princeton University Press.

Weber, Max. 1970. "Politics as Vocation." In *From Max Weber: Essays in Sociology,* edited by H. H. Gaert and C. Wright Mills. London: Routledge and Kegan Paul.

RESOURCES FOR FURTHER STUDY

Boix, Carles. 2015. *Political Order and Inequality: Their Foundations and Their Consequences for Human Welfare.* Cambridge, UK: Cambridge University Press.

Jessop, Bob. 1990. *State Theory: Putting Capitalist States in Their Place.* Cambridge, UK: Polity Press.

Levi, Margaret. 2002. "The State of the Study of the State." In *Political Science: State of the Discipline,* edited by Ira Katznelson and Helen V. Milner, 33–55. New York: Norton.

Mann, Michael. 2012. *The Sources of Social Power*. New ed., vols. 1–4. Cambridge, UK: Cambridge University Press.

Pierson, Christopher. 1996. *The Modern State*. New York: Routledge.

Poggi, Gianfranco. 1990. *The State: Its Nature, Development, and Prospects*. Cambridge, UK: Polity Press.

WEB RESOURCES

Brookings Institution Index of State Weakness in the Developing World

(https:www.brookings.edu/research/index-of-state-weakness-in-the-developing-world/)

Comparative Constitutions Project

(http://comparativeconstitutionsproject.org)

The Fund for Peace, Fragile States Index 2016

(fsi.fundforpeace.org)

The Heritage Foundation, Index of Economic Freedom

(http://www.heritage.org/index/ranking)

International Crisis Group

(http://www.crisisgroup.org)

Organisation for Economic Co-operation and Development (OECD), Better Life Index

(http://www.oecdbetterlifeindex.org)

Organisation for Economic Co-operation and Development (OECD), Country Statistical Profiles

(http://www.oecd-ilibrary.org/economics/country-statistical-profiles-key-tables-from-oecd_20752288)

Transformation Index BTI

(http://www.bti-project.org/home)

Transparency International, Corruption Perception Index

(http://www.transparency.org/policy_research/surveys_indices/cpi)

United Nations

(http://www.un.org/en)

The World Bank, Worldwide Governance Indicators

(http://info.worldbank.org/governance/wgi/index.aspx#home)

3 States, Citizens, and Regimes

The broom (to sweep away corruption) is the symbol of the new All Progressives Congress party in Nigeria. The new party was created by three opposition parties to challenge the ruling People's Democratic Party, which controlled Nigeria from 1999 to 2015. The new party gained power in a historic election in 2015, the first change in government via election in the nation's history, and won again in 2019.
AP Photo/Sunday Alamba

Key Questions

- How do different ideologies balance the rights of citizens with the state's ability to compel obedience?
- On what grounds do different regimes give citizens an opportunity to participate in politics? Who rules where citizens do not seem to have such an opportunity? Can this be justified?
- To what extent does ideology explain how different regimes are organized and justify themselves? What else helps explain how different kinds of regimes actually function?
- Where do different regime types emerge and why?

Learning Objectives

After reading chapter 3, you should be able to do the following:

3.1 Discuss the meaning of citizenship and its role in civil society

3.2 Explicate the relationship among citizens, ideologies, and regime types

The proper relationship between a state and its people, individually and collectively, is one of the most interesting and debated questions in political science. All successful modern states are able to compel their citizens to obey and to regulate many areas of their lives. No modern state can do this, however, without answering questions about the legitimate boundaries of such compulsion and regulation. States vary on how far and under what circumstances they can compel individuals and groups to obey those in authority, how extensively they can intervene in people's lives, and how and whether some areas of individual and collective life should not be subject to the state's power. These differences are embodied in what political scientists call regimes.

This chapter examines variations in the relationships between states and citizens embedded in different regimes. A **regime** is a set of formal and informal political institutions that defines a type of government. Regimes are more enduring than governments but less enduring than states. Democratic regimes, for example, may persist through many individual governments. The United States elected its forty-fifth presidential government in 2016, yet its democratic regime has remained intact for over two centuries. Similarly, a modern state may persist though many regime changes from democratic to authoritarian or the other way around. The state—the existence of a bureaucracy, territory, and so on—is continuous, but its key political institutions can change.

Political scientists categorize regimes in many different ways. We think it is most useful to define regimes primarily based on their distinct political ideologies, which are usually explicitly stated and elaborately developed. Among other things, political ideologies make normative claims about the appropriate relationship between the state and its people: who should be allowed to participate in politics, how they should participate, and how much power they should have. We will focus on the major political ideologies that have been used to underpin

regime: A set of formal and informal political institutions that defines a type of government

regimes over the last century. We will also examine the ways in which regimes diverge from their ideological justifications because no regime operates exactly as its ideology claims.

Citizens and Civil Society

Before we begin discussing any of this, however, it is helpful to understand the historical development of the "people" over whom modern states claim sovereignty. Ideas about how the people stand in relation to the state have evolved in tandem with the modern state described in chapter 2. At the most basic level, a **citizen** is a member of a political community or state. Notice that a citizen is more than an inhabitant within a state's borders. An inhabitant may be a member of physical and cultural communities, but a citizen inhabits a political community that places her in a relationship with the state. In the modern world, everyone needs to be "from" somewhere. It is almost inconceivable (although it does happen) to be a "man without a country." By this minimal definition, everyone is considered a citizen of some state.

citizen: A member of a political community or state with certain rights and duties

The word *citizen*, however, is much more complex than this simple definition suggests. Up until about two or three hundred years ago, most Europeans thought of themselves as "subjects" of their monarchs, not citizens of states. Most people had little say in their relationship with the state; their side of that relationship consisted of duty and obedience. The very nature of the absolutist state meant that few mechanisms existed to protect subjects and enable them to claim any "rights." If the king wanted your land or decided to throw you in jail as a possible conspirator, no court could or would overrule him.

Marianne is a key symbol of France. Representing liberty and reason, she was created during the French Revolution, which helped usher in liberalism and the modern conception of citizenship in Europe.
Art Media/Print Collector/Getty Image

This began to change with the transition to the modern state. As the state was separated from the person of the monarch and its apparatus was modernized, states gained both the ability and the need to make their people more than just subjects. The concept of sovereignty, like the state itself, was divorced from the person of the sovereign, and many European philosophers and political leaders began to toy with the idea that sovereignty could lie with the people as a whole (or some portion, such as male landowners) rather than with a sovereign monarch. This was an important step in the development of the concept of modern citizenship: citizens, unlike subjects, were inhabitants of states that claimed that sovereignty resided with the people. Thus, after the French Revolution overthrew the absolutist *ancien régime*, people addressed one another as "citizen."

Over time, as the modern state developed, people began to associate a complex set of rights with the concept of citizenship. In the mid-twentieth century, the philosopher T. H. Marshall (1963) usefully categorized the rights of citizenship into three areas: civil, political, and social. **Civil rights** guarantee individual freedom and equal, just, and fair treatment by the state. Examples include the right to equal treatment under the law, habeas corpus, and freedom of expression and worship. **Political rights** are those associated with political participation: the right to vote, form political associations, run for office, or otherwise participate in political activity. **Social rights** are those related to basic well-being and socioeconomic equality, such as public education, pensions, or national health care. Marshall believed that modern citizenship included basic legal (civil) status in society and protection from the state as well as the right to actively participate in the political process. He argued that full citizenship also requires enough socioeconomic equality to make the civil and political equality of citizenship meaningful. Modern conceptions of citizenship go beyond just the focus on rights, however. Many scholars argue that truly equal citizenship requires that citizens treat each other as equals, giving each other full respect as members of the community. As we will explore in chapter 4, gender, racial, ethnic, and religious differences, among others, often result in not all people being fully respected members of the political community, even when they are legally citizens. A citizen, then, is a member of a political community with certain rights, perhaps some obligations to the larger community, and ideally a fully respected participant in that community.

Participation, of course, typically happens in organized groups of one sort or another, what we call **civil society**. This is the sphere of organized, nongovernmental, nonviolent activity by groups larger than individual families or firms. In the United States, examples include interest groups like the Sierra Club or the Chamber of Commerce. Like citizenship, civil society in Europe developed in conjunction with the modern state. Absolutist states would not have conceived of such a realm of society separate from the state itself, for what would this have meant? If a monarch could dispose of lands and goods, grant monopolies on tax collection, and determine which religion the realm would follow, what could "society" mean apart from that? The rise of religious pluralism and of modern, capitalist economies alongside the modern state meant that there were now areas of social life outside the immediate control of the state.

This history should not be romanticized or thought of as a linear movement toward modern, democratic citizenship. Change was neither inevitable nor always positive. The same changes that gave us the modern state, however, also gave us the modern concept of the citizen and the modern concept of an independent civil society in which citizens could organize collectively for all sorts of purposes, from religious worship to charitable activity to political action.

Today, ideas of citizenship and civil society are connected to regime claims to legitimacy via the concept of "popular sovereignty." Recall that a claim to legitimacy is a key characteristic of modern states: all modern regimes make some claim to legitimacy, and most do so based on representing and speaking on behalf of "the people." Although it is a distinctly European and liberal democratic notion, the idea of popular sovereignty has deeply influenced all subsequent political ideologies. Even dictators claim to be working on behalf of the citizenry. They may claim that they must deny certain rights in the short term to benefit society as a whole in the long term (or, in the case of theocracy, that God has willed certain exceptions to citizens' rights), but they still lay some claim to working toward the well-being of the citizens.

civil rights: Those rights that guarantee individual freedom as well as equal, just, and fair treatment by the state

political rights: Those rights associated with active political participation—for example, to free association, voting, and running for office

social rights: Those rights related to basic well-being and socioeconomic equality

civil society: The sphere of organized, nongovernmental, nonviolent activity by groups larger than individual farms or firms

Immigrants and supporters demonstrate in front of the Greek parliament, demanding citizenship for children of immigrants who were born in Greece. Citizenship gives full rights to immigrants. Laws on who can be a citizen and how that happens vary from state to state and help define national identity.
George Panagakis/Pacific Press/LightRocket via Getty Images

Some argue that a "postnational" citizenship is now emerging as the latest chapter in this history, especially in the European Union (EU) (Lister and Pia 2008). We can see this in several major institutions around the world: the rights of citizenship are embedded in key United Nations documents, the International Criminal Court in the Hague exists to enforce those rights on behalf of the world community, the EU has a "social charter" that sets standards for treatment of citizens in all EU countries, and most EU members have a common immigration policy that allows people to travel freely within the Union as if they were traveling in only one country. The EU's difficulties, however, in responding to both the 2008–2009 financial crisis and the 2015–2016 refugee crisis raised serious doubts about the viability of this expanded concept of citizenship. In terms of participation, as international organizations such as the World Trade Organization become more important, citizens are forming international groups to try to influence those policies. Keck and Sikkink (1998) called this phenomenon "transnational civil society." These new trends are undoubtedly important and may still grow, but for now almost all citizenship in terms of core rights still resides within the nation-state. Even in the EU, one gains "European" citizenship only via citizenship in a member state.

In practice, regimes vary enormously in their relationships to both citizens' rights and civil society. Virtually no country fully provides all three types of rights described by Marshall. Similarly, the manifestation of civil society ranges from flourishing, lively groups of independently organized citizens, like the many interest groups and political movements in the United States or Europe, to highly controlled or actively repressed groups, such as the government-controlled labor union in China. In short, modern citizens and civil society are much like the modern state: the ideas represent an ideal type but are not universally implemented in contemporary societies. By looking at regimes' political ideologies, we can learn how they attempt to justify and legitimize their various relationships with their citizens.

Regimes, Ideologies, and Citizens

Not all political ideologies have been embodied in regimes, but virtually every regime has some sort of ideology that attempts to justify its existence in the eyes of its citizens and the world. Regimes are much more than just the legal and institutional embodiments of their ideologies, however. Although all regimes have formal rules and institutions that reflect, at least to some extent, their ideological claims to legitimacy, they also have informal rules and institutions, and these may conflict with their ideological claims. Informal institutions may be more important than formal ones; rulers may not actually believe the ideology they proclaim; or the realities of being in power, of trying to govern a complex society, may necessitate ideological modifications. As we noted in chapter 2, weak states in particular are characterized by relatively weak formal institutions. In these states, knowing the informal rules and institutions at work may be more important to understanding how their regimes actually function than knowing the formal institutions embodied in their constitutions.

Even where informal institutions predominate, though, ideologies are important. Four major political ideologies have defined the terms of the most important political debates of the past century: liberal democracy, communism, fascism, and theocracy. (These are described in the "Major Political Ideologies and Regime Types" box below.) Most regimes have come to power in the name of one or another of these ideologies, and many have made serious efforts to rule along the lines prescribed by them. We begin with liberal democracy. While it is certainly not universally accepted, it has become powerful enough that all regimes, implicitly

Major Political Ideologies and Regime Types

LIBERAL DEMOCRACY

ORIGINS Social contract theory. Legitimate governments form when free and independent individuals join in a contract to permit representatives to govern over them.

KEY IDEA Individuals are free and autonomous, with natural rights. Government must preserve the core liberties—life, liberty, and property—possessed by all free individuals.

CHARACTERISTICS Representative democracy. Citizens have direct control, and leaders can be removed. Separation of powers, federalism, and social citizenship supplement but are not essential to legitimate government.

WHO HAS POWER Legislature.

COMMUNISM

ORIGINS Marxism. Ruling class oppresses other classes, based on mode of production. Historical materialism means that material (economic) forces are the prime movers of history and politics.

KEY IDEA Proletariat will lead socialist revolution. Socialist society after revolution will be ruled as a dictatorship of the proletariat over other classes; will eventually create classless, communist society in which class oppression ends.

CHARACTERISTICS Lenin believed that the vanguard party can lead socialist revolution in interests of present and future proletariat. Vanguard party rules socialist society using democratic

(Continued)

(Continued)

centralism and is justified in oppressing classes that oppose it.

WHO HAS POWER Vanguard party now; proletariat later.

FASCISM

ORIGINS Organic conception of society. Society is akin to a living organism rather than a set of disparate groups and individuals.

KEY IDEA Rejects materialism and rationality; relies instead on "spiritual attitude."

The state creates the nation, a "higher personality"; intensely nationalistic.

Corporatism. The state recognizes only one entity to lead each group in society (for example, an official trade union).

CHARACTERISTICS The state is at the head of the corporate body. It is all-embracing, and outside of it no human or spiritual values can exist. "Accepts the individual only in so far as his interests coincide with those of the State" (Benito Mussolini, 1933).

WHO HAS POWER A supreme leader.

MODERNIZING AUTHORITARIANISM

ORIGINS End of colonialism and desire to develop; technocratic legitimacy.

KEY IDEA

Modernization theory. Postcolonial societies must go through the same process to develop as the West did. Development requires national unity; democracy would interfere with unity.

CHARACTERISTICS Four institutional forms: one-party regimes, military regimes, bureaucratic-authoritarian regimes, and personalist regimes. Neopatrimonial authority is common.

WHO HAS POWER A modern elite—a relatively few, highly educated people—who are capable of modernizing or "developing" the country; the claim to rule based on special knowledge is technocratic legitimacy.

PERSONALIST REGIME

ORIGINS One-party regime or military coup.

KEY IDEA Claims to modernizing authoritarianism but really based on neopatrimonial authority.

CHARACTERISTICS Extremely weak institutions, instability and unpredictability

WHO HAS POWER Individual ruler.

ELECTORAL AUTHORITARIANISM

ORIGINS Primarily failed transitions to democracy.

KEY IDEA Legitimacy is based on a combination of liberal democratic and modernizing authoritarian ideologies.

CHARACTERISTICS Allows limited freedoms of expression and association.

Allows limited political opposition to hold some elected offices but ensures ruling party/leader holds most power.

Informal institutions are often more important than formal institutions.

Contradictions exist between democratic and authoritarian elements.

WHO HAS POWER Ruling party.

THEOCRACY

ORIGINS Ancient religious beliefs.

KEY IDEA Rule is by divine inspiration or divine right.

CHARACTERISTICS Islamist version:

- *Islamism.* Islamic law, as revealed by God to the Prophet Mohammed, can and should provide the basis for government in Muslim communities.
- *Ijtihad.* The belief that Muslims should read and interpret the original Islamic texts for themselves, not simply follow traditional religious leaders and beliefs.
- *Sharia.* Muslim law should be the law of society for all Muslims.

WHO HAS POWER God is sovereign, not the people.

or explicitly, must respond to its claims. In fact, approximately 90 percent of the world's constitutions, including those of many authoritarian regimes, mention "democracy" somewhere (Elkins et al. 2014, 141).

Liberal Democracy

Democracy means different things to different people: many people find it hard to define, yet they think they know it when they see it. The word literally means rule by the *demos*, or the people, but that doesn't tell us very much. In this book, we will follow the main convention in comparative politics and use a "minimal definition" of the term, typically referred to as *liberal democracy*. The two words of the phrase are stated together so frequently that in many people's minds they have become one. The distinction between the two, however, is important to understanding both the development of liberal democracy and current debates over its expansion around the world, which we discuss in subsequent chapters.

Liberalism, the predecessor of liberal democracy, arose in the sixteenth and seventeenth centuries amidst the religious wars in England and the later revolution in France. The key liberal thinkers of the period created a model of political philosophy known as **social contract theory**. Although there are many variations, all social contract theories begin from the premise that legitimate governments are formed when free and autonomous individuals join in a contract to permit representatives to govern over them in their common interests. The originators of this idea, Thomas Hobbes and John Locke in England and the Baron de Montesquieu and Jean-Jacques Rousseau in France, started from an assertion that had not been part of Europe's political landscape since ancient Athens: all citizens should be considered free and equal. They theorized an original "state of nature" in which all men (and they meant men—women weren't included until much later) lived freely and equally with no one ruling over them. They argued that the only government that could be justified was one that men living in such a state of nature would freely choose.

Beginning with Locke, all social contract theorists ultimately came to the same basic conclusion about what such a freely chosen government would look like. Locke argued that in the state of nature, government would only arise if it helped preserve the core liberties of all free men: life, liberty, and property (a phrase Thomas Jefferson later modified as "life, liberty and the pursuit of happiness" in the Declaration of Independence). This became the central doctrine of liberalism: a regime is only justified if it preserves and protects the core liberties of autonomous, free, and equal individuals. A state can only infringe on these liberties in very particular circumstances, such as when an action is essential for the well-being of all or when a particular citizen has denied others their rights. Preservation of rights is essential and severely limits what governments can do.

Key Characteristics of Liberal Democracy

The classical liberal doctrine on the preservation of rights justifies limited government to enhance individual freedoms, but it says nothing about how a government will come to power or make decisions. Liberals argued that men in a state of nature would desire a government over which they had some direct control, with leaders they could remove from office if necessary, as protection against a state trying to destroy basic liberties. Representative democracy thus became the universal form of liberal governance. By voting, citizens would choose the government that would rule over them. Those chosen would be in office for a limited period, with some mechanism for removal if necessary.

social contract theory: Philosophical approach underlying liberalism that begins from the premise that legitimate governments are formed when free and independent individuals join in a contract to permit representatives to govern over them in their common interests

Some type of legislature would thus be essential and central to government, as the body in which elected officials would debate and decide the important issues of the day. While kings and courts had long existed in Europe as the executive and judicial branches, liberals argued that the most important branch ought to be the legislative, the body of elected representatives of free and equal citizens. For all of their forward thinking about equality, most liberals still conceived of the citizens to which these concepts applied as male property owners only. They argued that while everyone had some basic civil rights, only men who owned property were adequately mature, rational, and independent of the whims of others to be given the right to vote and participate in governing. Restricting full citizenship to this group meant that all citizens could be considered equal: different men held different amounts of property and had different abilities, but compared with the rest of society they were roughly similar. It was not long before groups not initially granted full citizenship, such as men without property, women, and racial minorities, began asking why they weren't considered as free and autonomous as anybody else. This question produced the largest political struggles of the nineteenth and twentieth centuries in Europe and the United States, struggles to fully democratize liberalism by expanding citizenship to include more and more groups. This slow expansion exposed real inequalities in social citizenship, leading many modern democracies to provide extensive government services to promote greater equality.

Modern liberal democratic regimes arose from this history. Political scientist Robert Dahl captured the essentials of the liberal democratic system of government by noting the eight key guarantees it provides: freedom of association, freedom of expression, the right to vote, broad citizen eligibility for public office, the right of political leaders to compete for support, alternative sources of information, free and fair elections, and institutions that make government policies depend on votes and other forms of citizen preferences. We include these in our working definition of **liberal democracy**. No liberal democracy fully achieves complete political or social citizenship for all, of course. Debates continue within democracies and democratic theory about how best to truly achieve the promises of liberal democratic citizenship.

Many of the most important developments in the history of liberal democracy occurred in the United Kingdom (UK). The earliest important milestone, long before liberalism as a philosophy developed, was the Magna Carta in 1215. It included the first right to trial by peers, guaranteed the freedom of the (Catholic) church from monarchical intervention, created an assembly of twenty-five barons that became the first parliament, and guaranteed nobles the right to discuss any significant new taxes. All of these rights and guarantees were strictly designed to preserve the dominance of the nobility, but they were a significant first step in limiting the monarch's individual power. The Glorious Revolution of 1688 saw Parliament's bloodless removal of King James II from the throne and the installation of a new king and queen, a dramatic expansion of parliamentary power over the monarch. The following year, Parliament passed a Bill of Rights that substantially expanded the rights of citizenship. From that point forward, Parliament gained increasing power vis-à-vis the monarchy. The British form of liberal democracy became unusually centralized, with Parliament having nearly unlimited formal powers within the confines of basic rights. The United States' Constitution in 1787 created another form of liberal democracy, one in which Montesquieu's idea of the separation of powers was entrenched and governmental power was divided among different levels of government, what we now call federalism. Although quite distinct, the United Kingdom and United States, as well as many other countries, have regimes that qualify as being liberal democracies.

liberal democracy: A system of government that provides eight key guarantees, including freedoms to enable citizen participation in the political process and institutions that make government policies depend on votes and other forms of citizen preferences

MAP 3.1

Spread of Democracy by Era

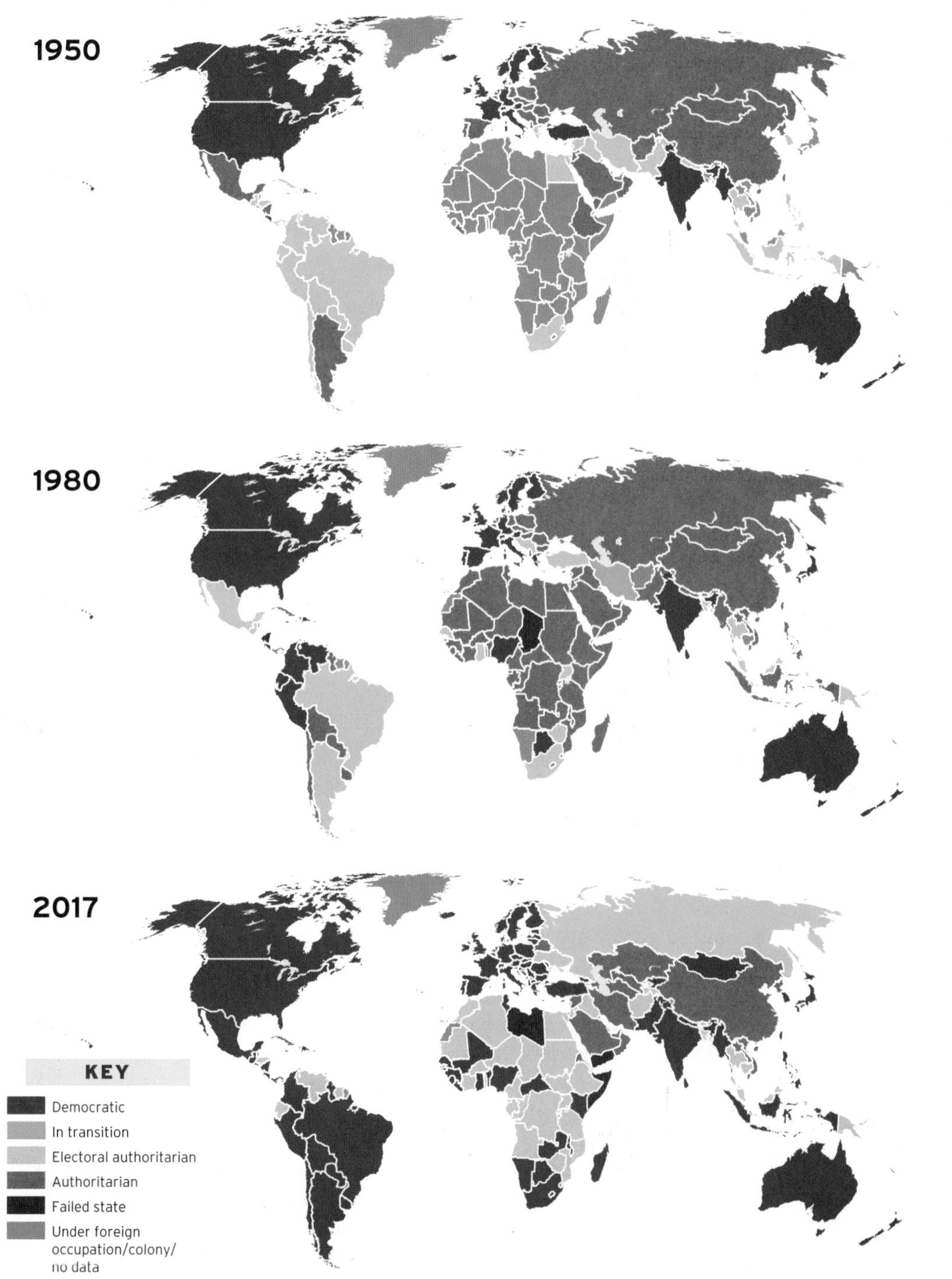

The idea of democracy that liberalism launched has spread widely, especially in recent years. Between 1950 and 1980, most colonial rule came to an end, but democracy did not spread very far. By 2017, however, many more countries had become democratic, and many authoritarian regimes had become somewhat more open electoral authoritarian regimes that allowed some limited political competition, as we discuss later in this chapter. Only a relative handful of purely authoritarian regimes remain.

Source: Data from Polity IV Project: Political Regime Characteristics and Transitions, 1800–2017 (http://www.systemicpeace.org/inscrdata.html). We code the variable "Polity" as follows: democracy (6 to 10); electoral authoritarian, (-5 to 5); authoritarian, (-10 to -6). "In transition" and "failed state" are classifications coded in the Polity IV database.

CRITICAL INQUIRY

What Makes a Democracy a Democracy?

The alternative definitions of democracy raise a set of important normative questions worthy of debate: What are the essential elements of democracy? Are Dahl's eight attributes of liberal democracy enough to give citizens true political equality? If not, what more is required? Are social democrats correct that a minimum level of social equality is necessary for true "rule of the people"? Is electing representatives to rule on behalf of citizens enough, or do citizens need to participate more actively in actual decision making? Should areas of life beyond what we normally think of as "political" be subject to democratic control as well?

Varieties of Democracy

Liberal democracy is not the only form of democracy that democratic theorists have imagined or advocated. Perhaps the best known alternative is **social democracy**. Advocates of social democracy argue that citizens should control not only the political sphere, as liberals believe, but also key elements of the economic sphere. They favor public ownership or at least extensive regulation of key sectors of the economy to enhance equal citizenship and the well-being of all. They believe in maintaining a market economy, but one that is regulated in the interests of the greater good of the citizens as a whole.

Social democratic parties emerged in the late nineteenth century to demand that all citizens gain Marshall's third category of rights, social citizenship: decent living standards so that they could be respected in their communities and fully participate in citizenship as moral equals. Social democratic ideology did not create a separate regime type, but it became an important variant in the internal debates of liberal democracy. Its proponents argue that without social citizenship, democracy is not yet achieved, in spite of the presence of basic civil and political rights.

Proponents of **participatory democracy** argue that real democracy must include far more than the minimal list of institutional guarantees. Real democracy requires direct citizen participation in the decisions that affect their lives. Therefore, advocates of participatory democracy support the decentralization of decision making to local communities to the greatest extent possible, with the goal of direct citizen involvement. Many also support the democratization of the workplace, advocating for worker participation in the key decisions of the companies for which they work.

social democracy: Combines liberal democracy with much greater provision of social rights of citizenship and typically greater public control of the economy

participatory democracy: A form of democracy that encourages citizens to participate actively, in many ways beyond voting; usually focused at the local level

historical materialism: The assumption that material forces are the prime movers of history and politics; a key philosophical tenet of Marxism

Communism

The first and most influential ideological alternative to liberal democracy was communism, which became the basis for regimes in Russia, China, and a number of other countries. Karl Marx, the originator of communism, grounded his philosophy on what he called **historical materialism**, the assertion that material (economic) forces are the prime movers of history and politics. He believed that to understand politics, one must first understand the economic structure of a society and the economic interests that arise from it. As the material forces in the society—technology, raw materials, and the way they are combined to make goods—change, so too will the political, social, and ideological systems.

Feudalism produced all-powerful lords and monarchs, with religious sanction from the church as the chief ideological justification, to keep the peasants in their place, producing a surplus for the lords. The shift to capitalism produced liberalism, in which political power shifted from the landed aristocracy to all men of property. This allowed the rising bourgeoisie, the owners of capital, to gain political power. Capitalism requires labor that is paid a wage and can move from place to place, so the feudal system that required peasants to stay on the land where they were born was abolished, and many peasants were forced off their land to work for a daily wage in cities.

Liberal democracy, according to Marx, is the political and ideological shell that allows capitalism to work and that serves the interests of the bourgeoisie, capitalism's ruling class. When Marx was developing his ideas, only men of property had full political rights in most countries. Even where those rights had expanded to others, as in the United States by the 1830s, Marx argued that this was only a charade. He called liberal rights "equal rights for unequal people," arguing that where workers did have the vote, it was virtually meaningless because those with wealth were the only ones with any real power. Civil society, he argued, was a realm dominated by capitalists as well, a sphere created to give capitalists independence from the state and a means by which they could control the state.

Marx saw the transition from one **mode of production** to another, such as from feudalism to capitalism, as a process of social revolution. He argued that all modes of production ultimately create contradictions they cannot overcome, leading to revolution. Capitalism, he believed, would be characterized by an ever greater division between the bourgeoisie and the proletariat, workers who must sell their labor for a wage to survive. Marx believed that as more and more wealth and power accrued in the hands of capitalists, the proletariat would become so poor that they would not be able to consume all of capitalism's products, creating an economic crisis that would usher in a new era of social revolution. Just as the liberal revolutions had been led by the bourgeoisie and had established liberal democracy, the next revolutions would be communist revolutions led by the proletariat. Marx called this the "specter haunting Europe" in *The Communist Manifesto* (1848/1888). He believed this revolution was inevitable and that it was communist movement's responsibility to recognize when and where social revolutions were emerging and bring them to fruition to create a new and better society and political system.

Marx believed that revolution would generate a communist society that would abolish class distinctions and collectively own the means of production. All people (or at least men—Marx was no more feminist than most other nineteenth-century philosophers) would be paid the same amount for the same work, and everyone would have to work. This he saw as the first stage of communism, which he also called socialism. Who would rule during this stage? Marx was clear: workers as a class would rule over all other classes in what he called the **dictatorship of the proletariat**. This was class dictatorship, not a one-man dictator, and it would control and ultimately eliminate all other classes. Political opposition and civil society distinct from this workers' state would no longer be needed. This was justified in Marx's view because all governments, including all liberal democracies, have been class dictatorships; liberal democracies are simply dictatorships of the bourgeoisie in disguise. As this socialist society developed, everyone eventually would become equal in the sense of all being part of the proletariat. At that point, the second, higher stage of communism would develop in which no state would be necessary because no class divisions would exist, and all dictatorships would end.

Marx believed that communism was both inevitable and the final stage of human historical evolution. Marx believed human nature, like political systems

mode of production: In Marxist theory, the economic system in any given historical era; feudalism and capitalism in the last millennium in Europe

dictatorship of the proletariat: In the first stage of communism in Marxist thought, characterized by absolute rule by workers as a class over all other classes and ideologies, is the product of economic forces. With class division and exploitation eliminated, he believed that human nature itself would change from being self-interested and greedy under capitalism to being what he viewed as more fully human under communism. This would facilitate the creation of his ultimate and, he believed, inevitable goal of a communist utopia.

Marxism is only one of many ideologies that liberal democrats see as justifying the violation of fundamental individual civil and political rights in the name of some ostensibly greater goal. They fear the dictatorship of the proletariat would result in simple, outright dictatorship. Postmodern theorists have argued further that Marxism or any theory claiming certainty about the "laws" of human history or promising an unreachable utopia inevitably will result in a **totalitarian state** that attempts to control every aspect of society in the name of its vision. Fascism, discussed below, is another twentieth-century example.

The history of communism in Russia illustrates the potential and pitfalls of the communist dream. Marx believed the communist revolution would start in the wealthiest and most advanced capitalist societies, such as the United Kingdom, Germany, and France, not a relatively poor country like Russia. As Russians writhed in the throes of World War I, however, Vladimir Lenin led his forces to victory in the October Revolution of 1917 and created the first Communist regime, the Soviet Union. Lenin knew that according to Marx, Russia was not ripe for revolution, but he argued that where capitalism had not developed sufficiently to produce the economic crisis and socialist revolution, a **vanguard party** could still lead a revolution. This party would take power and rule on behalf of the proletariat until the country was fully industrialized and therefore fully proletarian. Socialism, the first stage of communism, would last longer than Marx had envisioned, but the revolution could occur sooner. After Lenin's death in 1923, Joseph Stalin came to power and launched a plan to institute state control of the economy, taking ownership of virtually all land and extracting huge surpluses from agriculture to build industry. The result was rapid industrialization that transformed the Soviet Union from a poor agricultural country into an industrial powerhouse and superpower by World War II. Those who opposed Stalin's policies were ruthlessly suppressed; estimates of deaths under his reign range from two million to twenty million. He created a totalitarian state that he tightly controlled, eliminating all vestiges of civil society.

Stalin's policies had industrialized the economy, but the inefficiencies of central state control grew over time, and the wealth and productivity of the Soviet Union declined compared with that of Western countries. By the mid-1980s, Communist Party leader Mikhail Gorbachev launched modest economic and political reforms to improve the situation, but he eventually lost control of the process. In August 1991, the Soviet Union began to crumble, and in December 1991, it officially ceased to exist.

The Russian Communist Party set the basic model of communist rule that was copied, with some modifications, in China and elsewhere after World War II. Only China, Cuba, Vietnam, and North Korea still maintain a claim to communism, and only North Korea maintains the centralized economic system that was at the heart of the effort.

totalitarian state: A state that controls virtually all aspects of society and eliminates all vestiges of civil society; Germany under Hitler and the Soviet Union under Stalin are key examples

vanguard party: Vladimir Lenin's concept of a small party that claims legitimacy to rule based on its understanding of Marxist theory and its ability to represent the interests of the proletariat before they are a majority of the populace

Fascism

Fascism was the other major European alternative to liberal democracy in the early to mid-twentieth century. It was self-consciously both antiliberal and anticommunist. Fascist ideology conceives of society as being akin to a living organism rather than a set of disparate groups and individuals. The state is central to and dominant within this organic society; it regulates and ensures the smooth functioning of the organism, much as the brain does for the body. Italian fascist leader Benito Mussolini, in *Fascism: Doctrine and Institutions* (1933/1968), argued that "the State is all-embracing; outside of it no human or spiritual values can exist. . . . The Fascist State . . . interprets, develops, and potentiates the whole life of a people." He goes on to say that the state creates the nation (that is, the collective identity of the people), which is itself a "higher personality." Fascists are thus intensely nationalistic, but they conceive of the nation as created by and loyal to the state first and foremost. In contrast to liberals, fascists argue that the individual is and should be subsumed within the state. Mussolini, for example, said the fascist "accepts the individual only in so far as his interests coincide with those of the State, which stands for the conscience and the universal will of man as a historic entity." Thus, the interests of the state are justifiably dominant over both individual citizens and civil society. This state, in turn, is led by one man who becomes the supreme leader and head of the state, which itself is both the head and the spirit of the nation. He rules on behalf of the entire "body" of society so that it can function properly.

Fascist belief in society as an organic whole leads to the argument that society should not have competing organizations that could potentially work against one another. Fascists reject the liberal notion of civil society as a sphere of voluntary organizations independent of the state. Instead, just one organization, controlled by the state, should represent the interests of each component of society. This idea is known as **corporatism**. In fascist (and some other authoritarian) societies, the state creates one trade union to "represent" all workers—one business association, one farmers' association, one women's association, and so forth—all tightly controlled by the state.

Fascists also reject Marxists' emphasis on materialism and economic life. Instead, Mussolini calls fascism "a spiritual attitude," describing a fascist life as "serious, austere, religious." Fascists reject much of the rationality that is the basis for most of Western philosophy, appealing instead to spiritual principles and traditions of a nation as a living organism. Fascist doctrine sees life as a struggle and proclaims a life of action. It views each nation as a unique and historical force that must work to maximize its power and position in the world, and it accepts war as a part of this struggle for the glorification of the state, the nation, and the leader.

Fascists share the modern conception of citizenship in the sense of a direct relationship between citizens and a state. Like communists, however, they define citizens not as everyone legally in the state's territory but much more narrowly. Only those loyal to the state can be citizens, and even these citizens do not have rights in the liberal sense. Because individuals have no existence outside of the state, the concept of preexisting individual rights is nonsensical. Citizens are left only with duties, which they fulfill as part of achieving a more complete life. Fascists, like communists, thus justify the complete elimination of civil society, but in contrast to communists, Mussolini openly admitted that the fascist state was and should be totalitarian.

Fascist regimes took power in Germany, Italy, Spain, and Portugal in the 1930s. In Germany, the Nazi ideology combined fascism with explicit racism that was not part of the original doctrine. The horror of Nazi rule delegitimized fascist ideology the world over. No regime proclaims itself as fascist today. Many observers, however, argue that fascist tendencies still exist. Parties that espouse a virulent nationalism, often defined on a cultural, racial, or religious basis and opposed to immigrants they see as threats to the "soul of the nation," are frequently termed **neofascist**. These groups usually deny the label, however. The best-known example

corporatism: System of representation in which one organization represents each important sector of society; two subtypes are societal and state corporatism

neofascist: Description given to parties or political movements that espouse a virulent nationalism, often defined on a cultural, racial, or religious basis and opposed to immigrants as threats to national identity

of neofascism is France's National Front, which sees the immigration of Muslims, mainly from North Africa, as the greatest danger facing France. Although long a minor party, by 2014, the National Front came in first, with nearly a quarter of the vote, in elections for France's seats in the EU parliament and achieved a similar result in elections for France's regional governments a year later. In 2017, the party's presidential candidate came in second, receiving a third of the vote, the party's highest total ever, though it fared poorly in the subsequent legislative election. Since the 2008–2009 global financial crisis, extreme right-wing, anti-immigrant parties that many see as neofascist made significant electoral gains in the Netherlands, Finland, Austria, Hungary, Germany, and Greece as well. In the United States, a number of commentators saw President Donald Trump as espousing neofascist ideas as well, including opposition to immigration, banning or registering groups based on their identity, and claiming that national strength was the greatest of virtues. Although fascism is dead, many believe neofascism is not.

Modernizing Authoritarianism

While no regime currently uses fascism as an acceptable claim to legitimacy, the argument that the needs of the state and nation must take precedence over liberalism's individual rights remains common. Many regimes that arose after the end of colonial rule based their legitimacy on **modernizing authoritarianism**: their common claim to legitimacy was that they would modernize or "develop" their countries, and doing so required restricting or eliminating individual rights and elections. Modernizing authoritarianism is not as consciously elaborated as the other ideologies we have discussed, but it nonetheless appeals to a common set of precepts. Many postcolonial states are relatively weak, so the formal institutions based on modernizing authoritarianism may reveal less about how they actually rule than their informal institutions. All modernizing authoritarian regimes, however, share a set of core assumptions that underpin their official claim to legitimacy.

The first of these assumptions is that development requires the leadership of a "modern elite." In societies with relatively few highly educated people, the assumption is that power should be in the hands of those who understand the modern world and how to advance within it. They should be the ones who rule, at least until their societies are "ready" for democracy.

This assumption is an appeal to **technocratic legitimacy**, a claim to rule based on knowledge that was part of **modernization theory**. This theory of development argued that in order to develop, postcolonial societies needed to go through the same process of modernization that the West had undergone. Modernization theorists argued that the modern elite—a "new type of enterprising men" in the words of Walt Rostow (1960), a pioneer of the theory and a founder of the American foreign aid program—would lead the development process. Modernization theorists assumed that democracy would arise along with economic development. The leaders of the modernizing authoritarian regimes, however, recognized the contradiction between democracy and the idea that development requires the leadership of an educated elite. They believed that in a country in which a large percentage of the population was illiterate, democracy would not necessarily put the "right" people in power. In their eyes, this legitimized truncating democracy and limiting citizens' rights in favor of some form of authoritarian rule led by elites who claimed to have special leadership abilities based on their education.

The second common assumption of modernizing authoritarian regimes is that they can produce the benefits of "development." The word *development* means many things to many people (see chapter 11), but in political discourse throughout

modernizing authoritarianism: A claim to legitimacy based on the need to "develop" the country via the rule of a modernizing elite

technocratic legitimacy: A claim to rule based on knowledge or expertise

modernization theory: Theory of development that argues that postcolonial societies need to go through the same process that the West underwent in order to develop

the postcolonial world since the 1950s, for most people it means creating a wealthy society like those in the West. For the poorest countries, this meant transforming poor, overwhelmingly agricultural societies into urbanized, industrialized societies with dramatically higher productivity and wealth. For middle-income countries, such as Brazil, development meant continuing the industrialization that had already started, "deepening" it from relatively low-technology to higher-technology and higher-productivity industries. All of this required the application of modern science and technology, which the educated and technocratic elite claimed to understand and be able to employ on behalf of the entire country. The goal, and the main justification for authoritarian rule, was development.

Development also required national unity, the third assumption underpinning these regimes. Postcolonial elites argued that achieving the Herculean task of "catching up" to the West necessitated unusual measures. Their countries did not have time for lengthy debates about what policies to pursue. Instead, the modern elite should take control to move the country forward. Debate and democracy had to wait until the "big push" for development was completed or at least well underway.

Modernizing authoritarianism has taken different institutional forms. The most common civilian form is the **one-party regime**, once common in Africa and Asia. In many of these countries, a single party gained power after independence and systematically eliminated all effective opposition in the name of development and national unity. Some, such as Kenya and Côte d'Ivoire, achieved notable economic progress, while many others did not. **Military regimes** frequently took power in postcolonial states via coups d'état; they often justified elimination of the previous government in terms of modernizing authoritarianism. Often citing prolonged economic stagnation or growing social unrest as their impetus, military leaders argued that they would "clean up the mess" of the prior government and get the country at least started down the road to development before returning it to civilian and democratic rule. Brazil under military rule from 1964 to 1985 was a classic case of this type of regime. Fearing communism at the height of the Cold War, Brazil's military overthrew an elected, leftist government and used its "national security doctrine" to guide its rule. This included actively using the state to develop industry, allowing only government-controlled labor unions, and limiting political participation severely, all in the name of rapid economic growth, which it achieved in what came to be called the *Brazilian economic miracle* in the late 1960s and 1970s. Industrialization, though, produced growing demands for democratization, including the creation of independent labor unions, forcing the end of military rule in 1985.

Personalist Regimes

Modernizing authoritarian regimes arose primarily in postcolonial states, many of which are relatively weak states with weak formal institutions. Informal institutions are therefore often quite important to understanding how these regimes function. In the very weakest states, **personalist regimes** often arose. In these regimes, few if any institutions constrained the individual leader's power. Power can thus be quite personalized, and the rule of law is inconsistent at best. Personalist regimes can arise via either one-party rule or military coup, but either way a central leader comes to dominate. Even the military or party that helped bring him to power will lose power vis-à-vis the individual leader. These leaders not only eliminate all opposition but also weaken the state's institutions even more in order to centralize power in their own hands. Mobutu Sese Seko of Zaire (now

one-party regime: A system of government in which a single party gains power, usually after independence in postcolonial states, and systematically eliminates all opposition

military regime: System of government in which military officers control power

personalist regime: System of government in which a central leader comes to dominate a state, typically not only eliminating all opposition but also weakening the state's institutions to centralize power in his own hands

Tanzania's One-Party Regime

From the 1960s until the 1980s, the African state of Tanzania was an interesting example of a modernizing authoritarian one-party regime. Julius Nyerere, the president from 1962 to 1985, has been called Africa's "philosopher-king," in part because he was unusually self-conscious and explicit in justifying his regime. He argued that political parties in Western democracies are based primarily on social class divisions and that since Africa had few and minor class divisions, there was no need for opposing parties. He suggested that in Africa, "when a village of a hundred people have sat and talked together until they agreed where a well should be dug they have practised democracy" (1966). He thereby justified a one-party regime. His party, the Tanganyika African National Union (TANU), overwhelmingly won the country's first election on the eve of independence, and it didn't take much effort to change the constitution to legally eliminate the opposition.

Tanganyika African National Union (TANU) youth league members carry hoes in a parade in 1968. The youth league was an important element of the ruling party in Tanzania's modernizing authoritarian regime. The hoes symbolize agriculture, the backbone of the economy and key to the regime's claims to legitimacy based on "development."
Associated Press

In addition to his idea of "African democracy," Nyerere envisioned creating an "African socialism," dubbed *ujamaa* in Swahili. He argued that this would return the country to its precolonial origins but with distinctly modern additions. The centerpiece of the effort was the creation of *ujamaa* villages in which Tanzanians would live and work communally. This arrangement would also facilitate the provision of more modern social services such as schools, health clinics, and clean water. While Nyerere justified *ujamaa* as a return to precolonial "traditions," it was in fact an example of a modernizing authoritarian regime in action. It distorted precolonial practices and postcolonial realities against the will of the people in the interests of "development." Nyerere's vision of precolonial Africa was historically inaccurate, and the rural majority had no interest in farming communally or moving into villages. Nyerere ultimately turned to force to create his vision; the state moved millions into new villages and tried to force communal labor. The results were disastrous for agricultural production and the country's economy, though the government was able to improve health care and education, achieving the amazing feat of nearly universal literacy in one of the world's poorest countries.

Nyerere's commitment to village democracy ultimately proved limited as well; public debate became more and more circumscribed over time. His twin goals of African democracy and African socialism were contradictory. The bulk of the population didn't support Nyerere's vision of African socialism; had they been able to exercise full democratic rights, they would have voted against it. Throughout TANU's rule, however, the party did hold parliamentary elections once every five years, allowing two party-approved candidates to compete for each seat. Though the candidates could not question the ruling party's overall policies, they could and did compete over the question of who would best represent the area, so the elections were fair, if not free.

By 1985, Nyerere realized that his vision had produced a bankrupt country and that the key economic policies would have to change. He resigned the presidency voluntarily, only the third African president ever to do so, rather than implement a reversal of his vision. In the 1990s and following the trend across the continent (see chapter 9), Nyerere argued in favor of opening the country to multiparty democracy, saying the time for one-party rule was over. The country did allow full legal opposition, starting with the election of 1995, but TANU (renamed CCM, Chama Cha Mapinduzi, or Party of the Revolution in 1977) continues to rule against only token opposition.

the Democratic Republic of the Congo) and Ferdinand Marcos of the Philippines were classic examples of personalist regimes. They often justify their rule by using the arguments of modernizing authoritarianism, but they rarely put those ideas into practice. Instead, the arguments are simply a fig-leaf to justify centralizing power in the hands of one leader and his closest confidants. They rarely achieve any real development. Actual practice and informal rule typically trump ideology and formal institutions.

Comparativists studying Africa have suggested that many personalist regimes are imbued with **neopatrimonial authority**. German sociologist Max Weber (1925/1978) defined "patrimonial" societies as those in which rule is based on reciprocal personal ties and favors, not bureaucratic institutions or formal laws. Many African regimes combine the trappings of modern, bureaucratic states with underlying informal patterns of patrimonial authority that work behind the scenes to determine real power; hence, the term *neopatrimonial*. Constitutions, laws, courts, and bureaucracies all exist, but power really derives mainly from personal loyalty, personal favors, and patronage. Patron–client relations are central in these regimes. Personalist rulers maintain their power by distributing patronage to their followers, who are personally loyal to the rulers. Politics becomes a competition among key patrons for access to the state's resources that they then distribute to their supporters. Neopatrimonial authority can exist to some degree in a variety of regimes but is the hallmark of personalist ones. One of the most notorious and exceptionally brutal personalist rulers was Uganda's Idi Amin (1971–1979). Uganda gained independence from Britain in 1962, with deep political divisions between north and south. The first president, a northerner, gained office by forging an alliance with the king of the largest southern kingdom, the Baganda. Once in power, though, he slowly centralized power to himself, ultimately deposing the Bagandan king and creating a "republic" with a strong, centralized presidency. Idi Amin, a northerner but from a different ethnic group than the president, had risen to be head of the army and was increasingly a rival of the president. In 1971, he overthrew the government in a coup d'état and established an even more personalist regime than his predecessor. Amin purged many areas of the government of his predecessors' supporters and put members of his own ethnic group in power. He exiled the unpopular South Asian minority, who owned most of the major businesses in the country, and gave their assets to his supporters. Neopatrimonial authority was in full force. He also used the army to brutally suppress any and all opposition. After eight years of increasingly chaotic rule, Amin was overthrown by an invasion of forces from neighboring Tanzania and Ugandan exiles, leading to seven years of instability before a longer-term regime (still in power today) was established.

neopatrimonial authority: Power based on a combination of the trappings of modern, bureaucratic states with underlying informal institutions of clientelism that work behind the scenes; most common in Africa

Electoral Authoritarianism

Since the end of the Cold War and the wave of democratizations that followed, modernizing authoritarian regimes have become far less common. A related but distinct regime type, however, has become more common: **electoral authoritarian regimes**. These regimes "allow little real competition for power . . . [but] leave enough political space for political parties and organizations of civil society to form, for an independent press to function to some extent, and for some political debate to take place" (Ottaway 2003, 3). In electoral authoritarian regimes, opposition parties are allowed to exist and win some elected offices, but the ruling party manipulates electoral rules and processes enough to ensure that it maintains virtually all effective power. Such regimes typically allow some limited freedom of expression as well, but they ensure that this also does not threaten the ruling party's grip on power.

electoral authoritarian regime: Type of hybrid regime in which formal opposition and some open political debate exist and elections are held; these processes are so flawed, however, that the regime cannot be considered truly democratic

Some scholars have referred to electoral authoritarian regimes as "hybrid regimes" because they seem to combine some democratic and some authoritarian elements. This is clear ideologically: they attempt to legitimize themselves using a combination of democratic and modernizing authoritarian ideas. Unlike modernizing authoritarian regimes, they proclaim themselves democratic and point to democratic elements to justify this claim, in particular the presence of regularly scheduled elections (however flawed they are in practice). At the same time, electoral authoritarian regimes invoke ideas from modernizing authoritarianism as well, justifying limits on democracy as essential for national unity and development. This combination means that, as in modernizing authoritarian and personalist regimes, informal political institutions are often more important than formal institutions.

The spread of electoral authoritarian regimes in the last twenty years is undoubtedly due partly to growing international acceptance of liberal democratic norms: in the post–Cold War and postcommunist world, it is no longer legitimate to proclaim a regime as purely authoritarian (of whatever ideology). Electoral authoritarian institutions—such as minimally competitive elections and a national legislature in which opposition parties are allowed to hold a few seats and, within limits, criticize the ruling party—provide a veneer of democratic legitimacy to regimes that in an earlier era might have been modernizing authoritarian. This is especially true in states that at least began a transition to democracy, typically in the 1990s. Full reversion to modernizing authoritarianism is unacceptable to the citizenry and the international community, and even the beginning of a transition to democracy usually unleashes popular pressure that the regime can better manage by allowing some limited opposition to exist rather than repressing it entirely.

Russia is an example of this path to electoral authoritarian rule. After the collapse of its communist regime in 1991, Russia became a rather weak state with a fragile democratic regime under its first postcommunist president, Boris Yeltsin (1990–1999). Yeltsin's handpicked successor, Vladimir Putin (1999–2008, 2014–), openly proclaimed his desire to strengthen the state and began to systematically limit democracy. After a decade of chaos and weakness, the public was ready for order and strength, and Putin easily won the 2000 election. He rapidly put in place an electoral authoritarian regime, though he referred to it as "managed democracy," saying he supported democracy but only as long as it did not produce disorder and weakness. He created the new regime by (1) relying on his tight control of the security apparatus; (2) stripping key economic elites of their assets and handing those assets to his closest associates; (3) creating a dominant, ruling party; (4) centralizing Russian federalism; and (5) fostering an ideology of order and strength that became increasingly nationalist. An economic boom driven by high world oil prices gave Putin vast resources to expend in co-opting support to make all this happen.

Putin used his popularity (throughout his first two terms, his popular approval ratings rarely dipped below 70 percent) and his control over patronage to ensure that his party won control of parliament in 2003, a position it has never lost. By controlling most seats in parliament and in legislatures in virtually all eighty-nine regional governments, Putin has a vast array of offices to give to loyal supporters. He has also manipulated the electoral system to maintain that advantage. Barred by the constitution from continuing as president beyond 2008, Putin handpicked his successor and he himself became prime minister, the number two position in the government. He used his control of informal mechanisms of power, however, to maintain nearly total control throughout. When he declared he would run for the presidency again in 2012, large protests erupted in major cities. Two years of severe recession, caused mainly by declining oil prices, reduced his popularity, and by 2016, a poll showed support for his party at only 45 percent (Stratfor 2016). Nonetheless, further manipulation of the electoral system worked: his party won a supermajority of the parliament—343 of 450 seats—in 2016, and Putin handily won reelection as president in 2018 with 77 percent of the vote.

Theocracy

Theocracy is rule by religious authorities. They rule on behalf of God and following His dictates. It's very unlikely that you would have found theocracy included in a textbook on comparative politics forty years ago. If it were mentioned at all, it would have been in connection with the "divine right of kings" of medieval and early modern Europe under which the monarchy was thought to represent God on Earth, sanctioned as such by the universal Catholic Church. Today, the prime example of theocracy is not Christian but Muslim. Like other kinds of regimes, the Muslim theocracy in Iran is based on a well-elaborated political ideology. Iran currently is the world's only true theocracy, but political movements aimed at achieving similar regimes exist throughout the Muslim world. Some other countries, such as Saudi Arabia, have monarchies that are closely tied to and in part legitimized by Islamic religious authority, but their primary basis for legitimacy is the monarchy itself. We focus on Islamic theocracy as an ideology and regime type not because it is the only conceivable kind of theocracy but because it is the only contemporary example of a theocratic regime and because theocratic political ideology is an important challenger to liberal democracy today.

The political ideology that has inspired such fear in much of the West and such admiration in some of the Muslim world is typically known as "Islamic fundamentalism," a name that implies a set of ideas that is often quite different from what its adherents actually believe. The word *fundamentalist* implies "traditional" to many people, but nothing could be further from the truth in this case. "Traditional" Islamic beliefs, as developed over the centuries, hold that religious law ought to be the basis for government, but in practice local cultural traditions and rulers compromised these precepts significantly. In many countries in the twentieth century, traditional Muslim religious authorities compromised with modernity and the increasing secularization of the state by withdrawing from politics nearly completely and quietly accepting secular, modernizing authoritarian regimes. Indeed, many Islamists argue that the rise of a new, politicized Islamic movement over the past century, far from being "traditional," is in large part a reaction to twentieth-century Western imperialism (Abu-Rabi 2010). Bassam Tibi (2012) says it involves "the invention of tradition" rather than the re-creation of an actual tradition.

Most scholars therefore prefer the term **Islamism** to *Islamic fundamentalism*. While it has many variations, Islamism is generally defined as a belief that Islamic law, as revealed by Allah to the Prophet Mohammed, can and should provide the basis for government in Muslim communities, with little equivocation or compromise with other beliefs or laws. Islamism arose in the nineteenth and twentieth centuries with the goal of "purifying" Muslim society of the creeping influences of the West and secularism that traditional Muslim religious leaders had often been willing to accept. In line with this, most Islamists explicitly reject the Muslim concept of *taqlid,* the acceptance of all past legal and moral edicts of the traditional clergy, and instead embrace *ijtihad,* the belief that Muslims should read and interpret the original Islamic texts for themselves. They base their ideology on their interpretation of the Quran and Sunnah, the two holiest books of Islam, and take as their primary model the seventh-century Muslim society and state created by Mohammed and his immediate followers. Islamists vary in the degree to which

theocracy: Rule by religious authorities

Islamism: The belief that Islamic law, as revealed by God to the Prophet Mohammed, can and should provide the basis for government in Muslim communities, with little equivocation or compromise

they are willing to compromise with aspects of the contemporary world. Not all, for instance, support stoning as punishment for adultery, but most adhere to a fairly strict belief in Muslim law, **sharia**. Past compromises by traditional clergy are therefore unacceptable.

Islamists believe that sovereignty rests with Allah, so they ultimately reject democracy and its idea of popular sovereignty. Some, however, such as the early Palestinian leader Taqi al-Din al-Nabhani (1905–1978), reserve a place for *shura*, which means "consultation with the people." He believed the Muslim state should be led by a caliph, a supreme religious and political leader, but that the caliph should be acceptable to the population as a whole and be advised by an elected council. Some religious authorities have since used this concept to argue in favor of allowing an ideologically limited civil society, one that stays within the bounds of Islamic practices, ideas, and law. Much debate has arisen over how compatible Islamism is with democracy (Tibi 2012), but those who argue that the two can be combined base that argument on the concept of *shura*. Some Islamists, such as the Muslim Brotherhood in Egypt, have been willing to go a step further and participate in democracy as a means of gaining power. After the "Arab Spring" overthrew the regime of Hosni Mubarak, the Brotherhood created a political party and won the first presidential election, though it was overthrown in a military coup in 2013. Other Islamists reject the notion of democracy altogether, maintaining that any compromise with democracy violates Allah's sovereignty.

Iran shows the tension between the sovereignty of Allah and the idea of *shura*. The Islamist regime created by the Ayatollah Ruhollah Khomeini has a "supreme leader," who must be a major religious leader (Khomeini himself before his death), as well as an elected parliament and president. Elected officials make laws, but institutions controlled by the supreme leader can control who is allowed to run for office and can veto legislation the leader doesn't like. Iranian politics have swung between periods of relative openness, during which the supreme leader allows "reformers" to come to power, and subsequent periods in which he clamps down on the reformers, limiting what they can achieve and ultimately forcing them out of office. It is clear the population as a whole, especially in urban areas, supports the reformers, as was evident in reformist president Hassan Rouhani's reelection with 57 percent of the vote in May 2017, but the supreme leader and his allies can thwart the popular will for years at a time in the name of following Islamic law.

As the electoral participation of some groups demonstrates, while all Islamists place great significance on **jihad**, not all advocate violence. Jihad means "struggle," and, although it is not one of the "five pillars" of the faith, it is an important concept in Islam. The Quran identifies three kinds of jihad. The first and most important is the individual's internal struggle to renounce evil and live faithfully. The second is the struggle of the individual to right evils and injustice within the *umma*, the Muslim community. The third and least important is protection, armed and violent if necessary, of the *umma*. The most radical Islamists argue that the *umma* is under attack externally from the West and internally via secularization and Westernization. For groups like Al Qaeda and the Islamic State, this justifies violence outside and within the *umma*. Furthermore, following *ijtihad*, these individuals reject the traditional teaching that violent jihad should only be carried out on the orders of high religious authorities. They argue instead that individuals and religiously untrained leaders like Osama bin Laden can discern for themselves when and where violent jihad is not only a justifiable option but a moral necessity.

sharia: Muslim law

jihad: Derived from an Arabic word for "struggle" and an important concept in Islam; the Quran identifies three kinds of jihad

Conclusion

All political ideologies involve the question of the proper relationship between individual citizens and the state. Most citizens of established democracies probably consider liberal democracy's insistence on limited state power and citizens' rights, especially the right to participate in politics through voting, as the presumptive norm. Liberal democracy, however, is an outlier in this regard. Communism, fascism, modernizing authoritarianism, electoral authoritarianism, and theocracy all tilt the balance in varying degrees in favor of the state. Each finds some grounds for arguing that government should not rest in the hands of citizens or elected representatives alone. Most ideologies offer some sort of rationale for giving a select group, whether it's the working class, the fascist state itself, or a technocratic or religious elite, more say and limiting the participation of others. In these ideologies, real citizenship is thus restricted to members of the key party, those loyal to the nation, those capable of helping the country achieve development, or those who are part of the faithful. This was true for much of liberalism's history as well, of course, as male property owners were the sole citizens. Despite this history, all long-standing liberal regimes have been democratized over the last century as the formal rights of citizenship have expanded to include virtually all adults.

The question of who actually has power, though, may be less clear than formal ideological differences suggest. Pluralist theorists have argued that in almost all regimes, even some of the most totalitarian, factions exist. Elites clearly rule, but they do not rule in a fully united manner. They are divided into factions that vie for power, resources, and influence, often behind the façade of a united and repressive regime. And critics argue that elites often control real power in liberal democracies as well, despite widespread formal rights. Liberal equality of citizenship may exist legally, but it never exists in reality, even where fairly extensive social rights are practiced. The sharp distinctions between liberalism and its ideological alternatives may be less stark in practice than they are in theory.

Ideology offers what regimes hope is a compelling justification for their actions and often serves as a blueprint on which their formal institutions are based, but regimes rarely abide strictly by their ideologies. Democracies vary in their institutional structures, for instance, and even the most established ones have only relatively recently granted full citizenship rights to all adult citizens regardless of gender or race. Similarly, communist regimes modified Marx's ideal of rule by the proletariat in favor of Lenin's concept of rule by the vanguard party. In weaker, postcolonial states, some modernizing authoritarian regimes have failed to meet their own goals of technocratic government, or personalist regimes have ruled in the interests of the key leadership with only a façade of ideological legitimacy. In these regimes, informal institutions often explain more about how a regime actually works than the official ideology does. Because ideology alone does not explain how regimes arise and function, comparativists have used a wide array of theories to examine regimes. Political culture theorists, for instance, have argued that the first communist dictatorship emerged in Russia in part because of the long-standing authoritarian elements in Russian political culture, bred under centuries of tsarist rule. Marxists, of course, use their structural theory to explain the rise of particular regimes, arguing that ideology is simply a mask to justify class dictatorships of various sorts: liberal democracy emerged to serve the interests of the bourgeoisie and foster capitalism; modernizing authoritarian regimes further neocolonialism and the interests of both the budding capitalist elites in postcolonial societies and global corporations. Institutionalists, on the other hand, argue that what matter most are not just regimes' ideological blueprints but how well developed their formal institutions are—and, therefore, how important informal institutions and practices are. Ideology is important to understanding regimes' claims to legitimacy, but understanding why certain regimes arose in certain places and how they actually govern requires far more, which we discuss at length later in the book. First, though, we turn to another crucial issue for modern states: their relationship to identity groups. ●

Sharpen your skills with SAGE Edge at **edge.sagepub.com/orvisessentials2e. SAGE Edge for students** provides a personalized approach to help you accomplish your coursework goals in an easy-to-use learning environment.

KEY CONCEPTS

citizen (p. 56)
civil rights (p. 57)
civil society (p. 57)
corporatism (p. 67)
dictatorship of the proletariat (p. 65)
electoral authoritarian regime (p. 71)
historical materialism (p. 64)
Islamism (p. 73)
jihad (p. 74)
liberal democracy (p. 62)
military regime (p. 69)
mode of production (p. 65)
modernization theory (p. 68)
modernizing authoritarianism (p. 68)
neofascist (p. 67)
neopatrimonial authority (p. 71)
one-party regime (p. 69)
participatory democracy (p. 64)
personalist regime (p. 69)
political rights (p. 57)
regime (p. 55)
sharia (p. 74)
social contract theory (p. 61)
social democracy (p. 64)
social rights (p. 57)
technocratic legitimacy (p. 68)
theocracy (p. 73)
totalitarian state (p. 66)
vanguard party (p. 66)

WORKS CITED

Abu-Rabi, Ibrahim M. 2010. "Editor's Introduction." In *The Contemporary Arab Reader on Political Islam*, edited by Ibrahim M. Abu-Rabi, vii–xxv. New York: Pluto Press.

Elkins, Zachart, Tom Ginsburg, and James Melton. 2014. "The Content of Authoritarian Constitutions." In *Constitutions in Authoritarian Regimes*, edited by Tom Ginsburg and Alberto Simpser, 141–164. Cambridge, UK: Cambridge University Press.

Keck, Margaret E., and Kathryn Sikkink. 1998. *Activists Beyond Borders: Advocacy Networks in International Politics*. Ithaca, NY: Cornell University Press.

Lister, Michael, and Emily Pia. 2008. *Citizenship in Contemporary Europe*. Edinburgh, UK: Edinburgh University Press.

Marshall, T. H. 1963. *Class, Citizenship, and Social Development: Essays*. Chicago: University of Chicago Press.

Marx, Karl, and Friedrich Engels. 1888. *The Communist Manifesto*. Translated by Samuel Moore with Friedrich Engels. London: William Reeves Bookseller. (Originally published *as Manifest der Kommunistischen Partei* in London in 1848.)

Mussolini, Benito. 1968. *Fascism: Doctrine and Institutions*. New York: Howard Fertig. (Originally delivered as address to National Cooperative Council, Italy, in 1933.)

Nyerere, Julius K. 1966. *Freedom and Unity: Uhuru Na Umoja; A Selection From Writings and Speeches, 1952–65*. London: Oxford University Press.

Ottaway, Marina. 2003. *Democracy Challenged: The Rise of Electoral Authoritarianism*. Washington, DC: Carnegie Endowment for International Peace.

Polity IV Project. 2017. "Political Regime Characteristics and Transitions, 1800–2017" http://www.systemicpeace.org/inscrdata.htm.

Rostow, W. W. 1960. *The Stages of Economic Growth: A Non-Communist Manifesto*. Cambridge, UK: Cambridge University Press.

Stratfor. 2016. *A Subtle Manipulation of Russian Elections*. Retrieved from https://www.stratfor.com/analysis/subtle-manipulation-russian-lections.

Tibi, Bassam. 2012. *Islamism and Islam*. New Haven, CT: Yale University Press.

Weber, Max. 1978. *Economy and Society*. Edited by Guenther Ross and Claus Wittich. Berkeley: University of California Press. (Originally published as *Wirtschaft und Gesellschaft* in Germany in 1925.)

RESOURCES FOR FURTHER STUDY

Brownlee, Jason. 2007. *Authoritarianism in an Age of Democratization*. Cambridge, UK: Cambridge University Press.

Dahl, Robert A. 1971. *Polyarchy: Participation and Opposition*. New Haven, CT: Yale University Press.

Esposito, John L. 1997. *Political Islam: Revolution, Radicalism, or Reform?* Boulder, CO: Lynne Rienner.

Held, David. 1996. *Models of Democracy*. 2nd ed. Stanford, CA: Stanford University Press.

Husain, Mir Zohair. 2003. *Global Islamic Politics*. 2nd ed. New York: Longman.

Marx, Karl, and Friedrich Engels. 1978. *The Marx-Engels Reader*. Edited by Robert C. Tucker. 2nd ed. New York: Norton.

McCann, James A., and Jorge I. Domínguez. 1998. "Mexicans React to Electoral Fraud and Political Corruption: An Assessment of Public Opinion and Voting Behavior." *Electoral Studies* 17 (4): 483–503. doi:10.1016/S0261-3794(98)00026-2.

Mill, John Stuart. 1870. *The Subjection of Women*. New York: D. Appleton.

Moore, Barrington, Jr. 1966. *Social Origins of Dictatorship and Democracy: Lord and Peasant in the Making of the Modern World*. Boston: Beacon Press.

O'Donnell, Guillermo A. 1979. *Modernization and Bureaucratic-Authoritarianism: Studies in South American Politics*. Text ed. Berkeley: Institute of International Studies, University of California.

Pitcher, Anne, Mary H. Moran, and Michael Johnston. 2009. "Rethinking Patrimonialism and Neopatrimonialism in Africa." *African Studies Review* 52 (1): 125–156. doi:10.1353/arw.0.0163.

Roy, Olivier. 2004. *Globalized Islam: The Search for a New Ummah*. CERI Series in Comparative Politics and International Studies. New York: Columbia University Press.

Sargent, Lyman Tower. 1987. *Contemporary Political Ideologies: A Comparative Analysis*. 7th ed. Chicago: Dorsey Press.

Schedler, Andreas, ed. 2006. *Electoral Authoritarianism: The Dynamics of Unfree Competition.* Boulder, CO: Lynne Rienner.

Sherman, John W. 2000. "The Mexican 'Miracle' and Its Collapse." In *The Oxford History of Mexico*, edited by Michael C. Meyer and William H. Beezley, 537–568. Oxford, UK: Oxford University Press.

Suchlicki, Jaime. 2008. *Mexico: From Montezuma to the Rise of the PAN*. 3rd ed. Washington, DC: Potomac Books.

Tarrow, Sidney G. 1998. *Power in Movement: Social Movements and Contentious Politics*. New York: Cambridge University Press.

WEB RESOURCES

CIRI Human Rights Data Project

(http://www.humanrightsdata.com)

DataGov, Governance Indicators Database

(http://infor.worldbank.org/governance/wgi/index.aspx#home)

Freedom House, Freedom in the World Survey

(https://freedomhouse.org/report/freedom-world-2016/table-scores)

United States Citizenship, Involvement, Democracy (CID) Survey

(http://www.icpsr.umich.edu/icpsrweb/civicleads/studies/4607)

AP Photo/Sunday Alamba

4 States and Identity

University students in the Philippines march under a pride flag in support of gay rights. Gay rights movements are spreading rapidly in postcolonial countries around the world.
Noel Celis/AFP/Getty Images

Key Questions

- How and why do identity groups form and become politically salient?
- How does the social construction of identity groups influence who has power?
- What are the implications of identity groups' demands on the ideal of equal citizenship in the modern state?
- What are the different political issues faced by different types of identity groups?

Learning Objectives

After reading chapter 4, you should be able to do the following:

4.1 Provide specific examples of the role of identity in politics

4.2 Discuss the debate over group rights versus individual rights

4.3 Explain the various theories of nationalism and its role in contemporary politics

4.4 Explore the role of ethnicity in politics and society

4.5 Articulate how the concept of race influences political debates

4.6 Define and provide examples of social class within societies

4.7 Explain the potential conflicts and issues that arise between religious institutions and the state in secular societies

4.8 Explicate the importance of recognition and civil status for women and people who identify as LGBTQ

The great political battle of the second half of the twentieth century was between liberalism and communism, but nationalism won. Nationalist, ethnic, and religious movements seemed to be the main beneficiaries of the fall of communism, and they emerged as the greatest challenges to democracy. Since the end of the Cold War, an internationalist Islamist movement has rocked the world, nationalism has surged in parts of eastern Europe, such as Hungary and Poland, a resurgent Hindu nationalist movement governs India, and racial conflict has come to the fore in the United States. From the battles to create new governments in Iraq and Afghanistan to secessionist struggles in Chechnya and Ukraine to debates over same-sex marriage in many countries, identity politics are on the rise.

Comparativists studied political conflicts based on identity long before the post–Cold War era. As we noted in chapter 2, states and nations are intimately connected. Internationally, the state is seen as the representative and voice of the nation. Domestically, political leaders can gain legitimacy and power by proclaiming their nationalism and castigating their opponents as "traitors" to the nation. As modern states developed, many actively championed the creation of nations over which to rule. This process usually involved attempts to homogenize a disparate populace, which often led to the exclusion of certain groups from the "nation" or the rise of movements that claimed an identity distinct from the "nation" that the state was proclaiming.

We noted in chapter 3 that groups based on some sense of common identity are only one of many kinds of political groups, but they often have a particularly intense hold on people's loyalties. Few people would risk their lives defending the Sierra Club or Chamber of Commerce, but everyone is expected to do so for their nation, and many would do so for their ethnic or religious group as well. The potential for this ultimate political commitment means that states must and do care deeply about identity politics. All states seek to develop and gain legitimacy from some sense of identity, but the "wrong" identity can be the gravest threat a state can face.

Even when identity groups, such as women's or gay rights movements, do not threaten the existence of a state, they still raise fundamental questions about equal citizenship, particularly about individual versus group rights. States throughout the world have created new policies to try to address these concerns, and globalization has meant that even states with very little open political space or only weak demands for change have nonetheless felt pressure to address at least some of these issues.

These groups and debates raise a number of important questions in comparative politics. Why do identities emerge and become politically important? What do the demands of identity groups tell us about the ideal of equal citizenship and states' success in achieving it? In this chapter, we ask four key questions about identity politics, looking at groups based on nationalism, ethnicity, class, religion, gender, and sexual orientation.

Understanding Identity

Many people view their national, ethnic, religious, or gender identity as natural or even divinely ordained, but the intensity and political impact of those identities vary widely across countries and over time. While group membership of some sort may be natural to human beings, a particularly intense political loyalty to the nation, ethnic group, religion, class, gender, or sexual orientation is not, given how greatly it varies. The **political saliency**—the political impact and importance—of identity groups is created, not innate. Explaining this process is our first major task.

The oldest approach to understanding identity is now commonly called **primordialism**. It underlies many people's understanding of group origins and differences, and it is implicit in the arguments of most nationalist, ethnic, and racial leaders. The purest primordialists see identity groups as in some sense "natural" or God given; they have existed since "time immemorial"; and they can be defined unambiguously by such clear criteria as kinship, language, culture, sex, or phenotype (physical characteristics, including skin color, facial features, and hair). Few social scientists are pure primordialists today; virtually all have been convinced that group identities change enough that the argument that they are somehow natural is insupportable. However, the approach still holds important popular and political influence.

A more nuanced primordial argument is based on political culture or psychology. Because cultural values and beliefs are deeply ingrained, they can be the basis of seemingly immutable group identities. Religious tenets understood in this way served as the basis of an influential work by Samuel Huntington titled *The Clash of Civilizations* (1996/1997). Huntington argued the world can be divided into seven or eight major civilizations based largely on religious identity, and that major wars of the future will occur along the boundaries of these civilizations.

The currently dominant alternative to primordialism is **constructivism**. Like primordialism, it is based partly on political culture, but constructivism uses the

political saliency: The degree to which something is of political importance

primordialism: A theory of identity that sees identity groups as being in some sense "natural" or God given, as having existed since "time immemorial," and as defined unambiguously by such clear criteria as kinship, language, culture, or phenotype

constructivism: A theory of identity group formation that argues that identities are created through a complex process usually referred to as social construction

postmodern ideas of political culture outlined in chapter 1, emphasizing the shifting interpretation of symbols and stories. Constructivists argue that a complex process, usually referred to as **social construction**, creates identities. Societies collectively "construct" identities as a wide array of actors continually discuss the question of who "we" are. According to constructivism, this discourse is crucial to defining identities or "imagined communities" (Anderson 1991). Identity communities are "imagined" in the sense that they exist because people believe they do: people come to see themselves as parts of particular communities based on particular traits. These communities are flexible, though they typically change relatively slowly. Furthermore, individuals are members of a number of different groups at the same time. Elites can attempt to mobilize people using the discourse and symbols of any one of several identities in a particular time and place.

This creation of social and cultural boundaries, even where no legal ones exist, is central to the social construction of identity. As a group defines who "we" are, it also creates boundaries that define who "they" are. To take the most obvious example, the concepts and identities of "man" and "woman" could not exist without each other. If human beings were a species of only one sex, neither word would exist. On the other hand, the growing transgender movement has questioned the binary nature of the traditional gender division of "man" and "woman." Most theorists today see gender existing on a continuum; gender boundaries, like ethnic or racial ones, are set by society, not by nature.

Constructivists argue that identities and boundaries are created in part by the interpretation and reinterpretation of symbols and stories. Through families, the media, and the public education system in all countries, individuals develop a sense of identity as they learn the importance and meaning of key symbols and stories. The state always plays an important role in this process. As a government develops and implements educational curricula, it requires that children be taught the "national history," which can include only certain events interpreted in certain ways to support a specific national identity. The end result of this only partly planned and always amorphous process is adherence to certain beliefs, values, symbols, and stories that come to constitute an identity: for example, a flag, a monarch, the struggle for independence, the fight for racial equality, and monuments to fallen heroes.

Constructivism does not mean that individuals are free to choose any identity they wish. Kanchan Chandra (2012) distinguished usefully between "attributes" and "categories." Individuals have any number of attributes that give them nominal membership in a variety of identity categories, such as the national origin of their parents, skin color, or sexual preference. Identity categories are formed by political and social entrepreneurs using these attributes to create a social category that might then also become politically salient. The state uses education, censuses, elections, and various other official actions, to influence and constrain this process of category creation. Chandra argued that individuals can activate their membership in a particular category at a particular time, but they cannot create or significantly modify the categories individually. That can only happen socially, as the transgender movement has shown recently.

Gender identity plays a distinct role from most other identities in this process. Though rarely the source of demands for separation or territorial autonomy, social constructions of gender—in particular, symbols of what a "proper" woman is—are key ways in which national, ethnic, religious, and racial group boundaries are demarcated (Yuval-Davis and Anthias 1989). Women literally reproduce the community by giving birth, and, as the primary childcare providers in almost all societies, they also pass on key cultural elements to the next generation. Women

social construction: Part of constructivist approach to identity, the process through which societies collectively "construct" identities as a wide array of actors continually discuss the question of who "we" are

Pakistani transgender women henna their hands as they prepare to celebrate Eid al-Fitr, one of the most important Muslim holidays. Gender identity movements threaten all other identity categories and today most often conflict with claims based on religion.
A Majeed/AFP/Getty Images

also serve as symbolic markers of community identity and boundaries. Anne McClintock (1991), for instance, showed how the idea of a "pure" Afrikaner woman in South Africa under apartheid helped solidify Afrikaner nationalism, distinguishing Afrikaners from other white South Africans and creating a feminine ideal around which Afrikaner men could rally vis-à-vis the black majority. More recently, the wearing of the Islamic veil has become an issue of debate both in Europe and in several Middle Eastern countries. What women do, how they behave, what they wear, and where and how they are seen are often central to the social construction of not only gender but also other identities. Like most contemporary social scientists, in this text we adopt a primarily constructivist approach to understanding identity.

The Policy Debate

Once we have a framework for understanding how identity groups are constructed and evolve, we can examine why and how states respond to these groups, whose political demands can raise fundamental questions about equal citizenship or even threaten the existence of a state. States, whether to avoid greater conflict or to live up to their ideals, sometimes must recognize and grant groups some of what they demand. Making these concessions, however, can cause clashes with other groups with equally strong or opposing demands and values. Political autonomy for one ethnic group can lead others to demand the same. Equal treatment of all citizens regardless of gender or sexual orientation often conflicts with deeply held religious beliefs or long-standing cultural practices. Recent controversies over transgender rights are just the latest in a long history of clashes of deeply held values. Even when the principle of equal citizenship is not questioned, major controversies arise over what "equal treatment" means.

Much of the debate over how states should accommodate identity group demands has taken place in the context of normative democratic theory. At the heart of the debate is the question of individual versus group rights and recognition. Liberal democracy in its classic formulation is based on individual rights and the equal treatment of all citizens regardless of their personal, cultural, or social differences. Liberals have traditionally focused on equalizing political rights and assimilating new groups into the political status quo. Contemporary identity groups ask, Is that enough?

The Demands of Identity Groups

Before turning to the policy debate, we have to understand what identity groups demand. The universal demand revolves around what Charles Taylor (1994) called the "politics of recognition." They want the state and society to recognize them as distinct groups with unique and legitimate concerns. They usually seek legal rights at least equal to those of other citizens. Globally, the last vestige of legalized racial discrimination was eliminated with the end of apartheid in

South Africa in 1994. Legal discrimination against women, especially in areas of property ownership and family law, remains fairly common, however, and legal discrimination against homosexuals and transgender people remains the norm in most of the world.

Members of ethnic or religious groups sometimes seek **autonomy** to control their own affairs, either in a particular region where they are in the majority or over areas of their lives influenced by cultural traditions or religious beliefs, such as family law and property rights. If these demands are thwarted, ethnic or religious differences may result in demands for complete secession, which often leads to civil war. To mitigate this possibility, states may grant autonomy or group rights.

A third demand that many groups make is for representation and full participation in the political process. As long as they accept the basic integrity of the state and thereby view themselves as part of the political community, they will want representation and participation. This may appear to be a simple legal matter of ensuring basic political rights, but it often becomes more complicated and controversial as groups question whether they are truly allowed to participate on an equal footing with other citizens and whether institutional changes are necessary for them to achieve that equality.

A final demand is for better social status. Virtually all identity groups that mobilize to demand changes begin in a socially marginalized position: they are typically poorer and less educated than the average citizen and may be socially segregated as well. Harkening back to T. H. Marshall's (1963) ideas of the social rights of citizenship (see chapter 3), they argue that they need better education and economic positions and greater respect from and acceptance in society as a whole. How to achieve those improvements has proven quite controversial.

Arguments for Group Rights and Recognition

Some theorists argue that individual rights, no matter how fully respected, will never allow full inclusion of culturally distinct or socially marginalized groups. Social or cultural differences, as well as histories of exclusion and repression, mean that legal equality alone is not enough. More must be done, usually in the form of rights for or preferential policies that target the distinct needs and weak social positions of particular groups. Theorists making these arguments support policies of several types: (1) recognizing and actively supporting the preservation of distinct cultures; (2) granting some degree of governing autonomy to particular groups; (3) reforming representative institutions such as electoral systems and political parties to enhance or guarantee participation and representation for members of particular groups; and (4) actively intervening to improve the socioeconomic status of distinct groups, usually via government intervention in the market.

Political theorist Will Kymlicka contended that collective rights for minority cultures are justified "to limit the economic or political power exercised by the larger society over the group, to ensure that the resources and institutions on which the minority depends are not vulnerable to majority decisions" (1995, 7). He argued that most people find it very difficult to cross cultural barriers fully. Thus, without recognition and protection of their distinct cultures, they will not be able to participate completely in the larger society and make the choices on which democratic citizenship depends. **Assimilation**, as practiced in the United States and elsewhere, has the goal of eventually integrating immigrant or other minority cultures into the larger culture of the whole society and so would fail to guarantee

autonomy: The ability and right of a group to partially govern itself within a larger state

assimilation: A belief that immigrants or other members of minority cultural communities ought to adopt the culture of the majority population

equal rights and participation. In contrast, Kymlicka and Norman (2000) encouraged a policy based on **multicultural integration**, which

> does not have the intent or expectation of eliminating other cultural differences between subgroups in the state. Rather, it accepts that ethnocultural identities matter to citizens, will endure over time, and must be recognized and accommodated within [political] institutions. The hope is that citizens from different backgrounds can all recognize themselves, and feel at home, within such institutions. (14)

Critics have asked whether respecting cultural differences might undermine individual rights, especially freedom of expression and gender equality. Kymlicka and Norman, though, were clear that only cultural practices not violating fundamental liberal rights should be allowed and encouraged via multicultural integration.

Predating Kymlicka's arguments, an institutional expression of this general idea is **consociationalism** (Lijphart 1977). Consociationalism accepts ethnically or religiously divided groups and political parties, granting each some share of power in the central government. Switzerland, Northern Ireland, and Belgium are examples of this system. Power sharing can be done formally, as in Lebanon, where power is divided along religious lines: by agreement of all parties, the president is always a Christian, the prime minister a Sunni Muslim, and the Speaker of the parliament a Shiite Muslim. It can also be done more informally. The electoral system can be designed to encourage the formation of parties based on key identities. The parties, once elected, can then work out power-sharing arrangements in some type of government of national unity. Typically, each major ethnic or religious party will have, in effect, a veto over major legislation, so all must agree before laws are passed. Consociationalists also suggest using federalism by creating ethnically or religiously homogeneous states or provinces so that central governments can try to shift the focus of identity politics from the center to the regional governments (see chapter 5 for more on federalism). This type of federalism has been the most common response to identity-based conflicts in the post–Cold War era.

The best-known recent effort at consociationalism was the Belfast Agreement of 1998 that ended the religiously based conflict in Northern Ireland, which dated back to British colonial rule, when English and Scottish Protestant plantation owners oversaw a Gaelic, Catholic population. In the nineteenth century, an Irish nationalist movement arose, and most of Ireland gained independence in 1920. The six northern counties, however, remained part of Great Britain, gaining only limited local government under Protestant control. Nationalists continued to demand unification of the north with the Irish Republic throughout the twentieth century, and the conflict became particularly violent starting in the late 1960s. By the early 1990s, the nationalists recognized they could not militarily defeat the British, and the unionists—Protestants favoring continued union with Great Britain—acknowledged they could not continue to rule unilaterally without paying a steep price in terms of lives, political stability, and economic well-being.

This set the stage for the historic 1998 Good Friday agreement creating a consociational solution that, while far from perfect, is holding to date. Under the agreement, Northern Ireland remains part of Great Britain, and Ireland renounced its long-standing claim to the territory. Government would devolve, however, from direct rule from London to local rule in Northern Ireland. A National Assembly would be elected based on a proportional electoral system that ensured that nationalists and unionists would have seats in parliament equal to their share of the national vote. (See chapter 6 for details on proportional electoral systems that

multicultural integration: Accepts that ethnocultural identities matter to citizens, will endure over time, and must be recognized and accommodated within political institutions; in contrast to assimilation

consociationalism: A democratic system designed to ease ethnic tensions via recognizing the existence of specific groups and granting some share of power in the central government to each, usually codified in specific legal or constitutional guarantees to each group

produce this type of result.) The first minister and deputy first minister, who are elected by the National Assembly, share executive power. They must each win a majority vote of both the nationalist and unionist members of the National Assembly, and every member, once elected, must declare herself to be officially unionist, nationalist, or other. Cabinet positions are then shared among all parties in the assembly based on their share of the total seats. In this way, both sides of the sectarian divide must support the government. Despite a promising start, compromise between the main parties remained elusive, and the government collapsed from 2002 to 2007 and again since 2017. Several issues fueled ongoing disagreement in 2019 that prevented forming a new governing coalition. The most prominent was nationalists' demands that the Irish language (Gaelic) be recognized as an official language. Efforts to forge cross-community relationships in civil society and integrate institutions such as schools have begun, but they have been far from successful two decades on. Despite these problems, the consociational system has succeeded in ending almost all of the violent conflict and establishing a government in which the former antagonists have shared power peacefully for extended periods.

Arguments Against Group Rights

Critics of group rights argue that "special" group rights or preferences undermine the norm of equal citizenship, serve to perpetuate a group's distinct and therefore unequal position, and threaten the common identity and bonds on which citizenship and national identity are based. The classic liberal position is that only individuals can have rights and all individuals should have them equally. This implies support for government policies of nondiscrimination, but it does not justify giving distinct rights or preferences to members of particular groups or treating them differently in any other way, which would be beyond the state's rightful purview. Once legal equality is achieved, individuals are and should be free to pursue political participation as they desire and are able.

centripetal approach: A means used by democracies to resolve ethnic conflict by giving political leaders and parties incentives to moderate their demands

Classic liberals fear that group rights will undermine political stability and democracy, both of which, they argue, require a common identity and a shared set of values. Nationalism underlies the development of the modern state and of democracy, and each state is given international legitimacy as a representative of "a people." A sense of commonality, then, is essential to domestic and international legitimacy for all states. From this perspective, group rights and preferences will preserve group differences rather than encourage commonality, undermining political stability.

An institutionalist approach that attempts to get beyond group identities is known as the **centripetal approach**, championed most strongly by political scientist Donald Horowitz (1985). He argued that ethnic or religious conflict can best be resolved by giving political leaders incentives to moderate their demands and broaden their appeal beyond their particular groups. Certain electoral systems can encourage this by requiring winning candidates to gain votes over a broad

A radical Protestant mural in 2007, nearly a decade after the Belfast Agreement ended religious conflict in Northern Ireland. While the consociational agreement produced a new government and peace, popular sentiments on both sides remain a challenge.
AP Photo/Peter Morrison

geographic area containing multiple religious or ethnic groups, for instance. Also, rules for recognition of parties can require them to have representation and leadership across ethnic or other identity lines. Creating ethnically or religiously mixed states or provinces in a federal system can also encourage compromise within each one, moderating tensions. For instance, ethnically and religiously diverse Nigeria requires registered political parties to have broad membership across most of its thirty-six states, and the winning presidential candidate must not only win a majority of the votes but also at least 25 percent of the vote in two-thirds of the states to ensure support across ethnic and religious groups. Finally, all liberal theorists ask, To what extent can and should group rights be supported if those groups pursue goals contrary to a state's liberal ideals? Should a religious group that explicitly opposes equal rights for men and women not only be allowed to participate in the political process but also be given specific preferences? Nigeria, once again, provides an example of this issue, as some states in their democracy have instituted a form of Muslim sharia law that opponents see as violating core democratic values. We now turn to look at the debates in the context of each of the major identity categories of importance today: nation, ethnicity, race, class, religion, and gender and sexual orientation.

Nations, Nationalism, and Immigration

The nation remains a fundamental building block of the global political system and the starting place for any discussion of identity. Each state claims to be the sole legitimate representative of a nation, and each nation claims a right to its own state. Despite this, clearly defining the word *nation* is no easy task. In 1882, French theorist Ernest Renan concluded that no single cultural feature was crucial. Instead,

> a nation is a soul, a spiritual principle. Two things, which are really only one, go to make up this soul or spiritual principle. One of these things lies in the past, the other in the present. The one is the possession in common of a rich heritage of memories; and the other is actual agreement, the desire to live together, and the will to continue to make the most of the joint inheritance.

Renan's deduction strikingly resembles contemporary notions of social construction. A nation is an "imagined community," created through shared memories. All of those memories beyond the immediate experience of the individuals themselves are shared only because a group has learned to share them, in part through state-sponsored education.

The distinction between a nation and an ethnic group, in particular, is often not clear. The Irish are members of a nation, but when they immigrate to the United States, they become part of an "ethnic group." The Zulu in South Africa are an ethnic group, but the Palestinians, who are less culturally distinct from their Arab neighbors than are the Zulu from neighboring South African groups, are generally regarded as a nation. As Renan concluded, no particular set of cultural markers distinguishes a nation from an ethnic group. The only clear definition ties back to the state. A **nation** is a group that proclaims itself as such and has or seeks control of a state. This desire to be a nation and thus to control a national state is **nationalism**. Ethnic groups, on the other hand, do not think of themselves as nations and do not desire to control their own state. Clearly, and to the potential

nation: A group that proclaims itself a nation and has or seeks control of a state

nationalism: The desire to be a nation and thus to control a national state

detriment of states' territorial integrity, an unsatisfied ethnic group can develop into a nation demanding its own state.

Not surprisingly, most nationalist leaders are primordialists: each claims his nation has existed since the beginning of time as a mighty and proud people. As we saw in chapter 2, however, the history of nation-states suggests otherwise. States such as France and England propagated national identity to strengthen their legitimacy. As Italian nationalist Massimo d'Azeglio declared shortly after the unification of Italy in the 1860s: "We have made Italy. Now we must make Italians." While a few scholars argue that nations are inherently based on older ethnic groups (Gat 2014; Smith 1998), most support the idea that nations are modern entities tied in some way to the development of the modern state and economy.

Organizer Jason Kessler speaks at a Unite the Right rally for "white civil rights" across from the White House in 2018, attended by white supremacists, the Ku Klux Klan, and other hate groups. Such events, along with calls for President Trump's wall along the U.S. border with Mexico, deportation of millions of illegal immigrants, and a ban on Muslim immigration, led some observers to fear that a form of cultural nationalism—specifically, white nationalism—is eroding civic nationalism in the United States.
Mark Wilson/Getty Images

Nationalism has a complicated relationship with liberal democracy as well. At least until the mid-twentieth century, many nationalists saw themselves as carving democratic nations out of the remnants of feudal or colonial empires. Before "we the people" can declare ourselves sovereign, "we" must have a sense of "us" as a "people": who is and is not included in "us" defines who has the rights of democratic citizenship. In this context, two distinct forms of nationalism have crucial implications. **Cultural nationalism** is national unity based on a common cultural heritage. Cultural nationalists usually advocate a legal definition of citizenship based on **jus sanguinis**—blood rather than residence. For instance, prior to 2000, anyone whose parents were ethnically German could gain automatic German citizenship, whereas citizenship for all others was extremely difficult to procure. Cultural nationalism poses obvious challenges for democracy, for how can those lacking the "national" characteristics be full citizens with democratic rights? For this reason, most observers see **civic nationalism** as more supportive of democracy. In civic nationalism, the sense of national unity and purpose is based on a set of commonly held political beliefs. Those who share the beliefs are part of the nation. Civic nationalists typically support legal citizenship based on **jus soli**, or residence on the state's "soil," thus automatically conferring citizenship on second-generation immigrants, whatever their cultural characteristics, as is true in the United States.

Immigration is often the context in which debates about national identity are played out. States secure their sovereignty via physical control of their borders; nations define themselves by constructing conceptual borders between themselves and others, often including others living within the state's territory. Across Europe, the arrival of about a million Syrian refugees beginning in 2015 fueled a resurgence in popularity of cultural nationalist parties proclaiming their opposition to further immigration and their fear of "losing" their national culture. British voters chose to leave the European Union in 2016, desiring to assert their national identity and reduce the flow of immigrants into the country. Shortly thereafter, Donald Trump was elected president of the United States, in part by promising to build a wall the length of the U.S. border with Mexico and to ban all Muslim immigrants. Officially, the United States proclaims a civic nationalism based on the principles in the

cultural nationalism: National unity based on a common cultural characteristic wherein only those people who share that characteristic can be included in the nation

jus sanguinis: Citizenship based on "blood" ties; for example, in Germany

civic nationalism: A sense of national unity and purpose based on a set of commonly held political beliefs

jus soli: Citizenship dependent on "soil" or residence within the national territory; for example, in France

Declaration of Independence and Constitution. A recent survey, however, showed that 50 percent of Americans think that people were "true Americans" "only if they were Christian, spoke English, and had been born in the United States," while only 24 percent expressed civic nationalist ideas (the remaining quarter were "disengaged," with no strong opinion) (Bonikowski and DiMaggio 2017).

Ethnicity

Ethnic groups, like nations, see themselves as united by one or more cultural attributes or a sense of common history but do not have or seek their own states. Like all other identity categories, ethnic identity is imagined: people's perceptions are what matter, not actual attributes or some "objective" interpretation of history. Ethnic groups may be based on real cultural attributes, such as a common language, but even these are subject to perception and change. In the former Yugoslavia, Serbs, Croats, and Bosniaks all spoke closely related versions of what was known as Serbo-Croatian. As ethnic conflict and then war emerged in the early 1990s, each group began claiming it spoke a distinct language—"Serbian," "Croatian," or "Bosnian"—and nationalists in all three groups began to emphasize the minor linguistic differences among them.

If ethnic groups do not desire to have their own state, what do they want? All identity groups wish to be recognized. For ethnic groups, recognition may take the form of official state support of cultural events, school instruction in their language, official recognition of their language as one of the "national" languages, or inclusion of the ethnic group's history in the national history curriculum. In short, many ethnic group leaders demand the kind of policies Kymlicka and Norman (2000) envisioned with their notion of "multicultural integration." If an ethnic group resides primarily in one area, it also may demand some type of regional autonomy, such as a federal system of government in which its leaders can control their own state or province. The issue of federalism became so contentious in India in the 1960s that the national government created a commission to examine it. The commission recommended the creation of a number of new states based on linguistic boundaries. Even when an ethnic group is not regionally concentrated, it will typically demand greater representation and participation in government, perhaps especially when a federal option is not possible.

Unlike national identity, ethnicity is not always political. In the United States today, white ethnic identities have very little political content. Irish Americans, for example, may be proud of their heritage and identify culturally with Ireland, but few feel any common political interests based on that identification. This can change, of course: a century ago, many Irish Americans felt their identity was tied very strongly to their political interests. A crucial question, then, is when and why ethnicity becomes politically salient. Leadership can be a key catalyst. Because of the potential intensity of ethnic attachments, they are a tempting resource for ambitious politicians. A leader who can tie ethnic identity to political demands can gain tremendous support.

ethnic group: A group of people who see themselves as united by one or more cultural attributes or a sense of common history but do not see themselves as a nation seeking its own state

Constructivists point out, however, that leaders cannot do this at will. The context is important. If a group believes those in power have discriminated against it economically, socially, or politically, members may see their political interests and ethnic identity as one and the same. Their history, which they may pass from parent to child, is one of discrimination at the hands of the powerful "other." On the other hand, relative wealth can also lead to ethnic mobilization. If an ethnic group is based in a particular region that has a valuable resource such as oil, group members may feel that they should receive more benefits from what they see as "their" resource. This is a central issue in the ethnic and religious divisions in Iraq because the country's oil reserves are located in both Kurd and Shiite areas but not in Sunni areas. Sunni leaders, not surprisingly, want oil revenue fully controlled by the central government in Baghdad, not by regional governments; they fear being dominated by the larger groups within whose territory the oil is located. Fear, then, is also a common source of ethnic mobilization. With the fall of communism in eastern Europe and the former Soviet Union, many people felt great fear about the future. The old institutions had collapsed, and the new ones were untested. In this situation, it is relatively easy for a political leader to mobilize support with an ethnic or nationalist appeal that suggests that other groups will take advantage of the uncertain situation and try to dominate. Incentives facing political leaders can also shape when and why ethnicity becomes politically salient. Daniel Posner (2005) used a rational institutionalist argument to analyze ethnic politics in Zambia, arguing that political institutions, including electoral systems, help create both the range of possible ethnic identities available to mobilize and influence which ones leaders mobilize at a particular time.

Race

While the distinction between ethnic group and nation is relatively clear, the difference between ethnic group and race is much more ambiguous. In a particular context, it may seem obvious, but a consistent distinction is difficult to apply systematically. Following Stephen Cornell and Douglas Hartmann (2007, 25), we define a **race** as "a group of human beings socially defined on the basis of physical characteristics." Most ethnic identities focus on cultural rather than physical characteristics, though many do see specific physical characteristics as markers of particular groups as well. Most racial groups are distinguished by physical characteristics, though they and others may also perceive cultural distinctions. This distinction between race and ethnicity, then, is not perfect but is probably the best we can do.

Perhaps more important than the actual definitions of race and ethnicity are the differences in these identities' origins and social construction. Ethnic identity usually originates at least partially in a group's self-assertion of its identity. Most ethnic groups represent people who are themselves claiming an identity and the political demands that go with that claim. Race, in contrast, originates in the imposition of a classification by others. Race in its modern sense began with Europeans' expansion around the globe and their encounter with markedly different peoples. Primarily to justify European domination and slavery, European explorers and colonists classified the native populations of the lands they conquered as distinct and inferior races. Embedded within the very classification was an assertion of power (the third dimension of power outlined in chapter 1). This legacy continues today: almost every racial classification system marks current or quite recent differences in power along racial lines. Like race, ethnicity may also represent starkly different positions in a power structure, but as the case of German Americans or Italian Americans today shows, it does not always do so. Ethnicity and race, then, usually differ in how they are marked (culture versus physical characteristics), their origins (self-assertion versus external imposition), and the degree of power differences embedded in their contemporary social construction.

race: A group of people socially defined primarily on the basis of one or more perceived common physical characteristics

For the concept of race, just as for that of nation and ethnicity, we emphasize perception. Genetically, members of racial groups, such as white and black

Americans, have as much in common with one another as they do with members of their own groups: genetic variation is no greater across the two groups than it is within each. Races are constructed by focusing on particular differences, such as skin color, and ignoring the far more numerous similarities.

Like all socially constructed categories, racial identity varies across time and place, as the cases of the United States and Brazil demonstrate. In the United States, the infamous "one-drop" rule historically defined everyone with any African ancestry as black in order to ensure that children of black slaves and white masters were legally slaves. In contrast, Brazilians define race purely based on visual cues. The black–white dichotomy that characterizes U.S. racial history makes little sense to most Brazilians, where what Americans would call "interracial" marriage is quite common. Brazil's white population, facing a country in which at least half of the population was of slave descent, actively encouraged the creation of intermediate racial categories as buffers between them and poor, uneducated blacks. The result is more than a dozen unofficial racial categories between "white" and "black." In the last decade, an affirmative action program based on race for university admissions has become quite controversial. One of the main issues is the question of who is "black" and therefore deserves the admission preference.

Given the power dynamic inherent in racial classification, it is always political. Whether recognized or not, racial classifications give certain groups more power than others. Like ethnicity, however, whether this leads to conscious political mobilization on the basis of race depends on the ability of leaders to articulate a common agenda by using the symbols of racial identity or discrimination in a compelling way. A dominant group, such as white Americans, typically will not see itself as pursuing a common racial agenda, though their racial identity may nonetheless give them power and privilege. Groups in a minority or subordinate position are more likely to view their political interests as tied to their racial identity, in part because they face discrimination on that basis.

Politicized racial groups usually desire recognition, representation, and improved social status. Autonomy is a less common goal because racial groups usually do not share a distinct geographical home. Recognition usually means official governmental recognition of the race as a socially important group through such means as inclusion on a census form, the teaching of the group's historical role in the larger national history, and the celebration of its leaders and contribution to the nation's culture. In addition, racial groups desire representation in the sense of full formal and informal participation in their government and society, which in turn, they argue, requires improved social status. Thus, racial demands typically focus on inclusion in public and private employment, political offices, and the educational system. Frequently, as in the United States, groups may argue that past discrimination justifies some type of preferential system that works relatively rapidly to achieve representation equal to their share of the population and greater socioeconomic equality. Mechanisms to do this might include numerical targets or goals for hiring, increased funding for training and education, or adjustments to the electoral system that make the election of racial minorities more likely or guaranteed.

The United States shows that racial politics can be at least as intense as ethnic or national politics. Many heralded the election of Democrat Barack Obama as president in 2008 as the start of a new era in which the United States would become "postracial." By 2010, however, the anti-Obama and overwhelmingly white Tea Party had become a major new force in party politics, giving the Republican Party a massive electoral victory. Four years later, a series of highly publicized police killings of black men led to the creation of the Black Lives Matter movement

FIGURE 4.1

Percent Population with College Degree

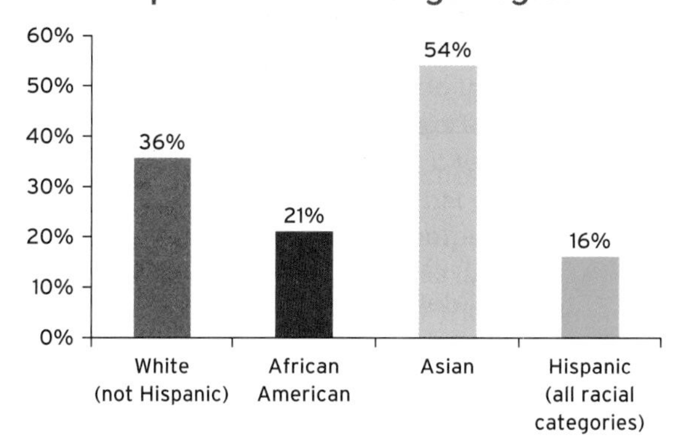

FIGURE 4.2

Median Household Income 2018 ($US)

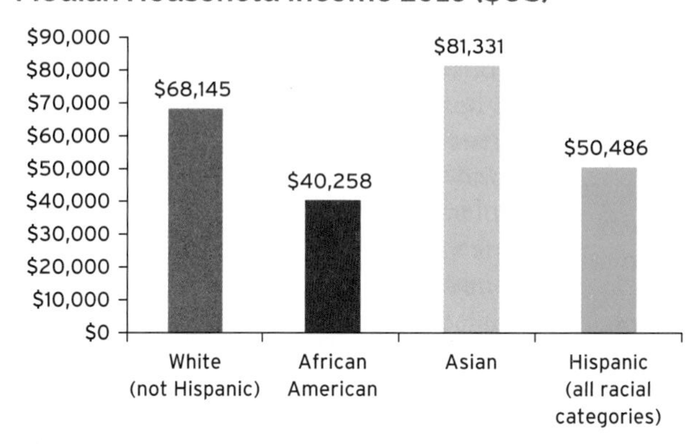

FIGURE 4.3

Racial Groups as Percentage of U.S. Population

As percentage of US population

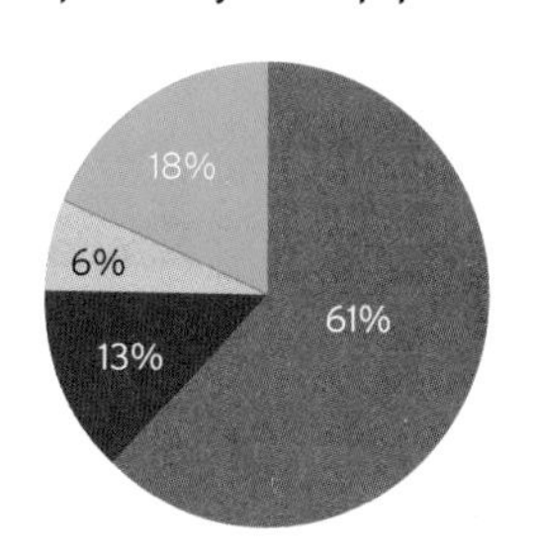

FIGURE 4.4

Racial Disparity in House of Representatives

As percentage of House

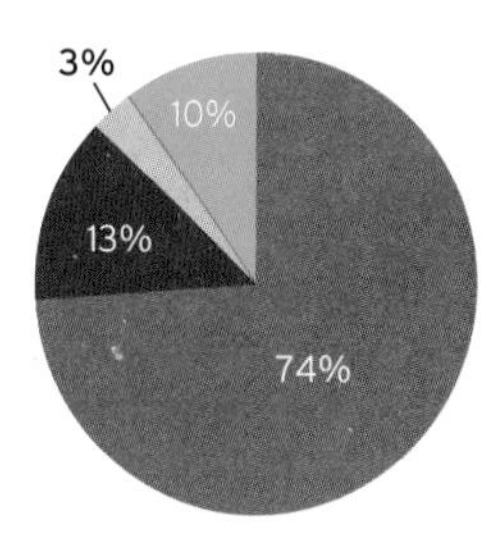

FIGURE 4.5

Racial Disparity in Senate

As percentage of Senate

3%

5%

3%

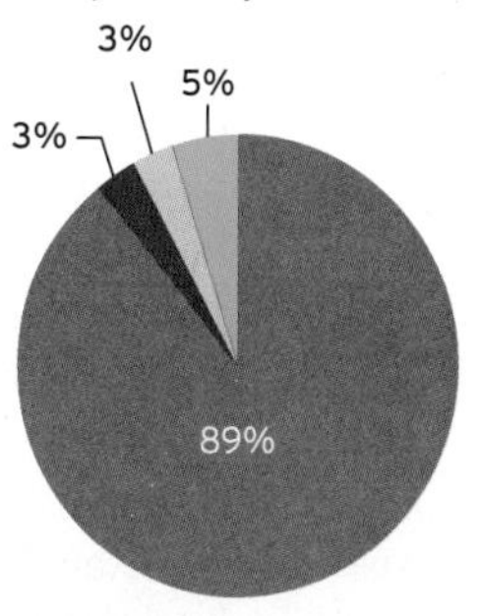

Sources: Income data are from "Income and Poverty in the United States: 2017," United States Census Bureau (https://www.census.gov/library/publications/2018/demo/p60-263.html); education data are from "Educational Attainment," U.S. Census Bureau (https://factfinder.census.gov/faces/tableservices/jsf/pages/productview.xhtml?pid=ACS_17_1YR_S1501&prodType=table); population data are from QuickFacts—United States Census Bureau (https://www.census.gov/quickfacts/fact/table/US/RHI125217); and political representation data are from "Membership of the 114th Congress: A Profile," Congressional Research Service (https://fas.org/sgp/crs/misc/R45583.pdf).

Note: There are 435 total seats in the U.S. House of Representatives and 100 seats in the Senate.

FIGURE 4.6

Racial Resentment, Economic Anxiety, and Support for Donald Trump in 2016

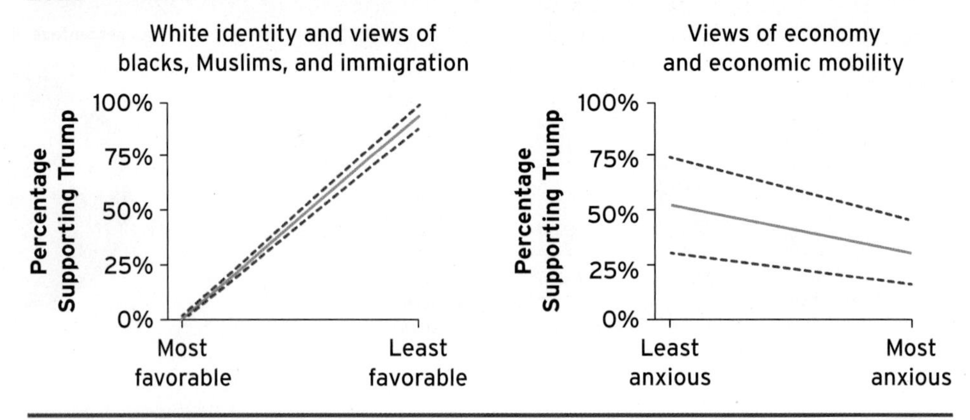

Source: adapted from Sides et al. *Identity Crisis: The 2016 Presidential Campaign and the Battle for the Meaning of America*, 91. Princeton University Press.

and hundreds of demonstrations across the country, the largest African American protest movement since the 1960s. And in 2016, Republican Donald Trump was elected president in spite of making several statements widely condemned as racist. As Figure 4.6 shows, when scholars used survey research to measure voters' economic concerns and racial resentment simultaneously (as well as other standard predictors of voting, such as party identity and ideology), they found that economic concerns had little effect on the likelihood of supporting Trump. Negative views of blacks, Muslims, and immigrants, however, strongly predicted the Trump vote. Attitudes aside, Figures 4.1 through 4.5 show that racial disparity in terms of education, income, and representation remains significant.

Social Class

Like other categories of identity, social class has been defined over time both by "objective" criteria and by the process of social construction. While virtually all analysts use social construction to understand other categories of identity, however, many analysts continue to define class based on objective characteristics. This is in part because it is possible to draw clear distinctions based on the common criteria used to define class. While no one can use a criterion like skin color to unambiguously delineate races, it is possible to use income, for instance, to unambiguously distinguish classes; draw a specific line for household income and all households will fall below or above it. Whether it is useful to do so, however, is another question. While **social class** can be defined relatively easily as a group of people who share or perceive themselves to share a social status based on some combination of a common level of wealth, income, type of work, or education, delineating classes clearly is difficult.

social class: A group of people who share or perceive themselves to share a social status based on some combination of a common level of wealth, income, type of work, or education

Karl Marx was one of the earliest theorists of class. As we discussed in chapter 1, he defined classes based on the criterion of their relationship to the means of production. Under capitalism, the most politically important classes were the bourgeoisie who own the means of production and the proletariat who don't and therefore must work for a wage. In post-industrial societies, it's far less clear that a unified proletariat exists; janitors and college professors both work for a wage and do not own the means of production, but is it useful to think of them in the same class? And who really "owns" the means of production when a substantial proportion of salaried employees own some corporate stock (typically via retirement funds), although a very small amount that gives them no actual control over a company?

With these problems in mind, most contemporary theorists who use "objective" criteria to analyze social class focus on income, education, or type of work. Income is the most straightforward in the sense that classes can be defined simply by creating what seem to be meaningful income categories, such as quartiles of the population, or other lines that define classes (for example: all households with incomes over US $150,000 are defined as "upper class"). Similarly, educational attainment can be categorized (e.g., less than high school, high school graduate, college graduate). Type of work is more complicated but typical divisions refer to (1) salaried employees (often called "white collar" in the United States) who do not work for an hourly wage, tend to be more educated, and have some control over their working time; (2) employees who get paid hourly and have less education and control over their work (often called "blue collar" in the United States); (3) farmers; (4) small business owners who work for themselves; and (5) large-scale business executives who own or control large corporations.

The question with all of these ways of defining class is where and why lines should be drawn? In the United States, much recent focus has been on the top 1 percent of households based on income. While they are far wealthier than other Americans, some analysts have questioned this focus, suggesting a broader group such as the top 10 percent really constitute a more important social class that controls significantly greater wealth and power than the other 90 percent and reproduces itself via access to elite higher education (Stewart 2018). Still others look at education itself as the key criterion, noting that in the United States today, college graduation is highly correlated with a whole set of socioeconomic outcomes in life: income and type of employment, life expectancy, stable marriage, voting, and participation in volunteer organizations. College graduates, approximately a third of the country, are the important "upper class" to understand, according to this argument. Implicit in these arguments about how classes are delineated are arguments about the social and political impact of these class distinctions, which leads us to the question of the social construction of class.

Proponents of a social construction understanding of class argue that class is just like other categories of identity: socially constructed through complex and evolving processes. It is certainly influenced by income, wealth, and education but also includes how people perceive themselves and others. We know a "middle class" person not by knowing their income or educational achievement but by a host of socially constructed symbols that define how a "middle class" person is supposed to behave in a variety of settings. Like other socially constructed identities, those that are dominant—the "upper" or at least "middle" class in wealthy societies—are the presumed norm to which all others are at least implicitly encouraged to aspire, not only in terms of income and education but also in terms of interests, speech, mannerisms, family life, and so forth. Social class power derives not only from the control of material and educational resources but also via the third dimension of power, a social process of convincing others that a particular way of being is superior and those who can't achieve it are somehow inferior.

However we delineate classes, we still have to ask about their political salience. Like ethnicity, class is often politically important, but it isn't always. Upper classes typically do not assert their political interests as a class publicly, especially in democracies in which equal citizenship is supposed to be a central element of the political system. Wealthy individuals, groups, and major businesses, of course, are very active everywhere in trying to influence governments. Conscious working-class political action has typically taken place via labor unions and allied political parties. The percentage of the population who are union members, however, has declined precipitously for decades: for the OECD (Organisation for Economic Co-operation and Development, a group that includes almost all wealthy democracies), the average declined from about 35 percent in 1985 to about 17 percent today. It varies from a high of 70 percent in some Scandinavian countries to just over 10 percent in the United States. Workers, who gained the right to vote in most countries only in the late nineteenth century, traditionally supported social democratic parties in Europe, which fought for greater government protections for manual laborers.

The most noted trend in class politics in the past generation, though, has been increased inequality, which has occurred in virtually every wealthy democracy. In the 1980s, the wealthiest 10 percent of the population in OECD countries had seven times the income of the poorest 10 percent; in 2016 they had nine and a half times the income of the poorest (OECD 2017). As the decline in trade unions shows, though, this has not translated into clear mobilization of workers along class lines. In fact, social democratic parties have lost support almost everywhere. With unions declining and social democratic parties seemingly unable to improve workers' well-being, many working-class voters have turned to supporting nationalism and right-wing parties, often seeing immigrants and "globalization" as the cause of their problems (see chapter 6). In effect, these voters have shifted their political activity from a class-based focus to a national, racial, or ethnic one, supporting the British vote to leave the EU, President Trump in the United States, and the National Front in France (which came in second in the 2017 presidential election). John Huber (2017) used a rational choice model to explain when leaders are able to mobilize voters on class versus ethnic/racial/national lines. He argued that political leaders seek to achieve a "minimum winning coalition" to gain power. When divisions based on ethnic or other identities can create majority support more efficiently—getting to a majority more easily—leaders will try to mobilize voters along those lines rather than class lines.

There is no better place to understand class politics than Britain. Anyone who has watched the historical drama *Downton Abbey* has at least a romanticized idea of class divisions in Britain in the early twentieth century. Traditionally, the British elite sent their children (initially, only boys) to the expensive private boarding schools (confusingly called "public" schools because for the aristocracy, they replaced having a private governess). These schools educated the students who would go on to Oxford and Cambridge universities, from which virtually the entire economic, social, and political elite of the country emerged. The non-elite majority were virtually entirely excluded from this realm. British political parties and voting patterns reflected the exceptionally strong influence of class. The Conservative Party was historically the party of the aristocracy, long proclaiming what it termed "Tory paternalism": the upper class would take good care of the rest of society. Trade unions created the Labour Party in 1900 to represent their interests, rejecting Tory paternalism; by the 1920s Labour was one of Britain's two main parties.

But the traditional working classes' share of the population dropped in half (to between 20 and 25 percent of the population) from 1930 to 2010 (Evans and Tilley, 2017, 7). By 2016, less than a quarter of the workforce was unionized. In this context, Labour Party activists forced unions to accept less control over the party, and the party shifted its ideology, moving to a more centrist position to attract more middle-class voters. In recent years, the nationalist United Kingdom Independence Party, which championed the "Brexit" vote to leave the EU in 2016, captured disproportionate working-class support, as many workers blamed the EU and immigrants for their woes. As in all wealthy countries, traditional class divisions and political allegiances have shifted over the last generation. At the same time, though, inequality climbed: prior to 1980s, the most common measure of inequality, the Gini Index, stood at about 0.25; since the late 1990s, it has been around 0.35. Britain is more unequal than almost all other European countries, although it is still significantly less unequal than the United States (where the Gini Index is about 0.45).

Demonstrators carry banners and portraits of Mao Tse Tung during a rally called by the Pakistani Workers' Union on May 3, 1970. Marxists may have seen this as the work of a "class for itself," but with hindsight, we know that the 1970s marked the decline of the traditional British working class and trade union membership. Class continues to be an important part of British identity, but it is no longer tied to the type of work one does. The politics of class have grown more complicated, as the Blairite Labour Party moved to the center to attract middle-class support, and many erstwhile factory workers and others in the traditional working class heeded nationalist calls for Brexit, feeling that globalization of the British economy had left them behind.
AP Photo/Dennis Lee Royle

Class divisions, of course, exist in postcolonial countries as well, though they are distinct from those in wealthy democracies. In Latin America, significant industrialization in most countries in the mid-twentieth century led to the rise of trade unions; many authoritarian governments, however, were able to control and limit their activities. As democratization spread in the 1980s and 1990s, trade union political activity grew. In Brazil, unions helped lead the movement to create democracy and founded the Workers' Party, which governed the country from 2002 to 2016. In poorer countries, where industrialization has advanced least, unions are typically smaller and weaker. A larger percentage of the population—a majority in many African countries—work in agriculture, many on their own small farms. Some politically organize on behalf of their interests as farmers, which may be distinct from industrial workers' interests. Many of these countries also have politically significant ethnic or religious divisions as well. In this context, the political salience of class is often far less than that of ethnicity, as John Huber's theory would predict.

Religion: Recognition, Autonomy, and the Secular State

Religion is both the oldest and, in a sense, newest basis for questions of inclusion and clashing values. As we noted in chapter 3, religious divisions within Christianity in early modern Europe led to civil wars and the emergence of liberalism. Eventually, secular states became universal in Western societies, which, at least in theory, relocated religion into the private sphere. The secular state reached its zenith after World War II and the onset of independence of numerous secular states across Africa and Asia. In the past generation, however, and with renewed emphasis since the terrorist attacks of September 11, 2001, religion has again become a major issue in almost all societies.

Religion as Group Identity

We can apply most of what we have learned about ethnic groups to religious groups as well. One might assume that religious group membership can be more inclusive and flexible than ethnicity, more like civic than cultural nationalism. Virtually all religions allow conversion to the faith, so while you may not be able to become Chechen, you can convert to Islam. In practice, this may be more difficult than in theory, however, especially where religious identity has become a divisive cultural marker and a basis for political mobilization. It is unlikely that members of other groups will want to convert at this point or be accepted if they did. Conversion is much more likely when the political salience of religious identity is relatively low.

While religious conflict is often based on a deep sense of religiosity, that is not always the case. The three major groups in the former Yugoslavia were defined primarily by religion: Serbs are Orthodox Christian, Croats are Catholic, and Bosniaks are Muslim. Ironically, because Communists had ruled the country since World War II, religious belief and practice were very low among all three groups prior to the conflict; religious affiliation was a marker of identity based on birth, not a matter of personal faith. As the conflict spread, religious observance increased within all three groups. Once people start shooting at you because of your religion, it starts to loom larger in your consciousness.

The demands of religiously mobilized groups are comparable to those of ethnic groups: they want some version of multicultural integration, involving recognition and often some autonomy. For religious groups, recognition certainly involves the right to practice one's faith openly, but it might also include demands that the state officially recognize the religion in the form of state-sponsored religious holidays or recognize and perhaps fund religious schools. A desire for autonomy could be expressed as a demand for federalism if the religious group lives in a particular region. Within its own province, the group could then practice its religion and use the provincial government to support it. Demands for autonomy can also take the form of asking that religious leaders and organizations be granted legal control over marriage, death, and other personal matters.

State Response to Religion: Differing Forms of Secularism

The vast majority of the world's states officially respond to religion by maintaining some version of secularism, with most of the exceptions being in the Middle East. In liberal democracies, few question the right of citizens to practice any religion they choose in the private sphere (with the possible exception of religious practices that break other kinds of laws, such as those against drug use or polygamy). In most societies, religious groups may organize, build houses of worship, and do charitable work as they desire. Controversies arise over what role, if any, the state should play in this process and what role, if any, the religious groups should play in secular politics and policy.

Current approaches to secularism reflect the broader debate over multiculturalism and group rights. The version of secularism most familiar to Americans we call the **neutral state model**: the state should be neutral about, but not opposed to, religion. The United States is a chief example of this form of secularism. Recent controversies have therefore involved actions that seem to question the state's neutrality, such as posting the Ten Commandments in courtrooms or public school classrooms or requiring children to pray in school

neutral state model: A model of secularism wherein the state is neutral about but not opposed to religion

or learn about creationism instead of the theory of evolution. Other controversies implicate the state in actively supporting religion, such as government funding for religious groups' charitable work or abstinence programs in schools in lieu of sex education courses.

A more absolute version of secularism the French call ***laïcité***. It developed in societies whose political origins lay in a battle to separate the state from a single, dominant religion. France, Turkey, and Mexico are all examples of this. The French and Mexican revolutions and the establishment of the modern state in Turkey after the demise of the Ottoman Empire each involved the creation of a secular republic independent of the politically powerful Catholic Church in France and Mexico and the Islamic caliphate in Turkey. The result was a secularism advocating that religion should play no part in the public realm. The state is not neutral toward religions but rather is actively opposed to religion having any role in the public sphere, and the state generally has the right to regulate religion as it deems necessary for the public interest. Private religious practice remains acceptable, as long as it is kept private. Religious references in political discourse, while not illegal in most cases, are nonetheless considered inappropriate.

Laïcité in Mexico dates back to Mexican independence and the long process of reducing the Catholic Church's public role. The PRI government after the revolution (1920–2000) increased the state's anticlericalism even more, stripping the church of much of its land and remaining influence. After democratization in 2000, some leaders of the main conservative party, the Partido de Acción Nacional (National Action Party), began to express their religious beliefs in public. When church leaders urged voters to elect people who opposed abortion rights, many Mexicans believed it had crossed a line that it should not have. Controversies arise in this type of secularism when a religious group seeks an independent public role for its religious beliefs; the case of Islamic girls wearing veils in France and Turkey provides another example of this.

A third variant of secularism Alfred Stepan (2011) termed **positive accommodation**, arguably the closest to the tenets of multicultural integration. It sees the state as neutral among but willing to support religions that it recognizes as important elements in civil society. Germany is the classic model of this type. Since the end of World War II, it has officially recognized various Judeo-Christian faiths, the leaders of which register with the government to gain recognition. The state even collects a tax on their behalf to help fund them, and they help administer some of Germany's extensive welfare programs. Controversies in this type of secular state involve deciding which religious groups gain recognition and how they have to be organized to do so. Most Sunni Islamic sects, for instance, are nonhierarchical, which means that each mosque is independent. This has raised questions about if the German state should recognize Muslim groups the way it has Jewish and Christian ones. Some individual German states have recognized some Muslim groups, but no national policy on the question exists.

Most postcolonial states are officially secular even while making various accommodations for religions. Perhaps the biggest difference between African and Asian states, in particular, and European states is that the former are much more religious. Rajeev Bhargava (2016) argued that India provides a model of secularism that is a variant of positive accommodations and would be useful in Europe as it deals with growing Muslim immigration, what he termed the "principled distance" model. Principled distance "interprets separation to mean not strict exclusion or strict neutrality, but . . . both engagement with and disengagement from [religion] and does so by allowing differential treatment

laïcité: A model of secularism advocating that religion should play no part in the public realm

positive accommodation: A model of secularism wherein the state is neutral among but willing to support religions that it recognizes as important elements in civil society

Islamic Headscarves in France and Turkey

France is at least nominally largely Catholic, but it is home to the largest Muslim population in Europe, most of whom are immigrants from North Africa. The population of Turkey is nearly all Muslim. Both countries have faced considerable controversy over young women wearing Islamic headscarves. The issue aroused such passion in part because each state's sense of national identity includes its particular conception of secularism; any questioning of it threatens national identity itself.

In 1989, the principal of a junior high school in a Paris suburb expelled three Muslim girls for wearing the *hijab*, the Muslim headscarf, in school. This ensuing national controversy pitted defenders of *laïcité* and feminists, who viewed the headscarf as a form of oppression, against defenders of religious freedom and multicultural understanding. The government ultimately determined that religious symbols could be worn in schools unless "by their nature… or by their ostentatious or protesting character … [they] disturb the order or normal functioning of public services" (Fetzer and Soper 2005, 79). Following this vague edict dozens of Muslim girls were expelled from school, so the heated controversy continued. In 2004, the French parliament banned the wearing of all "conspicuous religious symbols" in schools, and since then, more Muslim girls have been expelled for wearing the hijab. Critics contend that the law is an anti-Muslim attack on religious freedom, since students have long worn small crosses and yarmulkes to school without incident. Supporters argue that the law is essential to the preservation of a secular republic and to the French norm of gender equality. In 2017, the European Court of Justice weighed in, ruling that employers could ban religious symbols in the workplace as long as they did not discriminate against any particular religious group.

In 2010 Parliament banned wearing the burqa, the full-body and full-face covering worn by some Muslim women, in public places (except places of worship), saying it contradicted the French ideals of *laïcité*, equality between the sexes, and *fraternité* (brotherhood). Most Muslims argued that the ban would further marginalize them from mainstream French life. Noting that fewer than two thousand women in the entire country regularly wear the *burqa*, critics suggested that the ban was more about "Islamophobia" and appealing to nationalist sentiments to gain political support than about an actual policy problem. In 2016 a controversy paralleling earlier debates arose over Muslim women wearing the "burkini," a full-body swimsuit, on French beaches. (Ironically, the bikini, once a controversial symbol of sexual license, became a symbol of "traditional" French values in this debate.) And in 2019, a French sporting goods store dropped plans to market a "sports hijab" when it faced a major public backlash against the idea.

Kemal Atatürk founded the modern Turkish state after World War I based on an explicit campaign to modernize and Westernize the country, in part by eliminating the role of Islam in the former seat of the Muslim caliphate. Whenever Muslim parties that called for Turkey to recognize its place in the Muslim Middle East gained too much power, they were banned or the military carried out a coup. The Muslim headscarf on women, though, was not banned in universities and government offices until 1981, and the ban wasn't regularly enforced until after the military forced an Islamist government out of power in 1998.

A new Islamist party, the Justice and Development Party (JDP), arose in 2001, led by the popular, charismatic mayor of Istanbul, Recep Tayyip Erdoğan. The JDP modified past Islamist parties' demands, preserving its embrace of Islamic principles on social issues but also supporting globalization, economic modernization tied to the West, and Turkey's application to join the European Union. It won the 2002 national election and Erdoğan and the JDP have been in power ever since, surviving a failed coup attempt by some elements in the military in 2016.

The JDP came to power promising to allow women to wear headscarves more widely, including in universities, but it did not pass legislation to that effect until February 2008. The secular elite reacted swiftly. Millions of secularists held pro-ban demonstrations, and the Constitutional Court ruled in June 2008 that the new law was unconstitutional. After winning a referendum in 2010 to amend the constitution, the JDP government felt it had the political strength to stop enforcing the ban on headscarves in universities. While it has not changed the constitution further, women are now allowed to wear headscarves at universities. By 2017, women could wear headscarves in all governmental jobs, including the military and police.

France and Turkey have long envisioned a strictly secular public sphere, a vision challenged by rising Islamic sentiment. Both states have reacted by legislating women's ability to wear clothing that symbolizes their Islamic faith, though by 2013 Turkey was moving toward fewer restrictions while France was moving toward more.

[of different religious groups]" (Bhargava 2016, 174). Philosophically, it closely resembles Kymlicka's multicultural integration in the sense that particular groups may be given particular rights in the interests of both social harmony and their inclusion in the broader society. As India demonstrates, that can be a difficult process in practice.

Gender and Sexual Orientation: The Continuing Struggle for Recognition, Social Status, and Representation

The women's movement and changes in women's position, activity, and status have been the most dramatic social and political revolution of the last generation, especially in wealthy countries. There, the number of women in the workforce, in professional positions, and in higher education has skyrocketed since the 1960s. Jeane Kirkpatrick wrote in the early 1970s in her classic study of the United States, *Political Woman:*

> Half a century after the ratification of the nineteenth amendment, no woman has been nominated to be president or vice president, no woman has served on the Supreme Court. Today, there is no woman in the cabinet, no woman in the Senate, no woman serving as governor of a major state, no woman mayor of a major city, no woman in the top leadership of either major party. (1974, 3)

Today, every item on the list has been checked off. While still underrepresented in each of the offices Kirkpatrick mentions, women are present in noticeable and growing numbers. As of 2013, 52 percent of Americans were represented by at least one woman as governor, senator, or Congress member. In 2018, a record number of women were elected to the U.S. Congress, bringing the total to over 20 percent (though obviously still far below their share of the population). Hillary Rodham Clinton, the Democratic nominee for president in 2016, won the most votes but lost the election in the Electoral College. While this final, political "glass ceiling" remains to be shattered, women's participation in American politics has been transformed since Kirkpatrick's statement. Many other countries have already shattered that final ceiling and outstrip the United States in percentage of women in high offices.

While some might argue that what is commonly known as the "gay rights movement" has not achieved as much progress as the women's movement, it has nonetheless had a dramatic and rapidly growing impact. Particularly in Western countries, gays and lesbians are often comfortable living in the open, and, in many countries, they have successfully fought for the right to marry, to serve in the armed forces, and, like women, to not face employment discrimination. However, both of these interrelated movements continue to face opposition to their demands, greater in some countries than others.

Both the women's and gay rights movements emerged from the tumultuous 1960s in the West. Women active in other movements, such as the anti–Vietnam War effort, gradually began to demand equal treatment and recognition, both within the movement and in society more broadly. The gay rights movement burst forth much more suddenly and dramatically. While various countries had small "homophile" organizations earlier, the modern gay rights movement was born in New York City in 1969 when New York police raided a popular gay bar, the Stonewall Inn, setting off five days of sometimes violent defense of the bar in what became known as the Stonewall riots. In the context of the racial and feminist movements of the late 1960s, the effect of Stonewall was dramatic: "Literally overnight, the Stonewall riots transformed the homophile movement of several dozen homosexuals into a *gay liberation movement* populated by thousands of lesbians, gay men, and bisexuals who formed hundreds of organizations demanding radical changes" (Eskridge 1999, 99).

The women's and gay rights' movements have fundamentally challenged social and political norms. Norms of gender and sexuality, of course, are closely intertwined. What it means to be a "man" in every society is tightly woven with what it means to be a "heterosexual man." And because particular notions of gender help define what it means to be a member of a nation, ethnic group, race, or religion, challenging gender and sexual orientation norms challenges the validity of other identity groups. Women, gays, and lesbians who demand recognition of gender and sexual orientation as distinct categories of concern have thus come into conflict not only with nationalists in the West but also with postcolonial nationalists who demanded national unity to throw off colonial rule, leaders of racial or ethnic groups who demanded unity to overcome oppression, and religious groups who demanded recognition and autonomy.

Most recently, the transgender movement has questioned not only gender norms but the definition of gender itself. The success of the feminist and gay rights movements has empowered transgender people to demand recognition and equal social status. The "coming out" of Caitlyn Jenner as a transgender woman in 2015 was simply the most public event in a longer history. In 2016 the U.S. government issued guidance for schools suggesting that giving transgender students equal access to all facilities, bathrooms in particular, based on their self-declared gender identity was necessary to fulfill laws on gender equality (Title IX of the Educational Amendments of 1972, in particular), and the military began to allow transgender soldiers to serve openly, though both policies were reversed under the Trump administration in 2018. Germany in 2013 became the first European country to allow parents to designate a newborn's gender as something other than "male" or "female" and in 2018 allowed adults to apply to change their legal gender from "male" or "female" to "diverse." Doing so, however, required a doctor's support, and transgender activists argued it should be a matter of personal choice. On the other side of the debate was a leader of a far-right party who said, "Gender designation has been an objective fact since the beginning of history" (Eddy 2018). The debate around primordialism versus constructivism, especially when it comes to gender, is not over.

Transgender rights also posed some problems for elements of the women's movement, as it raised the question of who is a "woman." Women's colleges, for instance, struggled with whether they should accept transgender women, who were assigned the male gender at birth, as students, including whether they should accept transgender women who had or had not had surgery to change their anatomy. (Not all transgender people desire or are able to have surgery to reconcile their anatomy with their gender identity.) Some feminists also questioned whether transgender women who had spent most of their lives living as men could understand the discrimination women face and therefore be included as legitimate members of women's movements.

The question of exactly who should be included in the group has long been debated within the gay rights movement as well. Originally referred to as "homosexual," by the late 1960s, the group had adopted the term "gay and lesbian" in some countries, in part because "homosexual" had been a term used by psychiatrists to classify the practice as a mental disorder. By the 1980s, though, it was becoming clear that not all people who were not heterosexual identified themselves as gay or lesbian. Sex research has long shown that sexual preferences do not fit into absolute categories but rather extend along a continuum—from sole preference for the opposite sex on one end and for the same sex on the other and a range of variation in between. Eventually, the categories "bisexual" and "transgender" were added to produce "lesbian, gay, bisexual, and transgender" (LGBT). Even though transgender refers to gender identity rather than sexual orientation (transgender people can be of any sexual orientation), their movement arose within the "gay rights" movement, and they share the common issue of demanding to live their true identity in the public sphere rather than being forced to hide "in the closet." Recently, some activists and theorists have adopted the word *queer,* formerly considered derogatory, as an affirmative term to include the entire LGBT group or sometimes as an addition to the label, as in LGBTQ, the most common current designation in the United States.

Debating Goals

As they challenged other groups, feminists and LGBTQ rights advocates also debated among themselves what their agenda ought to be. This debate mirrors the broader debate on multiculturalism and group rights. Liberal feminists, like proponents of liberal equality more generally, focus on gaining equal rights with men as their main goal, and they tend not to challenge social or political norms beyond that, accepting existing political and economic systems but demanding equal treatment within them. Similarly, LGBTQ activists who favor what is known as an assimilationist approach seek equal civil and political rights but generally are willing to adopt the cultural norms of mainstream, heterosexual society: for instance, they favor same-sex marriage, the expansion of a heterosexual institution to include them.

Many feminist and LGBTQ theorists and activists demand more than just equal treatment in legal, political, and economic contexts. Like other proponents of group rights, many feminists have come to believe that major social and political institutions need to change if women are to truly realize legal equality. Philosopher Iris Marion Young argued that for women as well as other marginalized groups:

> Inclusion ought not to mean simply the formal and abstract equality of all members of the polity of citizens. It means explicitly acknowledging

> social differentiations and divisions and encouraging differently situated groups to give voice to their needs, interests, and perspectives. (Young 2000, 119)

This might require changes to electoral systems or various types of affirmative action programs to ensure that women and others have access to the power and resources needed to influence policy.

Similarly, the **liberationist** approach to LGBTQ rights seeks to transform sexual and gender norms, not simply to gain equal rights with heterosexuals but also to liberate everyone to express whatever sexual orientation or gender identity they wish. The goal is to gain social acceptance and respect for all, regardless of their conformity to preexisting norms or institutions. Those favoring a liberationist approach question the importance of same-sex marriage because they question the entire idea of marriage as a patriarchal, heterosexual institution from which everyone should be liberated. They certainly favor equal rights, but they seek much greater change than that, calling for a new "sexual citizenship" (Bell and Binnie 2000).

Objectives and Outcomes

Recognition

Both women and the LGBTQ community initially demand recognition of themselves as a group and their concerns as legitimate. Recognition is especially central to the LGBTQ community because they have been forced to hide throughout most of human history. In this context, being publicly recognized and "coming out" as gay or transgender is the first crucial political act. In gaining recognition, these groups have raised a fundamental question about how the state should regulate the "private" sphere. Liberal political debate is generally restricted to what is deemed "public," with private matters left to the individual, family, and religious institutions. Each society defines for itself, however, what is public and what is private. In most societies, including those in the West, men's treatment of their wives was long a private concern: verbal, physical, and sexual abuse, as long as it did not go as far as murder (and sometimes even when it did), was typically ignored and considered a private, family matter. On the other hand, the act of engaging in sex with someone of the same sex was considered morally offensive and therefore subject to public sanction. In reality, all liberal democracies regulate the "private" sphere in one way or another; the question is how they will do so. The women's and LGBTQ movements have demanded and, in many cases achieved, changes to this regulation.

Social, Legal, and Economic Status

While women have made many gains, their social and legal status is still not uniformly equal to men's. Women's groups worldwide have sought greater access for women to education and participation in the labor force at all levels, and while women have not achieved full parity, they have made tremendous gains. Many people have an image of Western women as having achieved nearly equal status with men while women in postcolonial countries continue to be mired in oppression. In fact, in many postcolonial countries, this image no longer applies. The gender gap in educational access and attainment has narrowed substantially in most Latin American and African countries and in some Asian ones as well, although,

liberationist: Member of the LGBTQ movement who seeks to transform sexual and gender norms so that all may gain social acceptance and respect regardless of their conformity to preexisting norms or institutions

as is true everywhere, professional status and labor force participation rates lag behind education. Aili Mari Tripp (2013) asked not what kind of country but what kind of regime produces the best outcomes for women, finding that even when controlling for the wealth of the country, democracies provided better outcomes for women overall, including in countries that recently went through democratic transitions. Map 4.1 displays gender inequality rankings around the world.

Concerns about achieving greater social and economic status have led women to demand reproductive rights and state support for childbearing and child rearing. Women's movements have successfully championed the spread of access to contraception in much of the world, and birth rates have fallen significantly in most countries over the last generation. Legalized abortion remains a controversial subject, with women successfully leading efforts in many societies to support it even as moral and religious objections keep it illegal in quite a few others. Women in approximately sixty countries currently have access to legal abortion. Women, especially in wealthier countries, have also demanded greater state support for childbearing and child rearing to facilitate their participation in the labor force and the public realm. Support has included paid and unpaid maternity leave, paid and unpaid paternity leave (for fathers to help with child rearing), and access to affordable and high-quality childcare.

A recent addition to the prominent goals involving women has been the "#MeToo" movement, which demands an end to sexual assault and harassment via greater exposure of men who perpetrate these crimes, better legal processes, and changes of institutional rules in a wide variety of settings in order to define assault and harassment more clearly and prevent it more successfully. While starting in the United States, it has spread rapidly, including to countries such as Denmark,

MAP 4.1

Gender Inequality

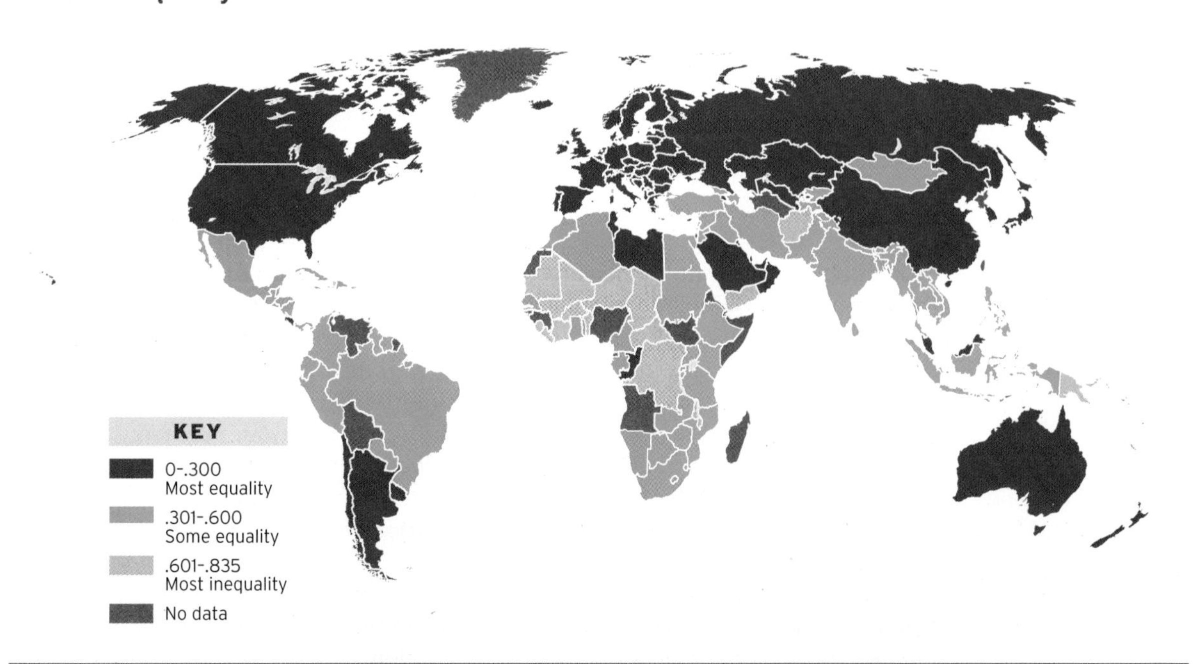

Source: Gender Inequality Index 2018. International Human Development Indicators, United Nations Development Programme (http://hdr.undp.org/en/composite/GII).

which in other areas is given high praise for its egalitarian gender relations but still has a serious assault and harassment problem (Sorensen 2019).

A key target of women's groups worldwide has been the achievement of legal status equal to that of men in areas of family law, including rights concerning custody of children, land ownership, and inheritance of family property. These gains have been achieved in virtually all wealthy countries but not in all postcolonial countries. In many of the latter, women still face various legal inequities vis-à-vis men that prevent them from independently owning land or inheriting property; in some cases, women are even restricted from having independent access to banking and travel. While virtually all countries have active women's movements working toward these goals, women in most postcolonial societies remain poorer and less educated, on average, than in wealthier countries, so their movements lack the resources that have helped wealthier women achieve many gains.

Members of the LGBTQ community cannot proclaim their identity publicly in most countries because of laws criminalizing their behavior, so repealing those laws is always one of the first priorities. Beyond decriminalization of their behavior, they have worked for passage of antidiscrimination laws that prevent government, employers, educators, and adoption agencies from discriminating based on sexual orientation.

States around the world have responded to the LGBTQ movement in various ways, as Map 4.2 demonstrates. Some have not only decriminalized homosexual activity but have legalized same-sex marriage; others have severe penalties for any homosexual activity. The biggest issue of recent years has been same-sex marriage. A handful of states have granted complete rights to marry, starting with the Netherlands in 2001 and by 2019 including twenty-five countries, as shown on Map 4.2. Proponents of same-sex marriage argue it is a matter of equal civil rights for all. Opponents disagree based on religious beliefs or on the argument that heterosexual marriage is a key building block of social order and should be preserved as such. In contrast to many of the debates over inclusion, in this case, those arguing for the status quo do so on the basis of preserving particular group rights (religious justifications for heterosexual marriages), while those seeking change argue for treating all individuals equally.

Although the LGBTQ movement began in the United States, its success there was comparatively slow. Sodomy laws against homosexual activity were not eliminated by the Supreme Court until 2003, gay men and lesbians were not allowed to serve openly in the military until 2010, and same-sex marriage was not legalized nationwide until 2015. It remains legal to discriminate on the basis of sexual orientation in the workplace in most of the country: twenty-one states have laws protecting against employment discrimination on the basis of sexual orientation (eighteen of which include gender identity as well), but no federal antidiscrimination legislation exists. The Employment Non-Discrimination Act (ENDA) to do so has been introduced in Congress every year since 1974 but has never passed. Its current version includes protection on the basis of gender identity. LGBTQ employees have reported facing discrimination on the job in numerous surveys. While it is difficult to obtain accurate data because many LGBTQ people do not reveal their identity to their employer, one survey found that gay and bisexual men earn between 10 and 32 percent less than heterosexual men in the U.S. workforce (Mezey 2017, 4).

Relatively few postcolonial societies have active LGBTQ movements. Higher levels of religiosity and cultural traditions in many of these societies mean greater social opposition to public proclamation of homosexuality, as Map 4.2

MAP 4.2

Gay Rights

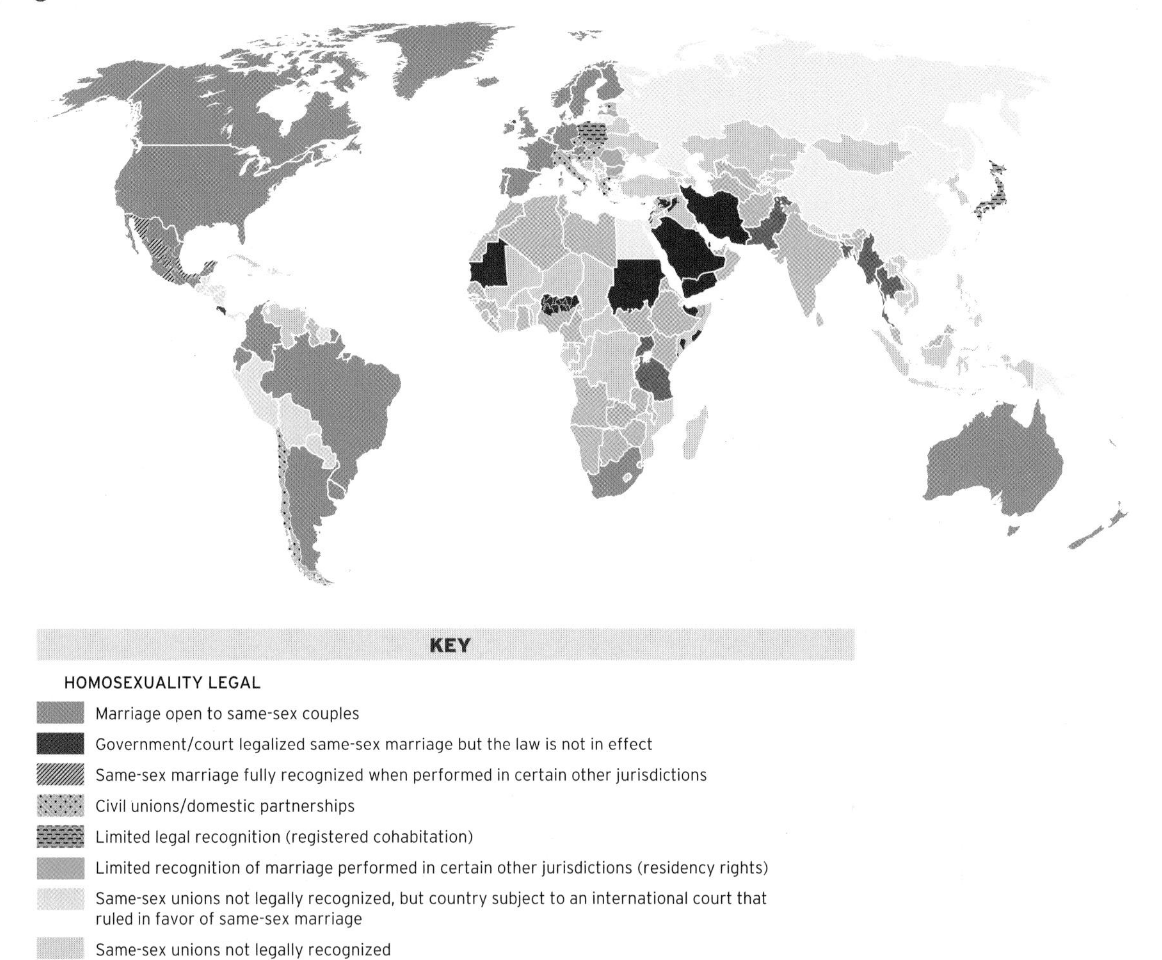

Source: Wikipedia, Homosexuality Laws (http://en.wikipedia.org/wiki/File:World_homosexuality_laws.svg); (https://www.washingtonpost.com/graphics/world/gay-rights/).

demonstrates. In a growing number of postcolonial countries, however, active gay rights movements have arisen. Indeed, South Africa became the first country in the world to include sexual orientation in its constitution as a category protected from discrimination. In 2005 a South African court interpreted this to apply to marriage, making it also one of the first countries to legalize gay marriage. Fledgling LGBTQ movements elsewhere in Africa, such as in Zimbabwe, Kenya, and Uganda, face much greater popular and legal resistance. In many African and Middle Eastern countries, homosexual activity remains explicitly illegal. Brazil is an example of a postcolonial society with an active LGBTQ movement that has had some notable policy successes, including legalizing gay marriage in 2013, though the election of the openly anti-gay rights president, Jair Bolsonaro, in 2018 raised questions about the future of gay rights in Latin America's largest country.

Political Representation

After a long struggle, women have gained recognition as a group with legitimate concerns and basic political rights in many societies (though not all). In terms of rights, members of the LGBTQ group are unusual in the sense that they secured basic political rights as individuals long before civil rights; that is, as individuals they could vote or run for office like any other citizen, as long as they kept their sexual orientation or transgender identity private. As a group, though, they were unwelcome until quite recently in all societies. Once they gain social and legal acceptance, the barriers to political participation are greatly reduced.

Women's movements, however, have focused great effort on improving their representation in the political process. Feminist scholar Jane Mansbridge (2000) argued that "descriptive representation"—representation by people who look like you and have similar life experiences—is particularly important when social inequality results in groups of citizens not trusting their elected representatives who hail from a different group, communication among members of different groups might be difficult, or unforeseen issues arise between elections. Tiffany Barnes and Stephanie Burchard (2013) used a statistical analysis of survey data to demonstrate that descriptive representation in the form of more women in legislatures produces greater female political engagement in the citizenry. Examining India, Simon Chauchard (2017) found that where so-called untouchables—the lowest caste in India (see chapter 6)—gained local political office, norms of how to treat them and relationships between them and the long-dominant higher castes improved.

While women have definitely gained ground, they remain just 24.1 percent of the total members of parliament worldwide (see Map 4.3), and only fifty-six countries have had a female head of government at some point in the last century (but only fifteen did in 2017). Parliamentary representation varies widely but not systematically by region. A number of postcolonial states have higher percentages of female representatives than do the United States or some European countries; Rwanda, Cuba, and Bolivia were the only countries above 50 percent in 2019. Women's movements in many countries have championed the creation of quotas for women's legislative participation, in the form of either rules that require a certain percentage of each party's candidates to be women or a certain percentage of women in the legislature itself. Quotas are typically set at anywhere from 25 to 50 percent of the total seats or candidates. While only ten states had any type of quota before 1980, over one hundred had them by 2010. The majority of these, however, have been voluntarily adopted within parties. Aili Mari Tripp and Alice Kang (2008) concluded from a large statistical analysis that quotas have a greater effect on the number of women in legislatures than do economic development, religion, or other commonly used explanations for why women gain representation. Quotas also are associated with greater substantive representation of women's issues (Krook and Schwindt-Bayer 2013, 565).

Quotas for women in legislatures, especially those mandated by law (more typical in Asia and Africa than in Europe), raise the key questions in the debate over

MAP 4.3

Percentage of Women in Legislative Seats Worldwide

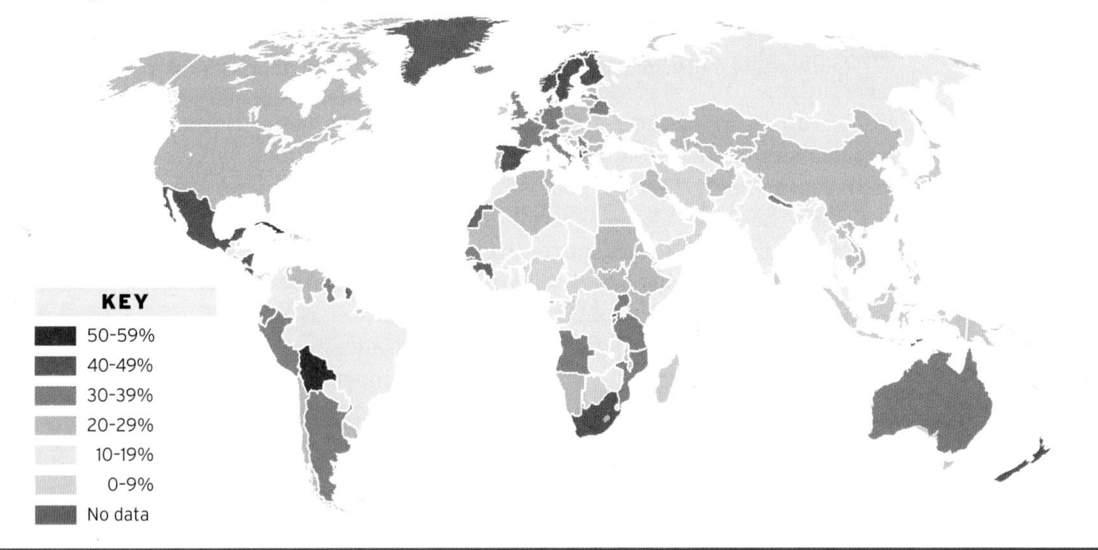

Source: Inter-Parliamentary Union, "Women in National Parliaments" (http://www.ipu.org/wmn-e/classif.htm).

Note: Bolivia, Rwanda, and Cuba are the only countries where women occupy 50 percent or more legislative seats. Percentages are for lower and single houses only. Data for upper houses, where available, can be found at the source website above. South Africa's estimate does not include the thirty-six special rotating delegates appointed on an ad hoc basis; all percentages given are therefore calculated on the basis of the fifty-four permanent seats.

multiculturalism and inclusion in democracies. Supporters of simple liberal equality argue that women are free to vote and run for office, and if they are elected, they are free to serve. Any type of quota violates the principle of equal citizenship for all. Supporters of quotas, on the other hand, argue for the group right of descriptive representation, following Iris Young's argument that democracies need to ensure that the voices of marginalized groups are included in policy discussions.

CRITICAL INQUIRY

The World Values Survey: Attitudes Toward Women, Religion, and Homosexuality

This chapter treats claims for inclusion by religious groups, women, and gays and lesbians separately, though we note that they share many similarities and can be understood using the same philosophical debate. The Critical Inquiry table provides data from the World Values Survey of attitudes toward all three groups and a few other key variables for a selection of countries. What patterns can you see in the data? Do attitudes for all three areas go together? Why or why not? What hypotheses can you generate to explain the patterns you find? Can you tie these hypotheses to some of the theories that explain political behavior that we've examined throughout the book?

(Continued)

(Continued)

	Importance of religion (% responding "very" and "rather important")	Membership in church (% active members)	Trust people of another religion (% responding "trust completely" and "trust somewhat")*	Importance of democracy (%)**	When jobs are scarce, men should have more right to a job than women (%)	Men make better political leaders (% responding "agree" and "strongly agree")	Homosexuality justified (% responding always justified) †***	Don't want homosexuals as neighbors (%)†
Argentina	56.1	17.0	53.1	71.6	15.0	26.9	28.4	11.0
Brazil	89.4	49.5	57.5	65.9	16.8	28.4	23.4	11.1
Colombia	85.4	49.1	28.6	70.3	22.4	27.4	11.6	34.6
Chile	50.3	23.1	40.8	72.8	17.6	27.0	29.1	25.7
Burkina Faso	94.8	23.8	52.3	58.8	50.5	57.6	3.9	80.5
Ghana	98.5	69.2	44.4	72.8	49.3	81.3	1.6	79.7
Rwanda	72.3	29.2	39.0	55.0	42.3	45.7	0.3	88.4
South Africa	83.9	56.2	53.8	55.2	30.0	51.6	17.2	37.9
Germany	38.0	14.1	50.0	84.6	15.5	19.8	36.6	22.4
France	40.8	4.3	75.0	77.2	18.1	20.7	47.8	28.8
United Kingdom	40.1	19.0	65.4	76.0	15.8	27.8	32.0	16.8
United States	68.4	34.5	69.0	72.7	5.7	19.4	31.9	20.4
Egypt	99.8	0.4	40.0	86.6	83.4	86.4	–	–
Iran	94.3	19.9	–	64.0	69.0	78.0	2.5	92.4
Iraq	97.5	7.0	32.8	66	65.2	79.3	1.2	80.3
Morocco	98.7	1.5	22.4	64.8	60.6	57.4	0.7	85.5
India	91.3	14.0	50.0	59.3	52.4	52.0	1.9	65.0
Indonesia	98.0	37.6	37.8	70.5	54.2	59.0	1.6	65.9
Japan	19.0	3.7	10.1	64.4	30.0	27.6	22.7	–

Source: World Values Survey (http://www.wvsevsdb.com/wvs/WVSAnalizeQuestion.jsp); selected samples: Argentina 2013, Brazil 2014, Colombia 2012, Chile 2011, Egypt 2012, Germany 2013, Ghana 2011, India 2012, Iraq 2013, Japan 2010, Morocco 2011, Rwanda 2012, South Africa 2013, United States 2011, Burkina Faso 2007, France 2006, Indonesia 2006, Iran 2005, United Kingdom 2005.

*Percentage combines answers "trust completely" and "trust a little" in the survey.

**Percentage combines answers 8–10 from the survey, where the survey used a scale of 1–10, with 1 being "not at all important" and 10 being "absolutely important."

***Percentage combines answers 8–10 from the survey, where the survey used a scale of 1–10, with 1 being "not at all justified" and 10 being "absolutely justified."

†World Values Survey notes that questions having to do with homosexuality were not asked in some countries for "cultural reasons."

Conclusion

Identity politics is so common and explosive in part because, as identity categories are created, a sense of superior and inferior status is often embedded within them. How a group is defined influences what it may claim in order to gain or enhance its power. In countries with significant immigration, like the United States and Germany, new immigrants continually raise new issues: their racial or ethnic categorization must be clarified, and the ongoing construction of their categories will influence their place and political power in the broader "nation" they are attempting to join.

Each person belongs to various identity groups, but whether people act politically based on these group memberships depends on a variety of factors. First, the group in question must have a sense of itself: it must be an "imagined community" with both perceived historic ties and a forward-looking agenda. Second, it must have some felt grievance. Finally, groups need political leadership, elites who can build on and strengthen the identity and link it to particular grievances and appropriate action.

Identity groups always pose challenges to the modern state. Under some circumstances, nationality, ethnicity, race, or religion can challenge the very existence of a state. Even when this is not the case, though, all identity groups raise questions of inclusiveness and equal citizenship. In liberal democracies, such challenges cut to the heart of one of the defining characteristics of the regime. Demands for inclusive citizenship can also raise challenges when they clash with the demands of other identity groups. States must then resolve the question of which groups' demands to meet. This can be particularly difficult when, for instance, women or LGBTQ groups demand individual civil rights in the name of equality, while a religious, ethnic, or other minority group claims a conflicting right to respect for its cultural practices.

The outcomes of protracted and intense political battles always reveal something about who rules in a particular political system. In the political disputes we examined in this chapter, a dominant group protecting the status quo exists in almost all cases. Lack of identity-based conflict may indeed reflect nearly complete domination by that group, as the "second face of power" (see chapter 1) would suggest. Where questions about the inclusion of minority or marginalized identity groups have become politically salient, those groups have at least gained enough power to raise their demands. Their success demonstrates growing power; continuing limitations on their demands equally demonstrate limits on their power. ●

KEY CONCEPTS

assimilation (p. 85)
autonomy (p. 85)
centripetal approach (p. 87)
civic nationalism (p. 89)
consociationalism (p. 86)
constructivism (p. 82)
cultural nationalism (p. 89)
ethnic group (p. 90)
jus sanguinis (p. 89)
jus soli (p. 89)
***laïcité* (p. 99)**
liberationist (p. 104)
multicultural integration (p. 86)
nation (p.88)
nationalism (p. 88)
neutral state model (p. 98)
political saliency (p. 82)
positive accommodation (p. 99)
primordialism (p. 82)
race (p. 91)
social class (p. 94)
social construction (p. 83)

WORKS CITED

Anderson, Benedict. 1991. *Imagined Communities: Reflections on the Origin and Spread of Nationalism.* New York: Verso.

Barnes, Tiffany, and Stephanie Burchard. 2013. "'Engendering' Politics: The Impact of Descriptive Representation on Women's Political Engagement in Sub-Saharan Africa." *Comparative Political Studies* 46 (7): 767–790. doi:10.1177/0010414012463884.

Bell, David, and Jon Binnie. 2000. *The Sexual Citizen: Queer Politics and Beyond.* Cambridge, UK, and Malden, MA: Polity Press and Blackwell.

Bhargava, Rajeev. 2016. "Is European Secularism Secular Enough?" In *Religion, Secularism, and Constitutional Democracy,* edited by Jean L. Cohen and Cecile Laborde, 157–181. New York: Columbia University Press.

Bonikowski, Bart, and Paul DiMaggio. 2017. "What 4 Types of Nationalism Can Tell Us About Trump Voters." *Washington Post,* February 6, 2017. https://www.washingtonpost.com/news/monkey-cage/wp/2017/02/06/true-or-false-real-americans-are-christian-speak-english-and-were-born-in-the-u-s/?postshare=3881487038528513&utm_term=.40a631caf979.

Chandra, Kanchan, ed. 2012. "Introduction." In *Constructivist Theories of Ethnic Politics,* 1–50. Oxford, UK: Oxford University Press.

Chauchard, Simon. 2017. *Why Representation Maters: The Meaning of Ethnic Quotas in Rural India.* Cambridge, UK: Cambridge University Press.

Cornell, Stephen, and Douglas Hartmann. 2007. *Ethnicity and Race: Making Identities in a Changing World.* 2nd ed. Thousand Oaks, CA: Pine Forge Press.

Eddy, Melissa. 2018. "Not Male or Female? Germans Can Now Choose 'Diverse," *New York Times.* December 14, 2018. https://www.nytimes.com/2018/12/14/world/europe/transgender-germany-diverse.html.

Eskridge, William N., Jr. 1999. *Gaylaw: Challenging the Apartheid of the Closet.* Cambridge, MA: Harvard University Press.

Evans, Geoffrey, and James Tilley. 2017. *The New Politics of Class: The Political Exclusion of the British Working Class.* Oxford, UK: Oxford University Press.

Fetzer, Joel S., and J. Christopher Soper. 2005. *Muslims and the State in Britain, France, and Germany.* Cambridge, UK: Cambridge University Press.

Gat, Azar. 2014. *Nations: The Long History and Deep Roots of Political Ethnicity and Nationalism.* With Alexander Yakobson. Cambridge, UK: Cambridge University Press.

Horowitz, Donald L. 1985. *Ethnic Groups in Conflict.* Berkeley: University of California Press.

Huber, John. D. 2017. *Exclusion by Elections: Inequality, Ethnic Identity, and Democracy.* Cambridge, UK: Cambridge University Press.

Huntington, Samuel P. 1997. *The Clash of Civilizations and the Remaking of World Order.* New York: Touchstone. (Originally published in 1996 by Simon and Schuster.)

Kirkpatrick, Jeane J. 1974. *Political Woman. New* York: Basic Books.

Krook, Mona Lena, and Leslie Schwindt-Bayer. 2013. "Electoral Institutions." In *The Oxford Handbook of Gender and Politics,* edited by Georgina Waylen, Karen Celis, Johanna Kantola, and S. Laurel Weldon, 554–578. Oxford, UK: Oxford University Press.

Kymlicka, Will. 1995. *Multicultural Citizenship: A Liberal Theory of Minority Rights.* Oxford, UK: Clarendon Press.

Kymlicka, Will, and Wayne Norman, eds. 2000. *Citizenship in Diverse Societies.* Oxford, UK: Oxford University Press.

Lijphart, Arend. 1977. *Democracy in Plural Societies: A Comparative Exploration.* New Haven, CT: Yale University Press.

Mansbridge, Jane. 2000. "What Does a Representative Do? Descriptive Representation in Communicative Settings of Distrust, Uncrystallized Interests, and Historically Denigrated Status." In *Citizenship in Diverse Societies,* edited by Will Kymlicka and Wayne Norman, 99–123. Oxford, UK: Oxford University Press.

Marshall, T. H. 1963. *Class, Citizenship, and Social Development: Essays.* Chicago: University of Chicago Press.

McClintock, Anne. 1991. "'No Longer in a Future Heaven': Women and Nationalism in South Africa." *Transition* 51: 104–123.

Mezey, Susan Gluck. 2017. *Beyond Marriage: Continuing Battles for LGBT Rights.* New York: Rowman & Littlefield.

OECD. 2017. *Understanding the Socio-economic Divide in Europe: Background Report.* January 26, 2017. https://www.oecd.org/els/soc/cope-divide-europe-2017-background-report.pdf.

Renan, Ernest. 1882. *What Is a Nation?* http://www.nationalismproject.org/what/renan.htm.

Smith, Anthony D. 1998. *Nationalism and Modernism.* New York: Routledge.

Sorensen, Martin Selsoe. 2019. "Denmark's 'Pervasive Rape Culture" Is Detailed in New Report." *New York Times.* March 4, 2019.

Stepan, Alfred. 2011. "The Multiple Secularisms of Modern Democratic and Non-Democratic Regimes." In *Rethinking Secularism,* edited by Craig Calhoun, Mark Juergensmeyer, and Jonathan van Antwerpen, 114–144. Oxford, UK: Oxford University Press.

Stewart, Matthew. 2018. "The Birth of a New Aristocracy." *The Atlantic*. June 2018. https://www.theatlantic.com/magazine/archive/2018/06/the-birth-of-a-new-american-aristocracy/559130/.

Taylor, Charles. 1994. "The Politics of Recognition." In *Multiculturalism: Examining the Politics of Recognition,* edited by Amy Gutmann, 25–74. Princeton, NJ: Princeton University Press.

Tripp, Aili Mari. 2013. "Political Systems and Gender." In *The Oxford Handbook of Gender and Politics,* edited by Georgina Waylen, Karen Celis, Johanna Kantola, and S. Laurel Weldon, 514–535. Oxford, UK: Oxford University Press.

Tripp, Aili Mari, and Alice Kang. 2008. "The Global Impact of Quotas: On the Fast Track to Increased Female Legislative Representation." *Comparative Political Studies* 41 (3): 338–361. doi:10.1177/0010414006297342.

Young, Iris Marion. 2000. *Inclusion and Democracy.* Oxford, UK: Oxford University Press.

Yuval-Davis, Nira, and Flora Anthias, eds. 1989. *Woman-Nation-State.* Consultant ed., Jo Campling. Basingstoke, UK: Macmillan.

RESOURCES FOR FURTHER STUDY

Baksh, Rawwida, and Wendy Harcourt, eds. 2015. *The Oxford Handbook of Transnational Feminist Movements.* Oxford, UK: Oxford University Press.

Brass, Paul R. 1991. *Ethnicity and Nationalism: Theory and Comparison.* Newbury Park, CA: Sage.

Brubaker, Rogers. 1992. *Citizenship and Nationhood in France and Germany.* Cambridge, MA: Harvard University Press.

Cordell, Karl, and Stefan Wolff, eds. 2011. *Routledge Handbook of Ethnic Conflict.* New York: Routledge.

Gellner, Ernest. 1983. *Nations and Nationalism.* Oxford, UK: Blackwell.

Ghai, Yash P., ed. 2000. *Autonomy and Ethnicity: Negotiating Competing Claims in Multi-Ethnic States.* Cambridge, UK: Cambridge University Press.

Gurr, Ted Robert. 1970. *Why Men Rebel.* Princeton, NJ: Princeton University Press.

Hobsbawm, Eric J. 1990. *Nations and Nationalism Since 1780: Programme, Myth, Reality.* Cambridge, UK: Cambridge University Press.

Hunter, Shireen T., ed. 2002. *Islam, Europe's Second Religion: The New Social, Cultural, and Political Landscape.* Westport, CT: Praeger.

Hutchinson, John, and Anthony D. Smith, eds. 2000. *Nationalism: Critical Concepts in Political Science,* vol. IV. New York: Routledge.

Ignatiev, Noel. 1995. *How the Irish Became White.* New York: Routledge.

Joppke, Christian, and John Torpey. 2013. *Legal Integration of Islam: A Transatlantic Comparison.* Cambridge, MA: Harvard University Press.

Juergensmeyer, Mark. 1993. *The New Cold War? Religious Nationalism Confronts the Secular State.* Berkeley: University of California Press.

Kaufman, Stuart J. 2001. *Modern Hatreds: The Symbolic Politics of Ethnic War.* Ithaca, NY: Cornell University Press.

Lovenduski, Joni, ed. 2005. *State Feminism and Political Representation.* Cambridge, UK: Cambridge University Press.

Lowe, Chris. 1997. "Talking About 'Tribe': Moving From Stereotypes to Analysis." With Tunde Brimah, Pearl-Alice Marsh, William Minter, and Monde Muyangwa. http://www.africaaction.org/talking-about-tribe.html.

Mazur, Amy G. 2002. *Theorizing Feminist Policy.* Oxford, UK: Oxford University Press.

Parekh, Bhikhu C. 2000. *Rethinking Multiculturalism: Cultural Diversity and Political Theory.* Cambridge, MA: Harvard University Press.

Sinno, Abdulkader H., ed. 2009. *Muslims in Western Politics.* Bloomington: Indiana University Press.

Taras, Raymond, and Rajat Ganguly. 2002. *Understanding Ethnic Conflict: The International Dimension.* 2nd ed. New York: Longman.

Van Deburg, William L., ed. 1997. *Modern Black Nationalism: From Marcus Garvey to Louis Farrakhan.* New York: New York University Press.

Wimmer, Andreas. 2013. *Waves of War: Nationalism, State Formation, and Ethnic Exclusion in the Modern World.* Cambridge, UK: Cambridge University Press.

WEB RESOURCES

Center for American Women and Politics

(http://www.cawp.rutgers.edu)

Conflict Analysis Resources, Royal Holloway, University of London

(http://www.rhul.ac.uk/economics/home.aspx)

Correlates of War

(http://www.correlatesofwar.org)

Fractionalization Data, The MacroData Guide

(http://www.nsd.uib.no/macrodataguide/set.html?id=16&sub=1)

International Lesbian, Gay, Bisexual, Trans and Intersex Association

(http://ilga.org)

OutServe-Servicemembers Legal Defense Network

(http://www.outserve-sldn.org)

Quota Project

(http://www.quotaproject.org)

The Religion and State Project, Bar Ilan University, Israel

(http://www.religionandstate.org)

Research Network on Gender Politics and the State

(https://pppa.wsu/research-network-on-gender-politics-and-the-state/)

UNDP Human Development Reports, Gender Inequality Index

(http://hdr.undp.org/en/statistics/gii)

World Values Survey

(http://www.worldvaluessurvey.org)

PART II

Political Systems and How They Work

5 Governing Institutions in Democracies

President Uhuru Kenyatta gives his first speech as president in April 2013. Kenya adopted a new constitution that changed its governing system from a British-style parliamentary system to a U.S.-style presidential system. The big question since is over institutionalization: Will the government really follow the new rules? Many critics argue that Kenyatta's government has violated it in numerous ways. Opponents have been unable to stop him, and he was reelected in 2017.
Billy Mutai/ Nation Media/Gallo Images/Getty Images

Key Questions

- A democracy must limit the power of its executives to provide accountability. Which institutional choices best ensure accountability, and how?
- How much power should a minority have in a democracy? How do different democracies seek to guarantee that minorities are protected from possible majority tyranny? Do some institutional choices seem to guarantee this better than others?
- Do greater participation and representation of many voices in government result in less effective policymaking?
- How can we explain why an institution that works well in one setting might not work as well in another?
- What explains why particular democratic institutions arise in particular countries but not in others?

Learning Objectives

After reading chapter 5, you should be able to do the following:

5.1 Delineate the difference between majoritarian and consensual democracies

5.2 Explain the similarities and differences among parliamentarism, presidentialism, and semipresidentialism

5.3 Explicate how accountability, policymaking, and stability vary across political systems

5.4 Understand the importance of the judiciary in upholding state institutions

5.5 Explain the positives and negatives of bureaucracies in politics

5.6 Define federalism and articulate its strengths and weaknesses

Schools in almost every country teach students about the formal institutions of their government and how they are supposed to work. Understanding politics requires knowing what powers are specifically allotted to different institutions, but it also requires far more. Social, cultural, and historical contexts can have significant bearing on how institutions function in practice. Presidents in different countries may have the same powers on paper, but one may be able to exercise them more effectively due to the context. Similarly, presidents in the same country at different times may have more or less actual power due to changing socioeconomic and cultural factors or because a particular leader helps strengthen or weaken an institution. To really understand politics, we must ask not just what a country's institutions look like on paper but to what degree a state's government processes and procedures are really honored in practice. This varies within and across all types of regimes. It is important to examine in democracies and even more important in authoritarian regimes, where it tends to vary more, as we'll see in chapter 8.

The study of institutions in democracies, which is the focus of this and the next chapter, raises other important questions for democratic theory and comparative politics. The first question involves who rules: Do certain institutional arrangements achieve greater **political accountability**, meaning the ability of the citizenry to directly or indirectly control political leaders and institutions?

political accountability: The ability of the citizenry, directly or indirectly, to control political leaders and institutions

Argentine political scientist Guillermo O'Donnell (1999) used the terms *vertical* and *horizontal accountability* to analyze the extent to which the power of key state institutions is under democratic control. **Vertical accountability** is

vertical accountability: The ability of individuals and groups in a society to hold state institutions accountable

the ability of individuals and groups to hold their state's institutions accountable directly. We examine participation and representation, the mechanisms of vertical accountability, in chapter 6.

This chapter focuses on **horizontal accountability**, the ability of the state's institutions to hold one another accountable. This is a type of indirect control on the part of the citizenry since institutions can act on behalf of the citizenry to thwart potential nondemocratic abuse of power by other institutions or leaders. Examples include the legislature's ability to ask the executive to justify his actions and ultimately to punish unconstitutional or unacceptable uses of power or the judiciary's ability to overrule legislative or executive actions as unconstitutional. In other words, we need to understand the relative balance of power among governing institutions.

You have probably already realized that the executive, legislature, judiciary, and so on are all types of governing institutions. Only one of these, the executive, is essential to a modern state as (see chapter 2). As sovereign entities that administer territories and people, all modern states need an executive and accompanying bureaucracy. The **executive** is the chief political power in a state, typically the single most powerful office in government. The position is filled through elections in a democracy, and is usually referred to as a president or prime minister. The executive of a modern state also requires a bureaucracy, a large set of lesser officials whose function is to implement the laws of the state, as directed by the chief executive. We explore both executive powers and modern bureaucracies in this chapter.

The idea of horizontal accountability suggests that a legislature and judiciary with autonomy from the executive are important institutions of democratization, even if not crucial to the modern state itself. The process of democratization is in part a matter of creating mechanisms through which the power of the executive is limited. In democratic theory, the **legislature** makes the law, and the **judiciary** interprets it. The power and autonomy of each, however, varies significantly in practice.

Many political scientists believe that forces in the modern world are strengthening the executive branch. The contemporary state has more sophisticated functions to carry out than in earlier eras. Legislators often delegate more technical decisions implied in particular laws to bureaucrats because the legislators lack the competence to make those decisions. As a result, the size and power of bureaucracies have expanded, making control of the executive paramount. Some political scientists also worry about a possible "judicialization" of politics in which courts and judges, the vast majority of whom are appointed, replace elected officials as key decision makers.

A second crucial question in democracies is, How much power should be given to the majority that, at least in theory, rules? Democracy implies majority rule, but how much power the majority has over dissident minorities remains a fundamental question. Some formal institutions give the representatives of the majority far greater power than do others. The United Kingdom and United States stand in sharp relief on this issue and illustrate the range of available options. As we discuss below, British parliamentary democracy gives the majority party much greater power than the divided and limited powers outlined in the U.S. Constitution does. Both countries are democracies, but they address the question of how formal institutions should protect minorities quite differently.

Finally we must ask, Is there a trade-off between popular participation in the government and representation of many viewpoints, on the one hand, and effective governance, on the other? If the institutions of a particular regime strongly limit one another and many different groups are represented in the decision-making

horizontal accountability: The ability of state institutions to hold one another accountable

executive: The chief political power and branch of government that must exist in all modern states; responsible for implementing all laws

legislature: Branch of government that makes the law in a democracy

judiciary: Branch of government that interprets the law and applies it to individual cases

FIGURE 5.1

Vertical and Horizontal Accountability

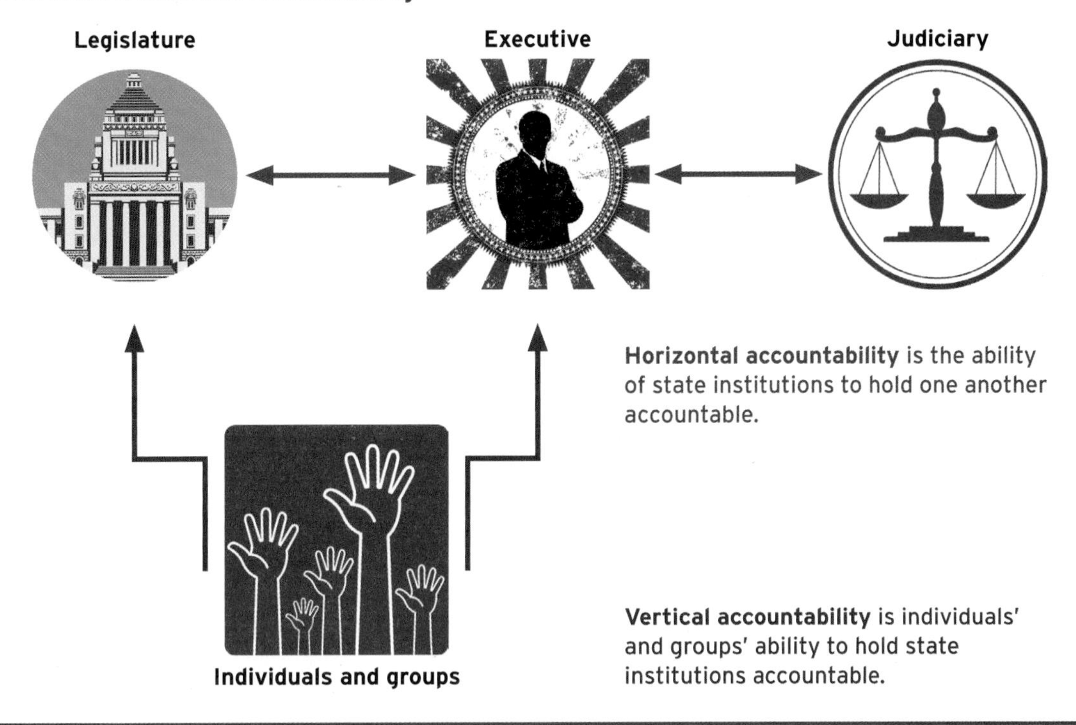
Legislature
Executive
Judiciary
Horizontal accountability is the ability of state institutions to hold one another accountable.
Vertical accountability is individuals' and groups' ability to hold state institutions accountable.
Individuals and groups

process, does this limit the government's ability to make effective policy? Arend Lijphart (1999) examined this question and suggested that we think of democracies on a continuum from what he termed "majoritarian" to "consensus." **Majoritarian democracies** concentrate power in a single place and office; they have a single-party executive, executive dominance over the legislature, a single legislative branch, and constitutions that can be easily amended. **Consensus democracies**, in contrast, have multiparty executives called a **coalition government** (in which at least two parties negotiate an agreement to rule together), executive–legislative balance, bicameral legislatures (with two roughly equally powerful houses), and rigid constitutions that are not easily amended. As Figure 5.2 illustrates, no democracy is perfectly majoritarian or consensus; rather, they lay on a continuum from one pole to the other. If a trade-off exists between representation and effective policymaking, majoritarian systems ought to be more effective because they have much more concentrated power. They seem likely to produce less horizontal accountability, however, since they have few institutions to check the executive.

George Tsebelis (2002) studied limits on effective policymaking as well. He argued that a key distinction among political systems and institutions is the number of veto players. A **veto player** is an individual or collective actor whose agreement is essential to effect policy change. The more veto players there are and the greater the ideological distance among them, the less likely policy change will be. Both institutional positions and structures defined by a constitution and more transient partisan battles and political support can create veto players. We will see how both the arrangement of governing institutions (examined in this chapter)

majoritarian democracy: A type of democratic system that concentrates power more tightly in a single-party executive with executive dominance over the legislature, a single legislative branch, and constitutions that can be easily amended

consensus democracy: A democratic system with multiparty executives in a coalition government, executive–legislative balance, bicameral legislatures, and rigid constitutions that are not easily amended

coalition government: Government in a parliamentary system in which at least two parties negotiate an agreement to rule together

veto player: An individual or collective actor whose agreement is essential for any policy change

FIGURE 5.2

Democracies on a Continuum

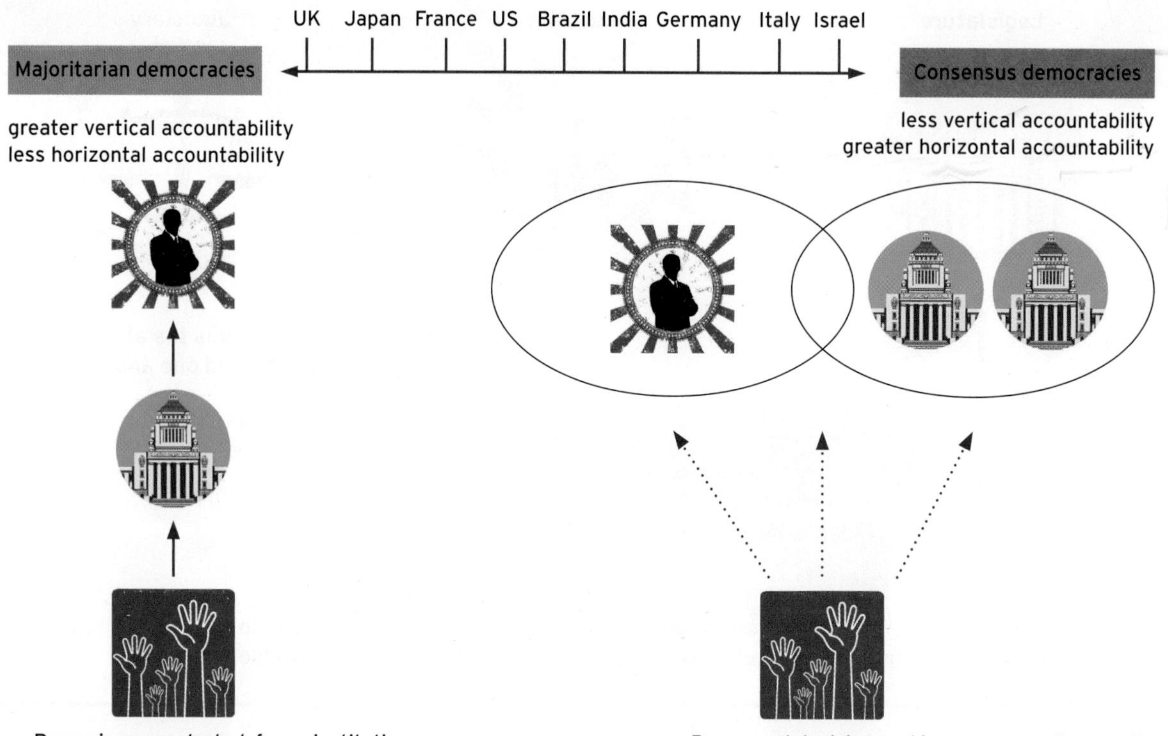

- Power is concentrated: fewer institutions to check executive power
- Single-party executive
- Executive dominance over legislature
- Single legislative branch
- Easily amended constitutions
- Key example = UK's Westminster

- Power and decision making are more dispersed
- Multiparty executives (coalition government)
- Executive-legislative balance
- Bicameral legislatures
- Hard-to-amend constitutions
- Key examples = coalition government in Israel or divided government in the US

and institutions of participation and representation (examined in chapter 6) create veto players. We will examine the trade-offs among horizontal and vertical accountability, representation, and effective policymaking in both chapters.

We begin with the relationship between the executive and legislative branches, which, more than anything else, distinguishes different kinds of democracies. We then examine the roles of the judiciary and the modern bureaucracy and their relationships to the executive and legislative branches. We also look at the question of federalism and the extent to which the overall power of the state is either centralized in national institutions or dispersed among subnational units of government; federalism can be another means of achieving accountability.

head of state: The official, symbolic representative of a country, authorized to speak on its behalf and represent it, particularly in world affairs; usually a president or monarch

Executives and Legislatures

The executive is indispensable to any state or regime and fulfills two very important roles. First, as **head of state**, the executive is the official, symbolic representative of a country, authorized to speak on its behalf and represent it, particularly in world affairs. Historically, heads of state were monarchs, who still exist as symbolic heads of state in a number of countries, including the United Kingdom and Japan. Second, as **head of government**, the executive's task is to implement the nation's laws and policies. The two parts of the executive function may be filled by one individual or two, but both are essential to any regime. Legislatures are less ubiquitous because authoritarian regimes can dispense with them. They are, however, crucial to democratic regimes because a legislature's very democratic function is to debate public policy and pass laws. We discuss the executive and legislature together because the relationship between them distinguishes three classic models of democratic government: parliamentarism, presidentialism, and semipresidentialism.

Parliamentarism: The Westminster Model

If you ask Americans to define democracy, many will start with the "separation of powers." The oldest model of modern democracy, however, does not separate the executive and legislature. Commonly known as the Westminster, or parliamentary, model, it originated in Britain. Lijphart called **parliamentarism** the purest form of his "majoritarian" model, in which power is concentrated in one place, creating very few institutional veto players. The fusion of the executive and legislative branches provides for an exceptionally powerful executive. This fusion exists in the office of the **prime minister (PM)** (in Germany, the chancellor), whose relationship to the legislature is the key distinguishing feature of the model. The PM is not only the executive but also a member of the legislature. She is the leader of the majority party or leading coalition party in the legislature. The PM, then, is not elected directly to executive office but rather is named after the legislative election determines the dominant party in parliament. Citizens cast one vote for a party or individual, depending on the electoral system, to represent them in parliament; the majority in parliament then names the prime minister. In practice, when citizens vote for parliament, they know who the PM candidate for each party is, so their vote for their preferred **member of parliament (MP)** or party is indirectly a vote for that party's leader to serve as PM.

Formally, the PM serves at the pleasure of parliament. Should a parliamentary majority lose confidence in the PM, members can cast a **vote of no confidence** that forces the PM to resign. At that point, the leading party in parliament can choose a new leader who will become PM, or the resigning PM will ask the head of state to call new parliamentary elections. Parliamentary systems often do not have fixed terms of office, and while the parliament can oust a prime minister if she loses the support of the majority of MPs, a PM can similarly dissolve parliament and call for new elections, as the Spanish PM did in February 2019 when parliament rejected his budget. In practice, votes of no confidence are usually called by the opposition party and are only successful in removing the government about 5 percent of the time, but they provide the opposition a means to highlight the government's weaknesses and usually result in opposition gains in the next election (Williams 2011).

Parliamentary systems separate the two functions of the executive. They have a "nonexecutive head of state," who embodies and represents the country ceremonially. Countries lacking a hereditary monarchy typically replace the monarch in this function with an elected head of state, whose title is often "president" but whose role, like the queen's in Britain, is small and ceremonial. Countries tend to elect esteemed elder political or cultural figures as presidents, who gracefully perform the ceremonial role while leaving all important executive functions to the head of the government, the PM. When a PM's party holds a majority of the seats

head of government: The key executive power in a state; usually a president or prime minister

parliamentarism: A term denoting a parliamentary system of democracy in which the executive and legislative branches are fused via parliament's election of the chief executive

prime minister (PM): The head of government in parliamentary and semipresidential systems

member of parliament (MP): An elected member of the legislature in a parliamentary system

vote of no confidence: In parliamentary systems, a vote by parliament to remove a government (the prime minister and cabinet) from power

in parliament and votes regularly as a bloc (as is almost always the case in parliamentary systems), the PM is an extremely powerful executive. Whatever legislation she puts forth is almost automatically passed into law by the legislature. A prime minister is in a somewhat different position if her party does not have a clear majority in parliament. In this situation, the PM will head a coalition government, in which at least two parties negotiate an agreement to rule together. A vote of no confidence is far more likely in a coalition government because if one party in the coalition is unhappy with a PM's policies, it can leave the coalition, causing the coalition to lose its majority. Smaller parties in the coalition often become partisan veto players; the PM must ensure that she has their support before she can get her legislation through parliament or even before she can form a government, a process that can involve extensive negotiations. After Sweden's 2018 election, it took 133 days for four parties to create a coalition that could gain enough support in parliament to govern.

The prime minister also appoints the other ministers (what Americans call "secretaries") to the cabinet, but the close executive relationship with parliament limits the PM's discretion in making these choices. The cabinet, especially in a coalition, serves as a check on the PM. Cabinet ministers must also be MPs, and in a coalition government, the prime minister must consult with the other parties in the coalition about the distribution of "portfolios" (cabinet seats). Normally, all parties in the coalition—and certainly the biggest ones—get some representation in the cabinet. The cabinet, then, is often the site of the most important negotiations over policy. When all cabinet members are from the same party, once they have agreed to put forth a piece of legislation, it should pass through the legislature quite easily.

FIGURE 5.3

Typical Parliamentary System

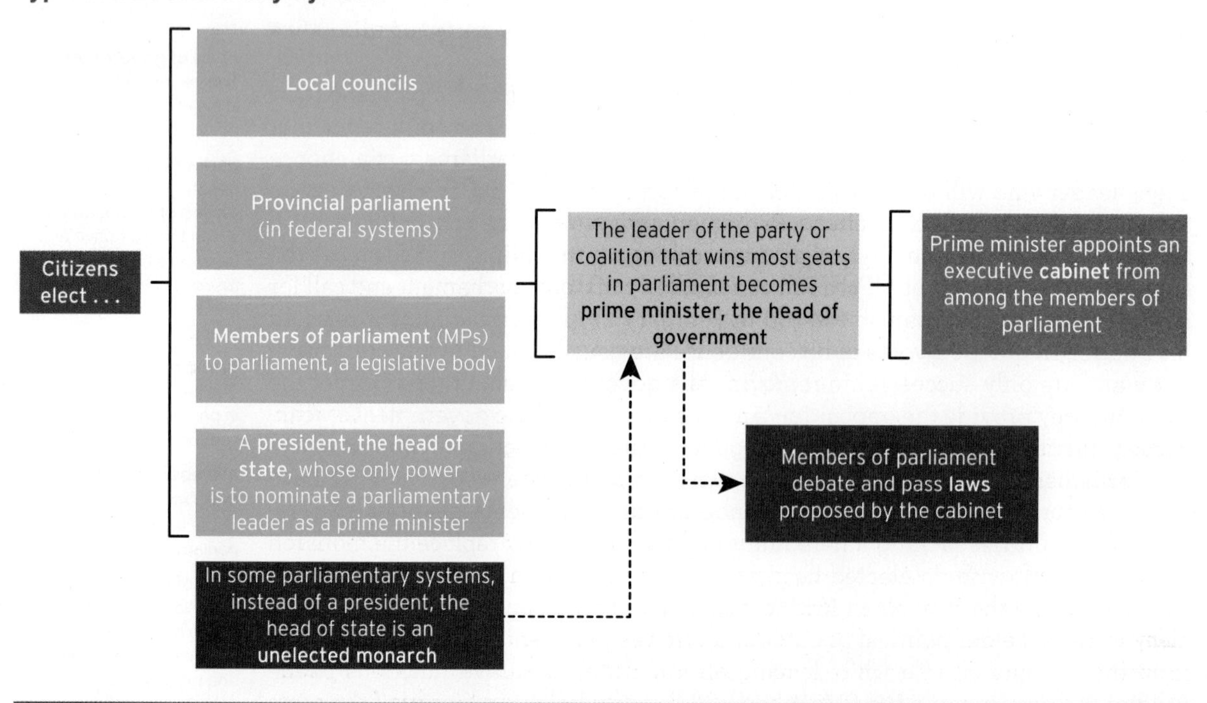

Of course, how these institutions work in practice depends on the context in each country, especially the nature of the electoral system and number of political parties (which we explore in detail in chapter 6). The parliamentary system was invented in Britain, which remains the classic case. Britain's prime minister is often called the most powerful democratic executive in the world. Like the United States, Britain has two major parties (Labour and Conservative) that almost always alternate in power: one or the other wins a majority of legislative seats in virtually every election. This means that coalition governments are very rare (the coalition government from 2010 to 2015 was the first since World War II). Unlike parties in the United States, British parties were traditionally highly disciplined in the legislature, meaning that MPs almost always voted in support of their party's position on legislation. This was partly an effect of the parliamentary system itself. Ambitious MPs want to become cabinet ministers, and the head of the party controls these positions; thus, MPs demonstrate loyalty to the party leadership. As head of the majority party, the PM could usually get legislation passed with ease. The system has very few veto players. Many argue that PMs have begun to look more presidential. The two most important PMs of the last generation, Margaret Thatcher (1979–1990) and Tony Blair (1997–2007), were charismatic leaders whose campaigns looked more like U.S. presidential campaigns than had prior British elections and who gave their cabinet ministers less of a role in setting policy. For the first time, the 2010 election even featured American-style televised debates among the three main contenders for PM.

The Brexit debate of 2018–2019 raised profound challenges for the traditional relationship of the PM and Parliament and seemed to undermine the PM's control. PM Theresa May had two years to negotiate the country's exit from the EU, as demanded by voters in a 2016 referendum. When May brought her plan, negotiated with the EU, to Parliament in early 2019, it suffered a humiliating defeat. The tradition of party discipline broke down dramatically, with Conservative members of Parliament repeatedly voting against their own party's PM. Parliament subsequently gave itself extraordinary powers to propose and vote on alternative possible Brexit plans, in open revolt against the PM's control. Both parties' MPs split on how, if, and when Brexit should happen. Party discipline and with it the PM's ability to set the agenda and pass legislation largely evaporated. May finally resigned in June 2019 and the Conservative party voted in a new prime minister, pro-Brexit Boris Johnson. This was the fourth time in twenty years that a new PM came to power not by a national election but by the majority party choosing to change leaders between elections.

India, a former British colony, has a nearly identical parliamentary system on paper, but it has functioned quite differently in a different context. For the first four decades after independence, one party dominated, winning every election. This left its leader as PM with very few constraints on her power. The dominant party's popularity declined over time, however, and from 1989 to 2014 every government was a coalition of multiple parties. Small parties that negotiated membership in these coalitions became quite important, requiring the PM to compromise with them. This has produced a predictable drop in stability, as seen in the number of PMs India has had: in its first thirty years of independence (1947–1977), the country had only three PMs; in its second thirty years (1977–2007), it had twelve, only three of whom served full terms. Coalition government also meant that parliament became less effective (Pelizzo 2010); it passed fewer laws than it did under the dominance of one party, and MPs spent far less time there. For all of these reasons, many Indians have bemoaned the "decline of parliament" as an institution, but the opposition in parliament has become more assertive, regularly introducing legislation, and sometimes even passing it with a coalition of small parties' support,

CRITICAL INQUIRY

Parliaments and Presidents

Map 5.1 shows how many parliamentary, presidential, and semipresidential systems exist today and where they are located. What patterns do you see in terms of where different systems have been adopted? What might explain those patterns? Which theoretical arguments from chapter 1 can help you explain the patterns? Choose a country that you think might not fit the patterns you've noticed, and do some background research to figure out why it's different. What does that tell you about why countries choose particular institutions and not others?

MAP 5.1

Three Major Types of Electoral Democracy

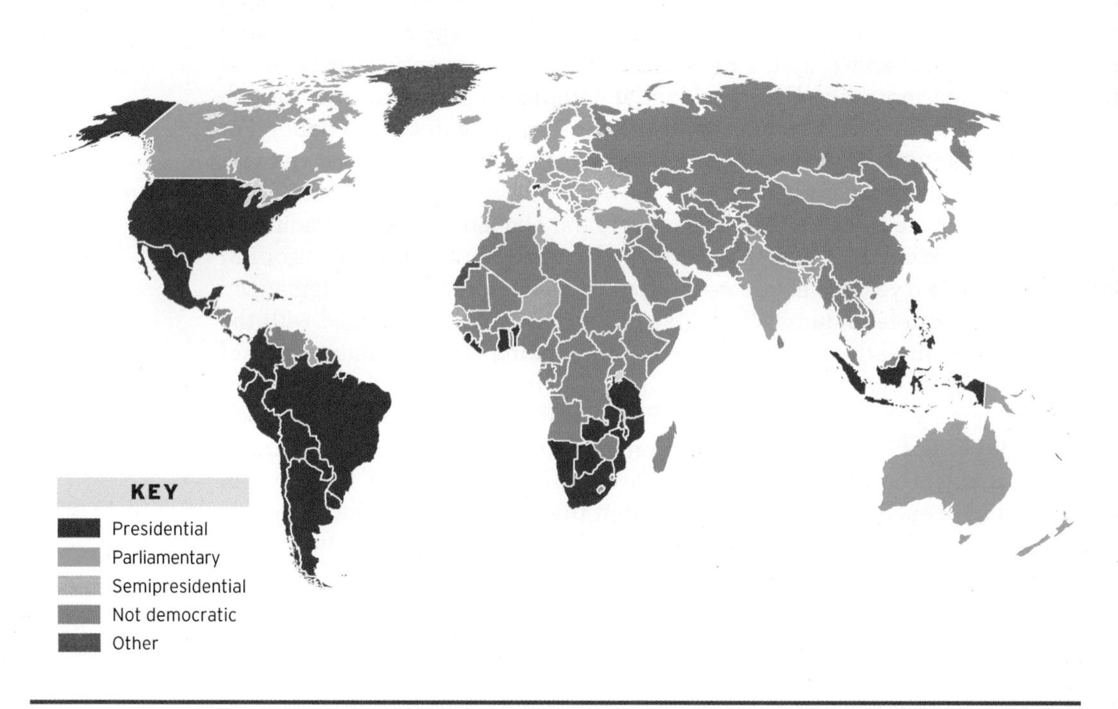

Source: Data are from Freedom House, Freedom in the World 2018 (https://freedomhouse.org/report/freedom-world/freedom-world-2018) and (http://en.wikipedia.org/wiki/File:Forms_of_government.svg). Modified by the authors.

something very rare in parliamentary systems. Narendra Modi's Bharatiya Janata Party (BJP) won an outright majority in parliament in 2014 and again in 2019, producing the first non-coalition governments since 1989.

presidentialism: A term denoting a presidential system of democracy in which the executive and legislature are elected independently and have separate and independent powers

Presidential Systems: The Separation of Powers

Presidentialism needs little introduction for American students because the best known and most enduring example is the United States. In a presidential system, the roles of head of state and head of government are filled by the same person, who is given the title "president." The crucial, defining aspect of a presidential system, however, is not this fusion of executive roles. Rather, it is the concept of **separation of powers**. The American founders, following the ideas of a French liberal political theorist, the Baron de Montesquieu, argued that the functions of the executive and legislative branches should be separate. Particulars of any specific constitution may differ, but everything about any presidential system reflects this choice. Thus, the executive and legislative branches are elected in separate (though possibly concurrent) elections, and the president must be independently and directly (or nearly directly) elected. Regardless of the electoral or party system in place, this institutional feature gives presidential systems an element of consensual democracy: institutional veto players are built into the founding documents of the system. The president and legislature are both legitimized independently by the electoral process, and creating laws requires the agreement, in some way, of both the president and a majority in the legislature (see Figure 5.4).

In contrast to parliamentary systems, presidents and their legislatures generally cannot interfere with one another's time in office. Presidents serve a fixed term, and it is very difficult for a legislature to remove the president from office. Most countries provide for some kind of impeachment process, but this usually requires extraordinary measures and can only be justified in extreme circumstances. Barring impeachment, no matter how much legislators disagree with the president or question his competence or policy, they cannot remove the executive from office. Similarly, legislators have fixed terms. In a bicameral legislature, terms may be different for each house. Regardless of the details, a president may not tamper with a legislature's sessions by forcibly shortening or lengthening them.

separation of powers: Constitutionally explicit division of power among the major branches of government

FIGURE 5.4

Typical Presidential System

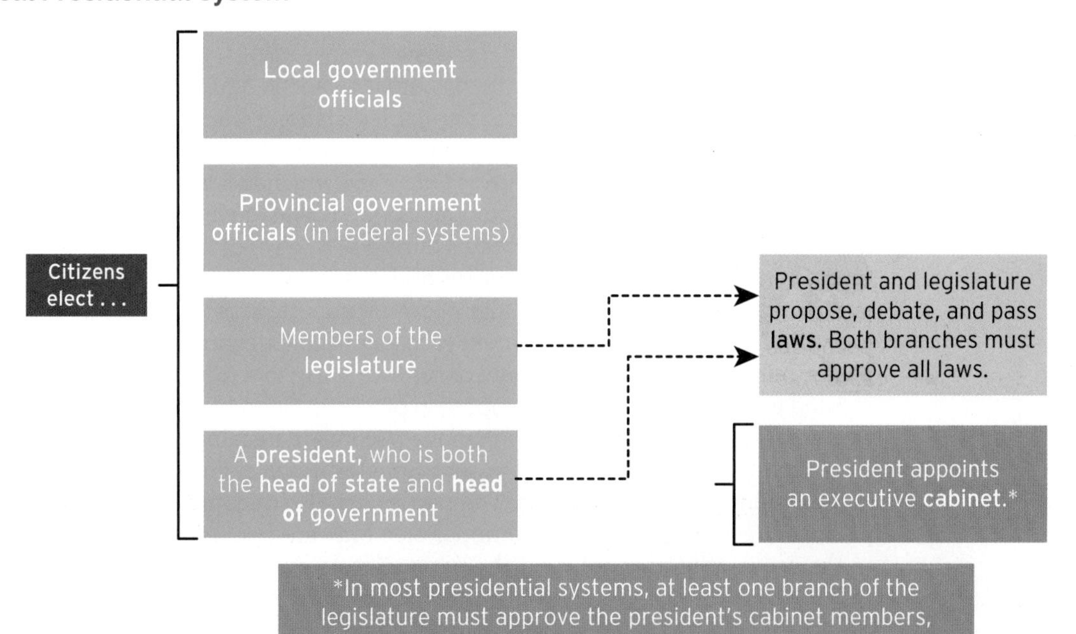

Finally, the separation of powers is clear in the president's powers of appointment. Although presidents may need the consent of the legislature, they are largely free to appoint their own cabinet ministers or secretaries. They may—and in many cases (including the United States) must—appoint individuals who are not in the legislature. They may also appoint people from any party they wish. Their appointments need not reflect the composition of the legislature in any way. Once appointed and confirmed by the legislature, the officers serve at the president's pleasure, and the legislature can interfere only minimally with their activities. In practice, of course, most presidents try to appoint to their cabinet a group of people more or less representative of the major political factions in their party. They only do this to the extent they think is politically expedient, however, rather than being required to in order to form a government, as prime ministers are. Thus, the cabinet is typically a far less important decision-making body than in a parliamentary system. Also, because members of the legislature are not vying directly for cabinet appointments, the president has less control over them than a PM does, so the legislature becomes a more important and independent decision-making body. Ironically, this means that legislatures in presidential systems are typically more powerful than legislatures in parliamentary systems.

The office of the president was one of the more controversial parts of the original U.S. Constitution. Many leaders, most notably Thomas Jefferson, feared that a single executive would inevitably become authoritarian. Although the formal powers are largely unchanged after 240 years, informal presidential power has certainly expanded. The president has become the symbolic leader of the nation, the undisputed leader of his party, and both the chief initiator and implementer of legislation. Members of Congress initiate considerable legislation, but the most important bills usually start as presidential initiatives. Nonetheless, most observers argue that the U.S. Congress is still the most powerful legislature in the world. It has perhaps the most extensive and expensive staffs of any legislature in the world. Committees and subcommittees are crucial in investigating, amending, and passing legislation. Individual members have great freedom to introduce legislation compared with members of most national legislatures, and it's entirely possible that individual legislation will become law.

One possible result of a strong executive balanced against a strong legislature is "gridlock," or the inability to pass major legislation, which has become an issue of great concern in recent years. Stalemates are most likely when one party controls the presidency and the other controls Congress, which has become the norm in the U.S. presidential system. Frank Baumgartner and colleagues (2014) compared legislative productivity in the United States during periods of divided versus united government (when the same party controls both the executive and legislative branches) and found that Congress is less likely to pass important legislation when power is divided. One of the president's main jobs has become trying to get his legislation passed, either by cajoling members of his own party to support him or by negotiating and compromising with the opposing party in Congress, especially when it is in the majority. Compromises, though, have become increasingly difficult to achieve. American parties appear to be gaining greater unity; their legislators vote more and more frequently in lockstep. The parties are also becoming more ideologically polarized (McCarty 2014) and national elections are becoming more competitive, in the sense of parties splitting the national vote evenly (Lee 2014). In the House of Representatives, fewer districts, though, are individually competitive; more and more have clear majorities for one party or the other, meaning individual legislators only need to worry about appealing to their party's supporters. These phenomena reinforce one another: as national competition increases, parties need to distinguish themselves from one another ideologically, leading to polarization. Individual congressional candidates use these ideological positions to gain the support of their party stalwarts in their relatively homogenous districts. Legislators therefore oppose the other party's proposals, not only because they disagree but also in order to gain an electoral advantage with their constituents. This would not produce gridlock in a parliamentary system; the majority party would simply have control of both the executive and legislature and be able to govern unimpeded, for better or worse. In a presidential system, though, it makes governing extremely difficult.

How easily a president can get her preferred policies approved by the legislature depends on whether she has majority support, via her own party or a coalition of parties, in the legislature as well as her ability to bargain with legislators. As democracy has spread around the world in the last thirty years, presidential systems have become more common but so has party fragmentation. A president facing a legislature made up of many parties, with her own party holding only a small percentage of the seats has become common. In this situation, the president has to form a coalition of parties in the legislature in order to pass laws, referred to as **coalitional presidentialism**. In these situations, presidents start to act a little more like prime ministers. While not required to in order to be in office like a prime minister, they nonetheless appoint members of other parties to their cabinet in order to secure those parties' support as part of a coalition that will pass the president's policy initiatives.

Brazil is a classic case of this relatively new and important variation on presidentialism, which produces a much weaker president. The Brazilian president's formal powers are actually greater than in the United States, including (1) the authority to issue provisional decrees (PDs), which become law for thirty days unless the National Congress approves them permanently; (2) a line-item veto, which allows her to eliminate individual measures in a bill sent from the National Congress without vetoing the entire law; (3) a monopoly over initiation of all legislation involving the budget; and (4) the ability to declare legislation urgent, moving it to the top of the National Congress's agenda.

The Brazilian president must operate, however, in a system with many fragmented parties. Brazil's electoral system gives politicians little incentive to form broad, inclusive parties or to follow party leaders once they are in the National Congress. Brazil's legislature therefore includes many parties, with the president's party typically controlling less than 20 percent of the seats. The only way for presidents to get their legislation passed is to build coalitions among several parties. Indeed, in the last few elections, several parties have supported the two major presidential candidates, a result of preelection negotiations regarding sharing power after the election. The president then appoints members of parties supporting her to the cabinet, like a prime minister would in a parliamentary system. Such presidential coalitions have been quite large and ideologically diverse, averaging nine parties each. Much of the debate over legislation, then, happens within the informal governing coalition rather than between them and the opposition. In the face of a massive corruption scandal, Brazilians elected "outsider" Jair Bolsonaro, from a tiny party, president in 2018. For the first time in twenty years, a president would have to try to make policy without a preexisting legislative coalition to support him, potentially weakening the Brazilian presidency anew.

coalitional presidentialism: A presidential system with many parties in the legislature, requiring the president to form an informal coalition of parties to pass legislation.

semipresidentialism: A term denoting a semipresidential system of democracy in which executive power is divided between a directly elected president and a prime minister elected by a parliament

Semipresidentialism: The Hybrid Compromise

The third major executive–legislative system is the most recently created. **Semipresidentialism** splits executive power between an elected president and a prime minister. The president is elected directly by the citizens as in a presidential system and serves as the head of state, but she also has significant powers in running the government. The official head of government is the PM, who is the leader of the majority party or coalition in parliament, as in a parliamentary system. The president appoints the PM, who must also obtain majority support in the parliament. Legislation requires the signature of the president, as well as support of the PM as head of the ruling party or coalition in parliament. The parliament can force the PM and cabinet to resign through a vote of no confidence. For semipresidentialism to be successful, the powers and duties of the president and PM as dual executives must be spelled out clearly in the constitution. For example, the president may be given power over military decisions (as in Sri Lanka) or foreign policy (as in Finland), whereas the prime minister typically concentrates on domestic policies. The specific division of powers varies greatly, however, and is not always clearly delineated.

The semipresidential system originated in France in the 1958 constitution establishing the Fifth Republic. Charles de Gaulle, a World War II hero and undisputed political leader of France at the time, envisioned the presidency as a stabilizing and powerful position, legitimated via national election. He assumed that the same party would win the presidency and a legislative majority. So long as it did, semipresidentialism gave the president, as head of the majority party who also appoints the PM, unparalleled power to govern.

cohabitation: Sharing of power between a president and prime minister from different parties in a semipresidential system

This worked as intended until the 1980s, when for the first time the president was elected from one party and the majority of the legislature from another, a situation the French humorously call **cohabitation**. Under cohabitation, the president must compromise with the legislature by appointing a PM from the majority party in the legislature rather than from his own party. A compromise had to be worked out regarding the specific powers of the president and the PM, since the French constitution did

FIGURE 5.5

Typical Semipresidential System

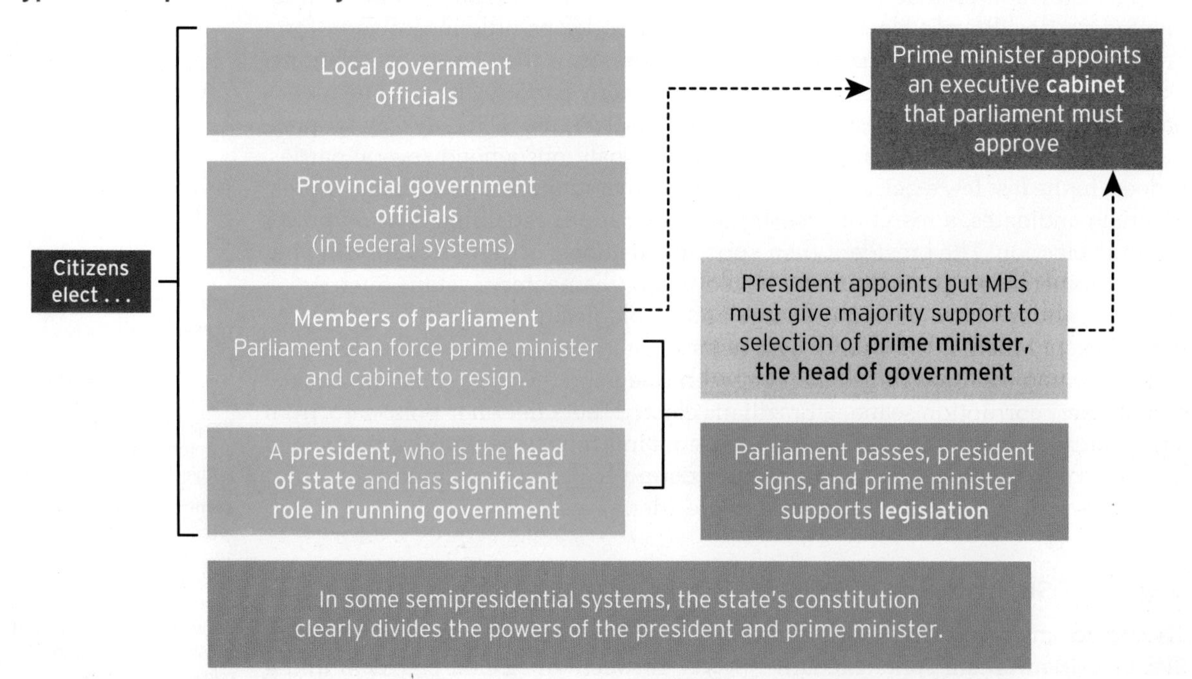

not draw clear boundaries. In practice, the compromise has been that the president runs foreign policy while the PM and the legislature control domestic policy. Critics of semipresidentialism fear that it gives the president too much power, but cohabitation clearly limits those powers significantly. If a majority in the legislature is elected in opposition to the president, he is forced to accept the results and live with cohabitation and the limits it imposes. However, cohabitation can also produce gridlock and inability to legislate effectively, as in a purely presidential system.

A second crucial institutional question in semipresidential systems is whether the president has the power to remove the PM. Robert Elgie (2011) argued that if he does, the semipresidential system is much less stable because neither the president nor the majority in parliament will have an incentive to compromise. If the president cannot remove the PM, the legislature has greater power, making the president more likely to compromise with it, which produces greater power sharing among contending factions. The semipresidential system, then, can produce stronger or weaker institutional veto players depending on the context: under cohabitation and with more limited presidential powers, veto players are stronger and compromise more likely.

Comparing Executive–Legislative Institutions

In comparing parliamentary, presidential, and semipresidential systems, we ask three major questions. Which system is most democratic in the sense of providing greatest accountability? Which system is most effective at making public policy? Which system provides the greatest political stability for a democratic regime? All three systems provide vertical accountability—the major leaders are subject to electoral sanction by voters. But how frequent and effective is this vertical accountability? And how much horizontal accountability exists? Recall that Lijphart (1999) argued that each system has trade-offs among accountability, efficiency, and stability. More majoritarian systems, with concentrated power and fewer veto players, may provide less representation and accountability but more efficient policymaking and perhaps fewer crises. More consensual systems tend to be just the opposite—the distribution of power among major parties and institutions makes more robust horizontal accountability but may threaten effective policymaking. In practice, the level of accountability, efficiency, and stability vary within each type of institutional structure, depending in part on the electoral system and the number and strength (discipline in voting together as a bloc) of political parties in a given country.

Accountability

The Westminster system, the most purely majoritarian system, is extremely democratic in theory because the legislature, the elected body of the people, is supreme. In multiparty systems such as contemporary India, parliamentarism may be more consensual, promoting negotiation, coalition building, and representation of a wide range of views in the cabinet. In a primarily two-party system like Britain's, however, in which one party almost always has a majority, the PM may be an unusually powerful executive because she is guaranteed legislative support. Some critics also argue that the modern world, especially with the rise of first television and now social media, is making prime ministers more similar to presidents who always have a legislative majority and therefore vest too much power in the hands of a single individual. On the other hand, Powell (2000) argued this can provide greater vertical accountability—at election time, citizens know whom to hold responsible for government policy.

Presidentialism seems to have greater horizontal accountability because the separation of powers gives legislatures more influence and greater ability to check the president. This is especially true where there are weaker parties (as in the United States) or divided government (with the presidency and legislature controlled by different parties). It may, however, interfere with effective policymaking, a problem analysts have seen in the United States in recent years. A presidential system with strong, disciplined parties and in which the president's party has a legislative majority, however, will look much like a parliamentary system with a strong majority party. Accountability in semipresidential systems depends not only on the strength and number of parties but also on the president's powers. If the president heads a strong party with a legislative majority, little horizontal accountability exists, though vertical accountability may be clearer. On the other hand, if a party opposed to the president controls the legislature, as under cohabitation in France in the 1980s, the president will have to compromise regularly with the prime minister. In this situation, horizontal accountability increases via more veto players.

Policymaking

In a review of the political science literature, David Samuels (2007) concluded that, overall, presidential systems are less likely to make policy that changes the status quo via legislation, and when they do, change will take longer and be more expensive than in parliamentary systems. In semipresidential systems, much depends on whether the president, PM, and parliamentary majority are from the same party. If so, little compromise will likely be necessary. If one or more are from different parties, compromise is more essential and successful policymaking less likely. This, of course, makes short-term horizontal accountability stronger.

Majoritarian systems with fewer constraints and veto players can change policy quickly and with little compromise, especially if they control a majority in parliament. In more consensual systems—parliamentary systems with coalitions, semipresidential systems with divided governments, presidential systems especially when different parties control the executive and legislature—compromise becomes more complex and time-consuming, making decisive policy changes is harder. Many observers contend this explains why PM Margaret Thatcher in the United Kingdom changed economic policies so much more successfully than did U.S. president Ronald Reagan, elected at about the same time and with a very similar ideology. Thatcher had a majority in Parliament who passed her proposals more or less without question, while Republican Reagan spent much of his two terms with a Democratic majority in Congress with whom he had to compromise.

Stability

The biggest debate over executive-legislative systems in recent years has been over whether one system is more stable than another. Political scientist Juan Linz (1990) initiated the debate. Looking mainly at new democracies, Linz argued that presidentialism has many potential disadvantages. The first is what he called "dual legitimacy." Since both the legislature and the executive are independently and directly elected, each has legitimacy. Since neither has a higher claim to legitimacy, there can be no democratic resolution of conflicts between them. He also argued that the direct election of the president could lead to chief executives with a "winner-take-all" mentality who would overemphasize their national mandate and be less willing to compromise; in this sense, he saw them as tending to be more majoritarian than consensual. Finally, Linz claimed that presidentialism is too inflexible. Fixed terms mean that any serious problem for which a president might need to be removed—or even a president's death in office—could provoke a political crisis, as happened in Nigeria in 2010 when an ailing president who could not carry out his duties refused to resign for months.

Much scholarship confirmed Linz's idea that presidentialism is likely to be more crisis-prone and threatening to the survival of a new democracy than is parliamentarism. This is much more likely to be true under coalitional presidentialism. The smaller the size of the president's party and the greater the overall fragmentation of the legislature, the greater the likelihood of regime collapse in presidential systems (Samuels 2007). More recent studies of coalitional presidentialism, though, have questioned this conclusion, showing that if presidents use the tools at their disposal well to maintain viable legislative coalitions, they can both remain in office and pass legislation. The greater the president's individual constitutional powers and the greater share of legislative seats their party controls, the more likely this will be (Chaisty, Cheeseman, and Power 2018). When the president has strong formal powers but does not have strong support in the legislature, crises of various sorts are more likely. The president will be tempted to use his formal powers to do whatever he wants, while his legislative opponents have the ability to resist that, including via mechanisms such as impeachment (Helmke 2017).

Semipresidentialism, with its combination of a parliament and president, seems more difficult to analyze. On the one hand, Linz argued semipresidentialism poses the dangers of the strong presidency—dual legitimacy and unwillingness to compromise. On the other hand, the PM's dependence on parliament means that her cabinet will, if necessary, reflect a coalition of parties in a fractionalized system and allow a degree of flexibility not found in pure presidential systems. Empirical research has found that while the specific powers of the president in semipresidential systems are important (presidents should not be allowed to override the legislature or dismiss the PM), these systems are no less stable than parliamentary systems, even under cohabitation (Schleiter and Morgan-Jones 2009). Furthermore, voters in semipresidential systems are quite capable of assigning responsibility for policies to particular officials, in spite of the dual executive, making accountability clear, and semipresidential systems seem just as capable of making policy decisions as other systems.

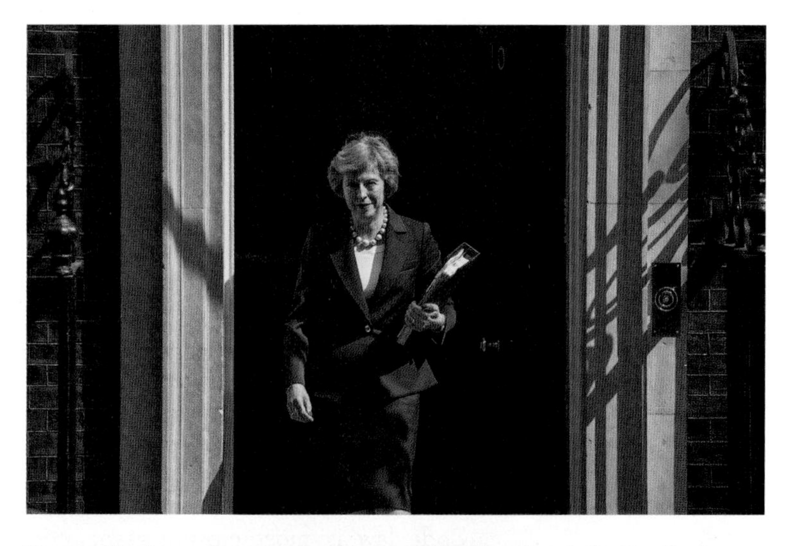

Theresa May leaves her official residence, 10 Downing Street, shortly after her selection as British prime minister in July 2016. She replaced David Cameron, who failed to defeat a referendum on Britain leaving the European Union and therefore resigned. The shift from Cameron to May, both in the Conservative Party that controlled a majority of Parliament at the time, was one of several changes of the head of the executive in Britain's parliamentary system that came without an election. Instead, the ruling party simply chose a new leader, who became prime minister. May herself was set to be replaced by someone internally selected by the party after she resigned in 2019.
Chris J Ratcliffe/Getty Images

Linz's critics argue that presidential institutions themselves are not the problem. After extensive quantitative analysis, political scientist José Antonio Cheibub concluded that the society, not the institution, is the problem. Presidential systems "tend to exist in societies where democracies of any type are likely to be unstable" (2007, 3). All of these concerns are relatively muted in a more established democracy in which regime collapse does not seem to be a real possibility. In those cases, the fixed terms of the presidential system, some argue, provide greater continuity and stability, especially compared with some of the more fragmented parliamentary systems with many parties, like Italy or Israel.

Executive–legislative institutions are at the heart of the biggest debates over how well democracies represent and govern their citizens. The effects of different institutional arrangements often appear reasonably clear in the abstract, but in practice the social, cultural, and political contexts make analysis much more complex. This complexity means that debates over democracies' varying effectiveness will continue to be a major subject of research in comparative politics.

Judiciary

The judiciary is the least studied branch of government in comparative politics, which is unfortunate since it is becoming more important in many countries. On a daily basis, the job of the judiciary is to enforce a state's laws. Its more important political role, however, is to interpret those laws, especially the constitution. Most democracies have some version of **judicial review**, the authority, vested in unelected judges, to decide whether a specific law contradicts a country's constitution. This makes the court a veto player in the political system. It is clearly a potential means to limit majority rule and achieve horizontal accountability, but it also raises a fundamental question: Why should unelected officials have such power? How much power they actually have, though, depends not only on formal rules but also on the strength of the judiciary as an institution. New democracies have often had to build new judicial institutions, and the weakness of these has become a major concern in comparative politics. **Institutionalization**—the degree which government processes and procedures are established, predictable, and routinized—is particularly important for the judiciary. Without it, judicial review can be meaningless in practice, even if clearly enshrined in a constitution. In this section, we discuss judicial review and its relationship to democracy, the judicialization of politics, and the question of judicial independence and institutional strength.

judicial review: The authority of the judiciary to decide whether a specific law contradicts a country's constitution

institutionalization: The degree to which government processes and procedures are established, predictable, and routinized

common law: Legal system originating in Britain in which judges base decisions not only on their understanding of the written law but also on their understanding of past court cases; in contrast to code law

code law: Legal system originating in ancient Roman law and modified by Napoleon Bonaparte in France, in which judges may only follow the law as written and must ignore past decisions; in contrast to common law

Judicial Review and the "Judicialization" of Politics

Two legal systems, common law and code law, emerged in modern Europe and spread to most of the world via colonialism (see Map 5.2). Common law developed in the United Kingdom and was adopted in most former British colonies, including the United States (it is sometimes referred to as Anglo-American law). Under **common law**, judges base decisions not only on their understanding of the written law but also on their understanding of past court cases. When a judge finds a law ambiguous, he can write a ruling that tries to clarify it, and subsequent judges are obliged to use this ruling as precedent in deciding similar cases.

Code law is most closely associated with the French emperor Napoleon Bonaparte, who codified it in what became known as the Napoleonic Code. (It is also known as civil law.) Under **code law**, which has its origins in ancient Roman law and was spread in modern Europe via Napoleon's conquests, judges may only follow the law as written, interpreting it as little as necessary to fit the case. Past decisions are irrelevant, as each judge must look only to the existing law. Like common law, code law spread globally via colonialism, especially to former French, Spanish, and Portuguese colonies.

MAP 5.2

Code- Versus Common-Law Countries

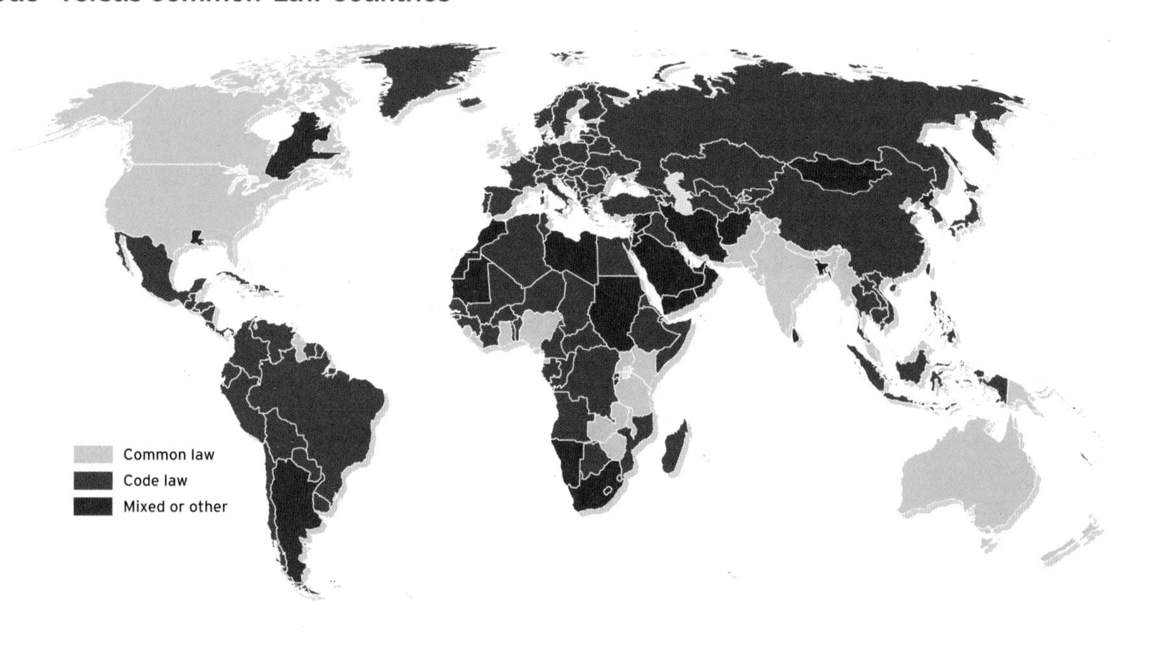

The two systems logically led to different kinds of judicial review. The United States provides examples of two practices typical of most common-law countries: decentralized judicial review and concrete judicial review. In decentralized judicial review, the same courts that handle everyday criminal cases also decide constitutional issues and can do so at any level. If a constitutional question begins in a lower court, it can be appealed upward, ultimately to the highest court. Concrete judicial means that only someone who has actually been negatively affected by the law in question can initiate a case. In contrast, code-law countries usually have centralized judicial review—a special court handles constitutional questions. Most also have abstract judicial review, meaning that certain public officials or major political groups can call on the courts to make a constitutional ruling even before the law is fully in effect. The length of appointments to whatever court handles judicial review is also important. Some countries have lifetime appointments; others limit judges' terms.

The fundamental question about judicial review in a democracy is why typically unelected judges, who are not subject to vertical accountability, should be allowed to make decisions with major political consequences. Proponents argue that the difference in democratic legitimacy between judges and elected officials is far less sharply defined than is often assumed. First, legislatures and executives are never perfectly representative or accountable, so the difference between them and the judiciary may be less than it appears. Second, the judiciary's horizontal accountability to executives and legislatures can be seen as an indirect source of democratic accountability. Judges are typically appointed by elected officials, so their stands on issues reflect the ideas of those officials and their constituents. Robert Dahl, one of the foremost scholars of democracy, argued in a widely read 1957 article that U.S. Supreme Court justices are part of political coalitions, just as elected officials are, and that they reflect the same political divisions that divide elected officials. Advocates of judicial review also argue that even if the judiciary is an imperfect democratic institution, it plays several crucial roles. It provides a check on executive and legislative power, serving as a mechanism of horizontal accountability. In the United States, many argue as well that judicial review exists to protect minority rights that might be trampled by a legislature or executive acting on majority opinion. In practice, however, most studies have shown that courts are more likely to rule in favor of those in power than on behalf of marginalized or oppressed minorities.

However one answers the questions raised by judicial review, it is certainly becoming more widespread. C. Neal Tate and Torbjörn Vallinder called this the "judicialization" of politics and argued that it is "one of the most significant trends in late-twentieth and early-twenty-first-century government" (1995, 5). Matthew Taylor (2008) argued that this is happening not only because the judiciary has chosen to act as a veto player but also because other political actors increasingly use the judicial system to conduct their policy battles, making the courts a "veto point." In the United States, as different judges have increasingly come to be seen as partisan in one way or another, political groups try to initiate cases strategically in particular courts because they believe a particular judge will be very likely to rule in their favor (Fernandez 2018).

Judicial Independence and Institutional Strength

Under any legal system, the judiciary must constitute a strong institution if it is to carry out its function properly in a system of horizontal accountability. Judicial review only matters in practice to the extent the key courts are willing and able to act independently of the other branches of government. This requires **judicial independence**, the belief and ability of judges to decide cases as they think appropriate, regardless of what other politically powerful officials or institutions desire. Judicial systems that lack independence are weak institutions in which corruption is common; judges may accept bribes to decide cases in a particular way or refuse to rule against powerful individuals. This can affect everyday criminal and civil cases as well as constitutional questions. No particular formal procedure or power guarantees judicial independence, though Ferejohn and Pasquino (2003) found that the distinct constitutional courts common in code-law countries are particularly independent and effective. Legal scholar Samuel Issacharoff (2015) argued that the creation of such courts in many new democracies over the last few decades facilitated the process of democratic transition by allowing political actors crafting new constitutions to leave some controversial problems for courts to decide later. The courts in turn have played a crucial role in helping young democracies resist efforts to undermine democratic rules.

What undoubtedly matters most to judicial independence, though, are informal factors that help make formal independence real in practice. The structure of political competition creates an important context. In fact, in new democracies, fragmentation and competition among political leaders create fear that their opponents will gain power and exclude them via extraconstitutional means, so they often support creating judicial review as a safety measure (Yadav and Mukherjee 2014). In both more and less established democracies, more fragmented political systems provide more political space for the judiciary to act independently. For instance, the possibility of divided government in a presidential system, multiparty parliamentary systems that require coalition building, and the existence of weak parties in which leaders have limited

judicial independence: The belief and ability of judges to decide cases as they think appropriate, regardless of what other people, and especially politically powerful officials or institutions, desire

control over legislators can all encourage judicial independence (Ferejohn, Rosenbluth, and Shipan 2007). Judges' beliefs may also be a crucial ingredient. Examining local courts' strength and independence in Brazil and Mexico, Matthew Ingram (2016) found that the presence of judges who were ideologically committed to reforms explained where reforms happened better than did the structure of political competition.

Because the judiciary lacks both military and financial resources, legitimacy is crucial to its institutional strength; without widespread legitimacy, the judiciary has little power. Judiciaries typically gain legitimacy only over time as the populace comes to understand their role more fully and is satisfied with key court decisions. Until then, they may use their powers rarely and warily. For example, many post-Communist countries have established judicial review in their constitutions, but their high courts have been reticent and cautious, believing they lack legitimacy and therefore cannot withstand pressure from more powerful officials (Gibson, Caldeira, and Baird 1998). Leading judges are often acutely aware of the court's position relative to other institutions and decide cases, as rational choice theory would predict, to enhance their own institutional strength (Hirschl 2009).

Brazil's judiciary in its relatively new democracy shows the trials and tribulations of establishing judicial independence. Brazil's 1988 constitution created a complex judicial system with constitutional protection for its autonomy in most personnel, budgetary, administrative, and disciplinary areas. The system is headed by the Supreme Federal Tribunal (STF), which hears constitutional cases. Judges to the highest courts are appointed by the president with approval of the Senate (the upper house of the legislature). Initially, Brazil's top judges seemed hesitant to use their independence vis-à-vis the president. By 1992, though, the STF had gained confidence, and its rulings helped lead to the president's impeachment on corruption charges, a watershed event in the four-year-old democracy. The top court has since ruled against a number of major political leaders on both constitutional questions and corruption charges, though in favor of the executive in other situations. The court's most prominent role began in 2014, as the giant scandal involving the national oil company exploded. The federal judge overseeing it, Sergio Moro, became something of a national hero as major political figures were indicted. As the breadth and depth of the scandal emerged, Brazilians increasingly saw the judiciary as a source of relative probity and therefore legitimacy: "For a public sick of corruption, [the judiciary] represented hopes that the old culture of impunity was finally over, that democratic institutions were growing stronger, that the division of powers was functioning and justice was being done" (Watts 2016).

Since 2016, though, the judiciary's legitimacy has been threatened. The impeachment of President Dilma Rousseff that year on relatively minor charges threatened the perceived impartiality of the judiciary's role in the broader scandal. In 2019, leaked emails showed that the one-time judicial hero, Sergio Moro, whom newly elected President Bolsonaro appointed as attorney general, had inappropriately coached prosecutors on how to pursue their cases while he was on the bench, again raising questions about the judiciary's impartiality. Finally, the judiciary's own lack of accountability has become a major problem. Virtually all observers view it as slow, inefficient, and corrupt. Scandals involving judges have sometimes gone unpunished, many courts have a backlog of cases stretching out for years, and Brazilian judges are some of the most highly paid in the world. Judicial independence has made it difficult to clean up corruption or reform the parts of the system that almost everyone agrees are not working.

Bureaucracy

As we noted in chapter 2, a state—of whatever regime type—will have greater capacity to rule its territory and people if it has an effective bureaucracy. All modern states have an executive branch that includes a bureaucracy. The ideal modern bureaucracy consists of officials appointed on the basis of merit and expertise who implement policies lawfully, treat all citizens equally according to the relevant laws, and are held accountable by the elected head of the executive branch. This ideal is an important component in the full development of an effective modern state, but it is particularly essential to liberal democracy because the ideals listed above insulate bureaucratic officials from the personal and political desires of top leaders. On the other hand, the power of unelected bureaucrats can be a threat to democracy, so they must be held accountable. Who will prevent them from abusing their independence and autonomy? Because vertical accountability does not exist, horizontal accountability is very important.

Bureaucracy can limit the executive in a number of ways, even as it enhances a state's capacity. Prior to modern reforms, bureaucratic positions in most societies were based on political patronage: leaders appointed all officials to suit the leaders' interests. (China was a major exception—Confucian ideas of merit in that country go back millennia.) Professionalization involved recruitment based on merit and a reduction of political patronage. It also came to mean that bureaucratic officials held technical expertise, on which political leaders often have to rely to make decisions in an increasingly complex world. Knowledge and expertise are key sources of bureaucrats' independent power. In this context, it is understandable that when President Trump entered office in 2017 with a goal of reducing the power of the Environmental Protection Agency, one of the first things his administration did was reduce the role of scientists in the agency's policymaking process. Modern bureaucracies developed into formal, hierarchical organizations in which career advancement, at least ideally, was based on performance and personal capability rather than on political connections.

Professionalization helps insulate bureaucrats from the whims of political leaders, but how will the political leadership hold the bureaucracy accountable? This can be understood as a **principal–agent problem**. The principal (the elected or appointed political leadership in the executive or legislative branches) assigns an agent (the bureaucrat) a task to carry out as the principal instructs; the problem is how the principal makes sure the agent carries out the task as assigned. Bureaucratic agents might well have strong incentives to deviate from their assigned tasks. Rational choice theorists argue that bureaucrats, however professional, are as self-interested and rational as any other actors. Bureaucrats' preferences are usually to expand their sphere of influence and the size of their organization to enhance their own prestige and salary. This can expand the size of the bureaucracy, create inefficiencies, and distort the principals' purposes. Self-interest can also lead to corruption, if bureaucrats exchange favorable treatment of political leaders or ordinary citizens for bribes or other advantages.

principal–agent problem: A problem in which a principal hires an agent to perform a task, but the agent's self-interest does not necessarily align with the principal's, so the agent may not carry out the task as assigned

political appointees: Officials who serve at the pleasure of the president or prime minister and are assigned the task of overseeing their respective segments of the bureaucracy

Numerous solutions to this problem have emerged over the years. In every state, the political leadership of the executive branch selects a certain number of **political appointees** to head the bureaucracy. These appointees, starting at the top with cabinet ministers, serve at the pleasure of the president or prime minister and, among other things, are assigned the task of overseeing their respective segments of the bureaucracy. Different countries allow different numbers of political appointees: the United States typically allows six or eight for each significant department in the federal government, whereas two are more typical for each ministry in the United Kingdom. (The United States uses the term *department* to designate the major agencies of the government, whereas most of the world uses *ministry* to mean the same thing, harkening back to the religious influence on the early modern state.)

Political appointees' power over professional bureaucrats is limited by the legal means through which the latter are hired, paid, and earn career advancement; bureaucrats, however, must answer to political appointees within those legal limits. In democracies, legislators can write laws that are as specific as possible to limit bureaucrats' discretion in implementing them. Whether they choose to do so, though, depends on a number of factors. If legislators trust bureaucrats or see them as sharing similar preferences, if they are not capable of writing detailed legislation, and if they can turn to the courts to control bureaucrats if necessary, then they are less likely to try to control bureaucratic behavior via detailed legislation (Huber and Shipan 2002). **Legislative oversight** is another key means of horizontal accountability; members of the legislature, usually in committees, oversee the bureaucracy by interviewing key leaders, examining budgets, and assessing how successfully a particular agency has carried out its mandate. Often, citizens use the judicial system to try to achieve accountability by taking individual officials or entire agencies to court, arguing that they have either failed to carry out their duties or have done so unlawfully.

None of these efforts at vertical accountability of the bureaucracy works perfectly, in large part because principals never know exactly what their agents within a bureaucracy are doing, especially as technocratic knowledge becomes more important. For most of the twentieth century, governments relied heavily on professional socialization to maintain standards. They recruited people who had been trained to abide by key professional norms of neutrality and legality, and they believed they could count on most of these recruits to behave in the general "public" interest. Some states, such as France and Japan, went so far as to recruit almost exclusively from one high-profile educational institution so that government bureaucrats garnered great prestige and professional status.

legislative oversight: Occurs when members of the legislature, usually in committees, oversee the bureaucracy

David Wildstein, a political appointee of New Jersey governor Chris Christie, looks toward his attorney at a hearing at the state assembly in 2014. A scandal over the closing of traffic lanes on the George Washington Bridge into New York City erupted that year, with many blaming Christie's political appointees for using the bureaucracy for partisan purposes, undermining bureaucratic autonomy. Hearings are a key element of legislative oversight of the bureaucracy.
Emile Wamsteker/Bloomberg via Getty Images

Rational choice theorists, however, argued that training could not overcome the incentives and self-interest inherent in the bureaucracy. Following this line of argument, the **New Public Management (NPM)** movement arose in the United States and United Kingdom in the 1980s and was associated with President Ronald Reagan and Prime Minister Margaret Thatcher. NPM advocates contended that inherent inefficiencies meant that the bureaucracy required radical reforms to make it operate more like a market-based organization. These included privatizing many government services so that they would be provided by the market, creating competition among agencies and subagencies within the bureaucracy to stimulate a market, focusing on customer satisfaction (via client surveys, among other things), and flattening administrative hierarchies to encourage more team-based activity and creativity. The ideas of NPM became widely popular and were implemented in many wealthy democracies to varying degrees. Some countries, such as the United Kingdom and New Zealand, cut the size of their bureaucracies extensively via NPM, while others, including Germany and Japan, implemented it slowly and partially. One of the few detailed studies of its effects, over thirty years in the United Kingdom, concluded that even though the size of the civil service was cut by one third, overall costs went up slightly and the quality and fairness of services (measured by the number of citizen complaints) declined slightly (Hood and Dixon 2015).

Bureaucracy and Corruption

One of NPM's main targets was bureaucratic corruption. Where the state and its institutions are generally weak, reform requires not only making the bureaucracy more efficient but also strengthening it as an institution. When bureaucratic rules and norms are extremely weak, corruption and massive inefficiency are likely (O'Dwyer 2006). Political elites may be able to use a weak bureaucracy to pursue personal or financial interests, citizens may be able to use bribery to gain favors from the state, and bureaucrats themselves may steal from the state. Bribery and rent seeking are two primary types of corruption in bureaucracies. In the least institutionalized bureaucracies, citizens often have to bribe officials to get them to carry out the functions they are mandated to do. The political leadership may not be interested in stopping this behavior because they benefit from their ability to purchase favors from bureaucrats. Alternatively, they may simply have lost all ability to control their agents in the bureaucracy, often because of very low bureaucratic salaries. **Rent seeking** is gaining an advantage in a market without engaging in equally productive activity; it usually involves using government regulations to one's own benefit. In weakly institutionalized bureaucracies, for example, businesses may be able to bribe officials to grant them exclusive rights to import certain items, thereby reaping huge profits for little effort.

The rent-seeking model of corruption is based on a rational choice theory of why corruption is greater in some countries than others (see Map 5.3). Rational choice theories, as always, focus on individual incentives, arguing that economic conditions are particularly important in explaining corruption: countries with more highly regulated economies and greater inequality are likely to be more corrupt. The former provides opportunities for corruption, as bureaucrats can demand bribes frequently; the latter means that average citizens have fewer resources to get what they want and therefore are more willing to pay bribes. Numerous other theories, however, have also sought to explain the puzzle of corruption.

One of the oldest theories is based on political culture—corruption is greater where societies lack shared values about the importance of the public sphere,

New Public Management (NPM): Theory of reform of bureaucracies that argues for the privatizing of many government services, creating competition among agencies to stimulate a market, focusing on customer satisfaction, and flattening administrative hierarchies

rent seeking: Gaining an advantage in a market without engaging in equally productive activity; usually involves using government regulations for one's own benefit

MAP 5.3

Annual Corruption Scores, 2018

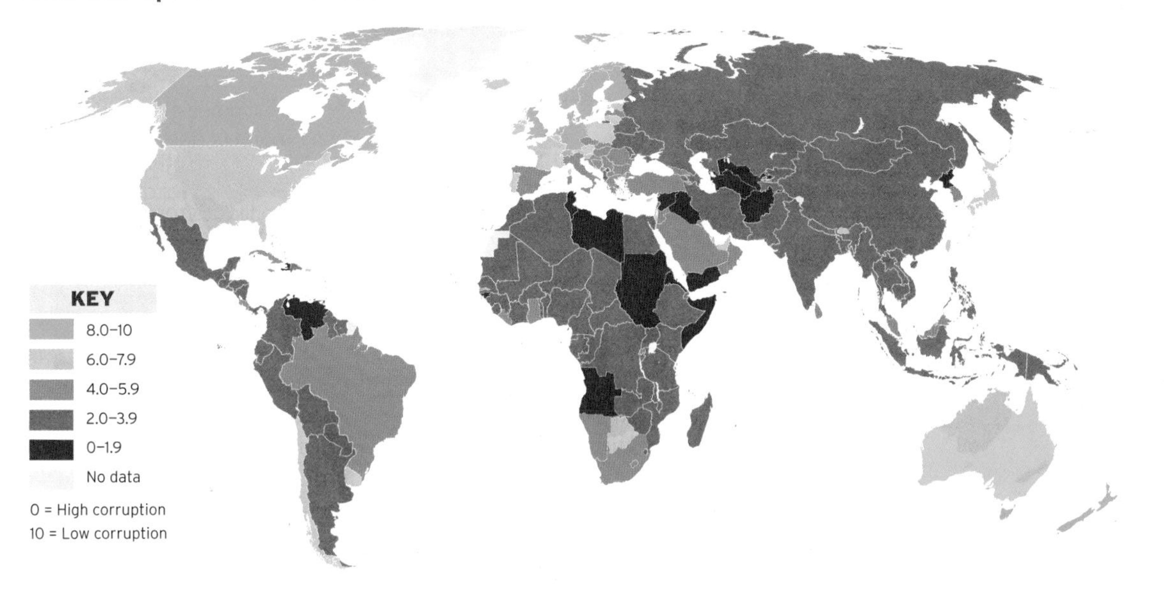

Source: Transparency International Corruption Perceptions Index Scores, 2018 (http://www.transparency.org/cpi2018).

instead placing personal, family, or ethnic interests above those of the society as a whole. Others have noted that greater corruption is found in postcolonial societies, and they contend that postcolonial states, with no firm roots in society, lack legitimacy, leading citizens to believe one should gain whatever one can from the public sphere. Nigerian sociologist Peter Ekeh (1975) argued that in Africa, two "publics" exist: a "primordial public," which includes ethnic, religious, and community identities in which people feel reciprocal moral responsibility toward one another and an amoral "civic public" involving the state, toward which people feel no obligation and therefore take from freely.

Much recent scholarship takes an institutionalist approach toward corruption. The general consensus has been that in democracies with stronger parties and greater political competition, corruption is lower. Leslie Schwindt-Bayer and Margit Tavits (2016) found that majoritarian democracies, in which clarity of responsibility for corruption is strongest, facilitated voters' ability to hold corrupt politicians responsible. Consensual democracies, they suggested, allow officials to blame each other for corruption, limiting voters' ability to know whom to hold responsible.

Michael Johnston (2005), one of the foremost scholars of corruption, combined theories based on economic factors and political institutions to argue that rather than trying to predict the total amount of corruption, we need to understand its variation in different kinds of societies. He elaborated four models of different types of corruption based on wealth level and the nature of the political system. Corruption in wealthy, established democracies is primarily based on "influence markets," in which corporations use access to politicians, usually via generous contributions to campaigns and parties, to gain preferential treatment from key bureaucracies, as in the case of Japan and the United States. In middle-income

CRITICAL INQUIRY

Wealth, Corruption, and Democracy

The table below shows the levels of wealth, corruption, and democracy for a selection of countries around the world. Michael Johnston argued that corruption isn't necessarily higher or lower in countries that are wealthier and more democratic but different. Based on the table, what trends do you see? Are wealthier countries clearly less corrupt? Are democratic countries clearly less corrupt? Which of the two (wealth or democracy) seems most influential in determining the level of corruption? What do your answers suggest for Johnston's argument?

Wealth, Corruption and Democracy

CORRUPTION PERCEPTIONS INDEX			
COUNTRY	GDP PER CAPITA, 2017 (U.S. $)	CPI (2018)	POLITY IV SCORE
Norway	$75,704.2	84	10
United States	$59,927.9	71	8
Germany	$44,668.5	80	10
United Arab Emirates	$40,698.8	70	−8
United Kingdom	$39,953.6	80	10
Japan	$38,430.3	73	10
Czech Republic	$20,379.9	59	9
Chile	$15,346.4	67	10
Russia	$10,749.1	28	4
Brazil	$9,812.3	35	8
Mexico	$8,910.3	28	8
China	$8,827.0	39	−7
Botswana	$7,595.6	61	8
Thailand	$6,595.0	36	−3
Colombia	$6,408.9	36	7
Iran, Islamic Republic of	$5,593.9	28	−7
Indonesia	$4,846.4	38	9
Georgia	$4,045.4	58	7
Philippines	$2,989.0	36	8
Vietnam	$2,342.2	33	−7
India	$1,979.4	41	9
Nigeria	$1,968.4	27	7
Congo, Democratic Republic of the	$1,654.0	20	−3

CORRUPTION PERCEPTIONS INDEX			
COUNTRY	**GDP PER CAPITA, 2017 (U.S. $)**	**CPI (2018)**	**POLITY IV SCORE**
Kenya	$1,594.8	27	9
Pakistan	$1,547.9	33	7
Rwanda	$784.3	56	–3
Uganda	$606.5	26	–1
Mozambique	$426.2	23	5
Niger	$378.1	34	5

Polity IV is a measure of how well institutionalized democracy is within a given country, with 10 being fully institutionalized democracy and -10 being fully institutionalized authoritarian regime.

CPI (corruption perception index) is a measure of the relative degree of corruption in any given country. A higher score indicates less corruption.

Sources: GDP data are from the World Bank, GDP per Capita (current US$). (http://data.worldbank.org/indicator/NY.GDP.PCAP.CD/countries); CPI scores are from Transparency International, Corruption Perceptions Index, 2018 (http://www.transparency.org/cpi2018#results; Polity IV scores are from Polity IV, Case Format (http://www.systemicpeace.org/inscrdata.html).

countries with newer and less well-institutionalized democracies, "elite cartels" emerge in which key political and business leaders form networks to gain control of the government and systematically use it to their joint political and financial benefit, as in Brazil. In middle-income countries that just recently became democracies, institutions are even weaker and political competition more intense, uncertain, and personal; in these countries, "oligarchs and clans" scramble for spoils in the system, as in Russia. In the least institutionalized (and often poorest) states with personalized or neopatrimonial rule, corruption often takes the form of the "Official Mogul," a strongman who uses the resources of the state as he pleases to favor his political allies and punish his enemies, as in much of Africa.

The extent of the problem and the possible remedies for corruption vary, Johnston argued, across these four types of countries, though corruption is an important issue in all of them. Johnston (2014) and other scholars (Börzel and van Hüllen 2014; Mungiu-Pippidi 2015) have argued that bringing corruption under control requires far more than simply reforming the bureaucracy via programs like NPM; instead, it requires a mobilized citizenry with adequate information to demand greater accountability.

Japan demonstrates both the power and limits of bureaucracy and the complex issues that arise when bureaucracy weakens. The Japanese bureaucracy was the only major political institution to survive the post–World War II U.S. occupation and political reforms, giving it a great advantage under the new democracy. The economy boomed for four decades after the war, thanks in part to economic guidance from the powerful bureaucracy. Until a 2014 reform, the prime minister only made around two hundred political appointments, as compared with the several thousand that a U.S. president makes, giving him little executive oversight. Combined with little legislative oversight, the bureaucracy was exceptionally powerful vis-à-vis the other branches of Japan's democracy. At the height of its power, most major legislative initiatives began not with the prime minister or the legislature but rather in the relevant bureaucracy.

Fears that the bureaucracy was becoming too powerful and corrupt were realized in a massive scandal in 1988, followed by numerous others since. In 2009, an opposition party surprised the long-ruling Liberal Democratic Party (LDP) and swept into power, largely on a promise to reform the bureaucracy. It centralized decision making in the cabinet and eliminated several important roles for senior bureaucrats, including what had been a crucial meeting of senior bureaucrats to coordinate policy across ministries, and instituted regular meetings of the elected cabinet, following the British model. These stark changes, though, left key decision makers inadequately informed on important issues and bureaucrats feeling marginalized (Shinoda 2012). Many citizens blamed the government and its reforms for its inept response to the 2011 earthquake and tsunami at Fukushima. Partially in response, the government reversed virtually all the reforms but lost the next election anyway. The LDP, back in power by 2012, created the Cabinet Bureau of Personnel Affairs to appoint over six hundred key political appointees, tripling the number of appointments the prime minister controlled, in a clear effort to control and curtail the independent bureaucrats. Whether this latest effort to rein in Japan's powerful bureaucracy will be successful remains to be seen.

Federalism

So far, we have only considered national institutions. In every country, of course, government institutions exist at lower levels as well, but their role and autonomy vis-à-vis the national government vary widely. The most important difference is between unitary and federal systems. In **unitary systems**, the central government has sole constitutional sovereignty and power, whereas in **federal systems** the central government shares constitutional sovereignty and power with subunits, such as states, provinces, or regions. Local governments exist in unitary systems, but they derive their powers from the central government, which can alter them as it pleases. In federal systems, some subnational governments have constitutionally derived powers that can only be changed via constitutional amendment.

The first modern federal system was the Dutch Republic of the United Provinces in what is now the Netherlands, but the best-known early example is the United States. Both federal systems were born when contiguous units within larger empires declared independence and banded together to form new states. In the case of the United States, separate and sovereign states—the original thirteen British colonies—formed a federation only after a looser union, a confederation, failed to produce a viable central state. Political scientist William Riker (1964) provided a now-classic rational choice explanation for how American federalism emerged, arguing that it resulted from a bargain among self-interested leaders of separate states, motivated primarily by the need to protect themselves from external threat.

Australia and Switzerland are also examples of federalism arising from separate states coming together to form a new state. Most modern federations, however, came about in exactly the opposite way: through states trying to remain together, often after colonial rule. In some cases, such as India, federations arose via implicit bargaining between regional elites and the central government. In other cases, such as Russia, authoritarian rulers imposed federalism to help them rule a vast, heterogeneous territory.

unitary systems: Political systems in which the central government has sole constitutional sovereignty and power; in contrast to a federal system

federal systems: Political systems in which a state's power is legally and constitutionally divided among more than one level of government; in contrast to a unitary system

Why Countries Adopt Federalism

While federal systems are a minority of the world's governments, they include most of its geographically largest countries. Larger countries tend to adopt federal systems in part to provide some level of government closer to the populace than the national government.

A second purpose of federalism is to limit the power of the majority by decentralizing and dividing governmental power. Federal systems usually have bicameral legislatures, with the second (usually referred to as the upper) house representing the interests of the states or provinces. They also have some sort of judicial review to settle disputes between the levels of government. Both institutions limit the power of the executive and the majority controlling the lower (and usually more powerful) house of the legislature. Federal systems, then, typically institutionalize several veto players that do not exist in unitary systems.

Finally, as we mentioned in chapter 4, federalism is often a means to protect the interests of religious or ethnic minorities. When regional minority communities feel threatened by other groups' control of the national government, a federal system that creates separate states or provinces with clear ethnic or religious majorities can ease tensions. This explains why some relatively small states have chosen federal systems. Belgium, for instance, was created in 1830 as a buffer against potential French expansion. Federalism there is combined with consociationalism: the national cabinet and many other appointments must be split 50–50 between the two major language groups, the Flemish and Walloons; separate elections and parties exist for each group; and governments are virtually always a coalition of the two largest parties from each side. Despite its prolonged existence as a nation–state, regionalism in Belgium has always remained strong and seems to be increasing. In 2010 a Flemish nationalist party that calls for Flemish independence won an unprecedented 30 percent of the Flemish vote to become the largest party in the Belgian parliament. It took a world-record 541 days for the ethnically divided political parties in parliament to form a coalition government after the election.

Federalism and Accountability

How much federalism limits majority power and provides accountability depends on the relative power and autonomy of the national and subnational governments. These factors, in turn, depend on the specific powers set out for each level of government in the constitution, the resources each level of government controls, and the composition and relative strength of the upper house in the legislature. The constitutions of all federal systems lay out the powers of both the central government and the states or provinces. Military, foreign, and monetary policies are always placed under the authority of the national level, as they are essential to the sovereignty of the modern state and a modern economy. States or provinces typically have power over education, transportation, and sometimes social services (at least partially). In more decentralized systems, like the United States and Brazil, states also have separate judicial systems that handle most criminal law.

However powers are distributed by the constitution, real power also depends on resources and bargaining among the units. In any federal system, the two key questions and areas of political combat between the levels of government are how much each can collect in taxes and how much they can spend. The power of taxation is particularly important, as it gives subnational units greater autonomy than they would have if they were wholly dependent on the central government for their revenue. In the most centralized unitary states, such as the United Kingdom and Ireland, the central government collects more than three-quarters of total government revenue; in the least centralized federal systems, such as Germany and Switzerland, the central government collects less than a third. Similarly, the central government in some unitary systems is responsible for around 60 percent of all expenditures, whereas in decentralized federal systems it is responsible for as little as 30 percent. During the twentieth century, revenue collection in federations became more centralized, reflecting the growing power of national governments over state or provincial ones.

The upper and weaker house of the legislature in a federal system is usually designed to represent the state or provincial governments, while the lower and more powerful house represents individual voters. The upper house's power and composition help determine the extent to which federalism limits majority rule. Its powers can be quite sweeping, as in the case of the U.S. Senate, which must approve all legislation, or much more limited, as in Germany's Bundesrat, which can only delay bills unless they directly relate to the *Bundesländer* (state governments). Because states or provinces are typically of different sizes, smaller ones are often overrepresented in the upper house. In the U.S. Senate, every state has two seats: in 2010 the twenty least populous states had just under 10 percent of the U.S. population but elected 40 percent of the senators. Given that Senate legislation requires the approval of 60 percent of the body on important issues, the representatives of just over 10 percent of the population can stop legislation, an unusually severe restriction on majority rule. Population shifts to cities are causing the population gap between large and small states to increase and leaving small states increasingly rural and conservative and larger states increasingly urban and liberal, meaning the representation gap has partisan implications favoring conservatives. The ratio of representation of the smallest states to the largest in the U.S. Senate is about 66 to 1. The same ratio in the German Bundesrat is only 13 to 1; this ratio, combined with the weaker powers of the Bundesrat, shows clearly that German federalism does not restrict majority rule nearly as much as American federalism does.

The degree of institutionalization in federal systems is also important to accountability, especially at the local level. Examining Latin America, Edward Gibson (2013) argued that especially in poorer and more rural states or provinces, a federal system can preserve nondemocratic rule within a national democracy. As the large, federal Latin American countries such as Mexico, Argentina, and Brazil, became democratic, some politically powerful "bosses" in particular states were able to use clientelism to maintain their rule largely unchallenged. In these cases, the new democratic institutions were not followed, so federalism allowed semi-authoritarian rule to continue at the state level, even though a democratic regime existed at the national level.

Federalism and Minority Rights

symmetrical federal system: A federal system in which all subnational governments (states or provinces) have the same relationship with and rights in relation to the national government

asymmetrical federal system: A federal system in which different subnational governments (states or provinces) have distinct relationships with and rights in relation to the national government

Most federal systems today exist in heterogeneous societies; part of their purpose is to give some local autonomy to ethnic or religious minorities. While all of the issues outlined above apply to these federal systems, other factors also come into play in preserving ethnic minority autonomy. The United States is an example of a **symmetrical federal system**: all states have the same relationship with and rights in relation to the national government. In contrast, many federal systems in ethnically divided societies are **asymmetrical**: some states or provinces have special rights or powers that others do not. These special relationships are often negotiated individually between the leaders of a particular group and the central government, sometimes at the end of a civil war or under the threat of civil war or secession. A recent comparative study concluded that federal systems on the whole help to accommodate ethnic and religious divisions, resulting in less conflict than occurs in unitary systems with heterogeneous populations. However, the study also found that federal systems work best where there has not been a history of severe repression of one group over another; in such cases, even the best designed federal institutions may not be able to overcome the tensions and lack of trust between a regionally based group and the central government (Amoretti and Bermeo 2004).

India is an example of an asymmetrical federal system designed to resolve ethnic conflict. Although most Indian states have the same basic powers, the central government has bargained with regional groups to create new states to enhance regional loyalty to the center. The designers of India's constitution specifically said they were not creating states along linguistic or ethnic lines, but over time, that is primarily what has happened. In the northeast, six new states were created along ethnic lines, and these have greater power and autonomy than do other states, including the freedom to respect local customary law and religious practices. Although few new states have been created in recent years, the issue remains very much alive: from 2011 to 2013 protests broke out and several MPs resigned over their demand to create a new state out of a region of Andhra Pradesh in southern India.

Indian federalism is unusually centralized. The national government has the right to create, eliminate, or change state boundaries as it pleases. It can also declare President's Rule in a particular state, under which the state government is dismissed and the prime minister in effect governs the state directly until he calls a new state election. The central government's greater taxing power, which has expanded over time, has given it great control over the policies of the states (Rao and Singh 2005, 172). Given this, federalism's ability to limit majority rule has varied over time, depending in part on the party system. When the Indian National Congress (INC) was the sole dominant party and controlled the national government between 1947 and 1977, it controlled virtually all state governments, so they generally did the bidding of the central government. From 1989 to 2014, however, India's national governments were coalitions between a major national party and several state-level parties. The state parties have used this to bargain with the national parties for greater state autonomy. Also, a 1994 ruling by India's Supreme Court limited the ability of prime ministers to declare President's Rule. Recent changes in economic policy have also strengthened some state governments: greater market freedoms have allowed certain state governments to attract capital from around the world, enriching those states and their tax base vis-à-vis the national government. Thus, state governments seem to be achieving some degree of institutional autonomy, and horizontal accountability may be increasing vis-à-vis national institutions.

Trends in Federalism

Ever since Riker's (1964) classic study, rational choice theorists have argued that federalism is inherently unstable. They view federalism as based on a negotiated agreement among political coalitions, and as those coalitions change over time, they will demand changes in the federal agreement. Federalism, then, always evolves, whether via constitutional amendment, as has happened in Germany, or via changing judicial interpretations of the constitution, as in the United States. In most cases, though, rational choice theorists argue that either a dominant majority is likely to centralize power, reducing the extent of or even eliminating federalism, or regional minorities will come to feel like they are not getting what they should from the system and demand greater autonomy, perhaps even secession. In Riker's classic analysis, this dynamic led to the American Civil War. More recently, a similar dynamic led to the collapse of the post-Communist federations of the

Soviet Union, Czechoslovakia, and Yugoslavia as the Cold War ended, producing twenty-three separate nation–states. One of those, Russia, is itself a federation that faced similar problems and has resolved them via extreme centralization and the effective end of both federalism and democracy (Filippov and Shvetsova 2013). Political parties that have a truly national reach can serve as integrative forces helping to limit the fragmenting tendencies of federalism, while parties that have only regional interests can exacerbate the problems (Thorlakson 2013).

In recent years, federal systems have tended to become more centralized as the federal governments have gained a greater share of total revenue and used it to override state prerogatives in areas such as civil rights, education, and even the drinking age. (Since the 1980s, the U.S. federal government has enforced the mandatory minimum drinking age of twenty-one by denying transportation funding to states that refuse to abide by it; therefore, all states comply.) In some unitary systems, such as in the United Kingdom, decentralization has taken place. This is often termed **devolution** because it devolves power from the center to the regions or subnational units. A British parliamentary report commented that devolution differs from federalism because parliamentary sovereignty means that devolution of power is reversible. The "devolved" institutions in Scotland, Wales, and Northern Ireland remain subordinate to the British Parliament. Interestingly, Britain is an example of "asymmetrical devolution," since each region has its own set of devolved responsibilities (Leeke, Sear, and Gay 2003). Devolution, though, hasn't fully satisfied the members of the Scottish National Party, in particular, who used their newly devolved powers to demand a referendum on independence. Though it failed in 2014, after Britain's vote to leave the EU in 2016, the party promised to hold another referendum, which most observers believed would succeed in creating a separate Scotland, disuniting the United Kingdom that was created in 1707.

Conclusion

Political institutions have an impact on who has the most power in a society and how they can exercise it. In strong institutions, the formal rules matter because on the whole they are obeyed. A crucial question for a democracy is how the executive power of the state can be effectively limited. Elections, of course, subject the executive to vertical accountability. Between elections, horizontal accountability depends greatly upon institutional choices. Does one set of governing institutions systematically hold executive power more accountable than other types of institutions? The answer in most cases depends on not only the formal governing institutions but also the broader political context in which they operate. The Westminster model seems to provide the weakest horizontal check on executive power, but only when the PM leads a cohesive majority party in parliament. And it arguably provides the clearest vertical accountability: voters know exactly who is responsible for government policy. Coalition governments provide a nearly constant check on the PM, as she must secure coalition partners' agreement to make any significant policy. The judiciary in most democracies is specifically tasked with horizontal accountability via judicial review, but we've seen that courts must assert their independence carefully, given their lack of democratic legitimation via elections and lack of other resources on which to base their power. Japan shows us that even when the elected executive is held accountable, an entrenched bureaucracy may wield great and unelected power and successfully resist reforms to democratize it.

devolution: Partial decentralization of power from central government to subunits such as states or provinces, with subunits' power being dependent on central government and reversible

Besides accountability, a second great question in liberal democracy is how to protect minority rights. Accountability is to the majority, which can and often does trample the liberal rights of minorities. Does one set of institutions help preserve minority rights better than others? Most Americans would immediately think of the Supreme Court as fulfilling this role, but political science research indicates that the judiciary upholds the interests of the dominant majority at least as often as it does the minority, and that is likely to be even more true when the judiciary as an institution is relatively weak (Chinn 2006).

More consensual democracies in which a variety of viewpoints are represented within the major governing institutions seem likely to enhance minority rights. One form of this is federalism, which is often designed specifically to protect ethnic and regional minorities. How well this works depends on how much real power—determined not only by formal rules but also by control of revenues—a federal system provides the national and regional governments. Again, the broader political context matters. For example, the strength of federalism in India has varied mainly due to changes in the party system.

A third major question for democracy involves the potential trade-off between representation and effective policymaking: Do some institutions provide more of one or the other, and does a clear optimum balance between them exist? Lijphart's consensual and majoritarian democratic models directly address this question. Majoritarian systems like the Westminster model ought to provide more effective policymaking at the expense of some immediate representation. Institutions that provide more horizontal accountability and require greater consensus, such as the U.S. or Brazilian presidential systems with weak parties and federalism, seem likely to slow down the policymaking process. Lijphart, though, argued that overall consensual models legislate nearly as effectively as majoritarian systems but add much greater representation. While Lijphart favored that balance, the debate is far from concluded. Political context matters here as well: the number and strength of political parties in office will affect how the institutions operate, as Indian history demonstrates—a subject we will examine in detail in the next chapter.

We can also ask why particular countries adopt particular institutions in the first place. Our cases suggest that wholesale change of institutions is difficult and unusual. Countries seem prone to follow what they know, as the examples of Britain's former colonies suggest. It is rare for a country to decide, as France did in 1958, that a complete change of institutions is in order, but countries transitioning to democracy face this choice as they write new constitutions. Cultural and historical institutional theories seem to explain best this continuity of institutions. Despite the elegant logic of rational choice arguments about which works best, deeply held values, socialized into the population over time, tend to preserve existing institutions unless they prove exceptionally dysfunctional.

No clear answer to the question of why an institution works better in one place than another is obvious, though certainly social, political, and ethnic contexts matter greatly. A society that is deeply divided by ethnic difference and other past conflicts is likely to benefit from a more consensual set of institutions that requires compromise at every step of the way. A majoritarian system or powerful single office like a presidency is likely to breed distrust, as no political actor in the system is willing to trust the others with such great power. Excessive fragmentation across political parties and local governments, though, may make policymaking nearly impossible or even threaten the continued viability of the state as a whole. Understanding how governing institutions in democracies actually function, though, almost always requires how political parties, participation, and representation work as well, a subject to which we now turn. ●

Sharpen your skills with SAGE Edge at **edge.sagepub.com/orvisessentials2e. SAGE Edge for students** provides a personalized approach to help you accomplish your coursework goals in an easy-to-use learning environment.

KEY CONCEPTS

asymmetrical federal system (p. 146)

coalition government (p. 121)

coalitional presidentialism (p. 129)

code law (p. 134)

cohabitation (p. 130)

common law (p. 134)

consensus democracy (p. 121)

devolution (p. 148)

executive (p. 120)

federal systems (p. 144)

head of government (p. 123)

head of state (p. 122)

horizontal accountability (p. 120)

institutionalization (p. 134)

judicial independence (p. 136)

judicial review (p. 134)

judiciary (p. 120)

legislative oversight (p. 139)

legislature (p. 120)

majoritarian democracy (p. 121)

member of parliament (MP) (p. 123)

New Public Management (NPM) (p. 140)

parliamentarism (p. 123)

political accountability (p. 119)

political appointees (p. 138)

presidentialism (p. 126)

prime minister (PM) (p. 123)

principal–agent problem (p. 138)

rent seeking (p. 140)

semipresidentialism (p. 129)

separation of powers (p. 127)

symmetrical federal system (p. 146)

unitary systems (p. 144)

vertical accountability (p. 119)

veto player (p. 121)

vote of no confidence (p. 123)

WORKS CITED

Amoretti, Ugo M., and Nancy Gina Bermeo, eds. 2004. *Federalism and Territorial Cleavages.* Baltimore, MD: Johns Hopkins University Press.

Baumgartner, Frank R., Sylvain Brouard, E. Grossman, S. G. Lazardeux, and J. Moody. 2014. "Divided Government, Legislative Productivity, and Policy Change in the USA and France." *Governance* 27: 423–447. doi:10.1111/gove.12047.

Börzel, T. A., and V. van Hüllen. 2014. "State-Building and the European Union's Fight Against Corruption in the Southern Caucasus: Why Legitimacy Matters." *Governance* 27: 613–634. doi:10.1111/gove.12068.

Chaisty, Paul, Nic Cheeseman, and Timothy Power. 2018. *Coalitional Presidentialism in Comparative Perspective.* Oxford, UK: Oxford University Press.

Cheibub, José Antonio. 2007. *Presidentialism, Parliamentarism, and Democracy.* New York: Cambridge University Press.

Chinn, Stuart. 2006. "Democracy-Promoting Judicial Review in a Two-Party System: Dealing With Second-Order Preferences." *Polity* 38 (4): 478–500. doi:10.1057/palgrave.polity.2300071.

Dahl, Robert. 1957. "Decision-Making in a Democracy: The Supreme Court as a National Policy-Maker." *Journal of Public Law* 6: 279–294.

Ekeh, Peter P. 1975. "Colonialism and the Two Publics in Africa: A Theoretical Statement." *Comparative Studies in Society and History* 17 (1): 91–112. doi:10.1017/S0010417500007659.

Elgie, Robert. 2011. *Semi-Presidentialism: Sub-Types and Democratic Performance.* Oxford, UK: Oxford University Press.

Ferejohn, John, and Pasquale Pasquino. 2003. "Rule of Democracy and Rule of Law." In *Democracy and the Rule of Law,* edited by José Maria Maravall and Adam Przeworski, 242–260. Cambridge, UK: Cambridge University Press.

Ferejohn, John, Frances Rosenbluth, and Charles Shipan. 2007. "Comparative Judicial Politics." In *The Oxford Handbook of Comparative Politics,* edited by Carles Boix and Susan Carol Stokes, 551–727. Oxford, UK: Oxford University Press.

Fernandez, Manny. 2018. "In Weaponized Court, Judge Who Halted Affordable Care Act Is a Conservative Favorite," *New York Times,* December 15, 2018.

Filippov, Mikhail, and Olga Shvetsova. 2013. "Federalism, Democracy, and Democratization." In *Federal Dynamics: Continuity, Change, and the Varieties of Federalism,* edited by Arthur Bens and Jorg Broscek, 167–184. Oxford, UK: Oxford University Press.

Freedom House, Freedom in the World 2018. http://www.freedomhouse.org/report/freedom-world-2018-table-country-scores.

Gibson, Edward L. 2013. *Boundary Control: Subnational Authoritarianism in Federal Democracies.* Cambridge, UK: Cambridge University Press.

Gibson, James L., Gregory A. Caldeira, and Vanessa A. Baird. 1998. "On the Legitimacy of National High Courts." *American Political Science Review* 92 (2): 343–358.

Helmke, Grethen. 2017. *Institutions on the Edge: The Origins and Consequences of Inter-Branch Crises in Latin America.* Cambridge, UK: Cambridge University Press.

Hirschl, Ran. 2009. "The Judicialization of Politics." In *The Oxford Handbook of Political Science,* edited by Robert E. Goodin, 253–274. Oxford, UK: Oxford University Press.

Hood, Christopher, and Ruth Dixon. 2015. *A Government That Worked Better and Cost Less? Evaluating Three Decades of Reform and Change in UK Central Government.* Oxford, UK: Oxford University Press.

Huber, John D., and Charles R. Shipan. 2002. *Deliberate Discretion? The Institutional Foundations of Bureaucratic Autonomy.* Cambridge, UK: Cambridge University Press.

Ingram, Matthew C. 2016. *Crafting Courts in New Democracies: The Politics of Subnational Judicial Reform in Brazil and Mexico.* Cambridge, UK: Cambridge University Press.

Issacharoff, Samuel. 2015. *Fragile Democracies: Contested Power in the Era of Constitutional Courts.* New York: Cambridge University Press.

Johnston, Michael. 2005. *Syndromes of Corruption: Wealth, Power, and Democracy.* New York: Cambridge University Press.

———. 2014. *Corruption, Contention, and Reform: The Power of Deep Democratization.* Cambridge, UK: Cambridge University Press.

Lee, Frances. 2014. "American Politics Is More Competitive Than Ever. That's Making Partisanship Worse." Monkey Cage. *Washington Post.* January 9, 2014. https://www.washingtonpost.com/news/monkey-cage/wp/2014/01/09/american-politics-is-more-competitive-than-ever-thats-making-partisanship-worse/.

Leeke, Matthew, Chris Sear, and Oonagh Gay. 2003. *An Introduction to Devolution in the UK.* Research Paper 03/84, November 17, 2003. House of Commons Library. http://www.parliament.uk/documents/commons/lib/research/rp2003/rp03-084.pdf.

Lijphart, Arend. 1999. *Patterns of Democracy: Government Forms and Performance in Thirty-Six Countries.* New Haven, CT: Yale University Press.

Linz, Juan José. 1990. "The Perils of Presidentialism." *Journal of Democracy* 1 (1): 51–69. doi:10.1353/jod.1990.0011.

McCarty, Nolan. 2014. "What We Know and Don't Know About Our Polarized Politics." Monkey Cage. *Washington Post*. January 8, 2014. https://www.washingtonpost.com/news/monkey-cage/wp/2014/01/08/what-we-know-and-dont-know-about-our-polarized-politics/.

Mungiu-Pippidi, Alina. 2015. *The Quest for Good Governance: How Societies Develop Control of Corruption.* Cambridge, UK: Cambridge University Press.

O'Donnell, Guillermo. 1999. "Horizontal Accountability in New Democracies." In *The Self-Restraining State: Power and Accountability in New Democracies,* edited by Andreas Schedler, Larry Diamond, and Marc F. Plattner, 29–52. Boulder, CO: Lynne Rienner.

O'Dwyer, Conor. 2006. *Runaway State-Building: Patronage Politics and Democratic Development.* Baltimore, MD: Johns Hopkins University Press.

Pelizzo, Ricardo. 2010. "Fragmentation and Performance: The Indian Case." *Commonwealth and Comparative Politics* 48 (3): 261–280.

Powell, G. Bingham, Jr. 2000. *Elections as Instruments of Democracy: Majoritarian and Proportional Visions.* New Haven, CT: Yale University Press.

Rao, M. Govinda, and Nirvikar Singh. 2005. *The Political Economy of Federalism in India.* Oxford, UK: Oxford University Press.

Riker, William. 1964. *Federalism: Origin, Operation, Significance*. Boston: Little, Brown.

Samuels, David. 2007. "Separation of Powers." In *The Oxford Handbook of Comparative Politics*, edited by Carles Boix and Susan Carol Stokes, 703–726. Oxford, UK: Oxford University Press.

Schleiter, Petra, and Edward Morgan-Jones. 2009. "Review Article: Citizens, Presidents and Assemblies: The Study of Semi-Presidentialism Beyond Duverger and Linz." *British Journal of Political Science* 39: 871–892. doi:10.1017/S0007123409990159.

Schwindt-Bayer, Leslie A., and Margit Tavits. 2016. *Clarity of Responsibility, Accountability, and Corruption.* Cambridge, UK: Cambridge University Press.

Shinoda, Tomohito. 2012. "Japan's Failed Experiment: The DPJ and Institutional Change for Political Leadership." *Asian Survey* 52 (5): 799–821.

Tate, C. Neal, and Torbjörn Vallinder. 1995. *The Global Expansion of Judicial Power.* New York: New York University Press.

Taylor, Matthew M. 2008. *Judging Policy: Courts and Policy Reform in Democratic Brazil.* Stanford, CA: Stanford University Press.

Thorlakson, Lori. 2013. "Dynamics of Change in Federal Representation." In *Federal Dynamics: Continuity, Change, and the Varieties of Federalism,* edited by Arthur Bens and Jorg Broscek, 229–248. Oxford, UK: Oxford University Press.

Transparency International. 2018. "Corruption Perceptions Index." http://www.transparency.org/cpi2018.

Tsebelis, George. 2002. *Veto Players: How Political Institutions Work*. Princeton, NJ: Princeton University Press.

Watts, J. 2016. "Brazil's Judiciary Faces Scrutiny as Rousseff's Government Teeters." *The Guardian*. March 30, 2016. https://www.theguardian.com/world/2016/mar/30/brazil-judiciary-dilma-rousseff-impeachment-corruption.

Williams, Laron K. 2011. "Unsuccessful Success? Failed No-Confidence Motions, Competence Signals, and Electoral Support." *Comparative Political Studies* 44 (11): 1474–1499.

Yadav, Vineeta, and Bumba Mukherjee. 2014. *Democracy, Electoral Systems, and Judicial Empowerment in Developing Countries.* Ann Arbor: University of Michigan Press.

RESOURCES FOR FURTHER STUDY

Cappelletti, Mauro, Paul J. Kollmer, and Joanne M. Olson. 1989. *The Judicial Process in Comparative Perspective.* Oxford, UK: Clarendon Press.

Cheibub, José Antonio, Zachary Elkins, and Tom Ginsburg. 2014. "Beyond Presidentialism and Parliamentarianism." *British Journal of Political Science* 44 (3): 515–544. doi:http://dx.doi.org/10.1017/S000712341300032X.

Frederickson, H. George, and Kevin B. Smith. 2003. *The Public Administration Theory Primer.* Boulder, CO: Westview Press.

Graber, Mark A. 2005. "Constructing Judicial Review." *Annual Review of Political Science* 8: 425–451. doi:10.1146/annurev.polisci.8.082103.104905.

Herron, Erik S., and Kirk A. Randazzo. 2003. "The Relationship Between Independence and Judicial Review in Post-Communist Courts." *Journal of Politics* 65 (2): 422–438. doi: 10.1111/1468-2508.t01-3-00007.

Mainwaring, Scott, and Matthew Soberg Shugart, eds. 1997. *Presidentialism and Democracy in Latin America.* New York: Cambridge University Press.

Mulgan, Aurelia George. 2002. *Japan's Failed Revolution: Koizumi and the Politics of Economic Reform.* Canberra, Australia: Asia Pacific Press.

Rosenbluth, Frances McCall, and Michael F. Thies. 2010. Princeton, NJ: Princeton University Press.

WEB RESOURCES

Binghamton University, The Institutions and Elections Project

(http://www.binghamton.edu/political-science/institutions-and-elections-project.html)

International Institute for Democracy and Electoral Assistance (IDEA), Democracy and Development

(http://www.idea.int/development/index.cfm)

Transparency International

(http://www.transparency.org)

Unified Democracy Scores

(http://www.unified-democracy-scores.org/index.html)

University of Bern, Comparative Political Data Sets

(http://www.cpds-data.org/)

6 Institutions of Participation and Representation in Democracies

Women wait to vote in state-level elections in West Bengal, India, in April 2016. India is the world's largest democracy and holds the world's largest elections in terms of voters and voting places. After long domination by a single party, India developed a multiparty system in which two large, national parties, and numerous regional ones that compete for voters' support. More recently, one national party's vote has plummeted, leading observers to question whether the party system is changing again.
Photo by Subhendu Ghosh/Hindustan Times via Getty Images

Key Questions

- Do some types of institutions in democracies provide better overall representation of and influence for average citizens?
- How do institutions affect the representation of ethnic, gender, religious, and other groups?
- Why do people join political parties and participate in other kinds of political activity?
- How do different electoral and party systems affect political leaders' behavior?
- Are there clear patterns of when and where particular party and electoral systems develop?

Learning Objectives

After reading chapter 6, you should be able to do the following:

6.1 Explain the various types of electoral systems and the advantages and disadvantages of each

6.2 Discuss the functions of political parties and systems

6.3 Provide a definition of modern civil society and explain how interest-group pluralism and corporatism differ

Virtually all regimes allow some participation and representation, if only to shore up their legitimacy or at least the appearance of it. Democratic regimes all claim to value and promote widespread participation and representation, which are especially vital to them as the core elements of vertical accountability. They differ significantly, however, in how they promote citizen involvement and fair and accurate representation of interests. Because institutions of participation and representation are vital to democracies, we examine institutions that shape political participation and representation in democracies in this chapter. In chapter 8, we examine and compare the same kinds of institutions in authoritarian regimes.

Participation and representation clearly have major implications for answering the question, "Who rules?" Different electoral systems embody different principles of representation and have different effects on accountability. We can demonstrate this by examining how well the systems represent those who have fewer economic resources in general and therefore seem likely to have less power in the society at large, such as women, racial, or ethnic minorities. Elite theorists argue that modern electoral democracies in reality give limited power to those in more marginalized positions; elites dominate the national discourse, control major institutions, and influence voters more than voters influence who is in office. If true, this allocation of influence obviously undermines vertical accountability, a crucial element of democracy. One question we ask is whether some systems of representation and participation give marginalized groups greater influence than do others.

Another central question is, Why do people participate in politics in the first place? This might seem obvious: people want to have power or influence, to make a contribution to their community and nation, or to gain recognition and status. While all this is undoubtedly true for some political activists, rational actor theorists long ago explained that for most people most of the time, there is no rational reason to participate in any political activity, including voting. Expending time or money to work toward any political goal, even just to go out and vote, is irrational, given the huge number of citizens and the correspondingly small impact of each individual and the costs (at least of time) of participating (Downs 1957). This is an obvious problem in a democracy, and it is exacerbated by the fact that members of the elite, with much greater direct access to key decision makers, have a greater incentive to participate and thus seem more likely to influence policy. Without any ameliorating circumstances, this would suggest that elite theory is correct: "democracies" are really elite controlled.

Democracies must resolve this **collective action problem**: individuals are unwilling to engage in a particular activity because of their rational belief that their individual actions will have little or no effect, yet when they all fail to act, all suffer adverse consequences (in the case of participation in democracy, losing control to the elite). If individuals participate in politics, they may be able to benefit collectively, but why would they do so when each one knows her individual impact will be negligible? While this is certainly a problem, it is equally clear that millions of people around the world do participate in politics. Besides achieving direct influence over government, which certainly motivates many in spite of the odds against individual influence, some citizens participate because they gain expressive or solidaristic benefits: they find satisfaction in the act of expressing their political beliefs publicly or in being part of a community of like-minded activists. The personal appeal or charisma of a particular leader can also inspire people to engage in the political process (Blondel et al. 2010). Recent psychological theories argue that emotions can also play an important role in explaining participation; people feel emotional costs from not participating in politics. Not voting or taking part in a political protest can result in negative emotions such as guilt or social exclusion from friends and neighbors. Thus, whether people participate depends on the relationship between the costs of participation and the emotional costs of not participating (Aytac and Stokes 2019).

Political institutions can affect the costs and opportunities of participating, intensifying or easing the collective action problem. Excessively complex political systems can discourage less educated citizens from participating compared to similar citizens in more accessible political systems (Gallego 2015). But well-designed institutions such as political parties and interest groups can help citizens identify their interests and then mobilize them to action. Different types of parties, party systems, and interest groups can have great influence over who participates and to what effect.

A final important question is, What influence do institutions—in this chapter, in particular, electoral and party systems—have on political leaders' behavior? What incentives do they give leaders? Do these incentives encourage leaders to promote more participation and representation, or less?

collective action problem: Individuals being unwilling to engage in a particular activity because of their rational belief that their individual actions will have little or no effect yet collectively suffering adverse consequences when all fail to act

electoral systems: Formal, legal mechanisms that translate votes into control over political offices and shares of political power

The Electoral System

Electoral systems are formal, legal mechanisms that translate votes into control over political offices and shares of political power. Different electoral systems provide distinct incentives to individual voters and political leaders and affect political parties' strengths and numbers, so they are crucial to understanding what opportunities parties provide for citizen participation.

In almost all elections, enfranchised citizens vote for people who will represent them rather than voting directly on policy. This raises a key issue for electoral systems: How are votes aggregated and counted, and which process provides the "best" representation? One common choice is for a country to divide its territory into geographic units, and each unit elects one or more representatives. This system assumes that citizens can best be represented via their membership in geographically defined communities. In contrast, some countries elect their legislatures nationally, or in very large districts. This system assumes that citizens' beliefs as espoused by parties or individual candidates rather than geographical community, are most important for representation. In rare cases, democratic countries choose to represent specific groups within society rather than or in addition to geographic districts or parties. After an ethnic conflict, for instance, a country may decide it needs to provide special representation for ethnic minorities. Several countries have also legally reserved seats in parliament specifically for women to ensure that they are represented. Ultimately, electoral system choice depends on an answer to the questions, On what basis do we wish to be represented? and With whom do we share our most important political interests or views?

In addition, electoral institutions often have important effects on governance because they affect the composition of legislatures and the executive branch. Gridlock in American politics or the legendary instability of Italian parliamentary regimes after World War II are familiar examples of this dynamic. These problems do not result from presidential or parliamentary institutions per se but rather from the ways in which those institutions interact with the electoral system. Electoral systems also help determine how majoritarian or consensual a particular democracy is. Systems that encourage many, fragmented parties are more consensual: they provide representation of diverse views in the legislature, but they may make effective government difficult due to gridlock (the U.S. presidential example) or the instability of coalition governments (in the Italian parliamentary example). Systems that encourage fewer parties tend to have the opposite effect and therefore are more majoritarian.

Single-Member Districts: "First-Past-the-Post" and Majoritarian Voting

Americans borrowed the **single-member district (SMD)** from Great Britain. In both countries, each geographic district elects a single representative. SMD can use plurality or majoritarian rules to determine who is elected. In a **plurality** system, whoever gets the most votes wins the election, even if they don't have majority. In a race with more than two contestants, the winner can be elected with a relatively low percentage of the vote total. This system is often called **"first-past-the-post" (FPTP)** because, as in a horse race, the winner merely needs to edge out the next closest competitor. In a majoritarian system, the winner must gain an absolute majority of the votes (50 percent, plus one) rather than just a plurality (the most). If no candidate wins an absolute majority, a second election takes place between the top two candidates to produce a winner. Because SMD systems produce one winner per district, they tend to be part of and support the majoritarian model of democracy; a single-party government is more likely to result.

Advocates of SMD systems argue they can give constituents a strong sense of identification with their representative. Each voter has a specific representative from his district to hold accountable for government actions. Even if you didn't vote for your representative and you disagree with her, she is still expected to work for you (as U.S. representatives often do by solving Social Security problems for constituents or writing letters of nomination to service academies). In theory, your most vital needs and interests are assumed to have been aggregated into those of your district. Empirical evidence, however, found no significant differences

single-member district (SMD): Electoral system in which each geographic district elects a single representative to a legislature

plurality: The receipt of the most votes but not necessarily a majority

"first-past-the-post" (FPTP): An SMD system in which the candidate with a plurality of votes wins

between SMD and other systems in terms of voters' level of contact with their representative, their knowledge of who their representative was, or their sense that their representative was representing them well (Curtice and Shively 2009).

Critics of the SMD system make two main arguments against it. First, many votes are "wasted," in the sense that the winning candidate does not represent the views of the voters who did not vote for him. This is especially true in systems with more than two viable parties. If only 30 or 35 percent of voters actually favored the winner, the votes of the majority were arguably wasted. This may be one reason why voter participation tends to be lower in countries with SMD than elsewhere. Minority voices are less likely to be heard. Voters—especially those who prefer minor parties—may find voting a waste of time; the system doesn't encourage them to overcome the collective action problem. Supporters of SMD argue, however, that even voters who have not voted for their representative are represented via **virtual representation**: candidates from their party are elected in other districts, and so their views are represented in the legislature, albeit not by their representative.

virtual representation: When voters' views are represented indirectly in the legislature by their chosen party's candidates who have been elected in districts other than their own

Second, this problem can be compounded by the under- or overrepresentation of particular parties. Consider a case in which a third party wins a significant share of the votes in many districts but a plurality in only one or two. The party would win a lot of votes but get only a couple of seats in the legislature. Conversely, if a large number of candidates from a particular party win by a very small plurality in their districts, that party's vote in the legislature will be inflated. The number of its representatives will suggest an overwhelming national consensus, when in fact the party may not even have won a majority of the vote nationwide. Figure 6.1

FIGURE 6.1

Results of the 2005 United Kingdom Parliamentary Election

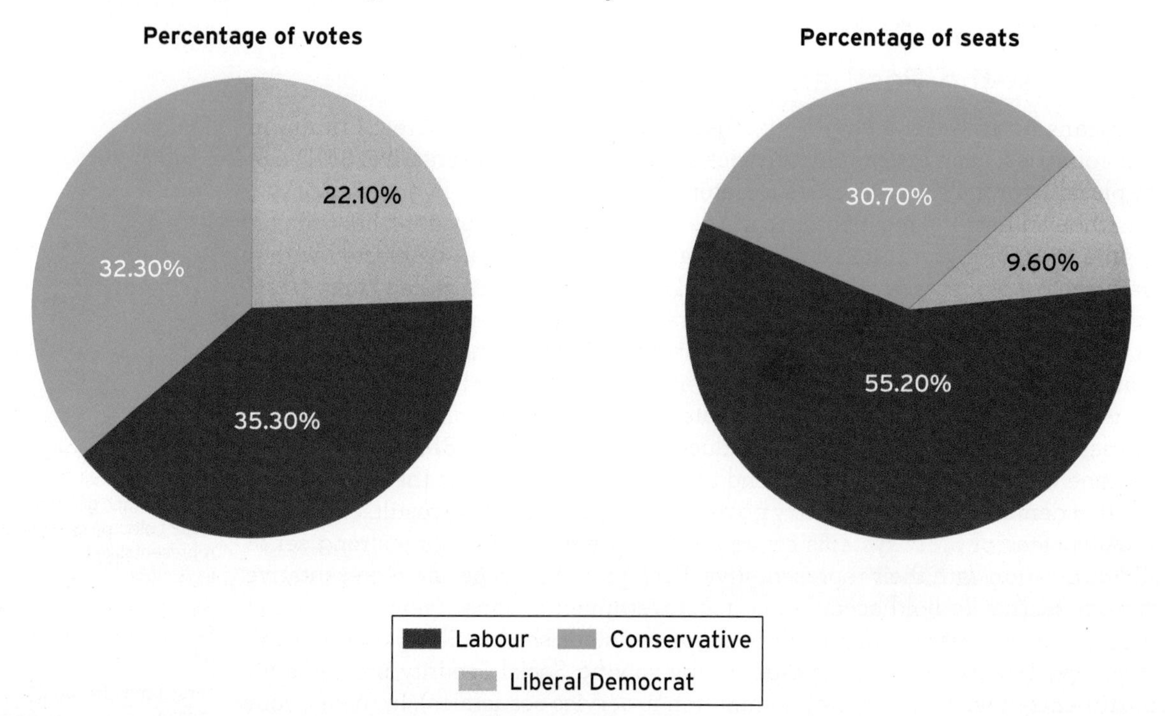

Source: BBC, "Election News, UK Results" (http://www.bbc.com/news/election/2005/results).

gives an example from Great Britain's 2005 election, in which the two major parties, Labour and Conservative, won similar vote shares but very different numbers of seats, and the third party, the Liberal Democrats, won a far larger share of votes than parliamentary seats. Even when there are only two parties, SMD lends itself to gerrymandering, the drawing of electoral districts to favor a particular party. Both major parties in the United States have done this over the years to varying degrees. Most recently, after the 2010 census, the Republican Party set out to gain control of state legislatures in order to redraw congressional districts in its favor. In the 2012 election, the popular vote for seats in the House of Representatives was a virtual tie, but Republicans won thirty-three more seats, and the biggest gaps between the popular vote and seats won were in states where Republicans controlled redistricting. In the ten most imbalanced states, Republicans won 7 percent more votes than Democrats but 76 percent more seats ("Imbalance of Power" 2013). SMD makes the system majoritarian—it may promote efficient, stable policymaking by allowing decisive legislative action—but it may come at the cost of accurate representation of the citizens' preferences.

Norbert Hofer, presidential candidate for Austria's Freedom Party, speaks to supporters in May 2016. Although the office of president is ceremonial in Austria's parliamentary democracy, the first-round election shook up the political establishment, as the right-wing Freedom Party and left-wing Green Party came in first and second. Although the Green candidate ultimately won, the election demonstrated the rise of right-wing parties that is common across Europe and the increasing difficulty that traditional, "mainstream" parties have in attracting voters.
Lisi Niesner/Bloomberg via Getty Images

Proportional Representation

Proportional representation (PR) differs from SMD in almost every way. In PR, representatives are chosen nationally or in large electoral districts with multiple representatives for each district. Thus, either a national legislature is simply divided on a purely proportional basis, or multiple representatives for large districts are allocated proportionally according to the vote in each district. Most PR systems include a minimal electoral threshold—for example, 3 or 5 percent of the vote—to gain representation in parliament, but any parties that cross that threshold can be certain that they will be represented. As Figure 6.2 demonstrates for the 2018 Swedish parliamentary elections, a PR system translates each party's share of the votes into almost exactly the same share of legislative seats (in stark contrast to the FPTP system in Britain, as a quick comparison of Figures 6.1 and 6.2 shows). PR systems tend to be part of and support consensus models of democracy; multiple voices via multiple parties are likely to be represented in the legislature, and coalition government is common.

proportional representation (PR): Electoral system in which seats in a legislature are apportioned on a purely proportional basis, giving each party the share of seats that matches its share of the total vote

If voters are not choosing among individuals running for a single seat, whom or what are they voting for, and who ends up in the legislature? The answer reflects a very different view of representation from SMD, because in PR systems, the voter is usually voting for a party, not an individual. PR assumes that voters primarily want their ideas and values represented. Voters are represented by the party they support in the legislature, regardless of the geographic origins of individual legislators.

closed-list proportional representation: Electoral system in which each party presents a ranked list of candidates, voters vote for the party rather than for individual candidates, and each party awards the seats it wins to the candidates on its list in rank order

In **closed-list proportional representation** (the version of PR most dissimilar to SMD), each party presents a ranked list of candidates for all the seats in the

FIGURE 6.2

Results of Sweden's 2018 Parliamentary Election

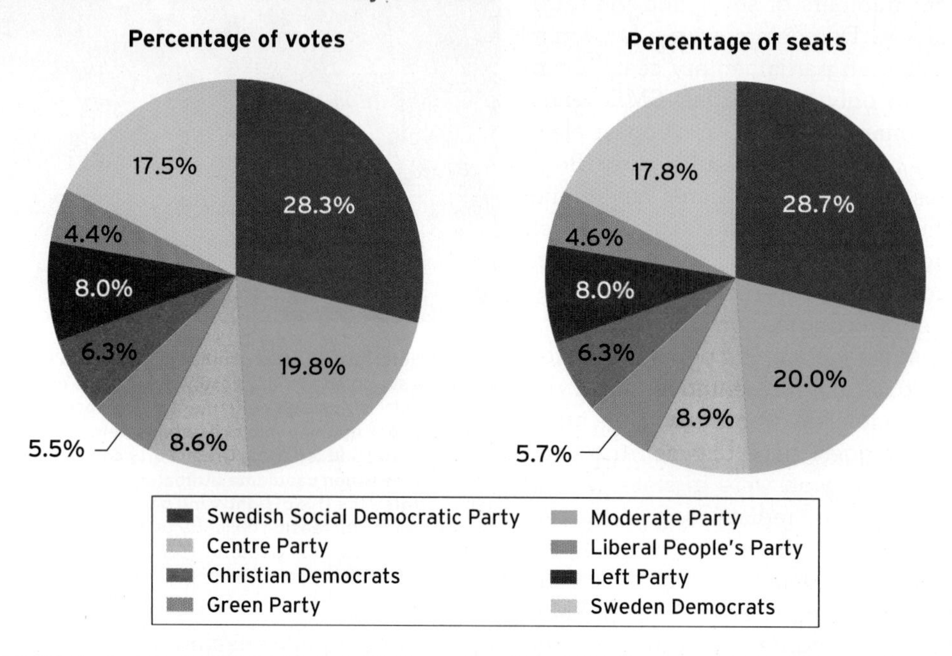

Source: Election Resources on the Internet, "Elections to the Swedish Riksdag," http://www.electionresources.org/se/riksdag.php?election=2018.

legislature. Voters can see the list and know who the "top" candidates are, but they actually vote for the party. If party X gets ten seats in the legislature, then the top ten candidates on the party list occupy those seats.

Another variant of PR is called **open-list proportional representation**. In this version, voters are presented with a list of candidates and vote for the candidate of their choice. When the votes are counted, each party receives a number of seats proportional to the total number of votes its candidates received. Those seats are then awarded to the top individual vote getters within the party.

open-list proportional representation: Electoral system in which multiple candidates run in each district, voters vote for the individual candidate of their choice, and the candidates with the most votes in the party get the seats the party wins

PR has some obvious advantages over SMD. First, very few votes are wasted because even small parties can gain some seats. To the extent that voters feel represented by a party, they know that someone in the legislature can give voice to their views—although realistically, smaller parties can usually only impact policy via coalitions with larger parties. Second, perhaps because fewer votes are wasted, participation rates in PR countries are higher, as Figure 6.3 shows. Proponents of PR argue that it is therefore more democratic and more broadly representative, since larger percentages of voters participate and virtually all have their views represented in the legislature. PR systems also tend to elect women and members of ethnic or racial minorities more frequently than SMD systems do, as party leaders often feel compelled (and in some countries are required by law) to include women or minority candidates on their party lists. Finally, PR systems that produce more parties may result in voters having more information available to them and faster changes to policies. Salomon Orellana (2014) examined

New Zealand, which switched from SMD to a partially proportional system, and the UK, which has SMD for its national elections but PR for elections to the European Parliament (the parliament of the EU). He found that the proportional systems in both cases provide a greater range of party positions and information for voters. He also used the World Values Survey to demonstrate that countries with proportional systems were more tolerant of diversity, more likely to adopt policy changes such as same-sex marriage, and more likely to have policies reducing inequality.

Critics of PR point to the "indirect" nature of PR elections: voters don't really choose individual representatives, even in an open-list system. In large, multimember districts, the individual voter does not have a unique, identifiable representative. And in a closed-list system, party officials are the ultimate arbiters of a candidate's fate because they assign the ranking. Because of this, legislators are less likely to open local offices and focus on local issues (Shugart 2005). Critics also question whether PR really results in voters expressing their beliefs more accurately. A rational choice model of voting developed by Orit Kedar (2009) argued that voters use their vote to ensure that their preferred policy would be carried out, not just to express their beliefs. In majoritarian, SMD systems, this is straightforward because the winning party will control government and can implement its preferred policy. In consensual PR systems with multiple parties, though, policy is based on negotiated compromises after the election, so voters compensate for this

FIGURE 6.3

Which System Increases Voter Turnout?

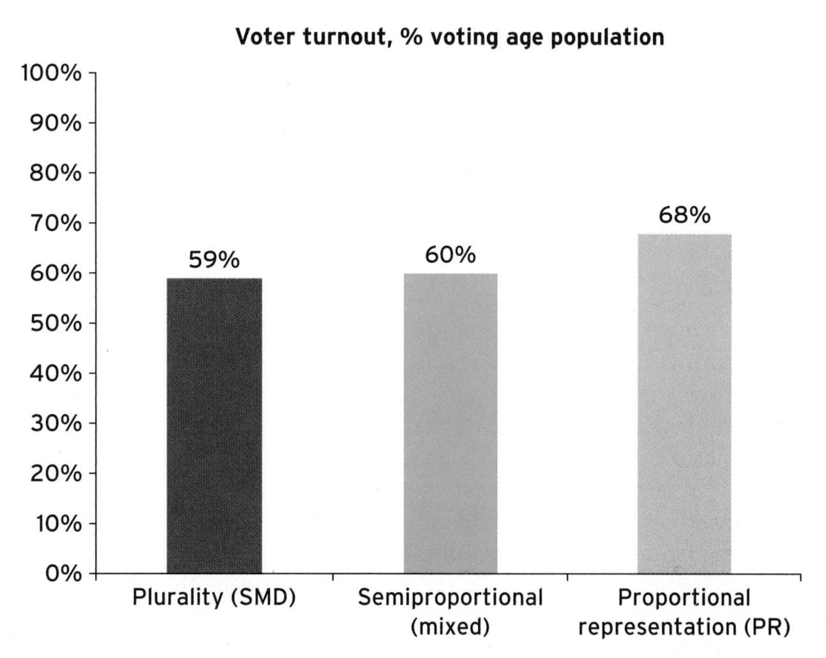

Source: Data are from International Institute for Democracy and Electoral Assistance, "What Affects Turnout?" Figure 25 (http://www.idea.int/vt/survey/voter_turnout8.cfm).

by voting for parties more ideologically extreme than their own positions, assuming negotiations will then result in their preferred and more moderate policy. She found, for instance, that voters in the UK choose the party closest to them ideologically at a much higher rate than do voters in most European countries with PR systems, where voters choose a more extreme party instead.

In addition, opponents of PR argue that having a broad range of parties in a legislature often has negative effects. Small parties, as noted above, often have little voice unless they join coalitions, but small extremist parties may gain inordinate power if they are able to negotiate key roles in ruling coalitions. Coalitions can be hard to form in such a fragmented environment, and where they do form, they may be unstable, as the case of Israel demonstrates.

Israel is a country of numerous ideological, religious, and ethnic divisions, so multiple parties compete in each election, and coalitions must band together to form a government in its parliamentary system. The country uses a pure, closed-list PR system: the entire country is one electoral district and citizens vote for their preferred party. The 120 seats in its parliament, the Knesset, are then allocated based on each party's share of the vote. Every party or coalition of parties that receives 3.25 percent of the national vote gets at least one seat in the Knesset. Most elections feature as many as two dozen parties, with at least a dozen winning seats in parliament. While two or three major parties have always existed, almost all governments are coalitions of one major party, which provides the prime minister, and at least three others—sometimes as many as six—who also receive cabinet seats to ensure their support in parliament.

The April 2019 election gave 11 parties seats in parliament. Prime Minister Benjamin Netanyahu's Likud bloc tied with the main centrist party, and he was asked to form a government. Failing to put together a coalition majority (61 of 120 seats) by the deadline, he dissolved parliament and set new elections for September. This time, the centrists edged Likud out by a couple of seats, but in the absence of a majority for either major party, Netanyahu was again asked to form the government.

Despite calls for a "national government" composed of both major parties, Netanyahu could not form a government by the deadline in October. The president asked Gantz to try and if that didn't work, Israelies would once again head to the polls for the third election in a year.

Mixed, or Semiproportional, Systems

Given the plusses and minuses of SMD and PR, it is not surprising that some countries have chosen to combine the two. The resulting hybrid is called a **mixed, or semiproportional**, system. A semiproportional system combines single-member district representation with overall proportionality. Voters cast two ballots: one for a representative from their district, with the winner being the individual who gains a plurality, and a second for a party list.

mixed, or semiproportional: An electoral system that combines single-member district representation with overall proportionality in allocation of legislative seats to parties; Germany is a key example

Under the compensatory mixed system in Germany, the legislature is composed by awarding seats first to all the district representatives, then adding members from the party lists until each party's seats approximate its share of the vote. So, for example, a very small party that crosses the 5 percent threshold required to enter parliament might send one or two representatives from its list to the legislature even though none of its candidates for individual district seats were elected. On the other hand, a large party that narrowly sweeps quite a few seats might gain no more from its list when proportional representation is factored in.

CRITICAL INQUIRY

Women in Power

Americans are used to considering themselves progressive when it comes to women's rights, yet in 2019, after a "female wave" election, only 23.4 percent of representatives in the House and 24 percent of senators were women, slightly below the global average for both. As Table 6.1b shows, in some democracies women constitute nearly half of the legislature, while others fare far worse than in the United States. What explains these disparities in how many women achieve power at the national level?

Table 6.1a suggests an initial hypothesis based on political culture because regional breakdowns seem to show that it plays a role. An alternative hypothesis is that the election of women is a case in which institutions matter. Table 6.1b suggests that PR systems are more conducive to electing women than are SMD systems. Because closed PR systems (most PR systems are closed) require parties to submit lists of candidates, more women are nominated. A party may be under some pressure to include at least some women on its list, since an all-male (or even overwhelmingly male) list could provoke negative reaction. Some PR systems include a quota system: parties must include a certain percentage of women candidates on their lists. A third hypothesis is that the longer a country is democratic, the more women will gain office; democracy provides an opportunity for underrepresented and marginalized groups to gain more influence, and the longer democracy lasts the more likely it will be that such groups will gain influence.

Look at the tables carefully. Based on the data, which of the hypotheses seems to be the best explanation for how many women are elected to national legislatures? Why do you come to the conclusion you do on this question? What implications does your answer have for which electoral system is most democratic?

TABLE 6.1A

Percentage of Seats in Lower House Occupied by Women, Regional Averages

REGION	% WOMEN
Nordic countries	42.5%
Americas	30.6%
Europe, OSCE member countries, including Nordic countries	28.6%
Europe, OSCE member countries, excluding Nordic countries	27.2%
Sub-Saharan Africa	23.9%
Asia	19.7%
Arab states	19.0%
Pacific	16.3%

Source: Data are from Interparliamentary Union, "Women in National Parliaments" (http://www.ipu.org/wmn-e/world.htm).

Note: OSCE is Organization for Security and Cooperation in Europe. It includes all European countries and the United States.

(Continued)

(Continued)

TABLE 6.1B

Women in World Legislatures

COUNTRY	% WOMEN IN LOWER HOUSE	TYPE OF ELECTORAL SYSTEM	LENGTH OF CURRENT REGIME IN YEARS
Bolivia	53.1%	Mixed	33
Mexico	48.2%	Mixed	18
Sweden	47.3%	PR	98
Namibia	46.2%	PR	25
Costa Rica	45.6%	PR	96
South Africa	42.7%	PR	21
Senegal	41.8%	Mixed	15
Finland	41.5%	PR	71
Spain	41.1%	Mixed	37
Norway	40.8%	PR	70
New Zealand	40.0%	Mixed	138
France	39.7%	SMD	46
Mozambique	39.6%	PR	21
Argentina	38.8%	PR	32
Belgium	38.0%	PR	71
Serbia	37.7%	PR	9
Denmark	37.4%	PR	69
Austria	37.2%	PR	69
Tunisia	35.9%	PR	1
Portugal	35.7%	PR	39
Italy	35.7%	PR	67
Switzerland	32.5%	Mixed	167
United Kingdom	32.0%	SMD	135
El Salvador	31.0%	PR	31
Latvia	31.0%	PR	24
Germany	30.9%	Mixed	25
Peru	30.0%	PR	14
Australia	30.0%	SMD	114
Philippines	29.5%	Mixed	28
Albania	29.3%	PR	18
Israel	29.2%	PR	67
Poland	29.1%	PR	24
Canada	26.9%	SMD	127
Bulgaria	25.8%	PR	25
Slovenia	24.4%	PR	24
United States	23.6%	SMD	206
Montenegro	23.5%	PR	9
Chile	22.6%	Other	26
Czech Republic	22.5%	PR	22
Ireland	22.2%	PR	94
Uruguay	22.2%	PR	30
Bosnia-Herzegovina	21.4%	PR	0
Lithuania	21.3%	Mixed	24
Bangladesh	20.7%	SMD	1
Romania	20.7%	Mixed	19
Slovakia	20.0%	PR	22
Guatemala	19.0%	PR	19
Colombia	18.7%	PR	58
Panama	18.3%	Mixed	26
Indonesia	18.2%	PR	16
Zambia	18.0%	SMD	14
Cyprus	17.9%	PR	41
Turkey	17.4%	PR	1
South Korea	17.1%	Mixed	27
Mongolia	17.1%	Mixed	23
Niger	17.0%	Mixed	4
Malawi	16.7%	SMD	21
Paraguay	15.0%	PR	23
Brazil	15.0%	PR	30
Georgia	14.8%	Mixed	24
Ghana	13.1%	SMD	14
India	12.6%	SMD	65
Hungary	12.6%	Mixed	25
Sierra Leone	12.3%	SMD	13
Ukraine	11.6%	Mixed	24
Japan	10.2%	Mixed	63
Botswana	9.5%	SMD	49
Benin	7.2%	PR	24

Source: Inter-Parliamentary Union, "Women in National Parliaments," World Classification Table (http://www.ipu.org/wmn-e/classif.htm). Based on figures for lower or single house.

Alternative-Vote, or Ranked-Choice, Electoral System

In November 2018, the state of Maine made U.S. history by electing the first members of the U.S. Congress by the **alternative-vote (AV) system**, more popularly known in the United States as "ranked-choice voting." AV is an SMD system in which voters rank all candidates rather than voting for just one, and the winning candidate must have a majority (not just a plurality) of the votes. When the ballots are counted and no candidate has over 50 percent, the first-place votes for the candidate with the least votes in a district are reallocated to those voters' second-choice candidates. If necessary, this process continues with the next lowest candidate, until a candidate gets to over 50 percent of the vote. In Maine's second district, Republican incumbent Bruce Polquin initially squeaked by his challenger by a vote of 46.1 to 45.9 percent. In most of the United States, the standard FPTP system would have declared him the winner. Under the AV system, though, the second-choices of voters who had voted for a third-party candidate as their top choice were reallocated to the two top candidates, and Democrat Jared Golden was declared the winner with a vote of 50.5 percent against Polquin's 49.5. Supporters of AV argue that it provides a single representative for each district who has the legitimacy of having won a majority of the votes, and it wastes fewer votes than does FPTP in a multiparty context because voters can vote for the candidate they truly like best rather than strategically voting for a party they think can win. This gives smaller parties a greater chance of surviving and expanding over time. It is likely to achieve greater proportionality than FPTP but certainly not as much as a simple PR system. Critics contend that AV's complexity make it difficult for voters to understand, thereby lowering its legitimacy in their eyes. For now, though, it seems popular in Maine, and some other states are considering it as well.

At the end of the day, the party composition of the legislature looks fairly similar to what it would have if it had been chosen based strictly on PR, but each district is also guaranteed its own, individual representative, as in a single-member system. In Japan, the noncompensatory mixed system reserves separate seats for representatives from the individual districts and from the party list vote. Parties get whatever the two seat totals happen to be, making Japan's system less proportional than Germany's.

In Japan's parliamentary system, a noncompensatory mixed electoral system awards three hundred seats in parliament via an SMD election, in which voters select individual candidates, and two hundred seats via a closed-list proportional election, in which voters select their preferred party. Because there are more SMD than PR seats, the system overall is more majoritarian than proportional. Japanese reformers created this system in 1993 after a series of corruption scandals, hoping to reduce the role of money in what had become the most expensive elections in the world and create a stable two-party system after the nearly continuous domination of the Liberal Democratic Party (LDP). Figure 6.4 shows the election results. Comparing the percentage of votes each party got overall with its share of SMD and PR seats shows once again how the PR system more accurately translates votes into legislative seats; small changes in a party's vote caused huge swings in the number of SMD seats it received. Until 2009, it appeared that the overall majoritarian nature of the system was creating two parties (the LDP and the Democratic Party of Japan [DPJ]), but the collapse of the DPJ's very unpopular government after the Fukushima tsunami disaster disrupted that trend by 2012. Since 2012, the long-ruling LDP has returned to power,

alternative-vote (AV) system: Single-member district electoral system in which voters rank all candidates rather than voting for just one

FIGURE 6.4

Japan's House of Representatives Election Result, 1996–2014

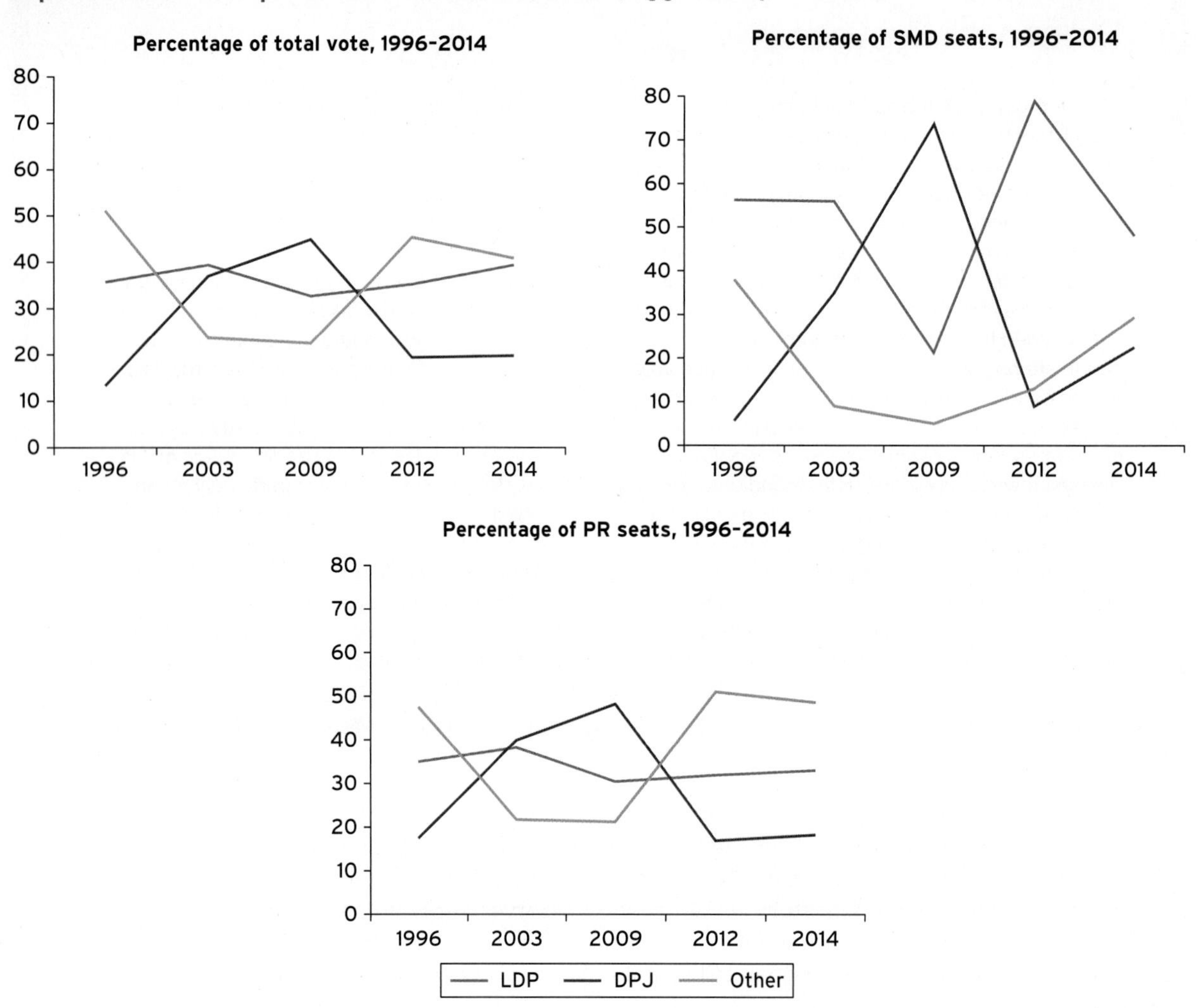

Source: Election Resources on the Internet, "Parliamentary Elections in Japan" (http://electionresources.org/jp).

largely on its ability to win SMD seats, even though its vote total didn't change all that much. The split of the DPJ into two parties in 2017 allowed the LDP to sweep three-quarters of the SMD seats even though it won less than 50 percent of the vote.

Mixed systems share some of the advantages of SMD and PR systems. Because they waste fewer votes, participation rates tend to be slightly higher, as in PR (see Figure 6.3), yet citizens are also guaranteed a personal representative to whom they can appeal. In addition, the single-district component of semiproportional systems tends to reinforce the dominance of a couple of large parties that find it easier to win a significant number of individual seats. Small parties

MAP 6.1

World Electoral Systems

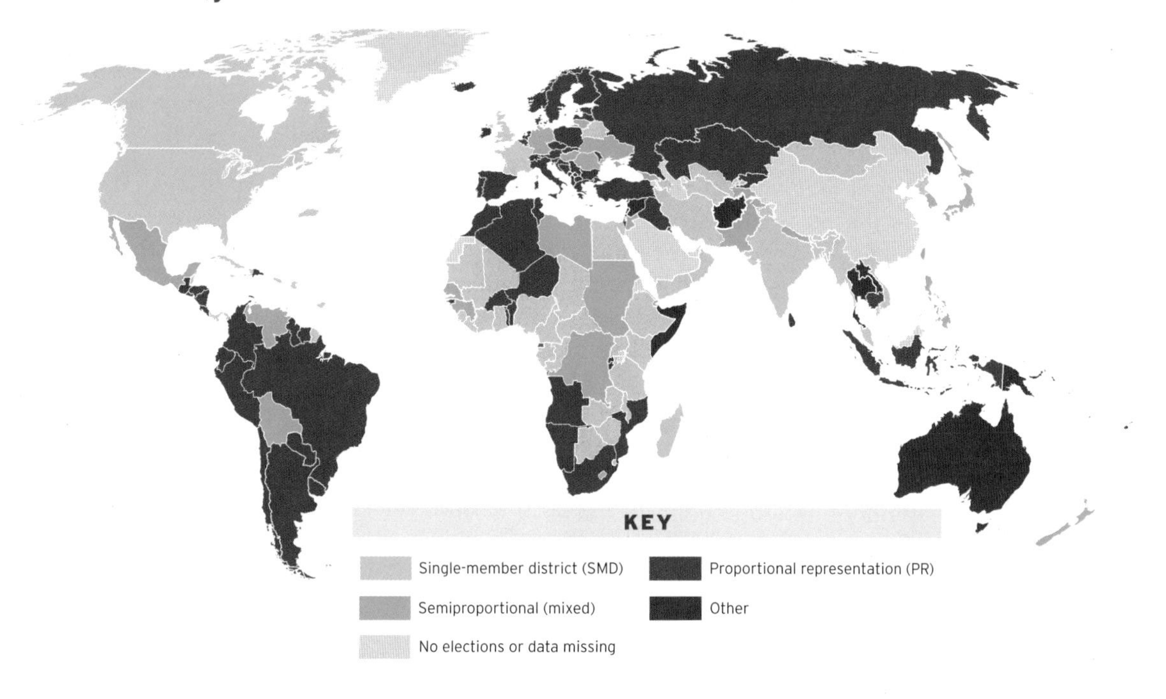

Source: International Institute for Democracy and Electoral Assistance (http://www.idea.int/esd/world.cfm). Modified by the authors.

also form and are represented, but the dominance of a couple of major parties facilitates coalition formation and stability.

Electoral systems clearly influence the type and extent of representation citizens in a democracy have, and all systems involve trade-offs to some extent. Electoral systems also have an important impact on two other institutions: political parties and party systems.

Formal Institutions: Political Parties and Party Systems

American political scientist E. E. Schattschneider wrote that "modern democracy is unthinkable save in terms of parties" (1942/2009, 1). Political parties are associations that seek to formally control government. In democracies, parties seek to control the government via elections and are limited in what they can do once they gain control. They bring together individual citizens and a number of discrete interests into a coalition of broadly shared interests that potentially helps to overcome the collective action problem. The number of parties and their relative institutional strength constitute a **party system**. Parties perform important functions in any democracy, such as mobilizing citizens to participate in the political process, recruiting and training political elites, clarifying and simplifying voter choices, organizing governments, and providing opposition to the current

party system: The number of parties and their relative institutional strength

government. Political scientists compare parties and party systems based on parties' ideologies, internal organization and strength, and number. These differences have important implications for where and how citizens can participate in a political system and the extent to which diverse interests are represented in a legislature. We begin our discussion with party systems because they interact closely with electoral systems and then turn to a closer examination of parties themselves.

Party Systems: Number and Strength

Comparativists categorize party systems by the number and relative strength of the parties within each system. By definition, democratic party systems include at least two parties, and nearly all have more, but they vary beyond that. At one extreme is the **dominant-party system**, in which multiple parties contest free and (more or less) fair elections following the electoral rules of the country, but one party is popular enough to win every election. In South Africa, for instance, the African National Congress (ANC), Nelson Mandela's party that led the struggle for liberation from apartheid, has won all six national elections easily. Numerous opposition parties exist, have some seats in the legislature, and are allowed to compete openly in the elections. The ANC remains dominant, though its vote share dropped to 57.5 percent in the 2019 national election, the first time it was below 60 percent. An earlier split in the party and its weaker showing in 2019 lead some analysts to predict an end to the dominant-party system, though that may still be a ways off. The line can be thin between a dominant-party system and an electoral authoritarian regime; in the latter, a dominant party maintains power not only via its popularity but also via manipulation of the electoral system, control of government resources, and intimidation of other parties (see chapter 8).

dominant-party system: Party system in which multiple parties exist but the same one wins every election and governs continuously

two-party system: Party system in which only two parties are able to garner enough votes to win an election, though more may compete; the United Kingdom and United States are key examples

multiparty systems: Party systems in which more than two parties could potentially win a national election and govern

In a **two-party system**, only two parties are able to garner enough votes to win an election, though more may compete. The United States is a classic case of a two-party system: no third party has had significant representation in government since the Republicans emerged in the 1850s. Third parties, such as H. Ross Perot's Reform Party during the presidential campaigns of the 1990s, arise to compete in particular elections, but they never survive more than two elections as a political force of any significance.

Finally, **multiparty systems** are those in which more than two parties could potentially win a national election and govern. In some of these, such as Italy for most of its post–World War II history, two of the parties are quite large but one of them almost always has to form a coalition with one or more of the smaller parties in order to gain a majority in parliament and govern. In still other multiparty systems, three or four relatively equal parties regularly contend for power, with a legislative majority always requiring a coalition of at least two of them.

So many individuals were seeking the Democratic nomination for president of the United States in 2019 that televised debates had to be divided into two large groups to accommodate them. In the two-party system, each party is likely to be home to a range of opinions. Candidates from different perspectives within the party can come forward to seek the nomination, but a successful candidate must be able to appeal broadly to party voters to win the nomination.
Saul Loeb/AFP/Getty Images

Origins of Party Systems

How and why did these different party systems emerge and change over time in different countries? The main explanations are sociological and institutional. Sociological explanations posit that parties arise to represent the various interests of self-conscious groups in particular societies. In nineteenth-century Europe, two types of conflicts emerged: economic and religious. The economic conflict between capital and labor became universal as industrialization expanded. All countries eventually had some sort of party defending business interests (usually called "liberal") and a party championing workers' concerns, usually socialist or social democratic. Religious divisions, on the other hand, existed in some places but not everywhere. For instance, Germany's Christian Social Union represents the Catholic minority in a Protestant country, but France, which was nearly universally Catholic, does not have a party with a primarily religious base of support. Where economic and religious divisions were politically salient, multiparty systems emerged; where only the economic division was important, two-party systems emerged.

Institutionalists, on the other hand, argue that a country's electoral system shapes both the number and strength of parties. Rational political leaders will create the types of parties that will help them gain power in the system in which they operate. One classic institutionalist argument is **Duverger's Law**. French political scientist Maurice Duverger (1969) contended that the logic of competition in SMD electoral systems results in the long-term survival of only two parties. Multiple parties are unlikely to survive because all political parties must gain a plurality or a majority in a particular district to win that district's legislative seat. Successful parties will be those with broad enough appeal to gain majority support. Relying on a small, ideologically committed core group will yield no legislative seats. Voters don't want to "waste" their votes on parties that can't win seats. Over time, ambitious politicians gravitate toward established major parties to win elections rather than joining small ones or creating new ones. Duverger's native France was one of the clearer examples of his law at work (see "France and the Shift Toward a Two-Party System").

Party systems have important implications for the stability of governments. Most analysts have argued that an SMD system with two broad parties makes governing easier and policy more coherent. Multiparty systems, on the other hand, give more formal voice to diverse opinions in the legislature but can produce unstable coalition governments. Lorelei Moosbrugger (2012), however, has argued that because politicians in SMD systems must appeal to a broad coalition of voters, even a small group in their electoral coalition can veto policy changes they oppose—even policies supported by a majority—by threatening to withdraw support from incumbents. In multi-party PR systems, on the other hand, politicians are less threatened by the loss of a particular, small group upset over one issue. Farmers, for example, were able to prevent widely supported environment policies more effectively in SMD than in PR systems.

In contrast, PR systems tend to create more parties and parties that are more ideologically distinct than SMD systems. Thus, in Germany's semiproportional system, the environmental movement was able to create a successful Green Party focused on the environment because the party could get enough votes to cross the minimum threshold and gain seats in parliament. Conversely, the United Kingdom's SMD system inhibited development of a strong Green Party because it could not compete for a meaningful number of seats with the Labour and Conservative parties.

The debate between sociological and institutional theories of party systems creates something of a "chicken and egg" question: Did political leaders create electoral systems to match the number and kinds of parties they led, or did the electoral systems provide incentives to create particular kinds of parties? Carles Boix's (2007) historical analysis brings the two approaches together. He argued

Duverger's Law: Institutionalist argument by French political scientist Maurice Duverger that SMD electoral systems will produce two major parties, eliminating smaller parties

France and the Shift Toward a Two-Party System

France provides a classic case of Duverger's Law, though the country's two-round system and multiparty heritage has meant that, even there, the law has not worked perfectly. France's Third (1871–1940) and Fourth (1946–1958) republics had parliamentary governing structures with PR electoral systems, multiparty systems, and unstable coalition governments. A crisis at the end of the Fourth Republic led to the creation in 1958 of the Fifth Republic, with a semipresidential system designed to end the instability.

The constitution of the Fifth Republic created an SMD two-round, majoritarian electoral system. For both legislative and presidential elections, a first-round election is open to all registered parties. If a candidate (for a legislative district or nationally, for the presidency) wins a majority in the first round, she is elected. If not, a runoff election is held two weeks later between the top two candidates in the first round, producing a majority winner. When a second round takes place, the losing parties usually support the candidate who is ideologically closest to them.

This system resulted in the creation of two "families" of ideologically similar parties, one on the left and one on the right, which were pledged to support each other in the second-round elections. By the 1970s, each party family consisted of two significant parties. Within each family, the two major parties were almost equally represented in the National Assembly, thus producing four major parties.

The system inched further toward two-party dominance in the 1980s and 1990s. By 1988, the Socialists held nearly 90 percent of the seats won by the left as a whole. On the right, once Jacques Chirac became president in 1995, his party gained nearly 90 percent of the seats on that side. By 2012, these two largest parties controlled 82 percent of the seats in the National Assembly, compared with only 56 percent in 1973. While the smaller parties continued to exist and gained some legislative seats, Duverger's Law worked in his own country; the shift from PR to a majoritarian system came close to producing a two-party system.

Institutionalist logic, though, is not set in concrete. France's party system collapsed in the 2017 election. The incumbent Socialist Party was extremely unpopular and the leading opposition candidate from the conservative Republican Party was mired in a major corruption scandal. Fed up, a majority of French voters supported Emmanuel Macron, a centrist who left the Socialist Party to form his own party only a year before the election. He and the leader of the far-right National Front won the top two slots in the first-round election and then Macron won a sweeping victory in the second round by a margin of two to one, becoming the youngest president in French history. The traditional left and right parties had their worst election ever. By the 2019 election for the European Union parliament, Macron's economic policies had become widely unpopular and the National Front gained the most votes. The future of France's party system remained uncertain. ●

that in almost all of Europe, parties began as "cadre" parties—one liberal and one conservative—among the elite, with tiny electorates in SMD systems. Where religious divisions grew, religiously based parties challenged and sometimes split the two established parties. With the rise of the working class and its enfranchisement in the late nineteenth century, socialist parties emerged as well. Where SMD systems were well entrenched, such as in the United Kingdom, the socialists tended to displace one of the prior parties, and both the two-party and SMD systems survived. Where religious divisions had already split the two parties—or in newer democracies in the early twentieth century that did not have well-institutionalized electoral systems—the socialists and religious parties successfully demanded a proportional system.

CRITICAL INQUIRY

What Explains Government Effectiveness?

This chapter and the last have discussed the relationship between the type of political system and effective policymaking. The data below allow us to examine this relationship ourselves. Table 6.2 lists a large set of electoral democracies. The first column is a measure of "government effectiveness" created by the World Bank. It assesses the quality of public services and the quality of policy formulation and implementation. The other columns identify key elements of the political systems: the electoral system, the executive–legislative system, and the number of "effective" political parties (a measure of the number and share of legislative seats of parties). Look closely at the table. Can you develop hypotheses for which elements of the political system produce more effective governance? Does a particular type of electoral system or executive–legislative system seem to be associated with more effective government? Do more parties or fewer create government effectiveness? Do you need to combine the variables to explain why some countries achieve more effective government than others? Finally, look at the list of countries and think about where they are in the world. Do other hypotheses emerge about government effectiveness that have nothing to do with the type of political system? What is your overall conclusion based on the table? ●

TABLE 6.2

Measures of Government Effectiveness

COUNTRY	EFFECTIVENESS (2017)*	ELECTORAL SYSTEM	EXECUTIVE–LEGISLATIVE SYSTEM	NUMBER OF EFFECTIVE PARLIAMENTARY PARTIES
Switzerland	2.06	Mixed	Presidential	5.57
Norway	1.98	PR	Parliamentary	4.39
Finland	1.94	PR	Parliamentary	6.47
Canada	1.85	SMD	Parliamentary	2.41
Netherlands	1.85	PR	Parliamentary	5.70
New Zealand	1.77	Mixed	Parliamentary	2.96
Liechtenstein	1.76	PR	Semipresidential	3.31
Germany	1.72	Mixed	Parliamentary	3.51
Japan	1.62	Mixed	Parliamentary	2.42
United States	1.55	SMD	Presidential	1.96
Australia	1.54	SMD	Parliamentary	3.23
Iceland	1.45	PR	Parliamentary	4.42
United Kingdom	1.41	SMD	Parliamentary	2.57
Israel	1.39	PR	Parliamentary	6.94
France	1.35	SMD	Semipresidential	2.83
Portugal	1.33	PR	Semipresidential	2.93

(Continued)

(Continued)

COUNTRY	EFFECTIVENESS (2017)*	ELECTORAL SYSTEM	EXECUTIVE–LEGISLATIVE SYSTEM	NUMBER OF EFFECTIVE PARLIAMENTARY PARTIES
Ireland	1.29	PR	Parliamentary	3.52
South Korea	1.08	Mixed	Presidential	2.28
Spain	1.03	Mixed	Parliamentary	2.60
Czech Republic	1.02	PR	Parliamentary	6.12
Lithuania	0.98	Mixed	Parliamentary	5.28
Mauritius	0.90	SMD	Parliamentary	2.0
Latvia	0.90	PR	Parliamentary	5.13
Chile	0.85	Other	Presidential	2.09
Slovak Republic	0.81	PR	Parliamentary	2.85
Poland	0.63	PR	Parliamentary	3.0
Croatia	0.58	PR	Parliamentary	2.59
Georgia	0.57	Mixed	Semipresidential	1.97
Hungary	0.51	Mixed	Parliamentary	2.01
Italy	0.50	PR	Parliamentary	3.47
Jamaica	0.49	SMD	Parliamentary	1.8
Botswana	0.43	SMD	Presidential	1.95
Uruguay	0.42	PR	Presidential	2.65
Greece	0.31	PR	Parliamentary	3.09
South Africa	0.28	PR	Presidential	2.60
Bulgaria	0.26	PR	Parliamentary	5.06
Costa Rica	0.25	PR	Presidential	4.92
Namibia	0.20	PR	Presidential	1.54
Serbia	0.19	PR	Parliamentary	4.87
Argentina	0.16	PR	Presidential	6.49
Montenegro	0.15	PR	Parliamentary	3.18
Macedonia, FYR	0.14	PR	Parliamentary	2.86
India	0.09	SMD	Parliamentary	3.45
Albania	0.08	PR	Parliamentary	2.78
Turkey	0.07	PR	Parliamentary	2.34
Panama	0.01	Mixed	Presidential	3.01
Mexico	–0.03	Mixed	Presidential	2.80

COUNTRY	EFFECTIVENESS (2017)*	ELECTORAL SYSTEM	EXECUTIVE–LEGISLATIVE SYSTEM	NUMBER OF EFFECTIVE PARLIAMENTARY PARTIES
Indonesia	−0.04	PR	Presidential	8.16
Tunisia	−0.07	PR	Semipresidential	4.62
Ghana	−0.11	SMD	Presidential	2.04
Peru	−0.13	PR	Presidential	3.97
Romania	−0.17	Mixed	Semipresidential	2.12
Brazil	−0.29	PR	Presidential	13.22
Senegal	−0.32	Mixed	Semipresidential	1.57
El Salvador	−0.37	PR	Presidential	3.31
Bolivia	−0.39	Mixed	Presidential	1.91
Ukraine	−0.46	Mixed	Semipresidential	3.3
Bosnia and Herzegovina	−0.48	PR	Parliamentary	7.60
Moldova	−0.51	PR	Parliamentary	4.80
Benin	−0.64	PR	Presidential	8.83
Niger	−0.67	Mixed	Semipresidential	4.64
Paraguay	−0.81	PR	Presidential	2.39
Mozambique	−0.89	PR	Presidential	2.16
Sierra Leone	−1.21	SMD	Presidential	1.9
Liberia	−1.37	SMD	Presidential	6.34

Sources: Government effectiveness data are from the World Bank, Worldwide Governance Indicators, "Government Effectiveness" (http://info.worldbank.org/governance/wgi/index.asp [http://info.worldbank.org/governance/wgi/wgidataset.xlsx]). Data for the degree of institutionalization of democracy are from Polity IV (http://www.systemic peace.org/inscr/inscr.htm). Data for number of effective parties are from Michael Gallagher, 2015, Election indices data set at http://www.tcd.ie/Political_Science/staff/michael_gallagher/ElSystems/index.php, accessed August 2016. These indices: data for electoral family are from IDEA (http://www.idea.int/uid/fieldview.cfm?id=156&themeContext=4). 350.

*Estimate of governance (ranges from approximately −2.5 [weak] to 2.5 [strong] governance performance).

Comparativists Robert Moser and Ethan Scheiner (2012) examined this "chicken and egg" question by focusing on countries with semiproportional systems. By comparing election results for the SMD and PR seats within the same country, they were able to see the effects of the two different electoral systems in a single sociological context. Scientifically speaking, this allowed them to hold constant sociological and other variables, while isolating the effects of the institutions. They found that SMD and PR systems had the effects institutionalists claim in long-established democracies such as those in western Europe. In newer democracies with less-institutionalized party systems, however, the electoral systems did not have any effect. SMD did not tend to produce two parties because voters were not very strategic. They might prefer to stick to an identity-based ethnic party, for example, even if it could not win. Leaders of such parties know they can count on that support, so they have less incentive to compromise. FPTP may produce a winning candidate with only 20 to 30 percent of the vote because many candidates are competing, but the number of parties does not drop over time. The ultimate question, perhaps, is whether the institutional logic will start having an effect over a longer time period as the democracies endure and parties become more institutionalized.

Political Parties: Members, Strength, and Ideology

Parties in wealthy democracies today face growing skepticism. A survey of citizens in twenty-one countries found that while 80 percent believed "democracy" to be a very good thing, only about 20 percent had confidence in parties (Scarrow and Webb 2017, 2). Support for "traditional" major parties has declined markedly in the last two decades in numerous countries, while new parties seen by many as "radical" or "anti-system" have risen rapidly. If parties are central to democracy, as political scientists have long claimed, any problems with their strength or legitimacy or major changes in their support will have major impacts on democracy as a whole. Hence, recent trends have raised great interest, and concern.

When most people think of parties, the first thing that comes to mind is ideology. Klaus von Beyme (1985) created an influential categorization of European parties based on their origins and ideologies. The most important categories are explained in Figure 6.5. They reflect the social and economic changes that characterized nineteenth- and twentieth-century Europe. For example, conservative parties defended the traditions and economic status of the landed elite against the liberals, who pressed for expanded rights for the bourgeoisie and the growth of market economies. Socialists and communists, meanwhile, tried to create mass parties to represent the interests of the emerging working class. These ideologies influenced parties that arose more recently in other places as well, especially in the Americas.

Many comparativists, however, think that differences in the way parties mobilize support is more important than ideology in understanding parties' role in democracy. All parties must mobilize citizens to support them, so how do they overcome the classic collective action problem of convincing the average citizen to participate? Most people would answer that citizens join parties because they agree with their ideas. Comparativists call this type of political mobilization **programmatic**. It can be based on economic or cultural appeals, but somehow party leaders mobilize support based on a set of ideas. This type of mobilization is generally seen as most common in wealthier societies.

Programmatic mobilization is implicit in liberal democratic theory: voters examine available alternatives and support the party that best represents their preferences. Christopher Achens and Larry Bartels (2016) called this the "folk theory" of democracy. In fact, they and other scholars have long argued that even in wealthy societies party support is far less rational than that. Most people are socialized to identify with and support a party: new voters join and support the party their families "have always supported" without necessarily making a conscious choice. Achens and Bartel argued that most voters in fact act in groups, based on important social identities. Voters are individually very poor at assessing detailed policy proposals or even accurately assessing a party's performance after it has been in office. Instead, they join and vote for parties they see as similar or representing "them" in the sense of one or more of their group memberships. While many people recognize this to be the case in ethnically or religiously divided societies, Achens and Bartel argued it is a key explanation of who supports which party nearly everywhere.

programmatic mobilization: Appealing to citizens on the bases of ideas, typically economic or cultural

In programmatic parties, whether based on rational evaluation among citizens or not, the internal organization among party members, political candidates, and

FIGURE 6.5

Von Beyme's Categorization of Political Parties

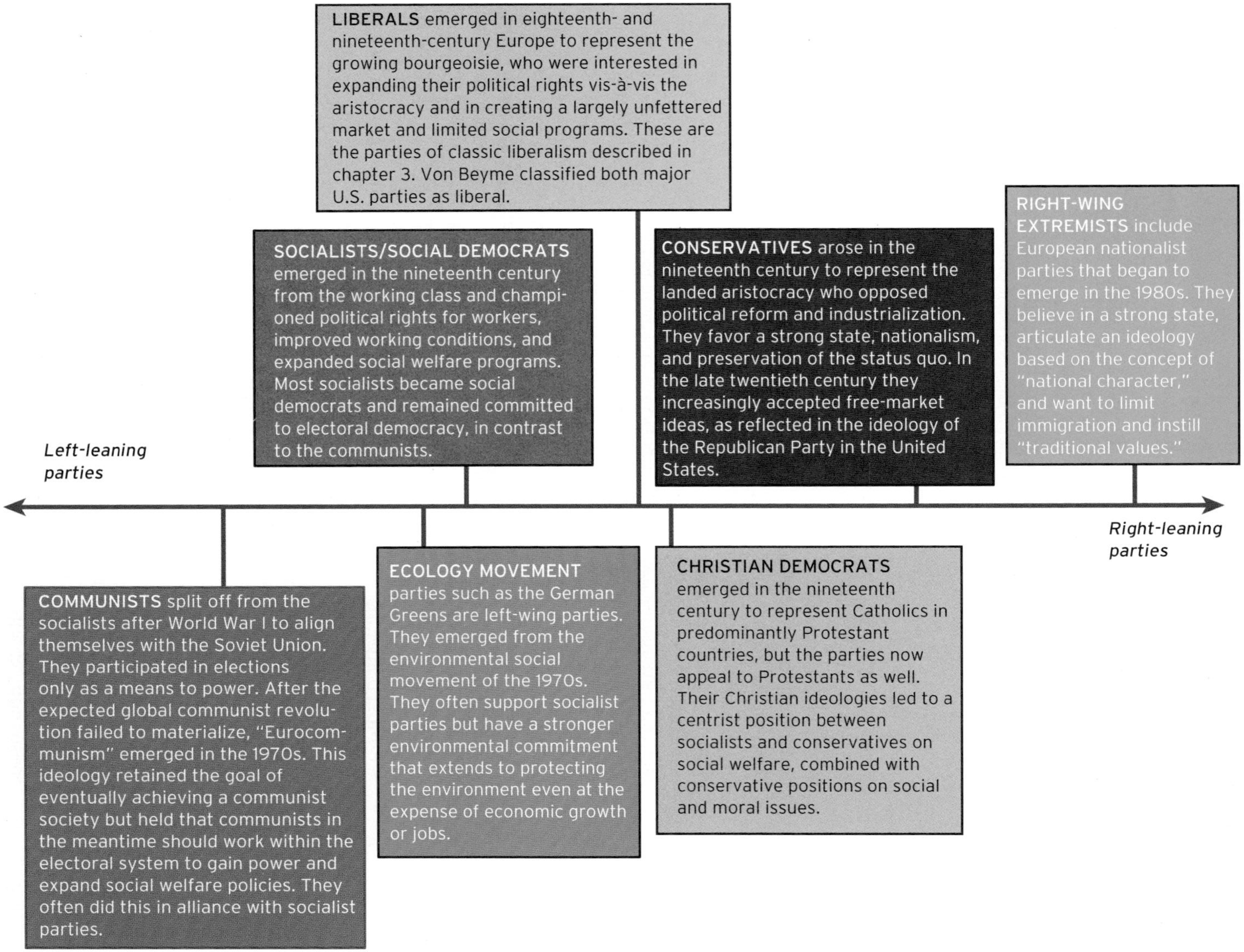

Left-leaning parties ←→ *Right-leaning parties*

COMMUNISTS split off from the socialists after World War I to align themselves with the Soviet Union. They participated in elections only as a means to power. After the expected global communist revolution failed to materialize, "Eurocommunism" emerged in the 1970s. This ideology retained the goal of eventually achieving a communist society but held that communists in the meantime should work within the electoral system to gain power and expand social welfare policies. They often did this in alliance with socialist parties.

SOCIALISTS/SOCIAL DEMOCRATS emerged in the nineteenth century from the working class and championed political rights for workers, improved working conditions, and expanded social welfare programs. Most socialists became social democrats and remained committed to electoral democracy, in contrast to the communists.

ECOLOGY MOVEMENT parties such as the German Greens are left-wing parties. They emerged from the environmental social movement of the 1970s. They often support socialist parties but have a stronger environmental commitment that extends to protecting the environment even at the expense of economic growth or jobs.

LIBERALS emerged in eighteenth- and nineteenth-century Europe to represent the growing bourgeoisie, who were interested in expanding their political rights vis-à-vis the aristocracy and in creating a largely unfettered market and limited social programs. These are the parties of classic liberalism described in chapter 3. Von Beyme classified both major U.S. parties as liberal.

CHRISTIAN DEMOCRATS emerged in the nineteenth century to represent Catholics in predominantly Protestant countries, but the parties now appeal to Protestants as well. Their Christian ideologies led to a centrist position between socialists and conservatives on social welfare, combined with conservative positions on social and moral issues.

CONSERVATIVES arose in the nineteenth century to represent the landed aristocracy who opposed political reform and industrialization. They favor a strong state, nationalism, and preservation of the status quo. In the late twentieth century they increasingly accepted free-market ideas, as reflected in the ideology of the Republican Party in the United States.

RIGHT-WING EXTREMISTS include European nationalist parties that began to emerge in the 1980s. They believe in a strong state, articulate an ideology based on the concept of "national character," and want to limit immigration and instill "traditional values."

campaign resources (mainly money) is important to a party's institutional strength. Parties that have internal mechanisms through which registered members select candidates, as they do in Britain, are likely to be stronger than those that select candidates via external processes, such as primaries in the United States. Candidates in Britain have an incentive to be loyal to the interests and demands of the party members who select them through a formal process and who provide the bulk of their campaign resources. Once elected, they are more likely to vote as a block in support of official party positions. In contrast, candidates in the United States raise most of their own campaign funds and gain their party's nomination via a primary election that is open to all voters in the party (or, in some states, to all voters regardless of party), not just formal party members who have paid dues and attended meetings. They are therefore much more independent of party leaders' demands, and can act more independently once in office. For these reasons, U.S. parties were traditionally less unified and weaker than many of their European counterparts.

Reforms within programmatic parties in recent years have moved many in a more "American" direction in this area. European parties have seen their official membership cut in half or more over the last generation. In response, they have tried to open themselves up to more member participation and often re-defined membership to make it a looser category. While none have moved to full U.S.-style primaries, many now let all of their members and other designated "supporters" (somehow officially registered as such) to help select candidates, rather than having just official members make the selections. The long-term implications of these organizational changes have yet to be seen.

Parties can also mobilize support via direct material benefits, what comparativists call **patronage-based mobilization**. Patronage is based on clientelism which we defined in chapter 2 as the exchange of material benefits for political support. It is one of the most widespread forms of mobilization. The party machines in early twentieth-century U.S. cities, for example, offered preferential treatment to party members when allocating jobs or awarding business contracts with city governments. In authoritarian regimes, formal institutions typically do not allow real citizen participation, and individual loyalty to a political leader can be the best means to survive and gain influence, as we will discuss in chapter 8. As the U.S. example show, parties can combine programmatic and patronage-based appeals or shift from one to another over time.

Most political scientists argue that in democracies, clientelism is more common in relatively poor societies and/or in new democracies in which parties are institutionally weak. In poor and unequal societies, citizens are more likely to need and accept material inducement in exchange for their political support, and inequality gives political leaders plenty of resources for patronage. But even when incomes rise substantially, if citizens remain vulnerable to economic crises—for instance, in countries with very weak welfare systems—clientelism can remain important because citizens turn to political leaders for individual help (Nichter 2018). In new democracies, political parties are typically new and often lack well-established bases of programmatic support so use patronage instead or in addition. Kitschelt (2014) found that parties use patronage most frequently in middle-income countries in which the state is typically very involved in the economy, which gives parties opportunities to share resources with their supporters, and plenty of poor people who will respond to these inducements (see Figure 6.6).

patronage-based mobilization: Appealing to citizens via provision of material resources in exchange for political support

Paul Kenny (2017) argued that a crucial element of the internal organization of patronage-based parties is the relationship between the parties' central authorities and patronage "brokers" lower in the system. Patronage is typically distributed from the center through regional or other lower-level officials, who serve as brokers

FIGURE 6.6

Clientelist Appeals and GDP per Capita

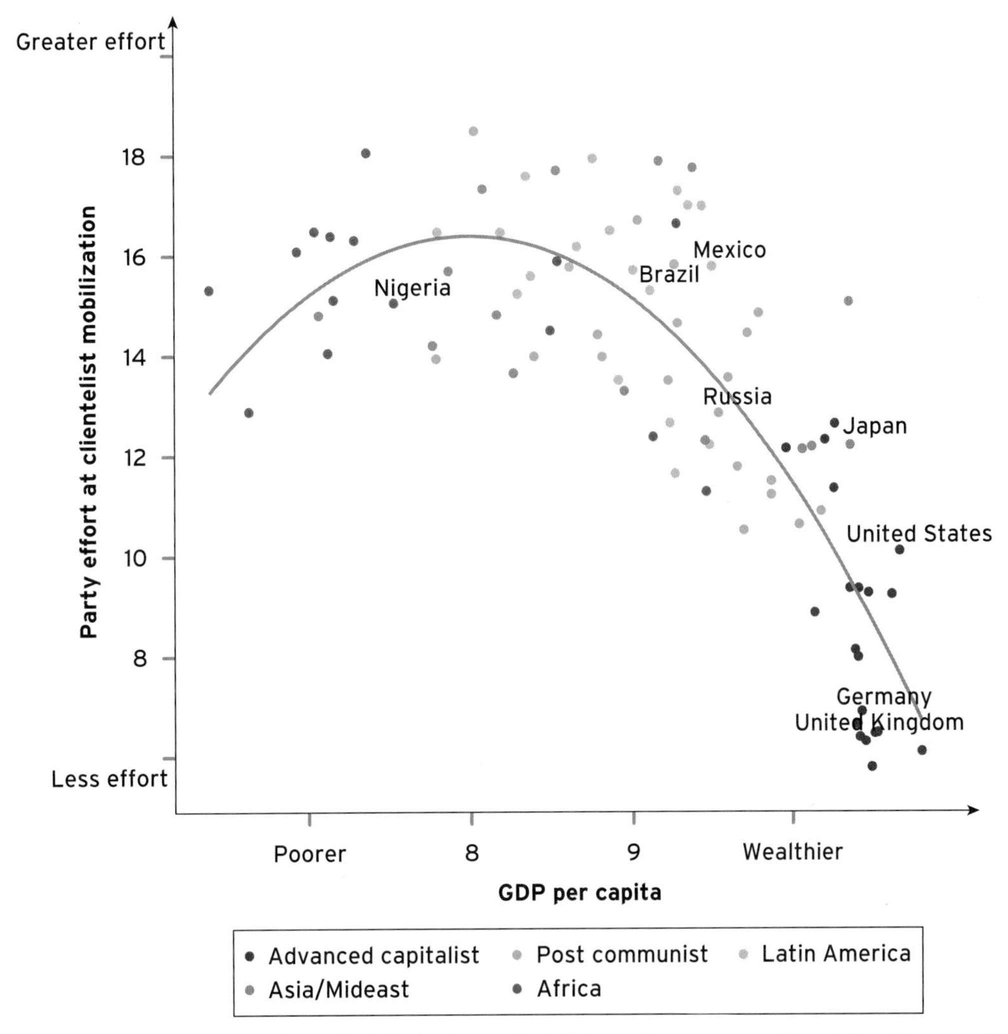

Comparativist Herbert Kitschelt measured the parties' efforts at using clientelist appeals and compared them to the GDP per capita, finding that parties in middle-income countries use clientelism the most and parties in wealthiest countries use it the least because in those countries programmatic and ideological appeals mobilize most voters.

Herbert Kitschelt, "Parties and Party Systems," p. 38, in Lawrence LeDuc, Richard G. Niemi, and Pippa Norris, eds. *Comparing Democracies: Elections and Voting in a Changing World*, (Washington, DC: SAGE, 2014), 32–57.

between the center and citizen supporters. If these brokers gain autonomy vis-à-vis central authorities, the parties will be weaker and might collapse into competing factions or entirely separate parties. This is one situation in which a third form of political mobilization might arise: populist mobilization.

populist mobilization: Appealing to citizens directly, often threatening established institutions, parties, and elites; emphasizing a united and morally superior "people" battling corrupt elites; engaging in "bad manners"; and focusing rhetoric around a sense of "crisis" that threatens "the people"

Populist mobilization involves a personalist leader appealing to voters directly, often threatening established institutions, parties, and elites. Populist leaders emphasize a united and morally superior "people" battling corrupt elites; engage in "bad manners" (behavior previously considered unacceptable for political elites); and focus their rhetoric around a sense of "crisis" that threatens "the people" (Moffitt 2016). Populist mobilization often arises when programmatic or patronage-based mobilization breaks down and at least some citizens no longer feel they are adequately represented by mainstream parties (Kenny 2017). Kirk Hawkins and colleagues (2017) provided a psychological explanation for why populism arises, arguing that some voters have latent populist attitudes that populist leaders can activate in a context of recognized elite failures, such as elite corruption (common in Latin America, where populism has also been common) or elite collusion to keep certain issues off the political agenda (more common in wealthy countries). These leaders might work within an older party, perhaps transforming the party itself in the process; create a new party; or rise to power without any party affiliation, at least in presidential systems in which party affiliation is not essential. The number of populist leaders in power has been increasing steadily since 1990, especially "cultural populists," who define "the people" in terms of "the native members of the nation-state, and outsiders can include immigrants, criminals, ethnic and religious minorities, and cosmopolitan elites" (Kyle and Gultchin 2018). Kenny demonstrated with a large quantitative analysis that populist leaders or parties in power are associated with a weakening of democratic norms and institutions, which has made them a subject of growing concern in recent years.

While we can often categorize individual parties as being based on one of these three forms of political mobilization, parties can and do combine them at times. A party may be able to make a programmatic appeal to some voters but use patronage to appeal to others. A populist leader might use patronage in addition to his populist appeals to cement support. Liberal democracy in its ideal form, as outlined in chapter 3, implicitly assumes programmatic parties, but patronage and populist forms of mobilization have existed and at times continue to exist in virtually all real-world democracies.

A Crisis of Party Democracy?

In the election for the EU parliament in May 2019, the total vote for the long-established parties that had supported the EU dropped, and critics from both the left and right increased their share of the vote to 25 percent. The far-right National Front came in first in France, while the "Brexit Party" that had only been created a few weeks before the election took first place in Britain. This was part of a longer-term trend: in the last thirty years, as shown in Figure 6.7, the long-established democracies have seen a drop in partisan loyalty to the traditional Christian democrat and social democratic parties; lower voter turnout; a dramatic decline in traditional parties' membership; increased electoral volatility (voters switch parties more frequently from one election to the next); more single-issue voting, especially on postmaterialist issues such as the environment or abortion; and greater focus on the personality of individual candidates rather than on parties and their ideologies.

As the traditional parties have declined, new parties, many considered populist and some considered "anti-system," have arisen on the ideological extremes. On the left, "green" parties focused on environmental and peace issues also emerged across Europe, especially in countries with PR electoral systems. Leftist parties questioning the continued benefits of the EU have also arisen in some countries, such as Greece and Spain. A more powerful trend, though, has been the emergence of "far-right" parties. While their precise ideologies vary, far-right parties generally focus on economic decline and oppose immigration, often blaming the EU and "globalization" for both. They have made major electoral gains over the last decade in Germany, France, Sweden, Denmark, the Netherlands, and Austria, and were part of a coalition government in Italy in 2018. In the United States, Donald Trump's

FIGURE 6.7

Voter Support for Populist Parties

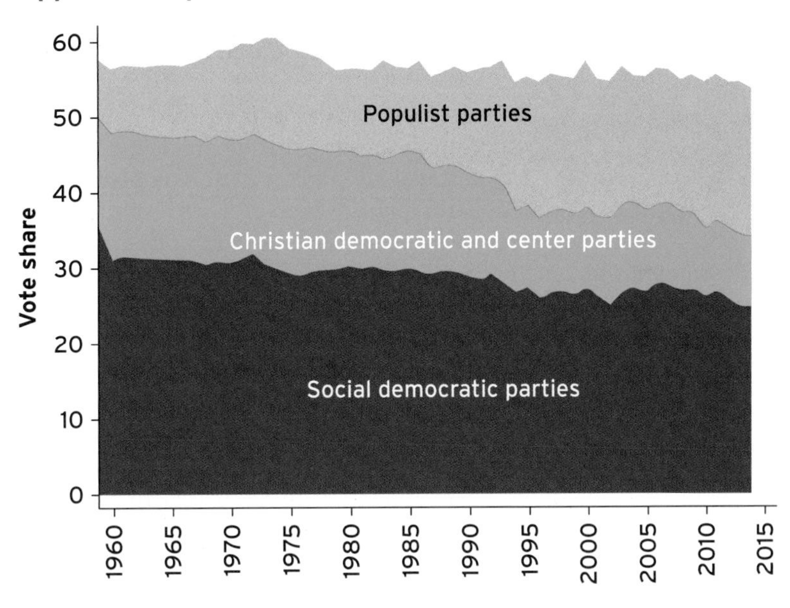

Source: Torben Iverson and David Soskice, *Democracy and Prosperity: Reinventing Capitalism Through a Turbulent Century* (Princeton, NJ: Princeton University Press, 2019), 130

successful campaign for president shared many elements with European far-right parties, as did Jair Bolsonaro's success in becoming president of Brazil in 2018.

Many far-right parties combine populist mobilization with nativism, an extreme form of cultural nationalism that sees the "people" as threatened by outsiders and demands a return to a more culturally pure nation. As we noted in chapter 4, this type of nationalism often envisions or argues for the re-creation of, traditional gender roles; in Europe, it has also included religious elements involving the image of "Christian Europe" versus Muslim immigrants. Critics argue that at least some of these parties champion policies that would undermine core democratic values, such as acceptance of diversity of opinion (populism defines "the people" as a homogenous whole) and of all residents as full citizens (immigrants are "outsiders" undeserving of inclusion). These parties generally gain most support among less-educated, white voters who seem to feel most threatened by economic and demographic changes. The newness of these parties and the focus in many of them on a charismatic leader raises questions about whether they do or can serve the traditional functions of parties in Western democracies—giving voters clear ideological choices, providing organizations within which citizens can usefully participate in politics, and creating stable coalitions of interests that can govern effectively.

The best known and one of the oldest far-right parties is the National Front in France. Its leader, Marine LePen, came in a close second in the first-round presidential election in May 2017. Although she was easily defeated by her centrist opponent in the second round, she nonetheless came closer to the presidency than the party ever had, capturing a third of the vote. In the parliamentary elections a month later, however, the party won only a handful of seats. Although the long-standing, "mainstream" parties also lost, they lost to the newly created party of the newly elected centrist president, who actively campaigned in favor of EU membership and globalization, in direct opposition to the National Front. In 2019, though, the National Front got the most votes, nearly a quarter, in the election for the EU parliament in France; it is far from defeated.

In Germany, the Alternative for Germany (AfD), a new right-wing party founded in April 2013, garnered 4.7 percent of the national vote in the September 2013 elections. The party initially focused on economic issues, criticizing Chancellor Angela Merkel's policies toward Greece and other bankrupt "eurozone" countries. By 2015, though, it shifted its focus to immigration, arguing that too many immigrants, particularly Muslims, were threatening national identity. In 2016 it gained representation in nine (of sixteen) German state parliaments. Much of the AfD's support is clearly a reaction to the government's response to the 2015–2016 refugee crisis in which the German government welcomed over 1.1 million Syrian and other refugees. The party has become more extreme, and though there is debate over whether it can be accurately described as a neo-Nazi party, several sectors of the party, including its youth wing, were put under surveillance by the Office for Protection of the Constitution in early 2019 because their "anti-immigration and particularly anti-Muslim attitude" are not aligned with German democratic principles. Although the AfD accepts democratic processes to achieve its goals and is not an imminent threat to democracy, it is antidemocratic in its rejection of pluralism and minority rights (Daehnhardt 2019, 104).

The decline of the traditional parties has produced significant debate among political scientists trying to explain why it has happened and where it might lead. A common explanation has focused on economic changes. The decline of manufacturing in wealthy democracies that accompanied globalization (see chapter 10) reduced job opportunities and incomes for less-educated, particularly male, workers, who not infrequently blamed immigrants and other countries for taking "their jobs." The European refugee crisis of 2015–2016 saw a million Middle Eastern refugees arrive in Europe in a matter of months, significantly strengthening far-right parties. Most traditional parties, of both the right and left, supported or at least accepted the economic changes that less-educated workers saw as hurting them; feeling abandoned, these voters supported the new, far-right parties, who tied their grievances to support for reduced trade, a reduced role for the EU, and reduced immigration in the name of "the people" and cultural nationalism. Dieter Rucht (2018) combined these explanations, arguing that the most "hard-core" supporters and activists of far-right, populist movements are people who feel they have lost out economically, are politically alienated from mainstream parties, and feel a "cultural disorientation" tied to immigration and other social changes such as around gender roles. Any of these might create sympathy and possibly support for far-right populism, but all three combined provide the strongest support.

Others saw social changes affecting the entire society as the underlying cause of the decline of traditional parties. Some scholars argued a fundamental partisan dealignment was occurring, as voters and parties disconnect, probably for the long term. They argued that major parties used to serve two key functions: educating voters about political issues and simplifying voters' choices. As voters have become more educated and media outlets (and now social media) have multiplied, they no longer need parties to educate them. The media changes have also prompted parties to campaign increasingly via national and social media rather than by mobilization of grassroots membership, and this has made it less important for them to maintain their membership base (Dalton and Wattenberg 2000). Other analysts, more optimistically, saw a less permanent realignment: voters' preferences changed, and the traditional parties didn't keep up. However, as parties changed or new parties emerged, voters and parties once again came into alignment. In particular, cleavages on cultural issues have expanded, creating space for emergent parties to appeal to voters on both the "left" and "right" on issues like the environment, race relations, and gender roles (Dalton 2018).

Another group of comparativists saw changes within the traditional parties themselves, rather than uncontrollable external social or economic changes as the source of their decline. At least since the 1980s, the ideological difference between the traditional "left" and "right" parties in most European countries has been shrinking (Maravall 2016, 52). While they remain distinct, they do not offer voters the stark choice they did a half century ago. Many parties became what are termed "catch-all" parties that appealed to voters not by their ideological distinctions but by offering more and more government aid and services to them, especially in Europe's more developed welfare states (see chapter 12). Political scientists Mark Blyth and Peter Mair (2017) argued that by the late twentieth century, this strategy was meeting budget constraints. Governments were no longer able to expand social benefits, so parties could no longer offer more to attract voters. They instead accepted market-oriented economic theories that argued for more limited government services (see chapter 10) and sold those to the electorate, lowering expectations about what was possible. Formerly catch-all parties became what they termed "cartel parties." Competition came to be about "managerial competence" rather than ideological differences or promises of benefits. In effect, major parties formed a cartel to maintain power, using media and money from the government to fund their own activities; all major parties implicitly came to agree on preserving the status quo. Among other things, this hurt citizens' sense of political efficacy, the feeling that their participation can have a political impact (Pardos-Prado and Riera 2016). In this context, populists had an opportunity to mobilize voters against an "elite" who was dividing power among themselves at the expense of "the people." The debate over what has caused the major changes in European parties and party systems in the last twenty years will continue; the answers seem likely to have major implications for the future of European democracy.

The idea of declining partisan loyalty and the rise of new parties may seem odd to most Americans, who see the two major parties maintaining their share of the national vote and see national politics as "too partisan." In spite of Donald Trump's successful populist campaign for president, the United States' party evolution is distinct from most other wealthy democracies. Between the 1950s and 1970s, America's two major parties were less ideologically divided than their European counterparts, "catch-all" parties from a much earlier period without a clear basis in a single core social group. The Democratic Party since the era of President Franklin Roosevelt brought together northern liberals and working-class voters in favor of government social programs, with southern whites committed to preserving Jim Crow. The Republicans mostly represented northern business interests opposed to social programs and other conservatives in the Midwest and western states. African American voters were divided between the two parties, though so many of them were disenfranchised that they did not have a major effect.

The civil rights struggle and enfranchisement of African American voters, combined with rapid immigration of Asians and Hispanics, fundamentally changed America's party coalitions. The parties' supporters became much more clearly "sorted" ideologically and racially into two distinct groups, spurring greater partisan polarization (Abramowitz 2018). From the 1960s to the 1980s, southern whites slowly but continuously shifted their allegiance to Republicans, blaming Democrats for the end of the Jim Crow era. Simultaneously, economic changes seemed to benefit urban and coastal areas over rural and interior ones and more-educated citizens over less-educated ones. Cities were also where most citizens of color and immigrants lived. By the 2000s, the Democratic Party had come to represent a multiracial coalition (about 40 percent of their voters are people of color and 60 percent are white) of primarily urban and coastal voters. The bulk of these voters were more educated and generally accepted and saw themselves as benefiting from the economic and social changes—for example, women's rights or LGBTQ rights—of the last few decades.

The Republican Party came to represent an overwhelmingly (90 percent) white electorate that is disproportionately southern, rural, less educated, and evangelical Christian. Their white, working-class, and evangelical Christian supporters saw themselves as having lost out on the economic changes brought on by globalization and their way of life and belief system threatened by immigration and recent social changes. This was the context in which Donald Trump mounted a successful populist campaign to capture the presidency, focused on immigration and restricting trade, and calling for a return to an earlier and better era. Based on surveys of a group of voters from 2012 to 2016, Diana Mutz (2018) argued that Trump's support was based on "issues that threaten white American's sense of dominant group status." Even though the recent history of America's party system is quite different from most of Europe's, questions about the stability of party systems are similar and raise potentially profound questions about the strength of long-standing democracies.

Civil Society

As we discussed in chapter 3, civil society arose in Europe with capitalism, industrialization, and democracy. It provides a space beyond the family or firm within which groups of citizens organize to influence government. As with parties, we ask questions about how organizations in civil society enhance democracy: Are their internal rules democratic? Do they represent their constituents accurately? Do they gain undue influence? Do they have beliefs and foster policies that enhance democracy or harm it?

Our definition of civil society includes all organized activity that is beyond the individual self-interest of the household or firm and is not controlled by the government. In most long-standing democracies, though, the term *civil society* typically connotes interest groups. These associations of individuals or businesses attempt to influence government, and most claim to represent clearly defined interests that their members share, such as protecting the environment, advancing civil rights, or representing various industries. They are formally organized, though their degree of institutionalization varies. They also are often regulated by the government and have to follow certain rules and procedures if they wish to be recognized as legitimate. Ideally, well-institutionalized interest groups are visible, have relatively large and active memberships, and have a significant voice on the issues in which they are interested. Less-institutionalized groups are less effective, and their legitimacy as representatives on various issues is often questioned. Similar to parties, interest groups bring together like-minded individuals to achieve a goal, but interest groups do not seek formal political power. In theory, if they are effective in carrying out their functions, the political system becomes more responsive and inclusive.

Modern interest groups emerged in the nineteenth century alongside mass electoral democracy. Labor, business, and agriculture became the key "sectoral" categories of interest groups; that is, they represented the three key sectors of the economy. As the bulk of the citizenry became more involved in the political process, other interest groups emerged as well, including groups focused on expanding participation rights for women and racial minorities. In postcolonial countries, similar groups emerged. In Latin America, unions and business associations arose with the beginning of industrialization in the late nineteenth century. In Asia and Africa, trade unions developed under colonial rule as colonial subjects began to work for wages and started to organize. Unions became important in the nationalist struggles for independence in most countries. In ethnically and religiously divided societies, though, ethnic or religious organizations are often more politically important than unions or other sectoral groups. As more and more different kinds of countries become democratic, more and more varied types of civil society organizations arise, making the study of their impact on democracy increasingly important and interesting.

Do all of these interest groups enhance democratic participation and representation? Ethnic and religious organizations may require members to be born into the groups represented. Such groups also often view any internal dissent as a threat to the group's sense of identity, resulting in an undemocratic internal organizational structure. Should democracies allow such organizations to exist, and does their existence contribute positively or negatively to participation and representation in democracy? Does the Ku Klux Klan (KKK)? It is clearly an organized group of citizens whose goals could certainly include trying to influence governmental policy. Its core beliefs, however, violate the basic tenets of liberal democracy, so we could liken it to a political party that runs on a platform that questions the legitimacy of democracy (as the Islamic Front did in Algeria in the early 1990s). The types and strength of different kinds of groups in civil society have important effects on the strength of a democracy.

India's long history of democratic rule provides a fascinating example of the complexity of civil society in postcolonial countries. The most important groups in Indian civil society are not trade unions and business associations. Both certainly exist, but they are relatively weak. Most workers are in the informal sector and are not members of unions. They do organize, however, and in India women in the informal sector in particular have formed associations to demand greater social services from the state rather than the traditional labor rights that typically interest unions (Agarwala 2013). Although these class-based groups certainly matter, they are ultimately overshadowed in civil society by groups championing ethnic, religious, or caste interests. Numerous movements initially arose around ethnic identity, based primarily on language. Movements based on religion, however, proved much more explosive. A Sikh movement in the 1970s ultimately turned violent. The government defeated it, but a Sikh nationalist subsequently assassinated Prime Minister Indira Gandhi. The largest religious movement now is Hindu nationalism. Its greatest cause became the destruction of a mosque and construction of a Hindu temple in its place in the northern city of Ayodhya in the 1990s. Occasional violent conflicts between Hindus and Muslims have occurred ever since, as religion has replaced language as the most volatile basis of political divisions. The current ruling party in India arose out of the Hindu nationalist movement; although it has pursued an aggressive economic development agenda, many observers fear it is trying to impose a more restrictive Hindu nationalist policy on India's secular democracy as well.

The Indian caste system has also been the basis of many movements in civil society. Traditionally, most of the distinctions among castes were based on occupation, with certain castes performing certain types of work. Along with these economic distinctions came strict social practices, such as not eating with, drinking from the same well as, or marrying a member of a caste beneath you. At the bottom of this hierarchy were the so-called untouchables, now known as dalits. Technological change, increased access to education, urbanization, and employment/education quotas for lower castes have changed the economic basis for caste divisions in recent decades. Brahmin (the highest caste) landlords no longer control land as completely and thoroughly as they once did; many of the lower-caste occupations no longer exist; and growing numbers of people of all castes have moved to cities, taking up new occupations at various levels of education and compensation. Nonetheless, caste remains very important. A 1999 survey found that 42 percent of Brahmins worked in white-collar professional positions or owned large businesses, as opposed to only 17 percent of middle castes and 10 percent of dalits, the so-called untouchables. Conversely, less than 4 percent of Brahmins worked as agricultural laborers, as opposed to 35 percent of dalits. Developing caste-based movements has involved shifting the social construction of caste identity. Traditionally, specific caste identities were very localized, and people mainly thought of themselves in relation to other local castes above and below them. Leaders of caste-based movements, though, have helped create a more "horizontal" understanding of caste, forging common identities among similar castes with different names in different locales. These movements created a new type of caste identity to which major parties had to respond if they wanted to win elections.

As is true for political parties, analysts have grown increasingly concerned about the strength of civil society, even in well-established democracies. Robert Putnam (2000) decried a decline in **social capital**—that is, social networks and norms of reciprocity that are crucial to democratic participation. Even apparently "nonpolitical" organizations (such as the local Little League or parent-teacher organization) in civil society, he argued, create social networks and mutual trust among members, which can be used for political action, but face-to-face organizations seem to be waning. Theda Skocpol (2003) argued that a system of mass-membership organizations in the United States arose in the nineteenth century and declined in the late twentieth century. "Managed advocacy" groups that rely on members for financial support and for occasional phone calls, emails, or presence at rallies, Skocpol argued, have replaced active local branches that bring members together on a regular basis.

What effect does this have on the quality of democracy? Critics of Putnam and Skocpol argue that while levels of trust and membership in formal organizations have declined, involvement in political activities has not (Dalton 2017). Rather, activity has shifted to new and different organizations and forms. Putnam's book was titled *Bowling Alone,* a reference to the decline of American bowling leagues; one of his best-known critics wrote an article titled "Kicking in Groups," a reference to the rise of the American Youth Soccer Organization at the same time bowling leagues declined (Lemann 1996). Citizens may participate in these new groups and perhaps influence government successfully, but they move relatively quickly among different issues and movements and may not develop strong ties with any particular group. Americans also volunteer more than ever before and join small groups such as self-help groups at higher rates than in the past. These scholars argue that new forms of activity have arisen to replace, at least in part, those that have declined. Much of this activity takes place via social movements and involves the use of social media, both of which we address in chapter 7.

Government–Interest Group Interaction: Two Models

social capital: Social networks and norms of reciprocity that are important for a strong civil society

No matter their origin, cause, or relative strength, the formal and informal relationships that interest groups have with government are crucial to how they operate and how effective they can be. The two major democratic models of government–interest group interaction are known as "corporatist" and "pluralist."

Interest-Group Pluralism

We used the word *pluralist* in chapter 1 to describe one of the major theories that attempts to answer the question "Who rules?"; here, however, **interest-group pluralism** means a system in which many groups exist to represent particular interests and the government remains officially neutral among them. Under a pluralist system in this sense, many groups may exist to represent the same broad "interest," and all can try to gain influence. The government, at least in theory, is neutral and does not give preferential access and power to any one group or allow it to be the official representative of a particular interest. The United States is the primary model of this pluralist system. The Chamber of Commerce exists to represent business interests, but so does the National Association of Manufacturers, the National Association of Realtors, and myriad other groups. Washington, D.C., contains literally thousands of interest groups, sometimes dozens organized around the same issue, all vying for influence over decision makers. This is repeated, on a smaller scale, in all fifty state capitals. The government of the day may listen more to one than another of these groups on a particular issue, but no official and enduring preference or access is given to one over others. Even when one large organization speaks on behalf of most of a sector of society—such as the AFL-CIO for labor—it is a loose confederation of groups whose individual organizational members can and do ignore positions and policies of the national confederation. Alternative groups have the right to organize as best they can. Figure 6.7 depicts this often-confusing system, with multiple groups interacting directly with the government as well as forming various loose affiliations (such as the AFL-CIO) that also interact with the government.

Corporatism

The major alternative to interest-group pluralism is corporatism. Unlike pluralism, which exists only in democracies, corporatism has more democratic (societal or neocorporatist) and less democratic (state corporatist) variants. We discuss the latter in chapter 8. **Neocorporatism**, also known as societal corporatism, is most common in northern Europe, where strong **peak associations** represent the major interests in society by bringing together numerous local groups, and government works closely with fewer, larger, and more highly institutionalized peak associations than under pluralism. Figure 6.8 depicts this more hierarchical system. In a neocorporatist system, peak associations maintain their unity and institutional strength via internal mechanisms that ensure local organizations will abide by the decisions of the national body. By negotiating binding agreements with them, the state in effect recognizes the peak associations as the official representatives of their sectors. Unlike **state corporatism**, however, no individuals or groups are required to belong to these associations, and they maintain internal systems of democratic control. Dissatisfied members may try to change the association's policies or found alternative organizations, but most do not pursue the latter option because membership in the main body provides direct access to government.

Germany is a prime example of the neocorporatist system. At its height in the 1970s, the German Trade Union Federation, the peak association for labor, claimed to represent 85 percent of the unionized workforce. Business is represented by three peak associations, each representing different-sized firms. From the 1950s through the 1970s, these peak associations worked closely with the major political

interest-group pluralism: Interest-group system in which many groups exist to represent particular interests and the government remains officially neutral among them; the United States is a key example

neocorporatism: Also called societal corporatism; corporatism that evolves historically and voluntarily rather than being mandated by the state; Germany is a key example

peak associations: Organizations that bring together all interest groups in a particular sector to influence and negotiate agreements with the state; in the United States, an example is the AFL-CIO

state corporatism: Corporatism mandated by the state; common in fascist regimes

FIGURE 6.8

Contrasting Models of State-Interest Group Interaction

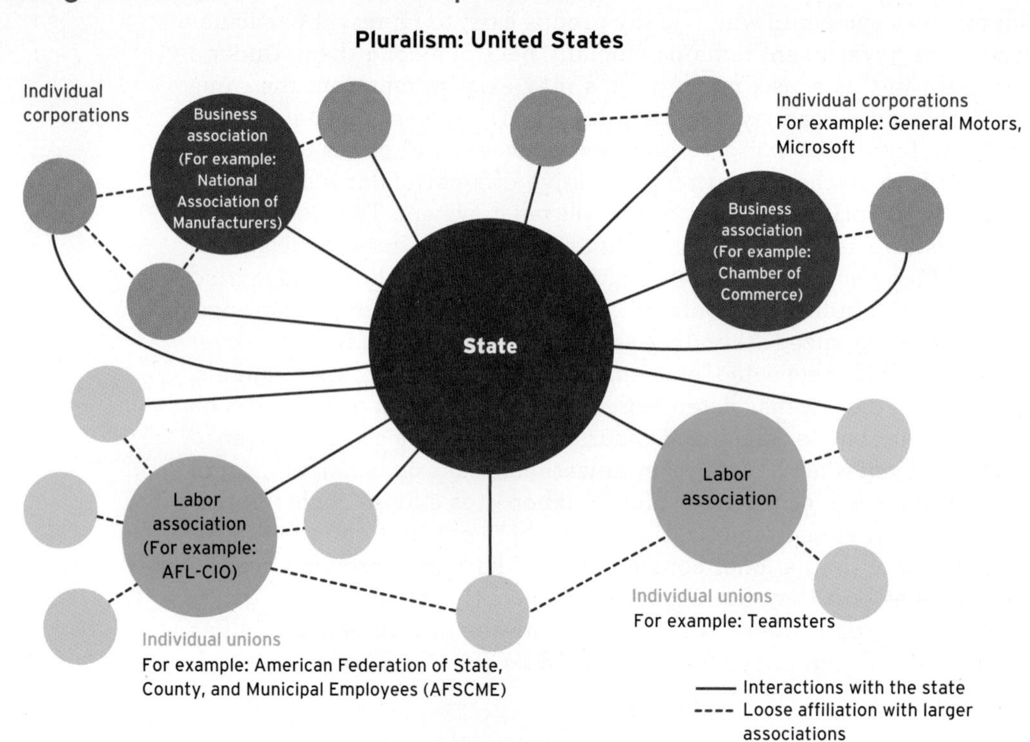

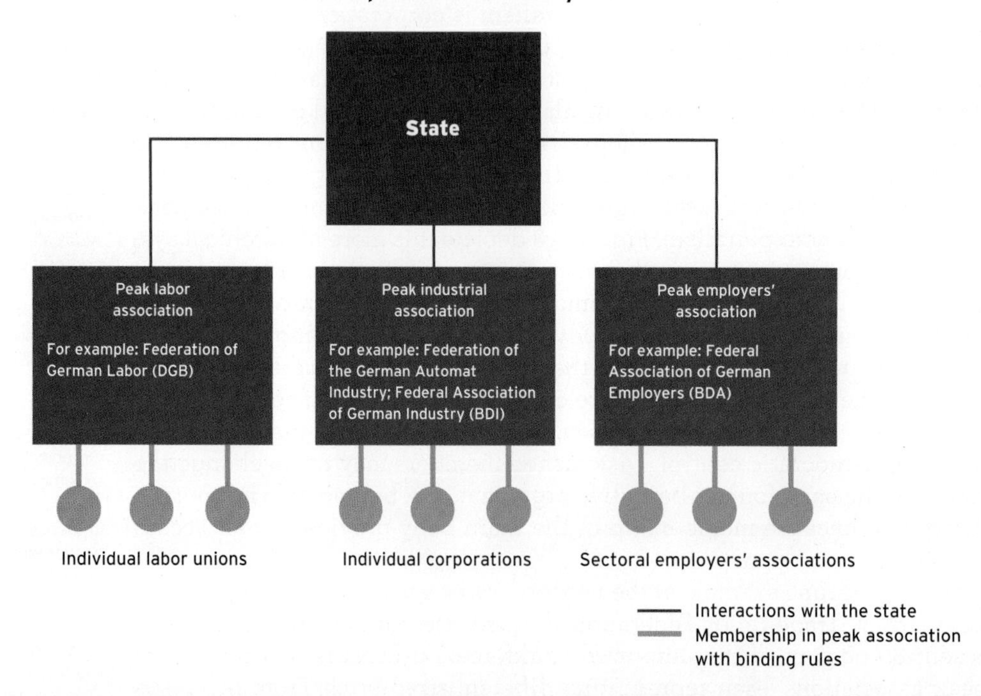

parties and the government to set wages and social policies. Most MPs on key committees were members of one of the peak associations, and many had worked professionally for them before entering parliament. Political scientists saw this model as a great success into the 1970s. Underlying it, however, were trends that would raise serious questions. Popular discontent became quite apparent by the late 1960s. A strong student movement arose that was opposed to the Vietnam War, German rearmament, the consumer culture, and Germany's support for the United States in the Cold War. Growing unemployment affected would-be middle-class college students and working-class young adults alike. All of this discontent culminated in widespread protests in 1968, which the government forcefully put down. The demise of this movement led young political activists to pursue several different paths. Some founded feminist, antinuclear, and environmental groups, whereas others formed what came to be known as "civil action groups." These were small, local groups of usually not more than thirty people that were focused on petitioning local government on issues such as building new schools or cleaning up pollution. By 1979, some 1.5 million Germans were participating in at least fifty thousand such groups. Some of the groups that focused primarily on the environment came together to form a national association. By 1980, this association helped create the Green Party, and in 1983 it became the first new party since 1949 to break the 5 percent vote barrier and gain seats in parliament.

A boy practices target-shooting via a video game at the National Rifle Association's Youth Day in 2013. The NRA is one of the most powerful interest groups in the United States. The pluralist U.S. system gives interest groups exceptional access to legislators, in particular. Critics argue these "special interest groups" unduly influence policy and help create the "gridlock" familiar to Americans.
AP Photo/Houston Chronicle, Johnny Hanson

Economic changes also weakened neocorporatism. The ability of the peak associations to enforce collective wage agreements was key to their power and influence. In the 1980s, these key associations began to weaken as unemployment rose and unions allowed greater flexibility in setting working conditions within firms. As control of working conditions became more localized, however, local unions had less reason to obey the dictates of the peak associations, thereby weakening their role. Facing rising costs from exporters elsewhere in the world, smaller businesses began leaving the employers' associations as well. The decline of traditional manufacturing, meanwhile, caused union membership to plummet by four million during the 1990s. The peak associations for both business and labor were speaking for and able to enforce central agreements on a shrinking share of the private sector, further weakening neocorporatism. New interests that felt they were not being represented in the neocorporatist system and economic changes have profoundly affected Germany's neocorporatist system; the traditional peak associations still exist and are important but perhaps not as exclusively important as they were a generation ago.

Pluralism and Neocorporatism Compared

Both pluralist and neocorporatist models have strengths and weaknesses. Pluralism allows greater local control and participation because any individual or group is free to start a new organization. National organizations have limited control over their local affiliates, so local members can work internally to move their local organization in whatever direction they wish. Because the state does not officially recognize any one group, there are fewer incentives for large organizations to maintain unity. This decentralization may limit the institutional strength and overall power of organizations in national politics. France is well known for its weak labor unions, for instance, in part because its two largest unions (one communist and one Catholic) are deeply divided over ideology.

Interest groups gain power vis-à-vis the state due to the resources they can bring to bear on the government. More centralized organizations have more resources and can legitimately claim to speak on behalf of more citizens. These factors increase their potential clout, although critics point out that no government treats each kind of group equally, at least in a market economy. Business interests are crucial for the well-being of the economy; therefore, the government in any market economy, even in the most pluralist systems, will pay more attention to business interests than to others, no matter how effectively others organize (Lindblom 1977). Critics of the pluralist model contend that groups such as workers are better off under neocorporatist systems, in which they are united in large, strong organizations that have a better chance of countering the always strong influence of business.

Because neocorporatist associations are so large and united, they typically have more direct influence on government than does any single national association in a pluralist system. The disincentives to creating new organizations, however, and the power that government recognition provides to the elite leadership of the peak associations, make neocorporatist associations seem less participatory. The incentives against starting alternative organizations are so strong that the vast majority of relevant constituents remain in the confines of already-established entities rather than starting new ones, no matter how dissatisfied they may be. A crucial question in these systems, then, is the degree of democratic control *within* the peak associations. If the association has strong mechanisms of internal democracy, such as open elections for leadership positions and constituent participation in setting organizational policies, its leaders can legitimately claim to represent members' views. If the association does not, it may have significant access to government and influence, but it may not really represent its members' views.

As the German case illustrates, neocorporatist institutions have declined in strength over the last two decades. Globalization has shifted economic interests, making many companies less willing to abide by corporatist agreements (see chapter 10). Labor unions' size and influence have also declined virtually everywhere, so social democratic parties that used to be closely tied to unions are no longer as dependent on them. These changes have meant that interest-group activity in many neocorporatist systems has shifted at least somewhat in a pluralist direction. More groups and less centralized groups are involved in the political process, and they now often seek influence directly with parliaments rather than relying on close ties to party leadership in the executive branch. Although distinctions with pluralist systems like that of the United States still exist, they are not as great as they were a generation ago.

Conclusion

Citizen participation and representation are at the heart of democracy, which ideally gives each citizen equal voice and power. The reality, of course, is that no set of institutions can translate participation into representation and power in a way that treats everyone perfectly equally. Different electoral, party, and interest-group systems channel participation and provide representation in different ways.

These institutions also interact with the governing institutions we outlined in chapter 5, creating yet more variation as we seek to understand who rules and what affects political behavior in democracies.

The most fundamental question about institutions of participation and representation is which system, if any, facilitates greater participation and better representation. Those systems that are more open to diverse organizations and viewpoints seem to create greater participation: multiparty systems, PR electoral systems, and pluralist interest-group systems. Whether they provide greater representation, however, depends on whether representation means only giving a set of people a voice or actually giving them influence. If the latter is a concern, then some would argue that a neocorporatist interest-group system that is based on stronger interest groups is better. While they may limit the ability to form new interest groups, neocorporatist systems arguably provide the greatest influence for recognized groups. Similarly, fewer and larger parties may provide less representation but more influence for their constituents than more numerous and smaller parties would.

This discussion raises the trade-off that Powell (2000) discerned between opportunities for participation and representation on the one hand and accountability on the other. Institutions that allow much representation of diverse interests often make it more difficult for citizens to know exactly whom to hold accountable for government action. More majoritarian systems, with a single ruling party at any given time, arguably provide less representation of diverse voices but make accountability more clear. Similarly, institutions of participation and representation influence the trade-off we discussed in chapter 5 between participation and effective governance. PR electoral systems that allow numerous, small parties to gain legislative representation arguably allow more distinct viewpoints to be expressed. The party coalitions that are then necessary to govern may make governing a challenge, though some political science research has questioned this conclusion.

Institutions affect the representation and participation of marginalized groups even more than they do average citizens. Ethnic or racial minorities and women are often unrepresented in large, catch-all parties or interest groups controlled primarily by the dominant groups in a society. One of the most robust findings in comparative politics is that PR systems provide greater representation of women in parliament. India is an example of going even further to ensure representation of minorities, reserving a specific share of legislative seats for them. While India does this on the basis of caste, several countries do it for women as well, as we discussed in chapter 4. Such laws implicitly assume that members of these groups can only be truly represented if members of their own groups are their official representatives. An SMD system without reservations, such as in the United States or the United Kingdom, assumes that people will be adequately represented by whomever voters collectively choose, regardless of the individual's own characteristics. In a two-party system, though, the choices are limited and disproportionately exclude women and racial or ethnic minorities.

The ultimate "Who rules?" question goes back to the classic debate between pluralist and elite theorists: Do modern democracies really provide government in which average citizens have effective power, or do elites' abilities to gain direct access to decision makers, shape the political agenda, and influence (or control) key institutions mean that they really rule? In the elite model, voters occasionally get a limited choice among a handful of alternatives, all of them led by elites and all typically within a relatively narrow ideological debate. Average voters have limited knowledge or interest and therefore limited influence. Declining partisan loyalty and social capital in recent decades simply strengthen these trends of elite control. Pluralists counter that institutions can and do make a difference in who is represented and in how much meaningful participation average citizens and especially more marginalized citizens can have. Regardless of institutional differences, liberal democracies ultimately provide all voters with the ability to organize and sanction leaders via the ballot box.

Most political participation happens within institutions. When citizens find that available parties, interest groups, and other institutions fail to represent them adequately, though, they may choose to make demands outside institutions' bounds, the realm of what comparativists refer to as "contentious politics," to which we turn next. ●

KEY CONCEPTS

alternative-vote (AV) system (p. 165)
closed-list proportional representation (p. 159)
collective action problem (p. 156)
dominant-party system (p. 168)
Duverger's Law (p. 169)
electoral systems (p. 156)
"first-past-the-post" (FPTP) (p. 157)
interest-group pluralism (p. 185)
mixed, or semiproportional (p. 162)
multiparty systems (p. 168)
neocorporatism (p. 185)
open-list proportional representation (p. 160)
party system (p. 167)
patronage-based mobilization (p. 176)
peak associations (p. 185)
plurality (p. 157)
populist mobilization (p. 177)
programmatic mobilization (p. 174)
proportional representation (PR) (p. 159)
single-member district (SMD) (p. 157)
social capital (p. 184)
state corporatism (p. 185)
two-party system (p. 168)
virtual representation (p. 158)

WORKS CITED

Abramowitz, Alan I. 2018. *The Great Alignment: Race, Party Transformation, and the Rise of Donald Trump.* New Haven, CT: Yale University Press.

Achens, Christopher H., and Larry M. Bartels. 2016. *Democracy for Realists: Why Elections Do Not Produce Responsive Government.* Princeton, NJ: Princeton University Press.

Agarwala, Rina. 2013. *Informal Labor, Formal Politics, and Dignified Discontent in India.* Cambridge, UK: Cambridge University Press.

Aytac, S. Erdem, and Susan C. Stokes. 2019. *Why Bother? Rethinking Participation in Elections and Protests.* New York: Cambridge University Press.

Beyme, Klaus von. 1985. *Political Parties in Western Democracies.* Aldershot, UK: Gower.

Blondel, Jean, and Jean-Louis Thiebault. 2010. *Political Leadership, Parties and Citizens: The Personalisation of Leadership*, with Katarzyna Czernicka, Takashi Inoguchi, Ukrist Pathmanand, and Fulvio Venturino. New York: Routledge.

Blyth, Mark, and Peter Mair. 2017. *Democracy and the Cartelization of Political Parties.* Oxford, UK: Oxford University Press.

Boix, Carles. 2007. "The Emergence of Parties and Party Systems." In *The Oxford Handbook of Comparative Politics*, edited by Carles Boix and Susan Carol Stokes. Oxford, UK: Oxford University Press.

Curtice, John, and W. Phillips Shively. 2009. "Who Represents Us Best? One Member or Many?" In *The Comparative Study of Electoral Systems*, edited by Hans-Dieter Klingemann, 171–192. Oxford, UK: Oxford University Press.

Daehnhardt, Patricia. 2019. "Tectonic Shifts in the Party Landscape? Mapping Germany's Party System Changes." In *Party System Change, the European Crisis and the State of Democracy*, edited by Marco Lisi, 98–114. London, UK: Routledge.

Dalton, Russell J. 2017. *The Participation Gap: Social Status and Political Inequality.* New York: Oxford University Press.

———. 2018. *Political Realignment: Economics, Culture, and Electoral Change.* New York: Oxford University Press.

Dalton, Russell J., and Martin P. Wattenberg. 2000. *Parties Without Partisans: Political Change in Advanced Industrial Democracies.* New York: Oxford University Press.

Downs, Anthony. 1957. *An Economic Theory of Democracy.* New York: Harper and Row.

Duverger, Maurice. 1969. *Political Parties, Their Organization and Activity in the Modern State.* London: Methuen.

Gallego, Aina. 2015. *Unequal Political Participation Worldwide.* New York: Cambridge University Press.

Hawkins, Kirk A., Madeleine Read, and Teun Pauwels. 2017. "Populism and Its Causes." In *The Oxford Handbook of Populism*, edited by Cristobal Rovira Kaltwasser, Paul Taggart, Paulina Ochoa Espejo, and Pierre Ostiguy, 267–286. Oxford, UK: Oxford University Press.

"Imbalance of Power." 2013. *New York Times*. February 2, 2013. http://www.nytimes.com/interactive/2013/02/03/sunday-review/imbalance-of-power.html?ref=sunday &_r=0.

Kedar, Orit. 2009. *Voting for Policy, Not Parties: How Voters Compensate for Power Sharing.* New York: Cambridge University Press.

Kenny, Paul. D. 2017. *Populism and Patronage: Why Populists Win Elections in India, Asia, and Beyond.* Oxford, UK: Oxford University Press.

Kitschelt, Herbert. 2014. "Parties and Party Systems." In *Comparing Democracies: Elections and Voting in a Changing World*, edited by Lawrence LeDuc, Richard G. Niemi, and Pippa Norris, 32–57. Thousand Oaks, CA: Sage.

Kyle, Jordan, and Limor Gultchin. 2018. *Populists in Power Around the World.* Tony Blair Institute for Global Change, November 7, 2018.

Lemann, Nicholas. 1996. "Kicking in Groups." *The Atlantic.* https://www.theatlantic.com/magazine/archive/1996/04/kicking-in-groups/376562/.

Lindblom, Charles E. 1977. *Politics and Markets: The World's Political Economic Systems.* New York: Basic Books.

Maravall, Jose Maria. 2016. *Demands on Democracy.* Oxford, UK: Oxford University Press.

Moffitt, Benjamin. 2016. *The Global Rise of Populism: Performance, Political Style, and Representation.* Stanford, CA: Stanford University Press.

Moosbrugger, Lorelei K. 2012. *The Vulnerability Thesis: Interest Group Influence and Institutional Design.* New Haven, CT: Yale University Press.

Moser, Robert G., and Ethan Scheiner. 2012. *Electoral Systems and Political Context: How the Effects of Rules Vary Across New and Established Democracies.* New York: Cambridge University Press.

Mutz, Diana C. 2018. "Status Threat, Not Economic Hardship, Explains the 2016 Presidential Vote." Proceedings of the National Academic of Sciences, May 8, 2018. *PNAS* 115 (19): E4330–E4339; published ahead of print April 23, 2018, https://doi.org/10.1073/pnas.1718155115.

Nichter, Simeon. 2018. *Vote for Survival: Relational Clientelism in Latin America.* New York: Cambridge University Press.

Orellana, Salomon. 2014. *Electoral Systems and Governance: How Diversity Can Improve Policy-making.* New York: Routledge.

Pardos-Prado, Sergi, and Pedro Riera. 2016. "The Attitudinal Implications of the Cartel Party Thesis: Ideological Convergence and Political Efficacy in Contemporary Democracies." In *Party Politics and Democracy in Europe: Essays in Honour of Peter Mair,* edited by Ferdinand Muller-Rommel and Fernando Casal, 83–100. New York: Routledge.

Powell, G. Bingham. 2000. *Elections as Instruments of Democracy: Majoritarian and Proportional Visions.* New Haven, CT: Yale University Press.

Putnam, Robert D. 2000. *Bowling Alone: The Collapse and Revival of American Community.* New York: Simon and Schuster.

Rucht, Dieter. 2018. "Right-Wing Populism in Context: A Historical and Systematic Perspective." In *Populism and the Crisis of Democracy: Volume 2: Politics, Social Movements and Extremism,* edited by Gregor Fitzi, Jurgen Mackert, and Bryan S. Turner, 67–84. New York: Routledge.

Scarrow, Susan E., and Paul D. Webb. 2017. "Investigating Party Organization: Structures, Resources, and Representative Strategies." In *Organizing Political Parties: Representation, Participation, and Power,* edited by Susan E. Scarrow, Paul D. Webb, and Thomas Poguntke, 1–30. Oxford, UK: Oxford University Press.

Schattschneider, Elmer Eric. 2009. *Party Government.* 3rd ed. New Brunswick, NJ: Transaction. (Originally published 1942 in New York by Holt, Rinehart and Winston.)

Shugart, Matthew Soberg. 2005. "Comparative Electoral Systems Research: The Maturation of a Field and New Challenges Ahead." In *The Politics of Electoral Systems,* edited by Michael Gallagher and Paul Mitchell, 22–55. Oxford, UK: Oxford University Press.

Skocpol, Theda. 2003. *Diminished Democracy: From Membership to Management in American Civic Life.* Norman: University of Oklahoma Press.

RESOURCES FOR FURTHER STUDY

Aldrich, John H. 1995. *Why Parties? The Origin and Transformation of Political Parties in America.* Chicago: University of Chicago Press.

Art, David. 2011. *Inside the Radical Right: The Development of Anti-Immigrant Parties in Western Europe.* New York: Cambridge University Press.

Avritzer, Leonardo. 2009. *Participatory Institutions in Democratic Brazil.* Baltimore, MD: Johns Hopkins University Press; Washington, DC: Woodrow Wilson Center Press.

Dalton, Russell J., David M. Farrell, and Ian McAllister. 2011. *Political Parties and Democratic Linkage: How Parties Organize Democracy.* Oxford, UK: Oxford University Press.

Green, Michael J. 2010. "Japan's Confused Revolution." *Washington Quarterly* 33 (1): 3–19. doi:10.1080/01636600903418637.

Levendusky, Matthew. 2009. *The Partisan Sort: How Liberals Became Democrats and Conservatives Became Republicans*. Chicago: University of Chicago Press.

Norris, Pippa. 2002. *Democratic Phoenix: Reinventing Political Activism*. New York: Cambridge University Press.

Pharr, Susan J., and Robert D. Putnam, eds. 2000. *Disaffected Democracies: What's Troubling the Trilateral Countries?* Princeton, NJ: Princeton University Press.

Putnam, Robert D., ed. 2002. *Democracies in Flux: The Evolution of Social Capital in Contemporary Society*. New York: Oxford University Press.

Rosenbluth, Frances McCall, and Michael F. Thies. 2010. *Japan Transformed: Political Change and Economic Restructuring*. Princeton, NJ: Princeton University Press.

Thomas, Clive S. 2001. *Political Parties and Interest Groups: Shaping Democratic Governance*. Boulder, CO: Lynne Rienner.

Tocqueville, Alexis de. 1969. *Democracy in America*. Garden City, NY: Doubleday Anchor. (Originally published in two volumes in 1835 and 1840, respectively, in London by Saunders and Otley.)

Ware, Alan. 1996. *Political Parties and Party Systems*. New York: Oxford University Press.

Wren, Anne, and Kenneth M. McElwain. 2007. "Voters and Parties." In *The Oxford Handbook of Comparative Politics*, edited by Carles Boix and Susan Carol Stokes, 555–581. Oxford, UK: Oxford University Press.

Wylie, Kristin N. 2018. *Party Institutionalization and Women's Representation in Democratic Brazil*. New York: Cambridge University Press.

WEB RESOURCES

Constituency-Level Elections Archive (CLEA)

(http://www.electiondataarchive.org)

Golder, Matt, "Democratic Electoral Systems Around the World, 1946–2011"

(http://mattgolder.com/elections)

Hyde, Susan, and Nikolay Marinov, National Elections Across Democracy and Autocracy (NELDA)

(http://www.nelda.co/#)

International Foundation for Electoral System, ElectionGuide

(http://www.electionguide.org)

International Institute for Democracy and Electoral Assistance (IDEA)

(http://www.idea.int)

Inter-Parliamentary Union, PARLINE Database on National Parliaments

(http://www.ipu.org/parline-e/parlinesearch.asp)

Johnson, Joel W., and Jessica S. Wallack, "Electoral Systems and the Personal Vote"

(http://thedata.harvard.edu/dvn/dv/jwjohnson/faces/study/StudyPage .xhtml?globalId=hdl:1902.1/17901)

University of California, San Diego, Lijphart Elections Archive

(http://libraries.ucsd.edu/resources/data-gov-info-gis/ssds/guides/lij/)

7 Contentious Politics

Social Movements, Political Violence, and Revolution

Black Lives Matter protesters meet in New York in July 2016, on the second anniversary of the death of Eric Garner, who famously said "I can't breathe" shortly before dying from a police officer's chokehold. The Black Lives Matter movement that began in 2013 in response to what organizers see as police brutality against African Americans is the largest black social movement since the 1960s and a prime example of what political scientists call "contentious politics."
Albin Lohr-Jones/Pacific Press/LightRocket via Getty Images

Key Questions

- How and why are people mobilized to participate in contentious politics?
- How do social movements and other forms of contentious politics function?
- What effects do contentious politics have on governments and policies?
- What effects have globalization and the advent of Internet-based communications and social media had on contentious politics?
- Why does contentious politics sometimes turn violent and take the forms of terrorism, civil war, or revolution?

Learning Objectives

After reading chapter 7, you should be able to do the following:

7.1 Elucidate why and how contentious politics arise

7.2 Articulate the major reasons why political violence occurs

7.3 Define the types of revolution that have led to regime change and explain why these revolutions succeeded

The year 2011 was a banner year for political protest; from the "Arab Spring" to the "Occupy" movement to protests against economic policies in Spain, Greece, and Italy, citizens everywhere seemed to mass in the streets demanding change. While not all of those protests succeeded, they gave new impetus to a long-standing area of interest in comparative politics, what most scholars refer to as "contentious politics." **Contentious politics** is political activity that is at least in part beyond institutional bounds. Groups form over grievances and demand change; they may work via elections and other institutions as well, but the hallmark of contentious politics is extra-institutional activity: petitions, protests, riots, violence, civil war, and revolution. Decades ago, political scientists often viewed such activity as a dangerous threat to political order (Huntington 1968). In the last several decades, most have come to see contentious politics, at least in nonviolent forms, as an important part of civil society and political participation, whether in a democracy where such activity is usually legal or an authoritarian regime where it is not.

The last chapter examined political participation within institutions; in this chapter, we will explore participation that goes beyond institutions—the realm of contentious politics. We will examine social movements and protests; political violence, including ethnic conflict, terrorism, and civil war; and revolution. Table 7.1 provides data on the number of protests, acts of political violence, and terrorist acts for a range of countries. While relatively few regime-threatening acts of political violence take place, hundreds and often thousands of protests occurred in many various countries over a fifteen-year period, both in democratic and authoritarian regimes. While formal elements of participation, such as voter turnout and party membership, have declined in wealthy democracies, informal forms of political participation have increased (Dalton 2017). Terrorist actions have also been common, and far more common in some poor countries like India and Nigeria than in the United States and other wealthy democracies. How regimes respond to violence varies greatly as well, with some engaging in far more repression than others. Finally, as a sign of the impact of globalization and technological change, the table also shows the ubiquity of cell phones around the world.

contentious politics: Political activity that is at least in part beyond institutional bounds, involving extra-institutional activity such as petitions, protests, riots, violence, civil war, and revolution

TABLE 7.1

Measures of Contentious Politics: Protests, Political Violence, and Acts of Terrorism: Contentious Politics

COUNTRY	POLITICAL PROTESTS (1990–2004)	EPISODES OF POLITICAL VIOLENCE FOCUSED ON REGIME CHANGE (1945–2006)	NUMBER OF TERRORIST INCIDENTS (2000–2017)	ACCESS TO SOCIAL MEDIA (MOBILE CELLULAR SUBSCRIPTIONS PER 100 PEOPLE [2017])
Brazil	797	2	26	113
China	898	15	137	104
Germany	2,012 (including East and West Germany)	2*	204	134
India	1,451	78	8,918	87
Iran	408	22	154	107
Japan	719	0	142	136
Mexico	902	15	120	89
Nigeria	456	27	3,826	76
Russia	1,160 (including USSR and Russian Federation)	20	1,866	158
United Kingdom	3,029	0	1,061	120
United States	5,722	0	475	121

Sources: Data for political protests are from J. Craig Jenkins, Charles Lewis Taylor, Marianne Abbott, Thomas V. Maher, and Lindsey Peterson, *The World Handbook of Political Indicators IV* (Columbus, OH: Mershon Center for International Security Studies, The Ohio State University) (https://sociology.osu.edu/worldhandbook). Data for episodes of political violence and response to violence are from Erica Chenoweth and Orion A. Lewis, *Nonviolent and Violent Campaigns Outcomes Dataset*, vol. 2.0 (http://www.du.edu/korbel/sie/research/chenow_navco_data.html). Data for terrorism are from the Global Terrorism Database (https://www.start.umd.edu/gtd/). Data for cell-phone penetration are from World Bank, "Mobile Cellular Subscriptions (per 100 People)" (http://data.worldbank.org/indicator/IT.CEL.SETS.P2/).

*Data for Germany are for East Germany to 1990 only.

Despite all this activity, participation outside institutional bounds faces the same collective action problem we outlined in the previous chapter. While many individuals may have grievances against their government, what incentives do they have to join a group, protest in the street, or throw a rock? Indeed, politics outside institutional channels is often risky and in some cases illegal; the collective action problem may be even greater than it is for voting. One of the key questions we ask, then, is, How and why are people mobilized to participate in contentious politics? Once they are, we ask, How do social movements and other forms of contentious politics function, and what effects do they have on governments and policies? We will also ask, What effects have globalization and the advent of Internet-based communications and social media had on contentious politics? Then we will turn to the question, Why do politics sometimes turn violent and take the form of terrorism or civil war? Finally, we will ask, Why do revolutions—contentious political episodes that change regimes—arise? We will start, however, with a brief examination of the role of contentious politics, particularly in its nonviolent forms.

Framing Contentious Politics

Political scientists have studied contentious politics for years, most commonly examining **social movements**, groups that have a loosely defined organizational structure and represent people who perceive themselves to be outside the bounds of formal institutions, seek major socioeconomic or political changes to the status quo, or employ sustained noninstitutional forms of collective action.

What we now call social movements arose at least a century ago, but they became much more common during and after the 1960s. In that decade in much of the Western world, growing numbers of citizens, particularly young "baby boomers," came to feel that their governments, political parties, and interest groups were not providing adequate forms of participation and representation. They viewed established political institutions as organs of elite rule, overwhelmingly controlled by white men. In response, "new social movements" led by racial minorities, women, antiwar activists, and environmentalists arose, challenging the status quo. These groups have since been joined by many others, such as the antiglobalization movement that proclaimed itself to the world in 1999 in protests in Seattle, the more recent "Occupy" movement that arose in 2011 in New York, and the "Black Lives Matter" movement in response to police violence against African Americans that began in Florida and Missouri.

While they exist throughout the world, social movements are most common and have arguably had the greatest impact in wealthy democracies. Social movements helped women enter public life to a degree never before seen. Racial minorities united to get many segregationist and discriminatory policies overturned and were able to enter public life to a much greater degree. Gay rights activists have succeeded in getting a number of governments to redefine marriage and international organizations to think of gay rights as part of universal human rights. And in the age of global climate change, environmentalists have put their concerns on the agenda of national and international institutions.

Social movements are generally seen as pursuing a "progressive" social change agenda based on ideas favored by the "left" of the political spectrum, usually in the name of less powerful members of society. Social movements can come from the conservative side of the political spectrum as well, however, as the Tea Party in the United States demonstrated. The Tea Party possessed all of the elements of a social movement: loose organization and leadership, opposition to what its members see as the status quo in both political parties and established interest groups, self-perception of its members as outsiders, and demands for fundamental change. It was a conservative movement, though, as it aimed to roll back many major policies of the last half-century and return to those of an earlier era. Similar movements have arisen in Europe as well, most recently in response to increased immigration from Muslim countries. Some of these movements support the far-right populist parties we discussed in chapter 6.

Given this history, comparativists have taken great interest in social movements and contentious politics more broadly. At one time or another, scholars have used almost all of the theoretical approaches we outlined in chapter 1 to try to understand contentious politics. The oldest theories used psychological or structuralist approaches to explain protest. More recently, scholars have looked at strategic interactions based loosely on rational actor models to analyze the dynamics of

social movements: Part of civil society; they have a loosely defined organizational structure and represent people who perceive themselves to be outside formal institutions, seek major socioeconomic or political changes, or employ sustained noninstitutional forms of collective action

how movements emerge and evolve. Finally, cultural theories have helped explain why and how movements gain supporters and effect change. We will examine this theoretical debate in this section, then turn to related debates about why people turn to violent political action in the next section.

Why Contentious Politics Happen

Why do contentious politics happen? Why do people mobilize to demand change and engage in protest or other actions beyond the day-to-day politics of elections and lobbying? The oldest theories are mostly psychological, focusing on why people develop grievances against their government. The best known is based on the concept of **relative deprivation**, a group's or individual's belief that they are not getting their share of something of value relative to their expectations or to what others have. Social psychology research suggests that relative deprivation produces demands for change, especially when members of a self-identified group believe they are not getting what they deserve in part because of who they are (Klandermans 2015, 220). Thus, the identities we discussed in chapter 4—race, ethnicity, gender, class, and so forth—can be powerful sources of contentious politics.

More recent research suggests that values and emotions, not just grievances, can lead people to participate in contentious politics. Using data from nearly ninety countries and 200,000 people in the World Values Survey, Christian Welzel found that "emancipative values"—values favoring greater individual freedom and equality of opportunity—generate social movements. As both individuals' and entire societies' emancipative values increased, so do participation in nonviolent social movements, in particular. Welzel used the postmaterialist thesis we outlined in chapter 1 (see pages 14–15) to argue that these values rise as people's basic needs are satisfied. Hence, social movements have been strongest and most effective in relatively wealthy countries, and even in those countries, support often comes not from the most deprived segments of society but from those at least somewhat better off and more educated (Welzel 2013).

Emotions can also be important values-related mobilizers. What scholars call "moral shock"—a sudden threat or affront to deeply held values about fairness or justice—can often produce grievance and then political action (Flam 2017). Surveys report citizens are more willing to participate in protests in the face of moderate levels of repression because of their outrage at the repression itself, as well as the negative emotions they might experience if they don't participate in something they support when their friends and neighbors join in (Aytac and Stokes 2019). Most scholars, though, argue that individual motivations—whether grievance, values, or emotions—do not fully explain contentious politics. People with grievances will not necessarily create or join a movement, protest, or rebellion; they may instead feel disempowered, unhappy, but unable to do anything about it. Overcoming the collective action problem requires something more. Scholars of contentious politics have pointed to several factors that explain how grievances lead to political mobilization. First, they examined what came to be known as "resource mobilization": What resources do groups and organizations have to effect change? These could include organizational capacity, money, or educated and effective leadership, among other things. The existence of seemingly strong organizations that at least appear to have the potential to succeed encourages people with grievances to join and support them.

Structuralist scholars argue that resources alone are not enough. A group with a grievance and resources must also have the **political opportunity structure**—a regime open to influence from social movements and other extra-institutional groups—to mobilize successfully. Consensual democracies are likely to be more

relative deprivation: A group's or individual's belief that they are not getting their share of something of value relative to their own expectations or to what others have

political opportunity structure: The extent to which a regime is open to influence from social movements and other extra-institutional groups

open than majoritarian ones, and both are generally more open than authoritarian regimes. Multiple and independent centers of power, openness to new actors, instability in political alignments, influential allies within the regime, and regime willingness to facilitate collective action all enhance the political opportunities social movements have (Tilly and Tarrow 2015, 59). Greater opportunities to succeed encourage people with grievances to mobilize to demand change.

Another group of scholars, mainly sociologists, have argued that networks are crucial to explaining why contentious politics happen. Network connections to a relevant group help overcome the collective action problem by providing potential group members personal connections to a group and direct information on the group's goals and activities. They can also serve as direct channels of recruitment into groups and help transform grievances in to action. Networks can also be closely related to identity, a powerful source of contentious politics: if you already identify with a particular ethnic or racial group, for instance, you are likely to have personal networks established within that group, both of which increase the likelihood of your engaging politically in what can be high-risk activities.

How Contentious Politics Happen

Once we have some ideas of why contentious politics happen, we can ask, What do social movements and other groups engaged in contentious politics actually do, and how can we understand variation in their behavior? Doug McAdam, Sidney Tarrow, and Charles Tilly, in their influential book *Dynamics of Contention* (2001), argued that we need to analyze contentious politics as a process involving multiple actors and mechanisms. Social movements and other groups have particular resources and act within a particular political opportunity structure and cultural context. As they act, however, other political actors and institutions respond, and the context can shift as a result, leading to changes in the way the social movements respond. This iterative process plays itself out in what they term "contentious episodes" of varying lengths.

Strategies and Repertoires

Social movements and other groups engage in a variety of strategic actions to demand change, from peaceful protest to acts of civil disobedience, such as sit-ins at lunch counters or the Black Lives Matter movement's blocking roadways. While contentious politics is partly outside institutional bounds by definition, social movements also use repertoires of working within institutions when possible and beneficial. In the United States, Doug McAdam and Katrina Kloos (2014) argued that both major political parties have been affected by "movementization"—the entry of powerful social movements into the party apparatus. On the other end of the spectrum, violent actions, which we discuss in more detail below, can also be strategic, even if they are typically condemned more quickly than other options. All of these are examples of "repertoires of action" that groups use in political performances to gain attention to their cause and demand change. Which repertoires a group chooses and which are more likely to be successful depend very much on context. Successful repertoires usually draw on meaningful past examples, often within a given society, though not always. Mahatma Gandhi's repertoire of civil disobedience—refusing to obey what he believed to be unjust laws, for instance—was consciously adopted by leaders of the American civil rights movement in the 1950s and 1960s (e.g., blacks riding in the "white" section of a bus), then taken up by the movement against the Vietnam War (e.g., burning draft cards).

Political Opportunity Structures

These can strongly influence how social movements engage in contentious politics, as the example of "movementization" within American political parties suggests. Consensual democracies with multiple-party systems are more likely to produce major candidates and/or parties that champion a social movement's demands, leading the latter to engage in electoral politics more readily. At the other extreme, repression under authoritarian regimes leads groups to engage in "repressive repertoires": often "underground" actions to preserve their group and plan for more overt action when the opportunity arises (Johnston 2015).

Discourse and Identity

Scholars examining cultural influences, often using a postmodern approach, analyze how social movements create meaning via discourses and constructing identities. Constructing stigmatized identities—such as identities based on ethnic, racial, or religious minorities—is particularly powerful in mobilizing support. These scholars often argue that constructing an identity, as we discussed in chapter 4, and giving the group political voice can be important ends in themselves (Scholl 2014). This was a key element of the "new social movements" that arose in the 1960s in Western countries, giving voice to women, gays and lesbians, and racial minorities.

New Communications Technology

The rise of new communications technology and especially social media has provided new repertoires for contentious politics and set off a debate about the effects of the new technology on movements' strength. In the previous chapter, we noted that some observers fear online communications erode social capital by isolating individuals, thereby limiting their likely participation in social movements and threatening the continued existence of the movements themselves. Other skeptics see online activity as "slacktivism"—low-cost, low-commitment activism that has little impact. At the other extreme, some scholars argue that "the networked social movements of the digital age represent a new species of social movement" (Castells 2012, 15). Social media, in particular, allows activists to bypass their traditional reliance on "mainstream media" to disseminate their ideas. It also allows all individuals, regardless of their past involvement or leadership, to express their grievances to larger audiences and find like-minded people with whom to form networks. This, supporters argue, means social media creates a more horizontal and potentially democratic public space in which social movements can form and act.

The web has two potentially transformative elements. First, it lowers the costs of creating and organizing movements; second, it aggregates individuals' actions into collective actions without requiring the participants to be in the same time and place. Lowering the costs of communication can help overcome the collective action problem. Seeing posts from people with similar grievances and knowing that others plan to show up to protest may help people overcome their fears and tendency to be free riders and join a movement themselves. Eliminating the need for activists to be in the same time and place can cut resource costs dramatically, perhaps even eliminating expensive infrastructure such as offices and paid staff (Earl and Kimport 2011). When movements are able to harness these benefits, they create new and powerful models of contentious politics.

Social and other digital media certainly played an important role in the 2011 event known as the Arab Spring. The world watched as seemingly out of nowhere tens of thousands of Tunisians took to the streets, demanding the ouster of the country's long-ruling president, Zine Ben Ali. Soon, Egyptians began flooding the main square in Cairo, demanding the ouster of their even longer-ruling president, Hosni Mubarak. In just six weeks, two of the oldest and seemingly most stable authoritarian regimes of the Arab world had fallen. As protesters tweeted out news of events on the ground and posted to Facebook, observers could hardly fail to perceive a new social movement tool at work. Tunisia and Egypt were among the countries with the highest levels of connectivity in the region, particularly via mobile phones, which had become nearly universal, especially in urban areas. Philip Howard and Muzammil Hussain (2013) found that social media was particularly important in helping activists share and spread their grievances, plan the protest itself, and ignite the spark that got people into the streets. Wendy Pearlman (2013) argued that shifting emotions played a crucial role in overcoming what seemed to be a lack of political opportunity: the regime's initial repression and the strength in numbers gained via social media spread transnationally from Tunisia to Egypt to other Arab countries, turning fear into anger, a powerful mobilizing emotion. While the outcomes varied widely—from electoral democracy in Tunisia to a return to military rule in Egypt to civil war in Syria and Libya—contentious politics affected the entire region. But the protests were not as spontaneous as they seemed; long-standing social movements used social media, their preexisting networks, and a common set of repertoires to mobilize people for effective action.

An Egyptian woman uses her cell phone to take a photo during a demonstration in Tahrir Square, Cairo, in January 2011. Mobile phone technology was a crucial tool used by organizers of the Arab Spring, especially in Egypt, where the rate of cell phone usage is quite high. On the ground, demonstrations were organized partially via social media and documented with cell phones for the world to see.
Marco Vacca/Contributor

More recently, the "Yellow Vest" movement in France in 2018–2019 made active use of social media. It began as a petition against a new gas tax on the website change.org that gathered a million signatures in less than six months. Two activists then called for demonstrations to block roads across the country on a Saturday morning in November 2018, and the movement was born, named after the yellow safety vests its members wore to the protests, which France requires all drivers to carry. Participants were mainly from rural and outlying urban areas, with the biggest events being driven by protesters coming into central Paris each Saturday morning. Journalists reported that participants were motivated not just by opposition to the gas tax but by a broader sense that small towns and outlying urban areas were losing jobs, services, and opportunities. Like the U.S.-based "Occupy Wall Street" movement of 2011, the group claimed to have no leadership. It used Facebook and other online media to coordinate strategy and refused to appoint particular leaders to negotiate with the government. Unlike Occupy, however, the movement had no clear ideology. A survey found that about a third of the participants voted for the far-right candidate and a third for the far-left candidate in previous presidential election. The group's main repertoire came to be protesting every Saturday morning, in Paris and towns across the country. In the first few weeks, hundreds of thousands joined, and some violence against property occurred, such as attacks on expensive retail outlets in Paris. By March 2019, though, the movement was fading, with much smaller turnouts. French president Macron had rescinded the gas tax and initiated a series of discussions across the country about how to respond to the movement. Polls showed popular support for it dropping quickly. While social media helped mobilize hundreds of thousands, lack of organization infrastructure may explain its inability to create a long-term movement, though it nonetheless had a noticeable impact on French economic policy—at least in the short term.

The new technologies can also have negative consequences. Authoritarian governments, most notably China (see chapter 8), have increasingly made use of new technology to surveil their population more effectively. Also, sustainable movements require organizations and leaders who have learned to work together, to strategize, and to shift tactics in the face of a changing environment. Zeynep Tufekci (2017) argued that while social media has many advantages for social movements, it can also create a "tactical freeze"—organizations that create large-scale movements very quickly via social media have no experience in changing tactics when needed, so they simply try to repeat the tactic that initially worked. She argued that the protesters that brought down the regime of Hosni Mubarak in Egypt in 2013 suffered from this problem. The initial mobilization brought down a dictator in six weeks, but the movement could not shift to effectively engage in the subsequent electoral process and instead continued to try to "fill Tahrir square" repeatedly, with less and less effect. Ultimately, this lack of focus helped the Egyptian military regain power two years later.

Transnational Activism

As global communication has become easier through the Internet and a growing number of issues (e.g., trade, human rights, environmental protection) seem to require global action, transnational social movements have arisen. One estimate counted 183 such groups in 1973 and over 1,000 in 2003 (Tarrow 2012, 187). Virtually all of these groups operate at both the national and global levels. Some groups, such as the global justice movement (GJM), launched in the "battle for Seattle" in 1999, explicitly target international organizations, while others simply use global resources to fight domestic battles. The Seattle protest at the 1999 meeting of the World Trade Organization (WTO) was the first of a series of protests targeting global organizations such as the WTO, World Bank, International Monetary Fund, and G8 (an annual meeting of the heads of government of the largest economies in the world, known as the G7 since the exclusion of Russia in 2014 following its annexation of Crimea). These actions brought together traditional movements like labor unions with "new" transnational networks of activists around issues of fair labor, environmental destruction, and indigenous rights, all connected together by a concern for the effects of globalization. Conflicts among the groups—between the older hierarchical organizations such as labor unions and the newer "horizontal" networks of activists and between violent and nonviolent groups—was a continuing problem, but these protests nonetheless represented a new level of global organizing and action (Fominaya 2014).

The GJM is only the best known of a set of new "transnational advocacy networks" of activists working together to use global resources to force policy change (Keck and Sikkink 1998). Transnational activism has created new political opportunity structures and new resources: groups can target international organizations instead of or in addition to national governments, and wealthy and more experienced groups can share their knowledge and resources with younger and weaker groups in other countries. Groups can also share repertoires of action across borders much more easily, as global norms around issues such as human rights create a sense of collective purpose. These changes have been particularly important for groups in poorer countries and under authoritarian regimes; their ability to appeal to and borrow repertoires and resources from groups in wealthier countries can be crucial to their survival and success. Entire networks of like-minded organizations have formed to engage in parallel actions around the world, as the Occupy movement briefly demonstrated in 2011.

On September 17, 2011, approximately a thousand activists descended on the little-known Zuccotti Park near Wall Street. In the name of "occupying Wall Street," they set up a camp in which they remained for two months. Occupy groups quickly emerged in other American cities and around the world, ultimately reaching 951 cities in 82 countries (Rogers 2011). Their grievances centered on the political and economic inequality that seemed to increase significantly after the recession of 2007–2009. The movement never became a single organization. Indeed, organizers declared it a new kind of movement based on a horizontal model of organizing and a new conception of participatory democracy. They in fact denied that any real "leaders" existed, though a key group of people planned the main events in New York and ran key social media sites.

The movement engaged in a new repertoire of action involving long-term occupation of space and active use of social media. Inspired by the Arab Spring and the massive movement of Indignados (the indignant) in Spain (who protested the economic policies imposed on Spain by the European Union in the European debt crisis), Occupy sought to establish a long-term encampment, like those in Tahrir Square in Cairo and Puerta del Sol in Madrid. The initial group fell far short of their goal of mobilizing twenty thousand protesters; for most of the two months of the encampment, a few hundred people were there. Prior to the encampment, activists primarily used Twitter to spread their message, eschewing Facebook as not trustworthy and too corporate. Gerbaudo (2012, 113–117) argued that the Twitter efforts had little effect because they did not make an appeal to people's emotions. Once the famous "we are the 99%" slogan crystallized and an online campaign of photos of people holding signs saying "I am the 99%" went viral on Facebook, support spread rapidly. Occupy groups sprang up across the country and around the world, occupying city squares, university campuses, prominent government headquarters, and financial institutions. Repertoires originating in Cairo and Madrid were adopted in New York and in turn spread to London, Paris, and beyond.

What Effects Do Contentious Politics Have?

The ultimate question about contentious politics may be, Does it matter? What impact has all this difficult political action had? Oddly, political scientists have examined this question far less than the questions of why and how. On the one hand, it seems obvious that contentious politics has mattered a great deal. For anyone living in "the West," the new social movements arising in the 1950s to the 1970s clearly have had an impact: attitudes and policies about racial minorities, women, and the environment—just to name a few—have changed dramatically. Similarly, authoritarian regimes around the world have fallen over the last thirty years as their citizens mobilized, demanding democracy (see chapter 9). On the other hand, how do we know that these changes were a result of the social movements' actions? Outcomes of contentious politics are particularly difficult to discern because many factors influence government policy, social attitudes, and cultural changes. And if we can figure that out, can we then determine why some forms of contentious politics are more successful than others?

Most social movements focus on changing government policy, but many outcomes are possible. In addition to policy changes, contentious politics can affect access to the political system, the political agenda, policy output (resources for and

CRITICAL INQUIRY

Are Nonviolent Movements More Successful Than Violent Ones?

The table below gives some examples of the cases on which Chenoweth and Stephan (2011) based their argument that nonviolent movements tend to be more successful than violent ones. What other hypotheses about why movements succeed or fail can you generate from the table? The table includes the years of the movement, so you can think about the era in which it took place and its length, as well as whether it used new media in the digital age and the level of repression it faced from the state.

COUNTRY	GROUP	YEARS	VIOLENT?	USE OF NEW MEDIA	REPRESSION	SUCCESS
Afghanistan	Taliban	1992–1996	Yes	No	Extreme	Yes
Burma	Karens	1948–2006	No	No	Extreme	No
China	Democracy Movement	1976–1979	No	No	Moderate	No
Colombia	FARC	1964–2006	Yes	Yes	Extreme	No
Czechoslovakia	Velvet Revolution	1989–1990	No	No	Mixed	Yes
Egypt	Kifaya	2000–2005	No	Yes	Moderate	No
Ethiopia	Eritrean Secession	1974–1991	Yes	No	Extreme	Yes
Georgia	Rose Revolution	2003	No	Yes	None	Yes
Great Britain	IRA	1968–2006	Yes	No	Extreme	No
India	Kashmir Separatists	1988–2006	Yes	Yes	Extreme	No
Indonesia	East Timorese Independence	1988–1999	No	No	Extreme	Yes
Kenya	Democracy Movement	1990–1991	No	No	Moderate	Yes
Mexico	Democracy Movement	1987–2000	No	Some	Moderate	Yes
Romania	Anti-Ceausescu	1987–1989	Yes	No	Extreme	Yes
Russia	Chechen Independence	1994–2006	Yes	Yes	Extreme	No
Spain	Basque Separatist	1968–2006	Yes	No	Moderate	No
Sri Lanka	Tamil Separatist	1972–2006	Yes	No	Extreme	No
West Papua	Anti-Occupation	1964–2006	No	Yes	Extreme	No

Source: Data are from Erica Chenoweth and Orion A. Lewis, *Nonviolent and Violent Campaigns Outcomes Dataset*, vol. 2.0 (http://www.du.edu/korbel/sie/research/chenow_navco_data.html).

implementation of policy), policy impact on people's lives, and more fundamental structural changes (Giugni 2004, 7). Contentious politics can also have indirect effects on policy by changing social or cultural attitudes and opinions or the practices of other important institutions such as large corporations. Participation in contentious political actions, even if they are not effective at changing policy, often affects those involved, giving them a greater sense of political efficacy and a set of political skills they can use in the future. Finally, particular episodes or groups can affect future contentious politics as social movements evolve or give rise to new ones. Thus, the study of the outcome of contentious politics is exceptionally complex.

Scholars are divided over what explains the outcomes of contentious politics. Some, following the political opportunity structure approach, argue that the context in which particular movements act is crucial. Marco Giugni (2004) argued that the presence of allies within the state and public opinion in support of a movement's goals are crucial to success—so is a state's capacity to respond by changing policy efficiently and effectively. If a state cannot adapt new policies with relative ease, no amount of pressure is likely to change policy.

Other scholars, however, argue that factors internal to movements themselves are crucial. Those following the resource mobilization school argue that only sufficient resources of all types will allow a group to succeed. William Gamson (1990)—and many scholars since—argued that strategy matters: disruptive tactics and even violence produce successful change; groups engage in these tactics because they work. Some scholars have suggested more recently that this argument applies to terrorism as well, a subject we address below. On the other hand, Erica Chenoweth and Maria Stephan (2011) used a quantitative analysis of a large data set covering the past century to examine movements demanding regime change. They argued that nonviolent civil resistance is more effective than violence in all cases except secessionist movements, primarily because nonviolent movements are more effective at mobilizing widespread popular support. Nonviolent movements that could not mobilize widespread support tended to fail, while the relatively few successful violent movements were those that did mobilize support. This was true even when facing authoritarian regimes and active repression.

Beyond policy and regime changes, social movements and their individual members evolve in response to their past activities, another set of potentially important outcomes. Some of their members go on to found or join formal interest groups, such as the National Organization of Women, or even political parties, such as the German Green Party. As social movements become more institutionalized, many become NGOs (non-governmental organizations), developing organizational imperatives to find funding and hire professional staff. In the process, they adapt both their goals and strategies to work within institutionalized political systems rather than challenging those systems more directly and may speak for rather than engage with the citizens whom they claim to represent (Lang 2013). New groups often emerge to replace them with newer and more challenging agendas. In the U.S. environmental movement, for example, older groups like

Activists take part in the International Day of Climate Action in Sydney, Australia. The event was organized by 350.org, a group working to bring attention to climate change around the world. It organizes primarily via the Internet and, while based in the United States, has spread throughout the world, an example of a transnational social movement using modern technology to coordinate contentious political action across time and place.
Janie Barrett/The *Sydney Morning Herald*/Fairfax Media via Getty Images

Friends of the Earth (FoE) became institutionalized as interest groups. This left the role of social movements open to new challengers like EarthFirst!, which engages in more provocative direct action tactics than FoE, and 350.org, which utilizes new technologies in a way the older organization did not. In contrast, where the electoral system permits, a movement may generate a political party. Proportional representation in Germany provided an opportunity for the environmental movement to form a Green Party that has had a significant electoral impact, in contrast to the much weaker Green Party that emerged in the first-past-the-post system in the United States. On the other hand, where the quality of democratic representation is low—where parties and elections do not represent popular opinion well—NGOs can have an important role in mobilizing protest; once again, the political opportunity structure matters (Boulding 2014).

Scholars of contentious politics have drawn from a wide array of political science theories—institutional, structural, and cultural—to try to understand why, how, and to what effect contentious political movements occur. Many of these theories were first developed in the context of iconic examples of contentious politics such as the American civil rights movement but can be applied to more contemporary contentious politics as well, such as the Occupy and Black Lives Matter movements.

Political Violence

Many people have sympathy for social movements that engage in peaceful protest but very different feelings toward groups that engage in violence. This is especially true in liberal democracies, where peaceful protest is a well-established action within the bounds of civil society but violence is seen as illegitimate; but even in authoritarian regimes, many people question whether violence is justified. Scholars of contentious politics, however, see violence as simply one more repertoire of action in which movements might engage. Rather than asking whether violence is ethically justifiable, comparativists in the field of contentious politics instead ask why and how groups choose to engage in violence. They note that many groups shift from nonviolent to violent tactics and back again, and they assert that the contentious politics framework we outlined above can help us explain why violence happens.

Scholars working in other subfields of comparative politics—such as security studies, ethnic conflict, terrorism studies, and revolution—also try to explain why violence occurs. Violence takes many forms, from small-scale protests using physical force to terrorism to ethnic conflict or genocide to full-scale civil war. These categories overlap and merge into one another at times, as particular situations evolve. Often, movement among these categories of violence does not depend on the intent of groups in society but instead on whether a regime splits in response, making a transfer of power possible (Tilly and Tarrow 2015, 172–175). We examine all of these situations briefly, using multiple perspectives from comparative politics.

Theories of Political Violence

Political violence is the use of physical force by nonstate actors for political ends. We include the term *nonstate* in this definition simply to distinguish political violence from war undertaken by states or states' claims to a "monopoly on legitimate violence" domestically. We make no assumption or argument here about the ethical superiority or justification of political violence vis-à-vis violence perpetrated by states, but it is analytically useful to distinguish the terms. Donatella della Porta (2013) used the contentious politics framework to explain why groups choose to

political violence: The use of physical force by nonstate actors for political ends

engage in violence. She highlighted the interactive processes between social movements and the state, and among competing movements. The political opportunity structure that groups face, she argued, is a key element. Scholars have long noted that social movements are likely to be more peaceful in democracies, where they have greater opportunity to achieve their goals. Repression, under whatever type of regime, can produce violent responses. It is likely to undermine the influence of or radicalize moderates within opposition groups, leading the groups in a more radical direction. If police escalate their response to peaceful protest and especially if protesters see that response as excessively brutal, a violent response is more likely. Even riots, which many people view as purely destructive and unjustified, typically occur in a situation in which grievances among a particular population have been growing, and a "spark," almost always involving state security forces using what some perceive as excessive force, produces a riot (Waddington 2017).

Competition among protest groups can also produce violence, as they compete for attention and support by engaging in ever more dramatic actions. Repertoires of action, however, also matter; past political violence in a society can serve as a model of acceptable and/or effective tactics, while certain forms of violence may be seen as beyond the bounds of moral acceptability, regardless of their effectiveness. Finally, emotions can be a powerful force as well; Seferiades and Johnston (2012) argue that violence can help turn emotions into a sense of meaning and purpose for activists. Della Porta and others using the contentious politics framework argue that we cannot explain violence by looking at the nature of the groups or individuals involved or their ideology. Rather, we have to understand the dynamic process that unfolds as groups engage in contentious actions and the state and other groups react, all within an evolving political system and cultural setting.

Conflicts among ethnic or other identity groups, as we discussed in chapter 4, are a particularly common source of political violence. Identity groups, like other social movements, may pursue their grievances in nonviolent ways initially and then choose to become violent. Comparativists studying ethnic and other types of identity conflicts, though, have developed several other theories for why these conflicts seem to generate so much violence. In a recent comparative analysis of several African cases, Scott Straus (2015) argued that the way in which the political community was socially constructed along lines of identity is central to understanding when the most horrific form of ethnic violence, genocide, happens:

> [G]enocide [is] more likely in those places where founding narratives establish a primary identity-based population whom the state serves. Such narratives thereby construct a group or groups within a territorial space that should not be dominant and in whose hands power should not reside. In a crisis, political elites are more likely to take actions that conform to the protection of the group that defines the nation and to construct the excluded group as having interests that are inimical to the primary group. (2015, 64)

He noted that genocide only happens in times of war: when faced with an extreme threat, elites follow the logic of socially constructed identities, protecting "their own" at the expense of "the other" when groups have been constructed in the manner he describes above.

The perception of threat is a long-standing explanation for ethnic violence via the concept of the **security dilemma**. This is a situation in which two or more groups do not trust and may even fear one another and do not believe that institutional constraints will protect them, often because the state is weak. In that context, the fear

security dilemma: A situation in which two or more groups do not trust and may even fear one another and do not believe that institutional constraints will protect them, increasing the likelihood that violence will break out between them

of being attacked leads people to attack first, believing that doing so is necessary to protect themselves. Stuart Kaufman (2001) joined the security dilemma and leaders' manipulation of ethnic symbols, arguing that violent ethnic conflict arises when the two combine in a vicious spiral. Straus's (2015) study of genocide reaffirms this general approach, arguing that it even explains the worst types of violence.

The security dilemma can be especially explosive when the boundaries of identity groups overlap other social, political, or economic cleavages. If an ethnic group, for instance, believes that as a group it is not getting its fair share of land, income, or political power, violence is often possible. The perception of injustice based on the unequal distribution of resources or power is reinforced by the symbolic importance of an identity group vis-à-vis others. Psychological theorists note that experiments regularly show that when people are put in groups, over time an "us versus them" attitude develops. Combined with perceived unfairness or inequality, this attitude can be explosive. Emotions can play an important role as well. Roger Petersen (2002) posited three emotions that lead to violence: fear, hatred, and resentment. Fear is a response to situations like the security dilemma in which a group's primary motivation is safety. Hatred is a motivation when an opportunity arises for violence against a group that has been frequently attacked in the past. Resentment motivates violence after a sudden change in status hierarchies among ethnic groups.

One of the most difficult tests of these theories in recent history is the genocide in Rwanda in 1994. In one hundred days, thousands of Hutu slaughtered 800,000 of their Tutsi compatriots in the worst genocide since the Holocaust. Genocide, the attempt to completely eliminate a people, is perhaps the most difficult political phenomenon to understand: why would large numbers of people, even when horrific leaders are encouraging them, slaughter people en masse based on who they are? In most cases of genocide, including Rwanda, people had been living together more or less peacefully (though not without resentment and memories of past violence) when, seemingly overnight, large numbers of one group started slaughtering people in a different group. While many people view Africa as full of "ancient tribal" animosities, no situation shows the inaccuracy of this primordial argument better than Rwanda. Hutu and Tutsi spoke the same language, lived in the same communities and neighborhoods, had the same customs, followed the same religions, and had lived for centuries in the same kingdom. Cultural differences between them don't exist. What did exist were several other elements commonly involved in political mobilization and violence: a potential battle over a key resource (land), a sense of relative deprivation, fear of attack in a situation of extreme political uncertainty, and an elite using a racist ideology to mobilize hatred of the "other" as part of an effort to build a strong state that it could control.

The Tutsi dominated the precolonial kingdom, but a Hutu-led government controlled the country from independence in 1960 to the genocide. Tutsi exiles who had long lived in neighboring Uganda invaded the country in 1990. By 1993 a cease-fire had been established, and democratic elections were planned. Elements on both sides, however, feared the results. Hutu leaders enjoyed the privileges of power and wanted to maintain them, and some Tutsi rebel leaders seemed unwilling to allow the majority (overwhelmingly Hutu) to rule, even via democratic means. A group of Hutu extremists in the government began propagating an anti-Tutsi ideology. They continuously told their followers that the Tutsi were trying to regain complete power, take away Hutu land, and kill them. In a very densely populated country dependent on agriculture, the threat to land ownership was particularly explosive. The Hutu extremists also created a private militia of unemployed and desperate young Hutu men, and when the

Hutu president's plane was shot down on April 6, 1994, the extremists and their armed militia swung into action. Barriers went up across streets all over the capital, and the militia began systematically executing "moderate" Hutu who might oppose the genocide (lists of the first to be killed had been prepared in advance), as well as any Tutsi they found. The extremist hate-radio directed much of the effort, telling the militia where Tutsi were hiding. Members of the militia demanded that other Hutu join them in identifying and killing Tutsi; those who refused would themselves be killed. The killing didn't stop until the Tutsi-led rebel army swept into the capital and took over the country—but only after three-quarters of the entire Tutsi population had been killed. Leaders took advantage of a situation of fear (the security dilemma) and relative deprivation to mobilize people around a socially constructed identity tied to claims on both sides that they should rightfully rule the nation. While crimes of this magnitude are still impossible to comprehend fully, we can see some patterns that help us find a rational explanation based on past theories.

A soldier stands at a checkpoint in Rwanda in 1994. Like all genocides, Rwanda's was planned in advance and led by a militia created for the purpose. Roadside checkpoints were a key location where Hutu militia members found and killed Tutsi.
Scott Peterson/Liaison/Hulton Archive via Getty Images

Civil War

The Rwandan genocide took place at the end of a three-year civil war. While not all civil wars occur along ethnic lines, many, as the Rwandan example suggests, do. **Civil war**, whether tied to ethnicity or not, has been a particularly common form of political violence in recent decades. It is distinguished from other forms of political violence by the nature of the conflict: two or more armed groups, at least one of which is tied to the most recent regime in power, fight for control of the state (Tilly and Tarrow 2015, 180). Since 1960, civil wars have constituted a significant majority of all wars worldwide (Tilly and Tarrow 2015, 182). This chapter cannot present all elements of the long-standing debate over civil war, much of which is the purview of the field of international relations. Comparativists, however, have increasingly examined civil war within the larger framework of political violence and contentious politics.

Groups that eventually become armed combatants in civil wars may well begin as nonviolent actors engaging in contentious politics. As in other situations, the state's use of force against a nonviolent group can often precipitate the first use of violence. Often, a situation of increasingly violent contention becomes a civil war, not because the groups involved are inherently different from groups competing in other situations of potentially violent contention but because the incumbent regime splits, with important regime supporters joining the opposition and thereby providing it with enough resources to challenge the regime's monopoly on violence. Sometimes, this comes in the form of regional elites attempting to secede, as happened in the American civil war. The groups that rebelled against the government of Bashar al-Assad in Syria in 2011 initially pressed their demands nonviolently as part of the Arab Spring. In contrast to Tunisia and Egypt, the Syrian regime had been so repressive that no prior organized protests had occurred; the initial protests were largely spontaneous and peaceful but not as well organized

civil war: Two or more armed groups, at least one of which is tied to the most recent regime in power, fight for control of the state

CRITICAL INQUIRY

Ethnic Fragmentation and Political Conflict

Collier and Hoeffler (2004) claimed that ethnicity has little to do with violent conflict; it is simply a way to justify conflict and mobilize supporters. Cederman et al. (2013), on the other hand, argued that ethnically based political exclusion and inequality do produce conflict. Map 7.1 provides measures of ethnic fragmentation and violent political conflict around the world. Comparing the two maps, what patterns do you see? Does it seem that countries with greater ethnic fragmentation also have a lot of violent political conflict? What hypotheses can you develop from the map to explain why political violence occurs more in some places than others? What do the maps suggest for the debate over what explains ethnically based violence?

MAP 7.1

Civil Wars and Ethnic Fragmentation

Ethnic fragmentation

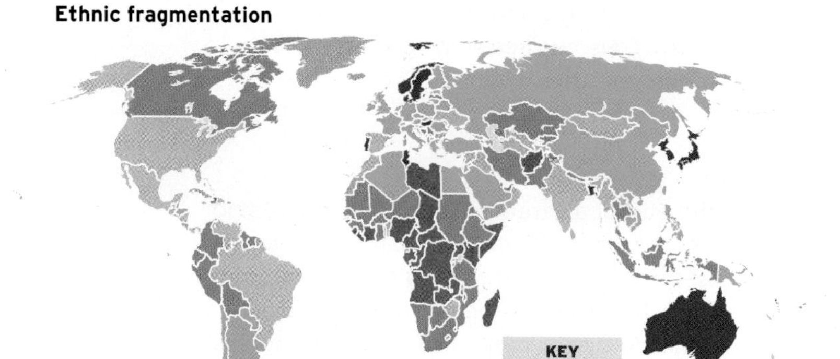

Source: Data for the ethnic fractionalization map are from Alberto Alesina et al., "Fractionalization," *Journal of Economic Growth* 8 (2003): 155–194.

Civil wars since 1960

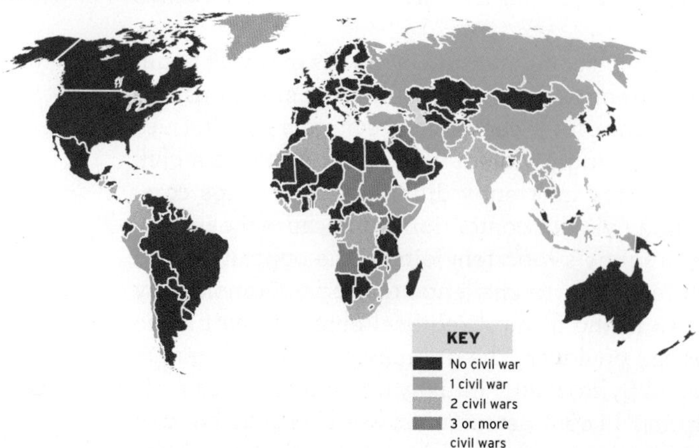

Source: Data for the civil war map are from Lars-Erik Cederman, Brian Min, and Andreas Wimmer, "Ethnic Armed Conflict dataset" (http://hdl.handle.net/1902.1/11797 V1 [Version]).

Note: No data available for French Guiana, Greenland, and Western Sahara.

Note: A rank of 1 equates to a highly diverse ethnic population, while a lower ranking signifies greater ethnic homogeneity. No data available for French Guiana, French Polynesia, Puerto Rico, U.S. Virgin Islands, West Bank, and Yemen.

as elsewhere. The regime responded with brutal repression, and the country was divided along religious lines. The result was not a united and peaceful rebellion but instead growing divisions within the military, partly along religious lines, and eventually defections from the military to create an armed opposition that had the support of a significant Syrian diaspora outside the country. Repression and internal divisions helped turn peaceful protests into civil war, as the contentious politics framework suggests.

Earlier nonviolent social movements and other networks of support can also explain why some violent insurgencies become strong and successful while others fail. Using an institutional approach, Paul Staniland (2014) argued that leaders of insurgent groups that have strong preexisting vertical and horizontal networks are able to create "integrated" groups that can wage successful wars, such as the Taliban in Afghanistan. Horizontal ties are networks among elites with shared interests; vertical ties are networks between elites and local communities that allow elites to mobilize support. Groups with only strong horizontal ties produce "vanguard" insurgencies that have few local roots and are relatively easily defeated. Groups with only strong vertical ties to local communities tend to be parochial and fragment, limiting their success. "Integrated" groups like the Taliban have strong prior networks in both directions. Pushed out of Afghanistan in the 1980s, the Taliban's future leaders created horizontal ties in the madrasas (Islamic schools) they attended and supported in northern Pakistan. Individually, they had strong vertical ties to the communities from which they came and in which they fought the wars of the 1980s. The combination allowed the Taliban to best rival Afghan factions, take over the country in the 1990s, and continually frustrate the U.S. military in what became America's longest war.

One type of tie that can inspire, strengthen, or fragment violent movements is ethnicity. Analysts long assumed a close connection between ethnic difference and civil war: groups forced to live together, typically in postcolonial states, had profound cultural, social, and political differences, and this inevitably led to secession and civil war. A group of economists led by Paul Collier, however, conducted a large, quantitative examination of all civil wars since 1960, finding that greed and opportunity were the key factors that led to violence, not ethnic difference (Collier and Hoeffler 2004; Collier, Hoeffler, and Rohner 2009). Where valuable resources such as minerals were available for groups to fight over and reap the rewards of, civil war was more likely, indicating greed is a major driving force. Civil war is also more likely in societies with large numbers of unemployed young men, available to join ethnic militias, and in societies with mountainous terrain in which rebels can hide, suggesting opportunity is also a major factor. In contrast, societies with greater ethnic fragmentation were not more likely to have civil wars, indicating these wars really weren't about identity politics at all, even if their leaders claimed that was what they were fighting over.

Political scientists Andreas Wimmer (2013) and Lars-Erik Cederman et al. (2013) used new data to challenge the economists' arguments. Their data measured not just the existence of ethnic difference but the degree to which ethnic groups were excluded from political power and the degree of economic inequality among groups. Wimmer (2013) argued that civil wars typically occur in the first few decades after the formation of a nation-state, when political institutions are often weak and ethnically divided elites cannot compromise on shared governance, and some groups may be excluded entirely. Cederman et al. (2013) found that both an ethnic group's political exclusion and relative poverty increased the likelihood of civil war. Thus, ethnic grievances do cause civil war, but not just because different ethnic groups exist (which is what Collier and colleagues measured), but rather because certain groups are excluded from power and perceive themselves to be denied their fair share of society's resources. These situations lead to mobilization of opposition as outlined in the contentious politics framework, which can and often does turn violent.

The rise of the Internet and social media may be affecting civil wars in ways similar to their effects on social movements. Barbara Walter (2017) noted that since 2003, the frequency of civil wars has increased compared to earlier decades, a much higher proportion of them involve radical Islamist movements, and more of the groups have transnational goals. She argued that the Internet and social media are important causes of these trends. The new technologies make it easier to organize rebellions, spread an ideology, raise funds, and recruit members, including transnationally as ISIS has famously done. The technologies that allow nonviolent social movements to organize to demand social changes may also be increasing political violence.

Terrorism

While civil war is unquestionably the form of political violence that has produced the most fatalities in recent decades, the most closely studied type of violence in the last fifteen years, of course, has been **terrorism**: "political violence or the threat of violence by groups or individuals who deliberately target civilians or noncombatants in order to influence the behavior and actions of targeted publics and governments" (Nacos 2012, 32). The key distinction between terrorism and other forms of political violence is who is targeted. Groups that become violent in opposition to some government typically target that government directly: the African National Congress in South Africa battled apartheid primarily by attacking the symbols and infrastructure of the state, such as police stations and the power grid. In civil war, the goal is to target and defeat the government, even if civilians are killed in the process. Terrorists, on the other hand, target civilians who are not directly responsible for the targeted state's policies; they try to sow fear in a general population via seemingly random acts of violence in order to influence a particular government or population. Terrorist groups are almost always clandestine, while other groups engaging in political violence are typically more public.

Since the attacks by Al Qaeda on September 11, 2001, the field of "terrorism studies" has exploded. About fifty books were published on the subject in the 1990s and over three thousand in the 2000s (della Porta 2013, 11). Like other forms of political violence, terrorism is a tactic, not a type of unchangeable group. Many groups that engage in terrorism began using other means to address their grievances, and some ceased using terrorism at some point. Many types of groups can and have used terrorism; one of the longest-standing "terrorist groups"—now no longer using violence at all—was the Irish Republic Army (IRA), which fought to free Northern Ireland from British rule. Today, of course, most attention is focused on religious terrorists, Islamist ones in particular.

Scholars working in "terrorism studies" explain the decision to use terrorism by looking at characteristics of individuals and groups who engage in it, structural preconditions that could make it more likely, and ideology. On the individual level, scholars have argued that emotions such as fear and humiliation motivate terrorism, particularly in the Middle East, where Muslim societies have gone from perceiving themselves as being the most "advanced" societies in the world a millennium ago to being colonized and exploited by the West over the last century. Numerous psychological theories have predicted certain personality types may be more prone to engage in terrorism, which may help explain individual behavior but

terrorism: Political violence or the threat of violence by groups or individuals who deliberately target civilians or noncombatants in order to influence the behavior and actions of targeted publics and governments

"Subcomandante Marcos," in ski mask, speaks with representatives of Mexican political parties in 1994. Marcos's erudition, anonymity, and effective use of Internet communication made him and the Zapatista movement a global phenomenon, drawing support from around the world for an indigenous movement in a small, poor state in southern Mexico.
Gerardo Magallon/AFP/Getty Images

not why a terrorist group arises in a particular time and place (assuming personality traits are fairly evenly distributed around the world and over time).

Structural theories look at both economic and political backgrounds that could induce the rise of terrorism. Weak states are characterized by limited control over borders and the means of violence, which provides at least an opportunity for terrorist groups to operate. State strength, measured in various ways, is generally associated with less terrorism. On the other hand, after the 2001 attacks, many observers asserted that terrorism ultimately stems from socio-economic factors: the poverty and lack of education in many Muslim societies, particularly among young men. In fact, numerous studies have shown that neither factor is associated with the decision to join a terrorist group; some have found that more education is associated with more terrorism, not less (Nacos 2012, 103). Ethnic diversity and urbanization have also been found in some studies to be associated with more terrorism. Rapid economic development, especially if accompanied by growing inequality, as it often is, also may foster terrorism (Chenoweth and Moore 2018, 164–165). At best, though, structural factors explain why terrorism might be possible in a particular place and time, not why particular groups arise when they do.

Ideology, of course, is another possible source for terrorism. Religious terrorism justifies acts of violence against what most people would see as "innocent" civilians in the name of God (or Allah) and His dictates. The leadership of Al Qaeda was heavily influenced by the Salafi form of Islam prominent in Saudi Arabia, in particular, which looks back to the founding of the religion as the golden age to which Muslims should adhere. Motivated by their opposition to Israel and Western support for it, the Iranian revolution, and the Soviet invasion of Afghanistan, some radical Salafis developed a "jihadist" version of Islam that justified terrorism in the name of ridding the *umma* (the Muslim community as a whole) of Western and Jewish influence. They look to the eventual re-creation of the caliphate, or single Muslim theocratic rule across the entire Muslim world. As we discussed in chapter 2, the Islamic State in Iraq and Syria (ISIS) tried to put that caliphate in place. Some scholars see religious terrorism as qualitatively different from older, secular forms, arguing that religiously inspired groups seem to desire to kill as many people as possible, apparently without limits.

Scholars using the contentious politics framework, though, question the utility of explaining terrorism via the traits of individuals or groups. They point out that, like many other episodes of contentious politics, even Al Qaeda evolved over time in response to its political context. Osama bin Laden and others officially founded Al Qaeda in 1988 as an offshoot of a broader jihadist movement whose main purpose was supporting the Taliban in its fight against the Soviet occupation of Afghanistan. The United States and Saudi governments, among others, actively supported the jihadists, including bin Laden, in their fight against the Soviets. Once the Soviets withdrew from Afghanistan, many jihadists, mostly from Saudi Arabia and Egypt, tried to return home to continue Islamist political activity, both peaceful and violent. They fought in Yemen and Bosnia in the early 1990s in defense of what they saw as Western or Soviet attacks on Muslims. Many of their governments, however, viewed the returning jihadists as threats to domestic stability; Egypt actively repressed them, while the Saudi government initially tried to co-opt them. When the Saudi government allowed U.S. troops into the kingdom in response to the Iraqi invasion of neighboring Kuwait in 1990, bin Laden broke with his government. By 1992, he had been forced into exile in Sudan and then in 1996 to Pakistan. It was in this period, facing repression, financial constraints, and competition for followers among competing Islamist groups, that Al Qaeda issued two key *fatwas*, or commands, in 1993 and 1996, identifying the United States as the primary enemy of the Islamic *umma* and instructing the faithful to kill all Americans. Al Qaeda's ideology had evolved from fighting to defend Muslim territory from direct invasion to indiscriminate terrorism on a global scale, in response to political opportunity structures, resources, and competition within the larger Islamist movement (Alimi, Demetriou, and Bosi 2015).

Revolution

In the first decade of the 2000s, what Charles Tilly (1978) called a "revolutionary situation" seemed to exist in northeastern Nigeria, where Islamic religious ferment grew in a context of poverty, marginalization and resentment. The radical Islamic group Boko Haram arose in this context. It hoped to overthrow Nigeria's democracy, but no revolution occurred. Revolutions are a form of contentious politics, but with a difference: they involve not just a mobilized group demanding change but the successful overthrow of a regime and, in some cases, an entire social order. The impetus behind revolutionary movements is often similar to the causes of other types of contentious movements, but the outcome—regime change—requires additional explanation. Social movements and other forms of contentious politics could become revolutionary movements demanding regime change, though only a handful do and even fewer succeed. Here, we address why revolutions occur and save their outcomes for chapter 9, where we discuss regime change more broadly.

Types of Revolution

As with so many terms in political science, scholars have debated endlessly how to define and classify *revolutions*. One way is to classify them by the ideologies that inspire them: the liberal revolution of France, the communist revolutions of Russia and China, and the Islamic revolution of Iran, for example. These ideological differences would seem to be crucial, yet most scholars of revolution argue just the opposite, that the ideological motivations and pronouncements of key leaders do not explain very much about revolutions. Typically, only the top leadership thoroughly understands and believes in the ideology in whose name the revolution is fought. As is true for all forms of contentious politics, many participants have other motivations for joining a revolution, and specific political circumstances must exist for revolutions to succeed. Ideology helps more to explain the outcomes of revolutions in that the subsequent regimes, as we discussed in chapter 3, arise out of the ideological commitments of the revolutionary leadership. However, ideology usually does not tell us much about why the revolutions happen in the first place.

Lech Walesa, the trade union leader who became the chief leader of the anticommunist movement in Poland, campaigns for president in 1989. The collapse of communism in Eastern Europe from 1989 to 1990 is the most recent example of social revolution: not only the regime but also the social and economic structures of society fundamentally changed. Some countries, like Poland, became fully democratic, while others did not; but they all profoundly changed via revolutions, the rarest form of regime change.
AP Photo/Czarek Sokolowski

We find it most useful to think of two key types of revolutions: political revolutions and social revolutions. A **political revolution** is the fundamental transformation of an existing regime, instigated and primarily carried out by a social movement or armed group. The key difference between a political revolution and a military coup or regime transition negotiated among elites (see chapter 9) is the role of at least one major social movement or armed group of citizens. Political revolutions are relatively rare, but much more rare are **social revolutions**: fundamental transformations of a regime and social structure, instigated and primarily carried out by a social movement or armed group of citizens. Social revolutions are so rare they are often historically important events, not only for their country but the world, such as in France (1789), Russia (1917), China (1911–1949), Cuba (1959), Iran (1979), and Eastern Europe (1989–1990).

Many revolutions, particularly social revolutions, are violent, though they need not be. For many years, analysts believed that violent movements were more likely to result in revolution, particularly social revolutions. The presumed scenario was an armed group overwhelming a weak and illegitimate regime, militarily removing them from power: storming the bastille in France is the classic image. Since the end of the Cold War, some theorists have reassessed that position. As we noted earlier, Chenoweth and Stephan (2011) found that nonviolent movements are actually more successful at achieving regime change than are violent movements. Not all regime changes are revolutions, though, as we will discuss further in chapter 9. Using a comparative case method, Sharon Nepstad (2011) argued that nonviolent movements achieve political revolutions when they convince a section of the regime's security forces to abandon the regime. It seems the state's monopoly over the use of violence has to be eliminated one way or the other, either by overwhelming it with an alternative force or by splitting it into factions.

political revolution: The fundamental transformation of an existing regime, instigated and primarily carried out by a social movement or armed group

social revolution: A fundamental transformation of a regime and social structure, instigated and primarily carried out by a social movement or armed group of citizens

Why Do Revolutions Happen?

Comparativists have developed several theories to explain why revolutions occur, using the full range of political science theory: Marxist analyses of the economic structure of the old regime, structural arguments focused on political opportunity structures and movements' resources, psychological theories of the motivation to revolt, and analyses of the process of modernization.

Scholars using the contentious politics framework have claimed that grievances, mobilization, resources, and political opportunity can all be important in producing a revolution. Using social-psychological theories, James Davies (1962) argued that revolutions occur at periods of rising expectations: people don't revolt when they are at their lowest point but rather when things have started to get better and they want more. This is closely related to Ted Robert Gurr's (1970) theory of relative deprivation, which can explain the motivation for revolution just as it can other contentious political actions. Nepstad (2011, 5–6) noted the factors involving grievances and mobilization that produce a revolutionary situation: widespread grievances against the state, some elites shifting allegiance from the state to the opposition, enough anger over regime injustices to motivate popular action, a unifying ideology of rebellion, and a mobilizing organization with adequate resources to coordinate and mobilize people.

Many argue, however, that a revolutionary situation will produce a revolution only when the political opportunity and/or economic structures are supportive. Theda Skocpol (1979) noted that a crucial ingredient for successful revolution is a state in crisis, often one that has been weakened by international events. She pointed to the effects of World War I on Russia as an example. A revolution can only happen where a state faces a severe crisis and lacks the resources to respond, creating a political opportunity. Jeff Goodwin (2001) also focused on the state but argued that certain types of states are prone to revolution: those with weak, neopatrimonial regimes that exclude major groups from a share of power. These regimes are not capable or willing to allow political opposition a role in politics, which forces the opposition to turn to revolution as the only option for change, and the states' weakness means it cannot resist revolutions once started.

Was the American Revolution Really a Revolution?

The careful reader might note that we have not mentioned the United States in our discussion of revolutions. This may come as a surprise to American students who are accustomed to thinking of the "American Revolution" as a pivotal historical event. It certainly was that, but whether it was a revolution in the sense that comparativists use the term has been subject to extensive debate. Barrington Moore (1966) argued that the real revolution in the United States was the Civil War, which ended slavery as an economic system and established the dominance of industrial capitalism. He was clearly thinking of a social revolution in arguing that the American Revolution did not qualify. Like any successful anticolonial movement based on a popular uprising, the American Revolution seems to qualify as a political revolution, in that the colonial regime was destroyed and a fundamentally new one put in its place. The crux of the debate over the place of the American Revolution in the broader understanding of revolutions is the question of whether it fundamentally transformed not just political institutions but the social structure as well.

One school of thought argues that the American War of Independence was led primarily by the colonial elite, who did not envision or implement a major redistribution of wealth. Granted, they eliminated British rule and created a new republic based on the republican ideal of equality of all citizens, but they defined citizens very consciously and deliberately as white male property owners. Wealth was actually distributed less equally after the war than it had been before—and, arguably, slavery was more entrenched (Wood 1992). Not only was slavery codified in the Constitution, but it expanded for several more decades. Indeed, the Constitution as a whole can be seen in part as an effort to limit the effects of egalitarianism in that it created an indirectly elected Senate to represent state governments rather than citizens and an indirectly elected president with the power to veto laws passed by the directly elected House of Representatives.

The chief proponent of the view that the American Revolution really was a social revolution is historian Gordon Wood. Wood argued that the American Revolution "was as radical and as revolutionary as any in history" (1992, 5). Though he readily conceded most of the points mentioned above, he argued that the egalitarian ideals of republicanism created not just a political but also a social and cultural revolution during and after the war. Republican thought did not deny the existence of all forms of superiority but instead argued that superiority should not come from birth but from talent and reason. Some men (women were not included) would rise to the top as leaders of the new society based on their abilities, their hard work, and the willingness of others to elect them to positions of leadership. Government was therefore to serve the public interest in a way that a monarchy never did or could.

This egalitarian ideal spread throughout society, Wood contended, leading to further questions about the prerogatives of rank and privilege. He noted numerous changes to social and cultural norms, such as pressure to end many private clubs, the taking of the titles "Mr." and "Mrs." that were previously reserved for the landed gentry, and the shift from reserving the front pews in churches for select families in perpetuity to selling rights to those pews to the highest bidders. As the latter suggests, the revolution caused commerce to expand rapidly as well; wealth became even more unequally distributed, but many new men gained it. This revolution of ideas and in the way men treated other men (the treatment of women changed little and wouldn't for well over a century) helped to create a new society never before seen in which inherited status was considered illegitimate and leadership and high status were to be based solely on merit and election.

In the long term, the American Revolution clearly had a profound effect, especially due to its notion of equal citizenship. As Wood rightly noted, its ramifications went far beyond what its original Founders intended. But most of the political and social elite before the War of Independence remained the elite after the war. As for the grand ideals of equality, they applied only within the very restricted realm of white, male property owners for another generation. As Crane Brinton (1965) noted in his classic study of revolutions, the American Revolution (which he included as one of his cases) is also quite peculiar in its evolution and result: no reign of terror occurred, as is so common in violent revolutions, and an authoritarian state did not ultimately result. While arguably beneficial, the absence of these elements, along with the other points above, raises questions about whether the first war of independence against European colonialism was also a social revolution.

The earliest theorist of revolution in the modern era was Karl Marx. As we explained briefly in chapter 3 (see p. 65), Marx believed that social revolution was the necessary transition from one mode of production to another and that the most important transition would be from capitalism to communism. Therefore, he thought the major revolutions of the future would be communist and would occur in the wealthiest, most advanced capitalist countries. Events would show that he was clearly wrong about where and therefore why revolutions would occur. Many social revolutions have been communist inspired, but they have not happened in wealthy capitalist societies or democracies. Instead, they have occurred in relatively poor countries with authoritarian regimes, most notably in Russia and China. Marx explained revolutions as the result of a particular economic structure. More recently, numerous scholars have viewed revolutions more specifically as part of the modernization process. Samuel Huntington (1968) saw them as being most likely to occur after economic development has raised popular expectations and political demands, but state institutions have not developed adequately to respond to them. Steven Pincus (2007) argued more narrowly that state modernization is the key: revolutions are most likely when the old regime is attempting to modernize the state, which brings new groups into contact with the state and expands its activities. If, in this process, it becomes apparent that the state may lack a full monopoly on the use of violence, revolutionary leaders will try to take advantage of the situation. Perhaps the most influential modernization approach, though, was Barrington Moore's *Social Origins of Dictatorship and Democracy* (1966). Moore set out to answer not only why revolutions occur but also why democracies emerge in some places and dictatorships (sometimes via revolutions) in others. He focused on the transition from agricultural to industrial society, arguing that if the landed elite commercializes agriculture by removing the peasants from the land and hires labor instead, as happened in Britain, the landed elite would ultimately become part of the bourgeoisie and demand liberal rights, putting the country on the path to liberal democracy. In contrast, if the peasantry remained on the land into the modern era, as in Russia and China, they continued to be affected by the commercialization of agriculture in ways that harmed them. In response, they provided the basis for revolutionary communist movements.

As with many areas of comparative politics, the theoretical debate over the cause of revolutions will undoubtedly continue. Some scholars see revolutions as products of particular historical epochs or transitional periods, which could help explain why there seem to be fewer of them now than in the past. Others see them as the result of forces and circumstances not tied to a particular era: rising expectations or particular political opportunities such as a severely weakened state.

The Iranian revolution of 1979 that created the Islamic Republic emerged from a sense of relative deprivation among many segments of the population despite a growing economy; an old regime weakened by at least the perception of a loss of international (especially U.S.) support; and a religious leader, Ayatollah Ruhollah Khomeini, who became the charismatic symbol of the revolution. The shah of Iran's government prior to the revolution had seemed to be a classic case of a modernizing authoritarian regime during the 1960s and 1970s. The regime's policies, however, did not benefit everyone equally. Although economic growth and personal incomes rose noticeably on average, what the poor saw was the elite's conspicuous consumption, which they compared with their own very meager gains. Modernization of agriculture drove rural migrants to the cities, and there they joined the long-standing bazaari groups (petty traders in Iran's traditional bazaars), who felt threatened by modernization as well (Clawson and Rubin 2005). Along with students and workers, these groups became key supporters of the revolution. Opposition to the shah was divided along ideological lines among nationalists who wanted greater democracy, Marxists, and religious groups.

A perception that the shah's regime was weak was a crucial element in igniting the actual revolution. U.S. president Jimmy Carter enunciated a new foreign policy based on human rights and noted the shah's regime as one that did not adequately protect such rights. The United States had strongly supported the regime for decades, so even the hint of U.S. willingness to consider regime change inspired the opposition to act. In January 1978, theology students organized a large demonstration in protest in the holy city of Qom. The shah's police responded with violence, and at least seventy people were killed. The religious opposition, joined by students and the bazaaris, then used the traditional mourning gatherings for those killed to organize greater demonstrations. By September, a demonstration of more than a million people took place in Tehran, and the shah once again reacted with the use of force, killing more than five hundred people. Continuing demonstrations demanded Khomeini's return from exile, a demand the government continued to resist until finally giving in on February 1. Khomeini immediately declared one of his supporters the "real prime minister," a claim the government rejected. The opposition mobilized its followers to invade prisons, police stations, and military bases on February 10 and 11 to take them over in the name of the revolution. After two bloody days in which hundreds more people were killed, the revolutionaries succeeded in gaining power. A sense of relative deprivation, a weak state, and religious leadership combined to produce an Islamist revolution.

Conclusion

The study of contentious politics has helped transform our understanding of political action outside formal institutional bounds. Political leaders and political scientists alike had earlier seen demonstrations, riots, sit-ins, and rebellions as nothing but threats to political stability. Starting in the 1960s, both activists and scholars began to argue that such contentious political acts could enhance democracy. At least in their nonviolent forms, they could express legitimate grievances that were not being met institutionally in a democracy, and they could seriously threaten authoritarian regimes. The original focus of the contentious politics framework was on social movements in Western societies, but scholars have expanded its use to examine various forms of political violence and even revolution. The study of both violence and revolution, though, includes scholars using other theoretical frameworks such as security studies.

Comparativists have examined individual motivations; internal group characteristics and dynamics; and the larger political, economic, and cultural context to try to understand contentious politics. Psychological theories are the primary means by which scholars try to explain individual motivation, focusing on why and how people form grievances and then choose to act on them. The latter, however, usually involves something beyond the psychological level. A relatively recent theory that is closely related to psychological theories focuses on emotion, particularly how anger arises. Beyond that, though, theorists have examined how and why aggrieved and angry people overcome the collective action problem. In this context, internal characteristics of mobilizing groups such as their resources and networks can be important, but so can the political and economic context. Political opportunities can lower the threat of repression from the state and increase the perceived odds of success, leading people to act. Groups' effective use of key cultural symbols and language can also help motivate action.

While nonviolent forms of contentious politics are widely accepted as legitimate in democracies and as legitimate opposition to authoritarian regimes, political violence is not. Indeed, since the September 11, 2001, terrorist attacks in the United States, political violence is most often associated with the killing of innocent civilians. In fact, other types of political violence have long existed and are far more common than terrorism. Ethnic and other types of identity movements can be particularly susceptible to becoming violent, in part because of the powerful connection between individuals' grievances and their identity. Where such violence leads—to small-scale armed rebellion, civil war, or revolution—depends as much or more on the context as it does the ideological motivations of the group in question. Groups often change repertoires, from nonviolent to violent and among violent options, depending on what is strategically advantageous and perhaps morally justified in their minds. Most scholars even see terrorism as a repertoire rather than a permanent characteristic of a group, though some groups such as ISIS seem to have placed terrorism at the heart of their ideology.

Revolutions are the rarest form of contentious politics, meaning a particular set of circumstances must account for them, but it is not always easy to determine what those circumstances are. A weakened old regime and state seem essential, as strong states can resist revolution no matter how many people are involved. A strong revolutionary organization that unites and mobilizes people's grievances also seems vital. Revolutions are known by their leaders' ideologies, but that does not always explain the motivations of the masses supporting them. The masses are often motivated by the failure of the old regime as well as a sense of relative deprivation, whether due to declining economic circumstances or rising expectations that have not been met.

The full range of political science theories have been employed to explain contentious politics. Theories focusing on individual motivation, both psychological and rational actors, try to understand the individual motivations behind contentious politics. Rational actor theorists have also looked at the strategic dynamics between the state and political movements to explain the evolution of particular episodes of contentious politics. Structural theories have long been used as well, looking at the economic structure of a society, the political opportunity structure, and the distribution of resources among groups to explain why some succeed while others fail. Finally, theorists using cultural models have sought to understand why particular symbols and language embedded in groups' repertoires are successful at mobilizing support and how these repertoires shift over time and place.

We turn next to political institutions and participation in authoritarian regimes. While scholars initially studied contentious politics mainly in wealthy democracies, many have done so in authoritarian regimes in recent years. With institutionalized participation severely limited, scholars have recognized the growing role of contentious politics, both in expressing citizens' grievances within authoritarian regimes and in demanding the end of those regimes, a subject to which we turn in chapter 9. ●

Sharpen your skills with SAGE Edge at **edge.sagepub.com/orvisessentials2e. SAGE Edge for students** provides a personalized approach to help you accomplish your coursework goals in an easy-to-use learning environment.

KEY CONCEPTS

civil war (p. 209)

contentious politics (p. 195)

political opportunity structure (p. 198)

political revolution (p. 215)

political violence (p. 206)

relative deprivation (p. 198)

security dilemma (p. 207)

social movements (p. 197)

social revolution (p. 215)

terrorism (p. 212)

WORKS CITED

Alimi, Eitan Y., Chares Demetriou, and Lorenzo Bosi. 2015. *The Dynamics of Radicalization: A Relational and Comparative Perspective.* Oxford, UK: Oxford University Press.

Aytac, S. Erdem, and Susan C. Stokes. 2019. *Why Bother? Rethinking Participation in Elections and Protests.* New York: Cambridge University Press.

Boulding, Carew. 2014. *NGOs, Political Protest, and Civil Society.* Cambridge, UK: Cambridge University Press.

Brinton, Crane. 1965. *The Anatomy of Revolution.* New York: Vintage Books.

Castells, Manuel. 2012. *Networks of Outrage and Hope: Social Movements in the Internet Age.* Cambridge, UK: Polity Press.

Cederman, Lars-Erik, Kristian Skrede Gleditsch, and Alvard Buhaug. 2013. *Inequality, Grievances, and Civil War.* Cambridge, UK: Cambridge University Press.

Chenoweth, Erica, and Pauline Moore. 2018. *The Politics of Terror.* Oxford, UK: Oxford University Press.

Chenoweth, Erica, and Maria J. Stephan. 2011. *Why Civil Resistance Works: The Strategic Logic of Nonviolent Conflict.* New York: Columbia University Press.

Clawson, Patrick, and Michael Rubin. 2005. *Eternal Iran: Continuity and Chaos.* New York: Palgrave Macmillan.

Collier, Paul, and Anke Hoeffler. 2004. "Greed and Grievance in Civil War." *Oxford Economic Papers* 56 (4): 563–595. doi:10.1093/oep/gpf064.

Collier, Paul, Anke Hoeffler, and Dominic Rohner. 2009. "Beyond Greed and Grievance: Feasibility and Civil War." *Oxford Economic Papers* 61 (1): 1–27. doi:10.1093/oep/gpn029.

Dalton, Russell J. 2017. *The Participation Gap: Social Status and Political Inequality.* Oxford, UK: Oxford University Press.

Davies, James C. 1962. "Toward a Theory of Revolution." *American Sociological Review* 27 (1): 5–19.

della Porta, Donatella. 2013. *Clandestine Political Violence.* Cambridge, UK: Cambridge University Press.

Earl, Jennifer, and Katrina Kimport. 2011. *Digitally Enabled Social Change: Activism in the Internet Age.* Cambridge, MA: MIT Press.

Flam, Helena. 2017. "Micromobilization and Emotions." In *The Oxford Handbook of Social Movements,* edited by Donatella della Porta and Mario Diani, 264–276. Oxford, UK: Oxford University Press.

Fominaya, Cristina Flesher. 2014. *Social Movements and Globalization: How Protests, Occupations and Uprisings Are Changing the World.* Basingstoke, UK: Palgrave Macmillan.

Gamson, William. 1990. *The Strategy of Social Protest.* 2nd ed. Belmont, CA: Wadsworth.

Gerbaudo, Paolo. 2012. *Tweets and the Streets: Social Media and Contemporary Activism.* London: Pluto Press.

Giugni, Marco. 2004. *Social Protest and Policy Change: Ecology, Antinuclear, and Peace Movements in Comparative Perspective.* New York: Rowman and Littlefield.

Goodwin, Jeff. 2001. *No Other Way Out: States and Revolutionary Movements, 1945–1991.* Cambridge, UK: Cambridge University Press.

Gurr, Ted Robert. 1970. *Why Men Rebel.* Princeton, NJ: Princeton University Press.

Howard, Philip N., and Muzammil M. Hussain. 2013. *Democracy's Fourth Wave? Digital Media and the Arab Spring.* Oxford, UK: Oxford University Press.

Huntington, Samuel P. 1968. *Political Order in Changing Societies*. New Haven, CT: Yale University Press.

Johnston, Hank. 2015. "'The Game's Afoot': Social Movements in Authoritarian States." In *The Oxford Handbook of Social Movements*, edited by Donatella della Porta and Mario Diani, 619–633. Oxford, UK: Oxford University Press.

Kaufman, Stuart J. 2001. *Modern Hatreds: The Symbolic Politics of Ethnic War.* Ithaca, NY: Cornell University Press.

Keck, Margaret, and Kathryn Sikkink. 1998. *Activists Beyond Borders.* Ithaca, NY: Cornell University Press.

Klandermans, Bert. 2015. "Motivations to Action." In *The Oxford Handbook of Social Movements*, edited by Donatella della Porta and Mario Diani, 219–230. Oxford, UK: Oxford University Press.

Lang, Sabine. 2013. *NGOs, Civil Society, and the Public Sphere.* Cambridge, UK: Cambridge University Press.

McAdam, Doug and Katrina Kloos. 2014. *Deeply Divided: Racial Politics and Social Movements in Post-War America.* Oxford, UK: Oxford University Press.

McAdam, Doug, Sidney Tarrow, and Charles Tilly. 2001. *Dynamics of Contention.* New York: Cambridge University Press.

Moore, Barrington. 1966. *Social Origins of Dictatorship and Democracy: Lord and Peasant in the Making of the Modern World.* Boston: Beacon Press.

Nacos, Brigitte L. 2012. *Terrorism and Counterterrorism.* 4th ed. New York: Longman.

Nepstad, Sharon Erickson. 2011. *Nonviolent Revolutions: Civil Resistance in the Late 20th Century.* Oxford, UK: Oxford University Press.

Pearlman, Wendy. 2013. "Emotions and the Microfoundations of the Arab Uprisings." *Perspectives on Politics* (June): 387–409.

Petersen, Roger. 2002. *Understanding Ethnic Violence: Fear, Hatred, and Resentment in Twentieth-Century Eastern Europe.* New York: Cambridge University Press.

Pincus, Steven. 2007. "Rethinking Revolutions: A Neo-Tocquevillian Perspective." In *The Oxford Handbook of Comparative Politics,* edited by Carles Boix and Susan Carol Stokes, 397–415. Oxford, UK: Oxford University Press.

Rogers, Simon. 2011. "Occupy Protests Around the World: Full List Visualized." *The Guardian*, October 17, 2011. http://www.theguardian.com/news/datablog/2011/oct/17/occupy-protests-world-list-map.

Scholl, Christian. 2014. "The New Social Movement Approach." In *Handbook of Political Citizenship and Social Movements,* edited by Hein-Anton van der Heijden, 233–258. Northampton, MA: Edward Elgar.

Seferiades, Seraphim, and Hank Johnston. 2012. "The Dynamics of Violent Protest: Emotions, Repression, and Disruptive Deficit." In *Violent Protest, Contentious Politics, and the Neoliberal State,* edited by Seraphim Seferiades and Hank Johnston, 3–18. Burlington, VT: Ashgate.

Skocpol, Theda. 1979. *States and Social Revolutions: A Comparative Analysis of France, Russia, and China.* New York: Cambridge University Press.

Staniland, Paul. 2014. *Networks of Rebellion: Explaining Insurgent Cohesion and Collapse.* Ithaca, NY: Cornell University Press.

Straus, Scott. 2015. *Making and Unmaking Nations: War, Leadership, and Genocide in Modern Africa.* Ithaca, NY: Cornell University Press.

Tarrow, Sidney. 2012. *Strangers at the Gates: Movements and States in Contentious Politics.* New York: Cambridge University Press.

Tilly, Charles. 1978. *From Mobilization to Revolution.* New York: McGraw-Hill.

Tilly, Charles, and Sidney Tarrow. 2015. *Contentious Politics.* 2nd ed. Oxford, UK: Oxford University Press.

Waddington, David. 2017. "Riots." In *The Oxford Handbook of Social Movements,* edited by Donatella della Porta and Mario Diani, 423–438. Oxford, UK: Oxford University Press.

Walter, Barbara F. 2017. "The New New Civil Wars." *Annual Review of Political Science* 20 (1): 469–486.

Welzel, Christian. 2013. *Freedom Rising: Human Empowerment and the Quest for Emancipation.* New York: Cambridge University Press.

Wimmer, Andreas. 2013. *Waves of War: Nationalism, State Formation, and Ethnic Exclusion in the Modern World.* Cambridge, UK: Cambridge University Press.

Wood, Gordon. 1992. *The Radicalism of the American Revolution.* New York: Knopf.

RESOURCES FOR FURTHER STUDY

della Porta, Donatella. 2015. *Social Movements in Times of Austerity.* Cambridge, UK: Polity Press.

della Porta, Donatella, and Mario Diani, eds. 2015. *The Oxford Handbook of Social Movements.* Oxford, UK: Oxford University Press.

Sadiki, Larbi, ed. 2015. *Routledge Handbook of the Arab Spring: Rethinking Democratization.* Abingdon, UK: Routledge.

Van der Heijden, Hein-Anton, ed. 2014. *Handbook of Political Citizenship and Social Movements.* Cheltenham, UK: Edward Elgar.

WEB RESOURCES

Global Terrorism Database

(https://www.start.umd.edu/gtd/)

The Nonviolent and Violent Campaigns and Outcomes (NAVCO) Data Project

(http://www.du.edu/korbel/sie/research/chenow_navco_data.html)

The World Handbook of Political Indicators

(https://sociology.osu.edu/worldhandbook)

8 Authoritarian Institutions

A man walks by a portrait of Syrian president Bashar al-Assad near the Syrian capital of Damascus. The Syrian civil war shows the potential conflagration that can occur when an authoritarian regime starts to lose control. Assad met a peaceful uprising as part of the Arab Spring in 2011 with violence and clung to power. The Syrian civil war ensued, sucking in international actors, including the United States and Russia, and provoking the largest humanitarian and refugee crisis since World War II, which rocked the foundations of the European Union. Assad regained control of Syrian territory, but an official settlement remained elusive in 2019.
Youssef Karwashan/AFP/Getty Images

Key Questions

- Some authoritarian regimes disperse power more widely than others. How can comparativists determine "who rules" and what limits executive power in an authoritarian regime?
- Authoritarian regimes come in several different subtypes: military, one-party, theocratic, personalist, and electoral authoritarian. In what ways do differences across these subtypes explain differences in leaders' actions, levels of repression, and types of popular participation?
- Why is clientelism so prevalent and important in authoritarian regimes? In what types of authoritarian regimes does it seem most important, and what might explain this?
- Some authoritarian regimes allow at least some institutionalized limits on rulers' power. What explains where and why this happens, or doesn't happen?

Learning Objectives

After reading chapter 8, you should be able to do the following:

8.1 Discuss current trends in authoritarian rule

8.2 Explain the "dictator's dilemma" and what it means for authoritarian regimes

8.3 Articulate the role of elections, parties, and legislatures in authoritarian regimes

8.4 Explicate the function of clientelism and civil society in authoritarian regimes

The spread of democracy in the aftermath of the Cold War led some to believe that democratic rule was irreversible; dictators were relics, soon to be relegated to the "dustbin of history." Many eastern European and African societies that threw off or severely challenged their authoritarian regimes, however, ended up creating new, albeit less repressive ones. Electoral authoritarian regimes, in which some opposition and participation is allowed but a key ruler or party firmly holds on to power, became more common. In other cases, especially in the Middle East, the winds of democratic change did not blow strongly enough to seriously challenge authoritarian regimes until the sudden outburst of popular opposition in the Arab Spring of 2011.

The answer to the question "Who rules?" seems like it ought to be particularly obvious in authoritarian regimes: the dictator does. Discerning who really has power and how much power they have, however, is not that easy. Authoritarian regimes tend to arise in relatively weak states that have weak formal institutions, and therefore informal institutions and processes are more important. A key difference among authoritarian regimes is how institutionalized they are. We defined institutionalization in chapter 5 as the degree to which government processes and procedures are established, predictable, and routinized. In the least-institutionalized personalist regimes, decisions truly can be made and implemented at the whim of the dictator. In other authoritarian regimes, the leader's power is still extensive, but it is somewhat curtailed by institutionalized checks, typically controlled by other elites.

Wide variation in institutionalization in authoritarian regimes also makes explaining political behavior challenging. In chapter 3, we outlined several subtypes of authoritarian regimes based on their origins and formal institutions: one-party, military, personalist, theocratic, and electoral authoritarian.

These subtypes have different governing institutions, but given that formal institutions in authoritarian regimes tend to be weak, how much does this really explain? Are one-party regimes as a group different in distinctive ways from military regimes? Does one subtype always provide greater levels of institutionalized limits on executive power? Is one subtype always more repressive?

Trends in Authoritarian Rule

While not the promised land of democracy that some analysts predicted, the era after the end of the Cold War certainly had a significant effect on authoritarian regimes. Their numbers declined from about 75 percent of all countries

MAP 8.1

Autocratic Regimes

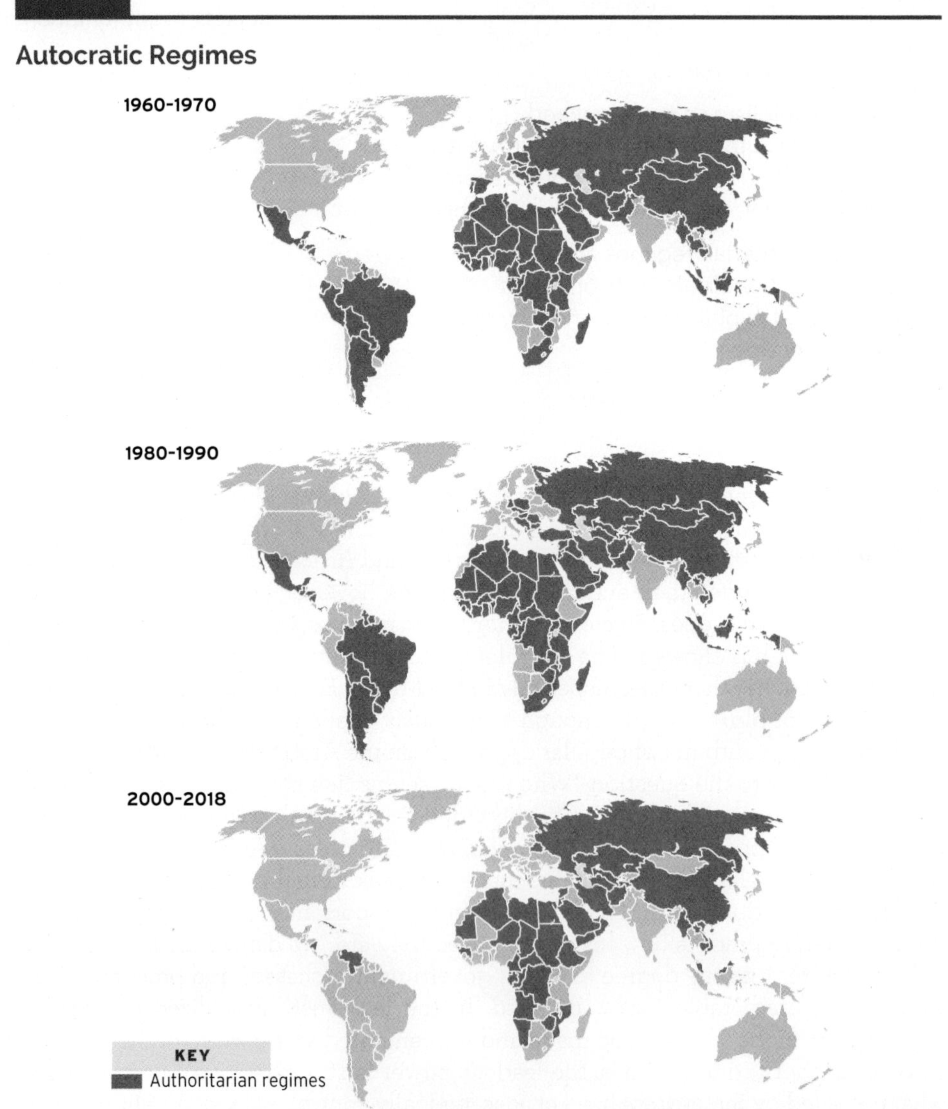

Source: "Autocratic Regime Data," National Science Foundation, https://sites.psu.edu/dictators/.

in the late 1970s to about 40 percent by 2008 (Svolik 2012, 25), and their institutions changed. In the last decade, however, the number of authoritarian regimes has increased slightly, as the degree of political freedom around the world has declined (see chapter 9). Map 8.1 shows the global decline of authoritarian regimes as a whole, as well as their concentration now in Africa, the Middle East, and Asia.

With the expansion of democracy as a global ideal, the number of purely authoritarian regimes fell, and more regimes attempted to legitimize their rule through the creation of electoral authoritarian regimes (see Figures 8.1 and 8.2). Most dramatic was the precipitous drop in one-party authoritarian regimes at the end of the Cold War and their replacement with multiple-party systems. Figure 8.2 demonstrates that over 80 percent of current regimes have elected legislatures of some sort, and about 60 percent allow multiple candidates per legislative seat, a good indicator of an electoral authoritarian regime. In about 40 percent, the ruling party controls less than three-quarters of the legislative seats, indicating it has allowed the opposition a significant (though still firmly minority) position. Today, most authoritarian regimes allow some sort of legislature and opposition parties to exist and participate in some form. A key question is why.

FIGURE 8.1

Restrictions on Political Parties, 1946–2008

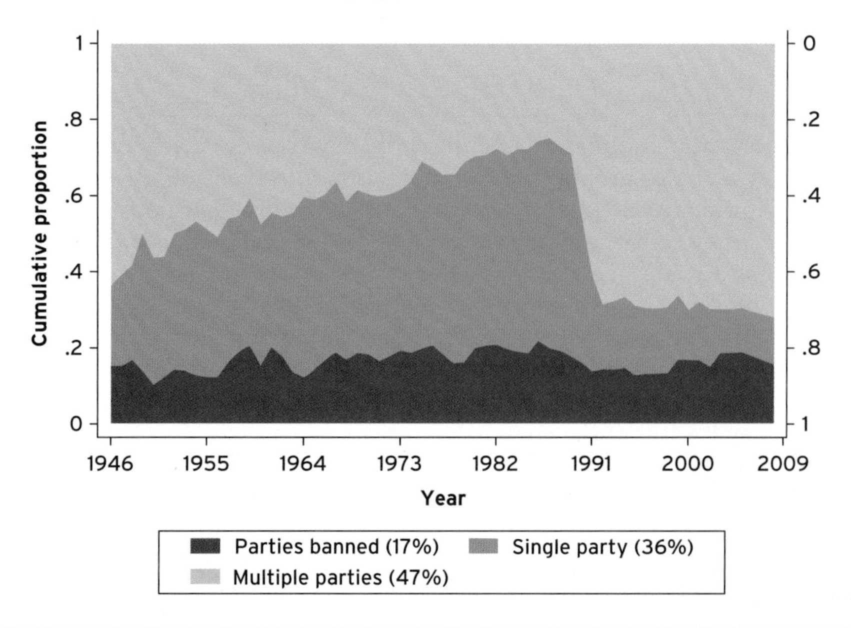

Source: Milan W. Svolik, "Figure 2.4, Restrictions on Political Parties in Dictatorships, 1946–2008," *The Politics of Authoritarian Rule* (Cambridge University Press), 35. © Milan W. Svolik 2012. Reprinted with the permission of Cambridge University Press.

Note: Overall distribution of individual categories in parentheses.

FIGURE 8.2

Legislative Selection in Dictatorships, 1946–2008

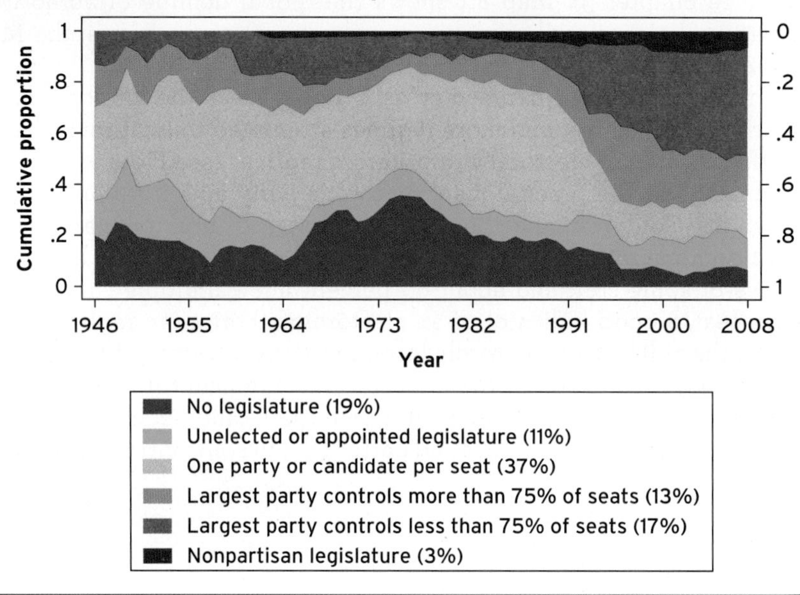

Source: Milan W. Svolik, "Figure 2.6, Legislative Selection in Dictatorships, 1946–2008," *The Politics of Authoritarian Rule* (Cambridge, UK: Cambridge University Press, 2012), 36.

Note: Overall distribution of individual categories in parentheses.

The Dictator's Dilemma: Governing Authoritarian Regimes

While authoritarian regimes around the world have a wide variety of formal institutions, they all rule through some combination of repression, co-optation, and efforts at legitimation. *Repression* is the popular image that pops into people's minds when they think of dictators, but it is an expensive way to rule. Even the most ruthless dictator needs to find other means by which to ensure citizens' loyalties. *Co-optation* via material inducements and official positions, which often goes hand in hand with corruption, is the most obvious alternative means of securing support. Most regimes also expend resources to try to instill loyalty in the citizenry to secure some actual legitimacy; if citizens believe in the regime, they will obey it without the costs of repression or co-optation. Communist parties use their well-developed ideology for this purpose to a greater extent than do most authoritarian regimes, but virtually all authoritarian regimes try to gain legitimacy in some way.

dictator's dilemma: An authoritarian ruler's repression creates fear, which then breeds uncertainty about how much support the ruler has; in response, the ruler spends more resources than is rational to co-opt the opposition

Repression, the universal tool (to varying degrees) of authoritarian regimes, produces what rational choice theorists term the **dictator's dilemma**: because of the repression they practice, dictators lack accurate information on how much political support they actually have. Repression breeds fear, which in turn breeds misinformation; the greater the repression, the greater the dictator's dilemma (Wintrobe 1998).

Uncertain of their position, dictators often try to co-opt potential rivals by purchasing their loyalty. They can never be certain, however, of how much they need to spend to purchase the loyalty they require, so they tend to overspend, lavishing resources on key sectors from which they believe threats may emanate. Various elements in the military often receive such attention. In ethnically divided societies, dictators may focus spending on their own ethnic group to maintain their core base of support. In a number of African authoritarian regimes in the 1970s and 1980s, you could tell who was in power by how well paved the roads were in different regions of the country. The current dictator would build infrastructure such as roads, schools, and hospitals mainly in his home area. As you drove from one region to another, you could literally see who ruled by the immediate and extreme change in the quality of the roads.

Stronger institutions have the potential to reduce the dictator's dilemma by providing regime leaders with better information on who supports them and who doesn't, as well as possibly increasing their legitimacy by providing services to the citizenry. Stronger institutions, though, can also be a threat to a dictator's power because they can enhance the power of potential rival elites who lead them, so dictators typically do not create them of their own free will (Migdal 1988). Rather, the relationships and relative power among key regime elites heavily influence how strongly institutionalized or how personalist a regime becomes and therefore how successful it is at overcoming the dictator's dilemma.

Virtually all authoritarian regimes recognize one supreme leader, even if he leads a larger ruling group, such as the politburo in a communist system or the ruling junta in a military government. This **supreme leader** typically wields executive power with few formal limits, though the extent of those limits varies and is crucial for understanding how different regimes function. No dictator gains power alone; all need the support of other key elites to gain power in the first place. Once they come to power, though, the group chooses a supreme leader, who will likely try to maximize his own power and will fear his allies might try to remove him, as they did the previous regime. The elites who helped put him in power, of course, fear the supreme leader will take all power so they will try to limit him.

Milan Svolik (2012) demonstrated that when there is a balance of power between the supreme leader and other key elites, the regime is more likely to create formalized institutions that limit the supreme leader's power. This balance of power, in turn, is most likely when the elites around the supreme leader are united, because their unity creates a credible threat that they could overthrow the supreme leader, forcing him to accept limits on his power. If key elites around the leader are factionalized, the leader will be able to overcome the limits they try to place on him more easily and the regime will become more personalist. If not checked, a fully personalist regime with very weak institutions can result from this process (Geddes, Wright, and Frantz 2018).

Barbara Geddes and colleagues (2018) created a data set on authoritarian rule to demonstrate that authoritarian regimes that emerge from disciplined militaries or long-standing political parties become more institutionalized because their elites are more unified due to the strength of the institutions from which they came. In Brazil, for instance, the modernizing authoritarian regime that the military established in 1964 was highly institutionalized with strict limits on and rotation of the supreme leader, at least in part because the military itself was highly disciplined and had a clear purpose when it came to power. Similarly, communist regimes that come to power via an established communist party often create more institutionalized regimes based on the prior institutionalization of the party.

Security is all regimes' top priority, and this is especially true for authoritarian regimes whatever their level of institutionalization, because they often have limited legitimacy. The loyalty of the military is, of course, crucial. Where elites

supreme leader: Individual who wields executive power with few formal limits in an authoritarian regime; in the Islamic Republic of Iran, the formal title of the top ruling cleric

have successfully limited the supreme leader, the regime will typically rely on the regular military, which they often control directly in a military government or control via a political party infiltrating the military, as in many communist regimes. In less-institutionalized regimes, personalist leaders often place close supporters, even family members, in key positions in the country's security apparatus. In ethnically divided societies, they often deputize people of their own ethnic group or even from their own hometown to ensure loyalty. For instance, Saddam Hussein in Iraq (r. 1979–2003) put not only his fellow Sunni Arabs but also people from his home village in positions of authority in his extensive security apparatus. Personalist leaders also frequently create entirely new security organizations, loyal only to them, as Muammar el-Qaddafi in Libya (r. 1977–2011) did. The creation of military organizations distinct from the national army and personally loyal to the supreme leader rather than to a broader institution of authoritarian rule such as a military junta or communist politburo is a tell-tale sign of the personalization of a regime.

Many authoritarian regimes also create vast networks of spies, both civilian and military, whose job is to gather intelligence on opponents, providing information that can help overcome the dictator's dilemma. For the supreme leader, the targets of this surveillance are likely to be the key elites surrounding him who might threaten his rule. For the regime as a whole, the targets are typically a broader set of lower-level and/or regional elites who could potentially threaten the regime. In the age of electronic surveillance technology and artificial intelligence (AI), surveillance threatens to become even more extreme, as AI can allow a regime to follow masses of people very quickly and correlate vast amounts of data to identify patterns that might threaten the regime, as China has begun to do. China has an estimated two hundred million cameras around the country to literally watch the population—one camera for every seven people (Economy 2019). It initiated a "social credit" system in 2014 that it hopes will include every citizen by 2020. This is a vast network of data collection that gives citizens "social credit" for positive behavior and statements of any type, including online, and demerits for poor behavior, whether economic, such as failing to repay loans, or political. Along with a growing collection of citizens' DNA and facial recognition technology, the system raises the possibility of using "Big Data" and AI to gather, retain, and use information on each citizen to ensure their behavior comports with regime edicts to a degree never before possible (Qiang 2019).

Virtually all authoritarian regimes can be threatened by the issue of succession of the supreme leader. Unlike electoral democracies, most authoritarian regimes have no standard procedure for changing leadership on a regular basis. Each regime must create its own system for choosing new leaders. Again, the degree of institutionalization matters greatly. Communist regimes, for instance, generally choose new leaders from among key contenders within the politburo. While the exact process is usually hidden from the general public, both regime leaders and citizens know that should a leader die, resign, or be forced from office, a pool of successors are available and top party leaders collectively choose one from among their own. China under Mao's long rule (1949–1976) did not deal with the succession issue seriously when Mao died in 1976. A two-year battle among factions ensued that created a period of great uncertainty. Ultimately, Deng Xiaoping and his allies emerged victorious, launching China on its current path of economic reform and growth. Deng anointed Jiang Zemin as his successor and systematically began transferring power to him in 1989, though the process took several years. In 2003 the transfer of power became regularized as Jiang chose Hu Jintao as his successor, though Jiang continued to be influential, including having a substantial role in choosing the new politburo and getting his protégé, Xi Jinping, appointed as supreme leader a decade later. China seemed to have institutionalized a form of leadership succession both for the very top posts and more broadly. The succession process promised some predictability and stability, though as the charismatic President Xi gained greater personal power than any leader since Deng, his strength raised a potential threat to the collective leadership (Minzner 2015). Xi broke with past precedent by not revealing his successor at the 2017 Party Congress, increasing speculation that he might try to hold power longer than the two terms that have become the norm. If he does, China could lose the stability and predictability it has achieved by institutionalizing the succession process.

In contrast to the Chinese example, personalist leaders often rule for life or until they are forced out of office. Many groom a successor as they age, simultaneously working to ensure that the successor does not become a threat before it's time to pass the baton. In the most personalist regimes, the leader grooms his own son to be his successor. The Somoza dynasty in Nicaragua (1936–1979) began with Anastasio senior, who was succeeded by his son Luis, who in turn was succeeded by his brother, another Anastasio. This was also the case in the regimes of "Papa Doc" (1957–1971) and "Baby Doc" Duvalier (1971–1986) in Haiti. Baby Doc was only nineteen years old when his father died and he became head of state. The death of a personalist leader often creates a crisis for the regime. The rise of electoral authoritarian regimes since the end of the Cold War reduced the likelihood of this type of succession crisis. During the Cold War, military coups were the most common way leadership changed in authoritarian regimes, but since then, nonviolent, internal means of leadership change, including elections, have become most common (Frantz 2018, 55–57).

While the heart of authoritarian regimes is the top leadership in and around the executive and supreme leader, other branches of government matter as well. Authoritarian regimes always curtail the rule of law and judicial independence, although some allow these institutions slightly more leeway, typically only in nonpolitical cases. Providing the political good of basic personal security to citizens who do not oppose the regime allows the regime to gain a degree of legitimacy. This type of limited judicial autonomy can also help top leaders gain information about how effectively their state functions on the ground, reducing the dictator's dilemma. Citizens can go to court to attempt to get local government to carry out its functions properly, revealing to leaders potential local problems.

Allowing courts to enforce property rights and contracts encourages domestic and foreign investment, which improves economic growth and therefore government revenue, potentially strengthening the regime. Even so, research on China found that authorities allowed judicial autonomy on economic issues only when organized investors could demand it and credibly threaten to take their assets elsewhere (Wong 2013). Ultimately, however, authoritarian leaders do not submit to the limitations of the rule of law: when necessary, they use the judicial system to repress their opponents and remove judges to ensure that the leader's will is done. In many authoritarian regimes, especially personalist ones, the judiciary becomes quite corrupt as well. Regime leaders and other wealthy people often bribe judges to rule in their favor; once this begins, more and more people recognize what "justice" actually requires, and corruption expands.

All states require a bureaucracy, and all leaders face the principal–agent problem we identified in chapter 5. In an authoritarian regime, though, the question is how strong and independent a bureaucracy the supreme leader wants and opponents can demand. A less-institutionalized bureaucracy, while not serving citizens' interests well, may have distinct advantages to the leader in the form of patronage opportunities it offers regime supporters. Bureaucratic positions provide opportunities for corruption. The top leaders can maintain loyalty by allowing officials to use their positions to their own benefit, weakening the institutions of the state but rewarding the loyalty of potential rivals. If this behavior is informally institutionalized, it can become somewhat predictable. Lesser officials will remain loyal because they believe they can rise to higher and more rewarding positions, which can lead to somewhat predictable career paths within key institutions. In more personalist regimes, like that of Mobutu Sese Seko in Zaire (see "The 'Politics of Survival' in Mobutu's Zaire"), bureaucratic appointments and corruption can be a means for the supreme leader to maintain personal power over potential rivals.

The level of institutionalization of authoritarian regimes, then, is crucial to how and how long they rule. More institutionalized regimes can regularize career paths for supporters and succession, increasing their longevity and support. More personalist regimes make all aspects of political life less certain, reducing support and increasing the chance the regime could be overthrown from within or collapse from a succession crisis. Ironically, a balance of power among the supreme leader and his key allies is more likely to result in institutionalized and therefore more enduring regimes. Dictators need to be saved from themselves. In contemporary electoral authoritarian regimes, institutions of participation such as elections and legislatures, even if severely limited, can play an important role in greater institutionalization.

CRITICAL INQUIRY

What Explains the Institutionalization of Authoritarian Regimes?

We have now become familiar with several of the leading theories of why authoritarian rulers do or do not create institutions and allow some opposition to have a voice. Map 8.1 and Figures 8.1 and 8.2 on pages 226–228 showed us the broad patterns of when and where authoritarian regimes have arisen and disappeared and the shifts in their use of particular institutions. Looking again at the map and figures, can the theories we've just discussed explain the patterns you see? What other hypotheses can you create that would explain the patterns you see in the map and figures?

The "Politics of Survival" in Mobutu's Zaire

Zaire (now the Democratic Republic of the Congo), under the dictatorship of Gen. Mobutu Sese Seko (r. 1965–1997), was a classic case of a corrupt, personalist regime in a weak state. His long rule shows the ability of a personalist dictator to survive, especially when he has external support, but it also demonstrates that a personalist dictator who does not allow real institutions to emerge ultimately is weak and in danger of being overthrown.

Mobutu came to power via a U.S.-supported military coup in the midst of a civil war and created the formal structures of a one-party state, as many personalist dictators do to try to limit factionalism among the elite. But he never allowed the party and other institutions any real autonomy or strength; his rule was always very personalist. As most personalist dictators do, he created a militia made up of close followers from his home area and personally loyal to him as a counterweight to the national army. All power and all major decisions went through him, and personal loyalty and patronage were the key elements of survival. To maintain personalist rule, he had to severely weaken virtually all institutions by following the logic of what political scientist Joel Migdal (1988) termed "the politics of survival."

A dirt street in a poor neighborhood of Kinshasa, Zaire's capital, at the end of Mobutu Sese Seko's rule. Mobutu's thirty-two-year reign destroyed both political institutions and infrastructure, as is typical for personalist rulers.
AP Photo/David Guttenfelder

Strong institutions can be sources of regime strength and longevity if the supreme leader is willing or is forced to allow them. A personalist regime is one in which the leader has managed to avoid that, perhaps to his short-term advantage of maintaining total power. In the long term, though, he comes to fear any potential source of opposition, including from those who control whatever institutions exist. Subordinates who lead state agencies can gain political support, potentially threatening the supreme leader, because they can solve people's problems or provide them valuable resources. Personalist leaders resist the logic of allowing limited institutionalization in order to co-opt opposition. Instead, they undermine institutions by, for example, frequently shuffling subordinates so that they can't build a following.

Mobutu was a master of this kind of politics. He ruled first and foremost by patronage, creating a regime that many referred to as a "kleptocracy," or rule by theft. A government appointment was a license to steal. He also shuffled personnel frequently, removing potential rivals from office only to return them to power shortly afterward. A famous case involved Nguza Karl-i-Bond, foreign minister and then head of the ruling party in the mid-1970s. After being mentioned as a possible successor to Mobutu, he was accused of treason in 1977, imprisoned, and tortured. A year later, Mobutu forgave him and restored him to the prominent office of state commissioner. Then, in 1981, Nguza fled into exile in Belgium, denounced Mobutu for his corruption and brutality, and even testified against him before the U.S. Congress. In 1986, however, Mobutu once again forgave him, and Nguza returned to Zaire to a hero's welcome; shortly afterward he was named to the prestigious position of ambassador to the United States. Examples like this proved to all that Mobutu could take people from a top position to prison and back again in the blink of an eye.

The politics of survival (along with generous Western support during the Cold War) kept Mobutu in power for three decades but weakened all institutions in Zaire. Even basic infrastructure declined as the state's resources and capabilities collapsed. When Mobutu's neighbor and ally, Rwandan president Juvénal Habyarimana, was facing an armed insurrection in the early 1990s, Mobutu is alleged to have told him, "Your problem is you built roads. They are coming down those roads to get you." Mobutu did not make that mistake: Zaire's road network deteriorated to almost nothing under his rule. Nonetheless, rebel forces eventually forced the aging Mobutu out of power, after the end of the Cold War deprived him of Western support. Without external support and lacking resources for patronage, loyalty to him evaporated, as did his regime and even his chosen name for his country.

Elections, Parties, and Legislatures

In electoral authoritarian regimes, the legislative branch and the elections and political parties that are part of it can help overcome the dictator's dilemma and provide greater stability. Even if the legislature has little power over policy and elections allow little actual competition, they can serve to provide information on local problems, regime support, and opposition; co-opt potential regime opponents; and provide at least a sheen of democratic legitimacy, domestically and internationally. If the legislature has any real power or elections permit any real competition, though, they could threaten the supreme leaders' power and perhaps the regime itself, so once again the question is, Why do these regimes increasingly allow parties, elections, and legislatures to exist?

Regimes that come to power on the basis of a pre-existing political party tend to be united, as noted above, and will understandably use their party to rule the country, whether they allow other parties or not. Parties and legislatures provide offices to use as patronage to maintain the loyalty of local-level and regional elites. Mexico's PRI politicians operated on the basis of patronage, and citizens in rural regions in particular understood that votes for the PRI could result in material benefits for their communities. Similarly, membership in the Communist Party is usually a prerequisite for many jobs in any communist regime. Top leaders also try to use ruling parties to implement their policies at the local level. Communist regimes have cells in government agencies, communities, and major organizations, such as state-run companies, to monitor policy implementation and regime loyalty.

Leaders in more factionalized regimes that did not come to power on the basis of a previously existing party, though, also create parties in some cases. As with other institutions, this is most likely when there is a relative balance of power between the supreme leader and other key elites, giving both sides incentives to allow some institutionalized restraints on their power. If either side is significantly more powerful than the other, however, the more powerful side will resist the institutionalized limits a ruling party might impose (Reuter 2017). A ruling party and its patronage opportunities build a base of support for the supreme leader and regularized access to the state's resources for other elites. Elections provide opportunities to spread patronage more widely among the population. Even in regimes where elections are not competitive, government spending goes up (Geddes et al. 2018).

Given these advantages of a ruling party, why would a regime allow competition that could threaten it? Once again, the dictator's dilemma provides the answer. Top leaders face a principal–agent problem as they try to ensure that local leaders in the ruling party provide them accurate information and implement polices correctly. Local leaders can benefit from opportunities for corruption that can undermine regime policies. They also have an incentive to hide bad news from top leaders for fear of losing their positions. Electoral competition from other parties can help rectify this. Competition incentivizes local leaders to provide resources and services to their constituents, potentially reducing corruption. Because opposition parties can voice local grievances that ruling party officials may prefer to hide from top leaders, the latter have an incentive to try to fix those problems. At the local level, the success of opposition parties can provide valuable information to top leaders.

Competition also helps ensure that the ruling party has local leaders with some basis of support. In Kenya's one-party state in the 1960s and early 1970s, individual legislators—typically leaders of local ethnic groups who won competitive elections within the sole, ruling party—were able to voice limited criticisms of the government, work on behalf of their constituents to gain resources for their home areas, and use their access to government to gain direct benefits for themselves and their closest associates via corruption. They became regional elites with some modicum of real support, spokesmen for their areas with access to the top leadership of the government. The parliament clearly served as a mechanism of co-optation and, occasionally, of limited policy discussion. When MPs criticized the dictator too much, though, he and his successor clamped down, and regime stability suffered. By the 1980s, the regime faced a coup attempt and an active underground opposition movement, and in the 1990s, it was forced to open up the regime to opposition parties, which finally took power via an election in 2002.

As noted previously, in the post–Cold War world, allowing limited opposition, elections, and a legislature can also provide some domestic and international legitimacy to the regime. Legislatures at times can actually provide a space in which policy compromise can occur: opposition groups can make their demands with less confrontation, and dictators can compromise without seeming to capitulate when they do so in the context of electoral institutions. Electoral authoritarian regimes spend less money on the military, have greater respect for human rights (Gandhi 2008), spend more on health care, and have lower child mortality than do authoritarian regimes that allow no opposition (Geddes et al. 2018), indicating that they are more responsive to their citizens and presumably more accepted by them as legitimate.

Opposition electoral success, though, cannot be too strong, or it will threaten the regime's hold on power. This requires the regime to keep competition within certain limits. For this reason, many regimes do allow competition for the legislature but not for the executive, keeping the supreme leader beyond possible threat. But many other options also exist to limit the regime's risk of losing power. Though rulers will certainly engage in electoral fraud if necessary, more sophisticated and institutionalized systems do not usually require it to keep the ruling party in power. Usually, some combination of the type of electoral system (typically a majoritarian one that favors the already large ruling party), gerrymandering constituency boundaries, vote buying, controlling access to the media, restricting civil liberties, using government resources for partisan purposes, and jailing opponents serve to keep the opposition under control. In Kenya in the 1990s, government civil servants openly campaigned for the ruling party during work hours, candidates handed potential voters gifts of cash or food, and opposition party rallies were denied permits or harassed by police. In Rwanda's 2010 presidential election, three opposition candidates ended up in jail by election day on various charges, allowing President Paul Kagame, in power since the genocide in 1994, to win 93 percent of the vote.

The complex theocratic regime in contemporary Iran shows both the limits and potential of a legislature in an authoritarian regime. The regime mixes appointed and elected offices to maintain the central control of the leading clergy while allowing some voice to other political forces, though within strict limits. Figure 8.3 provides an overview of these institutions. Elected officials are allowed to pass laws and voice some public criticism, but the authority of the Shiite clergy is final. The supreme leader, always a respected member of the clergy, has the power to appoint the heads of all the armed forces, the head of the judiciary, six of the twelve members of the all-important Guardian Council, and the leaders of Friday prayers at mosques. These powers mean that very little of significance can occur in Iran without at least the supreme leader's tacit consent.

FIGURE 8.3

Iran's Governing Institutions

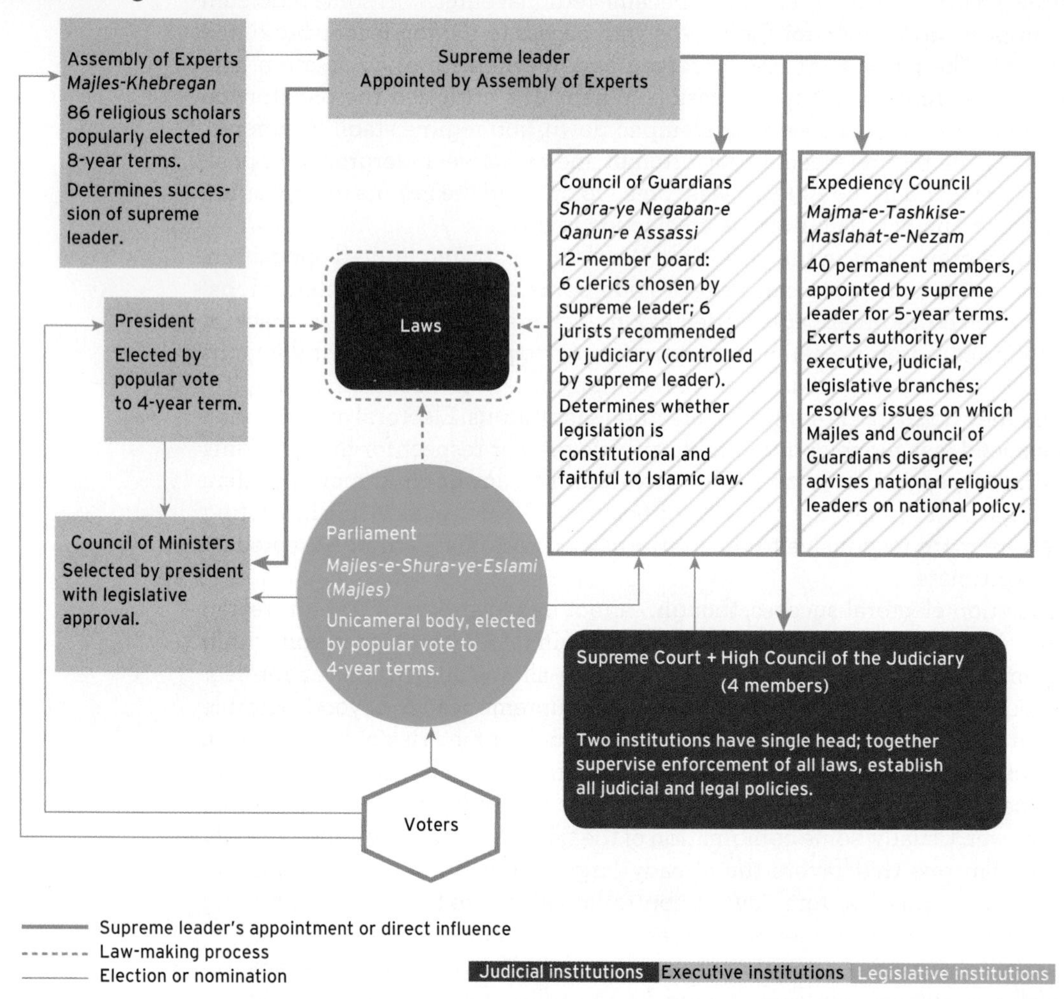

The supreme leader shares formal executive power with a directly elected president in a theocratic version of a semipresidential system. The elected president appoints a cabinet, which the parliament approves and can remove, and runs the daily affairs of government. The president is selected via a majoritarian election and can serve two four-year terms. The dual executive creates the possibility of tension between the supreme leader and president similar to tensions between the president and prime minister under cohabitation in semipresidential systems. When an avowed reformist was president from 1997 to 2005, he and his supporters in parliament initially passed significant reforms into law, but they increasingly clashed with the supreme leader and the Guardian Council. The Council, consisting of six clergy appointed by the supreme leader and six lay leaders nominated by the head of the judiciary and approved by parliament, must agree to all legislation. Given that all of its members are either appointed directly by the supreme leader or nominated by his appointed judiciary, it is a bastion of clerical authority that preserves the will of the supreme leader. It also must approve all candidates for election and has repeatedly banned candidates it has deemed unacceptable for president, parliament, and local government councils. In 2005, it banned most reform supporters from running for parliament, and a conservative candidate supported by the supreme leader won the presidential election. All authoritarian regimes, even those that make claims of democratic legitimacy and allow a legislature, have such mechanisms to limit the legislature's and therefore the opposition's power.

Even competitive elections for the executive may be beneficial to a regime. Successful campaigns and elections demonstrate the leader's continued strength and support (Geddes et al. 2018). During elections and at other times, regimes use large rallies and praise for the leader to show their strength. When Mexico's Partido Revolucionario Institucional (PRI) ruled as an electoral authoritarian regime, supporters would be trucked in from the countryside to rallies in the cities, where they would enjoy free food, drink, and entertainment. Cameroonian scholar Achille Mbembe (1992) called such huge but empty displays the "banality of power." Svolik (2012), however, argued that they actually serve a clear purpose by demonstrating the ruling party's strength and providing a warning to potential rivals.

All electoral authoritarian regimes limit competition, but how much and how successfully they limit it varies. Regimes with an alternative basis for legitimacy—notably monarchies—and regimes that control significant natural resources such as oil have less incentive to allow elections at all. Yonatan Morse (2018) argued that, in Africa, ruling parties with well-institutionalized and long-standing ties to the citizenry can easily win elections and so allow relatively open ones to occur, while weaker ruling parties must limit and manipulate elections in order to stay in power. Stronger, more united opposition parties might also force the regime to allow greater competition.

Political scientists originally saw electoral authoritarian regimes as temporary, likely to revert to more closed authoritarian rule or to democracy, but it's become clear that they are here to stay for some time. Figure 8.4 shows the growing share of authoritarian regimes that allow elections and the correlation between allowing elections and staying in power. Milan Svolik (2012) demonstrated that authoritarian regimes with strong ruling parties, whether ruling alone or allowing some limited opposition, survive longer than regimes without parties. In the post–Cold War world, most of these regimes are electoral authoritarian, allowing a modicum of opposition but nonetheless maintaining power.

Vladimir Putin's regime in Russia is the most prominent example of an electoral authoritarian regime today, one that is more restrictive than some. It developed out of the chaotic process of democratization in Russia in the 1990s. Putin's predecessor as president, Boris Yeltsin, refused to join a political party, trying to remain "above the fray" of party politics. This left him a weak leader, with little control over the legislature in what was a semipresidential system. He was also informally dependent on the wealthy oligarchs who captured control of major companies during the chaotic transition from a state-planned to a market economy. Facing a destabilizing succession battle among several close aides, in 1999 Yeltsin anointed the relatively unknown Vladimir Putin as his successor and resigned from office, so Putin could run as an incumbent in the 2000 presidential election.

Putin, a former KGB agent who led the security apparatus under Yeltsin, proved to be a much stronger president than his predecessor. He successfully undermined the power of both the parliament and regional governments in his first few years in office, effectively replacing Russia's nascent democracy with an electoral authoritarian regime. As the economy boomed, revenue poured into the central states' coffers as well. Putin distributed the funds to regions based on their political loyalty,

FIGURE 8.4

Electoral Authoritarian Institutions and Regime Durability, 1951–2008

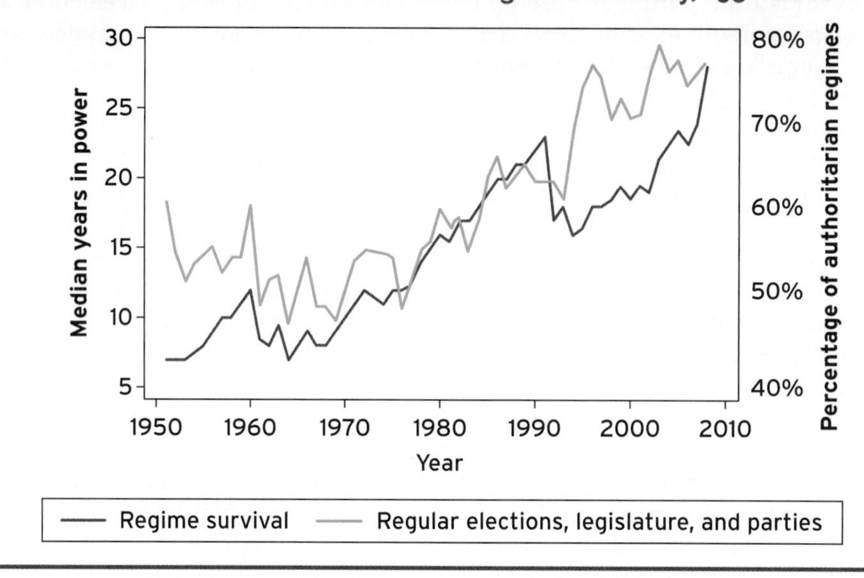

Source: Adapted from Erica Frantz, *Authoritarianism: What Everyone Needs to Know* (New York: Oxford University Press, 2018), 121.

removing any opposition to his gutting of federalism. Like all authoritarian rulers, Putin has used repression and co-optation when needed to maintain his power. This is particularly clear in his treatment of key economic players. He attempted to co-opt the "oligarchs," who were powerful under Yeltsin, but when he couldn't, he used his control over the judiciary to jail them or force them into exile. His allies or the state itself would then take ownership of key industries, especially natural resources, a key source of patronage and revenue.

Political scientists Hans Oversloot and Ruben Verheul (2006) argued that the most important party in Russia has long been the "party of power, the party that those around the president create to win as many seats as they can in the Duma, insuring support for the president's proposals." Yeltsin never fostered such a party, but Putin did, developing United Russia as his party of power. He used his greater popularity (throughout his first two terms, his popular approval ratings rarely dipped below 70 percent) and his control over patronage to ensure that United Russia won handily. Since 2003, United Russia has easily dominated the Duma, meaning the Duma has rubber-stamped everything Putin has proposed, even though small opposition parties exist and win a minority of legislative seats.

Police arrest a protester in December 2011 during the protests against fraud in the parliamentary election. The protests were the largest since the end of the Soviet Union, but Russia's electoral authoritarian regime withstood the opposition and continues to rule.
Sovfoto/UIG via Getty Images

Putin has also used electoral fraud, a common technique of electoral authoritarian regimes, to limit opposition when needed. The parliamentary elections in December 2011 included widespread fraud, some of it captured on video and posted on the Internet. After years of relative quiescence, Russian civil society awoke; protests of tens of thousands of people demanding fairer elections took place repeatedly from December 2011 to March 2012. The regime successfully resisted the protesters' demands, however, and Putin was duly elected (again, partly via fraudulent elections) president in March 2012. With another Duma election looming in 2016, Putin chose manipulation of the electoral system as a means of control, shifting from a PR to mixed electoral system. Since United Russia was the only party able to field winning candidates across the nation, it gained a supermajority of the Duma and the ability to change the constitution at will. Putin once again handily won reelection in 2018, securing 77 percent of the vote. His most serious rival, Alexei Navalny, known for organizing nationwide anticorruption campaigns, was barred from running. Putin's firm control of an electoral authoritarian regime leaves little doubt that he and his party will continue to rule for the foreseeable future.

Clientelism and Civil Society

Patronage to co-opt rival elites, often via ruling parties, is a central element of authoritarian regimes' survival. Not surprisingly, then, clientelism is a central means through which citizens participate in politics. Electoral authoritarian regimes provide some limited institutionalized means of participation, but the purpose of participation is often to gain positions and access to patronage, since only very limited policy impact is possible. In personalist and less-institutionalized regimes, even those avenues are mostly cut off. By becoming an individual client of a powerful patron, citizens can gain access to some resources, power, or influence. This occurs behind closed doors, of course, but as the patron gains power and position in the system, the clients gain also through special privileges and access to resources.

In the absence of other effective means of participation and representation, following a patron may be the best available option. A patron can represent a client's most immediate interests vis-à-vis the state. The problems in this type of system, though, are numerous. First, its informality means that no client is ever guaranteed anything. Each individual has a unique and largely private relationship with a patron, who will try to maintain the client's loyalty in the long term but who will not respond to every demand. Clients have no recourse unless an alternative patron is available. This is sometimes the case, but transferring loyalty is never easy or quick. Second, clientelism discourages citizens from organizing on the basis of collective interests. As long as citizens believe that following a personal patron is the most effective route to obtaining what they need from government, they have little incentive to organize collectively to change the government and its policies more broadly, with profound implications for civil society.

Even in authoritarian regimes that allow it to exist, civil society is extremely circumscribed and repressed. Civil society in a democracy, at least ideally, operates in a public sphere in which open debate is possible with few legal constraints on speech and nonviolent political action, even if cultural norms limit what is considered "acceptable" speech and actions. Civil society in authoritarian regimes must operate in what Alexander Dukalskis (2017) calls an "authoritarian public sphere." This is a public sphere tightly controlled and monitored by an authoritarian regime that uses it to try to gain legitimacy. The regime propagates messages that show their rule as all-powerful and inevitable, frame it as beneficial for the nation as a whole, and limit negative images of the regime. Under President Xi, the Chinese regime has actively used the authoritarian public sphere to propagate an official ideology. In contrast to his immediate predecessors, Xi began making major ideological pronouncements shortly after gaining power. He has tried to expand the role of nationalism and Confucianism as ideological supports for the regime. In 2017, the Party Congress enshrined Xi Jinping, *Thought on Socialism With Chinese Characteristics for a New Era* (known simply as *Xi Jinping Thought*), in the constitution, as Mao Zedong *Thought* and Deng Xiaoping *Thought* were earlier. In 2019, the regime created a smart phone "app" of *Xi Jinping Thought* that is interactive. Citizens are expected to interact with it frequently and many fear punishment if they don't.

Communist regimes such as the Soviet Union and China at their heights were totalitarian, as North Korea remains today. Totalitarian regimes completely eliminate civil society—the ruling party "represents" all interests that it believes deserve representation. Trade unions or youth or women's groups often nominally exist, but these mass organizations are always part of the Communist Party. They cannot be truly part of civil society, which by definition is autonomous from the state.

Noncommunist regimes often use state corporatism to control interest groups. Remember that corporatism is the idea that each component (or interest) in society should be represented by one organization. When a government legally mandates this, it is referred to as state corporatism because the state controls the interest groups and chooses the ones it wishes to recognize. Mexico's electoral authoritarian regime under the PRI was a classic example. The PRI recognized and included within the party a single labor organization, a single peasant association, and a single association for "popular groups"—small businesses, women's interests, and various others. These organizations were to represent their constituents within the party. Over time, however, they became increasingly corrupt and controlled by the elite at the top of the party hierarchy. The workers' organization, in particular, was very powerful within the party, and real wages rose for most of the PRI's long rule, even though the unions rarely contradict official party policies. In most of Asia and Africa, unions and other major interest groups arose with and were part of nationalist movements for independence. After independence, however, authoritarian regimes emasculated these organizations, often creating state corporatist systems in their place.

Often, observers assume that civil society, when not obviously controlled by a ruling party, will inherently resist authoritarian rule, but this is not always the case. Organizations in civil society need to survive if they hope to benefit their members, and cooperating with the regime even when not legally required to may be the best way to achieve that aim. Accepting regime patronage and therefore supporting the regime may gain organizations access to resources for their members, while a principled opposition in the name of democracy may prevent them from achieving anything (Jamal 2007). Religious organizations, for instance, often cooperate with authoritarian regimes to gain regularized status and material rewards, and authoritarian leaders may be willing to cooperate with them in order to gain prestige and possible legitimacy by association, especially when a particular religion has deep social roots, such as the Russian Orthodox Church (Koesel 2014).

Jessica Teets (2014) argued that in China this dynamic is producing a new model of state–civil society relations—"consultative authoritarianism"—that combines elements of liberal autonomy and state corporatism. Authoritarian regimes, she argued, increasingly allow civil society groups to operate to improve overall governance by helping overcome the dictator's dilemma and by providing services directly. On the other hand, the regimes must ensure civil society stays within certain bounds to maintain regime control, so they use a combination of positive and negative incentives to do so, minimizing repression to the extent possible.

The result is improved governance for citizens on a daily basis but little chance that civil society will foster regime change toward democracy.

Nonetheless, elements of civil society often do attempt resistance, as least when the opportunity arises. In Iran, the media, and women's and student groups have been key pillars of the reformist movements over the years. Whenever the government has allowed it, the media have expanded rapidly. Leading up to the 2000 *majlis* election, many newspapers emerged, and an exceptionally open political debate occurred. Since that time, religious authorities have again repressed newspapers, closing them down for criticizing the government too harshly and drastically reducing public debate. Women have become an important organized force over the last decade. They constitute 62 percent of university students, and a birth control policy has lowered childbearing and population growth rates dramatically. These changes have fostered the growth of women's organizations calling for even further change. All major politicians now court the women's vote during elections.

Civil society propelled the 2009 protests against in what was widely seen as fraudulent elections. Since then, numerous political activists and journalists have been arrested and jailed, and key journalistic and legal associations were banned. The government created a new "cyberpolice force" to monitor the Internet and disrupt bloggers and social media sites critical of the regime, and it officially banned Facebook and Instagram. These restrictions, however, have had modest effects; forty-five million Iranians have Facebook accounts, including, ironically, Supreme Leader Khamenei and President Rouhani (Milani 2015, 58). Antigovernment protests in January 2018 led authorities to slow down Internet connections, block servers outside Iran, and block Instagram and Telegram. After temporarily lifting both blocks, Telegram was declared a security threat and was permanently blocked in April 2018. The Iranian state does not appear to have the strength to restrict the Internet as effectively as the Chinese state, but it continues to exert control and block access, leading Freedom House to classify it as not free with a score only slightly better than China's (Freedom House 2018).

With civil society circumscribed, average citizens often find it rational to pursue individual clientelist relationships in order to participate and survive in authoritarian regimes. At times, though, grievances grow and opportunities for broader participation emerge, especially in electoral authoritarian regimes that allow some degree of openness. The emergence of truly independent social movements is often one of the first signs of a democratic opening. In Latin America in the 1970s, labor-based social movements outside the confines of the official corporatist unions began challenging the status quo and ultimately forced authoritarian regimes to move toward democratization, a subject we turn to in chapter 9.

Conclusion

By the dawn of the new millennium, it was clear that while democracy had expanded, authoritarianism was not about to disappear entirely. Since the end of the Cold War, electoral authoritarian rule has expanded, and more "closed" authoritarian rule that allows no formal opposition has been on the wane (with China clearly being the world's biggest exception to the trend). The differences between fully authoritarian and electoral authoritarian rule, though, aren't as great as they might at first appear. Understanding the opaque political dynamics of authoritarian and electoral authoritarian regimes will continue to be a concern for comparative politics for the foreseeable future.

On the face of it, dictators seem to control virtually everything in authoritarian regimes. The executive would seem to be all-powerful. As we've seen, though, this is often not the case, which makes figuring out who rules rather difficult. The key question is not just what formal institutions exist but how institutionalized they are. Ultimately, in authoritarian regimes, the supreme leader or a small coterie of leaders (such as a politburo) has final authority to decide as they will. Much of the internal politics and institutionalization of authoritarian rule is determined by the relationships between the supreme leader, on one hand, and the rest of the top elite, on the other.

Ruling by fiat and repression alone is both difficult and expensive. Holding a gun to every citizen's head, as well as maintaining the loyalty of those holding the guns, is not easy. All regimes, therefore, seek to gain some sort of legitimacy or at least to buy support via co-optation. A means to achieve both legitimacy and support is to limit the supreme leader's power in order to give others, especially key elites, some influence. Institutionalized and therefore predictable governing and limited participatory institutions can accomplish this. Examining those institutions and how strong they are can thus be a key means to understanding who really rules and how much influence they have. Even in the most personalist regimes with little institutionalization, patron–client relationships are important for co-opting opposition. More powerful individuals control more patronage, and on the other side, some clients are more powerful and thus more likely to have their requests attended to than others. Comparativists attempt the difficult task of understanding these informal networks and relationships to determine who rules in countries where institutions matter little.

Comparativists have long catalogued authoritarian regimes into various subtypes. It's clear, however, that certain commonalities exist in all authoritarian regimes. For instance, all dictators face the dictator's dilemma, though they attempt to solve it in different ways. All dictators also rule through some combination of repression, co-optation, and attempts at legitimation, but again in differing ways and amounts. Some of this variation is systematic across subtypes: different subtypes display consistent and distinct behavior. One-party and of course electoral authoritarian regimes provide opportunities for greater participation via formal institutions. Military regimes are less likely to do so, as political participation and open dissent are foreign to professional military culture. Following the logic of the dictator's dilemma, regimes that allow less participation are likely to require more repression and co-optation. Military regimes seem likely to use repression, given their inherent control of force. Personalist regimes that have weak institutions across the board focus mostly on co-optation via patronage, using repression as well but often in less institutionalized and therefore less effective ways. Such a personalist regime might have, for example, multiple and competing military agencies that are informally loyal to individual leaders rather than to the regime as a whole. The splits within the military in response to the 2011 uprising in Libya show the possible effects of this aspect of personalist rule. Personalist regimes that are able to establish institutions, usually because of a rough balance of power between the supreme ruler and other elites, are more likely to avoid Libya's fate.

The earliest theoretical approaches to understanding authoritarian regimes focused mainly on individual leaders or national cultures. Individual leaders are clearly crucial in such regimes, so scholars used psychological theories to understand their personal influences and motivations. More recently, scholars have used rational choice or historical-institutionalist models to understand authoritarian regimes. Dictators face a common set of governing problems. To overcome these, they engage in a combination of repression, co-optation, and legitimation. This behavioral pattern, rational choice theorists argue, is determined by the dictators' and their opponents' or allies' rational responses to their conditions, the most important of which are the relative strengths of the actors and the resources at their disposal. As with many arguments in comparative politics, institutionalist theories are at the forefront of the debate today but have not definitively proven their case. We turn next to another set of difficult questions about regimes: why and how they change from one type to another via military coup, revolution, or democratization. ●

KEY CONCEPTS

dictator's dilemma (p. 228)

supreme leader (p. 229)

WORKS CITED

Dukalskis, Alexander. 2017. *The Authoritarian Public Sphere: Legitimation and Autocratic Power in North Korea, Burma, and China.* New York: Routledge.

Economy, Elizabeth. 2019. "30 Years After Tiananmen: Dissent Is Not Dead." *Journal of Democracy* 3 (2): 57–63. *Project MUSE.* doi:10.1353/jod.2019.0024.

Frantz, Erica. 2018. *Authoritarianism: What Everyone Needs to Know.* Oxford, UK: Oxford University Press.

Freedom House, Freedom on the Net 2018. Retrieved May 3, 2019, from https://freedomhouse.org/report/freedom-net/2018/russia; https://freedomhouse.org/report/freedom-net/2018/iran.

Gandhi, Jennifer. 2008. *Political Institutions Under Dictatorship.* Cambridge, UK: Cambridge University Press.

Geddes, Barbara, Joseph Wright, and Erica Frantz. 2018. *How Dictatorships Work: Power, Personalization, and Collapse.* Cambridge, UK: Cambridge University Press.

Jamal, Amaney A. 2007. *Barriers to Democracy: The Other Side of Social Capital in Palestine and the Arab World.* Princeton, NJ: Princeton University Press.

Koesel, Karri. J. 2014. *Religion and Authoritarianism: Cooperation, Conflict, and the Consequences.* Cambridge, UK: Cambridge University Press.

Mbembe, Achille. 1992. "Provisional Notes on the Postcolony." *Africa: Journal of the International African Institute* 62 (1): 3–37. doi:10.2307/1160062.

Migdal, Joel S. 1988. *Strong Societies and Weak States: State-Society Relations and State Capabilities in the Third World.* Princeton, NJ: Princeton University Press.

Milani, Abbas. 2015. "Iran's Paradoxical Regime." *Journal of Democracy* 26(2): 52–60.

Minzner, Carl. 2015. "China After the Reform Era." *Journal of Democracy* 26(3): 129–143.

Morse, Yonatan L. 2018. *How Autocrats Compete: Parties, Patrons, and Unfair Elections in Africa.* Cambridge, UK: Cambridge University Press.

Oversloot, Hans, and Ruben Verheul. 2006. "Managing Democracy: Political Parties and the State in Russia." *Journal of Communist Studies and Transition Politics* 22 (3): 383–405. doi:10.1080/13523270600855795.

Qiang, Xiao. 2019. "The Road to Digital Unfreedom: President Xi's Surveillance State," *Journal of Democracy* 30 (1): 53–67. Project MUSE. doi:10.1353/jod.2019.0004.

Reuter, Ora John. 2017. *The Origins of Dominant Parties: Building Authoritarian Institutions in Post-Soviet Russia.* Cambridge, UK: Cambridge University Press.

Svolik, Milan W. 2012. *The Politics of Authoritarian Rule.* Cambridge, UK: Cambridge University Press.

Teets, Jessica C. 2014. *Civil Society Under Authoritarianism: The China Model.* Cambridge, UK: Cambridge University Press.

Wintrobe, Ronald. 1998. *The Political Economy of Dictatorship.* Cambridge, UK: Cambridge University Press.

Wong, Edward. 2013. "In China, Widening Discontent Among the Communist Party Faithful." *New York Times,* January 19, 2013. http://www.nytimes.com/2013/01/20/world/asia/in-china-discontent-among-the-normally-faithful.html?emc=eta1.

RESOURCES FOR FURTHER STUDY

Clapham, Christopher S. 1982. *Private Patronage and Public Power: Political Clientelism in the Modern State.* New York: St. Martin's Press.

Clapham, Christopher S., and George D. E. Philip, eds. 1985. *The Political Dilemmas of Military Regimes.* Totowa, NJ: Barnes and Noble.

Jahanbegloo, Ramin, ed. 2012. *Civil Society and Democracy in Iran.* New York: Lexington Books.

Mbembe, Achille. 2001. *On the Postcolony.* Berkeley: University of California Press.

McFaul, Michael. 2005. "Chinese Dreams, Persian Realities." *Journal of Democracy* 16 (4): 74–82. doi:10.1353/jod.2005.0068.

WEB RESOURCES

Quality of Government Institute, University of Gothenburg, the QoG Data

(http://www.qog.pol.gu.se/data)

World Bank, Database of Political Institutions

(http://go.worldbank.org/2EAGGLRZ40)

World Justice Project, Rule of Law Index

(http://www.worldjusticeproject.org/rule-of-law-index)

World Values Survey

(http://www.worldvaluessurvey.org)

Youssef Karwashan/AFP/Getty Images

9 Regime Change

Hundreds of thousands of Egyptians watch fireworks set off to celebrate the military's ouster of President Mohamed Morsi on July 7, 2013. The military coup came two and a half years after a political revolution that started a process of democratization. The tortuous route and uncertain outcome of Egypt's regime change is not unusual.
REUTERS/Amr Abdallah Dalsh

Key Questions

- Why does the military intervene in politics in certain countries and not in others?
- Why are some countries able to found and sustain democracies while others aren't?
- Why do authoritarian regimes take power and why do they end quickly in some places but last much longer in others?

Learning Objectives

After reading chapter 9, you should be able to do the following:

9.1 Explain how regime change has evolved since the end of the Cold War

9.2 Explicate the conditions under which non-democratic regimes make the transition to democracy

9.3 Explain how and why authoritarian regimes arise

Regime change is the high drama of comparative politics. Many of our most iconic political images are of regime change, from the "shot heard 'round the world" signaling the start of the American Revolution in 1776, to Nelson Mandela taking the oath of office in South Africa in 1994, to protesters in Tahrir Square in Egypt in 2011. They are often images of popular and charismatic leaders backed by the mobilized masses demanding a better world. But other images are less positive, like that of a general seizing power as tanks roll into the capital, as happened in Egypt in 2013, or the slow erosion of democracy under President Recep Tayyip Erdoğan in Turkey. Comparativists analyze all of these events, whether positive or negative, as **regime change**, the process through which one regime is transformed into another. The specific focus of our inquiry has always been influenced by the political context. During the Cold war, we focused on military coups d'état and revolutions; in the early post–Cold War years, we concentrated primarily on what Samuel Huntington (1991) called the third wave of democratization; and most recently, we have looked more closely at how democracies break down. All types of regime change remain important, however. Although the Arab Spring produced a democracy in Tunisia, coups have taken place in recent years in Guinea and Mali, and Turkey saw a failed coup attempt in in July 2016. In 2019, some analysts began talking about a "new Arab Spring," as massive protests in Algeria and Sudan forced long-reigning dictators out of power; they were removed by their own militaries, however, and it remained unclear what kind of regime would replace them. Often we can only distinguish the outcome of a regime process in retrospect.

The study of regime change raises several fundamental questions in comparative politics: Why do revolutions or military coups happen in some countries and not in others? Why are some countries able to found and sustain democracies while others aren't? Why do authoritarian regimes take power, and why do they end quickly in some places but last much longer in others?

Trends in Regime Change

Logically, any type of regime we have discussed earlier in this book could be changed into any other, giving many possibilities. Some changes, however, are more common than others. Regime change can occur via a number of mechanisms: military **coup d'état**, revolution, military insurgency, negotiated

regime change: The process through which one regime is transformed into another

coup d'état: When the military forcibly removes an existing regime and establishes a new one

transition to a democracy, slow erosion of democratic institutions ultimately producing an authoritarian regime, or foreign invasion. These mechanisms can produce various outcomes. Military coups, for instance, often result in military regimes but can produce new democracies. Revolutions, especially social revolutions, and insurgencies typically produce some type of authoritarian regime, but there are exceptions to that as well. In examining regime change, then, we need to distinguish between and analyze both mechanisms and outcomes.

The regime changes to which we will give most of our attention are changes from democratic to authoritarian regimes and vice versa. These are the dramatic beginnings of new democracies, mass uprisings to overthrow dictators, or the rolling of tanks down the streets of a nation's capital. But regimes can change from one authoritarian regime to another as well, such as when a faction of a military dictatorship decides to replace an incumbent military regime with a new but equally authoritarian one or when a social revolution overthrows a monarchy to install a communist regime.

The rarest type of regime change is from one democratic regime to another. Once democracies are established, they may weaken and ultimately be overthrown by the military, as in Brazil in 1964, or be transformed into authoritarian regimes as elected leaders amass nearly unlimited power, as Vladimir Putin did in Russia. Very rarely, however, does a nation decide to shift from one type of democratic regime to another. A rare exception was the transition from the Fourth to the Fifth Republics in France in 1958. In the midst of the Algerian war for independence from France, part of the French army rebelled against the democratic government by demanding that France continue to fight to preserve Algeria as part of France. World War II general and war hero Charles de Gaulle called for the dissolution of the government and a constitutional convention, to which parliament agreed. The parliamentary Fourth Republic was dissolved and the semipresidential system, a new type of democratic regime that we outlined in chapter 5, was established, ending the crisis in a very rare transition from one democratic regime to another.

Both the mechanisms and outcomes of regime change shifted with the end of the Cold War in 1990. As the Berlin Wall fell and the Soviet Union collapsed, one superpower was gone and the other (the United States) became much less concerned about propping up friendly dictators. Communism as an ideology was seen as largely bankrupt and liberal democracy the near-universal norm—with the major exception being defenders of monarchy or theocracy in the Middle East. We saw in chapter 8 that the post–Cold War era produced a shift from more closed to more open, electoral authoritarian regimes. Figure 9.1 shows a parallel trend toward democracy. The number of closed authoritarian regimes peaked in the late 1970s and shrank dramatically in the 1990s, while the number of democracies increased, then leveled off in the new millennium. During the Cold War, two-thirds of regime changes that ended authoritarian regimes ultimately created new authoritarian regimes; since the end of the Cold War, the ratio has flipped, with two-thirds of those regime changes creating democracies (Conroy-Krutz and Frantz 2017, 11). Figure 9.2 shows a change in the mechanisms of regime change as well, looking specifically at the fall of authoritarian regimes. Coups have become a far less common mechanism for ending authoritarian regimes while elections, military insurgencies, and popular uprisings increased.

Clearly, the international context affects both the mechanisms and outcomes of regime change, but it doesn't determine them. Military coups still happen since the Cold War, and some democracies were created during the Cold War. As comparativists, we need to examine the internal dynamics of regime change. We will do that first by looking at regime changes that replace authoritarian rule with

FIGURE 9.1

Regime Types, 1946–2017

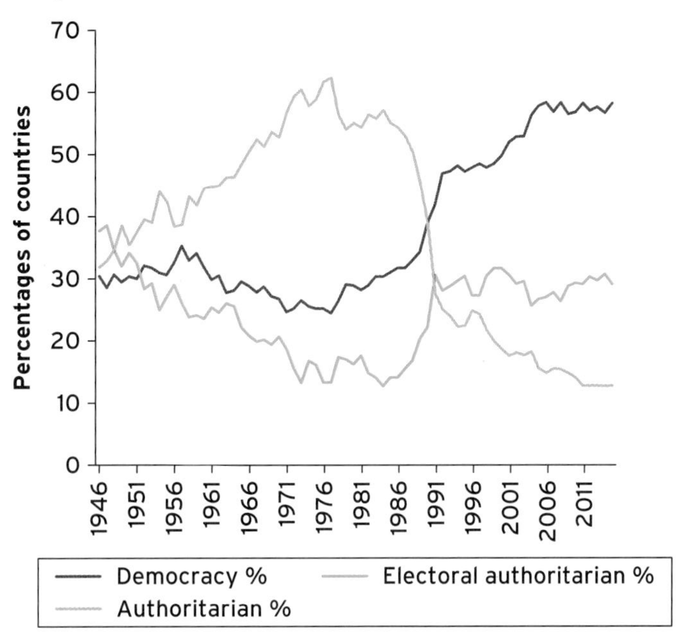

Source: Data are from the Polity Project's Polity IV data set, Center for Systemic Peace, http://www.systemicpeace.org/polityproject.html

Note: Electoral authoritarian regimes are regimes with scores between −5 and 5. Authoritarian regimes score between −10 and −6 and democracies rate between 6 and 10. The labels shown above have been modified from the original by the authors to conform to terminology used in this book. Polity IV's label of "anocracy" we referred to as "electoral authoritarian," and Polity IV's label of "autocracy" is labeled here as "authoritarian."

FIGURE 9.2

How Authoritarian Regimes Fall

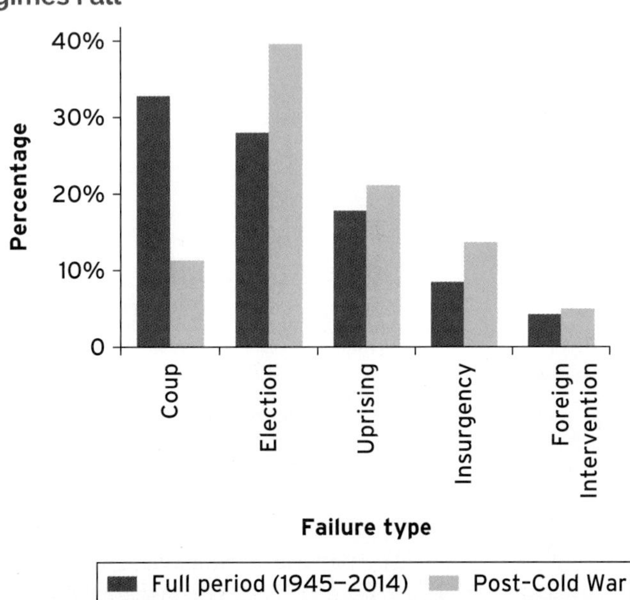

Source: Adapted from Erica Frantz, *Authoritarianism: What Everyone Needs to Know* (New York: Oxford University Press, 2018), 125

democracy and then at changes that create authoritarian regimes, including those that end democracies.

Regime Change: Transitions to Democracy

In 1972 Freedom House, a nongovernmental organization (NGO) that analyzes the level of political and civil rights in countries around the world, classified forty-four countries as "free," meaning that they were fully functioning liberal democracies. In 1990 the number of "free" countries rose to sixty-one, and in 2019 it had grown to eighty-six. In the new millennium, though, progress has slowed and even reversed. Freedom House reported that 2019 was the thirteenth straight year in which the number of countries that became less free was greater than the number that became more free. A recent review of the third wave of democratization found that of ninety-one transitions to democracy since 1974, thirty-four had reverted to authoritarian rule and thirty remained democracies but "low-quality" ones in terms of fair elections, protections of rights, and the rule of law. Only twenty-seven countries were "high-quality" liberal democracies as of 2017 (Mainwaring and Bizzarro 2019). Map 9.1, using a different data set, shows the spread of electoral democracy over time. Democracy has clearly advanced, but reversal is possible, and the 1990s image of global mass rebellion overwhelming dictators and establishing lasting democracy was, alas, overly simplistic.

As discussed in chapter 7, political revolutions in which popular uprisings overwhelm a dictator happen but are rare. The fall of Ferdinand Marcos in the Philippines in 1986 and Nicolae Ceauşescu in Romania three years later are classic examples that captured the world's imagination. Much more common, though, are negotiated changes from an authoritarian to a democratic regime, like the four-year process in South Africa from anti-apartheid leader Nelson Mandela's release from prison in 1990 to his election as president in 1994. One study found the average length of a transition to democracy was 6.1 years (Conroy-Krutz and Frantz 2017, 6). Regime changes that create democracies are typically long, complicated

MAP 9.1

Democratic Institutionalization

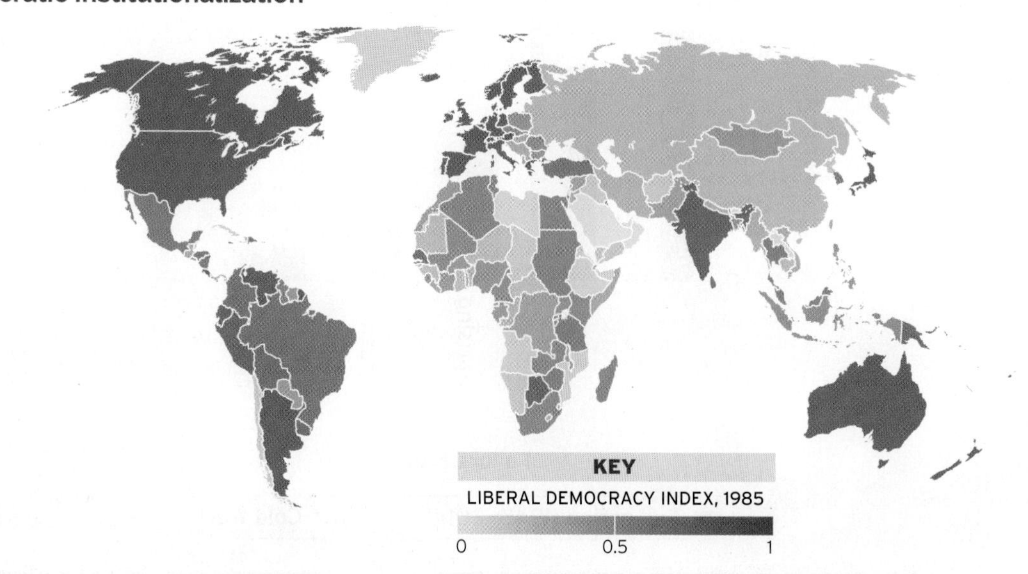

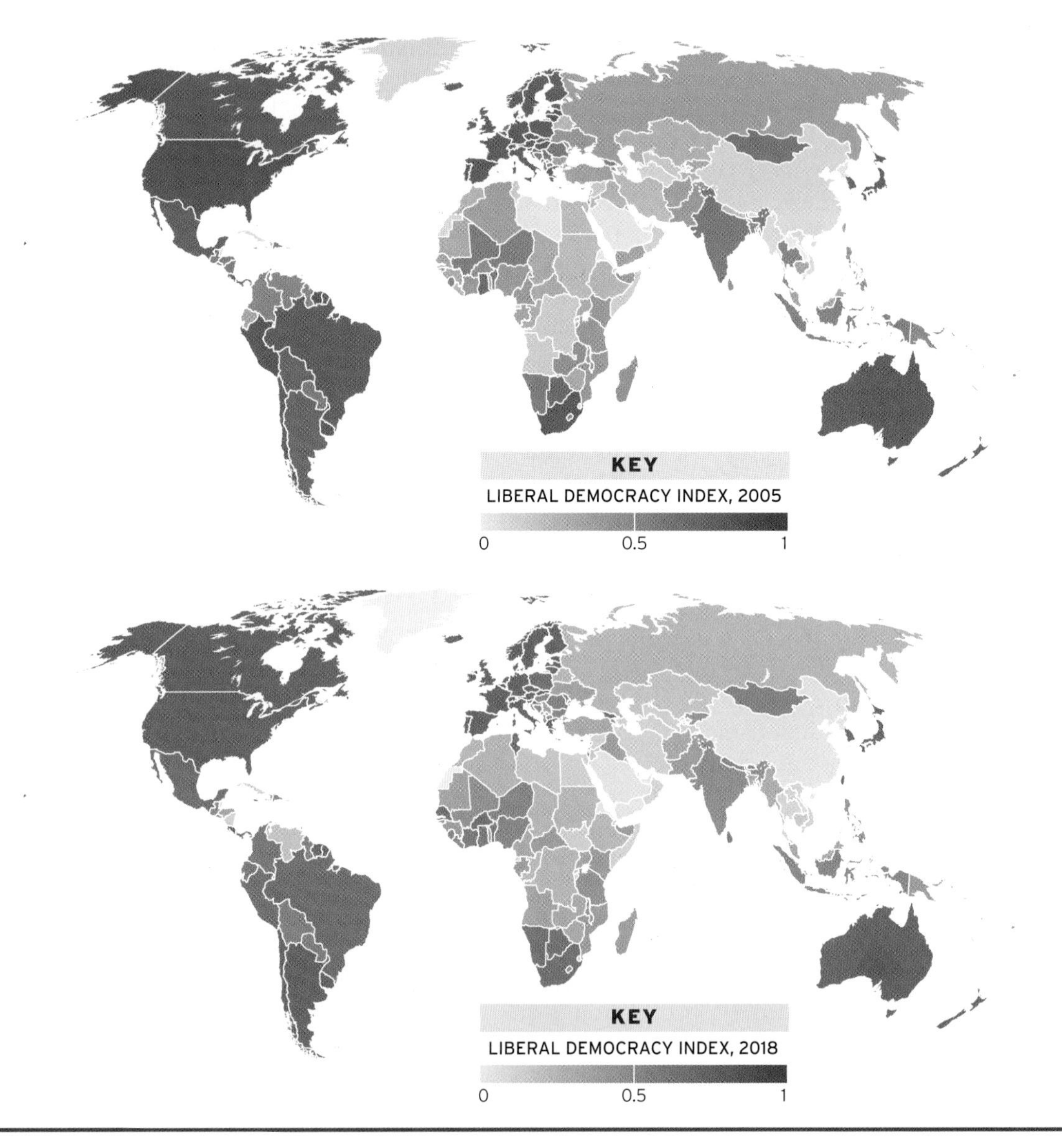

Source: https://www.v-dem.net/en/analysis/MapGraph/

affairs involving significant bargaining among major political actors, all set in a particular economic, cultural, and international context. Comparativists have tried to understand the expansion of democracy and its more recent stagnation by asking why and how countries become democratic, what obstacles they face, how democratic they are, how likely they are to stay democratic, and how they can become more democratic.

Transitions to Democracy, Democratic Consolidation, and Democratic Backsliding

A **transition to democracy** is a regime change that results in a democracy, typically involving a negotiated process among major political actors in an authoritarian regime and their opponents who demand democracy. Transitions are often triggered by some particular event, such as a natural disaster, economic

transition to democracy: A regime change typically involving a negotiated process that removes an authoritarian regime and concludes with a founding election of a new, democratic regime

crisis, major change in the international context or international support of the old regime, massive civilian protests, or death of a personalist dictator. Reaction to the triggering event can come from within the regime or from society at large. Some of the elite supporting the existing authoritarian regime may decide to split from it if they see the costs of loyalty to the regime increase while the costs and risk of rebellion decrease. If a regime's inadequate response to a natural disaster, for instance, leads to massive protests in the streets, or if an economic crisis starves the regime of the resources it needs to co-opt key elites, a regime split may occur, and this is often the first step in a transition process. If opposition in society, motivated by some triggering event, coalesces into a large and well-organized social movement for democracy, the regime may split or may conclude that staying in power is no longer viable and attempt to negotiate a peaceful and safe exit for themselves.

In what many theorists consider the ideal model, reaction to the triggering event leads to a process of negotiation that results in a **pact**, an explicit agreement among the most important political actors in the regime and civil society to establish a new form of government. Whether this occurs depends in part on the relative strength of the key actors. If, for instance, a military regime does not split, it can often dictate the terms of its own exit; in Chile, for instance, General Augusto Pinochet agreed to return the country to democracy in 1989 but wrote a constitution that gave the military continued control over its own budget, the central bank, and 20 percent of the national Senate. A pact, or imposed democratic system like in Chile, ideally produces a new democratic constitution and founding election, the first democratic election in many years (or ever) that marks the completion of the transition process.

Creating a democracy is one thing; sustaining it over the long term is another. Political history is littered with democracies that reverted to authoritarian rule, from the Nazi takeover of Germany in 1932 to the military coup in Egypt in 2013 or President Viktor Orbán's slow undermining of democracy in Hungary in the early years of the twenty-first century. Transition theorists developed the concept of **democratic consolidation** to help analyze the sustainability of democracy, but there has been much dispute over the definition and utility of the concept. Intuitively, democratic consolidation is simply the idea that democracy has become widely accepted as the permanent form of political activity in a particular country. It has become "the only game in town," and all significant political elites and their followers accept democratic rules and are confident that everyone else does as well. This is important, because democracy requires faith that, in the future, any significant party or group might gain power via an election. If some major political actors do not believe that, they might be tempted to use nondemocratic means to gain power, fearing that their opponents will not give them a chance to win via free and fair elections in the future.

Knowing when a country has reached the point of democratic consolidation, however, is quite difficult. How can we know whether all the actors in the country have accepted democracy unquestionably? Huntington (1991) argued that a country must pass the "two-turnover test" before we can consider it a consolidated democracy: one party must win the founding election, and then a different party must win a later election and replace the first party. By this strict standard, West Germany did not become a consolidated democracy until 1969, India until 1980, Japan until 1993, Mexico until 2012, and South Africa still does not qualify. Other scholars rely on surveys to demonstrate that the elite and population as a whole express support for democratic values and democracy in their country in particular. Whatever measure is used, it's clear that many new democracies have not fully consolidated, and doing so can take not just years but decades.

pact: In a transition to democracy, a conscious agreement among the most important political actors in the authoritarian regime and those in civil society to establish a new form of government

democratic consolidation: The widespread acceptance of democracy as the permanent form of political activity; all significant political elites and their followers accept democratic rules and are confident everyone else does as well

Transition theorists look for evidence of democratic consolidation because they fear **democratic backsliding**: a decline in the quality of democracy, including the extent of participation, the rule of law, and vertical and horizontal accountability. This can ultimately result in democratic breakdown: the rise of a new authoritarian regime. During the third wave of democratization and since, few countries that have completed a transition to democracy have reverted to closed authoritarian regimes that allow no opposition. Some hold reasonably free and fair elections but do not abide by the full array of liberal rights and the rule of law, while others become electoral authoritarian regimes in which a ruling party rigs elections and manipulates institutions as necessary to stay in power, like Putin's regime in Russia. Questions about the quality of democracy, of course, apply to all democracies, not just recent ones. Two major NGOs, using distinct measures, both found in 2019 that democratic quality was actually declining most in long-established democracies in Europe and North America (Freedom House 2019; Lührmann et al. 2018).

Explaining Democratization, Consolidation, and Backsliding

Political scientists have used the full array of theories outlined in chapter 1 to try to explain democratic transitions and consolidation. As is so often the case, we can usefully divide the theoretical debate into approaches based on structures, culture and beliefs, and individual action. Structural arguments have focused on economic factors, political institutions, and international context.

Structures: Economic

Prior to the third wave, all but a handful of democracies were wealthy, Western countries. In the 1950s and 1960s, political scientists understandably followed the ideas of modernization theory, arguing that democracy could be sustained only in certain types of societies. Seymour Martin Lipset (1959) saw economic structure as the most important element, arguing that democracies arise only in countries with reasonably wealthy economies and a large middle class that is educated and has its basic needs securely met. In these societies, political competition is not too intense and therefore compromise, an essential component of democracy, is easier. Other scholars argued that political developments must occur in a particular sequence; for instance, a strong state and sense of national identity must emerge before a democracy can succeed.

During the third wave, democracy began breaking out in unexpected places. First southern European and then Latin American military dictatorships gave way to democracy. Then the end of the Cold War unleashed a new round of democracy creation, first in the former Communist countries of Eastern Europe and then in Africa and parts of Asia. According to modernization theories, these countries were far too poor, still faced questions about the strength of their state and national identity, and seemed not to have democratic cultures, yet here they were writing constitutions, holding elections, and establishing democracies. The limited success of many of these new democracies, however, led comparativists in the new millennium to revisit some of the ideas of modernization theory, using new and much more sophisticated research methods, as well as examining other economic variables such as economic crises and inequality.

Adam Przeworski and colleagues (2000) created a data set of 141 countries from 1950 to 1990, revisiting the key structural arguments: did socioeconomic

democratic backsliding: A decline in the quality of democracy, including the extent of participation, the rule of law, and vertical and horizontal accountability

development predict whether countries have transitions to democracy and how long those new democracies survive? They found a strong statistical relationship between development and the sustainability of democracy, arguing that "democracy is almost certain to survive in countries with per capita incomes above $4,000" (Przeworski et al. 2000, 273) but a very weak relationship between development and the likelihood that a country would have a transition to democracy. They concluded that in terms of predicting transitions, "modernization theory appears to have little, if any, explanatory power" (Przeworski et al. 2000, 137). Carles Boix and Susan Stokes (2003) challenged these findings, however. They used the same data but removed states that, during the Cold War, were tightly controlled by the Soviet Union and countries that were heavily dependent on oil wealth. They argued that both of these factors would prevent democracy from occurring and therefore should not be included in a test of modernization theory overall. Removing these countries from the data, they concluded that, for the countries on which the theory focuses—poor and middle-income countries—development does indeed make transitions to democracy more likely.

Many postcolonial countries going through transitions to democracy simultaneously went through market-oriented economic reform (see chapter 11), which, in the short term, often causes economic decline before it brings benefits. Theorists feared that negative economic effects might undermine popular support for democracy after a transition. Nancy Bermeo (2003) examined this hypothesis, looking at the breakdown of democracy in Europe before World War II and in Latin America in the 1960s. She found that the populace as a whole did not reject democracy in times of economic crisis, but, instead, key elites did. The military in Latin America, for instance, feared economic instability and put an end to democracy despite a lack of public support for their actions. A global quantitative analysis of third-wave democratization efforts found that poor economic performance of the incumbent regime was associated with both democratization and reversions of democracy to authoritarian rule—economic crisis produced regime change in either direction as the incumbent regime lost support (Haggard and Kaufman 2016). Crises can lead to regime change, but popular pressure is very rarely in favor of authoritarian rule. Rather, elites sometimes create authoritarian rule in the midst of a crisis.

Other theorists debated the effects of economic inequality on democratization. One school of thought argued that relatively unequal societies are unlikely to democratize because elites fear that if the impoverished majority gains the vote, they will use it to redistribute income, so the elites will fight to maintain authoritarian rule. In more equal societies, the elite will fear redistribution less, so they will be more willing to allow democratization (Acemoglu and Robinson 2006; Boix 2003). Stephan Haggard and Robert Kaufman (2016) examined this question in detail using a quantitative analysis of third wave democracies and found that inequality had no effect on the likelihood of successful democratization or democratic backsliding. Instead, institutional factors such as the old regime's repressiveness, the capacity of social movements to protest, a history of military coups, and the strength of political institutions, explain when protests demanding democracy arise and when democratization succeeds.

Structures: Political Institutions

Political institutions, then, in both the old regime and the new democracy, can affect both the transition to democracy and consolidation. Since World War II, military regimes have been shorter lived than other types of authoritarian regimes, increasing the possibility of democratic transition in those countries. They have been twice as likely to collapse as personalist regimes and three times as likely to collapse as dominant-party regimes (whether single-party or electoral authoritarian). Figure 9.3 shows what has happened when these different types of authoritarian regimes collapse. The collapse of military regimes is far more likely to result in democracy than the collapse of other types of authoritarian regimes. The explanation for these patterns rests in the domestic support the differing regimes typically have, their coercive ability, and the likely result they face if they leave office. Personalist leaders, for instance, are far more likely to face death, jail, or exile after a transition and therefore cling to power as long as possible, but they often have genuine support among particular sections of the country, sometimes due to ethnic or religious ties, that helps them stay in office. Ruling parties, in both one-party and electoral authoritarian regimes, often foster some institutionalized or ideological legitimacy that allows them to resist opposition longer. Military regimes are more likely to lack domestic support to help them stay in power but also are more likely to control effective repressive power and use it to negotiate a safe retirement for themselves and, as the Chilean example preceding showed, perhaps even a role in the new democracy (Escriba-Folch and Wright 2015, 42–64). Many more authoritarian regimes were military led during the Cold War than since, when electoral authoritarian regimes became the most common. This may help explain the dramatic success of the transitions to democracy in the 1990s as the Cold War ended. It may also explain the more meager gains in the new millennium, since the remaining electoral authoritarian regimes seem less likely to fall and less likely to become democratic if they do.

Weak political institutions in the old regime can also make a transition to democracy difficult. In the neopatrimonial regimes with exceptionally weak

FIGURE 9.3

What Happens After Authoritarian Regimes Fall

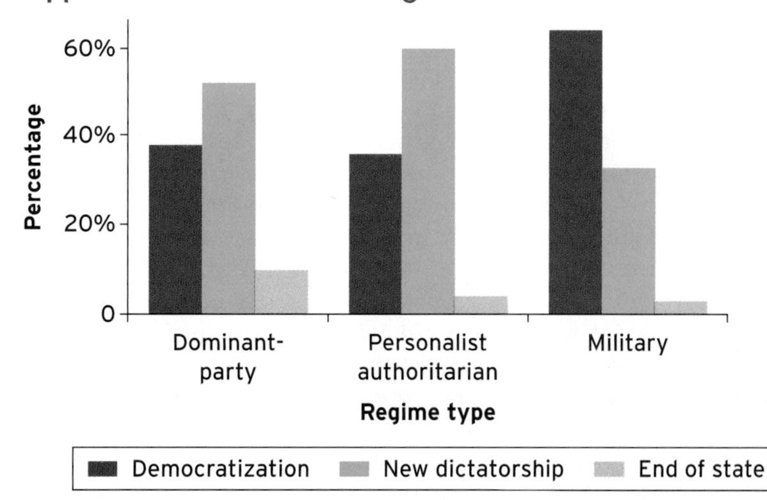

Source: Adapted from Erica Frantz, *Authoritarianism: What Everyone Needs to Know* (New York: Oxford University Press, 2018), 140

institutions in much of sub-Saharan Africa (see chapter 3), political competition was primarily about securing access to government resources for patronage. Pacts almost never happened because parties were little more than temporary vehicles for shifting coalitions of patrons trying to gain power, so parties had neither sufficient ideological disagreements nor enough stability to provide the credible commitments that pacts require. In the absence of pacts, incumbents typically did not liberalize their regimes completely, instead holding elections that were only partially free and fair. More often than not, they won those elections. Even when the opposition won, it was likely to create an electoral authoritarian regime in order to maintain its access to key resources (Bratton and van de Walle 1997). While almost all African countries experienced at least an attempted transition in the 1990s, only eight were "free" in 2019, while twenty-one were "partly free" and eighteen were "not free" (Freedom House 2019).

Kenya exemplifies the problems that Bratton and van de Walle delineated. A single ruling party, under two different presidents, controlled the country continuously from independence in 1963. By the mid-1970s, it had become a one-party, authoritarian regime. When the third wave came ashore in Africa in 1990, protests broke out in the capital demanding a return to multiparty politics. President Daniel arap Moi initially resisted forcefully, but when Western aid donors threatened to cut off foreign aid, he capitulated, allowing other parties to form and calling an election for December 1992. No negotiations or pact occurred, and Moi did not change any other aspect of the authoritarian regime, including partisan use of government resources and security forces. Moi handily won what Joel Barkan (1993) termed a "C- election" against an ethnically divided opposition. Civil society continued to demand a more complete transition, including a new constitution. Moi resisted but did agree to modest reforms with moderate members of the opposition ahead of the 1997 election, which he also won, though the quality of the election improved. The battle over the rules continued.

In 2002, Moi surprised many observers by retiring, but he tried to handpick his successor. Opposition forces finally coalesced across ethnic lines and defeated the incumbent party; power changed hands via the highest-quality election in the country's history. The ethnic coalition that came to power, however, quickly divided over sharing the spoils of office, and in 2007 the incumbent president rather obviously "stole" the election via fraudulent ballot counting. The worst ethnic violence in the country's history ensued, killing thousands and displacing hundreds of thousands. Ultimately, the UN brokered a negotiated agreement that avoided civil war and required writing a new constitution, put in place in 2010. In the 2012 election, the incumbent president completed his maximum two terms and retired. His preferred replacement won the election under the new constitution, keeping power in the hands of the same ethnic group, and the government since has reduced civil and political rights substantially in spite of the new constitution. It has also been at least as corrupt as prior governments. The 2017 election was even worse, with the supreme court ruling it unconstitutional and demanding it be rerun. The major opposition leader, however, refused to participate in the rerun because he said none of the problems in the process had been fixed, so the incumbent won handily, but his electoral legitimacy was severely undermined. By 2019, the same opposition leader came to a vague agreement to support the government, probably to gain access to patronage resources. Opposition parties and civil society have long demanded improved adherence to the rule of law and basic rights, which have never been firmly established in a country imbued with neopatrimonial patterns of authority, despite twenty-five years of electoral democracy.

The type of political institutions that are adopted during the transition can also affect the success of democratization. Juan Linz (1990) argued that the "perils of presidentialism" (see chapter 5) are particularly important in new democracies. Because new democracies are often deeply divided and competing elites do not fully trust one another or the new democratic institutions, consensus democracies with power-sharing mechanisms, such as coalition governments in parliamentary systems, are likely to help preserve democracy. In Africa, Jaimie Bleck and Nicholas van de Walle (2019) pointed to continued presidentialism as a key explanation for why multiparty elections have not produced improved democracy: incumbent presidents, many in power before competitive elections began, have used the resources of the executive branch to maintain power in ways that would be less likely in parliamentary systems. In other regions, though, presidential systems have succeeded, and differences among them may be important in explaining successful democratic consolidation. Latin American countries that adopted a two-round majoritarian system for electing the president in the early 1990s had stronger democracies twenty years later than neighboring countries with plurality elections for president. Cynthia McClintock (2018) argued this was because having a majority gave the president greater legitimacy and the system encouraged ideological moderation among candidates.

Longtime Kenyan opposition leader and presidential candidate Raila Odinga, far left, meets with the Independent Electoral and Boundaries Commissions to submit his candidacy papers for the August 8, 2017, election. Most observers saw Odinga's loss in 2007 as fraudulent. It set off weeks of violence that came close to civil war.
AP Photo/Sayyid Abdul Azim

Chapter 6 demonstrated the importance of political parties to any democracy. In new democracies, strong parties can form the basis of coherent and powerful opposition to the ruling party, before and after an initial transition. In Africa (Lebas 2011) and Eastern Europe (Gherghina 2015; Tavits 2013), historical legacies and conscious choices party leaders made to build their organizations made a difference to how strong parties were during and after a transition. Ironically, in Africa, stronger authoritarian leaders who were able to control the democratization process more fully provided incentives for opponents to form more institutionalized parties. The result was greater accountability and stability in the post-transition era (Reidl 2014). In Latin America, the most successful parties were forged in deep and sometimes violent conflict during the transition, or had strong historical legacies from earlier eras in the country (Levitsky et al. 2016).

After the initial transition, elections themselves may promote further democratization. Staffan Lindberg (2009) showed how elections in Africa can shift the balance of power between the ruling party and its opposition. Even limited elections allow the opposition to win some share of power. This gives dissidents within the ruling party a viable alternative and thus an incentive to defect to the opposition. When political leaders think an opposition coalition has a real chance to win, they become even more likely to join it, further strengthening its chances until a tipping point is reached at which a large opposition coalition emerges to win an election despite the incumbent's manipulation of the system, as in Kenya in 2002 (van de Walle 2006). But systematic analyses both in Africa and globally have found that more elections, even high-quality ones, do not improve the overall quality of democracy (Bleck and van de Walle 2019; Flores and Nooruddin 2016). Flores and Nooruddin argued that not just holding elections but the quality of the elections is important to democratic consolidation. As elections took place in poorer countries with less revenue, more ethnic heterogeneity, and less history of democracy, they were of lower quality and did not improve democracy.

Providing an overall assessment, Grigore Pop-Eleches and Graeme Robertson (2015) looked at structural factors in electoral authoritarian regimes—income level, ethnic and religious cleavages, and state capacity—and found that those with structural advantages on these key dimensions (more wealth, ethnic and religious homogeneity, and state capacity) are more likely to transition to democracy while those with structural disadvantages will more typically oscillate between democracy and some type of authoritarian rule.

Structures: International Context

The international context of any democratization process can be a structural factor helping or hindering a particular country's transition. As noted previously, the end of the Cold War resulted in a burst of democratization, in part because it removed the incentive for the superpowers to support "friendly" dictators. Some dictators, such as Mobutu Sese Seko in Zaire, lost power in part due to a dramatic decline of U.S. support. Others, such as the self-proclaimed Marxist regime in Ethiopia, lost power after their Soviet patrons literally disappeared.

Other, less direct international factors also affected democratization. Regimes more closely linked to the West tended to have more successful transitions (Levitsky and Way 2010), and a process of diffusion from one country to another also occurred. Democracy activists in one country would see and copy the successful practices in others, especially other countries with which they had a connection. Barbara Wejnert (2014) used a statistical modeling approach to demonstrate that diffusion was more important than any characteristics of individual countries in predicting democratization. Particularly in poorer countries, proximity to other democracies and interactions with neighboring countries significantly increased the likelihood of countries becoming democratic. International structure matters more, she argued, than domestic structures or culture.

Cultures and Beliefs

In *The Civic Culture* (1963, 1989), Gabriel Almond and Sidney Verba presented a culturalist version of modernization: democracy thrives only in countries that have "civic" (or democratic) political cultures. Citizens must value participation but defer to elected leaders enough to let them govern (see chapter 1). Ronald Inglehart and Christian Welzel (2005) used data from a global survey of citizen beliefs and concluded that culture, specifically "emancipative values" that emphasize freedom of expression and equality of opportunities, helped sustain democracy. Even controlling for earlier experience with democracy and prior economic development, countries with higher emancipative values in the early 1990s were much more likely to have stronger democracies after 2002. Hadenius and Teorell

(2005), however, using a different measure of democracy and different data set, found no relationship between emancipative values and levels of democracy. Clearly, the debate over modernization theory in both its structural and cultural forms remains unresolved.

As noted before, many scholars argued that another aspect of culture, ethnic division, produces a weaker sense of national unity and often bitter political intergroup competition that threatens to undermine democratic norms and institutions. These theorists predicted the third wave democracies were unlikely to last due to their ethnic diversity. A study by Steven Fish and Robin Brooks (2004) across approximately 160 countries, though, found no correlation between ethnic diversity and the strength of democracy. Christian Houle (2015), however, found that economic inequality among ethnic groups, not just the existence of ethnic diversity, harms democratic consolidation.

Individual Action

A long-established theory of which countries successfully established democracies focused on great democratic leaders who, especially at their outset, had the foresight to create democratic norms and processes. The American founding fathers, especially George Washington, and South Africa's Nelson Mandela are examples these theorists point to. Today, most political scientists reject these "great man" theories of democracy. Some, though, continue to point to the importance of leaders' attitudes and actions. Scott Mainwaring and Aníbal Pérez-Liñán, in a quantitative study of Latin America (2013), found that leaders' preferences for radical (of either the left or right) or moderate policies and normative commitment to democratic values predicted whether a democracy would survive better than measures of economic modernization did. Countries with leaders who had moderate policy preferences and strong commitments to democratic values had democracies that survived longer.

Rational choice theorists also argued that individual preferences and actions best explain how democracies emerge and survive. Well-institutionalized democracy provides all major political actors with a degree of participation, protection from the worst forms of repression, and the possibility that they can gain power at some point. Based on the experiences of the third wave, rational choice theorists argued that major political elites might choose democratization regardless of whether they really believed in democracy, so long as it served their interests. Even in the most recalcitrant authoritarian regime, some elites might see democratic transition as a viable choice if the stakes were high enough.

As we noted, transitions often begin with a triggering crisis of some kind that produces a surge of activity by civil society groups demanding fundamental political reforms. In response, regime elites often split internally, with hardliners wanting to repress any opposition and preserve the status quo, while softliners are willing to consider compromising with civil society groups to survive the crisis. Civil society itself often divides between radicals demanding immediate and complete democratization, and moderates, who are willing to compromise with the authoritarian government to make some gains. Rational choice models suggest that the calculus of a successful transition to democracy requires the softliners in the regime and the moderates in civil society to each gain the upper hand over their internal opponents and then negotiate with one another to establish new rules of the game. If regime hardliners or civil society radicals are too strong, democratization will fail.

TABLE 9.1

Theories of Democratic Transition

THEORY	EXPLANATIONS	KEY EMPIRICAL EVIDENCE
Structures: Economic	• Wealth and large middle class reduce stakes of politics and encourage democracy • Simultaneous democratization and market-oriented economic reform undermines democracy because economic reform is painful to citizenry • Inequality makes elites fear redistribution and therefore oppose democracy	• Democracy sustainable with per capita income above $4,000 • Wealth does predict democratization for countries not dependent on oil or the Soviet Union during the Cold War • Economic reform produces regime change, both toward and away from democracy • Inequality does not seem to reduce chances of democratization
Structures: Political Institutions	• Type and strength of prior regime affects democratization • Type of new democracy affects consolidation of democracy • Continued elections, even if flawed, can strengthen democratic consolidation	• Military regimes more likely to transition to democracy than authoritarian regimes with a ruling party • Presidentialism hurts democratic consolidation in Africa but not in Latin America with two-round elections • Strong political parties strengthen democratic consolidation • Elections strengthen democratic consolidation only if they are of high quality
Structures: International Context	• End of Cold War facilitated democratization • Diffusion from neighboring democracies helps democratic consolidation	• Third wave of democratization happened as Cold War ended • Diffusion of democratic models from neighboring countries increases likelihood of democratization
Culture and Beliefs	• Civic culture prerequisite for democratic consolidation • Ethnic diversity threatens democratic consolidation	• Evidence that emancipative values in 1990s produced democracy in the 2000s is ambiguous • Inequality among ethnic groups, not just ethnic diversity itself, threatens democratization
Individual Action	• Key leaders have to have democratic values to achieve democracy • Rational choice theory: Negotiated agreement among elites that creates institutions that all benefit from can create and sustain democracy in any context	• Latin American leaders' ideology and democratic values predicted democratic consolidation • Transitions in the third wave that involved pacts and cooperation produced higher quality and longer-lasting democracy

Most theorists argue that the regime and civil society have to be of roughly equal strength for the transition process to produce a full democracy as well. Softliners and moderates need to be real partners, or the transition may be merely superficial or weak. Sujian Guo and Gary Stradiotto (2014) examined the effects of the type of transition a country went through on the quality and durability of the subsequent democracy over its first ten years. Undertaking a quantitative analysis of all transitions since 1900, they found that those that they term "cooperative"—those that involved pacts and in which the opposition had enough power to influence the outcome of the pact—were of significantly higher quality and more likely to survive, as the rational choice approach would suggest.

African National Congress (ANC) supporters await the start of a campaign rally in 2016. South Africa's transition to democracy from 1990 to 1994 is seen as a model of the transition paradigm. Nelson Mandela's party, the ANC, has remained in power ever since, though, raising concerns about limited democracy in a dominant-party system. Opponents criticize the ANC for placing limits on political competition and for allowing corruption, but Freedom House still rates the country as "free." South African voters' allegiance to the party credited with ending apartheid is being tested, but the ANC won the 2019 general election, albeit with a diminished majority.
John Wessels/AFP/Getty Images

South Africa's transition to democratic rule in 1994 is a classic case of the transition process unfolding in a way these theorists saw as ideal. In the 1980s, the apartheid regime faced both widespread international sanctions and an increasingly violent and radical uprising on the streets of the black townships. It had tried modest liberalizations, such as allowing mixed-race people some minimal political participation, but this was met with more resistance. In 1990, newly elected President F. W. de Klerk shocked the nation and the world by announcing he was freeing Nelson Mandela from prison and lifting the ban on Mandela's party, the African National Congress (ANC). Faced with a crisis his government could not contain, de Klerk became a softliner who, after secret negotiations before the public announcement, came to see Mandela as a moderate with whom he could negotiate. Three years of negotiations for a new constitution ensued, with white hardliners and black radicals frequently and sometimes violently attacking the process and both political parties involved. Ultimately, though, Mandela and de Klerk held majority support of their respective communities and agreed on a pact, a new constitution that was then ratified by the population. On April 27, 1994, Nelson Mandela was elected president, ending the world's last bastion of legal racial segregation. The ANC has ruled ever since, though, which has raised questions about how fully democratic the society has really become. Nonetheless, Freedom House has continuously rated it as "free."

Modernization theorists might say that South Africa's successful transition was not surprising: as a middle-income country its level of socioeconomic development made democracy plausible. A much more surprising African success story was Ghana, a country with a history of military coups and a gross national income of only $1,590 per capita in 2016. As the third wave of democratization washed over Africa, Ghanaian military ruler Jerry Rawlings agreed to allow multiparty competition based on a new constitution that he and his aides wrote. Its presidential system concentrated power in the hands of the president. Rawlings won the subsequent election, which involved significant electoral fraud, and many feared Ghana's transition was following the typical path of a neopatrimonial regime toward electoral authoritarianism, not democracy. After that founding election, however, the electoral commission brought the major political leaders together to discuss rules for future elections. With the support of external aid, the leaders strengthened the national election commission itself. Ghana did not have a full pact, but working together to create electoral rules helped opposing leaders build trust in each other and in the political process in general. The next election in 1996 was fairer, reinforcing this trust. In 2000 Rawlings was constitutionally barred from running for a third term. He left office without resisting, and without Rawlings on the ticket, his party lost the election. Power changed hands from one elected leader to the next for the first time in Ghana's history. It passed the two-turnover test when power changed hands again via razor-thin election victories in 2008 and 2016. In contrast to many African countries, Ghana's democracy, though imperfect, is functioning well; Freedom House has long rated it as fully "free."

The 1980s and 1990s were the halcyon days of democratization, when it seemed that democracy was spreading to nearly every corner of the globe. Most Latin American countries and some Asian and African countries made apparently long-term transformations toward consolidated democracy. In many other cases, though, initial transitions have produced electoral authoritarian regimes, so the debates about democratic transitions, consolidation, and backsliding are far from settled, and comparativists have used our full array of theoretical approaches to try to understand these processes.

Regime Change: Transitions to Authoritarian Rule

In the new millennium, China has defied predictions by surviving and getting stronger as a fully authoritarian regime. Vladimir Putin has turned Russia's democracy into an electoral authoritarian regime and Turkey, Hungary, and Venezuela have followed a similar path to varying degrees. A recent quantitative analysis of increasing democratic backsliding, in fact, declared that a "third wave of autocratization" began shortly after the third wave of democratization did, and has expanded notably in the last decade (Lührmann and Lindberg 2019). Just as the third wave of democratization focused attention on democratic transitions, the third wave of authoritarianization has heightened attention to transitions back to authoritarianism. We noted earlier that democratic regimes virtually never directly replace prior democratic regimes. The same cannot be said for authoritarian regimes; new ones regularly replace prior ones. In fact, regime changes that replace one authoritarian regime with a new one are more common than changes in which an authoritarian regime replaces a democracy. In the post–Cold War era, though, the latter is becoming more common. Figure 9.4 shows us the mechanisms by which authoritarian regimes gain power. Coups are most common, but their frequency has declined in the post–Cold War era. Armed insurgencies, popular uprisings, and **authoritarianization**, the creation of an authoritarian regime via the undermining of democratic institutions by elected incumbents, have all become more common.

authoritarianization: The creation of an authoritarian regime via the undermining of democratic institutions by elected incumbents; has become more common.

Many of the theories that try to explain democratization may also explain the rise of authoritarian regimes. For modernization theorists, if income above a

FIGURE 9.4

How Authoritarian Regimes Seize Power

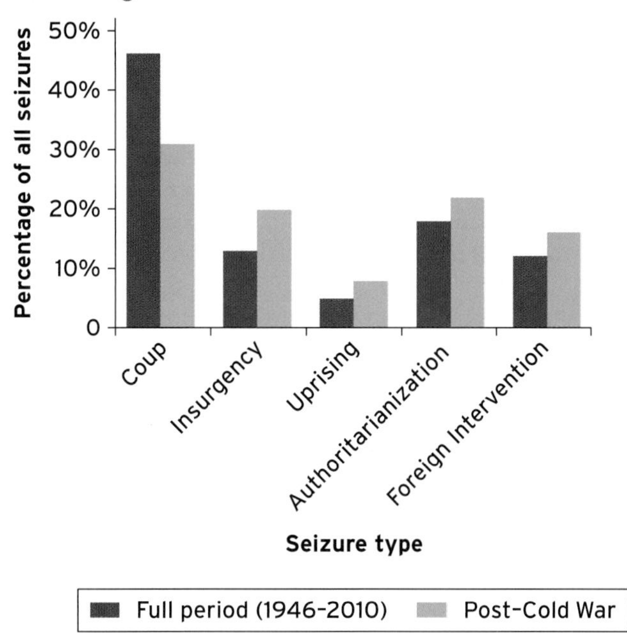

Source: Adapted from Erica Frantz, *Authoritarianism: What Everyone Needs to Know* (New York: Oxford University Press, 2018), 90.

certain level makes democracy more likely, income below that level makes authoritarian rule more likely. Political culture theorists argue that a lack of democratic culture would make it more likely that elites would want to overthrow a democracy and more likely that they would succeed because the bulk of the citizenry might not care. Rational choice theorists argue that if a balance of power doesn't exist and a successful bargain is not struck between an old regime and civil society groups demanding democracy, a new authoritarian regime is a likely outcome. All these theories, though, have also been applied in more specific ways to the main mechanisms that produce authoritarian rule: military coups, revolution (which can encompass both military insurgencies and popular uprising in Figure 9.4), and authoritarianization—the potential end result of democratic backsliding.

Military Coups

All modern states must have a military and maintain effective control over it to maintain sovereignty. Americans generally view the military as an apolitical organization firmly under civilian control. In reality, no military is completely apolitical. When President Barack Obama decided that he wanted to get the U.S. military out of Iraq and reduce its presence in Afghanistan, various military leaders made it clear they disagreed with those decisions. When congressional committees consider the U.S. defense budget, they hold hearings and listen to the advice of top military leaders, among others. These are both examples of the military engaging in political activity. The key is that a regime with effective control over the military, whether democratic or authoritarian, keeps such activities within institutionalized limits: the military does not go beyond the bounds set by the civilian leadership.

When it does, a constitutional or political crisis can arise. We now examine the most flagrant military intervention in politics, the coup d'état, in which the military forcibly removes the existing regime and establishes a new one.

When American students are asked why the military does not stage a coup in the United States, the first answer is usually that the Constitution prevents it. The elected president is commander in chief, and the military must obey him. But given that the Constitution is a piece of paper and the president is one unarmed person whereas the U.S. military is arguably the most powerful force on the planet, there must be more to it. In fact, civilian regimes, whether democratic or authoritarian, go to great lengths to ensure that their militaries are loyal to the regime's ideals and institutions. Civilian leaders try to inculcate the appropriate values in the military leadership, either professional values specific to the military or more general values that are supportive of the regime and that reflect the broader political culture. Well-established democracies train military leaders carefully in military academies, such as West Point in the United States or Sandhurst in Britain, to instill professional values that portray the military as prestigious and apolitical. Since military personnel come out of society as a whole, a strong system of political socialization throughout the society that ingrains respect for the major political institutions also helps to ensure that military leaders have those same values. Communist systems attempted to achieve the same ends via direct Communist Party involvement in the military, mandatory party membership for the military leadership, and, like democracies, political socialization in the broader society.

Less-institutionalized authoritarian regimes often lack these types of generally effective and systematic mechanisms. As we saw in chapter 8, military leaders often control what are in effect armed factions. They represent the threat of a regime change from the existing authoritarian regime to a new one, with a new supreme leader. Supreme leaders therefore must engage in what is known as "coup-proofing": co-opting major armed factions, counterbalancing them by creating multiple military institutions, or relying on informal ties of loyalty within the military, such as ethnic affiliations. Many African personalist rulers created a well-equipped and well-paid presidential guard from the same ethnic group or region as the president, which was personally loyal to the president as an individual patron. The job of this presidential guard was mainly to protect the president from his own army.

Military coups occur when all efforts to keep the military loyal to (or at least under the control of) the regime fail. When coups first became common in postcolonial countries in the 1960s, the dominant explanation followed modernization theory, focusing not on the military itself but instead on the societies and political systems in which the coups occurred. Samuel Huntington contended that "the most important causes of military intervention in politics are not military . . . but the political and institutional structure of the society" (1968, 194). The military, these theorists argued, intervened to restore order when civilian leaders had weakened the civilian regime via corrupt and incompetent rule. They saw the military, with its training and hierarchical organization, as one of the few modern institutions in postcolonial societies and believed it could rule in the national interest, reestablishing order and restarting development, as modernizing authoritarianism regimes promised (see chapter 3).

A second school of thought looked not at society but within the military as an institution. These theorists argued that a military engages in a coup to advance its own institutional interests, such as getting larger budgets, higher pay, or better equipment (Huntington 1964; Janowitz 1964). Military leaders may also instigate a coup in response to what they perceive as unjustified civilian intervention in military matters, such as the appointment of top officers without the military's approval. Military leaders may see a coup in these situations as a defense of their professional status vis-à-vis civilian leaders. In effect, the military in this theory is just another interest group clamoring for power and position within the government, but one with guns.

A third major explanation for coups, originally focusing on Africa, sees coups as coming from factional divisions not only between civilian and military leaders but within the military itself. Samuel Decalo (1976, 14–15) described the typical African military as "a coterie of distinct armed camps owing primary clientelist allegiance to a handful of mutually competitive officers of different ranks seething with a variety of corporate, ethnic and personal grievances." Decalo argued that most coups occurred because particular military leaders wanted to gain power for their own interests, those of their ethnic group or region, or those of their faction within the military. Coups were about gaining a greater share of power and resources for the coup leaders and their clients, not about the interests of society as a whole or even "the military" as an institution. Barbara Geddes and colleagues (2018), using a quantitative analysis of a new data set on authoritarian rule and how it arises, also concluded that coups arise from military officers' own interests, whether institutional or based on factions. Regimes, whether democratic or authoritarian, in which the top leadership shared "experiences, values, ideas, or friendship" (57) with key military leaders were less likely to suffer coups. Ethnic heterogeneity in the military, on the other hand, produced more coups, reflecting likely divisions and factions within the military.

All of these theories provide motives for why coups are attempted. Naunihal Singh (2014) pointed out that only about half of all coups succeed. Coups require a high-risk conspiracy to overthrow a regime. Singh argued they are "coordination games": military leaders are most likely to support a coup if they think it will be successful, regardless of their personal opinions. He showed that coups led by the top of the military hierarchy succeeded about two-thirds of the time, those led from the middle ranks succeeded 42 percent of the time, and those from the lower ranks only 28 percent of the time (Singh 2014, 71). He argued that this is because top leaders can control communications and convince the rest of the military they will succeed. Similarly, past successful attempts, especially recent ones, will lead them to believe the new attempt will succeed. Lower-level military leaders are rebelling against not just the government but the military hierarchy itself, making it more difficult for them to convince their fellow members of the armed forces that they will be successful, so they have less support and therefore fail more often. Similarly, coup-proofing by creating multiple and rival military groups makes coups less likely to succeed (DeBruin 2017).

The coup attempt in Turkey in 2016 illustrates this dynamic. Prior to that attempt, Turkey had seen numerous coups over the years, most recently in 1997. Typically, the military has seen itself as defender of the secular tradition established by the country's founder, Kemal Atatürk, after World War I. Whenever an Islamist-oriented group gained too much power, the military would step in to remove it and restore democracy relatively quickly, after suppressing Islamist groups. The top of the military hierarchy led most of the coups, so they were both successful and bloodless; little opposition was possible. The Islamist party in power since 2003, however, managed to avoid military intervention, initially by being more moderate than past Islamists and then by a successful purge of much of the military leadership, replacing its secularist officers with those more willing at least to tolerate the moderate Islamist government. As the party's leader, Recep Tayyip Erdoğan, became more autocratic, secularists became increasingly concerned.

While the exact leadership and intent of the coup attempt in July 2016 is unclear, the top military leadership did not take part. Middle- and lower-level officers

CRITICAL INQUIRY

Coups and Coup Attempts Around the World

Naunihal Singh (2014) argued that coups are more likely to succeed when they are led by top military leaders and in countries that have had successful coups in the past. Map 9.2 shows coups and coup attempts around the world since World War II. The maps use categorized data, but the detailed data show Iraq leading the world with sixteen coup attempts but only one success; Sudan is second with eleven attempts and four successes. Other countries, such as Colombia, have had only one attempt, but it was successful. Also note the countries that are gray in both maps, meaning they

MAP 9.2

Coup and Coup Attempts, 1946-2015

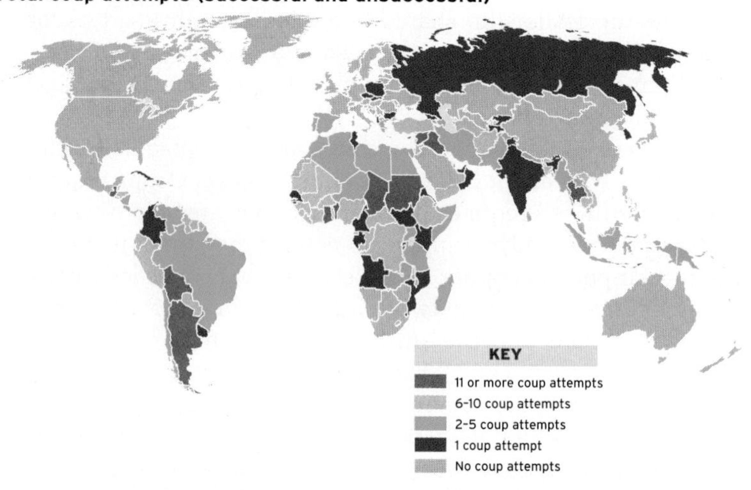

Successful coups

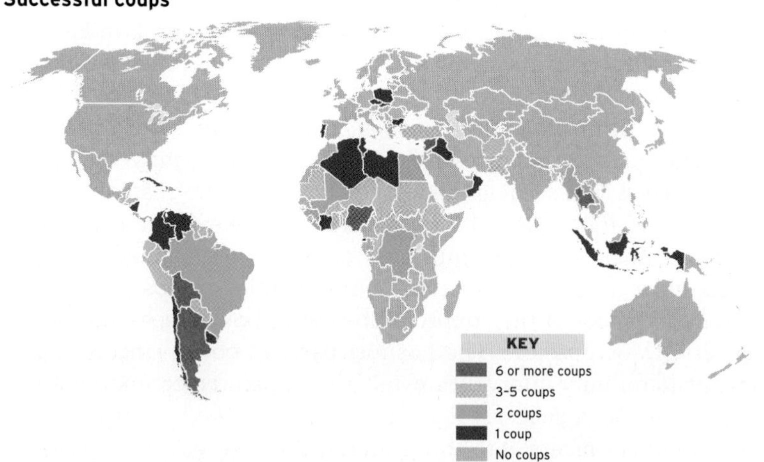

Source: Data for the maps are from Monty Marshall and Donna Ramsey Marshall, "Coup D'Etat Events, 1946-2015," Center for Systemic Peace, http://www.systemicpeace.org/inscrdata.html

have had no attempts or no successes. Compare the two maps for specific countries, especially those that have had more attempts than successes. What trends do you see in terms of where and when coups have happened and their success rates? Can you formulate hypotheses other than Singh's to explain these trends? How would you try to determine which hypothesis best explains why coups occurred and when, where, and why they succeeded or failed?

were leading the rebellion and were met with armed opposition from other military forces loyal to the president. The government reportedly knew in advance of the coup plot, so the rebels were forced to launch the coup earlier than planned. They failed to capture Erdoğan or all of the media outlets, allowing Erdoğan to speak with the media initially via FaceTime on his cell phone. He urged his civilian supporters to pour into the streets to oppose the coup and was able to communicate with top generals as well. In less than twenty-four hours, the coup was defeated. Within a week, at least fifty thousand government employees—in the military, judicial system, and education system—were arrested, with an estimated eighty thousand eventually losing their jobs. Erdoğan blamed supporters of a former ally who were known to hold positions throughout the government, including the military. Indeed, some of the rebellious military leaders rose in the ranks after Erdoğan's earlier removal of more secular officers he didn't trust (Arango and Yeginsu 2016). Whatever the motives for the coup, though, the rebels conspicuously failed at the "coordination game": Erdoğan was able to communicate strength rather than the rebels doing so, and most of the military and civilians (including opposition parties) supported the government against the coup.

As Turkey demonstrates, it is often difficult to discern which theory best explains a particular coup. Military leaders invariably claim that they intervened to save the nation from corruption and incompetence and to provide unity to pursue development. Their subsequent rule often betrays them as having other motives. Once again, the distinction between mechanisms and outcomes of regime change matters. A coup by an institutionalized military is likely to produce an institutionalized and relatively united military regime. A coup coming from a more factionalized military is likely to produce a more personalist regime. In some of these cases, as we argued in chapter 8, the new supreme leader may ultimately create a ruling party to co-opt potential rival elites, leading to a one-party or electoral authoritarian regime.

The complexities of explaining coups is clear in the classic case of Brazil. The origins of its 1964 coup can be traced to the creation of an elite military academy after World War II, the Escola Superior de Guerra (ESG), or Superior War College. Its faculty developed what came to be known as the National Security Doctrine in the 1950s, which envisioned national security as including not just protection from foreign aggression but also economic development and prevention of domestic insurrection. In 1961 leftist president João Goulart seemed intent on reforming Brazil's very unequal society: strengthening labor unions, redistributing land, and providing greater benefits to the urban working classes. He clashed with both the military elite and the conservative majority in the National Congress. As he failed to get his policies passed through the National Congress and faced growing opposition within the military, he became more populist. To try to gain greater military loyalty, he replaced several senior military officers who opposed him with others who were more supportive, thus dividing the military itself. When junior navy

Turkish prime minister Tayyip Erdoğan attends a ceremony with his top military leadership in 2010. After the failed July 2016 coup attempt, led mostly by midlevel officers, Erdoğan conducted a major purge of the military. He detained as many as ten thousand military personnel and dishonorably discharged nearly two thousand in the first two weeks after the coup attempt. Turkey has the second largest military in NATO after the United States and has been actively involved in the Syrian civil war, making instability in its military and government of great concern around the world.
Adem Altan/AFP/Getty Images

officers revolted against their superiors, demanding the right to unionize, Goulart supported them.

The night after Goulart proclaimed his support for the naval officers, the military moved to take over the reins of government in a largely bloodless coup it dubbed the "Revolution." The coup clearly was led from the top as a united effort, and with quiet U.S. support, meaning coordination of its efforts was easy. The regime it subsequently created was strongly institutionalized and based heavily on the National Security Doctrine. Several explanations for the coup have been put forward. The best known is Guillermo O'Donnell's (1979) argument that the coup came about because of economic contradictions that the democratic government could not resolve. If capitalist industrialization was to continue, it required a repressive government to force a growing working class to accept low wages. An elected government could not do this politically, so the military stepped in, under the auspices of its National Security Doctrine, to take the necessary steps. Other analysts, however, have noted that the coup itself was caused just as much by Goulart's direct threat to the military hierarchy. By removing military officers who opposed him and especially by supporting junior officers who wanted to unionize, Goulart was interfering with the autonomy of the military itself (Roett 1978). It is entirely possible, of course, that these two sets of factors (economic pressures plus threats to the autonomy of the military) dovetailed, coming together to give the military the incentive and justification to intervene and set Brazilian politics on a fundamentally different course.

Revolution

In chapter 7, we defined a political revolution as a fundamental transformation of an existing regime, instigated and primarily carried out by a social movement or armed group. Social revolutions go even further, transforming not just a regime but the entire social order. Both are regime changes, often but not always violent. Revolutions are a rare mechanism of regime change; on the continent of Africa alone, there have been more than eighty military coups since 1960, whereas only a small number of revolutions have occurred anywhere in the world. We examined the explanations for why revolutions occur in chapter 7; here, we discuss their outcomes.

Aside from some of the former Communist countries of eastern Europe, the general outcome of social revolutions has been fairly consistent: authoritarian rule and the creation of stronger states. Postrevolutionary governments have taken various forms, based in part on the ideological beliefs of their revolutionary leaders, but few have become enduring democracies directly after the revolution. This was

The Arab Spring: Revolution, Democratization, or None of the Above?

In chapter 7, we briefly discussed the Arab Spring as a case of contentious politics, trying to explain why and how protests suddenly exploded across the region. Here we look at the outcomes of those protests: what regime changes did they produce, and why? By 2019, Tunisia was seen as the "success story" in that it had an elected government; Freedom House rated it as "free," and Polity IV scored it as a democracy, though barely. Egypt initially appeared to be following a similar, though less certain, path until the military coup of 2013 created a new authoritarian regime that Freedom House rated as "not free" and Policy IV as an electoral authoritarian regime (though just one point from fully authoritarian). Syria, Libya, and Yemen descended into civil wars. Protests broke out in other Arab countries as well, but as the table shows, none saw a regime change or war; instead, the old regime successfully repressed the protests. How can we explain the different trajectories regime change took in these countries?

Outcomes Since 2011

	FREEDOM HOUSE SCORE, 2019	POLITY IV DEMOCRACY SCORE, 2017*	REGIME TRANSITION SINCE 2011
Algeria	Not free	3	Coup to stop uprising (2019)
Bahrain	Not free	0	None
Egypt	Not free	0	Electoral democracy (2011–2013) Electoral authoritarian (2013–)
Iran	Not free	0	None
Iraq	Not free	6	None
Jordan	Partly free	2	None
Kuwait	Partly free	0	None
Lebanon	Partly free	6	None
Libya	Not free	Interregnum	Civil war
Morocco	Partly free	1	None
Oman	Not free	0	None
Qatar	Not free	0	None
Saudi Arabia	Not free	0	None
Sudan	Not free	0	Coup to stop uprising (2019)
Syria	Not free	0	Civil war
Tunisia	Free	7	Electoral democracy (2013)
Turkey	Not free	4	Electoral authoritarian (2017–)
United Arab Emirates	Not free	0	None
Yemen	Not free	Interregnum	Civil war

*Higher number means more democratic.

(Continued)

(Continued)

A key element was the role of negotiations and the ability of opposing political forces to create a pact. Key actors in most of the countries of the Arab Spring included the military, secular opposition forces, and Islamist groups who, to varying degrees, seemed willing to participate in a democratic process. The transition in Tunisia came to be known as the Jasmine revolution and could certainly be considered a political revolution, in that a movement from within society forced fundamental regime change. But in fact, negotiations were crucial to establishing a democracy. While the dictator did flee in the face of a massive uprising, democracy emerged from a subsequent pact creating a new constitution. Stepan (2012) noted that exiled secular and Islamist opposition leaders had been meeting secretly in Europe for several years and therefore knew and trusted one another. This allowed them to negotiate a pact with the military that created the new regime relatively seamlessly, creating a PR electoral system that ensured all significant parties would be well represented in parliament. While the process had tense moments, it ultimately produced a new constitution and democracy in which elections have been free and fair, though not all individual rights are fully respected and the rule of law remains weak.

In Egypt, military leaders initially took full control after the dictator was forced out. The military pushed through enough constitutional changes to hold elections but preserved significant control for themselves. The secular and Islamist forces (the Muslim Brotherhood) had not worked together at all and did not trust one another or the military. The single-member district (SMD) elections gave the Muslim Brotherhood dominant power in the elected bodies, but the military still retained great autonomy, and the judiciary—still full of the appointees from the old regime—ruled important elements of the new constitution illegal. Crucially, the Supreme Constitutional Court annulled the initial parliamentary election and forced the parliament to disband. In response, President Mohamed Morsi, a member of the Muslim Brotherhood, declared in November 2012 that he would rule by decree until the new constitution was fully implemented and new elections held. The Brotherhood's opponents ultimately walked out of the negotiations for a permanent constitution, which the Morsi government nonetheless completed and the citizenry ratified via a referendum.

At this point, the legitimacy of all political institutions was seriously questioned by at least some major political actor, and a deep chasm had clearly developed between the Muslim Brotherhood and more secular political forces. In response to Morsi's pushing through a new constitution, the military intervened in July 2013, ousting Morsi from power and severely constricting civil and political rights, including banning the Muslim Brotherhood and arresting most of its leaders. The secular forces that initiated the original uprising in 2011 at least initially supported the coup, fearing the Muslim Brotherhood more than they did the military.

Clearly, the military was a crucial player in both countries. Both Egypt's and Tunisia's authoritarian regimes were relatively institutionalized, with coherent militaries. The Mubarak regime gave top military elites significant business opportunities so they initially wanted to defend him, but lower-ranking officers were not benefiting, and the top military leaders realized they could not completely control their troops if they tried to defend the regime against the mobilized populace. The Tunisian military had not benefited nearly as much from Ben Ali's rule so were more willing to move against him (Nassif 2015). In both cases, the old rulers gave up power, not when the protesters went into the streets but when the military decided to support the protesters to protect its own interests vis-à-vis the regimes' top leaders. The willingness or ability of the military to negotiate a pact with opposition forces ultimately determined the different outcomes in the two cases.

The regimes in Libya and Syria were both much more personalist and divided. When protests broke out in Libya, the regime responded with repression, but in the eastern region, which had never supported the dictator Muammar el-Qaddafi, protesters took over the major city and essentially declared themselves free of the regime. The military, like society at large, was divided by regional and kinship loyalties. Qaddafi responded with military force, knowing he had the personal support of at least some of the military, but other elements of the military broke off and formed independent militia, igniting the civil war. With Western support, the militia eventually gained control of the entire country. A new government was put in place and elections held, but it remained extremely weak, ultimately descending into renewed civil war, in large part because many of the militia remained independent; the state had not fully restored its monopoly on the legitimate use of force.

The Syrian regime responded forcefully to protesters as well, which led to the creation of independent militia and the start of the civil war. Syrian society was divided along sectarian lines and some military personnel broke with the regime but most did not, enabling the regime to hold out much longer than in Libya (and the West, for strategic reasons, chose not to intervene). In still other countries, such as Bahrain, the military held firm with the regime and was united, so protests were crushed.

The Arab Spring produced different outcomes in different places in part because of the nature of the authoritarian regimes and particularly the militaries at the heart of them. The rather modest differences in the socioeconomic and cultural characteristics of the countries in the region lend little support to modernization theory as an explanation of the different types of regime change. The distinct paths taken by the transitions to new regimes in Tunisia and Egypt, though, demonstrate key elements of the transition paradigm, particularly the importance of a pact to establish a new order to which all major political forces could agree.

true even in countries such as France, where many of the revolution's leaders were liberals. Political revolutions' outcomes vary a little more; some lead to democracy, though that is by no means certain, even though it is often the stated goal of the key revolutionary groups.

Scholars account for these outcomes by pointing out the extremely difficult political circumstances facing postrevolutionary governments. The entire regime and sometimes the social structure have been overthrown, so new ones must be created. Many revolutions are at least partly violent, and the new regime must re-create the state's monopoly on the use of force. Postrevolutionary societies are almost by definition deeply divided along ideological lines; the new leadership is committed to a particular ideological blueprint of what the new regime should look like, while many followers do not fully share this commitment. All of these factors lead post-revolutionary leaders to brook little dissent and to view any opposition as a threat to the revolution. As revolutionary leaders consolidate their power and eliminate their enemies, they create stronger states as well, at least in the short to medium term.

Political revolutions have more mixed results than do social revolutions. The former do not overthrow the entire social order and are often less violent, so many postrevolutionary divisions are not as difficult to overcome. One key question is the military's response to popular uprisings. If the military remains united and favors or opposes the revolutionary forces, they are likely to determine the success of the revolution. In the Arab Spring of 2011, the militaries of both Egypt and Tunisia remained united and turned against the old dictators, but the Egyptian military had long had a much stronger political role than the Tunisian one. Egypt's military overthrew its nascent democracy in 2013, while Tunisia's military allowed its democracy to survive. Militaries that are more unified help prevent civil war; those that have benefited from the old regime are less likely to side with a potential revolution; and those that view the old regime as increasingly illegitimate, especially in the face of large-scale protest, are more likely to side with protesters and help remove the dictator (Barany 2016). As Egypt and Tunisia show, however, the ultimate outcome remains uncertain. In 2019, military leaders forced long-standing dictators in Algeria and Sudan out of office in the face of massive popular uprisings, but it remained unclear what new regimes would ultimately replace them.

When the military does support a revolution, new political institutions have to be put in place quickly, making regime outcomes uncertain. The "color revolutions" that peacefully replaced several sitting governments between 2000 and 2005, most famously in Ukraine and Georgia, are good examples. In Ukraine, the "Orange Revolution" averted what appeared to be a deterioration of a minimally democratic regime and installed a more popular leader. It also eventually resulted in a Russian annexation of the disputed region of Crimea and "soft invasion" of a larger section of the eastern part of the country, instigating a war of secession that crippled the state in that region. The "Rose Revolution" in Georgia seemed more successful, helping to move Georgia from what had become an electoral authoritarian regime to a flawed but nonetheless democratic one, including making significant constitutional changes. It also, however, lost effective sovereignty in part of its territory to Russian-backed separatists.

Authoritarianization

Authoritarianization of an existing democracy is a more common mechanism of regime change than revolution but less common than coups; it is also becoming more frequent as the third wave of democratization ebbs. It involves a typically slow erosion of democratic institutions by an elected leader or party. It begins with democratic backsliding, under which initial changes in democratic institutions or norms lower the quality of democracy but do not destroy it. Democratic backsliding does not always result in authoritarianization. It can, however, as the undermining of key elements of democracy accumulates, resulting in increasing power in the hands of the incumbent executive and his key allies. While the distinction between a very weak democracy and an electoral authoritarian regime is not always clear, at some point, often after the fact, it becomes clear that the supreme leader and ruling party cannot be removed from office; the process of authoritarianization is complete.

Authoritarianization can take various paths but almost always includes institutional changes such as (1) undermining institutions, especially the judiciary, by placing individuals personally loyal to the chief executive in key positions; (2) controlling the media either directly via regime suppression of free expression or, more typically, manipulating laws to ensure the leader's allies gain control of major media outlets; (3) manipulating electoral rules to favor the leader and ruling party; (4) changing the constitution to give the leader more power, such as the ability to declare emergency decrees or a lengthened term in office; and (5) harassing civil society and opposition parties via lawsuits to undermine them and deplete their resources (Frantz 2018, 94–97).

Authoritarianization, though, can also begin with the undermining of informal norms of democracy, not just formal institutions. In *How Democracies Die*, Steven Levitsky and Daniel Ziblatt defined norms as "shared codes of conduct that become common knowledge within a particular community or society—accepted, respected, and enforced by its members" (2018, 101). They argued that written rules and formal institutions can never regulate every situation or ensure that all elements of democracy remain strong. The acceptance of key norms, especially among the political elite, is essential to the prevention of democratic backsliding that can ultimately become authoritarianization. In the case of the United States, for instance, they saw two norms as key: (1) mutual toleration, "the understanding that competing parties accept one another as legitimate rivals," and (2) forbearance, "the idea that politicians should exercise restraint in deploying their institutional prerogatives" (2018, 8). Without these, they suggested, partisan rivalry will become more extreme and efforts to use institutions for partisan purposes will undermine democratic legitimacy. They pointed to examples such as the use of the filibuster in the Senate, when the minority party seeks to prevent almost all majority legislation from passing; the removal of the filibuster when doing so favors the majority party; and presidential executive orders to enact policies when Congress is unwilling to do so.

As part of their examination of political culture and norms, Levitsky and Ziblatt's argued increasing polarization undermines the norm of mutual toleration, weakening democracy. Milan Svolik (2018) showed that a rational choice approach can help explain why polarization undermines democracy, using data from Venezuela, a country that went through the process in the new millennium. He argued that as voters become more polarized, their preference for their preferred candidate increases. When those candidates undermine democratic institutions, for example by manipulating the electoral system in their favor, their voters face a dilemma: supporting their preferred candidates or their professed democratic norms. Greater polarization means greater preference and loyalty to their candidates and opposition to their opponents, which Svolik found leads even those with strongly stated democratic values to support their candidates even when the candidates have undermined democratic institutions.

These processes of polarization, democratic backsliding, and ultimately authoritarianization typically start with a particular leader, often a populist. Populism (see chapter 7) propagates the beliefs that traditional political elites are unpatriotic and corrupt, that the country therefore faces a crisis, that the media and experts cannot be trusted, and that therefore only a strong leader can save the country (Frantz 2018, 99–101). Recep Erdoğan of Turkey and Viktor Orbán of Hungary are two such leaders.

In 2019, Freedom House lowered Turkey's rating from "partly free" to "not free" and Hungary's from "free" to "partly free." The two countries are at different places on what seems to be a similar path of authoritarianization. Both of their leaders, Erdoğan in Turkey and Orbán in Hungary, were elected prime minister when their parties won "landslide" victories during economic crises that destroyed the political support of the previous governments. While Turkey had a proportional representation electoral system and Hungary had a mixed system similar to Japan's (see chapter 6), both were designed in ways that made them significantly disproportional, producing their "landslides." Erdoğan's party won about 34 percent of the votes in 2002, and Orbán's party won just over half the votes in 2010, but both garnered about two-thirds of the parliamentary seats. Both rode to power on the basis of local versions of populist ideology. Erdoğan championed a moderate Islamism popular with many lower-income and less-educated Turks against the secularism of the country's elite. Orbán championed an anti-EU, anti-Semitic, and anti-immigrant Christian nationalism.

Once in power, both leaders set out to reduce the power of possible opponents, who were divided among many small parties. Many initially saw Erdoğan as improving democracy because he expanded devout Muslims' ability to express their faith publicly and reduced the power of Turkey's military, which had carried out several coups in the name of preserving secularism. His success in removing military leaders, however, allowed him to put his own loyalists in their place, which would help him survive the 2016 coup attempt we discussed earlier. The first signs of democratic backsliding came in 2009 but accelerated after large demonstrations against Erdoğan's government in 2013. In 2014, his parliamentary majority successfully silenced a corruption inquiry that threatened the government, effectively eliminating the parliament's role in holding the executive accountable; Erdoğan was then able to remove dozens of police officers and prosecutors who had pursued the inquiry.

Having served as prime minister since 2002, Erdoğan passed a referendum through parliament and a popular vote in 2010 that created a directly elected president, a position that he won in 2014. His party lost an outright majority in parliament in 2015, indicating the possibility of continued democracy, but a divided opposition could not form a government, so Erdoğan continued to rule. After the 2016 coup attempt, he again succeeded in amending the constitution, this time more fundamentally, creating a presidential system with very strong presidential powers. The 2016 coup attempt, which was widely unpopular, enhanced his power, allowing him to declare a state of emergency, remove tens of thousands of perceived opponents from government positions, replace them with his loyalists, and shut down numerous media outlets. By the 2017 referendum on the new presidential system, his opponents had little media access; Erdoğan won both that and the 2018 presidential election. While his margins of victory were not large, divided opposition and his control over most media assured his victories. In 2019, his party lost an election for mayor of Istanbul, one of the most important offices in the country and a base of Erdoğan's support. Rather than accept the results, he challenged it with the electoral commission, run by his supporters, and the election was re-done, but the opposition still won. It was a rare and important loss for Erdoğan. While he faces an active opposition protesting the decline of democracy, and a major rival in the new mayor of Istanbul, he still has the tools needed to stay in power for a long time.

Viktor Orbán wasted little time in moving to change the Hungarian constitution the year after he gained power. His two-thirds majority in parliament wrote an entirely new constitution in 2011 that expanded the Constitutional Court so Orbán could appoint his loyalists to it and strengthened the executive's power over the judiciary, the Central Bank, and the media. Orbán has since been able to replace many retired judges with new ones loyal to him. His allies and government pressure via a new media regulatory body purchased or forced the closing of many independent media outlets, leaving most of the press supporting the ruling party. A law restricting foreign-funded NGOs reduced the power of major groups in civil society, and a similar one closed the country's most prestigious university, founded by émigré George Soros. The government also revised the electoral system to make it more majoritarian, enhancing the electoral prospects of Orbán's party, the biggest in the country. By the time of the 2014 and 2018 elections, in which Orbán preserved his two-thirds parliamentary majority, the media landscape heavily favored the ruling party, and the party used government resources in its campaign. Both Orbán and Erdoğan were elected in to power and have been reelected. Both clearly have popular support in significant parts of society. But both used that support to undermine democratic institutions and weaken opposition to their continued rule.

Conclusion

Regime change is a difficult process to understand and predict. By definition, it lies outside the realm of "normal" politics. Instead, it is a period of intense politicization and rapidly unfolding events. This makes it an exceptionally fascinating area of comparative politics to study, and many comparativists have done so. Many questions remain, however.

Regime change affects who rules, but not only in the ways that might be expected. At least in theory, democratization produces regimes in which citizens rule. How true that is, of course, depends on the quality of the democracy that emerges. Sometimes, though, a democracy does not emerge at all. Similarly, a seemingly united revolutionary front in the interests of the people can result in leaders imposing their own vision on society and demobilizing popular participation in the new regime. In politics, those who fight for change do not necessarily get what they seek. The military holds the guns on which the state and regime rely and therefore can intervene directly if it chooses, putting itself in power. But militaries, even highly institutionalized ones, are not designed to rule. Every military regime relies on civilian support to some extent, especially within the state itself.

The often chaotic process of regime change continues to limit comparativists' predictive powers. Some cases, such as Ghana, defy the odds, producing democracy where theorists would least expect it. Consolidating a new democracy is an extremely challenging process. Partly for this reason, comparativists for years believed that democracy would only survive in very specific kinds of countries. That position was challenged by the "transition paradigm," which argued that democracy could survive anywhere. More careful recent scholarship suggests that while democracy can arise anywhere, its chances of survival are definitely higher in favorable cultural and economic contexts. The process can be easily undermined by institutional breakdowns of all sorts. An increasingly common result of these breakdowns, especially in the former Soviet Union and much of Africa, seems to be electoral authoritarian regimes, whose future will have a major impact on the future of democracy around the world.

In the last decade, growing concern has arisen that democracy is declining or at least threatened. This has led to renewed interest in regime changes that create authoritarian regimes rather than end them. The traditional and most common form of this was the military coup, which certainly still happens but less often than it used to. More frequent and receiving greater scholarly attention has been authoritarianization, the slow erosion of democratic norms and institutions by elected leaders. In places like Turkey and Venezuela, this has clearly produced electoral authoritarian regimes, but in other countries, including many long-established democracies, the erosion of norms and institutions has weakened democracy but not eliminated it—or at least not yet. Studying authoritarianization is important not only to understand the countries that have gone through it but others that might be threatened by it.

Regime change is such a large and important topic that virtually all major theories of comparative politics have been used to explain it. Political-culture theorists long argued that attributes of particular cultures set the stage for particular kinds of regimes. Some analysts of democratic transition argued as well that individual actors' belief in democracy matters. Influenced by rational choice theory, the transition paradigm argued that neither culture nor ideology is particularly important in understanding when a transition will occur; transitions take place when political elites see the acceptance of democratic institutions to be in their rational self-interest. Modernization theorists have responded, with growing evidence, that even if transition is possible, either culture or a structural condition—such as economic development—is necessary to preserve democracy in the long run. ●

Sharpen your skills with SAGE Edge at **edge.sagepub.com/orvisessentials2e. SAGE Edge for students** provides a personalized approach to help you accomplish your coursework goals in an easy-to-use learning environment.

KEY CONCEPTS

authoritarianization (p. 262)
coup d'état (p. 247)
democratic backsliding (p. 253)
democratic consolidation (p. 252)
pact (p. 252)
regime change (p. 247)
transition to democracy (p. 251)

WORKS CITED

Acemoglu, Daron, and James A. Robinson. 2006. *Economic Origins of Dictatorship and Democracy.* New York: Cambridge University Press.

Almond, Gabriel A., and Sidney Verba. 1963. *The Civic Culture: Political Attitudes and Democracy in Five Nations.* Princeton, NJ: Princeton University Press.

——. 1989. *The Civic Culture Revisited.* Newbury Park, CA: Sage.

Arango, Tim, and Ceylon Yeginsu. 2016. "With Army in Disarray, A Pillar of Modern Turkey Lies Broken." *New York Times.* July 29, 2016. http://www.nytimes.com/2016/07/29/world/europe/turkey-military-coup.html?smprod=nytcore-ipad&smid=nytcore-ipad-share&_r=0.

Barany, Zoltan. 2016. *How Armies Respond to Revolutions and Why.* Princeton, NJ: Princeton University Press.

Barkan, Joel D. 1993. "Kenya: Lessons From a Flawed Election." *Journal of Democracy* 4 (3): 85–99.

Bermeo, Nancy Gina. 2003. *Ordinary People in Extraordinary Times: The Citizenry and the Breakdown of Democracy.* Princeton, NJ: Princeton University Press.

Bleck, Jaimie, and Nicholas van de Walle. 2019. *Electoral Politics in Africa Since 1990: Continuity and Change.* New York: Cambridge University Press.

Boix, Carles. 2003. *Democracy and Redistribution.* New York: Cambridge University Press.

Boix, Carles, and Susan Carol Stokes. 2003. "Endogenous Democratization." *World Politics* 55 (4): 517–549. doi:10.1353/wp.2003.0019.

Bratton, Michael, and Nicholas van de Walle. 1997. *Democratic Experiments in Africa: Regime Transitions in Comparative Perspective.* New York: Cambridge University Press.

Conroy-Krutz, Jeffrey, and Erika Frantz. 2017. *Theories of Democratic Change Phase II: Paths Away From Authoritarianism.* DRG Center Working Paper Research and Innovation Grants Working Papers Series, December. https://www.iie.org/Research-and-Insights/Publications/DFG-MSU-TOC-Publication.

DeBruin, Erica. 2017. "Preventing Coups d'état: How Counterbalancing Works." *Journal of Conflict Resolution* 62 (7): 1433–1458. https://doi.org/10.1177/0022002717692652.

Decalo, Samuel. 1976. *Coups and Army Rule in Africa.* New Haven, CT: Yale University Press.

Escriba-Folch, Abel, and Joseph Wright. 2015. *Foreign Pressure and the Politics of Autocratic Survival.* Oxford, UK: Oxford University Press.

Fish, M. Steven, and Robin S. Brooks. 2004. "Does Diversity Hurt Democracy?" *Journal of Democracy* 15 (1): 154–166.

Flores, Thomas Edward, and Irfan Nooruddin. 2016. *Elections in Hard Times: Building Stronger Democracies in the 21st Century.* New York: Cambridge University Press.

Frantz, Erica. 2018. *Authoritarianism: What Everyone Needs to Know.* Oxford, UK: Oxford University Press.

Freedom House. *Democracy in Retreat: Freedom in the World 2019.* https://freedomhouse.org/report/freedom-world/freedom-world-2019/democracy-in-retreat.

Geddes, Barbara, Joseph Wright, and Erica Frantz. 2018. *How Dictatorships Work: Power, Personalization, and Collapse.* Cambridge, UK: Cambridge University Press.

Gherghina, Sergiu. 2015. *Party Organization and Electoral Volatility in Central and Eastern Europe.* New York: Routledge.

Giraudy, Agustina. 2015. *Democrats and Autocrats: Pathways of Subnational Undemocratic Regime Continuity Within Democratic Countries.* Oxford, UK: Oxford University Press.

Guo, Sujian, and Gary A. Stradiotto. 2014. *Democratic Transitions: Modes and Outcomes.* New York: Routledge.

Hadenius, Axel, and Jan Teorell. 2005. "Cultural and Economic Prerequisites of Democracy: Reassessing Recent Evidence." *Studies in Comparative International Development* 39 (4): 87–106.

Haggard, Stephan, and Robert R. Kaufman. 2016. *Dictators and Democrats: Masses, Elites, and Regime Change.* Princeton, NJ: Princeton University Press.

Houle, Christian. 2015. "Ethnic Inequality and the Dismantling of Democracy: A Global Analysis." *World Politics* 67 (3): 469–505. doi:http://dx.doi.org/10.1017/S0043887115000106.

Huntington, Samuel P. 1964. *The Soldier and the State: The Theory and Politics of Civil-Military Relations.* New York: Random House.

——. 1968. *Political Order in Changing Societies.* New Haven, CT: Yale University Press.

——. 1991. *The Third Wave: Democratization in the Late Twentieth Century.* Norman: University of Oklahoma Press.

Inglehart, Ronald, and Christian Welzel. 2005. *Modernization, Cultural Change, and Democracy: The Human Development Sequence.* New York: Cambridge University Press.

Janowitz, Morris. 1964. *The Military in the Political Development of New Nations: An Essay in Comparative Analysis.* Chicago: University of Chicago Press.

Lebas, Adrienne. 2011. *From Protest to Parties: Party-Building and Democratization in Africa.* New York: Oxford University Press.

Levitsky, Steven, James Loxton, Brandon van Dyck, and Jorge I. Dominguez. 2016. *Callenges to Party-Building in Latin America.* New York: Cambridge University Press.

Levitsky, Steve, and Lucan Way. 2010. *Competitive Authoritarianism: Hybrid Regimes After the Cold War.* New York: Cambridge University Press.

Levitsky, Steven, and Daniel Ziblatt. 2018. *How Democracies Die.* New York: Crown Publishing Group.

Lindberg, Staffan I. 2009. "The Power of Elections in Africa Revisited." In *Democratization by Elections: A New Mode of Transition,* edited by Staffan I. Lindberg, 25–46. Baltimore, MD: Johns Hopkins University Press.

Linz, Juan. 1990. "The Perils of Presidentialism." *Journal of Democracy* 1 (1): 51–69. doi:10.1353/jod.1990.0011.

Lipset, Seymour Martin. 1959. "Some Social Requisites of Democracy: Economic Development and Political Legitimacy." *American Political Science Review* 53 (1): 69–105. doi:10.2307/1951731.

Lührmann, Anna, Sirianne Dahlum, Staffan I. Lindberg, Laura Maxwell, Valeriya Mechkova, Moa Olin, Shreeya Pillai, Constanza Sanhueza Petrarca, Rachel Sigman, and Natalia Stepanova. 2018. *V-Dem Annual Democracy Report 2018. Democracy for All?* May. https://www.v-dem.net/media/filer_public/68/51/685150f0-47e1-4d03-97bc-45609c3f158d/v-dem_annual_dem_report_2018.pdf.

Lührmann, Anna, and Staffan I. Lindberg. 2019. A Third Wave of Autocratization Is Here: What Is New About it?, *Democratization*. doi: 10.1080/13510347.2019.1582029.

Mainwaring, Scott, and Fernando Bizzarro. 2019. "The Fates of Third-Wave Democracies." *Journal of Democracy* 30 (1): 99–113. doi:10.1353/jod.2019.0008.

Mainwaring, Scott, and Aníbal Pérez-Liñán. 2013. *Democracies and Dictatorships in Latin America: Emergence, Survival, and Fall.* New York: Cambridge University Press.

McClintock, Cynthia. 2018. *Electoral Rules and Democracy in Latin America.* New York: Oxford University Press.

Nassif, Hicham Bou. 2015. "Generals and Autocrats: How Coup-Proofing Predetermined the Military Elite's Behavior in the Arab Spring. " *Political Science Quarterly* 130 (2) 2015: 245–276.

O'Donnell, Guillermo A. 1979. *Modernization and Bureaucratic-Authoritarianism: Studies in South American Politics.* Berkeley: Institute of International Studies, University of California Press.

Pop-Eleches, Grigore, and Graeme B. Robertson. 2015. "Structural Conditions and Democratization." *Journal of Democracy* 26 (3): 144–156. http://www.journalofdemocracy.org/article/structural-conditions-and-democratization.

Przeworski, Adam, Michael E. Alvarez, José Antonio Cheibub, and Fernando Limongi. 2000. *Democracy and Development: Political Institutions and Well-Being in the World, 1950–1990.* Cambridge, UK: Cambridge University Press.

Reidl, Ruth Betty. 2014. *Authoritarian Origins of Democratic Party Systems in Africa.* New York: Cambridge University Press.

Roett, Riordan. 1978. *Brazil: Politics in a Patrimonial Society,* rev. ed. New York: Praeger.

Singh, Naunihal. 2014. *Seizing Power: The Strategic Logic of Military Coups.* Baltimore, MD: Johns Hopkins University Press.

Stepan, Alfred. 2012. "Tunisia's Transition and the Twin Tolerations." *Journal of Democracy* 23 (2): 89–103.

Svolik, Milan. W. 2018. *When Polarization Trumps Civic Virtue: Partisan Conflict and the Subversion of Democracy by Incumbents.* Working Paper, Department of Political Science, Yale University, August.

Tavits, Margit. 2013. *Post-Communist Democracies and Party Organization.* New York: Cambridge University Press.

van de Walle, Nicolas. 2006. "Tipping Games: When Do Opposition Parties Coalesce?" In *Electoral Authoritarianism: The Dynamics of Unfree Competition,* edited by Andreas Shedler, 77–92. Boulder, CO: Lynne Rienner.

Wejnert, Barbara. 2014. *Diffusion of Democracy: The Past and Future of Global Democracy.* New York: Cambridge University Press.

RESOURCES FOR FURTHER STUDY

Ackerman, Peter, and Jack Duvall. 2000. *A Force More Powerful: A Century of Nonviolent Conflict.* New York: St. Martin's Press.

Casper, Gretchen. 1995. *Fragile Democracies: The Legacies of Authoritarian Rule.* Pittsburgh, PA: University of Pittsburgh Press.

Dahl, Robert. 1971. *Polyarchy: Participation and Opposition.* New Haven, CT: Yale University Press.

Diamond, Larry, and Leonardo Morlino. 2005. *Assessing the Quality of Democracy.* Baltimore, MD: Johns Hopkins University Press.

Finer, Samuel E. 1962. *The Man on Horseback: The Role of the Military in Politics.* New York: Praeger.

Fish, M. Steven. 2005. *Democracy Derailed in Russia: The Failure of Open Politics.* New York: Cambridge University Press.

Fishman, Robert M. 2019. *Democratic Practice: Origins of the Iberian Divide in Political Inclusion.* . Oxford, UK: Oxford University Press.

Haggard, Stephan, and Robert R. Kaufman. 1995. *The Political Economy of Democratic Transitions.* Princeton, NJ: Princeton University Press.

Moore, Barrington. 1966. *Social Origins of Dictatorship and Democracy: Lord and Peasant in the Making of the Modern World.* Boston: Beacon Press.

Morgenstern, Scott, and Benito Nacif, eds. 2002. *Legislative Politics in Latin America.* New York: Cambridge University Press.

O'Donnell, Guillermo. 1999. "Horizontal Accountability in New Democracies." In *The Self-Restraining State: Power and Accountability in New Democracies,* edited by Andreas Schedler, Larry Diamond, and Marc F. Plattner, 29–51. Boulder, CO: Lynne Rienner.

O'Donnell, Guillermo A., and Phillipe Schmitter. 1986. *Transitions From Authoritarian Rule: Tentative Conclusions about Uncertain Democracies.* Baltimore, MD: Johns Hopkins University Press.

Pinkney, Robert. 2003. *Democracy in the Third World.* Boulder, CO: Lynne Rienner.

Przeworski, Adam. 1991. *Democracy and the Market: Political and Economic Reforms in Eastern Europe and Latin America.* Cambridge, UK: Cambridge University Press.

Reynolds, Andrew. 2002. *The Architecture of Democracy: Constitutional Design, Conflict Management, and Democracy.* New York: Oxford University Press.

Rios-Figueroa, Julio. 2013. "Effectiveness and Accessibility of Justice System Institutions in Mexico's Transition to Democracy." In *Representation and Effectiveness in Latin American Democracies: Congress, Judiciary and Civil Society,* edited by Moira B. MacKinnon and Ludovico Feoli, 143–159. New York: Routledge.

Schedler, Andreas. 2006. *Electoral Authoritarianism: The Dynamics of Unfree Competition.* Boulder, CO: Lynne Rienner.

Van Inwegen, Patrick. 2011. *Understanding Revolution.* Boulder, CO: Lynne Rienner.

Webb, Paul, and Stephen White, eds. 2007. *Party Politics in New Democracies.* Oxford, UK: Oxford University Press.

Wegren, Stephen K., and Dale R. Herspring, eds. 2010. *After Putin's Russia: Past Imperfect, Future Uncertain.* New York: Rowman and Littlefield.

Welzel, Christian. 2013. *Freedom Rising: Human Empowerment and the Quest for Emancipation.* New York: Cambridge University Press.

Zakaria, Fareed. 2003. *The Future of Freedom: Illiberal Democracy at Home and Abroad.* New York: W. W. Norton.

WEB RESOURCES

Freedom House, Freedom in the World, 2018

(https://freedomhouse.org/report/freedom-world/freedom-world-2018)

Global Integrity

(http://www.globalintegrity.org/)

Polity IV Project, 2016, "Global Trends in Governance, 1800–2014"

(http://www.systemicpeace.org/polityproject.html)

Transparency International, Corruption Perceptions Index

(http://www.transparency.org/research/cpi/overview)

Unified Democracy Scores

(http://www.unified-democracy-scores.org)

PART III

Political Economy and Policy

10 Political Economy of Wealth

A woman holds a sign opposing possible trade deals with Canada and the United States at a demonstration outside European Union (EU) headquarters in Brussels, Belgium, in 2016. Although members of the EU have yielded more economic sovereignty to a transnational organization than any other countries in the world, opening up further to the global economy remains controversial.
John Thys/AFP/Getty Images

Key Questions

- How and why should states intervene in the market economy?
- In what ways do economic policies reflect the relative power of different groups in a society?
- How important is globalization in determining the economic policies of individual countries?
- Why have some wealthy states intervened in the market economy more than others?

Learning Objectives

After reading chapter 10, you should be able to do the following:

10.1 Explain the function of a market economy in a modern state

10.2 Articulate the key debates over the role of economics in society

10.3 Define and differentiate the types of capitalist economies

10.4 Explore how globalization has affected wealthy economies

10.5 Explain how different economic theories and practices affect national politics in contemporary states

The Great Recession that began in the United States in 2007 and spread across the globe in 2008–2009 caused not only massive economic upheaval but major political changes as well. In the decade that followed, governments changed hands in France, Greece, Iceland, Ireland, Italy, Japan, Portugal, Spain, the United Kingdom, and the United States, among other countries. In all of those contests, the state of the economy was a major factor in the incumbent party's loss. Many analysts saw the effects of the recession as a major cause of the rise of the anti-establishment populism we discussed in chapter 6, including the British vote to leave the European Union, and the American election of Donald Trump as president. As Bill Clinton's 1992 presidential campaign put it, "It's the economy, stupid!" Political leaders in democracies across the globe rise and fall on the basis of citizens' perceptions of the economy and their own economic well-being.

Market economies have become nearly universal since the end of the Cold War. States no longer control the economy as the communist governments did in the past, but governments can and do intervene in the economy to try to encourage economic growth and influence how economic benefits are distributed. Therefore, the relationship between the state and the market and the debates surrounding it are crucial to understanding modern politics virtually everywhere. This is the realm of political economy, which we introduced in chapter 1 as the study of the interaction between economics and politics. We will examine it in detail in this and the next two chapters. As Table 10.1 (page 284) demonstrates, even though virtually all countries are now market economies, different histories, positions in the global economy, and economic policies produce dramatically different levels of wealth, economic growth, unemployment, inequality, and poverty.

This chapter examines the fundamental economic concepts that will help us understand the enduring relationship between the state and the market and the long-standing debates over that relationship. We ask how, why, and to what effect states intervene in market economies. We also examine various models of state–market relationships in wealthy democracies. Finally, we examine how the forces of globalization have challenged long-established models and theories and how

TABLE 10.1

Economic Outcomes Around the World

COUNTRY	AVERAGE GDP GROWTH (ANNUAL %),[1] 1980–2017	AVERAGE UNEMPLOYMENT (% OF TOTAL LABOR FORCE),[2] 1980–2018	AVERAGE INFLATION (% CHANGE),[3] 1980–2017	ABSOLUTE POVERTY, 2007–2017 (% OF POPULATION BELOW $1.90 PER DAY)[4]	INEQUALITY (GINI COEFFICIENT),[5] 2005–2018
Brazil	0.75	8.46	277.32	4.8	52.7
China	8.4	3.9	4.48	0.7	41.2
Germany	1.59	7.38	1.73	N/A	31.1
India	4.61	2.7	7.96	21.2	35.5
Iran	1.22	11.25	18.68	N/A	40.1
Japan	1.70	4.0	1.02	N/A	32.1
Mexico	0.94	3.99	23.41	2.5	47.6
Nigeria	0.58	4.16	17.57	53.5	45.0
Russia	0.67	7.51	73.24	N/A	40.2
United Kingdom	1.70	6.57	2.56	N/A	34.10
United States	1.57	5.95	3.20	N/A	41

[1]World Bank, GDP per capita growth (annual %) (http://data.worldbank.org/indicator/NY.GDP.PCAP.KD.ZG); data for Russian Federation between 1980 and 1990 not available.

[2]World Bank, World Development Indicators, average total unemployment (% total labor force) (https://databank.worldbank.org/data/source/world-development-indicators#). Data missing for: Brazil (1991, 2018)

[3]World Bank, World Development Indicators, inflation (% change), (https://databank.worldbank.org/data/source/world-development-indicators#). Data between 1988 and 1989, 2002, and 2003 are missing for all countries. Data missing for Brazil (1980); China (1980–1986); Germany (1980–1991); Russian Federation (1980–1992); United Kingdom (1980–1987).

[4]Human Development Reports, "Multidimensional Poverty Index" (http://hdr.undp.org/sites/default/files/mpi_2019_publication.pdf).

[5]Human Development Reports, "Gini coefficient" (http://hdr.undp.org/en/media/HDR_2010_EN_Table3_reprint.pdf).

wealthy states are responding. We will return to these themes in chapter 11, where we look at economic issues in middle- and low-income countries.

The Market, Capitalism, and the State

market economy: An economic system in which individuals and firms exchange goods and services in a largely unfettered manner

A **market economy** is an economic system in which individuals and firms exchange goods and services in a largely unfettered manner. To most people, this seems like a natural state of affairs, but until fairly recently, it was the exception, not the norm. In many preindustrial societies, people subsisted on the fruits of their own labor and engaged in very limited trade. In feudal Europe, most people were legally bound to a particular lord and manor and could not exchange their labor for a wage anywhere they pleased. The creation of the modern market economy required that feudal bonds restricting labor be broken so that most people would become dependent on market exchanges. In modern industrial and postindustrial societies, virtually the entire population depends on earning a wage or receiving a share of profit via the market.

Capitalism

Capitalism is not exactly the same thing as a market economy, though the terms are typically used interchangeably. Rather, capitalism is the combination of a market economy with private property rights. In theory, one can imagine a market economy without individual property rights. For example, collectively owned firms could be free to produce whatever they could for a profit in an unfettered market. Yugoslavia under the communist rule of Josip Tito attempted but never fully implemented a modified version of such a system in the 1960s and 1970s.

Virtually all countries have some form of a capitalist economy today, although the degree to which the market is unfettered and the precise nature of private property rights vary widely. There is no absolute law in economics about how "free" market exchanges or private property must be for a capitalist economy to function. The debates over the extent to which the state should intervene to limit and shape market exchanges and property rights are at the core of many of the most important political issues around the globe. The end of the Cold War eliminated the communist command economy—an economic system in which most prices, property, and production are directly controlled by the state—as a viable political economic model, but it did not end the debate over what ought to be the relationship between the market and the state.

Because people tend to see the capitalist market economy as somehow natural, they also see it as existing independently of government. Nothing could be further from the truth. Command economies were ultimately of limited efficiency, but they proved that a state can exist for a long time without a market economy. Advanced capitalism, on the other hand, cannot exist without the state. In a situation of anarchy—the absence of a state—the market would be severely limited; without state provision of security, property and contract rights, and money, exchange would be limited to bartering and would require extensive provision of private security forces. Mafias are examples of this kind of capitalism, which arises where states are weak or absent; they provide their own security and enforce their own contracts. While this can create some productive economic activity, the uncertainty of property rights and contracts and the costs of private security limit economic growth and create a society in which few would like to live. Steve Vogel argued that, in fact, creating "free" markets requires more government oversight than less free markets do: "If markets are institutions, then cultivating markets requires building institutions more than destroying them. In short, liberalizing the economy does not mean liberating it" (Vogel 2018, 4). Without regulations to maintain competition, businesses naturally tend to grow toward collaboration and oligopoly if not outright monopoly. This points to one of several important roles the state must play in a capitalist economy: preventing monopolies that destroy markets. The modern state typically intervenes in the market economy to perform three distinct roles: those that are *essential, beneficial,* or *politically generated.*

capitalism: The combination of a market economy with private property rights

public goods: Goods or services that cannot or will not be provided via the market because their costs are too high or their benefits are too diffuse

Essential Roles

The state's essential roles are providing security, establishing and enforcing property and contract rights, and creating and controlling currency. Most essential roles and many of the beneficial ones as well involve the provision of **public goods**: goods or services that cannot or will not be provided via the market because their costs are too high or their benefits are too diffuse. National security is an excellent example of a public good. Individual provision of security is extremely expensive, and if any one company could pay for it, the benefits would accrue to everyone in the country anyway, not allowing the company to generate revenue sufficient to cover the costs. The state must provide this service if the market economy is to thrive.

Protection of property and contract rights is also an essential state function in a market economy. Capitalism requires investing now with the expectation of future gains. Some uncertainty is always involved, but if potential investors have no means of ensuring that the future gains will accrue, no one will invest. Property rights protect not only property legally purchased in the market but also future property—the profits of current investment and productive activity. Similarly, profits require honest market exchanges: if a ton of cotton is promised for delivery at a set price, it must actually be delivered at that price. Details can vary significantly, but some legal guarantee that current and future property and exchanges will be protected is essential to achieving the productivity associated with modern market economies.

The modern state must also provide a currency to facilitate economic exchanges. States did not always print or control currency. Prior to the American Civil War, for instance, private banks printed most currency in the United States (hence the old-fashioned term *banknote*). When the state took over this process and created a uniform currency, exchanges across the entire country were eased. This happened transnationally as thirteen countries adopted the euro as the single currency of the European Union (EU) in 2002, greatly easing exchange across much of the continent.

Beneficial Roles

Several other roles the state commonly plays in the modern market economy are not absolutely essential, but most analysts consider them beneficial. These include providing infrastructure, education, and health care, and correcting market failures. The first three are all examples of public goods. Roads are a classic example of infrastructure as a public good. Private roads can and sometimes do exist, but governments build the bulk of all highway systems. Public provision of a road network lowers the cost of transporting goods and people, which improves the efficiency and profitability of many sectors of the economy.

Similarly, most economists and business leaders see an educated populace as beneficial to economic efficiency. Workers who can read, write, and do arithmetic are far more productive than those who cannot. Companies could provide this education themselves, but because education is a lengthy process, because children learn many things more efficiently and effectively than do adults, and because workers can switch jobs and take their company-provided education with them, providing basic education is not a profitable endeavor and is therefore a nearly universal function of the state.

In most countries, the provision of basic health care is seen in similar terms. Obviously, a healthy workforce is more productive than an unhealthy one, and investment in health is most productive in the early stages of life; the economic benefits of high-quality prenatal and early childhood health care are far greater than the benefits of health care for the elderly. Most countries, therefore, consider health care a public good. At the very least, the government aggressively intervenes in the health care market to ensure that such care is provided to all.

Today, vigorous debates about the state's role in providing public goods and services continue in many countries. While virtually all agree that basic education is beneficial and ought to be provided by the state (the United Nations has officially endorsed education as a right for all), that still leaves a great deal open to dispute: how much secondary and higher education should the state provide? Should the government pay for all or most of a person's higher education, as is the case in most of Europe, or should the individual pay a substantial share, as in the United States? Health care is even more controversial. While most agree that a healthy workforce enhances a market economy, how to achieve such a healthy population is the subject of near-constant debate. These issues are analyzed in greater depth in chapter 12.

The fourth beneficial economic function of the modern state is intervention to correct market failure. **Market failure** occurs when markets fail to perform efficiently. The primary justification for a market is efficiency: a well-functioning market maximizes the efficient use of all available resources. Three common causes of market failure are **externalities** (transactions that do not include the full costs or benefits of production in the price), imperfect information, and monopolies in which one seller can set prices. Advocates of an unfettered market recognize market failures as something governments should try to correct, but exactly when such intervention is justified and how governments should respond remain controversial.

Market externalities occur when a cost or benefit of the production process is not fully included in the price of the final market transaction, thereby reducing efficiency. Environmental damage is a common externality. If a factory pollutes the air as it makes a product, costs are incurred at least by local residents. The factory owners, however, do not have to pay those costs as they make and sell their products, and the price charged customers doesn't include those costs. The factory will pollute more than it would if it and its customers had to pay the costs of that pollution. Many economists argue, therefore, that the state should intervene to make the producers and consumers of the product bear its full costs.

Markets can also only maximize efficiency when buyers and sellers know the full costs and benefits of their transactions. Economists call this having "perfect information." In our financially and technologically complex societies, market actors often lack perfect information. The financial collapse that caused the 2008–2009 recession resulted in part from a set of transactions in which consumers and investors did not fully know what they were purchasing. The first breakdown in information came as many Americans purchased homes during the housing boom earlier in the decade. Potential buyers were desperate to purchase as home prices rose rapidly. Some lenders, especially in the "hottest" markets, offered buyers variable-rate mortgages with payments and interest that were low in the short term but that increased dramatically later. Many buyers seemed not to understand how high the payments would go, and some lenders used aggressive or fraudulent techniques to sell mortgages to uncreditworthy buyers, seeking to earn loan-processing fees and interest in the short term and not caring whether the borrowers would be able to pay back the loans in the long term (a practice known as predatory lending).

The second set of transactions in which buyers lacked perfect information occurred on Wall Street, where major banks sold investments called "mortgage-backed securities" (MBS), which were basically bundles of these high-risk mortgages. Theoretically, these investments helped to spread out the risks of these high-risk mortgages across many investors. Banks tried to reduce risk further by

market failure: Phenomenon that occurs when markets fail to perform efficiently or fail to perform according to other widely held social values

externality: A cost or benefit of the production process that is not fully included in the price of the final market transaction when the product is sold

selling MBS investors a kind of insurance called credit default swaps (which are part of a broader investment category called derivatives), which would compensate them if the mortgage holders defaulted on their loans. However, the Wall Street banks selling these investments and the companies that rate the risks did not fully disclose or realize the level of risk in the mortgages, so investors did not fully understand the risks involved in their investments. Once housing prices began to fall significantly in 2008, the most heavily involved Wall Street banks, most notably Lehman Brothers, faced bankruptcy as their investors tried to sell the MBS as quickly as possible but found no buyers, so the value of those investments collapsed. Even worse, the banks had to pay off those investors who had bought credit default swaps. Bankruptcy ensued for some of the banks, and investors in the United States and around the world (often unknowingly via instruments like pension funds) faced a massive loss of wealth. The result was the biggest economic downturn since the Great Depression. The market failure embedded in this series of transactions in which buyers of all sorts lacked "perfect information" led to renewed debate over how much government regulation is necessary in the mortgage and financial markets.

The third common market failure is **monopoly**—the control of the entire supply of a valued good or service by one seller. In a market economy, competition among alternative suppliers is a key incentive for efficiency. Because monopolies eliminate this incentive, the state may intervene to prevent them. It may do so in three ways: by making the monopoly government owned and therefore (in theory) run in the interest of the general public, by regulating the monopoly to ensure that its prices are closer to what they would be in a competitive market, or by forcing the breakup of the monopoly into smaller, competing entities.

Some monopolies are considered **natural monopolies**; these occur in sectors of the economy in which competition would raise costs and reduce efficiency. Where a natural monopoly exists, it makes more sense to regulate or take control of it rather than force a breakup. A good example of a natural monopoly is the history of telephone service. A generation ago, every phone had to be hardwired into a land line, and all calls traveled over wires; this meant that competition would have required more than one company to run wires down the same street. This obviously would have been prohibitively expensive and inefficient. Britain, like many other countries, chose the first option to deal with this natural monopoly: it created the government-owned company, British Telephone. The United States, by contrast, chose to heavily regulate a privately owned monopoly, and all services were provided by "Ma Bell" (as AT&T was nicknamed). By 1984, however, new ways to deliver voice and high-speed data transmission reduced the "natural" quality of the monopoly. A lawsuit led to the breakup of AT&T, spawning several local phone companies. With the advent of satellite and wireless technology, the natural monopoly evaporated; around the world, governments have privatized or deregulated phone services, and consumers now have a choice of providers.

monopoly: The control of the entire supply of a valued good or service by one economic actor

natural monopoly: The control of the entire supply of valued goods or services by one economic actor in a sector of the economy in which competition would raise costs and reduce efficiency

The most recent major debate about monopolies has focused on the biggest technology companies, such as Google and Facebook, that dominate their markets. Some argue these are natural monopolies: the more people use Google's search engine, the more accurate its algorithm becomes and the better it works, so even more people use it. Similarly, the more people who use Facebook or any other social media site, the more people will want to use it. The EU has passed various regulations and imposed fines on both companies for monopoly behavior and infringement of individuals' privacy. As of 2019, the United States had done far less of this. Chris Hughes, one of the founders of Facebook, argued in 2019 that the company ought to be split up, at a minimum separating ownership of its major segments—Facebook, Whatsapp, and Instagram—to reduce its power. The question of how governments should reduce monopoly power to ensure competitive markets remains an ongoing debate.

A worker stands in a construction site for a new sewage processing facility in St. Petersburg, Russia. Without facilities treating sewage, companies and households will dump their waste into rivers and lakes, destroying the environment, likely sickening people who live near the waterways and harming fishing. The people polluting the water, however, may well not pay the cost of the damage they are causing. Externalities like this are a primary justification for state intervention in a market.
Peter Kovalev\TASS via Getty Images

Politically Generated Roles

All the economic functions of the state discussed to this point are economically required or at least beneficial to the market. The final category of state functions in a market economy are those that are politically generated by citizens demanding that a state take action. Most economists do not see these functions as essential or perhaps even beneficial to creating an efficient market, but states have taken on these roles because a large section of the populace has demanded them. Karl Polanyi argued in his 1944 book, *The Great Transformation,* that the rise of the modern industrial economy produced political demands to limit what many people saw as the negative effects of the market. This led to what is now termed the "modern welfare state." Through the democratic process in European countries and the United States, in particular, citizens demanded protection from the market, and governments began to provide it to a greater or lesser extent. Primary examples of these politically generated state functions are government regulations requiring improved working conditions and policies that redistribute income.

Because these state interventions are the results of political demands, they remain very contentious and vary greatly from country to country. In wealthy industrial economies, modern working conditions—including a minimum wage, an eight-hour workday, and workers' health and safety standards—are largely the product of labor union demands. Yet labor policies in wealthy countries vary significantly, particularly in areas such as the length of the workweek, job security, the length of maternity leave, and the amount of paid vacation time that employers are required to give. In countries that have begun industrializing more recently, such as Brazil and China, labor unions are recent creations that have not had the opportunity to successfully champion the same reforms that are now taken for granted in countries that industrialized much earlier. Minimum wages may be low or nonexistent, workdays may be as long as twelve hours, and paid vacations are rare. This disparity between wealthier and poorer countries is at the core of the controversies surrounding globalization.

Similar controversy and variation exist around income redistribution policies. Typically referred to as "welfare" in the United States (though Social Security, which is not usually seen as welfare, is also an income redistribution policy), these policies exist to mitigate the effects of unequal income distribution that markets generate. Markets can provide great economic efficiency and growth, but they have no rules for how wealth is distributed. As social and economic inequality expanded in the late nineteenth and early twentieth centuries, reformers began to demand that the state take action to help those who were gaining little or nothing in the market. For reasons we explore in chapter 12, the extent to which the early industrializing countries in Europe and the United States pursued income redistribution and poverty amelioration varied considerably. As with proper and regulated working conditions, income redistribution policies barely exist at all in the poorest countries; the poorest people are left to survive in the market as best they can.

U.S. economic history illustrates the three types of government interventions in the market. The modern U.S. economy emerged in the late nineteenth and early twentieth centuries as rapid industrialization transformed the country from a primarily agricultural and rural society into a rapidly growing urban and industrial economy. Like all reasonably well-functioning modern states, the United States provided adequate security for business to operate and a court system that, as corruption dropped over time, provided at least some protection for contracts. Infrastructure expanded, particularly via the railway, but much of this was privately owned. The country was a pioneer of universal education in the nineteenth century, producing a literate workforce for the new economy, but otherwise had very little involvement in the economy until the end of the century. The first changes to this were aimed primarily at ensuring that the market would remain as free as possible by eliminating or regulating monopoly control of key sectors of the economy. This started with regulation of the railways and then expanded with the landmark Sherman Antitrust Act of 1890. In 1913 the government addressed other crucial needs of a modern economy, creating both the nation's first central bank to control monetary policy (the Federal Reserve) and the income and corporate tax systems.

The Great Depression, which produced 25 percent unemployment at its peak in 1933, shook the foundations of the nation's belief in the free market. During this time of rapidly rising union membership and radical political demands, Franklin Roosevelt won the presidency in 1932 with a promise of a "new deal." The fruition of this was a program of unprecedented government spending on public works projects that employed large numbers of workers to improve the nation's infrastructure. It also created policies that protected workers from the worst effects of the market, which the growing labor unions had long demanded: a federally mandated eight-hour workday, collective bargaining rights for workers, a minimum wage, protection against unfair labor practices, federal subsidies for farmers, a pension plan for the elderly (Social Security), and federal income support for poor, single mothers.

The New Deal era in which the government actively worked to improve economic growth and expand employment resulted in unprecedented growth. In the 1960s, Lyndon Johnson's administration initiated the "Great Society" to complete the goals of the New Deal. The pillars of this effort were the creation of Medicare, medical insurance for Social Security recipients; Aid to Families with Dependent Children (AFDC), a much-expanded welfare program for poor mothers; and Medicaid, health care for AFDC and other welfare recipients. These programs, along with the earlier Social Security system, helped reduce poverty from 25 percent of the population in 1955 to 11 percent by 1973. However, slower economic growth and waning political support subsequently led the government to reduce the real value of these antipoverty programs, contributing to a rise in the poverty rate to around 14 percent by the 1990s.

The symbiotic relationship between the modern state and the market economy provides a means to analyze state interventions in modern economic life.

The state must carry out certain roles if capitalism is to survive and thrive. Political leaders know that much of their popularity rests on the ability to generate goods and services, jobs, and government revenue. In the modern economy, states pursue various policies and market interventions beyond those that are the bare essentials for the survival of capitalism. Some of these are widely recognized as beneficial to contemporary economies, though the details of how and how much to pursue them remain controversial. Other policies, however, are generated primarily by political demands emanating from society, especially in democracies. These policies remain the most controversial and vary the most from state to state, as we will see in chapter 12.

Key Economic Debates

Understanding political economy and the relationship between the state and the market requires the application of both political science and basic economics. Major economic theories lie behind the debates over how governments should intervene in the market. The first, central debate that must be understood is between Keynesian and neoliberal theories of when, why, and how the state ought to attempt to guide the economy. Prior to the Great Depression, Western governments engaged in minimal intervention in the economy. Economists and government officials recognized that during economic downturns, unemployment rose and people suffered, but they believed that in the longer term, unemployment lowered wages until labor was cheap enough that businesses started to invest and employ people again, thus creating a new cycle of economic growth. Therefore, during economic downturns, government should do little but wait.

THE ROLE OF THE STATE IN THE MARKET		
ESSENTIAL FUNCTIONS OF THE STATE	BENEFICIAL FUNCTIONS OF THE STATE	POLITICALLY GENERATED FUNCTIONS OF THE STATE
Provide national and personal security: Failure to do so produces anarchy or the creation of a mafia.	**Provide public goods:** These are goods or services not provided via the market because their costs are too high or their benefits are too diffuse, such as public education.	**Improve working conditions:** Examples include health and safety standards, eight-hour workday, minimum wage.
Protect property and contract rights: These are essential for investments to produce profits over time.	**Mitigate market failures**: These are interventions when the market fails to allocate resources efficiently. Examples include environmental regulations and laws limiting monopolies.	**Redistribute income**: Examples include retirement benefits, unemployment compensation, welfare.
Provide a currency: Facilitates widespread exchange.		

Keynesianism

Keynesian theory: Named for British economist John Maynard Keynes, who argued that governments can manage the business cycles of capitalism via active fiscal policy and monetary policy, including deficit spending when necessary

John Maynard Keynes, after whom **Keynesian theory** is named, revolutionized economics after watching his native Britain enter the Great Depression in the 1930s. Keynes argued that the state could and should do more to manage economic crises. In an economic downturn like the Great Depression, the main problem was a lack of demand for goods and services, and he believed that through **fiscal policy**—or management of the government budget—government could revive demand and stimulate the economy. He suggested that the government could and should engage in **deficit spending**—that is, it should spend more than it collected in revenue to stimulate demand. To do this, it would borrow money. By creating new programs and hiring people, the government would put that money into people's hands; they in turn would start to buy other goods and services, and the economy would start to rebound. Similarly, **monetary policy**—the amount of money a government prints and puts into circulation and the basic interest rates the government sets—can stimulate the economy. Central banks (called the Federal Reserve in the United States) should lower interest rates to stimulate borrowing in an economic downturn. When the downturn is over, the government can reduce spending to pay off the debt it had taken on and raise interest rates. These policies would slow demand in the economy, as too much demand can cause inflation. Keynes believed that in this way the state could manage the economy, smoothing out the cycle of economic expansion and contraction—known as the business cycle—that seemed inherent in unchecked capitalism. Done properly, such management might even achieve continuous full employment.

Keynesians also recognized market failures and believed that governments had an important role to play in correcting them. This combined with growing political demands in areas like environmental pollution to produce a more activist state that regulated a variety of economic activity. From the 1940s to the 1970s in the United States, for instance, numerous regulatory agencies were created to protect consumers from harmful food and drugs, reduce pollution, and protect workers' safety. The state also regulated monopolies or oligopolies in areas like telephone communications and airlines. Fearing financial collapses like the one that produced the Great Depression, governments also regulated the banking industry more tightly; in the United States, rules required banks serving average consumers to remain entirely separate (and insured their deposits against bank failure) from banks engaged in stock market transactions. David Kotz (2015) termed this era "regulated capitalism."

Keynesianism (and the onset of World War II) offered governments a way to help their economies out of the Depression, and most Western governments adopted it either explicitly or implicitly. Growth rates and average incomes rose significantly throughout the Western world in the 1950s and 1960s. The power of the economic theory alone, however, was not the only reason why Keynesian policies became so popular. Deficit spending allowed elected politicians to create programs to benefit their constituents without having to raise taxes to pay for them. The appeal for politicians facing reelection is obvious. In Europe, Keynesianism also gave social democratic parties economic justification for a significant expansion of social spending and welfare policies after World War II. This political logic led to frequent distortion of pure Keynesian policies—deficit spending continued in many countries even in times of economic growth in contradiction to Keynes's idea that when the economy improved, a government would pay off its debt.

By the 1970s, Keynesian policies came under sustained questioning, first by economists and then in the political arena. Due partly to the quadrupling of oil prices in 1973, most Western countries faced a new economic situation: stagflation, meaning simultaneous high inflation and high unemployment. Keynes's prescription

fiscal policy: Government budgetary policy

deficit spending: Government spending that is more than what is collected in revenue

monetary policy: The amount of money a government prints and puts into circulation and the basic interest rates the government sets

of more government borrowing to reduce unemployment was seen as potentially disastrous in this situation because it was likely to produce more inflation. Growth slowed, unemployment grew, and incomes stagnated.

Neoliberalism

In this context, an alternative economic theory gained popularity. What came to be known as **neoliberalism** (the "liberalism" refers back to nineteenth-century liberal ideas in favor of individual freedom and open markets rather than modern, American liberalism associated with the Democratic Party) argued that government intervention to steer the economy was at best ineffective and often harmful. Instead, neoliberal economists such as Milton Friedman and Friedrich Hayek argued that government should minimize intervention in the free market so that the market can allocate resources as efficiently as possible to maximize wealth generation. They believed market failures are rare and most government regulation is therefore harmful. Friedman argued that fiscal policy does not stimulate economic growth. Rather, government borrowing and deficit spending simply "crowd out" private-sector borrowing, impeding the ability of businesses to invest and thereby reducing long-term growth. The key to economic growth, Friedman argued, is simply monetary policy. Inflation, he and other neoliberals asserted, is caused chiefly by excessive government printing of money, and low growth is due in part to government borrowing. Achieving continuous full employment, they claimed, was impossible and produced inflation. Defeating stagflation and restoring growth would therefore require reducing the amount of money in circulation, raising interest rates, and reducing deficit spending.

Because they believe market failure is relatively rare and government spending harms the ability of businesses to invest, neoliberal theorists also favor cutting back most government regulations. Government efforts to reduce pollution, protect consumers' and workers' safety, and regulate business activities such as banking put constraints on businesses' ability to invest wisely and wasted precious resources. They call for a reduction in regulations and the overall size of government, in addition to balancing government budgets by eliminating deficit spending.

Neoliberalism became the theoretical justification for the economic policies of U.S. president Ronald Reagan and British prime minister Margaret Thatcher. Both set out to radically reduce the size and scope of government intervention in the economy in the early 1980s. The economic boom that followed was seen as a vindication of neoliberalism more broadly, which became the "conventional wisdom" in economic theory, at least until the recession of 2008–2009. Even when the Democratic and Labour Parties came to power in the United States and United Kingdom in the 1990s, they continued to pursue mostly neoliberal policies: deregulation of the financial sector in the United States, for instance, was completed by Democratic president Bill Clinton in 1999. Neoliberal ideas and policies spread, with varying levels of adoption, to many other countries. They became particularly powerful in poorer countries, a subject to which we turn in chapter 11.

neoliberalism: An economic theory that argues government should balance its budget and minimize its role in the economy to allow the market to allocate resources to maximize efficiency and thereby economic growth

Keynesianism Versus Neoliberalism: An Ongoing Debate

The 2008–2009 Great Recession and its aftermath led to the most significant debate on economic policy in a generation. As the economy collapsed, most states, including the previously neoliberal United States, first turned to Keynesian policy to try to restart economic growth; governments engaged in significant deficit spending to stimulate the economy. Neoliberal restrictions on government spending collapsed in the face of the highest unemployment rates since the Great Depression and the political pressures that they had produced. As a slow recovery set in, however, governments on both sides of the Atlantic returned to greater fiscal austerity; fear of excessive debt became greater than desire for more short-term growth. Keynesian economists lambasted this move as happening far too early, pointing to similar policies in the mid-1930s that are believed to have lengthened the Great Depression. Neoliberals, on the other hand, saw the move back in their direction as a wise reversal after the Keynesian panic of 2009. The United States pursued somewhat more aggressive deficit spending in response to the crisis in 2009 and did not reverse it until 2012, a year after the EU did. Similarly, the U.S. Federal Reserve cut interest rates more quickly than did the European Central Bank (ECB) and began "quantitative easing"—a means of pumping money into the economy—earlier as well. In 2017, President Trump and the Republican majority in Congress passed a major tax cut, significantly expanding deficit spending and thereby stimulating the economy at a time when the recession was long over, going against both Keynesian and neoliberal theories. From 2016 to 2019, the U.S. economy was growing significantly faster than the European one was. While the debate continues, it seems that the more aggressive stimulus in the United States resulted in a somewhat stronger recovery, though even in the United States the recovery was slower than in past recessions. Eventually, of course, governments must reduce deficit spending by some combination of tax increases and expenditure decreases.

The recession also initiated a renewed debate about government regulation, especially of the financial sector. Neoliberal economist Alan Greenspan, chair of the U.S. Federal Reserve from 1987 to 2006, believed that private competition in the market for investments like mortgage-backed securities and credit default swaps would produce better security than would government rules. Investors could be counted on not to take on more risk than was prudent, meaning the government would be wasting money if it were constantly watching over investors' shoulders. Many Keynesians, on the other hand, believe regulation to be especially appropriate in the financial sector, since they see it as unusually prone to irrational and inefficient booms and busts. In the years following the crisis, both the United States and ECB put in place new regulations to monitor the largest banks considered "too big to fail" and reduce the risks they could take.

Crises such as the Great Recession can be what institutionalists call "critical junctures," moments when societies move in entirely new directions. Many initially believed the Great Recession would be such a critical juncture: after three decades of the dominance of neoliberal economic theory, governments rapidly shifted toward Keynesian policy in response to the crisis. Some analysts saw a potential shift back to the "golden age" of Keynesianism, while others wondered if a new model of economic policy might emerge (Kotz 2015). Nearly everyone saw a stronger role for the state as a likely outcome. By 2019, expanded regulations on finance were in place but were modest, and many governments had reduced deficit spending (with the United States being a major exception), suggesting they had not abandoned neoliberalism yet. A decade after it began, the Great Recession did not appear to have reset economic policies fundamentally in Western countries.

KEY ECONOMIC THEORIES		
	KEYNESIANISM	**NEOLIBERALISM**
Architect	John Maynard Keynes	Milton Friedman/Friedrich Hayek
Role of governments	Governments should actively manage business cycles	Governments should play diminished role in economy; open economies to global trade
Key instruments	Fiscal policy, including deficit spending; regulation; looser monetary policy	Monetary policy; deregulation; privatization
Criticisms	Deficit spending reduces private investment and growth and causes inflation; regulation limits business investment	Neoliberal restrictions on government spending slow growth during recession; deregulation creates boom and bust; increases inequality

Types of Capitalist Economies

Now that we have outlined the fundamental relationships between states and markets and the economic theories that guide government policies, we can examine the various models of capitalism among wealthy countries. While the state must perform certain core functions to sustain capitalism, this leaves much possible variation. Wealthy countries have created distinct models of capitalism that involve significant differences in how the state intervenes in the market. A recent, influential school of thought known as the **varieties of capitalism (VOC)** approach attempts to analyze these differences systematically. It focuses primarily on business firms and how they are governed in terms of their interactions with government, one another, workers, and sources of finance, such as banks and stock markets. Proponents of this approach distinguish between two broad types of economies among wealthy capitalist countries: liberal market economies and coordinated market economies.

varieties of capitalism (VOC): School of thought analyzing wealthy market economies that focuses primarily on business firms and how they are governed; divides such economies into liberal market economies and coordinated market economies

Liberal Market Economies

Liberal market economies (LMEs), such as the United States and the United Kingdom, rely more heavily on market relationships, meaning that firms interact with other firms and secure sources of finance through purely market-based transactions. They know little about one another's inner workings, which leads them to focus primarily on short-term profits to enhance stock prices, a key source of finance. Such firms' relationship to workers is also primarily via open markets: rates of unionization are low and labor laws are flexible, allowing firms to hire and fire employees with ease. The government's role in such economies is focused on ensuring that market relationships function properly through, for instance, fairly stringent antimonopoly laws and rules governing stock exchanges that guarantee that all buyers are privy to the same information.

liberal market economies (LMEs): In the varieties of capitalism approach, countries that rely heavily on market relationships to govern economic activity; the United States and United Kingdom are key examples

Coordinated Market Economies

Coordinated market economies (CMEs), by contrast, involve more conscious coordination among firms, financiers, unions, and government. Many firms and banks hold large amounts of stock in one another's operations, which gives them inside

coordinated market economies (CMEs): In the varieties of capitalism approach, capitalist economies in which firms, financiers, unions, and government consciously coordinate their actions via interlocking ownership and participation; Germany and Japan are key examples

information on how the others operate. This, in turn, encourages firms to coordinate their activities and establish long-term relationships in terms of finance and buying inputs. Firms are able to focus on longer-term initiatives because financiers have inside information about the potential for long-term gains. CMEs tend to have stronger unions and higher levels of unionization, and worker training is focused within sectors of the economy and within related firms. The government is involved in negotiating agreements among firms and between firms and unions, and it allows or even encourages the close relationships that might be termed "insider trading" or quasi-monopoly situations in an LME. Germany is a prime example of a CME.

The logic of the VOC approach also suggests that LMEs and CMEs are likely to pursue distinct fiscal and welfare policies. At first glance, it might seem that CMEs, with their high levels of government involvement in coordinating the economy, would be likely to pursue more interventionist, Keynesian fiscal policies, but VOC theorists argue exactly the opposite. Because CMEs have built-in ways to stabilize the labor market to maintain employment, they are less likely to need or want to pursue fiscal stimulation. LMEs, on the other hand, have far more flexible labor markets; therefore, unemployment is likely to go up more quickly in a recession, and their governments will need to pursue more Keynesian stimulation to reduce unemployment.

Scholars also noted a relationship between varieties of capitalism and the two types of democracies we outlined in chapter 5: majoritarian and consensus. Majoritarian democracies tend to have LMEs, while consensus democracies have CMEs. Japanese political scientist Masanobu Ido (2012), among others, argued that in consensus democracies, mostly with PR electoral systems, parties representing business interests must negotiate policies with parties representing labor so businesses become more adept and willing to negotiate with labor generally in CMEs. Consensus democracies also provide greater policy stability because of the many veto points in the system. This makes workers more willing to invest in the sector-specific skills typical of a CME; they are assured that government support for the particular sector—and therefore their skills—will continue. In majoritarian democracies, on the other hand, policy can change more quickly and workers will be reluctant to invest heavily in a particular sector. Businesses in majoritarian democracies, meanwhile, prefer to gain majority control of the government via the parties that represent them and create policies they favor rather than negotiating with labor, thus creating an LME.

Britain and Germany are major exemplars of the two models. Prior to World War II, Britain was a typical LME, with limited involvement in the economy. The Labour Party, which directly represented unions, took power for the first time after World War II and nationalized several major industries, created the National Health Service (see chapter 12), and built government-owned housing for millions of working-class people. In spite of this government activity, coordination was minimal. Nationalized firms ran independently, though became increasingly unprofitable over time. Britain was an LME like the United States but with a larger welfare state. A strong economy in the global boom after World War II fell apart in the 1970s. As inflation grew, unions demanded that wage increases keep up, which fueled more inflation. About half of the British labor force belonged to a union, an unusually high level for an LME, but the peak labor association, the Trade Unions Congress (TUC), did not have the power to impose wage restraints. In an LME such as Britain, neither unions nor businesses have a history of or an incentive to negotiate agreements to moderate wages. The crisis ultimately culminated in the "winter of discontent" in 1978–1979, when massive strikes occurred.

Out of this crisis rose a new, neoliberal manifestation of the Conservative Party, which Margaret Thatcher led to victory in the 1979 election. She won on promises of implementing a completely new approach to economic policy, unions, and the welfare state. In Britain's majoritarian system, under which Thatcher's Conservative Party fully controlled parliament, she passed legislation to implement major neoliberal policies, starting with reducing unions' ability to organize and strike. By 1995, union membership had dropped from half of all employees to only a third and is now down to about a quarter. When facing global economic pressure, LMEs look to reduce labor costs and increase flexibility to compete more effectively. Thatcher also began selling off state-owned companies to private investors, which increased unemployment as the unprofitable companies laid off workers: unemployment rose from an average of 4.2 percent in the late 1970s to 9.5 percent in the 1980s (Huber and Stephens 2001, A11). She successfully reduced inflation by reducing the money supply and budget deficit, increased the tax burden on lower-income groups, and lowered it on business and the wealthy. The share of the population living on less than half of the average national income increased from 9 to 25 percent (Ginsburg 2001, 186). Regional inequality increased a great deal as well. Deindustrialization (caused in part by the government selling off unprofitable industries) increased unemployment and poverty in the north, while the south, especially London, became one of the wealthiest regions in Europe and a global financial center. Thatcher's reforms reshaped the British economy by making it a purer LME, and subsequent British governments have not fundamentally changed that.

As a divided Germany emerged from World War II, its CME was created. The Christian Democratic Union (CDU) under Konrad Adenauer governed West Germany from its first election in 1949 until 1966. Though a "conservative" party, the CDU developed its CME. Christian Democrats generally saw protection of workers as part of their Christian ideology. The other major party, the Social Democrats, often wanted more social spending, but both major parties agreed with the basic premises of the system: a form of capitalism in which close relationships and interpenetration between the private and public sectors have shaped economic and social policies. Following the CME model, German banks rather than the stock market long provided the bulk of corporate finance. Banks lent money to companies and often had representatives on those companies' boards, so they knew how their money was being used. Unions were crucial in negotiating binding wage agreements with employers' associations, which all employers in a given sector had to follow in Germany's strongly corporatist interest group system (see chapter 6). Unions are also represented on the supervisory boards of all German firms with more than two thousand employees. This system, known as codetermination, gives unions power to influence employers' policies and facilitates close interaction between business and labor. Close interaction among large businesses, unions, and the government was the norm. This economic model made West Germany one of the

British commuters in the City of London, Britain's financial district. Under the country's LME, London's financial sector is second only to New York's. The Brexit vote to leave the EU in 2016, though, threatened that success. A number of large banks were considering moving to somewhere in continental Europe to stay within the EU.
Richard Baker/In Pictures via Getty Images

most successful economies in the world from the end of World War II until the 1980s. Although Germany today remains one of the wealthiest countries in the world and a clear leader of the EU, the CME model faced significant challenges with the merger of West Germany and the much poorer East Germany at the end of the Cold War.

The distinct models of capitalism in different wealthy countries developed after World War II and arguably came to full fruition by the 1970s and 1980s. They then faced what many analysts saw as a set of forces that threatened each model's ability to maintain its distinctive qualities and even the states' powers to set economic policy generally: globalization.

Globalization: A New World Order, or Déjà Vu All Over Again?

The 2008–2009 recession showed the negative elements of globalization clearly: a financial crisis based in the United States quickly spread around the world. Major European investors had stakes in the high-risk securities that collapsed on Wall Street, causing European banks to face possible bankruptcy and Cyprus, Greece, Ireland, Italy, Portugal, and Spain to come close to default. Export markets for developing economies like China and India plummeted, and a brief era of economic growth in Africa was nipped in the bud. These global effects all started with average people in places like Arizona and Florida buying homes with risky, variable-rate mortgages.

Globalization has become perhaps the most frequently used and abused term in political economy. It first gained prominence in the 1990s, and since then, hundreds of books and countless articles have been written about it. It has cultural as well as economic and political implications, but we will focus on the latter two in order to understand its effects on the relationship between the state and the market. That economic activity across borders has increased over the last generation is beyond question: between 1980 and 2010, trade as a share of global GDP increased from 30 percent to 56 percent, foreign direct investment more than quadrupled, and annual minutes of international phone calls from the United States went from two billion to seventy-five billion (Dadush and Dervis 2013).

Globalization has many definitions. We define it as a rapid increase in the flow of economic activity, technology, and communications around the globe. Three key questions have arisen about globalization: (1) Does it represent a brave new world in which the fundamental relationship between the state and the market has changed forever, or is it simply the latest phase in that relationship—something new and interesting but not fundamentally different? (2) What caused it in the first place? (3) What can and should be done about it, if anything?

globalization: A rapid increase in the flow of economic activity, technology, and communications around the globe, and the increased sharing of cultural symbols, political ideas, and movements across countries

A Brave New World?

Globalization's earliest adherents saw it as a portent of fundamental change. Japanese scholar Kenichi Ohmae (1995) argued that globalization would result in the "end of the nation-state," claiming that the rapid flow of money, goods and services around the globe will eventually make the nation-state irrelevant. Regional if not global management will have to fill the role currently played by the state. The flow of ideas and culture will severely weaken national identity, as the Internet in particular will allow people to form identities not linked to territories and their immediate local communities. All of these changes ultimately will require political responses in the form of strengthened international organizations for global governance and a new global civil society to respond to global problems with global solutions.

Since the initial separation of the economic and political spheres in early modern Europe, capital's greatest weapon has been its mobility: business can often threaten to move if it does not receive adequate treatment from a state. The state, in sharp contrast, is tied to a territory. Ohmae and other prophets of change argued that globalization significantly increased capital mobility so that businesses can credibly threaten to leave a country much more easily now than they could a generation ago. This mobility increased capital's power in relation to states. In trying to manage their economies, policymakers must be actively concerned about preserving the investments they have and attracting new ones, and with business able to move relatively easily, states increasingly must compete to attract it.

Similar changes in global finance—the flow of money around the world—also have weakened the state. Most countries now allow their currencies to be traded freely. Electronic communications have made currency transactions nearly instantaneous. For a government trying to pursue sound monetary policies through control of its money supply and interest rates, this new world of global currency flow can be problematic. The collapse of many Southeast Asian economies in 1997 was caused at least in part by currency speculators, traders who purchase a country's currency not to buy goods in that country but simply to try to buy it at a low valuation and sell it later at a higher valuation. When the speculators, led by international financier George Soros, found the Southeast Asian economies were weaker than they had believed, they began to sell the currencies. This led to a classic market panic in which virtually all international traders sold those currencies, causing immense economic loss and political instability in the region and, ultimately, in developing countries worldwide. States, especially in small and poor countries, must base monetary and fiscal policy not only on domestic concerns but also on how global markets might react.

Skeptics of the impact of globalization question the assertion that states are no longer relevant or even any less powerful. Torben Iversen and David Soskice (2019) challenged the key assumption of the globalization argument: that capital is more mobile than it used to be and therefore states are weaker. They argued that the new, knowledge-based economy that arose with the communication and technology revolutions is based most fundamentally on particular kinds of skilled labor, and that those skills cluster in certain places (such as Silicon Valley) and are not particularly mobile. Multinational companies certainly move capital around the world, mainly among advanced capitalist societies, but they do so in search of the skills they need. The skilled knowledge workers are most productive when working together in agglomerations that have come to reside in a series of major cities.

Iversen and Soskice argued that governments in advanced capitalist societies have created policies to facilitate this not, because capital is all powerful but because the growing workforce that benefits from these economic changes supports policies to further them. This has produced greater openness to allow capital to flow, but states remain powerful in establishing the policies that enhance their position in these new markets, supported by their educated citizens who benefit. At the same time, deindustrialization occurred as trade policies allowed older industries to take advantage of lower production costs in developing countries

Workers sit in protest in Italy, demanding the reopening of an Alcoa (an American company) aluminum plant. Globalization has shifted manufacturing jobs around the world in particular, leading to workers in some areas losing jobs while large numbers are hired elsewhere. Those on the losing end often fight politically against the changes, reflected in this kind of protest as well as the "Brexit" vote in the United Kingdom.
Photo by Andrea Ronchini/Pacific Press/LightRocket via Getty Images

and move manufacturing plants out of wealthy countries. Hundreds of thousands of workers, long reliant on relatively well-paying and secure jobs in such industries as automobile manufacturing and steel, faced unemployment and bleak prospects. These were the losers in the process, but their fellow citizens who were winners in the new economy actively supported the policies that benefited them, at the expense of the "old economy" of manufacturing. The new era is certainly a significant shift, but it was driven not by the power of capital but by the votes of the winners in the process, at the expense of the losers. States and democratic politics still matter.

In the new millennium, the scholarly consensus has moved away from Ohmae's view of globalization toward a more modest assessment of its effects. Certainly all of the trends described above exist, and many agree that globalization is likely to weaken the nation-state, but few now believe that globalization will destroy it. Even the most ardent skeptics of the "end of the nation-state" thesis recognize that major economic changes have taken place. Any state interested in the economic well-being of its populace must negotiate the rapidly expanding global markets as well as possible, bargaining for the best deal for its people, but how easy that is depends on the resources at its disposal. Iversen and Soskice's argument defends the continuing power of states in wealthy capitalist countries. A country like El Salvador, however, has none of the advantages the new knowledge economy can bring. Investments there are in agriculture and "light manufacturing," which involve a large amount of cheap, unskilled, and easily replaceable labor. The Salvadoran government is in a significantly weaker bargaining position vis-à-vis likely international investors than is, for example, the German government.

Causes of Globalization

What factors facilitated this weakening of the state vis-à-vis capital? The causes of globalization are undoubtedly multiple, but two major answers to this question have competed for attention. The first one is that technology is the driving force of globalization. The costs of communication and transportation have dropped dramatically. Air travel, once a luxury good for the elite, is now a common practice for citizens of wealthy countries. Advances in containerization and just-in-time manufacturing have allowed more rapid and efficient shipment of goods. And as we all know, the personal computer, the mobile phone, and the Internet have created instantaneous global communications capabilities while reducing costs. All of this has allowed businesses to expand across national borders at unprecedented rates and created a new set of highly skilled, knowledge-based workers. Those arguing that globalization does represent a new era point out that this communications and transportation revolution allows transnational corporations to coordinate complex production processes for both goods and services across multiple countries in a manner that is entirely new. Shoes may be designed in Portland, Oregon, but produced in Malaysia using Bangladeshi labor and material inputs from Vietnam and

China, all coordinated by "just-in-time" manufacturing to deliver just the number of shoes that are likely to sell in your local shopping mall this month.

A second school of thought argues that while technology was necessary for globalization, government policies made globalization a reality. The shift to neoliberal economic policies significantly reduced the role of most governments in regulating economic transactions, especially across their borders. The creation of the World Trade Organization (WTO) in 1995 accelerated a process, started after World War II, of lowering tariffs on imports and exports. Removing government controls on exchange rates allowed money to travel around the world without limit, seeking the best return at the least risk.

It is difficult to disentangle technological and policy changes to find a single cause of globalization. Iversen and Soskice (2019) argued the technological changes created new groups of beneficiaries among highly educated citizens who demanded policy changes to facilitate the process—technological changes laid the groundwork for political demands for policy changes, but the latter were not inevitable. The different answers have important implications. If technology is the primary cause, then globalization is inevitable and irreversible. If policies play an important role as well, then globalization, or at least its effects, may be subject to change.

Globalization and the European Union

The creation of the EU (see Map 10.1) and especially of its common currency, the euro, raised fundamental questions about globalization and state sovereignty over economic policy. On the one hand, the existence of the EU arguably limits globalization because it creates a regional market as an alternative. On the other hand, EU member states have given up far more economic sovereignty to a transnational organization than have any other modern states, and EU membership requires they follow many of the policies that Iversen and Soskice (2019) saw as facilitating the new, knowledge-based economy.

Initially, EU member states did not yield substantial sovereignty because each state retained an effective veto over Europe-wide policies. That changed with the Single European Act of 1987, which limited a single state's veto power; not even Germany, the biggest state, can veto decisions. Instead, several states must vote together to block a decision, which means that individual states have given up their individual sovereign right over key economic decisions. The next and biggest step was the Maastricht Treaty of 1992, which created the euro, controlled by a new European Central Bank (ECB). The seventeen states that have so far agreed to participate (the EU has twenty-seven members, but only seventeen have adopted the euro so far) gave up their ability to control their own monetary policy and agreed to limits on their fiscal policy, severely limiting their ability to set their own economic policies. The ECB controls the money supply and therefore monetary policy for these states. Crucially, however, each state continues to control its own fiscal policy; the disjuncture between monetary and fiscal policy and limited EU power over the latter was at the center of the "euro crisis" that began in 2009.

The Great Recession hit the EU and especially the euro extremely hard. Maintaining the limits on debt required by euro rules has always been hard, even for the healthier economies such as Germany and France. In the economic boom that preceded the crisis, several of the weaker economies ran up debts and deficits; their booming economies and use of the euro attracted capital from economically stronger countries in northern Europe, allowing them to borrow money cheaply and fueling exports from wealthy countries like Germany to poorer southern ones

MAP 10.1

The European Union

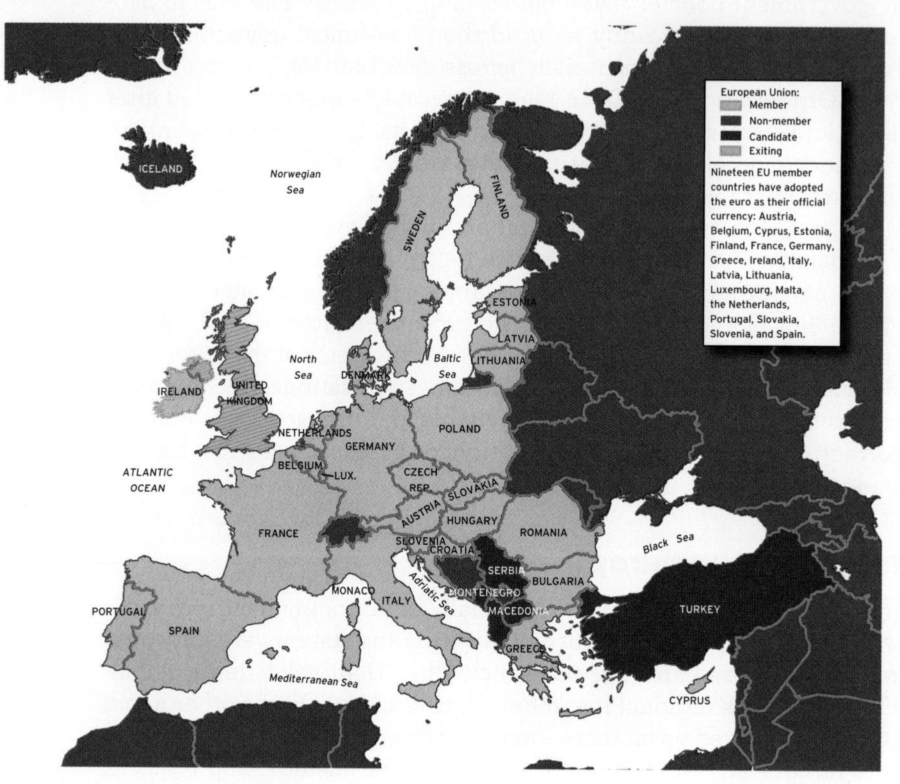

Source: Adapted from European Union (http://europa.eu/about-eu/countries/index_en.htm)

like Greece. Others, such as Spain and Ireland, had fiscal surpluses before the crisis, but the recession hit the countries' banking sector so hard that their tax revenue plummeted, creating a fiscal crisis. In some countries, such as Ireland and Cyprus, the banking sector constituted a huge share of the entire economy, setting off a severe recession when the financial crisis hit. The crisis revealed the problems created by EU control of monetary policy while fiscal policy remained at the national level and member countries' economic strength varied greatly. In 2010 private international creditors began to doubt the weaker states' ability to repay their debts and, therefore, started refusing to buy their government bonds. The worst hit were Greece and Ireland, followed by Portugal, Italy, Spain, and Cyprus. Usually, countries in this situation would allow the value of their currencies to drop to encourage exports and restart growth. This was not an option, however, because the countries use the euro and its value is tied to the strength of the entire EU. The value of the euro was not dropping fast enough to spur exports because of the continuing economic strength of the larger countries—especially Germany, which, as the strongest exporter in the region, had long been advantaged by the euro.

Debt crises for entire countries are usually resolved at the expense of both the debtors and creditors. Debt-ridden governments have to institute severe fiscal policies to reduce their deficits, cutting government employment and raising taxes, and creditors have to forgive part of a debt that is too big to ever pay back—essentially a bad loan. As the old joke goes, if you owe your bank $10,000 and can't pay it back, you're in trouble; if you owe your bank $10 million dollars and can't pay it back, your bank is in trouble. In the euro crisis, the wealthier, creditor countries were able to impose almost all of the costs on the debtors in the form of severe deficit reduction. Bailout packages funded by the ECB and International Monetary Fund (IMF) were put in place in 2010 for Greece and Ireland, with Greece requiring two more in 2012 and 2016. The bailouts gave those countries new funds to pay their debt but only very slightly forgave any debt (Frieden and Walter 2017). Alternatives, such as raising taxes on banks and the wealthy across Europe to help fund the weaker governments, were proposed but never seriously considered by the ECB or IMF (Cafruny and Talani 2013). Widespread protests turned violent in Greece and toppled the governments in Ireland and Italy. By 2018, modest economic growth had returned to Greece, but unemployment remained at 22 percent; in Italy, voters put a government led by openly anti-EU parties in power.

EU institutions also moved to prevent future crises. By 2013, the ECB had agreed to buy member government bonds if necessary (thereby protecting them from the worst effects of the markets) and had placed one hundred to two hundred of the largest European banks under its direct supervision to help ensure their integrity; the EU had created a permanent fund to support countries in financial crisis, and it had initiated policies to give stronger incentives to governments to stick to the official limits on their debts and deficits. All of this was an effort to reassure investors about the long-term stability of the euro.

For the first time since the creation of the euro, the crisis produced open discussion (especially in Greece) about whether continuing to use the common currency was wise. Critics of the EU have long opposed the fiscal and monetary policies required to join the euro, seeing them as forcing every member country to follow the neoliberal economic orthodoxy that they believe is undermining European social welfare policies. The crisis reinforced these arguments, calling into question the benefits that a single currency was supposed to provide while requiring even more unpopular fiscal policies. Nonetheless, the long-term benefits of remaining in the eurozone led governments in all the debtor countries to accept paying the costs of resolving the crisis.

In the aftermath of this crisis, the British passed "Brexit" with 52 percent of the vote in 2016, declaring their intention to leave the EU entirely. Britain had long only partially participated in the EU. It never adopted the euro and in 2015 refused to accept new rules on fiscal policy. Nonetheless, a long-standing movement led by the right-wing UKIP (see chapter 6) called for leaving the EU entirely; the euro-crisis helped it finally succeed. Despite promises of a "deal or no deal" Brexit by October 31, 2019, Prime Minister Boris Johnson asked for yet another extension when MPs failed to approve his proposed settlement. He called for a new election to take place a month before the new deadline (January 2020), in hopes the results would give the Conservatives a solid majority to finally quit the EU.

Political Responses to Globalization

The expanded global market and capital mobility also raise questions about the level at which political responses to economic problems can and should occur. As we noted above, individual states are still important, as they navigate global markets the best they can via their economic policies. More and more analysts argue, however, that new global problems such as climate change require global political solutions. As we discussed in chapter 7, many groups in civil society are not waiting for states to implement globally coordinated policies on their own. Citizens' groups are actively organizing across borders to put pressure on governments or international bodies such as the WTO, the IMF, and the World Bank to enact global measures to address global problems. Domestically, the Great Recession has led growing numbers of citizens to blame trade and immigration (aspects of the reduced border controls of globalization) for their problems and to support the populist, far-right parties and movements we discussed in chapter 6. These movements focused very much on the level of the nation-state and on the most visible signs of globalization: trade and immigration.

Two schools of thought have debated how wealthy governments should or must respond to globalization. According to the **convergence** thesis, the distinctions among different models of capitalism that we discussed above will tend to disappear as all governments are forced to conform to the logic of attracting global capital. In effect, they must pursue even more neoliberal policies. They must keep inflation low so prices are stable, which requires restraining government spending and the money supply. They must keep corporate taxes low so that businesses will want to invest, but if taxes are low, then spending must be low as well, meaning that social welfare programs also have to be cut. They must ensure that labor is flexible and relatively compliant, and they must do what they can to keep labor unions from making too many demands because rigid contracts and rules that guarantee jobs or benefits for long periods discourage investment. And, of course, they must keep tariffs and other barriers to the entry and exit of capital at a minimum. This raises profound questions about democracy: if governments have little choice in which economic policies they must pursue under globalization, do elections, parties, and voters' choices still matter, or do they matter only for noneconomic issues?

Comparativists using the varieties of capitalism approach, on the other hand, suggest that while globalization applies pressure toward convergence, long-established political and economic institutions heavily influence how each country can and will respond. They argued that the various institutionalized relationships in each kind of economy are complementary, which they term **comparative institutional advantage**. The institutions work together to provide greater benefits than any single institution could alone. It is difficult, they argued, to change one particular institution, such as corporate finance, without changing many others. Consequently, firms have interests in maintaining the institutions in which they operate, and they will be reluctant to change them in response to globalization. Firms in CMEs benefit from the various institutions that help them coordinate their activities, train their workers, and secure the services of employees over the long term. A more rigid labor market that does not make it as easy for workers to move from firm to firm, for instance, complements a training system in which firms invest in educating their workers for specific tasks. If workers could quickly move from job to job, the firms would lose the benefits of their investment in training. In LMEs, by contrast, more flexible labor markets give firms little incentive to train employees. Workers and the public education system therefore invest in more general skills that workers can transfer from firm to firm, meaning that firms don't have to invest directly in employee training.

convergence: Argument that globalization will force similar neoliberal policies across all countries

comparative institutional advantage: Idea in the varieties of capitalism school of thought that different kinds of capitalist systems have different institutional advantages that they usually will try to maintain, resulting in different responses to external economic pressures

The comparative institutional advantage of LMEs is in their flexible market relationships. In response to globalization, they tend to strengthen market mechanisms even more. Governments work to decrease union influence, provide broad-based education for an ever more flexible workforce, and increase the variety and efficiency of open-market sources of finance such as stock markets. Their typical majoritarian democracies help ruling parties institute these changes relatively quickly. The comparative institutional advantage of CMEs, on the other hand, is

FIGURE 10.1

Globalization's Effects on Economic Policies: Two Views

Convergence thesis

Hypermobile capital flows affect wealthy economies the same way.

Wealthy economies attract capital by lowering inflation, corporate taxes, and social spending, and implementing minimal tariffs and trade barriers.

They tend to converge regardless of type. Policies become increasingly similar in order to attract capital and respond effectively to globalization.

The convergence thesis focuses primarily on state-based responses to globalization and views all types of wealthy economies as having the same reaction to globalization.

The varieties of capitalism model

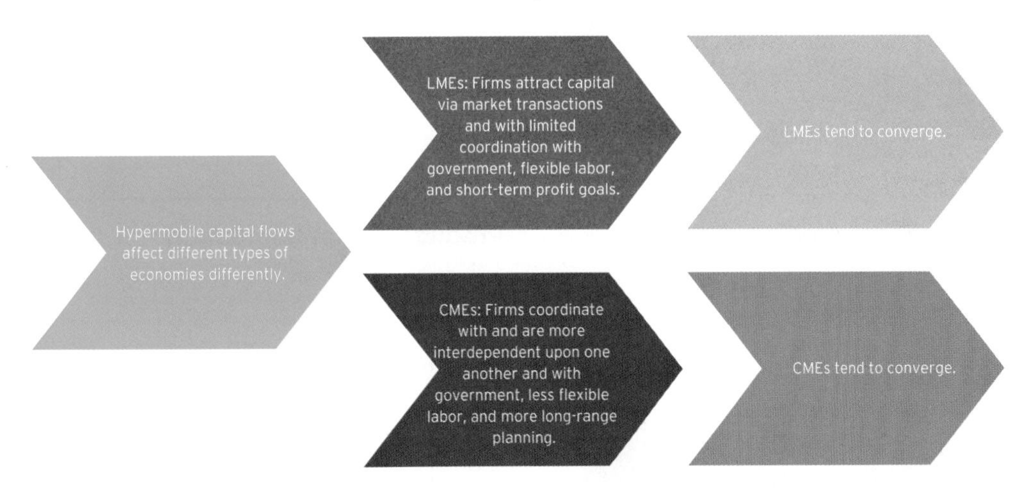

Hypermobile capital flows affect different types of economies differently.
LMEs: Firms attract capital via market transactions and with limited coordination with government, flexible labor, and short-term profit goals.
LMEs tend to converge.
CMEs: Firms coordinate with and are more interdependent upon one another and with government, less flexible labor, and more long-range planning.
CMEs tend to converge.

The varieties of capitalism model focuses on how firms interact with government, other organizations, and their workers and anticipates that different kinds of economies will respond differently to globalization. Convergence will occur within each type of economy, a "dual convergence."

CRITICAL INQUIRY

How Useful Is the Varieties of Capitalism Model?

The varieties of capitalism model argues that two types of advanced capitalist economies exist, are affected by globalization differently, and respond to globalization differently. Figures 10.2 to 10.7 provide a broad comparison of CMEs and LMEs over time, as globalization unfolded since the 1970s. Do the data agree with the arguments of the VOC model? What does the model accurately predict in the figures and what does it not? What might explain the areas in which the VOC model does not hold up?

(Continued)

(Continued)

FIGURES 10.2–10.7

Comparing Coordinated Market Economies and Liberal Market Economies

FIGURE 10.2

Union Density

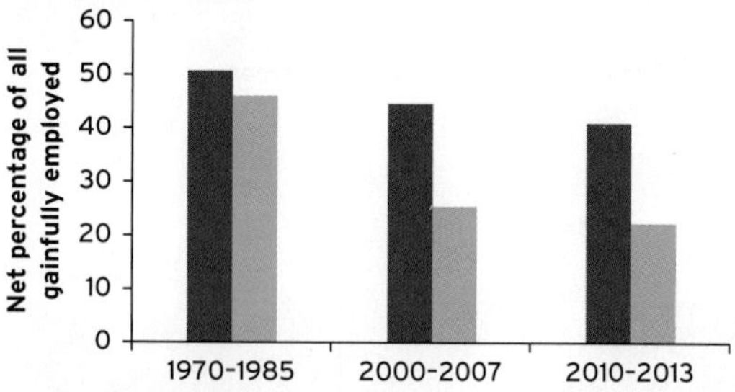

Net percentage of all gainfully employed

60, 50, 40, 30, 20, 10, 0

1970–1985 2000–2007 2010–2013

FIGURE 10.3

Strikes

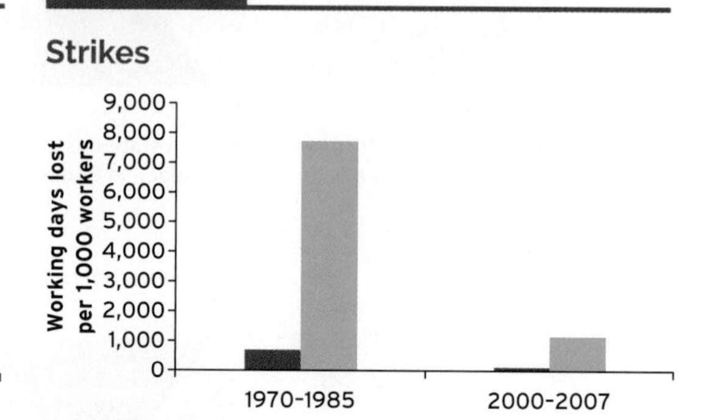

FIGURE 10.4

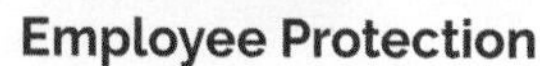

Employee Protection

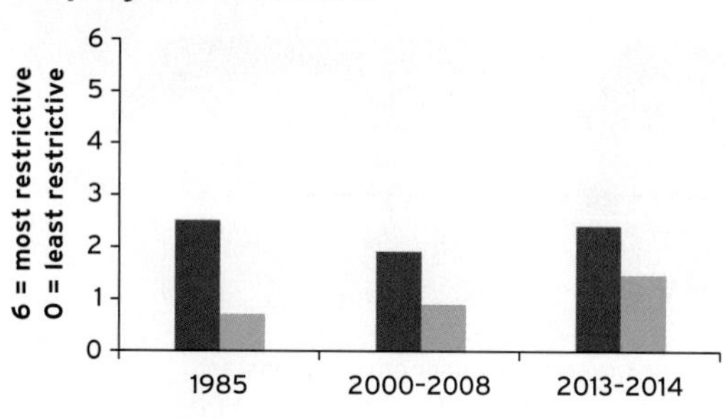

FIGURE 10.5

Product Market Regulation

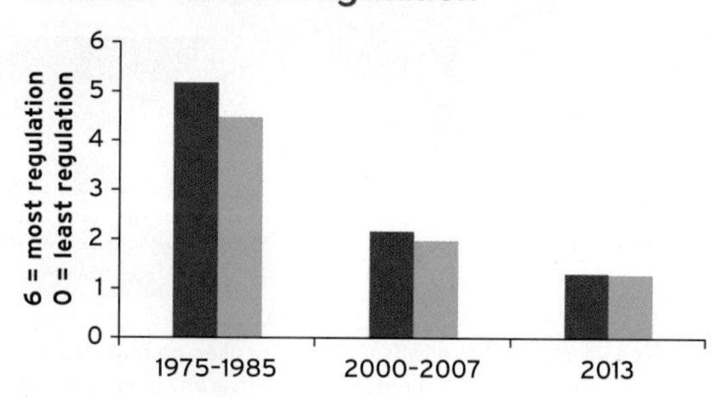

FIGURE 10.6

Trade Openness

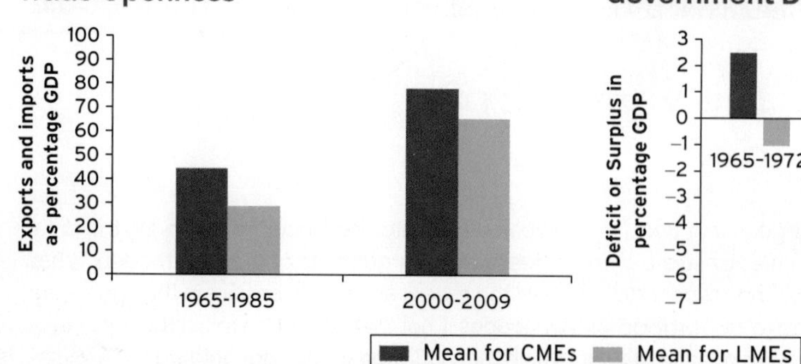

FIGURE 10.7

Government Deficit

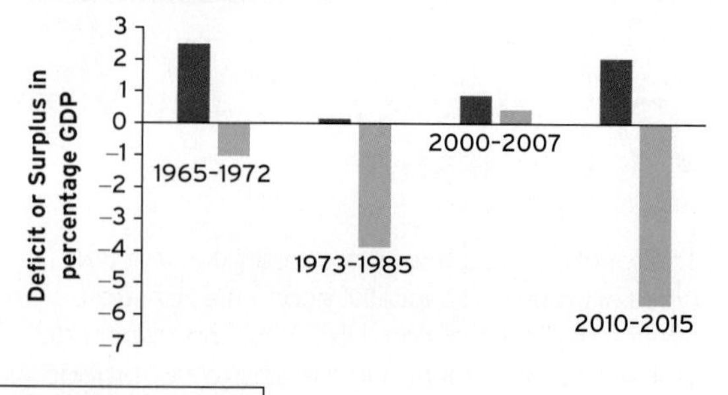

Source: All data are from the Organisation for Economic Co-operation and Development (OECD).

in their ability to adjust but maintain their coordination mechanisms. Firms do not abandon countries with CMEs because doing so would cause them to give up the institutional advantages they have there, advantages in which they have long invested. Their consensus democracies mean that policy change is slower. Management and workers have incentives to make marginal changes to improve the performance of the firms in which they have a long-term interest.

Hall and Gingerich (2009) tested the VOC approach with a series of extensive statistical techniques. They found that the patterns outlined by the approach held up empirically. Each type of economy (LME and CME) can be discerned by a set of complementary practices across a variety of statistical measures. Comparative institutional advantage holds up as well, in the sense that countries that more closely conform to one of the two models achieved higher growth rates. Countries with more mixed systems and therefore less reinforcing comparative institutional advantages grew more slowly. Across a variety of measures, however, they also found that most wealthy economies are moving in the direction the forces of globalization would suggest: protection of labor is down, social spending is down, and flexibility has increased. Iversen and Soskice (2019) argued that this reflects all advanced capitalist governments pursuing their interest in long-term growth by creating policies that serve the interests of the new, knowledge-based economy and its educated workforce. A quantitative analysis of election surveys in Europe found parties in more globalized countries still respond to voters' opinions, voters still make choices between parties on the left and right economically, they still believe they can hold their governments accountable, and they still believe in the value of their democracy (Vowles and Xezonakis 2016).

Japan has faced particular challenges dealing with globalization. Its economic model from the 1950s through the 1990s was the **developmental state** (Johnson 1982). It was a type of CME but with far less labor involvement than in European CMEs. A developmental state consciously seeks to create national strength in particular economic areas, taking an active and conscious role in the development of specific sectors of the economy. The Japanese government did this via two key bureaucratic agencies, the Ministry of Finance (MOF) and the Ministry of International Trade and Industry (MITI). The MOF had extensive influence over the banking sector via its control over interest rates and over the role of banks in the keiretsu, Japanese corporate families like Toyota and Mitsui. At the center of most keiretsu is a major bank, which lends money on favorable terms to its keiretsu members and typically sends representatives to work in the firms to which it has lent money to ensure that its loans are being used wisely. By guaranteeing the key bank loans, the MOF had substantial influence over where and how they lent. MITI influenced industrial policies more specifically through extensive licensing of technology and "administrative guidance," the bureaucracy's practice of informally and successfully suggesting that an industry or firm pursue a particular endeavor.

The developmental state created the "Japanese miracle," the sustained growth that made the Japanese economy six times larger in 1975 than it had been in 1950. Table 10.2 illustrates the sharp difference between the last twenty-five years in Japan and earlier decades. Economic growth has dropped substantially, unemployment has risen, and prices fell nearly continuously for fifteen years, a sign of serious economic stagnation. The economic miracle ended in 1990; on the first business day of that year, real estate and stock prices, which had been climbing rapidly, plummeted and the bubble burst. In the 1980s, the system of guaranteeing bank loans led Japanese corporations to take on excessive debt, which they invested

developmental state: A state that seeks to create national strength by taking an active and conscious role in the development of specific sectors of the economy (Ch 10)

TABLE 10.2

Profile of Japan's Economy, 1970–Most Recent Available

STATE	1970	1980	1990	2000	2011	MOST RECENT
GDP growth (annual %)	10.7	2.8	5.2	2.9	−0.7	1.7% (2017)
Social expenditures (total, as % of GDP)	..	10.3	11.2	16.1	23.1	21.9 (2018)
Gross national savings (as % of nominal GDP)	..	..	33.2	27.5	22	28 (2017)
Share of income or consumption, ratio of richest 20% to poorest 20%	..	..	4.3	3.4	3.4	6.2 (2015)

Sources: Data are from World Bank Indicators (all data except Social Expenditures), OECD (Social Expenditures).

in real estate and other unproductive areas. Simultaneously, the more successful Japanese companies, such as Toyota and Nissan, fully entered the age of globalization, investing elsewhere in the world so that instead of exporting cars from Japan, they began building them in the United States and Europe. This reduced Japan's key source of growth: exports. All of this reduced the extent to which keiretsu members continued to coordinate their activity, as the corporate structure of the Japanese economy in the 1990s and 2000s moved perceptibly toward a more LME model of vertically integrated, globally active corporations (Lincoln and Shimotani 2009). The economic base of Japan's CME profoundly shifted, largely due to the forces of globalization; Japan continues to struggle to adjust.

Globalization and Inequality

A growing concern in the era of globalization is increasing economic inequality. Capitalism inherently produces inequality, as some people benefit from the market and private property more than others, but the level of inequality varies over time and across countries, even among successful advanced capitalist economies. Thomas Piketty (2014) famously argued that inequality inherently grows under capitalism because the return to capital exceeds the growth of the economy as a whole. Growing equality from World War I to about 1980 was caused, he argued, by the devastation of two world wars and their political implications; growing inequality since then is a return to the normal effects of capitalism.

Excessive inequality has long been a concern because it is associated with greater poverty and because of its effects on the notion of equal citizenship in a democracy (see chapter 12). Figure 10.8 portrays what has come to be called "The Great Gatsby Curve," showing that countries with higher inequality have lower intergenerational mobility; the rich stay rich and the poor stay poor, which many associate with support for the far-right populist parties discussed in chapter 6. A team of economists at the IMF demonstrated that greater inequality also results in slower economic growth (Ostry et al. 2019). Since the 1980s, when the current era of globalization began, the Gini index, the most common measure of inequality, increased across all OECD countries from 0.29 to 0.33 in 2016, an increase of about 10 percent (OECD 2011, 2019). In 1980, the poorest half of the population in OECD countries had a slightly larger share of after-tax national income than the richest 10 percent; by 2017, the richer group had 5 percent more than the bottom

FIGURE 10.8

The Great Gatsby Curve

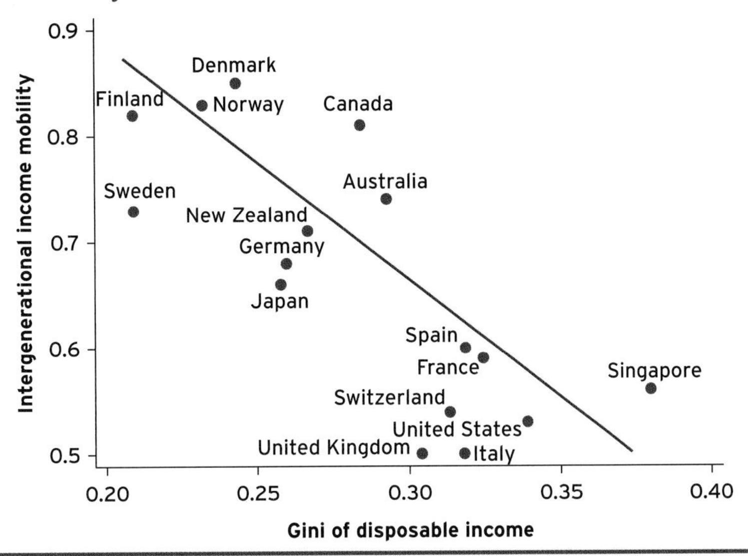

Source: Adapted from Torben Iversen and David Soskice, *Democracy and Prosperity: Reinventing Capitalism Through a Turbulent Century* (Princeton, NJ: Princeton University Press, 2019), 221

half (World Inequality Database 2019). In the most unequal countries, such as the United States, inequality has returned to levels not seen since a century ago.

That inequality is growing in wealthy countries is beyond dispute; why that is happening remains a major debate. The trend has clearly coincided with greater globalization, so many analysts point to a connection. As noted above, as globalization has freed capital to move around the world, relatively high-paying manufacturing jobs have disappeared from wealthy countries as factories opened up in lower-cost countries such as China. Former factory workers in wealthy countries typically have had to seek low-skilled employment in the growing service sector, such as retail, at lower wages. Meanwhile, technological changes, especially the rise of information and computer technology, has put a premium on highly educated workers needed in the new industries, so the earnings gap between the poorly educated and highly educated—those with and without college degrees—has increased.

Other analysts point to the neoliberal policies that helped foster globalization as leading to inequality, especially reduced trade barriers that encouraged deindustrialization and fiscal austerity that cut government services, including education, for lower-income citizens. Iversen and Soskice (2019) argued that in the pre-globalization era of greater manufacturing, skilled and unskilled workers shared a common interest in gaining higher wages from their common employers, unionized to do so, and supported government policies that benefited them all, such as social security. In the new knowledge economy, highly educated workers who benefit from policies that opened up the economy have no reason to support low-skilled workers who provide them services; the former provide political support for the policies that foster greater globalization and inequality. A recent IMF study found that computer technology, greater trade, and government policies such as fiscal austerity contributed roughly equally to greater inequality (Ostry et al. 2019).

No country has seen inequality increase more than the United States. Its level of inequality is now on par with many middle-income countries—what used to be called "Third World levels" of inequality—and well above all other high-income countries. Along with that, individual economic mobility has declined and is now lower than most European countries. Many analysts saw inequality as one of the causes of the rise of populist Donald Trump to the presidency in 2016. President Trump has questioned key tenets of neoliberal policy underlying globalization more than any other Republican has and more than many Democrats. He has championed restricting immigration and increased tariffs to force major trading partners, China in particular, to make concessions in an effort to reverse the deindustrialization that has long characterized the U.S. economy. His critics argued these policies would not work in the globalized economy. In response, Democrats, who have championed most aspects of globalization since the era of President Bill Clinton in the 1990s, have adopted positions that were once considered "extreme," such as substantially raising the minimum wage and providing tuition-free public university educations. The problem of inequality is implicitly recognized by all; the solutions remain subject to intense debate.

The influence of globalization seems clear. Capital's greater mobility ought to give it greater power vis-à-vis immobile states and less-mobile workers. Most scholars agree that this has happened to some extent over the past thirty to forty years, but the changes may not have been as dramatic as the convergence thesis asserted. VOC theorists argue that notable differences in how capitalism operates remain clear. Common trends toward greater openness to the market, however, seem equally clear. Figures 10.9 to 10.14 provide key data for the two LMEs (the United States and United Kingdom) and two CMEs (Germany and Japan) we mentioned earlier, giving us an overall review of their economic status and evolution in the era of globalization. The United States has produced the greatest wealth but also the greatest inequality. Although poverty is similar for all four countries (and quite low compared to much of the world), inequality is higher in the LMEs. The CMEs produced greater economic growth until the mid-1990s and recovered more quickly from the Great Recession, though the LMEs now appear to be doing better in the longer-term recovery. Reflecting the influence of neoliberalism, inflation fell across the board since 1980 and has remained very low ever since. The European countries long struggled with higher unemployment than the United States or Japan, but since the Great Recession, the LMEs have had higher unemployment, perhaps reflecting their response to the crisis, which involved greater flexibility in labor markets.

Conclusion

The extension of the market economy to nearly every corner of the globe has raised a universal set of issues involving the relationship between the market and the state. The state must perform certain tasks so that the market can function efficiently and in turn produce revenue for the state. The market is likely to generate greater wealth if the state is able to go beyond these essential functions by establishing policies to encourage investment and growth. Political pressure can lead to yet other policies, as organized groups in society demand particular state intervention in the market in their favor. Clear and consistent economic theories of how and why the state should intervene serve as intellectual guides for state actions. However, no government's policies follow these blueprints perfectly.

FIGURES 10.9–10.14

Economic Overview

FIGURE 10.9

GDP per Capita, 2017

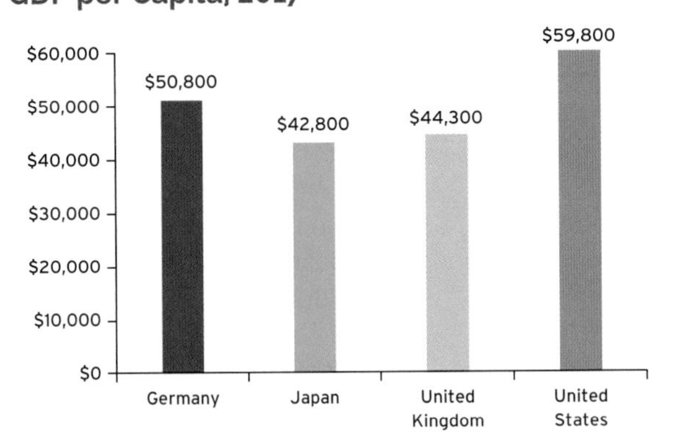

FIGURE 10.10

Inequality, GINI Index

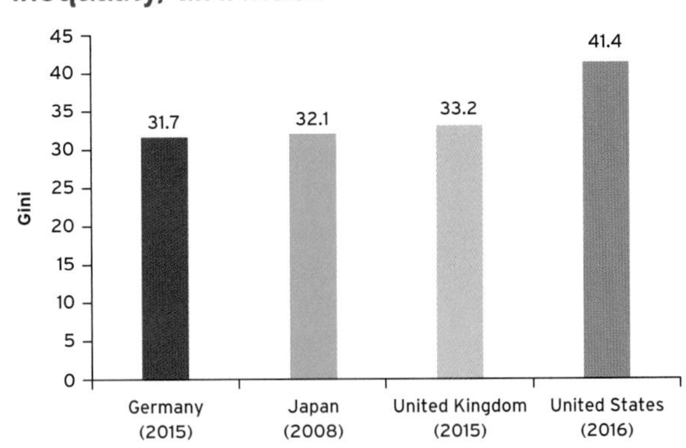

FIGURE 10.11

Population Living Below National Poverty Line (%) (2010–2015)

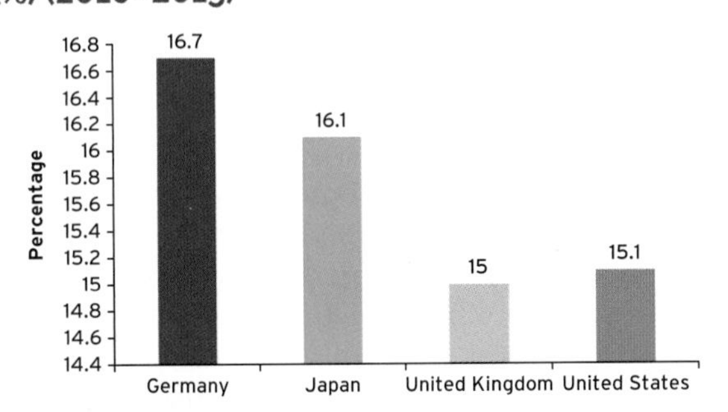

FIGURE 10.12

GDP Growth, 1980 to 2017 (%)

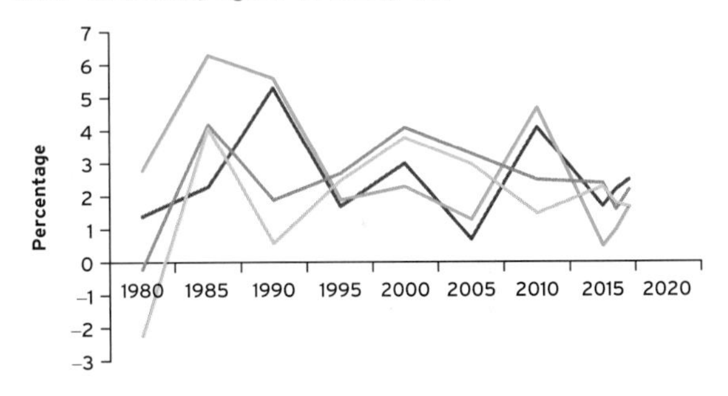

FIGURE 10.13

Unemployment Rate, 1990 to 2017 (%)

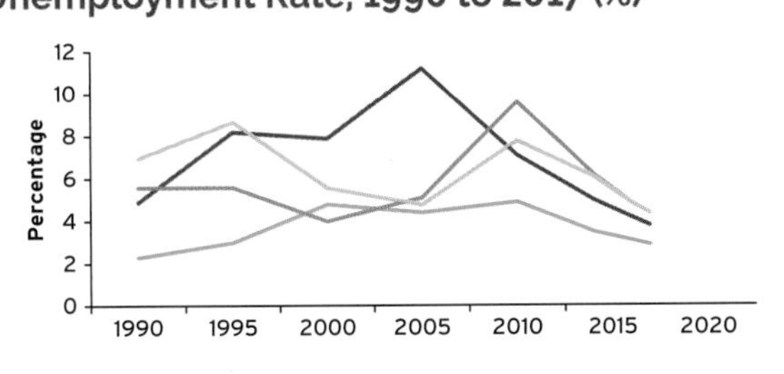

FIGURE 10.14

Inflation Rate, Consumer Price Index, 1980 to 2017 (%)

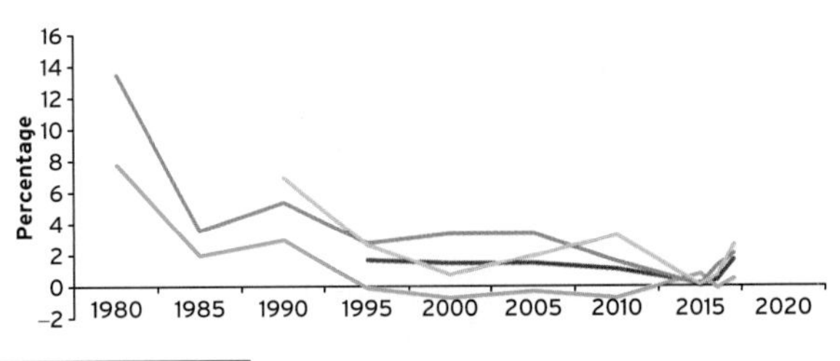

Germany
United Kingdom
Japan
United States

Sources: Figure 10.9: *CIA World Factbook*, Country Comparison: GDP per Capita, 2017 Estimates (https://www.cia.gov/library/publications/the-world-factbook/); Figure 10.10: World Bank, Gini Coefficients—Most Recent Measures per Country (https://data.worldbank.org/indicator/SI.POV.GINI?name_desc=false); Figure 10.11: *CIA World Factbook*, "Population Below Poverty Line" (https://www.cia.gov/library/publications/the-world-factbook/); *CIA World Factbook*, "GDP Growth, 1980–2017" (https://www.cia.gov/library/publications/the-world-factbook/); Figure 10.12: World Development Indicators From World Bank, GDP Growth (annual %) (https://www.cia.gov/library/publications/the-world-factbook/); Figures 10.13 and 10.14: *CIA World Factbook* (https://www.cia.gov/library/publications/the-world-factbook/).

Great variation exists even among the wealthiest in the relationship between the state and the market economy. The United States and United Kingdom are the paradigmatic LMEs, the models of a free-market economy with limited state intervention, though as we have seen, even here the state has intervened and expanded over the past century to try to improve economic outcomes and limit negative market effects. Germany's CME represents the common European alternative, while Japan's variant on the CME model, the developmental state, provides yet another alternative, one toward which a number of poorer countries have gravitated, which we discuss in chapter 11. Like most countries after the first wave of industrialization, Germany and Japan also used state intervention to guide investment into particular sectors.

Globalization has challenged all past economic models. Whether these models were successful or not in earlier decades, they now face rapidly moving capital that seems to limit their options and pushes them all in the direction of greater openness to the market. But states have not all responded to globalization in the same way. Economic sovereignty, while clearly reduced, still exists. Among the wealthy countries, LMEs have intensified their openness to the market to varying degrees, whereas CMEs have moved in that direction much more slowly, preserving some aspects of their distinct model. Despite challenges, wealthy countries have benefited more from globalization than they have been hurt by it.

Explaining the variation in state intervention in the market has long been a preoccupation of comparativists. Marxist analysts, whose theories of the dominance of the bourgeoisie are challenged by the existence of extensive welfare states such as Germany's, argue that the elite in capitalist societies sometimes sacrifice the short-term interests of particular businesses in order to preserve the system as a whole. A more widely accepted explanation of variation in state intervention is a pluralist one: countries with stronger workers' movements and unions have created the policies these groups favor.

Weak unions are just one example of weak institutions, which institutionalists argue are the key to explaining the economic paths of different countries. Institutionalists, including the varieties of capitalism approach, see key institutions developing in particular historical junctures and evolving slowly from there, only fundamentally disrupted at times of profound change. The ability of stronger institutions in Germany to discipline their members produced a less confrontational environment that allowed stronger coordination of economic policies. As globalization has weakened those institutions, German economic and social policy has shifted, largely toward a more market-oriented model. Strong bureaucratic institutions similarly help explain the rise of the developmental state in Japan. Globalization also made those institutions weaker over time, helping to undermine what was a widely admired model of economic growth. ●

KEY CONCEPTS

capitalism (p. 285)

comparative institutional advantage (p. 304)

convergence (p. 304)

coordinated market economies (CMEs) (p. 295)

deficit spending (p. 292)

developmental state (p. 307)

externality (p. 287)
fiscal policy (p. 292)
globalization (p. 298)
Keynesian theory (p. 291)
liberal market economies (LMEs) (p. 295)
market economy (p. 284)
market failure (p. 287)
monetary policy (p. 292)
monopoly (p. 288)
natural monopoly (p. 288)
neoliberalism (p. 293)
public goods (p. 285)
varieties of capitalism (VOC) (p. 295)

WORKS CITED

Cafruny, Alan W., and Leila Simona Talani. 2013. "The Crisis of the Eurozone." In *Exploring the Global Financial Crisis*, edited by Alan W. Cafruny and Herman M. Schwartz, 13–34. Boulder, CO: Lynne Rienner.

Dadush, Uri, and Kemal Dervis. 2013. "The Inequality Challenge." *Current History* 112 (750): 13–19. http://www.brookings.edu/research/articles/2013/01/inequality-challenge-dervis.

Ginsburg, Norman. 2001. "Globalization and the Liberal Welfare States." In *Globalization and European Welfare States: Challenges and Change*, edited by Robert Sykes, Bruno Palier, and Pauline M. Prior, with Jo Campling, 173–192. New York: Palgrave.

Hall, Peter Andrew, and Daniel Gingerich. 2009. "Varieties of Capitalism and Institutional Complementarities in the Political Economy: An Empirical Analysis." *British Journal of Political Science* 39 (3): 449–482. doi:10.1017/S0007123409000672.

Huber, Evelyne, and John D. Stephens. 2001. *Development and Crisis of the Welfare State: Parties and Policies in Global Markets*. Chicago: University of Chicago Press.

Ido, Masanobu. 2012. "Party System Change and the Transformation of the Varieties of Capitalism." In *Varieties of Capitalism, Types of Democracy and Globalization*, edited by Masanobu Ido, 55–79. New York: Routledge.

Iversen, Torben, and David Soskice. 2019. *Democracy and Prosperity: Reinventing Capitalism Through a Turbulent Century*. Princeton, NJ: Princeton University Press.

Johnson, Chalmers A. 1982. *MITI and the Japanese Miracle: The Growth of Industrial Policy, 1925–1975*. Stanford, CA: Stanford University Press.

Kotz, David M. 2015. *The Rise and Fall of Neoliberal Capitalism*. Cambridge, MA: Harvard University Press.

Lincoln, James, and Masahiro Shimontani. 2009. "Whither the *Keiretsu*, Japan's Business Networks? How Were They Structured? What Did They Do? Why Are They Gone?" Working Paper Series, Institute for Research on Labor and Employment, University of California, Berkeley. http://www.escholarship.org/uc/item/00m7d34g.OECD. 2011. *An Overview of Growing Income Inequalities in OECD Countries: Main Findings*. https://www.oecd.org/els/soc/49499779.pdf.

OECD. STAT. 2019. *Income Distribution and Poverty*. https://stats.oecd.org/Index.aspx?DataSetCode=IDD.

Ohmae, Kenichi. 1995. *The End of the Nation State: The Rise of Regional Economies*. New York: Simon and Schuster.

Ostry, Jonathan D., Prakash Loungani, and Andrew Berg, 2019. *Confronting Inequality: How Societies Can Choose Inclusive Growth*. New York: Columbia University Press.

Piketty, Thomas. 2014. *Capital in the Twenty-First Century*. Cambridge, MA: Harvard University Press.

Polanyi, Karl. 1944. *The Great Transformation*. New York: Farrar and Rinehart.

Vogel, Steven K. 2018. *Marketcraft: How Governments Make Markets Work.* Oxford, UK: Oxford University Press.

Vowles, Jack and Georgios Xezonakis, eds. 2016. *Globalization and Domestic Politics: Parties, Elections, and Public Opinion.* Oxford, UK: Oxford University Press.

World Inequality Database. 2019. https://wid.world/data/. Consulted May 13, 2019.

RESOURCES FOR FURTHER STUDY

Bates, Robert H. 2001. *Prosperity and Violence: The Political Economy of Development.* New York: W. W. Norton.

Friedman, Milton. 1962. *Capitalism and Freedom.* Chicago: University of Chicago Press.

Gilpin, Robert. 2000. *The Challenge of Global Capitalism.* Princeton, NJ: Princeton University Press.

Heilbroner, Robert L. 1985. *The Nature and Logic of Capitalism.* New York: W. W. Norton.

Keynes, John Maynard. 1935. *The General Theory of Employment, Interest, and Money.* New York: Harcourt Brace.

The Levin Institute, the State University of New York. "Globalization 101: A Student's Guide to Globalization." http://www.globalization101.org.

Lijphart, Arend. 1999. *Patterns of Democracy: Government Forms and Performance in Thirty-Six Countries.* New Haven, CT: Yale University Press.

Rothstein, Bo, and Sven Steinmo, eds. 2002. *Restructuring the Welfare State: Political Institutions and Policy Change.* New York: Palgrave Macmillan.

Siebert, Horst. 2005. *The German Economy: Beyond the Social Market.* Princeton, NJ: Princeton University Press.

Sykes, Robert, Bruno Palier, and Pauline M. Prior, eds. 2001. *Globalization and European Welfare States: Challenges and Change,* with Jo Campling. New York: Palgrave.

Woo-Cumings, Meredith, ed. 1999. *The Developmental State.* Ithaca, NY: Cornell University Press.

WEB RESOURCES

International Labour Organization, LABORSTA Internet

(http://laborsta.ilo.org)

International Monetary Fund, World Economic Outlook Database

(https://www.imf.org/external/pubs/ft/weo/2016/01/weodata/index.aspx)

Organisation for Economic Co-operation and Development (OECD), Stat Extracts

(http://stats.oecd.org)

UNDP Human Development Reports, International Human Development Indicators

(http://hdr.undp.org/en/statistics)

The World Bank, Economic Policy and External Debt

(http://data.worldbank.org/topic/economic-policy-and-external-debt)

John Thys/AFP/Getty Images

11 Political Economy of Development

Middle-school students use virtual reality devices in Beijing, China. While economic inequality has increased markedly, China's economic development model has transformed the country, moving more people out of poverty faster than any other country in history.
Zhao Yuhong/VCG via Getty Images

Key Questions

- What is development, and why does it matter?
- What should be the role of the state in the development process?
- What explains the ability of states to pursue development in the context of globalization?
- What types of regimes are able to pursue development more effectively, and why?

Learning Objectives

After reading chapter 11, you should be able to do the following:

11.1 Articulate the Western concept of development and explain how it affects the Global South

11.2 Explain the connection between development and globalization

11.3 Discuss the major debates that inform development in the modern world

In 1995 the average Brazilian was four times wealthier than the average Nigerian or Chinese citizen, who were about equal. By 2017, the Chinese was wealthier than the Brazilian, while the Nigerian lagged far behind both. You can see this story in the first column of Table 11.1 on page 318, which shows GDP per capita at "purchasing power parity," meaning it takes into account the differences in the cost of living in different countries. The tale is striking: how did one country, China, increase its wealth so dramatically, and why can't others do the same?

The word *development* conjures up images of impoverished children in Africa and gleaming new skyscrapers in China. "Underdeveloped" or "developing" countries are typically thought of as those that are or recently were poor on a global scale, the countries that during the Cold War were known as the "Third World" but are now more commonly referred to as the "Global South." As Table 11.1 shows, though, dramatic variation and change over time exist within the Global South, which is the subject of this chapter. The political economy of development examines the interaction of political and economic development. As in chapter 10, to do this we must understand the economic theories behind various models of development. These economic models, though, include prescriptions for states' roles in the process, and some argue that particular types of regimes can better achieve "development" than others. Since World War II, an entire industry and several major international organizations—the International Monetary Fund (IMF) and World Bank in particular—have arisen to try to help poor countries "develop." Governments of the Organisation for Economic Co-operation and Development (OECD), the wealthy countries of the world, spent $147 billion on foreign aid toward this effort in 2017, and that doesn't even include the money spent by international organizations.

But what is "development"? What we mean by it and why it is important are the first questions we must address. In the era of globalization, we must also ask what the effects of globalization are and how states in the Global South can navigate globalization to pursue development. That will lead us to the economic theories that have informed the "development debate" over the last half century. The various theories in that debate ask how states can best pursue policies that enhance development and how outside help like foreign aid, if used at all, can be effective. Some argue that democratic or authoritarian regimes are better able to "develop" their societies, a question to which we will also turn.

TABLE 11.1

Economic Development Around the World

	PER CAPITA GDP (PPP)[1]		HUMAN DEVELOPMENT INDEX[2]		NET FOREIGN DIRECT INVESTMENT (FDI) INFLOWS AS PERCENTAGE OF GDP[1]		EXPORTS AND IMPORTS OF GOODS AND SERVICES AS PERCENTAGE OF GDP[1]		PORTFOLIO INVESTMENT EQUITY AS PERCENTAGE OF GDP[1]	
Country	1995	2017	1990	2017	1995	2017	1995	2017	1995	2009*
Brazil	6,622.2	14,137.1	0.608	0.761	0.63	3.4	18.5	24.2	0.36	2.36
China	980	15,038.7	0.501	0.752	4.92	1.4	39.9	37.8	0.00	0.56
Germany	19,032.7	45,446.2	0.801	0.936	0.48	2.1	46.5	86.5	0.48	0.35
India	1,146	6,513.6	0.428	0.640	0.60	1.5	24.2	40.8	0.45	1.61
Iran	6,575.6	18,892.9	0.567	0.798	0.02	1.1	26.1	48.7	0.00	–
Japan	19,229.7	39,010.6	0.814	0.909	0.00	0.04	15.8	34.4	0.96	0.25
Mexico	6019.3	17,330.7	0.648	0.774	3.32	2.8	58.4	77.6	0.18	0.48
Nigeria	1,958.7	5,351.1	–	0.532	3.84	0.9	84.2	26.4	0.00	0.3
Russia	8,012.8	24,790.4	0.729	0.816	0.52	1.8	51.9	46.8	0.01	0.27
United Kingdom	17,446.3	39,993.8	0.773	0.922	1.88	2.5	56.8	61.4	0.70	3.52
United States	23,954.5	54,470.8	0.859	0.924	0.79	1.8	24.3	26.9	0.22	1.14

*Data are from 2009, the latest year for which data are available.

[1]Data on per capita GDP (PPP), stock of FDI, imports and exports of goods and services as a percentage of GDP, and portfolio investment equity are from World Bank. Per capita GDP (PPP) are available at http://data.worldbank.org/indicator/NY.GDP.PCAP.PP.CD; FDI data are available at http://data.worldbank.org/indicator/BX.KLT.DINV.WD.GD.ZS; exports data are available at http://data.worldbank.org/indicator/NE.EXP.GNFS.ZS; imports data are available at http://data.worldbank.org/indicator/NE.IMP.GNFS.ZS.

[2]Human Development Index data are from the UN Human Development Reports (http://hdr.undp.org/en/composite/trends).

What Is "Development"?

Before trying to explain how to achieve something, we need to know what we aim to achieve. That is particularly tricky for the idea of "development." The origin of the concept in its modern usage was connected to modernization theory (see chapter 3). Put simply, social scientists and policymakers at the time saw "development" as being about the poor countries of the world—what they called the "Third World"—looking more like wealthy, Western countries. Politically, this meant becoming independent, democratic states. Economically, it meant becoming wealthier, which meant industrializing and urbanizing. Chapters 3 and 9 discussed the long, difficult, and still incomplete road to democracy, leaving aside the assumption that everyone should or would want to live in a democracy. The economic road has been equally rocky. Some countries have been spectacularly successful: South Korea went from being part of the "Third World" to being a member of OECD, officially a member of the wealthy world. More recently, China's economic growth has helped make it a global superpower, though it remains only a "middle-income" country. Others, such as Zimbabwe, have barely nudged per capita income over decades.

As we discussed in chapter 3, the economic assumption of modernization theory assumed that poor countries would largely go through the same process to achieve wealth that the West had in an earlier era. Modernization theorists also assumed that those in the West knew how to help poor countries follow that path, thus justifying foreign aid. Critics questioned those assumptions in the 1960s and 1970s, wondering if poor countries in a different era in the global economy could really follow the same path as the West had and wondering if wealth generation—economic growth—should be the primary goal. We discuss the first of these concerns below when we turn to globalization. The second, that growth alone should not be the goal, led to a focus on poverty by the 1970s. Economic growth that did not reduce poverty, critics argued, should not be seen as development; instead, development should focus on the "poorest of the poor." Figuring out how the state and external aid could reduce poverty became the goal.

Economist and philosopher Amartya Sen (1999) profoundly influenced thinking on the concept of development in the new millennium with his focus on human capabilities. He argued that neither growth nor poverty reduction alone were adequate goals. The real goal of development anywhere in the world (including in wealthy countries) should be enhancing the capabilities of individuals to lead fulfilling lives as they define them. Economic growth that provides higher incomes and reducing poverty would certainly be part of that, but helping people achieve greater capabilities also meant they needed to be healthy, educated, and free. Many economists had long recognized that health and education were important parts of developing "human capital," the store of productive labor that would enhance economic growth. Sen, though, argued that health and education were important not only to enhance economic growth but also to allow individuals to maximize their own capabilities. Similarly, freedom is essential. Indeed, his book was titled *Development as Freedom*. He argued that people need to be free politically in democracies—only then could they define for themselves what a fulfilling life would be—and they needed to be free from social restrictions such as traditional gender norms that might limit their capabilities.

Sen's theory has become the leading conceptualization of development. It lay behind the creation of what became a widely used index of development, the UN's Human Development Index (HDI), which combines measures of health, education, and income. Table 11.1 shows the difference between this measure and wealth alone: India's per capita GDP is less than half of China's, but the difference in their HDI scores is much closer, while the United States is wealthier than Germany but Germany has a higher HDI score. In practical terms, policymakers still focus on economic growth extensively, as well as poverty, but health and education are also quite important. These tend to go together as well, as Figure 11.1 demonstrates, comparing a basic measure of health (life expectancy at birth) with GDP per capita. The democratization process we discussed in chapter 9 has also been tied to development, at least via foreign aid efforts. Many, though not all, theorists see democratic regimes with strong institutions as most likely to provide the conditions for the greatest development of human capabilities.

While Sen's capabilities theory is certainly the leading understanding of development today, critics of the entire idea of development have also arisen. Using postmodern theories, they argue that the very idea of "development" is an effort by the wealthy countries to control the Global South. They argue that development is still conceived as something the West has and countries of the Global South lack,

FIGURE 11.1

The Global Relationship Between Wealth and Life Expectancy

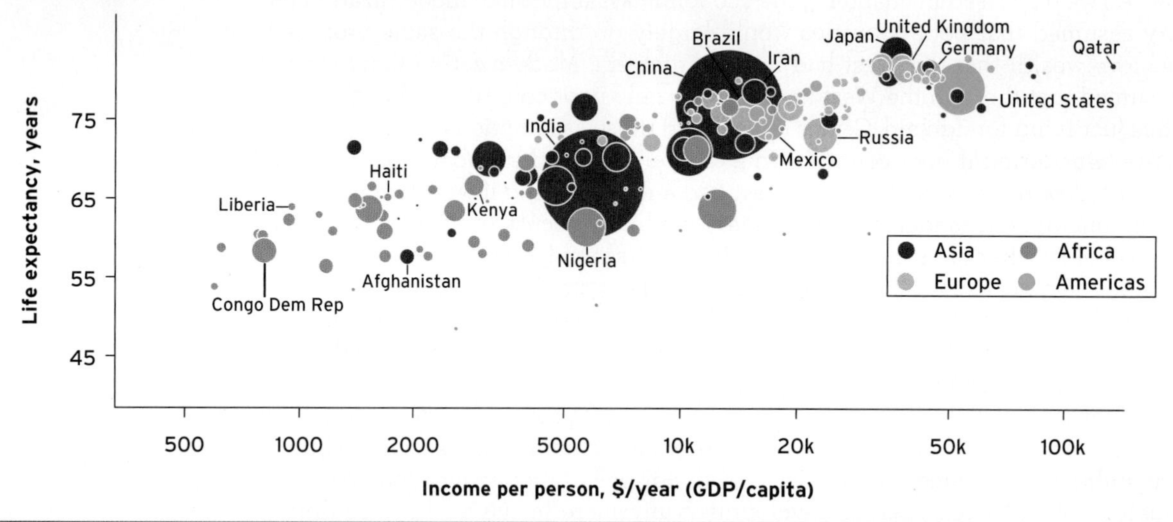

Source: Based on a free chart from www.gapminder.org.

Note: Data are from 2018. The relative size of the circles corresponds to the size of a country's population.

measured on various scales as deficiencies to be overcome. This, they claim, allows the West to insert itself into domestic economic and political processes in the Global South via foreign aid and other "development" efforts, to impose the West's vision of how these societies ought to be structured. Cast primarily in economic and technical terms, "development" also attempts to depoliticize the process of social and political change in the Global South, removing agency from local actors to chart the course for their own societies. Rather than an effort to improve people's lives, development as it is conceived and practiced is a continuation of colonialism in a new form (Weber 2014). While this is certainly a minority view, it nonetheless raises profound questions for development practitioners to consider.

Development and Globalization

In chapter 10, we saw that globalization has clearly affected the ways in which wealthy and powerful states guide their economies. If this is true for those states, it seems likely to apply even more to poorer and less powerful states. Poor countries' relationship with globalization is intimately connected with development: In this section, we examine the effects of globalization before turning to the "development debate" in the next section, which addresses what economic policies states should pursue.

foreign direct investment (FDI): Investment from abroad in productive activity in another country

trade: The flow of goods and services across national borders

international capital flows: Movements of capital in the form of money across international borders

One thing is certain: Table 11.1 shows key aspects of globalization: **foreign direct investment (FDI)**, foreign investment in directly productive activity; **trade**, exports and imports of goods and services; and **international capital flows**, the movement of money across national borders. In most countries, all three areas show marked increases. The greatest increases, though, are in the final column, portfolio investment equity, which partially measures the effects of international capital flows. These have expanded dramatically in almost all countries. The virtual elimination of barriers

FIGURE 11.2

The Effects of Economic Globalization

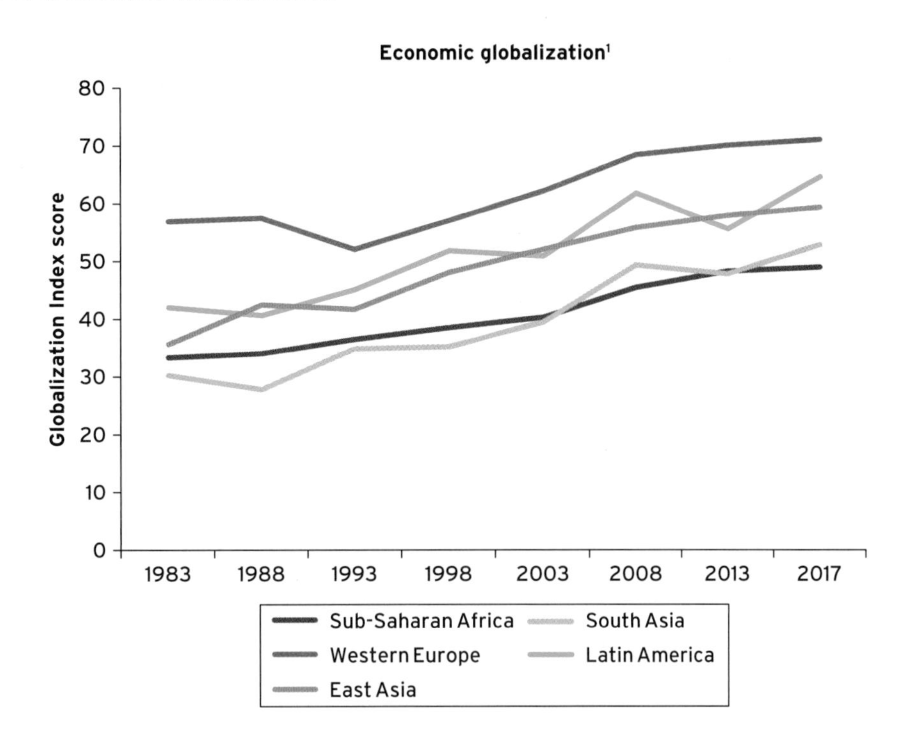

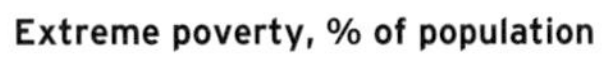

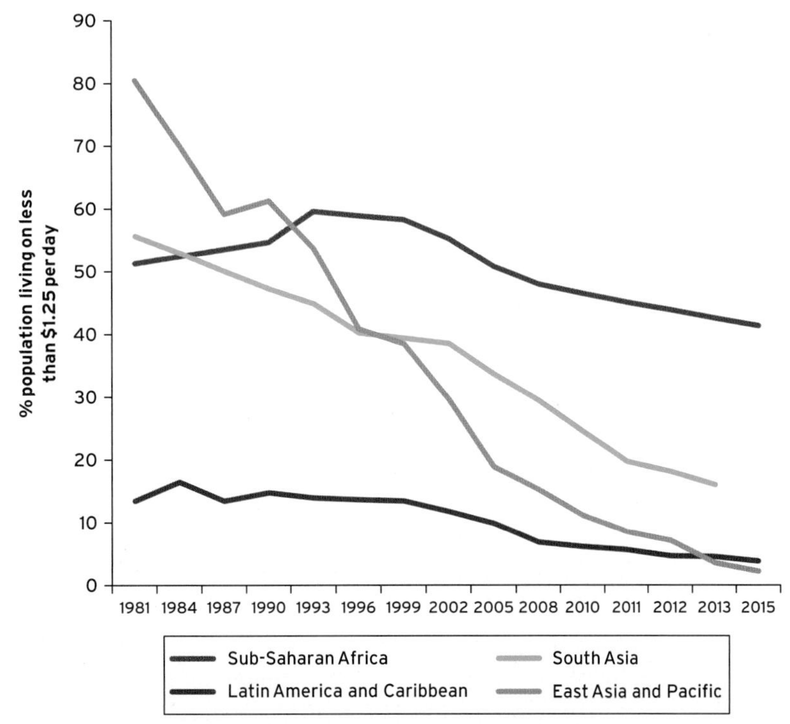

(Continued)

(Continued)

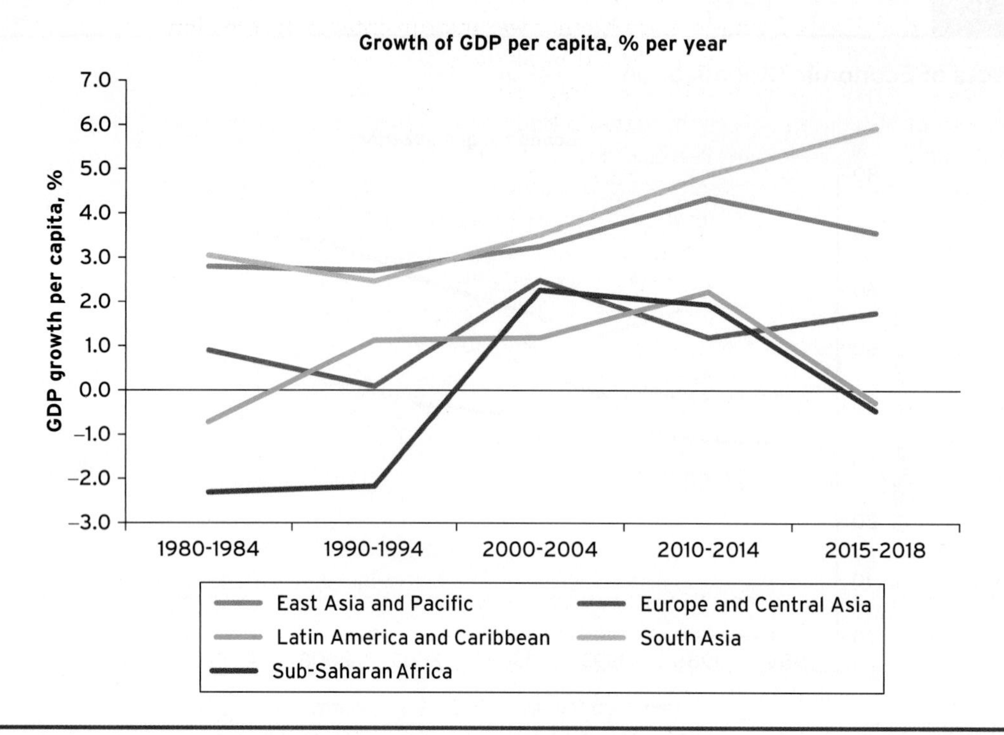

Source: Data for the Globalization Index are from the KOF Index of Globalization, "Economic Globalization" data (http://globalization.kof.ethz.ch/query). Data on GDP growth and extreme poverty are from the World Bank (http://data.worldbank.org)

[1] Composite of data on openness to and flows of trade, foreign direct investment, and portfolio investment.

to moving money across borders and improvement in global communications have resulted in more than $1 trillion crossing international borders daily.

Virtually all governments have followed neoliberal policies to some degree over the last two decades, opening their economies to the global market, but the results have not been consistent. Figure 11.2 compares each region's Economic Globalization Index score—a measure of economies' interactions with the global market—to growth rates and poverty rates since 1981. All regions have become more globalized over time, and the gap between the wealthier regions (Europe, East Asia, and Latin America) and the poorer regions (South Asia and Africa) has increased slightly. Economic growth and poverty reduction vary dramatically by region, though. Greater globalization has not systematically produced greater growth, but it appears to be loosely associated with poverty reduction. The rate of poverty reduction varies dramatically as well, even though change in the level of globalization does not. The question is, What explains this variation, and what can be done to improve the effects of globalization in the countries that are falling behind?

The Development Debate

The development debate over the last century has tried to answer this question: what explains the success of different development policies, and what should be the role of the state in development in a particular global context? The neoliberal–Keynesian debate that we discussed in chapter 10 also had an influential role in development policy in the Global South. John Maynard Keynes was instrumental in the creation after World War II of the IMF and the World Bank. One basic assumption of the postwar global economic order was that free trade should be as widespread as possible. The economic argument in favor of this is known as **comparative advantage**. It holds that well-being will be maximized if each country uses its resources to produce whatever it can produce relatively efficiently compared with other countries (i.e., it should produce the items that it can produce most efficiently compared with how well other countries produce them, even if it is not the most efficient at anything). It then trades with other countries for goods it does not produce, and all countries gain because they are using their resources as efficiently as possible. What this meant in practical terms was that the poor and agrarian countries of Asia, Africa, and Latin America would, for the foreseeable future, produce primarily agricultural products and raw materials. Their industries, where they existed, were quite new and therefore were not likely to compete successfully against the well-established industrial conglomerates of the wealthy countries.

The ISI Era

Leaders in the Global South and the economists who supported them, however, were not willing to have their countries relegated to producing only agricultural products and raw materials. The new field of "development economics," then, came to be about how a state could intervene in the economy to stimulate rapid industrialization and growth. This meshed with early ideas of development being about economic growth and industrialization, as well as the general Keynesian theory that the state could manage capitalism to enhance growth. In "developing countries," this management would simply take somewhat different forms than in industrialized countries. The central policy that developed out of these ideas was **import-substitution industrialization (ISI)**, which stated that a developing nation should protect its new industries by placing restrictions on international trade, thus allowing its new industries to grow until they were strong enough to compete on the international market. By limiting the number of imported manufactured products or placing tariffs on them, postcolonial governments could encourage domestic and international investment in new industries in their countries. Most countries in the Global South pursued these policies, with the support of Western governments and the World Bank, from the 1950s to the 1970s. In many countries where new industries had not yet begun, governments even took on the role of business owner, creating wholly or partly government-owned industries that supplied the domestic market with key goods.

At first, ISI was relatively successful in creating new industries. Countries such as Brazil, Mexico, and Turkey saw rapid economic growth throughout the 1950s and 1960s. By the 1970s, though, momentum was waning. Protecting industry from competition helped them get started, but in the long run it resulted in inefficient industries that could not compete on the international market. These industries and their employees, however, put political pressure on governments to preserve the protections that they enjoyed. When oil prices quadrupled in 1973, non-oil producers had to pay a lot more for oil and other key imports, but because their industries could not compete globally, they could not export enough goods to pay for the imports. They were forced to take out international loans to cover the resulting trade imbalance. When oil prices increased again in 1979, governments had to borrow even more money from international lenders. Some reached the

comparative advantage: Theory of trade that argues that economic efficiency and well-being will be maximized if each country uses its resources to produce whatever it produces relatively well compared with other countries and then trades its own products with other countries for goods it does not produce

import-substitution industrialization (ISI): Development policy popular in the 1950s–1970s that uses trade policy, monetary policy, and currency rates to encourage the creation of new industries to produce goods domestically that the country imported in the past

brink of bankruptcy, and Mexico's declaration in 1982 that it was unable to meet its international debt obligations began a global "debt crisis," which ushered in a new era in development policy.

The SAP Era

The growing problems with ISI were emerging at the same time that economists and policymakers in the West were shifting from Keynesian to neoliberal ideas and becoming increasingly skeptical of the ability of governments to manage the market. The World Bank abruptly shifted its development agenda and prescriptions in 1980, embracing a neoliberal development model. This was partly induced by what collectively came to be known as the "East Asian miracle": the great economic success of a handful of East Asian countries, in contrast to most of the postcolonial world, these rapidly growing countries, most notably South Korea, Taiwan, Singapore, and the city of Hong Kong, either had never adopted ISI or had abandoned it early on in favor of focusing on exporting in sectors in which they were competitive. Their success, especially in light of the problems ISI policies had begun to face, suggested to many policymakers that a new approach to development was needed.

The neoliberal model that emerged by 1980 shared neoliberals' skepticism of state interventions in the market. Neoliberal economists argued that developing countries were no different from wealthy ones and, as such, should follow the same basic neoliberal policies. These economists compiled a package of policies that came to be known as **structural adjustment programs (SAPs)**. These included directives to end government protection of industries and other restrictions on free trade, privatize (sell off) government-owned industries, and reduce fiscal deficits. SAPs required a drastically reduced government that would participate far less in the economy; this would allow comparative advantage and the market to signal how resources should be invested, which would maximize efficiency and therefore economic growth.

structural adjustment programs (SAPs): Development programs created in the 1980s; based on neoliberal principles of reduced government protection of industries, fiscal austerity, and privatization

The debt crisis that began in 1982 meant that many governments had to ask the IMF for emergency financial assistance. Working in tandem, the IMF and World Bank demanded that the governments receiving assistance in the 1980s and 1990s implement SAPs, effectively imposing this model on the Global South. This was a slow process in many countries; the necessary steps were politically unpopular because they initially resulted in high inflation, increased unemployment, and drastic cuts in government services, including education and health care. The promise was that if a country could endure these short-term pains, the new policies would maximize efficiency and encourage new investment, producing economic growth in the long term.

By the 1980s, ISI was becoming discredited, and neoliberals were advocating that developing countries should instead emulate the East Asian miracle by promoting export-led growth. In China, workers like these produce millions of pieces of clothing for export annually, helping spur the country's economic transformation over the last generation.
STR/AFP/Getty Images

Many analysts agree that SAPs were successful in certain cases, such as in Chile and several countries in Southeast Asia, but on the whole, their effects were mixed. On the most common measure of development, gross domestic product (GDP) per capita, developing countries grew more quickly than wealthy countries from 1965 to 1980, indicating that development policies prior to SAPs were helping them "catch up" to earlier developers. In the 1980s and 1990s, however, they grew more slowly than wealthy countries, suggesting SAPs might have made things worse or at least did not help them overcome other factors slowing their growth (Ocampo and Vos 2008, 10). Regional differences, however, were stark, as demonstrated in Figure 11.3. On the one hand, East Asia grew many times faster than the world average. On the other hand, Africa suffered economic contraction through most of the period, and Latin America contracted in the 1980s and saw very low growth of only 1.3 percent per year during the 1990s. Changes in poverty mirrored the changes in growth. The percentage of the world's population living in extreme poverty (earning less than a dollar per day) was cut in half over the two decades, from just over 40 percent to about 22 percent. Virtually that entire decline, however, took place in East and South Asia. Given population growth, the total number of people living in extreme poverty actually increased in Africa and Latin America and very slightly declined in South Asia, while it was cut by nearly three-quarters in East Asia. East Asia, of course, includes rapidly growing China, Taiwan, and South Korea. While the latter two served as one of the initial models for SAPs, we will see below that they in fact did not follow the neoliberal model very closely. Many analysts argue that the model was implemented most closely in Latin America, where growth declined and poverty changed little.

Mexico illustrates the evolution from ISI to SAP and the problems that it entailed. During the ISI period (1940–1982), economic growth averaged a relatively strong 3.1 percent. This success was in large part funded through Petróleos Mexicanos (PEMEX), the company that oversaw all of Mexico's oil production. The authoritarian government used the oil sector as revenue to fund public programs, as part of a clientelist effort to maintain popularity and legitimacy. Growth was relatively high, but so was inequality and inefficiency. Mexico's 1982 debt crisis began with falling oil prices, a recession in the United States, and massive,

FIGURE 11.3

Growth and Poverty Reduction in the SAP Era

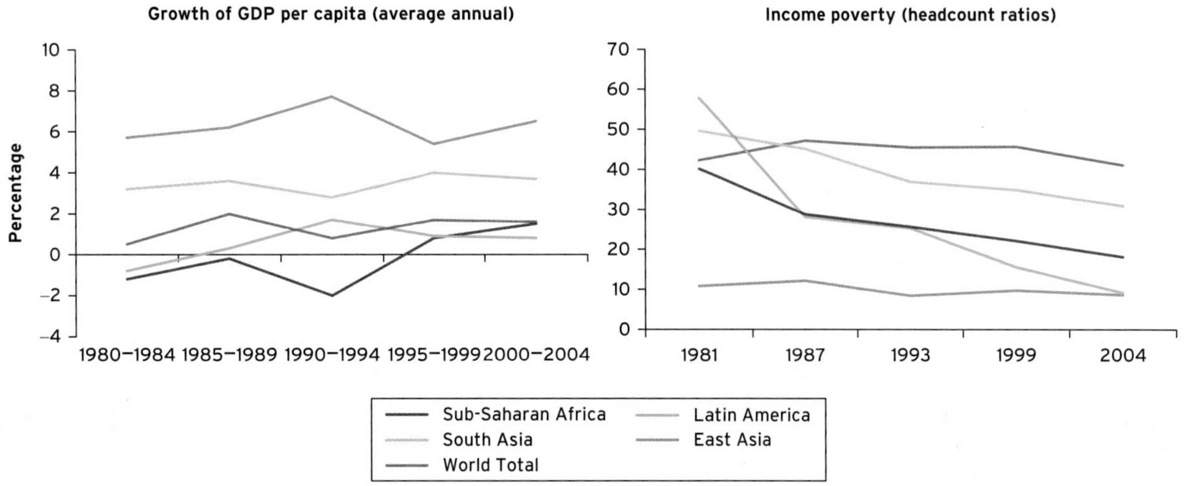

Growth of GDP per capita (average annual)

Income poverty (headcount ratios)

Percentage

1980–1984 1985–1989 1990–1994 1995–1999 2000–2004

1981 1987 1993 1999 2004

Sub-Saharan Africa
South Asia
World Total
Latin America
East Asia

Data for the figures are from Tables 11.1 and 11.3. Jeffrey Round, "Globalization, Growth, Inequality, and Poverty in Africa: A Macroeconomic Perspective," in *The Poor Under Globalization in Asia, Latin America, and Africa*, M. Nissanke and E. Thorbecke,, eds., (Oxford, UK: Oxford University Press, 2010), pp. 330, 334.

dollar-denominated debt. Declining oil revenue and the American recession caused the Mexican peso to fall sharply in relation to the dollar, making it much more expensive for Mexico to pay back its debt. As this happened, capital began to flee the country in the billions of dollars. The crisis ushered in what became the global debt crisis, and it put the IMF and U.S. government in a position to demand fundamental changes in economic policy. Foreign-educated experts took control of economic policy, strongly supported by the IMF and U.S. government. The country joined the General Agreement on Tariffs and Trade (GATT, the predecessor of the WTO) in 1986 and signed NAFTA in 1992.

In the late ISI period (1970–1985), GDP growth averaged 4.5 percent per year in the best-performing Mexican states; this figure dropped to only 2.5 percent during the early free-market period (1985–1992). Although NAFTA increased productivity, unemployment changed little and Mexico remains one of the most unequal societies in the world. Indeed, inequality increased as the wealthy benefited from the new business opportunities neoliberal policies provided while the average wage dropped 40 percent over the 1980s and 1990s. Exports, however, rose from 15 percent of GDP in 1985 to 35 percent in 2015. As the economy became more dependent on trade, regional disparities also became more pronounced, with northern states most able to exploit their proximity to U.S. markets. The less-developed southern states have lagged behind. In the free-trade economy, cheap, state-subsidized corn from the United States displaced traditional and less-developed agriculture meant for local consumption. The largely agrarian southern states became the chief source of migrant laborers destined for the United States. Neoliberal policies have also left Mexico more vulnerable to global economic trends, especially those emanating from the United States. It felt the full effect of the Great Recession and recovery since, closely paralleling its powerful northern neighbor.

A large theoretical and policy debate arose over what caused this mixed success among those who (1) viewed the failure of SAPs in some countries as a failure of implementation, (2) believed that the model was applicable only in certain political or economic circumstances, and (3) saw fundamental flaws in the model itself. To secure essential debt relief, poor countries had to accept the policy requirements that the IMF and World Bank imposed. States agreed to make certain policy changes over a period of about three years, and the IMF/World Bank subsequently monitored how the countries followed through on their promises. Often, political leaders only partially fulfilled their obligations, so everything went back to the drawing board. This resulted in very slow and partial implementation of neoliberal policies as countries went through several rounds of negotiation and implementation with the IMF/World Bank. One body of critics, including the IMF/World Bank, concluded that the model's limited success was due to failure of political will. Success happened when top political leaders took "ownership" of the ideas, understood their importance, and committed themselves to accomplishing them. In the absence of this, no amount of external arm-twisting would do the job, and partial implementation often made little economic sense. Chile's government in the 1980s actively embraced the neoliberal model without having it imposed and had the fastest growing economy in Latin America. In contrast, Kenya's leaders were forced to accept Africa's first ever SAP in 1983 and negotiated and renegotiated numerous packages with the IMF over the years but only very slowly and reluctantly liberalized their economy, resulting in economic stagnation for most of the period.

Lack of implementation came not just from lack of understanding and commitment but also from the rational actions of self-interested political leaders. Where leaders' political survival depended on their ability to provide supporters with patronage, they were reluctant to implement SAPs that reduced the size and scope of government and therefore their sources of patronage. Kenya was a prime example. Institutionalists contended that markets only work well when embedded in strong institutions, such as clear property rights and contracts. The ultimate goal of the neoliberal model is to improve efficiency to encourage investment and thereby future growth. Weak states that have weak institutions and leaders who rely on patronage will never gain greater investment because investors cannot be certain their investments and future profits will be secure. The initial neoliberal model ignored this essential area entirely and so was successful only where key institutions were already relatively strong, such as in Chile.

Another group argued that SAPs worked only in certain economic circumstances. A leading theory for East Asian economic success is the "flying geese" theory (Ozawa 2010). It argues that, like flocks of geese, when one economy in a region is successful, others can follow in its wake by producing goods that the newly wealthy country needs. In East Asia, the original "lead goose" was Japan, followed by South Korea and Taiwan, and later by China. Without a regional leader like Japan, the policies produced few benefits in Africa. Related to this, some analysts argued that the neoliberal model suffered from a *fallacy of composition:* just because something is true in one case does not mean it will be true when applied to all cases. In relation to SAPs, it suggests that market-friendly policies designed to attract investment will succeed in some cases, probably the earliest ones and those with other attractions to investors. When the same policies are extended to all countries, however, there will not be enough investment capital available to respond. Furthermore, the earliest success cases will be likely to attract even more investment, leaving the latecomers empty-handed. Even if later or less attractive states pursue the "right" policies, they still may not see the investment necessary to spark economic growth.

A final school of critics argued that the neoliberal model undermines the real fundamentals of long-term development: infrastructure and human capital. They contended that states succeed at instigating economic development by providing key political goods that investors will need: infrastructure, especially efficient transportation and communications systems; and human capital, an educated and healthy workforce. They pointed out that these were exactly the advantages with which East Asian countries, including China, began. SAPs demand fiscal austerity, typically meaning cuts to government spending in all three areas. For countries with weak infrastructure, education, and health care, these policies were a disaster.

A study of Latin America, the region most heavily affected by SAPs, found that in the new millennium, provision of enhanced social policies (1) did not reduce economic growth, as the neoliberal theory argued, and (2) did reduce poverty more than growth alone did (Ocampo and Gomez-Arteaga 2018). A broader review of the effect of neo-liberal policies—the overall SAP framework—concluded that "liberalizing countries see significant poverty reduction if and when they have beneficial initial conditions: good geography, large endowments of low-skilled labor (rather than unskilled labor), and strong institutions (e.g., property rights, flexible labor markets, rule of law)" (Rudra and Tobin 2017, 302). Without these conditions, success was limited, so development economists and practitioners began modifying the model. The World Bank, in particular, articulated an agenda of "good governance," arguing that states need to have more of a role in reform than the neoliberal model allows. First, they need to effectively and efficiently provide the key requisites for capitalist development that we outlined in chapter 10: security, property rights, contract enforcement, and infrastructure. Second, they need to enhance human capital and development potential via providing essential health and education services to the poor, which is also supported by Sen's capabilities conception of development. Virtually all major Western development agencies continue to support the basic principle that states should not distort markets (as they did under ISI), but many now believe that the state does have a role to play in simultaneously attracting capital and alleviating poverty.

Several more significant alternatives, though, have also gained popularity. One is derived originally from the Japanese developmental state model. It has been most prominent in a number of successful Asian developing economies. In Latin America, a leftist alternative to parts of the neoliberal model arose in the new millennium in several countries. Finally, in response to the failure to reduce poverty in the poorest countries—what Paul Collier (2007) called the "bottom billion"—policy alternatives involving large investments via aid have gained currency. All of these alternatives accept many of the core neoliberal recommendations for macroeconomic policies and believe that global market forces cannot be ignored but also that even the poorest states can and must play a significant role in harnessing those forces for the benefit of their citizens.

The Developmental State

We outlined the key elements of the developmental state in our examination of Japan in chapter 10. A number of other Asian countries adopted and modified the model, starting with South Korea. Developmental states consciously intervene in the market via an aggressive industrial policy: a policy aimed at strengthening particular industries. In contrast to the earlier ISI model, though, developmental states encouraged **export-oriented growth (EOG)**, growth via exports of goods and services, usually starting with light manufactures such as textiles. They tried to "pick winners," subsidizing and protecting new industries but demanding high performance from them and opening them up to global competition as soon as possible. The key aim was not to provide manufactured goods for the domestic market, as under ISI, but manufactured exports for wealthier countries. Light manufacturing is typically labor-intensive, so the new investments employed large numbers of people; Asian developmental states, in particular, used EOG to take advantage of their comparative advantage in large amounts of cheap labor.

export-oriented growth (EOG): Development policy based on encouraging economic growth via exports of goods and services, usually starting with light manufacturing such as textiles

CRITICAL INQUIRY

Structural Adjustment Programs

SAPs were intended to correct economic imbalances in developing countries in order to encourage investment, renew economic growth, and thereby reduce poverty via a shift from the protectionism of ISI to more open economy and export-oriented growth. The IMF along with the World Bank were the major organizations that imposed SAPs on often reluctant governments around the world. Table 11.2 presents the number of IMF agreements between 1980 and 2000 (the era in which structural adjustment was pursued most actively) for a selection of countries. While this alone does not tell us everything we might want to know about how much individual countries pursued SAPs, it is an indication of the influence of the IMF's policies. The question is, Do these SAPs lead to better economic outcomes? The table also provides data on GDP per capita, trade, poverty, and infant mortality (the best measure of overall health). Based on this table, what trends do you see? Can you use the data to come to conclusions about who is correct in the debate over SAPs? Did they enhance economic growth and improve well-being in developing countries? Did they create even greater poverty, as their critics asserted? What other information would you like to have to answer these questions even better?

TABLE 11.2

Effect of SAPs on Development: Changes in Key Indicators, 1980–2000

COUNTRY	# IMF AGREEMENTS, 1980–2000	GDP PER CAPITA (CONSTANT DOLLARS PPP), 1980	GDP PER CAPITA (CONSTANT DOLLARS PPP), 2000	TRADE SURPLUS OR DEFICIT (CURRENT ACCOUNT BALANCE, % OF GDP) 1980*	TRADE SURPLUS OR DEFICIT (CURRENT ACCOUNT BALANCE, % OF GDP) 2000*	ABSOLUTE POVERTY LEVEL (POVERTY GAP AT $1.25 A DAY PPP, %) 1980	ABSOLUTE POVERTY LEVEL (POVERTY GAP AT $1.25 A DAY PPP, %) 2000	INFANT MORTALITY RATE (PER 1,000 LIVE BIRTHS) 1980	INFANT MORTALITY RATE (PER 1,000 LIVE BIRTHS) 2000
Argentina	7	10,075	10,282	–1.23	–3.15	0.0 (1986)	2.8	173	95
Ghana	9	993	1,067	–0.21	–6.56	18.0 (1988)	14.4 (1998)	95	64
Indonesia	2	1,323	2,623	3.36	4.84	21.4 (1984)	12.5 (1999)	76	38
Kenya	9	1,375	1,283	–10.72	–2.31	15.4 (1992)	16.9 (2005)	69	70
Mexico	5	10,238	11,853	–4.61	–2.78	3.0 (1984)	1.5	55	24
Nigeria	3	1,645	1,469	8.85	12.47	21.9 (1986)	28.7 (2004)	129	113
Pakistan	8	1,224	1,845	–3.19	–0.29	23.9 (1987)	6.3	111	76
Peru	4	6,083	5,543	–5.06	–2.90	3.0 (1986)	4.6	79	30
Philippines	6	2,827	2,697	–6.91	–2.75	10.3 (1985)	5.5	53	29
Tanzania	4	823 (1998)	868	–7.69	–4.30	29.7 (1992)	41.6	105	78
Zambia	5	1,532	1,028	–15.08	–18.34	40.0 (1991)	26.9 (1998)	98	91

Sources: Data are from International Monetary Fund (number of SAPs, changes to trade surplus and deficit) and World Bank (GDP per capita PPP, absolute poverty rate, infant mortality rate).

*Positive numbers show exports are greater than imports and negative numbers show imports are greater than exports.

While developmental states intervened in the economy, subsidizing and guiding investments into particular areas rather than letting the market fully determine investment patterns, they usually followed neoliberal fiscal and monetary policy, keeping inflation low and their currencies stable and realistically valued vis-à-vis others, thus encouraging investment and exports. Their successes were also based on the fact that their high-quality education systems had produced a highly literate and therefore productive workforce. Another key component was a strong state, one in which economic bureaucracies were insulated from short-term political pressures so that they could pursue consistent, long-term policies. Several major analysts determined that this was a key factor for other states that wanted to pursue similar policies; weaker states that succumbed to short-term domestic pressures were far less successful (Haggard and Kaufman 1995).

China, of course, is the single biggest success of the East Asian miracle, though its development policies have only partially followed the developmental state model. It shared the developmental state's focus on EOG and initial growth via light manufacturing and was driven by a relatively strong and politically insulated state. Its stunning economic growth (see Table 11.1) began after Deng Xiaoping became leader in 1978 and set about dismantling the completely state-controlled economy. A series of reforms introducing markets in the agricultural sector was followed by the creation of a "dual-track" market system in 1984 under which state-owned enterprises (SOEs) were free to sell their surplus production at whatever market price they could get. Prior to reform, the government had set all retail prices. Over time, a larger and larger share of products were sold at market prices, reaching 95 percent by 1999. Throughout the 1990s, the government gradually but systematically lowered tariffs on imports and loosened restrictions on companies' rights both to import and export, a process that culminated in China's joining the World Trade Organization (WTO) in 2001. The result has been an explosion of international trade for the country: its exports and imports increased nearly tenfold between 2000 and 2014.

In 1995 the government started selling off the vast majority of SOEs to private investors. A decade later, the private sector constituted 70 percent of the economy and the state-owned sector only 30 percent. SOEs still control virtually entire sectors that are natural monopolies or considered strategic, such as energy and military industry. They continue to exist but are much smaller and must compete with private firms in sectors such as pharmaceuticals and chemicals, and they have been eliminated in highly competitive sectors, such as light manufacturing (Pearson 2015). SOEs are often inefficient and in debt, a problem the Chinese government still must deal with (Bradsher 2015). The government also controls much of the banking system and uses it, as other developmental states have, to guide investment where it wants. Many banks are troubled by outstanding debt to loss-making SOEs. Unlike Taiwan and South Korea, Chinese development has been accompanied by rapidly growing inequality, leading to demands for and government policies to enhance social services for the poor.

By 2015, economic analysts became increasingly concerned about whether China could maintain its exceptional economic development model. Rising wages in the manufacturing sector threaten China's status as the world's chief producer of low-wage goods. Like the other East Asian developmental states, China faced the need to transition to higher-value production. It launched a plan to navigate this economic transition in mid-2015, called Made in China 2025 (MIC2025). The plan outlined an ambitious agenda focused on developing Chinese national firms in high-tech fields, including pharmaceuticals, robotics, IT, autos, and aerospace. It brought objections, however, from the Trump administration, with bipartisan support in Congress. From the U.S. perspective, Chinese government support for developing tech and other firms constituted unfair trade competition and, in some cases, such as development of 5G technology, a potential security threat. Although China's partial developmental state has moved more people out of poverty faster than any other country in history, it faces challenges that other middle-income developmental states have also faced as it attempts to move into the ranks of the truly wealthy countries.

Thai farmers step on sheets of rubber to stretch them. The Asian financial crisis that harmed the developmental state model in 1997–1998 began in Thailand when international currency investors decided the country would not be able to pay its debts. The crisis was the largest loss of wealth in the world between the Great Depression and the Great Recession of 2008–2009.
Madaree Tohlala/AFP/Getty Images

Despite its success, the developmental state model came under intense scrutiny in the wake of the 1997–1998 East Asian financial crisis. The crisis started when the government of Thailand was forced to "float" its currency, the baht. The Thai economy had been booming: international capital poured in, factories opened, and the real estate market soared. Much of this activity, however, went through unregulated banks in a relatively weak state, which may be why international investors began to doubt the stability and long-term prospects of the Thai economy. The famous venture capitalist George Soros was one of the first to sell his Thai currency, and as more investors sold their currencies rapidly, getting out of the currency market the way investors get out of a stock market when they think it's about to crash, real estate prices and company profits collapsed. Economies that had been booming went into steep decline, and unemployment soared. The economic contagion spread rapidly from Thailand to Indonesia, Malaysia, the Philippines, and South Korea, and later to other developing economies like Brazil and Russia.

The massive loss of wealth in Asia ultimately brought down the government of longtime Indonesian dictator Suharto and produced recession and instability for many other developmental states, though most recovered and were growing substantially a decade later. In spite of this recovery, the crisis revealed that many states' regulation of the financial sector in particular was very weak. Banks took on unsecured international loans and lent money for dubious investments, often to companies with which they had close, even familial, ties. When the crisis hit, the banks rapidly sank into bankruptcy since their creditors could not repay them, and in turn, they could not repay their own international loans. Neoliberals argued that in spite of East Asia's rapid success, the state's role was not as beneficial as had been assumed. Many began to argue that economic growth would have been even more rapid without state credit and subsidies to key industries. Critics of neoliberalism made the opposite argument: lack of controls of the flow of money across borders allowed the speculative boom and subsequent bust.

Even taking the crisis into account, the developmental state has been the most successful developmental model of the last generation, but it seems difficult to imitate in contexts other than where it began. Even in Asia, countries like Thailand and the Philippines, while achieving significant success and becoming middle-income countries, have not duplicated the success of South Korea or Taiwan. This has come to be known as the *middle-income poverty trap*: with the exception of South Korea, Taiwan, and Singapore, even "successful" developmentalist states have only become middle income; no others have broken into the ranks of the wealthiest countries. This is the challenge China faces today.

Brazilian economist Luiz Carlos Bresser Pereira (2010) proposed a "new developmentalism" based on a modified version of the developmentalist state to try to overcome the middle-income poverty trap. He argued that globalization puts states into intense competition with one another for capital so, in contrast to neoliberal policies, states need to create active national development strategies. For middle-income countries, these should include a balanced budget to keep inflation under control and trade liberalization to encourage exports for growth, as neoliberalism recommends, but not full financial liberalization. He argued that middle-income countries, because they are typically dependent on a handful of key exports, tend to have what is called "Dutch disease": an overvaluation of their currencies because foreign capital flows into the country to buy the key exports. This makes their other exports less competitive and their citizens unable to purchase imports. The neoliberal policy of no government intervention in currency markets leaves these countries vulnerable to Dutch disease and to dramatic swings in the value of the currency, as in the Asian crisis. To avoid this, middle-income states should intervene when necessary to ensure their currency does not become too overvalued. For years, the United States complained that China kept its currency "artificially low" to benefit its exports; Bresser Pereira argued this is wise development policy for a middle-income country. Finally and in contrast to China, middle-income countries should work to ensure that wages rise with productivity in the country, so their workers have the purchasing power to help stimulate demand in the economy. Domestic demand, as Keynes, argued, can fuel growth. Bresser Pereira recommended this "new developmentalism," in particular, for Latin American countries, which had mostly followed neoliberal policies imposed by the IMF. Or they did until a new group of leftist governments came to power around the turn of the millennium, in what came to be known as the "pink tide."

The Pink Tide in Latin America

The neoliberal model and the IMF probably influenced Latin America more than any other region. The debt crisis that began in Mexico in August 1982 quickly spread to Brazil and Argentina, and the 1980s became known as the "lost decade" in Latin America because of the severe economic downturn that followed the debt crisis. By the mid-1990s, most Latin American countries had engaged in extensive privatization of state-owned activities, reduction of trade barriers, and fiscal restraint. Neoliberal reform, though, did not produce notable improvement in growth or reduction in poverty. Not surprisingly, this produced a political backlash. Citizens in Argentina, Bolivia, Brazil, Chile, Ecuador, and Venezuela elected leftist critics of neoliberal reforms in the new millennium, creating what many called Latin America's pink tide (Wylde 2012).

The pink tide governments varied widely. Some, such as Argentina and Brazil, preserved the major macroeconomic foundations of neoliberalism but implemented greater social programs aimed at the poor. Others, most famously that of Hugo Chávez in Venezuela, intervened in the economy in ways that more seriously challenged the market model, including heavily subsidizing certain sectors, such as food and fuel, and nationalizing key industries, especially minerals. Neoliberals feared that the pink tide would undermine what they saw as the gains of neoliberalism, including fiscal austerity and control of inflation. Most of the pink tide governments, though, preserved many neoliberal macroeconomic policies, maintaining more or less balanced budgets and keeping the economy open to trade and investment. Through 2007, they achieved slightly higher growth rates and greater fiscal surpluses than other Latin American governments, with only slightly higher inflation (Moreno-Brid and Paunovic 2010). Coupling this with expanded social services resulted in the rate of poverty in Latin America being halved in the new millennium.

The pink tide in Brazil began with the inauguration of Luiz Inacio "Lula" da Silva as president in 2003. He was a union leader who helped lead the democratization movement in the 1980s and helped found the Workers' Party (PT) that ruled the country from 2003 to 2016. During the 2002 presidential campaign, domestic and international business leaders feared a PT government, so the party wrote a manifesto stating that "social development," focused on reducing poverty and inequality, was crucial but that it would be coupled with neoliberal policies to keep inflation low and the government budget in surplus. Lula tried to do these two things sequentially by first securing economic stability and business confidence and then focusing on social programs. While progress was slow, by 2010 unemployment had dropped from 9 percent to under 6 percent, and poverty was cut roughly in half. Lula's government had achieved these gains for the working class and poor via increased and regionally widespread growth and new social programs (see chapter 12).

Newly sworn-in president Luiz Inacio Lula da Silva (R) speaks with Venezuean President Hugo Chavez 02 January, 2003 at the Palacio de Planalto, in Brasilia. Numerous heads of state and some 150 million people attended Lula's swearing-in ceremony 01 January. While both were part of the "pink tide," Chavez more directly challenged market forces, while Lula focused on coupling neoliberal policies with efforts to reduce poverty and inequality. Both economies suffered from slowing global growth and falling mineral prices in the 2010s, but Venezuela's collapsed catastrophically.
Mauricio Lima/AFP/Getty Images

Growth in Latin America as a whole and most pink tide countries peaked in 2010 as the effects of the Great Recession spread. The region entered recession in 2015–2016, followed by a weak recovery, with growth just over one percent, through 2019. Most analysts pointed to falling prices for key exports, especially minerals, as the main reason why. Brazil's economy collapsed in 2015, dropping 3.8 percent, while Venezuela's entered full-scale crisis, producing massive protests against the government of Hugo Chávez's successor and by 2019 a humanitarian crisis, as over a million people left the country for neighboring states, who themselves were struggling with sluggish economies. The exceptional growth before the Great Recession had relied heavily on selling raw materials, especially to China. As Chinese growth slowed and global mineral prices fell, so did Latin American growth and the pink tide experiment, a victim of the effects of globalization. The result was leftists being removed from power in several countries and others being forced to scale back their social programs as government revenue plummeted.

The Bottom Billion

Economist Paul Collier (2007) coined the term the *bottom billion* to refer to the population of the poorest countries on Earth, most of them in Africa, which seemed to be left behind by globalization. Being poor and heavily indebted, many of these poorest countries were forced to implement structural adjustment in the 1980s and 1990s. The results, however, were even more disappointing than in most Latin American countries. Of 189 countries on the Human Development Index in 2017, some 22 of the bottom 25 were African (the exceptions were Haiti, Yemen, and Afghanistan). By the new millennium, the continent had become the poster child of economic failure and the subject of growing attention from global development agencies, charitable foundations, and even rock stars. The failure of globalization and neoliberal policies to create growth and reduce poverty in the poorest countries produced a new development debate about both the causes of this failure and what to do about it.

As noted earlier, the World Bank and others began advocating for developing stronger state institutions and human capital. Following an institutionalist approach, they argued that the absence of strong, market-friendly institutions is the problem in the poorest states, in which neopatrimonial forms of authority harm investment and markets by exacting implicit taxes, distributing the revenue gained via patron–client networks, and weakening the rule of law. The World Bank prescribed the creation of effective and efficient governing institutions that help provide strong rule of law, political stability, and key public goods such as infrastructure, education, and health care. At least implicitly, this theory argued that these goals can best be achieved via a democratic regime.

Other analysts, such as Jeffrey Sachs, argued that specific conditions limit growth in the poorest countries, and external aid can help overcome these constraints. Sachs (2005) pointed to geography, disease, and climate as key issues in Africa in particular. Low population densities, few good ports, long distances to major consumer markets, many landlocked countries, and the ravages of tropical diseases all reduce Africa's growth potential in the absence of major foreign assistance. Sachs called for a massive inflow of aid, arguing that a large-enough volume targeted the right way could end African poverty in our lifetime. This approach led to the creation of the United Nations' **Millennium Development Goals (MDGs)**, a set of targets to reduce poverty and hunger, improve education and health, improve the status of women, and achieve environmental sustainability, all fueled by a call for a large increase in aid.

Neoliberal critics of this approach, such as William Easterly (2006) and Dambisa Moyo (2009), pointed to the fact that Africa has a long history as the world's largest aid recipient and yet has failed to achieve substantial development. Easterly argued that the result of misguided efforts such as Sachs's will be that "the rich have markets" while "the poor have bureaucrats." The former, he suggested, is the only way to achieve growth; the latter will waste and distort resources and leave Africans more impoverished and dependent on Western support. Moyo argued that microfinance and the global bond markets would be better means to finance development than continued dependence on aid. If poor countries had to use global bond markets to finance investment the way wealthier countries do, they would be forced to implement better policies, and these would foster growth. The punishing discipline of the international bond market (the same discipline that Greece faced in the eurozone crisis) would create the incentives governments in poor countries require to develop both stronger institutions and better policies.

Collier (2007) argued for a more nuanced approach, suggesting that different countries were poor for different reasons. Some faced a problem of bad governance, as argued above, while others faced being landlocked, a resource curse, or civil war; each problem, he argued, requires focus on that issue, with aid playing a part but targeted specifically to that problem. A higher percentage of countries in Africa are landlocked than on any other continent. Landlocked countries, especially if dependent on neighboring countries with poor infrastructure, have limited options, given constraints on their exports that they can do little about. Developing sectors like tourism and information or communications technology that don't rely as heavily on movement through the neighboring country may be their only option. Rwanda in the new millennium has been trying to develop into a "technology hub" for its region for this very reason.

We discussed the resource curse in chapter 2, noting it was a potential source of state weakness, meaning weak political institutions that can make

Millennium Development Goals (MDGs): Targets established by the United Nations to reduce poverty and hunger, improve education and health, improve the status of women, and achieve environmental sustainability

development difficult. The resource curse can also cause direct economic problems. Dutch disease, discussed above, is a key problem, as investment in the key resource and a rising currency value undermine growth in other areas of the economy. Collier argued for aid targeted at strengthening institutions and diversifying investment in the countries facing the resource curse. Empirical studies, though, show mixed evidence of the resource curse; some countries that depend on natural resource exports seem to avoid the curse. A key way is by creating sovereign wealth funds, which are funds from export revenues that are invested internationally and ideally managed independently of the government. They are essentially "rainy day" funds that can be used when a resource bust occurs, used to invest in other sectors of the economy, and used to build infrastructure, all to the long-term benefit of the country's development. While the most effective sovereign wealth funds were created in countries like Norway, which already had strong states and political institutions, the funds have been shown to be beneficial in countries with weaker institutions as well (Murshed 2018).

As this debate over how to help Africa overcome poverty was unfolding in the first decades of the new millennium, some analysts, including a number of African leaders, began to talk of an "African Renaissance." Overall economic growth improved significantly, averaging nearly 5 percent from 2000 to 2007 and 4.1 percent from 2010 to 2017, in spite of the Great Recession and subsequent decline in commodity prices. The population living in absolute poverty across the continent dropped from 51 percent in 2005 to 39 percent in 2012 (African Development Bank Group 2013, 2019). Much of this was fueled by rising prices for Africa's raw materials. In 2017 and 2018, though, countries that did not export raw materials grew faster than those that did. Whether this improvement can be sustained over the long term in the face of declining commodity prices will determine whether Africa can finally begin to see the benefits of globalization, or whether the bottom billion will remain so.

Even though it is a major oil producer, Nigeria, Africa's giant, illustrates many of the issues surrounding the bottom billion. In 1961 money from oil exports constituted less than 8 percent of Nigeria's government revenue; by 1974, it was 80 percent. The military governments of the 1970s used oil wealth to invest in large-scale infrastructure projects, borrowing money against future oil revenues to do so. When the oil market collapsed in the mid-1980s, the government was unable to pay back its loans and faced bankruptcy. Nigeria had to turn to the IMF to negotiate an SAP. The politically painful reductions in the government's size and activity that the IMF required were more than even the military governments could bear, and the process of instituting neoliberal policies was long and remains incomplete.

People gather near pieces of art exhibited in the new museum of black civilizations, in Dakar, Senegal, during the opening ceremony and inauguration in 2018. Institutions like this may be signs of an "African Renaissance," if growth can be sustained in the long run.
Seyllou/AFP/Getty Images

The democratic government that came to power in 1999 used its international support to gain financial aid and debt relief from Western donors but in turn was required to make substantial progress in moving its economic policies in a neoliberal direction. By 2006, the country's overall debt had dropped to less than one-tenth of what it had been two years earlier (Gillies 2007, 575). Donors responded to the neoliberal policies, not only with debt relief but also with a massive increase in aid, from less than $200 million in 2000 to more than $6 billion in 2005. All this combined with rapidly increasing world oil prices to substantially improve economic growth; per capita GDP more than doubled from 2000 to 2014, but because most of the gains in wealth remain in the oil sector, they have not been distributed widely. In 2018, Nigeria overtook India to become the country with the largest number of people living in extreme poverty in the world.

Recently, the economy was devastated by the drop in oil prices that began in 2014. Nigeria had created a sovereign wealth fund but had never seriously funded it, spending the revenue instead. With global oil prices falling by 50 percent, the country entered a recession, and the government, facing a revenue crisis, was considering selling off some of its ownership of the oil sector. Nigeria faces at least two of the problems Collier (2007) saw as plaguing the bottom billion: a resource curse and bad governance. Although the latter appears to have improved somewhat, dependence on the fickle world oil market continues to wreak havoc on the country, especially the substantial share of the population that remains poor in spite of the massive oil wealth.

After a half century of debate, no single development theory has proven itself as the key answer to the problem. Most analysts agree with a number of the fundamentals of neoliberalism, at least regarding the need to keep fiscal deficits and debt limited and inflation low to encourage investment. Most also now recognize the importance of the state creating (1) strong institutions providing the core functions we outlined in chapter 10: security, property, and contract rights; and (2) key public goods, such as infrastructure, education, and health care. All of these are now seen as essential to achieve both economic growth and enhanced human capabilities. It remains unclear, however, how states with varying levels of wealth and state strength can achieve these goals, especially in the face of globalization and dramatically shifting prices for the goods they export that help finance development. It is also far from clear how much the wealthy countries can and should help. What is clear is that a handful of countries, almost all in Asia, seemed to have figured out a way to pursue successful development, and they account for the vast majority of the success so far.

Regime Type and Development Success

Whichever developmental model seems most effective at navigating globalization to achieve growth and reduce poverty, a subsequent question is, What type of government is most likely to pursue beneficial policies? The classic question in this area has been, Do democracies or dictatorships produce better economic development? Most theorists initially asserted that democracy provides incentives for politicians to pursue policies that will gain them support so they can win elections and citizens will demand good economic policy. On the other hand, some of the primary development success stories such as South Korea, Taiwan, and China achieved much of their success under authoritarian regimes. Pundits and policymakers argued that strong states need to be created, as well as healthy economies, before democracy is viable. Sen (1999), of course, argued that democracy is not just a means to development; rather, the freedom democracy provides is part of the definition of development.

Those arguing that democracy enhances growth and reduces poverty focus mostly on accountability, stability, and the rule of law. They hold that democracies provide greater popular accountability, so citizens will demand that their governments pursue beneficial economic policies. Sen famously noted that no democracy has ever had a famine; the need for popular support ensures that democratic governments will not let their people starve en masse. Once consolidated, democracy also enhances political stability; while changes of governmental leaders still occur, elections regularize the process so change does not threaten the ability of investors to predict future returns, and the investment that is the basis of growth will continue to flow. Finally, democracies better protect the rule of law, including the property rights and contracts that are essential elements of capitalist growth.

Opponents of this view hypothesize that democracy impedes growth because democratic governments must follow political demands that favor consumption over investment. Long-term economic growth depends on investment, which can only happen if some of society's resources are not consumed. Democracies, this school of thought argues, have to bow to the will of the citizens, and citizens typically want more consumption now and are unwilling to invest and wait for future benefits. This is especially true in poorer societies, where more impoverished people understandably demand consumption now. Furthermore, in democracies with weak institutions and weak political parties, these demands are based on patronage, giving political leaders an incentive to control as many resources as possible. This has the effect of expanding the role of the state, harming the business climate, and again, discouraging investment. Dictatorships, the argument goes, can resist pressure for greater consumption by repressing citizens' demands and can follow more consistent policies over time, as the East Asian success stories demonstrate.

Despite this extensive debate, empirical findings, many using quite sophisticated statistical techniques, have been rather ambiguous. Przeworski et al. (2000) and Yi Feng (2003) analyzed the relationship between regime type and economic growth, taking into account numerous economic factors that influence growth in an effort to isolate the independent effect of regime type. Using somewhat different methodologies, both found no relationship between regime type and growth: democracies and dictatorships did not vary significantly in their ability to achieve development.

Regime type alone, however, may not be the determining variable in achieving growth and reducing poverty. The type of democracy and other aspects of the state may matter as well. Lijphart (1999) argued that consensual democracies produce greater well-being because the compromise they require forces leaders to distribute resources more equitably, which provides greater stability, encouraging investment and growth. Others have argued that strong political parties are a key ingredient to pursuing growth-enhancing and poverty-reducing policies in both Latin America (Flores-Macias 2012) and Africa (Pitcher 2012). Pippa Norris (2012) pointed to the state's bureaucratic capacity as the missing explanatory factor. Her quantitative analysis found that we need to distinguish between what she called "bureaucratic democracies," with high capacity to implement policies and "patronage democracies," lacking such capacity. Similarly, "bureaucratic autocracies" are more successful than "patronage autocracies," though not as successful as "bureaucratic democracies." Figure 11.4 provides the growth rates of each type of government. Even when controlling for many other factors that affect growth, democracy and state capacity, when considered together, make a difference. These distinctions within both democracies and autocracies, she argued, explain the ambiguous results of prior studies that focused on regime type alone.

These arguments return us to the issue of strong institutions. We discussed in chapter 2 the theory that modern states developed out of self-interested elite compromise to limit violence and its costs, ultimately leading to the creation of the impersonal institutions of the state. Two major studies have extended this general idea to explain why some states create prosperity and others don't. They argued that prosperity requires "open-access orders" (North et al. 2013) or "inclusive political and economic institutions" (Acemoglu and Robinson 2012). Both saw elite

FIGURE 11.4

Mean Economic Growth by Type of Regime

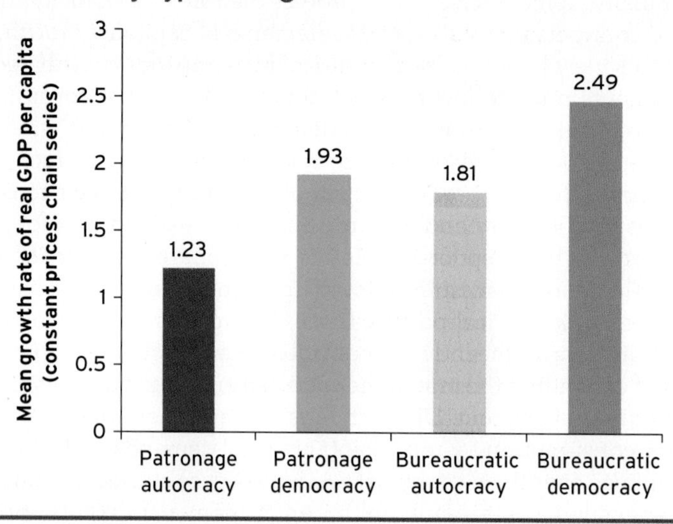

Source: Pippa Norris, Figure 5.1, "Mean Economic Growth by Type of Regime," Making Democratic Governance Work: How Regimes Shape Prosperity, Welfare, and Peace (Cambridge, UK: Cambridge University Press, 2012), 115.

compromise as crucial to establishing institutions that allow and secure incentives for wealth creation (property rights, contracts, the rule of law) and broad political participation that allows those gaining wealth to ensure an extractive state does not take it from them. Inclusive or open political and economic institutions can create a "virtuous circle" of success once created. The inability to achieve this could be a major cause of the "middle income poverty trap." Indeed, Acemoglu and Robinson asserted that China's growth, however impressive it appears, will be limited until more open political and economic institutions arise. These authors took a very long look at historical development to argue that institutions matter to achieving a truly wealthy society, and high-quality democracy is ultimately an important component of this process, even in situations where "bureaucratic dictatorships" seem to be successful for quite some time.

Conclusion

"Development" has been an important political and economic concept since World War II. For most people, it still means creating greater wealth—a process of poor countries becoming more like rich countries over time. Numerous scholars, though, have questioned whether that should be the goal, as well as how it should be achieved. Theories of economic development, in particular, have closely followed the broader debate over economic policy we discussed in chapter 10, including dramatic changes in prescriptions for how the state should be involved in the process.

Poorer countries have virtually all moved in the general direction of economic liberalization, but whether this has been a blessing is not always clear. Various analysts have argued that geography, resource endowment, distance from markets, government policies, and regime type all have a role in explaining why some countries, particularly the bottom billion, continue to struggle in the face of globalization, while others thrive. The closest thing to consensus is around recommendations for macroeconomic stability, strong institutions, and investment in human capital.

Even with this consensus, though, it isn't always clear why some states have been more successful in the era of globalization than others. Neoliberal policies have often not reduced poverty and have sometimes led to repeated financial crises. In this context, several alternative models have arisen. While pursuit of export-oriented growth in East Asia has generated strong growth and reduced poverty, the developmental state model is based on a strong state that not all countries have. The Great Recession was only the latest in a series of economic crises in the era of globalization. Each has shaken the foundation of one or another economic development model and has raised questions about who weathers a crisis best and why. The latest crisis has shown perhaps more clearly than ever the force of the global market in limiting states' responses. While most middle-income and poor countries were not as dramatically affected initially, a decade after the crisis, the continuing stagnation in the global economy raised questions even in China about how long high growth and poverty reduction could continue. A key question in both wealthy and poor countries is how effectively a state can intervene in the market to pursue goals such as greater equality, health, and environmental protection—subjects to which we now turn in chapter 12. ●

KEY CONCEPTS

comparative advantage (p. 323)

export-oriented growth (EOG) (p. 328)

foreign direct investment (FDI) (p. 320)

import-substitution industrialization (ISI) (p. 323)

international capital flows (p. 320)

Millennium Development Goals (MDGs) (p. 334)

structural adjustment programs (SAPs) (p. 324)

trade (p. 320)

WORKS CITED

Acemoglu, Daron, and James A. Robinson. 2012. *Why Nations Fail: The Origins of Power, Prosperity, and Poverty.* New York: Crown Publishing.

African Development Bank Group. 2013. *Annual Development Effectiveness Review 2013: Toward Sustainable Growth for Africa.* Tunis, Tunisia. July, 2013.

——. 2019. *African Economic Outlook 2019.* https://www.afdb.org/en/knowledge/publications/african-economic-outlook/.

Bradsher, Keith. 2015. "China Turned to Risky Devaluation as Export Machine Stalled." *New York Times.* August 17, 2015. http://www.nytimes.com/2015/08/18/business/international/chinas-devaluation-of-its-currency-was-a-call-to-action.html?smid=nytcore-ipad-share&smp rod=nytcore-ipad.

Collier, Paul. 2007. *The Bottom Billion: Why the Poorest Countries Are Failing and What Can Be Done About It.* Oxford, UK: Oxford University Press.

Easterly, William. 2006. *The White Man's Burden: Why the West's Efforts to Aid the Rest Have Done So Much Ill and So Little Good.* New York: Penguin Press.

Feng, Yi. 2003. *Democracy, Governance, and Economic Performance: Theory and Evidence.* Cambridge, MA: MIT Press.

Flores-Macias, Gustavo A. 2012. *After Neoliberalism: The Left and Economic Reforms in Latin America.* Oxford, UK: Oxford University Press.

Gillies, Alexandra. 2007. "Obasanjo, the Donor Community and Reform Implementation in Nigeria." *The Round Table* 96 (392): 569–586. doi:10.1080/00358530701625992.

Haggard, Stephan, and Robert R. Kaufman. 1995. *The Political Economy of Democratic Transitions.* Princeton, NJ: Princeton University Press.

Lijphart, Arend. 1999. *Patterns of Democracy: Government Forms and Performance in Thirty-Six Countries.* New Haven, CT: Yale University Press.

Moreno-Brid, Juan Carlos, and Igor Paunovic. 2010. "Macroeconomic Policies of the New Left: Rhetoric and Reality." In *Latin America's Left Turns: Politics, Policies, and Trajectories of Change*, edited by Maxwell A. Cameron and Eric Hershberg, 193–232. Boulder, CO: Lynne Rienner.

Moyo, Dambisa. 2009. *Dead Aid: Why Aid Is Not Working and How There Is a Better Way for Africa.* New York: Farrar, Straus and Giroux.

Murshed, Syed Mansoob. 2018. *The Resource Curse.* Newcastle upon Tyne, UK: Agenda Publishing.

Norris, Pippa. 2012. *Making Democratic Governance Work: How Regimes Shape Prosperity, Welfare, and Peace.* Cambridge, UK: Cambridge University Press.

North, D. C., Wallis, J. J., Webb, S. B., and Weingest, B. R. 2013. *In the Shadow of Violence: Politics, Economics, and the Problems of Development*. Cambridge, UK: Cambridge University Press.

Ocampo, José Antonio, and Natalie Gomez-Arteaga. 2018. "Social Protection Systems in Latin America: Toward Universalism and Redistribution." In *The Welfare State Revisited*, edited by José Antonio Ocampo and Joseph E. Stiglitz, 230–257. New York: Columbia University Press.

Ocampo, José Antonio, and Rob Vos. 2010. *Uneven Economic Development*. New York: Zed Books.

Ozawa, Terutomo. 2010. "Asia's Labour-Driven Growth, Flying Geese Style: Types of Trade, FDI, and Institutions Matter for the Poor." In *The Poor under Globalization in Asia, Latin America, and Africa*, edited by Machiko Nissanke and Erik Thorbecke, 87–115. Oxford, UK: Oxford University Press.

Pearson, Margaret M. 2015. "State-Owned Business and Party-State Regulations in China's Modern Political Economy." In *State Capitalism, Institutional Adaptation, and the Chinese Miracle*, edited by Barry Naughton and Kellee S. Tsai, 27–45. Cambridge, UK: Cambridge University Press.

Pereira, Luiz Carlos Bresser. 2010. *Globalization and Competition: Why Some Emergent Countries Succeed While Others Fall Behind.* Cambridge, UK: Cambridge University Press.

Pitcher, M. Anne. 2012. *Party Politics and Economic Reform in Africa's Democracies.* Cambridge, UK: Cambridge University Press.

Przeworski, Adam, Michael Alvarez, José Cheibub, and Fernando Limongi. 2000. *Democracy and Development*. Cambridge, UK: Cambridge University Press.

Round, Jeffrey. 2010. "Globalization, Growth, Inequality, and Poverty in Africa: A Macroeconomic Perspective." In *The Poor under Globalization in Asia, Latin America, and Africa*, edited by M. Nissanke and E. Thorbecke, 327–367. Oxford, UK: Oxford University Press.

Rudra, Nita, and Jennifer Tobin. 2017. "When Does Globalization Help the Poor," *Annual Review of Political Science*. 20: 287–307.

Sachs, Jeffrey D. 2005. *The End of Poverty: Economic Possibilities for Our Time*. New York: Penguin Books.

Sen, Amartya K. 1999. *Development as Freedom*. New York: Anchor Books.

Weber, Heloise, ed. 2014. *The Politics of Development: A Survey*. New York: Routledge.

Wylde, Christopher. 2012. *Latin America After Neoliberalism: Developmental Regimes in Post-Crisis States*. New York: Palgrave Macmillan.

RESOURCES FOR FURTHER STUDY

Cameron, Maxwell A., and Eric Hershberg, eds. 2010. *Latin America's Left Turns: Politics, Policies, and Trajectories of Change*. Boulder, CO: Lynne Rienner.

Evans, Peter B. 1995. *Embedded Autonomy: States and Industrial Transformation*. Princeton, NJ: Princeton University Press.

Ferreira, Francisco H. G., and Michael Walton. 2005. *Equity and Development*. Washington, DC: World Bank.

Jha, Prem Shankar. 2002. *The Perilous Road to the Market: The Political Economy of Reform in Russia, India, and China*. London: Pluto Press.

Jones, R. J. Barry. 2000. *The World Turned Upside Down? Globalization and the Future of the State*. Manchester, UK: Manchester University Press.

Kohli, Atul, Chung-in Moon, and Georg Sørensen, eds. 2003. *States, Markets, and Just Growth: Development in the Twenty-first Century*. New York: United Nations University Press.

MacIntyre, Andrew, T. J. Pempel, and John Ravenhill, eds. 2008. *Crisis as Catalyst: Asia's Dynamic Political Economy*. Ithaca, NY: Cornell University Press.

Nissanke, Machiko, and Erik Thorbecke, eds. 2010. *The Poor Under Globalization in Asia, Latin America, and Africa*. Oxford, UK: Oxford University Press.

Van de Walle, Nicolas. 2001. *African Economies and the Politics of Permanent Crisis, 1979–1999*. Cambridge, UK: Cambridge University Press.

World Bank. 1993. *The East Asian Miracle: Economic Growth and Public Policy*. New York: Oxford University Press.

WEB RESOURCES

CountryWatch

(http://www.countrywatch.com)

KOF Index of Globalization

(http://globalization.kof.ethz.ch). Based on data from Axel Dreher, "Does Globalization Affect Growth? Evidence from a New Index of Globalization," *Applied Economics* 38, no. 10 (2006): 1091–1110; updated in Axel Dreher, Noel Gaston, and Pim Martens, *Measuring Globalisation: Gauging Its Consequences* (New York: Springer, 2008).

UN Millennium Project, Millennium Villages: A New Approach to Fighting Poverty

(http://www.unmillenniumproject.org/mv/mv_closer.htm)

United Nations University, World Institute for Development Economics Research, World Income Inequality Database

(http://www.wider.unu.edu/research/Database)

World Bank, Economic Policy and External Debt

(http://data.worldbank.org/topic/economic-policy-and-external-debt)

Zhao Yuhong/VCG via Getty Images

12 Public Policies When Markets Fail

Welfare, Health, and the Environment

Rapid economic growth and industrialization have caused dangerously high levels of air pollution in major Chinese cities. Wearing face masks has become quite common. These women in Hong Kong are paying the costs of pollution other people are creating and profiting from: a classic externality.
Lam Yik Fei/Getty Images

Key Questions

- What do policy outcomes tell us about who has effective representation and power in a political system?
- Why do states intervene in the market via social, health, and environmental policies?
- Why have many governments pursued significant reforms to welfare states in the era of globalization?
- Why have states found it so difficult to reform health policy and control costs?
- Where and why did more effective welfare and health systems emerge, and can the most effective ones be replicated in other countries?

Learning Objectives

After reading chapter 12, you should be able to do the following:

12.1 Define social policy and its various elements and explain how and why it varies among nations

12.2 Explain the current debates on health policy and the different health systems currently employed in various states

12.3 Explicate the relationship between climate change and the role that market economics plays in environmental policy

As globalization spreads through the market economy, the issues raised in chapters 10 and 11 about the relationship between the state and the market loom ever larger. The long-standing debate over how much governments ought to intervene in the market in an effort to maximize citizens' well-being continues unabated. This chapter addresses three key areas that have long been subjects of debate in virtually every country: welfare, health care, and the environment. The common thread among them is the call for government to intervene in response to market failure.

We defined market failure in economic terms in chapter 10: markets fail when they do not maximize efficiency, most commonly because of externalities, monopolies, or imperfect information. Environmental damage is a classic example of a market failure to allocate resources efficiently. Markets can also fail, however, in the sense that they don't achieve the results a society collectively desires. In this chapter, then, we broaden the definition of market failure to a more general understanding that markets fail when they do not perform according to widely held social values. For instance, markets do not necessarily reduce inequality or end poverty, even though the alleviation of both is often a widely held social value. Governments develop what Americans call "welfare" policies to respond to market failures to distribute wealth in socially acceptable ways.

Government interventions of this type raise a host of interesting questions because they pit various groups of citizens against one another. The policy outcomes often tell us much about the classic "Who rules?" question. They also raise major questions focused on why government intervenes in the first place. In recent years, governments in all wealthy countries have reformed welfare policies substantially and tried, with limited success, to reform health care policies as well. Why have these trends been so widespread over the past twenty to thirty years, and why have some states been more successful than others at achieving reforms? Great variation exists in these policy areas around the world. Welfare systems vary from quite extensive to nonexistent, with dramatically different effects on the level of poverty. Key health care indicators like life expectancy and infant mortality vary dramatically as well. The wealthy countries achieve roughly similar health outcomes but at very different costs, while poor countries' health fares far worse.

"Welfare": Social Policy in Comparative Perspective

Most Americans think of welfare as a government handout to poor people. Being "on welfare" is something virtually all Americans want to avoid, as a certain moral opprobrium seems to go with it. Partly because of this and partly because different countries relieve poverty in different ways, scholars of public policy prefer the term **social policy** to welfare. Social policy's primary goals are to reduce poverty and income inequality and to stabilize individual or family income. Most people view a market that leaves people in abject poverty, unable to meet their most basic needs, as violating important values. Similarly, when markets produce inequality that goes beyond some particular point (the acceptable level varies widely), many people argue that it should be reversed. Markets also inherently produce instability: in the absence of government intervention, capitalism tends to be associated with boom-and-bust cycles that result in economic insecurity, especially due to unemployment. Reducing this insecurity has been one of the main impetuses behind modern welfare states.

Various philosophical and practical reasons justify social policies. On purely humanitarian grounds, citizens and governments might wish to alleviate the suffering of the poor. States might also be concerned about social and political stability: high endemic poverty rates and economic instability often are seen as threats to the status quo, including a state's legitimacy, and poverty is associated with higher levels of crime almost everywhere. Keynesians argue as well that policies to reduce poverty and stabilize incomes are economically beneficial for society as a whole because they help increase purchasing power, which stimulates market demand.

Opponents of social policy disagree, criticizing it primarily for producing perverse incentives. Markets maximize efficiency in part by inducing people to be productive by working for wages, salaries, or profits. Neoliberal opponents of social policy argue that providing income or other resources for people whether they are working or not gives them a disincentive to work, which reduces efficiency, productivity, and overall wealth. Critics also argue that financing social policy via taxes discourages work and productivity because higher taxes reduce incentives to work and make a profit.

In liberal democracies, the debate over social policy also raises a fundamental question over the trade-off between citizens' equality and autonomy. According to liberalism, citizens are supposed to be equal and autonomous individuals, yet in a market economy, it's difficult to achieve both. Citizens are never truly socioeconomically equal. As we saw in chapter 3, T. H. Marshall (1963) argued that social rights are the third pillar of citizenship because without some degree of socioeconomic equality, citizens cannot be political equals. Following this line of thought, when the market fails to create an adequate degree of equality, governments should intervene to preserve equal citizenship. On the other hand, in market economies, market participation is a primary means of achieving autonomy. The founders of liberalism believed only male property owners could be citizens because they were the only ones who were truly autonomous; women and nonproperty owners were too economically dependent on others to act effectively as autonomous citizens.

social policy: Policy focused on reducing poverty and income inequality and stabilizing individual or family income

All liberal democracies have modified this position, but the fundamental concern remains. Many citizens view only those who participate in the market—whether by owning capital or working for a wage—as fully autonomous. Welfare policies that provide income from nonmarket sources can then be seen as problematic. Traditional liberals argue that social policy undermines equal and autonomous citizenship by creating two classes of citizens: those who earn their income in the market and those who depend on the government (funded by the rest of the citizens). This argument typically makes an exception for family membership: an adult who depends on other family members who participate in the market is implicitly granted full autonomy and citizenship. Social democrats argue, to the contrary, that citizens should be granted full autonomy regardless of their source of income and that social policies that keep income inequality and poverty below certain levels are essential to preserving truly equal citizenship. Different kinds of welfare states are in part based on different values in this debate.

Figure 12.1 demonstrates that these debates matter. It correlates "social protection expenditures"—a measure of overall spending on social policy—and the Gini coefficient—the most widely used measure of inequality. Countries that spend more on social expenditures have less inequality, as the dotted line indicates. The spread of the dots representing the individual countries, however, shows that some countries achieve much lower inequality than others with the same level of social expenditure. This suggests that social policy has an impact, but different kinds of social policies must have greater impact than others, to which we now turn.

FIGURE 12.1

Public Social Protection Expenditure (Percentage of GDP) and Income Inequality, 2014

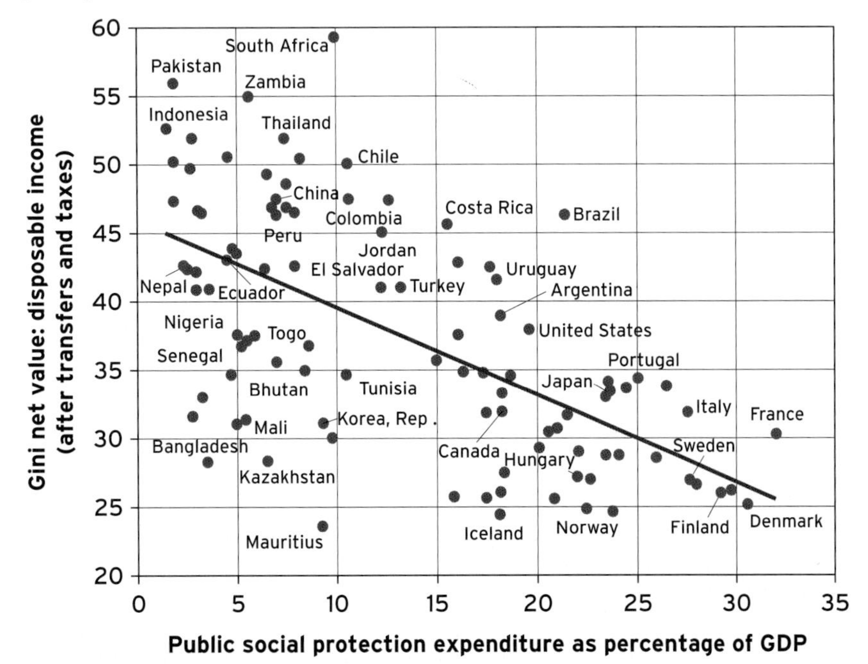

Source: Adapted from José Antonio Ocampo and Joseph E. Stiglitz, eds., *The Welfare State Revisited* (New York: Columbia University Press, 2018), 76. Original source from International Labor Organization; Gini Index from World Bank Development Indicators

Types of Social Policy

Whatever their justification, social policies can be categorized into four distinct types—universal entitlements, social insurance, means-tested public assistance, and tax expenditures. **Universal entitlements** are benefits that governments provide to all citizens more or less equally, usually funded through general taxation. The only major example in the United States is public education. All communities in the United States must provide access to public education for all school-age residents without exception, making it a universal benefit. Many European countries provide child or family allowances as universal entitlements—all families with children receive a cash benefit to help raise the children. Universal entitlements by nature do not raise questions about equal and autonomous citizenship, even when individual citizens may choose not to take advantage of them. No one questions the equal citizenship of public versus private school graduates in the United States or those who do not have children and therefore don't get child allowances in the Netherlands. Critics, on the other hand, argue that universal entitlements are wasteful because much of the money goes to relatively wealthy people who do not need the benefits.

The advantages of universal entitlements have led some to call for a much more expanded option: **universal basic income (UBI)**. UBI would give each individual member of a political community (presumably citizens of a nation-state) a guaranteed cash income from birth to death without conditions of any sort. It would be a social right of citizenship. Most proposals would set it at around the poverty level. Much impetus for it comes from the fear that artificial intelligence will reduce employment permanently, requiring some means of creating dignified lives for a growing population of unemployable citizens (van Parijs and Vanderborght 2017). Like other universal entitlements, it would not raise questions of unequal citizenship because every individual would receive it. Supporters claim it would also allow people to pursue educational opportunities to enhance their skills, increasing human capital and well-being. Critics argue that, like other universal entitlements, it would be inefficient in that it would give money to wealthy people who don't need it. They also argue that it would be prohibitively expensive (estimated at $3 trillion in the United States, more than half the current federal budget) and that it would provide disincentives from employment, for which there is some evidence (McGahey 2018). It is a proposal that would transform the standard models of the welfare state (discussion following), in that, if set at a near-poverty level, it would have to replace most existing social programs.

Social insurance provides benefits to categories of people who have contributed to a (usually mandatory) public insurance fund. The prime examples in the United States are Social Security, disability benefits, and unemployment insurance. In most cases, both workers and their employers must contribute to the funds. Workers can then benefit from the fund when they need it: after retirement, when temporarily unemployed, or when disabled. Because only those who contribute can gain benefits, fewer questions arise about the beneficiaries deserving their benefits, even though there is usually only a very general relationship between the size of a person's contribution and the amount of his benefit. The average American retiree, for instance, earns substantially more in Social Security benefits than the total of his lifetime contributions with interest, but that gap has never raised questions of equal citizenship. In addition, by covering entire large groups of people—all workers or the spouses of all workers—social insurance is not seen as undermining equal citizenship because it covers things nearly everyone expects (retirement) or hopes to avoid (unemployment).

universal entitlements: Benefits that governments provide to all citizens more or less equally, usually funded through general taxation; in the United States, public education is an example

universal basic income: A universal entitlement that would provide a guaranteed income to each individual citizen from birth to death

social insurance: Provides benefits to categories of people who have contributed to a (usually mandatory) public insurance fund; typically used to provide retirement pensions

Means-tested public assistance is what most Americans think of as "welfare." The Supplemental Nutrition Assistance Program (SNAP; also commonly known as "food stamps"), subsidized public housing, and Temporary Assistance to Needy Families (TANF) are examples in the United States. These are programs that individuals qualify for when they fall below a specific income level. Some countries impose additional requirements for public assistance, such as work requirements or time limits, but income level is the defining characteristic. Means-tested programs target assistance at the poor in contrast to the broader distribution of universal entitlements or social insurance, so they may be the most efficient means of poverty relief, though the administrative costs of determining who deserves the benefits are substantial. Their disadvantage, though, is their impact on recipients' status as equal and autonomous citizens. Because only those below a certain income level can benefit and benefits are typically financed from general taxation, recipients may be seen as somehow less deserving or not fully equal with other citizens who are paying taxes and not receiving benefits.

Tax expenditures, targeted tax breaks for specific groups of citizens or activities, have only been included as part of social policy fairly recently. To most people, tax breaks—not collecting taxes from someone—seem different from government spending. The net effect of the two, however, is quite similar. When the government selectively lowers the tax someone would otherwise pay, it is increasing that person's disposable income. Tax expenditures can be restricted to people with low incomes or provided much more widely, with different effects on reducing poverty and inequality. The tax deduction for interest paid on home mortgages, for instance, subsidizes all but the most expensive home purchases; it is a social policy designed to encourage home ownership (presumably improving standards of living and economic security) that provides greater benefits to the middle and upper classes than to the poor. A tax break for people with lower incomes, on the other hand, has the same general effect as the same amount of social spending targeted at that group.

Tax expenditures are an important part of social policy, especially in the United States. They can be restricted to people with low incomes or provided much more widely, with different effects on reducing poverty and inequality. In the United States, for instance, the Earned Income Tax Credit (EITC) aimed at lower-income families has become one of the largest poverty-reduction programs in the country, larger in fact than TANF, the program most Americans think of as welfare. The tax deduction for interest paid on home mortgages, on the other hand, subsidizes all but the most expensive home purchases; it is a social policy designed to encourage home ownership (presumably improving standards of living and economic security) that provides greater benefits to the middle and upper classes than to the poor.

Different types of social programs are often associated with particular kinds of benefits or groups of recipients. Workers are often covered by social insurance, for instance, while public housing is typically means tested. What is true for tax expenditures, however, is true for all types of social programs; any of them could be used for any type of benefit. For instance, unemployment insurance is fairly restricted in the United States, benefiting only long-term employees and usually for only six to nine months after a worker becomes unemployed; elsewhere, similar programs are more extensive and less distinct from what Americans call "welfare." Preschool is a universal entitlement in France but is means tested via the Head Start program in the United States. Retirement benefits also could be means tested so that when older people no longer earn a market-based income, only those below a certain income level would qualify for benefits. This would target retirement benefits more

means-tested public assistance: Social programs that provide benefits to individuals who fall below a specific income level; TANF is an example in the United States

tax expenditures: Targeted tax breaks for specific groups of citizens or activities designed to achieve social policy goals

efficiently at reducing poverty but might raise questions of equal citizenship common to means-tested programs, questions that retirees currently don't face.

Types of Welfare States

Governments combine social programs in different ways and with different levels of generosity, creating distinctive **welfare states**. Evelyne Huber and John Stephens (2001), modifying the pioneering work of Gøsta Esping-Andersen (1990), classified wealthy countries into three main types of welfare states: social democratic, Christian democratic, and liberal. **Social democratic welfare states** strongly emphasize universal entitlements to achieve greater social equality and promote equal citizenship. Governments typically provide universal entitlements in a wide array of areas, including paid maternity leave, preschool, child allowances, basic retirement pensions, and job training. They use high rates of general taxation to fund their generous social benefits and typically redistribute more income (taxing the wealthy more and giving equal universal entitlements to all) than do other welfare states. Social insurance programs, such as employment-based retirement pensions, also exist, but these usually just supplement the universal entitlements. The primary examples of social democratic welfare states are the Scandinavian countries.

Sweden is a prime example of a social democratic welfare state. From its start in the 1920s, Sweden's welfare state established basic services such as unemployment benefits and retirement pensions as universal social rights of citizenship. In the late 1950s, it added extra benefits that were tied to earnings and replaced as much as 90 percent of workers' wages when they were unemployed, disabled, or retired. In the 1970s, the government expanded services designed to induce women into the workforce and support them once they were employed, including the world's most generous maternity and sick-leave policies. The state combined these benefits with very high tax rates on income (60 percent of the economy at their peak in the 1970s), but it used low corporate tax rates to encourage investment in export industries and had one of the most open trade policies in the world. At its height in the 1970s, Sweden was the world's second-wealthiest country, with robust growth, strong export levels by brand-name companies such as Volvo, virtually no unemployment, and the world's most generous social services. Although globalization forced changes in later years, even after reforms in the 1990s, Sweden's social services and taxes remain among the world's highest. Unemployment benefits still cover about 80 percent of wages and have virtually no time limit. Parental leave provides sixteen months of paid leave at any time during the first eight years of a child's life at 80 percent of full salary. Parents get ten paid "contact days" per year to spend time in their children's schools as volunteers, up to sixty days of benefits per year to care for sick children, and access to a day care system that enrolls 75 percent of preschoolers, with more than 80 percent of the cost funded by the state (Olsen 2007, 147–151).

welfare states: Distinct systems of social policies that arose after World War II in wealthy market economies, including social democratic welfare states, Christian democratic welfare states, and liberal welfare states

social democratic welfare states: States whose social policies strongly emphasize universal entitlements to achieve greater social equality and promote equal citizenship; Sweden is a key example

Christian democratic welfare states: States whose social policies are based on the nuclear family with a male breadwinner, designed primarily to achieve income stabilization to mitigate the effects of market-induced income insecurity; Germany is a key example

Christian democratic welfare states primarily emphasize income stabilization to mitigate the effects of market-induced insecurity. Their most common type of social program, therefore, is social insurance, which is designed to replace a relatively high percentage of a family's market-based income when it is disrupted through unemployment, disability, or something similar. Benefits are usually tied to contributions, and financing is mainly through employer and employee payroll taxes rather than general taxation. This means that redistribution is not as broad as under social democratic welfare states. Most Christian democratic welfare states also feature corporatist models of economic governance; that is, social insurance programs tend to be administered by and through sectoral-based organizations such as unions, though under the state's guidance. Germany is a prime example of this system.

Demonstrators in Sweden protest cuts in public health care in September 2016. Sweden's exceptionally generous social democratic welfare state, while requiring some reforms to control costs over the last two decades, remains very popular.
Tommy Lindholm/Pacific Press/LightRocket via Getty Images

Otto von Bismarck created the world's first social insurance program in Germany in 1883. Most of the country's modern Christian democratic welfare state still relies primarily on social insurance. Programs are paid for mainly by roughly equal employer and employee contributions. Prior to reforms in 2003, the core social insurance system provided nearly complete income replacement in case of illness, at least 60 percent of an unemployed worker's salary for up to thirty-two months, and a retirement pension that averaged 70 percent of wages. These benefits continue to constitute the great majority of German social spending. Those unemployed for periods longer than three years received unemployment assistance at about 53 percent of their most recent salary, with no time limit. Others who had never worked a full year still received social assistance, a means-tested system that indefinitely provided enough support to keep them above the poverty line. Originally, the system assumed a male breadwinner could support his wife and children. As women entered the workforce, they supported reforms to make the system less focused on male breadwinners, including adding maternity benefits of fourteen weeks that covered full income, child benefits, and benefits to allow parents to take time off from work to care for young children.

German reunification in 1990 dramatically increased the costs of the system: unemployment rates skyrocketed in the former East Germany, and massive transfers of funds from the former West Germany were essential to pay social insurance benefits to these workers. The Hartz IV reforms in 2003 limited unemployment benefits to twelve months (rather than limitless), after which an unemployed worker would be placed on a fixed income (not connected to past earnings). Benefits for the long-term unemployed switched from social insurance to a means-tested benefit more typical of a liberal welfare state. Retirement pensions were reduced from 70 percent of retirees' wages in the 1980s to what will eventually be about 45 percent. As is often the case with means-tested programs, some stigma that could be undermining a sense of equal citizenship seems to be attached to the reforms: they were known as the Hartz reforms and the new verb *hartzen* means "to be unwilling to perform any work" (Grässler 2014). The reforms, though, helped lower social expenditures from 27 percent of GDP to 25 percent in 2018.

Liberal welfare states focus on ensuring that all who can work and gain their income in the market do so; they are more concerned about preserving individual autonomy via market participation than reducing poverty or inequality. They emphasize means-tested public assistance, targeting very specific groups of recipients for benefits. The emphasis on ensuring that only the truly deserving receive benefits often means that some poor people don't get assistance, and the desire to provide incentives for people to work can mean that benefits do not raise people out of poverty. But not all programs are means tested in these countries; retirement benefits are typically provided via social insurance.

liberal welfare states: States whose social policies focus on ensuring that all who can do so gain their income in the market; more concerned about preserving individual autonomy than reducing poverty or inequality; the United States is a key example

Most social policy in the United States' liberal welfare state began in the Great Depression as part of President Franklin D. Roosevelt's New Deal. The Social Security Act of 1935 was a social insurance retirement program similar to Germany's: pensions are tied to individuals' previous earnings and are financed by mandatory employer and employee contributions. Social Security is the country's most successful antipoverty program, and though not as generous as most European pension systems, it nonetheless dramatically reduced poverty among the elderly. Combined with Medicare, the health care plan for the elderly, it reduced American inequality by nearly 10 percent in 2000. (In contrast, public assistance—what most Americans think of as welfare—reduced American inequality by only 0.4 percent.) Prior to Social Security, the elderly had one of the highest rates of poverty, but now they have one of the lowest. President Lyndon Johnson's War on Poverty in the 1960s produced the second major expansion of American social policy. It created Aid to Families with Dependent Children (AFDC), which became the main means-tested entitlement benefit for the poor, with each state legally obligated to indefinitely provide a minimum level of support, primarily to poor, single mothers with resident children. By 1975, the poverty rate hit a low of about 12 percent of the population, half of what it had been in 1960.

In spite of notable success in reducing poverty, these programs were not widely accepted. Pressure for reform began as early as the late 1960s but grew significantly in the 1980s. In 1996, President Clinton signed the most important reform of social policy since the 1960s. The legislation replaced AFDC with Temporary Assistance for Needy Families (TANF), which limited recipients to two years of continuous benefits and five years over a lifetime, and required virtually all able-bodied recipients to work to keep their benefits. The number of people receiving benefits fell 75 percent from 1995 to 2014 (Edin and Shaefer 2016). The overall number of people in poverty, though, did not change markedly. Some families were able to get out of poverty with the help of the Earned Income Tax Credit (EITC), a major tax expenditure that aims to benefit the "working poor" and has been the fastest-growing social program in the country since 1990. Households making less than about $20,000 per year receive a tax credit each spring worth several thousand dollars, substantially more than they paid in taxes, which has become a key source of income for many.

By 2014, the U.S. government was spending six times more on EITC than TANF. In 2012 EITC and SNAP each lifted approximately 10 million people out of poverty, while TANF lifted only 1.3 million out of poverty (Sherman and Trisi 2015). Sarah Halpern-Meekin and colleagues (2015) argued that because EITC is a tax refund that recipients get simply by going through the same tax-filing process that other Americans do, it preserves their sense of citizenship much better than programs like TANF, which hand them money distinct from what others receive. Those who didn't or couldn't work, though, fell deeper into poverty: the number of children living in "deep poverty" (in households with incomes less than half the official poverty level) rose from 1.5 to 2.2 million between 1995 and 2005 (Greenstein 2016). In 2018, President Trump signed an executive order declaring that poverty had been successfully eliminated in America and increasing work requirements to receive assistance. A more stringent SNAP work requirement and more leeway for the states to increase work requirements for Medicaid were included in the order, and funding reductions and work requirements were in the proposed 2020 budget. The impact of these policies will be a major question going forward.

The Development, Evolution, and Crises(?) of Welfare States

Welfare states exist to mitigate the risks inherent in the market. Whether from sudden unemployment, an overall economic decline, low wages, inflation, sickness, or old age, without some type of social policy, individuals and families would be on their own to cope with crisis. As capitalism emerged, it created greater wealth but also winners and losers. The latter demanded help, forcing democratic regimes to respond, and states could use some of the wealth capitalism generated to provide that help. Marxist scholars argued that the welfare state allowed capitalism to postpone social revolution; reducing the misery capitalism created for the poor kept them from pursuing a socialist revolution. But welfare states vary in how and how much they reduce risk, prompting comparativists to instigate why these differences emerged and how they have responded to the profound economic changes brought on by globalization.

Origins

The most influential explanation of the rise of the distinct types of welfare states is known as "power resources theory" (Esping-Andersen 1990; Huber and Stephens 2001). It combined a structural argument based on class and an institutionalist argument. Welfare states, this approach argued, primarily reflect the strength and political orientation of the working and lower-middle classes. In countries where these classes were able to organize into strong labor unions and powerful social democratic parties, social democratic welfare states emerged that emphasize wealth redistribution and gender equality. Countries with more Catholics and stronger Christian democratic parties that appealed successfully to working and lower-middle classes saw the emergence of Christian democratic welfare states that emphasize social and family stability, rather than resource redistribution and women's participation in the workplace. Where the working classes were not strong enough to organize to gain political power, liberal welfare states emerged that provide minimal support only for those who are truly unable to work. Proportional electoral systems facilitated the creation of the more generous social democratic and Christian democratic systems by allowing social democratic parties to be part of a coalition in power in support of social policies, whereas liberal welfare states emerged in countries, such as the United States and United Kingdom, with majoritarian electoral systems that tended to be dominated by more conservative parties.

Cultural theorists, on the other hand, have pointed to long-standing values, religion, and ethnic or racial diversity to explain differences in welfare states. Anglo-American countries, they argue, have stronger liberal traditions emphasizing the importance of the individual and individual autonomy. Numerous surveys have shown, for instance, that despite upward social mobility being about the same in the United States and Europe, Americans are much more likely than Europeans to believe that people can work their way out of poverty if they really want to (Alesina and Glaeser 2004, 11–12). Similarly, countries more influenced by Protestantism, especially Calvinism, may see the wealthy as morally superior and have less sympathy for the poor, whereas countries with more Catholics may be more generous due to their beliefs in preserving social and family stability.

Alberto Alesina and Edward Glaeser (2004), among others, claimed that racial diversity partly explains the striking difference in the generosity of social spending in the United States and Europe. Surveys show that people (not only Americans) are less sympathetic to those of different races, and in the United States, many whites incorrectly perceive the poor as being mostly black or Hispanic. As a result, Americans are relatively unwilling to support policies to assist them. As immigration has diversified in many European countries, similar phenomena may be arising there as well. Immigrants within the European Union (EU) have the right to the same social benefits as citizens of the countries to which they have immigrated. If those citizens don't feel the immigrants are part of a deserving community who should be supported when need be, the legitimacy of general social benefits could be undermined (Cappelen 2016). In an extensive quantitative study, though, Dennis Spies (2018) found that while the attitudes of Europeans are similar to those of Americans about providing welfare benefits to people not like them, this has not resulted in less support for social spending because more European policies are universal, with substantial benefits for the middle class. Like Social Security in the US, they continue to receive public support even as the populace diversifies.

Evolution and Crises(?)

Globalization and the shift to neoliberal economic policy has raised the same question about modern welfare states that they raised about the liberal market economies (LME) and coordinated market economies (CME) discussed in chapter 10: will the different models survive or converge to a new, more neoliberal norm? To the extent that states have to compete for investment from mobile capital by lowering taxes, they will face pressure on social expenditures. That pressure, though, also comes from demographic changes: as populations age and birth-rates drop (as they have in virtually all wealthy countries over the past generation), fewer workers must somehow pay the benefits for larger dependent populations, particularly the elderly. Governments have also responded to globalization by reducing regulations on labor to allow businesses greater flexibility in hiring and firing. This has produced more part-time and temporary workers who often were not covered under the original welfare-state models, especially the Christian democratic ones focused on the stable employment of the male breadwinner. The result is often called *dualization* of the workforce: one, traditional segment of the workforce enjoys relative long-term, stable employment with union-negotiated protections and relatively generous social benefits such as unemployment insurance and retirement pensions; the other, newer and growing segment of the workforce is outside this model, typically not protected by unions, facing greater risk of unemployment, and not entitled to many of the traditional social benefits. These "outsiders" tend to be younger, less skilled, and more female than the traditional "insider" workforce.

As we suggested in chapter 10, though, even in the face of this combined fiscal, demographic, and labor-force pressure, few countries have fundamentally altered their social policies. Indeed, social expenditures in wealthy countries as a whole increased slightly, from about 18 percent to 20 percent of GDP, from 1980 to 2018. Institutionalist theorists argued that the welfare state created institutions and their beneficiaries, which then constituted powerful coalitions blocking reform (Pierson 1996). Nonetheless, all welfare states had to respond to the pressures of globalization and demography. Most reduced benefits to lower the costs of the traditional programs by raising the minimum age at which people can retire; reducing the length of unemployment benefits and the percentage of salary that is replaced; raising employee contributions to social insurance programs; and removing guarantees of benefits so that they can reduce them in the future if necessary (Bonoli, George, and Taylor-Gooby 2000). This trend accelerated after the Great Recession, with per capita social benefits dropping notably, particularly in countries hit hardest by the eurozone crisis that were forced to absorb almost all of the costs (Stetter 2018).

Simultaneously, many welfare states have placed greater emphasis on "social investment policies" aimed at encouraging employment and greater flexibility in the labor market (Gingrich and Ansell 2015). While traditional retirement pensions may be lowered, governments may spend more on childcare and family leave to encourage women to enter the workforce and job training for the unemployed. These policies, proponents argue, benefit the growing number of part-time and female workers who typically benefit less from traditional social policies. David Rueda (2015), however, demonstrated that the combination of cuts to traditional programs and social investment policies has lowered welfare states' effects on inequality overall, which has risen substantially in almost all wealthy countries, as we noted in chapter 10.

As the power resources theory would suggest, different types of welfare states responded differently to the pressures of globalization, though their differences were diminished compared to earlier eras (Huber and Stephens 2015). Some politicians were able to put together new coalitions of support for welfare reforms with parties of the left and right emphasizing differing kinds of social investment in line with their ideologies. Social democratic parties in many countries now receive most of their support from middle-class voters rather than their traditional working-class constituencies. This helps explain the shift to more social investment that benefits middle-class workers. Where there was little partisan competition for working-class support, it also produced significant cuts to traditional social programs, whereas if alternative parties had to compete for working-class support, cuts to traditional programs were less severe (Hausermann 2018). Similarly, countries with stronger women's movements tended to produce earlier, universal benefits that need not go through a male breadwinner and policies that support women entering the workforce, such as child allowances and universal childcare. They were thus more able to support the new types of workers that emerged with globalization (Sainsbury 2013).

Comparing Welfare States

The different types of welfare states initially created significantly different societies in terms of how much of the national income passes through government coffers and how much is redistributed from the rich to the poor. Tables 12.1 and 12.2 provide data comparing the three types of welfare states. Social democratic welfare states used to take the biggest share of the national economy as government revenue to provide extensive social services, reflected in their high social expenditures. In recent years, however, the Christian democratic systems have spent almost as much, as the costs of their extensive income-maintenance programs for the unemployed and elderly have risen rapidly, while the liberal welfare states spend significantly less.

Table 12.2 shows that when we compare gross (meaning just government expenditures) and net (taking into account receipts of social expenditures paid back to the government) we see a somewhat different picture. While the liberal welfare states still spend the least, the differences between them and the other two models are significantly reduced. A group of scholars (Alber and Gilbert 2010; Garfinkel, Rainwater, and Smeeding 2010) has argued that the three models of the welfare state are not as distinct as has been suggested. While Sweden spends generously

TABLE 12.1

Comparison of Welfare State Outcomes

	SOCIAL EXPENDITURE AS % OF GDP				GDP GROWTH %				UNEMPLOYMENT AS PERCENTAGE OF CIVILIAN LABOR FORCE			WOMEN'S LABOR FORCE PARTICIPATION (% OF FEMALE POPULATION AGES 15 + IN LABOR FORCE)			
	1980	1995	2010	2018	1981–1990	1991–2000	2001–2010	2011–2017	1991–2000	2001–2010	2011–2018	1990	2000	2010	2018
Social democratic welfare states	21.2	28.3	27.2	27.0	2.51	2.72	1.55	1.62	8.38	5.95	6.53	59.48	58.72	59.1	58.58
Christian democratic welfare states	20.6	24.1	26.7	24.4	2.29	2.16	1.26	1.2	7.49	6.49	7.0	43.31	47.99	51.73	52.69
Liberal welfare states	14.6	17.6	20.8	18	3.16	4.03	2.06	3.23	8.58	6.26	6.13	50.6	54.75	57	58.87

Sources: Data for social expenditures are from Organisation for Economic Co-operation and Development (http://stats.oecd.org/Index.aspx?QueryId=4549#); data for GDP growth, unemployment, and women's labor participation are from World Bank (http://data.worldbank.org/indicator/NY.GDP.MKTP.KD.ZG/countries?display=default), (http://data.worldbank.org/indicator/SL.UEM.TOTL.ZS/countries?display=default), and (http://data.worldbank.org/indicator/SL.TLF.CACT.FE.ZS).

on universal programs, for instance, it also has high taxes on consumption (e.g., sales tax), so some of the spending on the poor comes back to the government in taxes. The United States, on the other hand, has very low social spending but much higher tax expenditures targeted at people with low incomes. This helps explain the convergence among all wealthy countries in the size, if not the type, of their welfare states over the past three decades (Obinger and Starke 2015).

The extensive social policies of the social democratic and Christian democratic welfare states did not lower economic growth significantly at their height in the 1980s, though liberal welfare states seem to have grown faster recently. Similarly, more generous welfare states actually achieved lower levels of unemployment until recently. Figure 12.2 shows that all three types of welfare states distribute enough

TABLE 12.2

Social Expenditure, in Percentage of GDP

	GROSS PUBLIC SOCIAL EXPENDITURES	NET PUBLIC SOCIAL EXPENDITURES
	2017	2015
Social democratic welfare states	27.1	24.3
Christian democratic welfare states	24.9	24.86
Liberal welfare states	18.0	22.1

Source: Organisation for Economic Co-operation and Development (http://stats.oecd.org/Index.aspx?datasetcode=SOCX_AGG#).

FIGURE 12.2

Poverty and Inequality in Welfare States

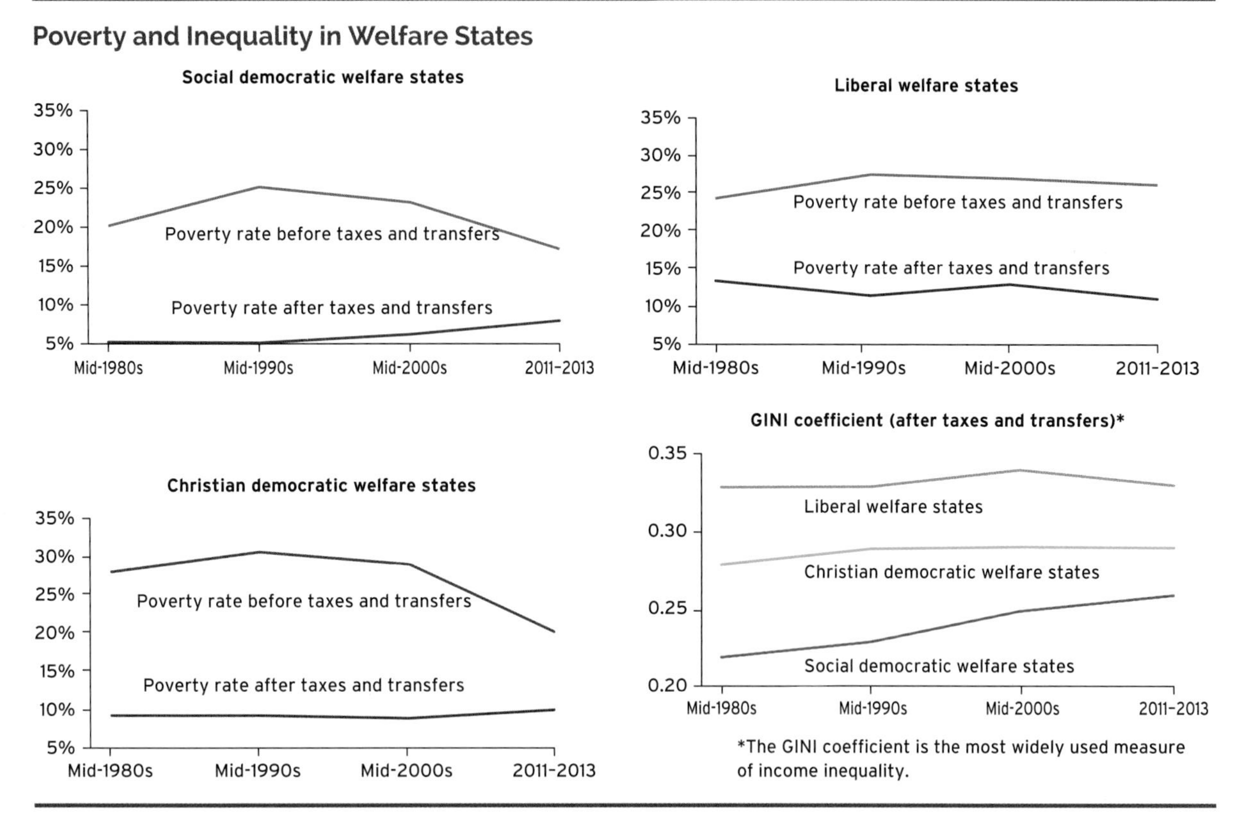

Source: All data are from OECD.Stat. Data for most current date range (shown as 2011–2015 averages) are poverty rate before and after taxes and transfers, all working-age household types, working age population eighteen to sixty-five. Data for GINI coefficient are Gini (market income, before taxes and transfers), calculated using the classifications of the three welfare states (liberal welfare state, Christian democratic welfare state, social democratic welfare state) as defined in Evelyne Huber and John D. Stephens, *Development and Crisis of the Welfare State* (Chicago: University of Chicago Press, 2001).

income to lower poverty substantially, but the reductions were greatest in social democratic states, followed by Christian democratic states, until recently, when liberal welfare states have improved, though they still tolerate more poverty and inequality among their citizens. Note, however, that differences in poverty have narrowed and inequality has increased in all three types of welfare states, reflecting the effects of globalization and demographic pressures in all wealthy countries. Table 12.1 demonstrates differences as well in terms of gender inequality, at least as measured by participation in the paid labor force. Social democratic welfare states facilitated greater female participation via such policies as universal child allowances, paid maternity leave, and subsidized preschool. Liberal and especially Christian democratic states lagged behind, though recently the liberal welfare states have caught up and the Christian democratic states have nearly done so.

Social Policy in the Global South

A welfare state requires a state capable of implementing fairly complex policies. In the weakest states, therefore, social policy is minimal, often involving little more than retirement pensions for the relatively small share of the population employed in the government and large companies. Many governments in the Global South provided benefits for the poor by regulating or subsidizing prices of basic goods they required, particularly food. Neoliberal development strategies have long focused on achieving high economic growth as the best means of reducing poverty. Their implementation, especially in the 1980s and 1990s (see chapter 11), almost always involved cuts to both social services and government subsidies, reducing the minimal programs many states had in place. Ian Gough (2014) terms social provision in most of these societies as "informal security regimes" in which people's social needs are provided mainly by a combination of private markets, formal and informal community organizations, and family networks. Patron–client relationships often are crucial to people's well-being in these societies and therefore also politically influential. Nongovernmental organizations (NGOs) typically provide a large share of whatever formal social services exist, as the state is too weak and poor to do so.

Neoliberalism's limited success, however, led to the emergence of social policy as an important issue in developing countries in the 1990s, especially in middle-income countries. The East Asian developmental states of Taiwan and Korea, for instance, had minimal social welfare states through the 1980s. Their development model produced far less inequality than most have, and their rapid growth reduced poverty substantially. In the 1980s and 1990s, though, as they democratized, popular demands rose for more social services and expenditures; both countries put many elements of Western-style social welfare states in place by the new millennium (Huber and Niedzwiecki 2015).

Democratization also played an important role in improving social policies in Latin America. Older social programs in Latin America were almost all social insurance systems benefiting only workers in the formal sector of the economy, disproportionately in the public sector. These workers are in fact a relatively well-off group in Latin America; the truly poor are in the informal sector (e.g., workers in small enterprises not recognized by the government, street vendors, and day laborers) and agriculture. In the new millennium, most countries in the region expanded their social spending and created programs that reached a significantly larger share of the population. Between 1990 and 2013, the region increased social spending by 5 percent of GDP, which helped reduce poverty from 43 percent of the population in 2003 to 28 percent a decade later (Ocampo and Gomez-Arteaga 2018).

The most innovative, though not the only, element of the changes in Latin America was the creation of **conditional cash transfer (CCT)** programs, which provide cash grants to the poor in exchange for recipients sending their children to school and to health clinics. These programs, pioneered in Brazil and Mexico, are means tested and target the poorest households to gain the maximum impact. CCT programs in Latin America reduced poverty by 4 to 8 percent, depending on the country, and have increased both school enrollment and use of health care services (Ferreira and Robalino 2011). CCTs have spread to a number of Asian and African countries as well, though they have not been as extensive or effective as in Latin America. They have been adopted primarily by middle-income democracies and by countries with a neighbor such as Brazil who modeled the system early on (Brooks 2015).

By 2015, Brazil's CCT, probably the most successful, was providing grants to nearly fifty-five million people, about a quarter of the entire population. The best estimates are that it is responsible for one-sixth of the 12 percent drop in poverty in the new millennium and a third of the drop in extreme poverty (Barrientos et al. 2016). It is also credited with playing a major role in the 50 percent drop in infant mortality and child malnutrition over the same period. The recession since 2015 in Brazil has caused poverty to increase slightly, but nonetheless even conservative president Jair Bolsonaro, elected in 2018, called for expanding Brazil's CCT. Because the cash grants are so small, the program costs only 0.5 percent of GDP, making it one of the most efficient poverty-reduction programs in the world.

conditional cash transfer (CCT): Programs that provide cash grants to the poor and in exchange require particular beneficial behavior from the poor, such as children's attendance at school and visits to health clinics

Health Care and Health Policy

While social policy generates philosophical debate over the proper role of government in most societies, much of the world has adopted the idea that health care is a social right of all citizens. Carsten Jensen (2014) pointed out that health policy is less partisan in most countries than social policy because of the different kinds of risk involved: social policies such as unemployment insurance and social assistance address labor market risks, which many people believe they are unlikely to face, while health policy addresses a life-cycle risk—everyone will get sick. Wealthy countries have the resources to attempt to realize a social right to health via interventions in the health care market, but most others lack the resources to make it a reality. A few countries, notably the United States, do not embrace health care as a social right but nonetheless claim the provision of the best health care possible to the largest number of people as a legitimate political and social goal.

Health Care and Market Failure

Social values are not the only reason for policy intervention in health care markets, however. Market failure takes distinct forms in health care that are based on specific characteristics of the health care market. The key problems are very high risk and poor consumer information, both of which produce inefficiency and misallocation of resources. People will do almost anything—pay any price or undergo any procedure—to restore their health when it is seriously threatened. On the other hand, healthy people need very little medical care. Those who lack the resources to pay for care when sick may face severe harm or even death. Insurance is the typical solution to such high-risk markets. It spreads risks across many people. Paying smaller, regular premiums more or less fixes the cost for each individual in the insurance pool, so catastrophic illness does not mean catastrophic bills. This principle also underlies homeowner's or auto insurance. Governments or private companies can provide insurance as long as a relatively large group of people with diverse risks pool their resources to cover emergencies as necessary.

Although insurance is a potential market-based solution to high risk, it creates its own potential market failure: **moral hazard**. Moral hazard occurs when parties to a transaction behave differently than they otherwise would because they believe they won't have to pay the full costs of their actions. In health insurance, this results from the gap between paying a fixed premium for health care and the costs of the care itself. If insurance covers the full cost of the care, patients have no incentive to economize because their costs (the insurance premium) will not change regardless of how much health care they use. Moreover, many insurance systems pay medical providers for each procedure, giving providers an incentive to oversupply procedures just as the patient has an incentive to overuse them. The obvious results are excessive medical procedures and rising costs. Governments intervene in health care in part to attempt to limit the effects of the moral hazard inherent in an insurance system.

Another market failure, poor information, compounds the problem of overuse. Patients generally rely on medical professionals to know what procedures or drugs are needed to get well. Even highly educated patients usually agree to their doctors' recommended treatments, especially if they are insured and face little direct cost. In the extreme case, a completely unregulated market with poor information can produce the iconic image of nineteenth-century American medical quackery, the "snake-oil salesman," a charlatan selling false remedies to

moral hazard: Occurs when parties to a transaction behave in a particular way because they believe they will not have to pay the full costs of their actions

desperate people. To avoid this, virtually all governments regulate both pharmaceuticals and medical practitioners.

Health Care Systems

Wealthy countries have developed three distinct types of health care systems to address these problems. These have served as models for poorer countries as well, though poor countries are severely limited by lack of resources. The earliest and still most common system in wealthy countries is **national health insurance (NHI)**. In an NHI system, the government mandates that virtually all citizens have insurance. NHI countries typically allow and encourage multiple, private insurance providers, while the government provides access to insurance to the self-employed or unemployed who do not have access via family members. Since the government mandates the insurance, it also regulates the system, setting or at least limiting premiums and payments to medical providers. In many NHI systems, access to health care is not specific to a particular employer, so workers can keep their insurance when they switch jobs. Germany pioneered this system in the late nineteenth century and continues to use it today, as do many other European countries and Japan. Few poor countries attempt to implement NHI because many of their citizens simply cannot afford insurance, although some do use a limited form of it for wealthier segments of the population, such as civil servants or employees of large corporations.

"Sickness funds," nonprofit organizations run by boards of employers and employees, are the key organizations in the German NHI. They are connected to employer, profession, or locale and are autonomous from the government in setting most of their policies and prices, though the services they must offer are uniform across the country. They negotiate services and payments with regional physician associations; doctors who wish to participate in the system (about 95 percent of them do) must be members of their regional association and abide by the negotiated agreements. All but the wealthiest Germans must belong to a sickness fund; in this way, Germany has long achieved universal coverage. The unemployed must belong to a fund as well, the costs of which are covered by federal and local governments. The wealthiest individuals may opt out of the system and purchase private insurance, though more than 90 percent of the population use the sickness fund system. Residents can also purchase supplemental insurance to give them greater choice in where and how they are treated, and about 10 percent of sickness fund members do so (Adolino and Blake 2001, 225; Green and Irvine 2001, 57). The biggest concern and subject of several reforms over the last couple of decades is rising costs. Some reforms have increased individuals' costs to access care, but nonetheless, under 2 percent of Germans reported missing medical examinations due to cost, distance, or wait time—less than half the EU average.

national health insurance (NHI): A health care system in which the government mandates that virtually all citizens must have insurance

national health system (NHS)/single-payer system: A government-financed and managed health care system into which all citizens pay, either through a separate insurance payment or via general taxation, and through which they gain medical care

A **national health system (NHS)** is the second most common type of health care system in wealthy countries and the most common type worldwide. Frequently called a **single-payer system**, NHS is a government-financed and managed system. The government creates a system into which all citizens pay, either through a separate insurance payment (like Medicare in the United States) or via general taxation. In most NHS countries, the majority of medical professionals gain their income directly from the government, which implicitly controls the cost of medical care via payments for procedures, equipment, and drugs. Most poor countries have an NHS through which the government provides most medical care via hospitals and local clinics and in which doctors are direct government employees. With limited resources in poor countries, however, clinics and doctors are few, and many people lack access to or must wait long periods for what is often low-quality care.

The classic example of this type of system is in the United Kingdom, which established its NHS after World War II. The British NHS traditionally signed contracts with general practitioners (GPs) in each region of the country to deliver primary services to patients. Each region served as one large insurance pool, with an average of about half a million patients. GPs are paid on a combination of fee-for-service and capitation basis, and British patients can sign up with the GP of their choice, usually in their neighborhood, who provides basic care and functions as a gatekeeper, referring them to a specialist or hospital as needed. The NHS regional and district health authorities received government revenue to provide hospital and specialist services, and most services (except for some pharmaceuticals) are free to the patient at the point of service, having been paid for by general taxes. Waiting times for seeing GPs are very low, but waiting times for specialists and nonemergency hospital stays are among the world's highest. No one can opt out of the NHS because it's funded by general taxes, but patients can purchase private supplemental insurance that allows them to see private doctors and get hospital services without the long waits of the public system. As Britons have grown wealthier and have demanded more health care, a growing number supplement NHS coverage with private insurance; in 2012 about 11 percent of the population had private insurance. These patients can use the NHS for routine illnesses and private insurance for procedures that have long waiting lines in the NHS.

The third system, a **market-based private insurance system**, is the least common. Although NHI and NHS countries typically permit some private insurance as a supplement for those who can afford it, the United States, Turkey, and Mexico are the only OECD countries that rely on private insurance for the bulk of their health care. In the United States, citizens typically gain insurance through their employment, and medical care is provided mostly by for-profit entities, such as private clinics and hospitals. Government programs often exist in market-based systems to cover specific groups without private insurance, such as the poor, the unemployed, and the self-employed. Market-based systems, though, do not guarantee access to health care to all citizens, and even in the wealthiest of these countries, a sizable minority lacks any insurance.

In the American market-based system, citizens typically gain insurance through their employment, and medical care is provided mostly by for-profit entities such as private clinics and hospitals. Extensive government health programs only began in 1965 with the creation of Medicare (for the elderly and disabled) and Medicaid (for the very poorest, mostly TANF recipients). In 1997 the State Children's Health Insurance Program (SCHIP) was created to provide insurance for poor or low-income children. The combination of SCHIP and an expansion of Medicaid coverage reduced the percentage of low-income children who were uninsured from 22.3 percent in 1997 to 14.9 percent in 2005 (CBO 2007, 8). The market-based system, though, still left a substantial minority without secure access to health care.

The Affordable Care Act (ACA, commonly known as "Obamacare") of 2010 sought to address this. It expanded insurance coverage by mandating that virtually everyone must obtain insurance (those who do not must pay a tax penalty) and expanding Medicaid to subsidize premiums for people with low incomes. It created insurance "exchanges" in each state that are available to all those who don't have insurance through their employers. Private insurance companies offer plans in these exchanges that must meet certain minimum standards of service coverage.

market-based private insurance system: Health care system that relies on private insurance for the bulk of the population

The exchanges created large pools of previously uninsured people, allowing them to obtain much cheaper coverage than they each could individually. Medium and large employers must offer minimal health insurance to their employees; those who don't must pay a fine that helps pay for the subsidies for the uninsured. The ACA also prevented insurance companies from denying insurance to people with preexisting medical conditions and allowed young adults to remain on their parents' insurance until age twenty-six to keep them in insurance pools (thereby increasing the diversity and health of the pools). The ACA reduced the number of uninsured people by twenty million in its first two years, from about 15 to 9 percent of the population (CDC 2016). After the election of Donald Trump as president, the Republican majority in Congress eliminated the mandate that everyone had to have insurance, and then Republican state attorneys general filed a lawsuit, which the Trump administration did not contest, arguing that without the mandate the ACA as a whole was invalid. The decision was appealed to the Fifth District Court in 2019, but no matter what the outcome, it will almost certainly be appealed to the Supreme Court.

Common Problems

Almost all countries face a common set of problems, regardless of the system they use. The most evident are rising costs (especially in wealthy countries), lack of access to care, and growing public health concerns.

Controlling Costs

Wealthier countries are most concerned about cost because as wealth increases, health care costs rise faster than incomes. This is because wealthier people demand more and better care, and improved but often expensive technology emerges to help provide that care. Wealthier countries also have relatively low birth rates and high life expectancies, so the proportion of the population that is elderly increases over time and needs more health care. From 2000 to 2009, expenditures grew at an annual average of 4 percent, well above overall economic growth, though they slowed considerably after the Great Recession. People in almost all wealthy countries use more and more of their income for health care, regardless of the system in place.

Wealthy countries use several means to try to control costs. A key factor is the size of insurance pools. Larger and more diverse pools of people lower costs because a larger number of healthy people (especially young adults) cover the costs of those (often the elderly) who use health care more heavily, thereby lowering premiums for everyone. NHS and NHI systems that group many or all of a country's citizens into one insurance pool gain a cost-saving advantage. In market-based systems, on the other hand, the risk pools are much smaller (usually the employees of a particular company), so costs tend to be higher. Governments in these countries spend less tax revenue on health care than do other governments, but citizens may spend more on health care overall via private insurance premiums and direct fees. The United States, which depends heavily on private insurance and has very low government expenditures on health care, has by far the highest overall health costs, both in terms of dollars spent per capita and as a share of GDP (see Table 12.3 in the Critical Inquiry box that follows).

Other cost-saving measures focus on limiting the effects of moral hazard. For example, paying doctors on a capitation, or per patient, basis rather than for each procedure creates an incentive to limit unnecessary procedures. Critics, however, argue that this gives providers an incentive to underprescribe, which endangers patients' well-being. A second strategy, "gatekeepers," can limit patients' demands for expensive treatments. Typically, a general practitioner serves as a gatekeeper who must give approval before patients can consult specialists, in order to limit unnecessary trips to expensive specialists and procedures. A third approach is to require patients to make copayments, small fees that cover part of the cost of each service. If kept to moderate amounts, copayments can theoretically discourage unnecessary or frivolous procedures; if set too high, however, they may discourage poorer patients from getting medically necessary care.

Clearly, a trade-off exists between cost containment and achieving a healthy population. Meeting all demands for health care instantly might produce the healthiest possible population, but it would be prohibitively expensive and would aggravate moral hazard. No society ever does this; instead, all choose to ration health care in some way, though many people may not perceive it as rationing. NHS countries can control costs most directly simply by limiting the overall health care budget, the payments to medical providers, purchases of new equipment, and/or drug prices. The result can be relatively low-cost but sometimes limited care. Limits typically take the form of patients waiting for certain procedures rather than getting them on demand. NHI countries can set insurance premiums and medical payments as well; they usually don't do so as universally as NHS countries, though Germany has experimented with greater regulation in recent years. Some countries, including the United States (the only wealthy country in this category), provide insurance only to a segment of the population, who thereby have access to fairly extensive care; those without insurance have very limited or no access to care. This is another way to ration.

The data in the Critical Inquiry box (page 364) suggest that the form of rationing does not make a substantial difference to achieving a healthy population among wealthy countries, though it does have a significant effect on costs. Those with the lowest costs, such as Britain, do not have significantly lower health outcomes overall, measured by key data such as infant mortality or life expectancy.

Access to Health Care

Access is a much greater problem than rising costs for the very poorest countries, where limited resources mean much smaller numbers of doctors, hospitals, and clinics per capita. Even though individuals may be nominally covered by a government health plan, they cannot access health care if facilities and providers are not available. While many have NHS systems, most health care funding still comes from private financing, often direct payments to providers without even the benefit of insurance. As a result of limited access and costs too high for the poor majority, preventable and easily treatable diseases continue to shorten life spans and cause loss of income and productivity in much of the world. The problem of access in wealthy countries with NHS or NHI systems has been virtually eliminated; those systems provide insurance coverage for nearly everyone, and medical facilities and doctors are plentiful. For the OECD as a whole, well under 5 percent of people reported not receiving adequate care for financial reasons in 2013 (OECD 2015). The only access problem typically is waiting times for some procedures. In market-based systems in wealthy countries, on the other hand, access is not universal: those without health insurance have only very limited access to care because they can't afford to pay for it.

CRITICAL INQUIRY

Comparing Health Care Systems in Wealthy Countries

Germany, the United Kingdom, and the United States illustrate the differences among health care systems in wealthy countries. Costs, in particular, vary dramatically, whereas outcomes are similar. Access to doctors, hospitals, and technology depends on how each country chooses to spend its health budget.

The data in Table 12.3 suggest that in these three cases, the type of health care system does not make a substantial difference to achieving a healthy population among wealthy countries, though it does have a significant effect on costs. Those with the lowest costs, such as Britain, do not have significantly lower health outcomes overall, measured by key data such as infant mortality or life expectancy. Germany's NHI provides more doctors and hospital beds, but wait times are lower in Britain's NHS (except for elective surgery). The American market-based system fares poorly on most measures of outcome and access, in spite of its exceptionally high costs.

TABLE 12.3

Comparing Health Care in Germany, the United Kingdom, and the United States

	GERMANY (NHI)	UNITED KINGDOM (NHS)	UNITED STATES (MARKET-BASED)	OECD AVERAGE
Costs				
Health care expenditures per capita ($), 2018	$5,986	$4,070	$10,586	$3,992
Health care expenditures as percentage of GDP, 2018	11.2	9.8	16.9	8.8
Public share of total health expenditures (%), 2014	77	83.1	48.3	72.4
Physicians' remuneration (ratio to average wage), 2009	3.3	4.2	3.7	NA
Outcomes				
Life expectancy at birth (years), 2017	81.1	81.3	78.6	81.4
Infant mortality rates (per 1,000 population), 2015	3.1	3.5	5.6	5.9
Childhood measles vaccination rate (%), 2014	97	93	91	94
Access				
Practicing physicians (per 1,000 population), 2017	4.3	2.6	2.9	NA
Acute care hospital beds (per 1,000 population), 2014	5.34	2.28	2.48	NA
Access to doctor or nurse (% waiting longer than six days), 2009	16	8	19	NA
Wait times for elective surgery (% waiting longer than four months), 2008	0	21	7	NA

Sources: Organisation for Economic Co-operation and Development (https://data.oecd.org/), (http://www.oecd-library.org/docserver/download/8115071ec025.pdf?expires=1475518210&id=id&accname=guest&checksum=C466A7111E38C2FF49DFD719EC25CA46), (http://data.worldbank.org/indicator/SH.IMM.MEAS); World Bank (http://data.worldbank.org/indicator/SH.XPD.PUBL); access to specialists: Commonwealth Fund (2008).

TABLE 12.4

Comparing Health Care in NHI, NHS, and Market-based Systems

	NHI	NHS	MARKET-BASED
Costs			
Health care expenditures per capita	$4,946.00	$3,700.77	$5,935.85
Health care expenditures as percentage of GDP (2016)	11.71	9.33	11.30
Outcomes			
Life expectancy at birth	82.5	82.1	79.1
Infant mortality	2.85	3.57	6.0
Life expectancy at age 65 (2014)	22.3	21.8	20.2
Access			
Medical doctors (per 1,000 population) (2009)	3.03	2.93	1.7
MRIs (per one million population) (2009)	19.67	8.43	25.9*

Source: All data are from World Bank (2019).

Note: All data are for 2017, unless otherwise noted. Countries in the sample are, for NHS: New Zealand, Spain, and the United Kingdom; for NHI: France, Germany, and Japan; for market-based systems: Chile and the United States.

*United States only; data not available for Chile.

Now, take a step back from the examples of Germany, the United Kingdom, and the United States and look broadly at the costs and outcomes of the three distinct models of health care: NHI, NHS, and market-based. In Table 12.4, we see key data on access and cost of health care along with basic health outcomes for all three.

Comparing the three, which do you think is the best overall model of health care? What are the principles or goals on which you base your assessment? Looking at the data, why do you come to the conclusions you do?

Public Health

The third major common problem is public health concerns. These are common to all countries but vary greatly. In the poorest countries, access to enough food and clean water remains a public health issue. Without access to clean water, populations continue to be plagued by a variety of contagious diseases. Furthermore, malnourishment exacerbates the effects of waterborne contagions, as immune systems are weak and resistance low. The health effects in terms of core indicators such as infant mortality and life expectancy are clear.

The wealthiest countries face a different kind of malnutrition: obesity. The highest rates of obesity in the OECD are in the United States and Mexico and now include more than 30 percent of the population. Obesity rates are rising in almost all wealthy countries: food is inexpensive compared with incomes, so people overconsume it.

Other public health issues resulting from affluence—alcohol and tobacco consumption—have seen positive change recently. Rates of alcohol use in the OECD declined by 9 percent from 1980 to 2009, while rates of tobacco use declined by about 18 percent from 1999 to 2009. Active public health education programs, along with legal limits and higher taxes on alcohol and tobacco consumption, reaped impressive results in many wealthy countries. Unfortunately, alcohol and tobacco consumption rates are increasing in many poorer countries, as their populations become wealthier and as alcohol and tobacco producers actively market in developing countries to compensate for shrinking consumption in their traditional markets.

Environmental Problems and Policy

Climate change is only the latest and largest environmental problem confronting governments around the world. Environmental problems became a significant policy issue later than either health care or welfare, perhaps in part because the environment, in contrast to the other two, is a classic postmaterialist concern, becoming more widespread as wealth rises. Early industrializers in Europe and the United States weren't very concerned about environmental degradation until the 1960s (with the exception of preservation of public land, which began much earlier), when people began to look at the effects of long-term pollution from the new context of economic security. Today, increasing wealth and security in some more recently industrialized countries also seem to be stimulating interest in clean air, water, and other environmental concerns.

The Environment and Market Failure

Environmental damage is an exceptionally clear case of market failure in the form of externalities. No form of pollution is without cost. When a factory pollutes a river with sewage, people downstream get sick and need costly health care while fish and other aquatic life die, raising the cost of fishing and reducing ecosystem diversity. Vehicle exhaust produces cancer-causing smog that results in millions of dollars of health care costs annually. Polluters rarely pay the cost of their own pollution in an unfettered market: many commodities cost less than they would if their true environmental costs were internalized in the production process. The market therefore devotes more resources to those undervalued products than it ought to, creating inefficiency. Meanwhile, other people bear the costs of the pollution produced, a classic externality.

Many environmental goods are inherently public and often free. Unregulated use of free goods like air, water, or public land can lead to the **tragedy of the commons**. This is an old idea. If free public grazing land exists in a farming area, all farmers will use it to graze their herds, and none will have an incentive to preserve it for future use; collectively, they will likely overgraze the land and destroy it so that they all lose out in the end. In wealthy industrial countries, a more current example is clean air, a completely "common" good we all breathe and pollute. Without a collective effort to limit use and abuse, no individual has the incentive or ability to preserve it, so it's likely to be overused. The free market grossly undervalues (at zero cost) a valuable public good.

tragedy of the commons: No individual has the incentive or ability to preserve a common, shared good that is free, so without collective effort, it is likely to be overused and perhaps ultimately destroyed

Beyond the national arena, globalization has created new environmental concerns. Globalization has produced industrialization in many new countries, which increases pollution in previously agrarian societies. Many observers fear that the dynamics of global competition will produce a "race to the bottom," as countries use lax environmental rules to attract foreign capital. They argue that wealthy countries are not only outsourcing factories and jobs but pollution as well. For example, the quality of the air and water around Pittsburgh has dramatically improved as the city's steel industry has declined, while China, now the world's largest steel producer, faces a massive pollution problem. The southeastern region of Nigeria is dotted with nearly 1,500 oil wells, which for many years provided an estimated 40 percent of U.S. oil imports. Estimates suggest as much oil is spilled annually in Nigeria as was spilled by the disastrous Exxon *Valdez* oil spill in Alaska in 1989. Citizens of one of the poorest regions of a poor country thus pay a large share of the environmental costs of U.S. oil consumption.

Opponents of the race-to-the-bottom thesis argue that postmaterialist values will be key: as globalization produces more wealth, it will help lower pollution because wealth and environmental concerns seem to increase in tandem. Analyzing the World Values Survey, however, Dunlap and York (2012) found little correlation between wealth and environmental concerns; citizens of poor nations expressed somewhat different but just as strong (and sometimes stronger) concern for the environment as citizens of wealthier countries. Using a large, quantitative analysis, Gabriele Spilker (2013) found that while higher GDP, trade, and foreign direct investment are associated with more pollution in developing countries, this effect was mitigated by (1) membership in key international organizations that could help the government respond to environmental problems, and (2) well-established democracy, in which people could demand and politicians would be forced to supply some regulation of environmental damages. Once again, national governments can at least partly mitigate the worst effects of globalization. Whichever argument proves more accurate in the long term, rapidly industrializing countries now face dramatically expanding environmental problems.

China illustrates this issue best. Its environmental degradation and problems are breathtaking, no pun intended. Besides urban air pollution, 30 percent of the nation's water is unfit for human or agricultural use, almost 90 percent of the country's grasslands and forests are suffering degradation, and the Yellow River now dries up before it reaches the ocean, becoming an open sewer (Ho and Vermeer 2006; Morton 2006, 64–65). Severe soil erosion and desertification have doubled since the 1970s and are degrading an area the size of New Jersey each year (Economy 2010, 66). The result of all of this is skyrocketing health problems: air pollution in northern China is estimated to have caused 1.2 million premature deaths by 2010, lowering life expectancy by five years vis-à-vis the less polluted southern China, and cancer rates increased by 30 percent over the past thirty years. In Beijing, where the most polluted days reach forty times the internationally recommended maximum level of air particulates, residents regularly wear face masks to protect them from air pollution. Those who can afford to do so will choose apartments and schools based partly on the quality of the air filtration system they use.

Concern about the environment among Chinese citizens has grown over the years, with three-quarters saying air and water pollution and climate change were "very big" or "moderately big" problems in 2015 (Gao 2015). Reflecting these concerns, environmental NGOs had grown substantially, from the first one legally registered in 1994 to more than 2,000 by 2018, and estimates of thousands more that were unregistered. The government often tolerates environmental NGOs and local-level protests, because top officials see them as pushing recalcitrant local officials to enforce environmental policies better while doing little harm on the national level. In 2012, three days of massive demonstrations ultimately stopped the construction of a petrochemical plant in a coastal city that the local government strongly supported. Facing mounting public pressure, the national government announced a major new initiative in September 2013 that set upper limits on air particulate levels in major cities. By 2015, air pollution had dropped slightly in most cities, mainly due to reductions in the use of coal, but Beijing still faced its first "red alert," a day so polluted that the government shut down schools and offices and advised citizens to remain indoors. Although the government has begun to take steps to improve the environment, whether public pressure forces enough change quickly enough to counter the devastating environmental problems globalization and industrialization have produced remains to be seen.

Also tied to globalization are what many term "third-generation" environmental problems: these problems are global and therefore require global responses. Air and water pollution have always crossed borders, but this new concern is distinct. The source of the pollution matters little because the effects are truly global. Scientists have demonstrated measurable effects of China's air pollution on the west coast of the United States. The major third-generation problem, though, is climate change, which we address below.

Developing countries have long struggled to achieve sustainable development: economic development that can continue over the long term. Development always involves increased use of resources, but if nonrenewable resources are being used quickly, development won't be sustainable. As demand for food and land increases, for instance, farmers and ranchers clear forested areas throughout the tropics. This gives them nutrient-rich soil on which to grow crops and graze cattle as well as valuable wood to sell on the global market, but tropical rainforest soils are thin and are quickly depleted when put to agricultural use. After a few years, new land must be cleared as the old is exhausted. The result is rapidly disappearing forests and development that is unsustainable in the long run. Deforestation also increases global warming because trees absorb and retain carbon. Farmers' and ranchers' rational response to growing global demand for agricultural products, then, has created unsustainable development and more global warming. Globalization-induced pollution of air and water and rapid use of nonrenewable resources make the goal of sustainable development ever more challenging for many poor countries.

Risk and Uncertainty

While most analysts agree that environmental damage is an externality that must be addressed, a vociferous debate thrives about the uncertainty nearly always present in environmental issues. Scientists can rarely tell us exactly what a particular form or amount of pollution will do. The top climate scientists in the world won the Nobel Peace Prize for their 2007 *IPCC Report,* but even their most certain predictions were termed "very likely" (90 percent certainty) or "likely" (66 percent certainty) outcomes of climate change. Environmental policy everywhere has to be based on **risk assessment** and **risk management**. Risk assessment tells us what the risks of damaging outcomes are, and risk management is policy used to keep those risks to acceptable levels. The costs of reducing risks must be weighed against the potential (but always uncertain) benefits.

risk assessment: Analysis of what the risks of damaging outcomes are in a particular situation

risk management: Policy used to keep risks to acceptable levels

precautionary principle: A policy that emphasizes risk avoidance even when the science predicting a risk is uncertain

Much of the debate, of course, is over what level of risk is "acceptable." In recent years, the EU and its member states have employed the **precautionary principle**, which emphasizes risk avoidance even when the science predicting the risk is uncertain. This principle lies behind the EU ban on genetically modified organisms (GMOs) in food. With limited scientific evidence on whether GMOs are harmful or benign, the EU errs on the side of caution, banning them until the science is clarified. The United States typically errs more toward reducing the costs of environmental fixes. For example, the United States currently allows extensive use of GMOs in the absence of greater scientific evidence of harm.

Policy Options

How do governments respond when they decide that environmental damage is an unacceptable risk? Several approaches exist. The oldest is known as **command and control policies**, which involve direct government regulation. These were the first type of policies most wealthy countries enacted in the 1970s. Based on assessments of health and other risks, a government simply sets a level of pollution no one is allowed to surpass or requires companies to pay a penalty if they do. Businesses must reduce production or find ways to produce the same goods with less pollution. Command and control policies require governments to set very specific limits on many pollutants from many sources and to inspect possible polluters to ensure they are following the regulations. Both of these tasks are expensive, leading many analysts to argue for what they see as more efficient means of pollution control in the form of incentive systems.

The best-known incentive system is the **cap and trade system**, in which a government sets an overall limit on how much of a pollutant is acceptable from an entire industry or country and issues vouchers to each company that give it the right to a certain number of units of pollution. The individual companies are then free to trade these vouchers. Companies that face high costs to reduce their pollution levels will be interested in buying additional pollution rights, while those that can more cheaply invest in new and cleaner technology will sell their rights. In theory, pollution is reduced in the most efficient way possible and at the least cost. Critics point out that cap and trade can result in high levels of pollution at particular sources. If you live downriver from the factory that purchased a large number of pollution rights, your water will be particularly polluted, while the water in other locations gets cleaner.

Simply taxing pollution directly is another way to provide an incentive to reduce it without dictating specific levels from specific sources. The most widely discussed tax policy today is a possible carbon tax. Carbon creates climate change, so the proposal would simply be to tax each ton of carbon produced by any economic activity. This tax would ripple through the economy, raising prices on activities that produce a lot of carbon, such as gasoline, moving heavy items long distances, and coal-fired electricity generation. Higher prices for carbon-intensive goods and services would result in less use of them, reducing the amount of carbon produced. Both cap and trade and taxation systems require the government to set an overall cap or tax at a level that will reduce pollution by the desired amount. While perhaps less complicated than specifying pollution levels from each source, this is still a complex and uncertain task.

Tax or cap and trade systems attempt to set a direct cost on pollution, forcing polluters to internalize an externality. A similar goal is embedded in policies to control use of what otherwise could be free goods, such as public land and the minerals under it, to avoid the tragedy of the commons. User fees on public land exist to limit use so that the overuse inherent in free public goods does not occur. Similarly, governments can charge for access to minerals, including oil. Given that minerals and fossil fuels are nonrenewable, their depletion contains an intergenerational externality: future generations will pay the price of finding alternatives to the finite resources current generations use. Many economists argue that this justifies government intervention to tax mineral extraction, raising the internal cost of mineral production. In practice, many governments, including the United

command and control policies: Pollution control system in which a government directly regulates the specific amount of pollution each polluting entity is allowed

cap and trade system: Market-based pollution control system in which the government sets an overall limit on how much of a pollutant is acceptable and issues vouchers to pollute to each company, which companies are then free to trade

States, pursue exactly the opposite strategy, subsidizing mineral exploration and development in order to maximize production and lower consumer costs in the present. Cheaper minerals and fuels spur economic growth, which all legitimate states strive to achieve. Subsidizing mineral exploration, however, encourages rather than discourages the tragedy of the commons in nonrenewable resources.

Climate Change

Burning fossil fuels—full of previously trapped carbon—has pumped excess carbon and other greenhouse bases (GHG) into the atmosphere. Virtually all scientists now agree that this has increased the entire planet's ambient temperature by an estimated 1.0°C (1.8°F) since the dawn of the industrial age, and the pace is accelerating. A series of reports by the Intergovernmental Panel on Climate Change (IPCC) put together by a large group of the world's top climate scientists has recommended that the world keep the temperature increase to no more than 2°C. The 2018 report drew headlines by demonstrating the difference between allowing an increase of 1.5°C and 2°C. That difference is estimated to result in an additional 23 percent of the population being exposed to extreme heat once every five years, an additional 50 million people facing drought, and an additional 1–11 million people suffering from rising sea levels. Restricting temperature increases to 1.5°C, the report predicted, will require achieving zero additional carbon production by about 2050; restricting the planet to a 2°C increase would require getting to zero additional carbon production by about 2070. The report suggests, "[p]athways limiting global warming to 1.5°C with no or limited overshoot would require rapid and far-reaching transitions in energy, land, urban and infrastructure (including transport and buildings), and industrial systems. These systems transitions are unprecedented in terms of scale, but not necessarily in terms of speed, and imply deep emissions reductions in all sectors" (IPCC 2018).

Two areas of policy response to climate change are possible, and most experts argue both are necessary. *Mitigation* involves reducing the cause of the problem: GHG production. This has been the central focus of efforts at creating international climate change accords over the past twenty years. *Adaptation* involves policies to adapt to the effects of climate change, such as building seawalls to keep rising sea levels from destroying property, farmers switching crops as local climates change, and island nations in the Pacific proposing to move en masse to other countries because their countries are projected to be completely underwater by the end of the century.

In spite of the international scientific consensus that dramatic action is required and clear ideas about what policies are needed, both national and global efforts have been modest to date. Thomas Rudel (2019) argued that major changes in environmental policy occur when dramatic events such as droughts or hurricanes make people feel trapped in a "cage" that threatens their well-being, leading to major shifts in public opinion and political mobilization in favor of environmental protection. Connecting climate change to particular events is difficult for scientists and impossible for the average person to experience, and such events, while increasingly frequent, occur in various places to varying degrees, limiting the extent to which large groups of people feel threatened. Social movement theorists have used social movement theory (see chapter 7) to argue that the uncertainty about the short-term effects of climate change, hostility of conservative political forces reducing political opportunity, and the difficulty of framing the issue as an imminent threat to individuals have limited the ability of social movements focused on climate change to gain strength (McAdams 2017).

The Kyoto Protocol, signed in 1997, was the first major international effort to address climate change. It included mandated targets for developed countries but no mandates on developing countries, which led the United States, the world's largest carbon producer at the time, to reject it. It ultimately only covered 15 percent of global carbon emissions because of the refusal of the United States to participate and the absence of binding agreements on large, developing countries like China and India. The Paris Agreement completed in December 2015 was the first climate change agreement that was signed by virtually every country in the world. Rather than legally binding agreements, however, every nation pledged to implement its own national policy to help the world keep temperature rise to less than 2°C in the twenty-first century and ideally below 1.5°C. The countries agreed to meet regularly to share and assess progress, but the agreement is ultimately a "name and shame" one: no enforcement mechanisms exist to ensure countries create and meet adequate targets. The Paris Agreement was supposed to reduce GHG emissions by 26 to 28 percent by 2025. President Barack Obama's Climate Action Plan, announced in 2013, was designed to reduce GHG emissions by about one-quarter by 2025. This was to be America's way of complying with the Paris Agreement. In 2017, President Trump revoked Obama's plan and withdrew the United States from the Paris Agreement, though all other countries remain in it. By late 2018, the initial round of national plans was estimated to leave world carbon emissions well above what would be needed to achieve the goal, with estimates of warming still reaching about 3°C by 2100.

In October 2016, an additional climate accord was reached in Kigali, Rwanda, to reduce hydrofluorocarbons (HFCs), powerful GHG used in refrigeration. Unlike the Paris Agreement on carbon emissions, the Kigali Accord is legally binding and includes enforcement mechanisms, meaning it may have more effect on climate change than the Paris Agreement. The accord was reached via a compromise between wealthy and poorer countries under which the wealthier countries will reduce HFC production sooner than the poorer countries, which will have more time to make the switch to alternative refrigerants. It is binding in part because it is actually an amendment to the binding Montreal Protocol of 1987 that lowered production of gases that created the ozone hole and, if fully implemented, could reduce global warming by nearly one-half of a degree by 2100. By early 2019, seventy-two countries had ratified it, though over one hundred still had failed to do so.

The battle between wealthy and poorer countries is at the heart of global climate change debates. Figure 12.3 and Maps 12.1 to 12.3 illustrate what this debate is about. Figure 12.3 shows that since the dawn of the industrial era, the wealthy, Western countries have produced the great bulk of carbon emissions. Because these gases do not dissipate, wealthy countries have produced the vast majority of the total GHG to date. The United States alone is estimated to account for nearly 30 percent of the total since 1850. Map 12.1, however, shows that while wealthy countries remain major carbon producers, a few rapidly industrializing countries account for a significant share of CO_2 emissions as well, especially China, the world's biggest producer currently. Map 12.2 demonstrates, on the other hand, that in per capita terms, the wealthy countries still produce far more even than China, let alone other developing countries. Each American citizen produces far more carbon annually than does each Chinese citizen. Finally, comparing Maps 12.1 and 12.3 also shows that the countries that produce the least carbon are the most vulnerable to the effects of climate change.

These data make the battle lines of the debate clear. The wealthy countries, led by the United States, argue that they cannot reduce global warming without all of the biggest polluters, including China and India, agreeing to curb their emissions

FIGURE 12.3

Share of Cumulate Global CO2 Emissions, 1850–2011 (Percentage of World Total)

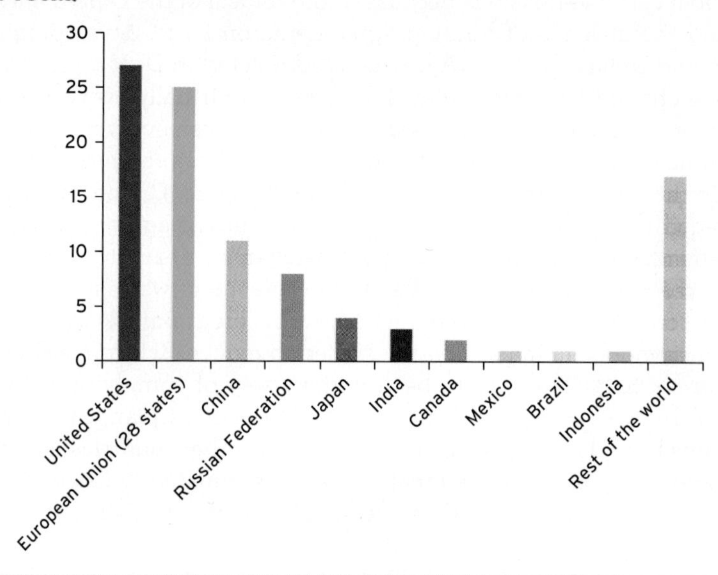

Source: Data are from World Resources Institute, "6 Graphs Explain the World's Top 10 Emitters," http://www.wri.org/blog/2014/11/6-graphs-explain-world%E2%80%99s-top-10-emitters.

significantly. The developing countries, led by China, counter that the wealthier countries are the main source of the total excess carbon in the atmosphere and that each individual in wealthy countries produces far more carbon than each individual Chinese or Indian does. Therefore, the wealthy countries have an obligation to reduce emissions the most. Moreover, denying countries now industrializing the right to pollute will doom them to inferior status forever. The wealthy countries benefited from unlimited carbon pollution while they were industrializing, for which the entire world will pay the price, and it is unethical to ask countries now industrializing to curb their development prematurely. Furthermore, the poorest countries argue that they have not caused the problem but will suffer the greatest effects, making a moral claim on the major polluters to reduce pollution and pay for adaptation for climate change's worst effects.

Given this structure of interests, numerous formulas for how to share the cost of reducing carbon emissions have been developed. Wealthy countries argue for grandfathering, the basis for the Kyoto Protocol, under which all countries reduce their emissions relative to a baseline year, so their past emissions are "grandfathered" in. The most common proposal from poorer countries is a per capita contraction and convergence principle: every person on the planet would be given the same rights to emissions, which would be reduced over time to lower overall emissions. Countries that exceed their rights would have to reduce their total and/or purchase excess rights from other countries; those with surplus rights could sell them. While not making up for the full historical legacy, this would place much greater burden on wealthier countries (Parks and Roberts 2009). Paul Baer et al. (2009) argued for what they term Greenhouse Development Rights based on countries'

MAP 12.1

Global Variations in CO2 Emissions, 2013

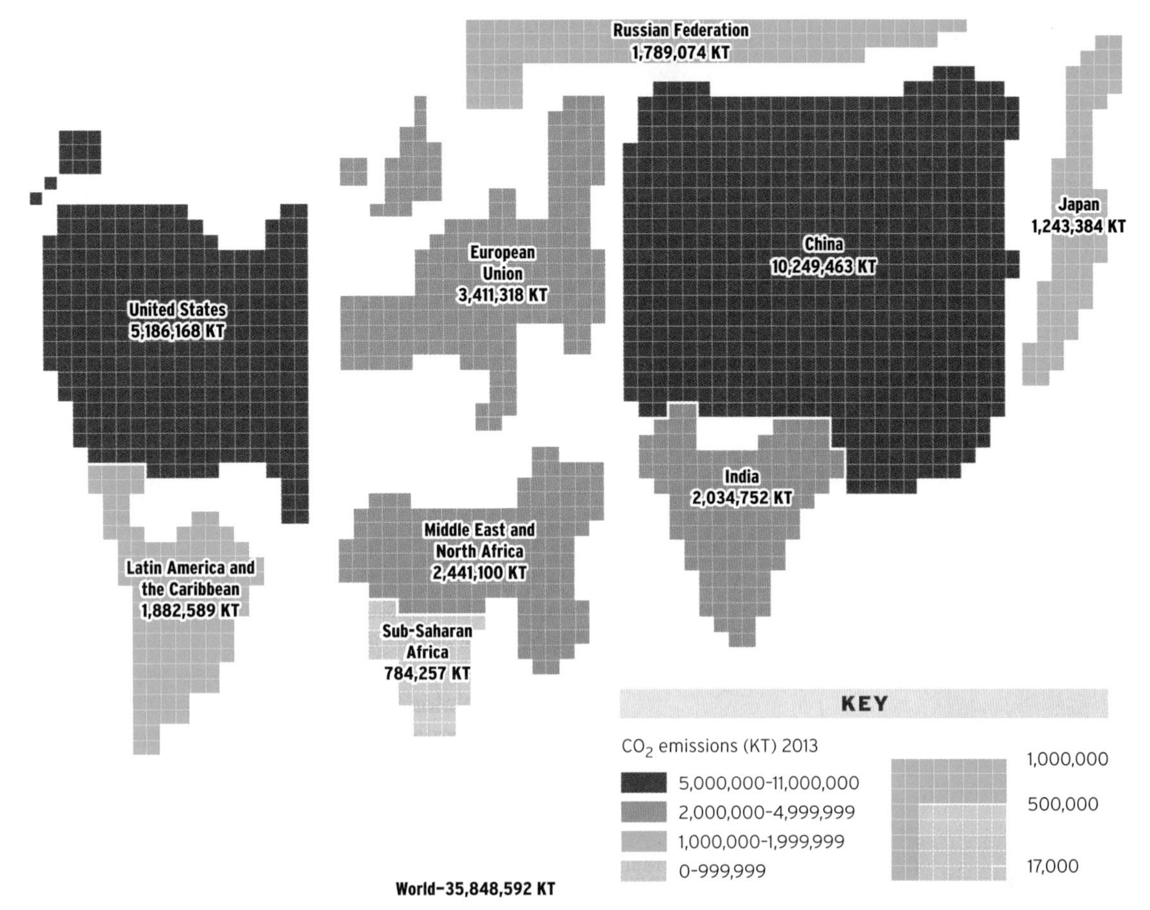

Source: Data for Maps 12.1 and 12.2 are from the World Bank (http://data.worldbank.org/indicator/EN.ATM.CO2E.PC) and (http://data.worldbank.org/indicator/EN.ATM.CO2E.KT).

capacity to pay (defined as the percentage of their population with incomes above $7,500 per year, chosen as a level that satisfies basic human needs) and responsibility for emissions (based on per capita emissions since 1990). The result in 2009 places about two-thirds of the burden on the wealthy countries, of which the United States would pay 27 percent, while China would be responsible for about 15 percent (Global Development Rights 2013).

Whoever pays the cost, no international consensus exists on exactly which policy mechanisms should be used to reduce greenhouse gases. The most common solutions are a cap and trade system for carbon or a carbon tax. The EU already instituted its own cap and trade system to help it comply with the Kyoto Protocol. It was estimated to have reduced emissions at participating facilities (utilities, factories, etc.) by 2 to 5 percent (Ellerman et al. 2010). The Kyoto Protocol also included the Clean Development Mechanism (CDM), a system that allows companies and countries to gain emission credits by investing in projects that reduce

MAP 12.2

Total Emissions per Capita, 2013

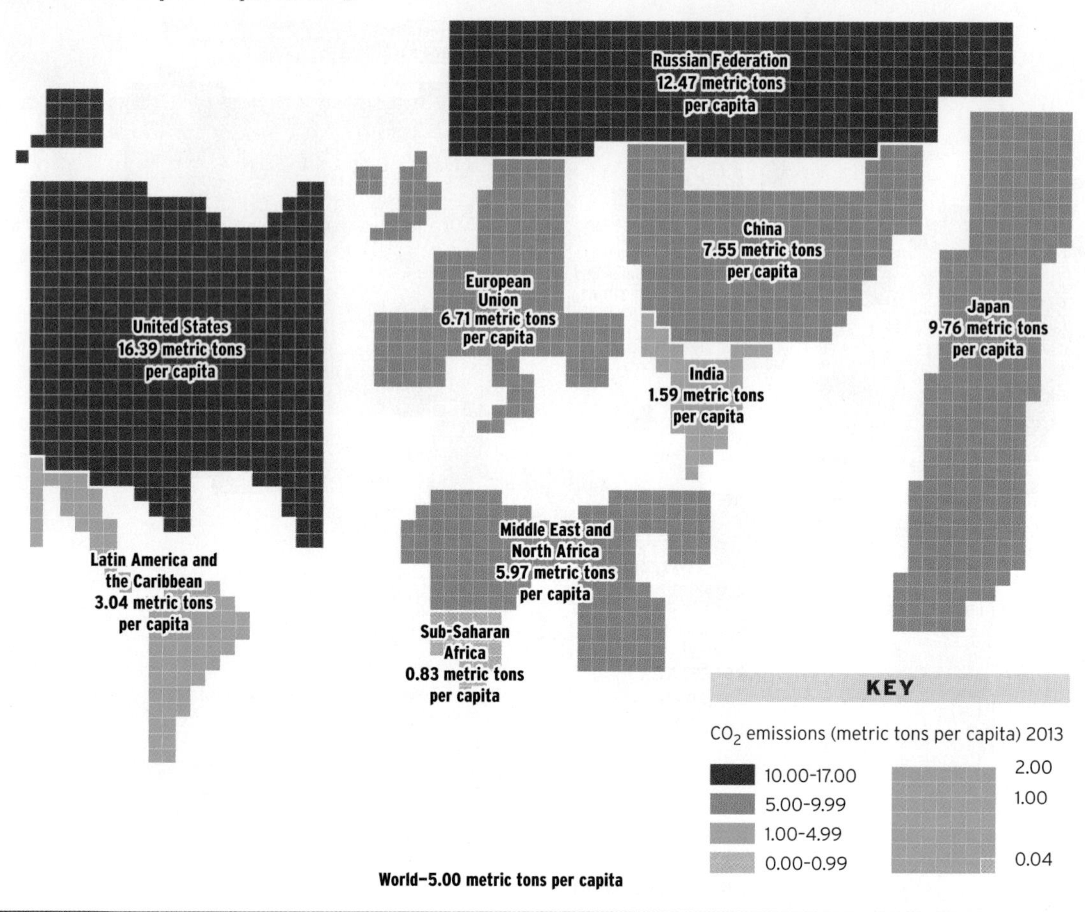

Source: Data for Maps 12.1 and 12.2 are from the World Bank (http://data.worldbank.org/indicator/EN.ATM.CO2E.PC) and (http://data.worldbank.org/indicator/EN.ATM.CO2E.KT).

emissions elsewhere in the world. Because many factories in the developing world use older technology, it's cheaper to reduce emissions there than in wealthy countries. A rapidly growing market has emerged that now includes several thousand emissions reduction projects globally, with over half of them located in China. The organization in charge of monitoring it estimated that the CDM had reduced carbon emissions by a billion tons by 2011 (Benney 2015, 42).

Of the three policy areas we discuss in this chapter, the environment is the easiest area in which to justify government intervention in markets. Environmental damage is clearly an externality that should be internalized for efficient allocation of resources and long-term sustainability. This has become particularly clear and urgent in the face of climate change, which threatens to wreak havoc on the lives of millions in the relatively near future. A number of clear policy choices exist as well. Their implementation, however, has been limited and slow. Different policies internalize costs in different ways, resulting in different people paying those costs. Both within individual countries and on a global scale, individual polluters and national governments strive to minimize the costs they will have to pay.

MAP 12.3

Climate Vulnerability

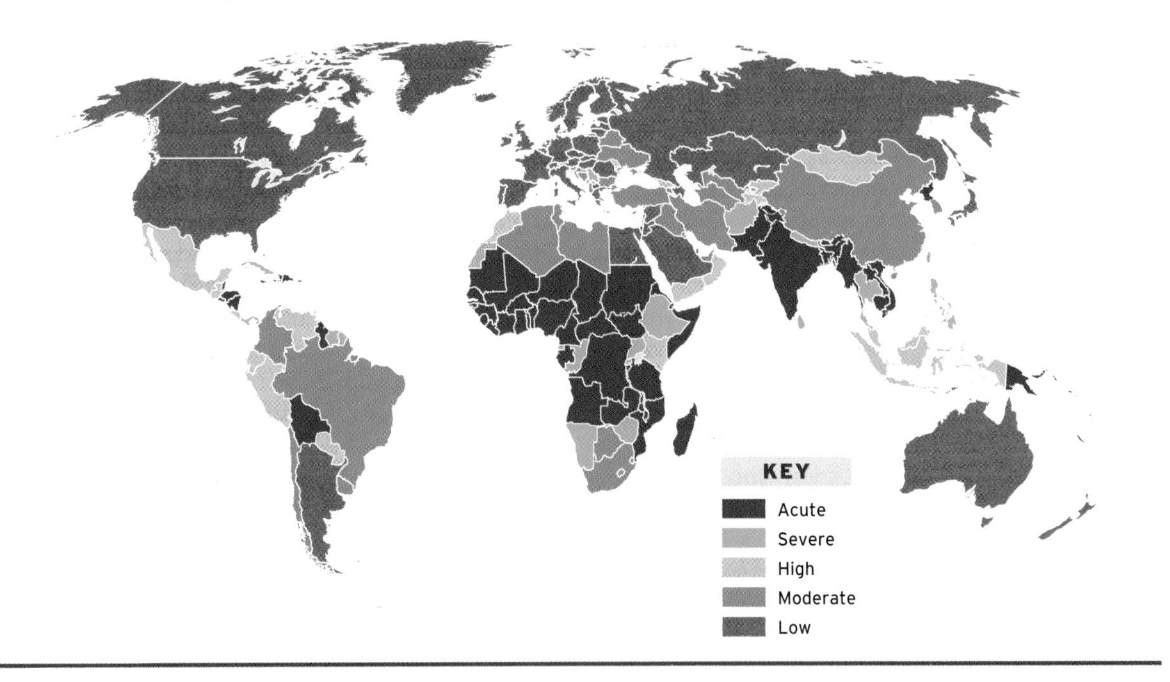

Source: DARA, *Climate Vulnerability Monitor, 2nd Edition: A Guide to the Cold Calculus of a Hot Planet*, 2012. Reprinted with permission.

Conclusion

The outcomes of policy battles can tell us much about "who rules." Policy outcomes reflect the relative strength of various groups in a given political system. More extensive welfare states, especially prior to the 1990s in Europe, likely reflected the greater power of workers and unions in those countries, in contrast to the United States. European countries for the most part have reduced welfare benefits in recent decades, though, suggesting that workers' power is declining relative to other forces, domestic and international. In poorer countries, the poor who would benefit most from social welfare and health care interventions seem to lack significant power, as those countries pursue few such policies, either because the governments are not interested or because they lack the resources. Innovative social policies in Brazil and elsewhere in Latin America, though, suggest that in a democratic setting, it is possible for the poor to overcome these problems at least partially and gain greater benefits.

Environmental policies, which usually assign clear costs and benefits to particular groups, perhaps demonstrate relative power most directly. Self-interested actors are likely to resist paying the costs of environmental improvement, at least until a broader consensus emerges that change is essential for all to survive. For most environmental issues, including climate change, the least powerful player in the game is future generations, who lack any political clout now. They may well end up paying the greatest costs for internalizing externalities in the long run.

State intervention in each of the three policy areas has its own rationale, but in all three, market failure of some sort offers a reason for the state to modify pure market outcomes. States don't intervene solely because they recognize market failures, however. Normative and political motivations also need to be present. Markets can create powerful veto players, which can only be overcome via collective action and/or consensus on the part of broader and usually more diffuse actors who believe they will benefit from intervention. For instance, the Great Depression and World War II helped bring the value of reducing poverty to the fore and led to the growth of modern welfare states. Similarly, wealthy industrial countries have led the way in environmental intervention, reflecting a classic postmaterialist value. Middle-income and rapidly industrializing countries may be attempting to join the bandwagon, but in the very poorest countries, it is difficult to argue convincingly that resources are something to be conserved rather than depleted to meet immediate human needs.

Globalization, too, has had an impact on policies in all countries. On social policy, our cases show a persistence of diverse models but a trend toward at least limited reform in the direction of a more liberal welfare state. Across all three types of welfare states, for instance, workers and the poor have seen social policy benefits reduced, work requirements and limits on social assistance increased, and their contributions to social insurance systems increased.

Globalization, increasing wealth, and an aging population make reform of health policy particularly urgent and difficult. While significant changes occurred in a number of countries after about 2005, they do not represent wholesale shifts from the long-standing systems in each country. Health care systems create their own institutionalized interests that resist change, from medical practitioners' support of the NHS in the United Kingdom to American insurance companies' opposition to a single-payer model. Health care, perhaps because it affects everyone, including relatively wealthy and powerful players, seems particularly difficult to reform.

In general, wealth seems to raise the prospect that countries can and will act effectively on value consensus in these three policy areas, but we need to explain significant variation among wealthy countries as well. The most widespread explanation for why some governments intervene more extensively than others is implicitly pluralist: in some countries, politically weaker groups have organized better and have more power, and policy reflects this. Institutions can matter as well, though. They create veto players that can be particularly powerful at blocking policy change, toward either more or less intervention. Germany's federal system and less centralized parliament, for instance, seem to make policy change there more incremental than in the more majoritarian United Kingdom.

Judging which set of policies is most "successful" in each of the three issue areas must in part be based on normative values, especially in social policy. If reducing poverty is the key goal, social democratic welfare states seem to be best; if ensuring people are employed is most important, though, a liberal welfare state may seem to be better. In health policy, what is "best" may be a little clearer. If the key criterion is gaining the most health at the least cost, it seems clear that market-based systems fare poorly, and well-established economic arguments explain why. Judging environmental policy success also depends on values: How much do we value clean air and water? How much do we value the well-being of future generations versus our own, right now? In terms of economic theory, environmental policy seems the easiest area in which to justify government intervention, but how much and how it should be done depend very much on larger value questions, including about who should pay how much of the costs, and when. ●

KEY CONCEPTS

cap and trade system (p. 369)

Christian democratic welfare states (p. 350)

command and control policies (p. 369)

conditional cash transfer (CCT) (p. 358)

liberal welfare states (p. 351)

market-based private insurance system (p. 361)

means-tested public assistance (p. 349)

moral hazard (p. 359)

national health insurance (NHI) (p. 360)

national health system (NHS)/single-payer system (p. 360)

precautionary principle (p. 368)

risk assessment (p. 368)

risk management (p. 368)

social democratic welfare states (p. 350)

social insurance (p. 348)

social policy (p. 346)

tax expenditures (p. 349)

tragedy of the commons (p. 366)

universal basic income (p. 348)

universal entitlements (p. 348)

welfare states (p. 350)

WORKS CITED

Adolino, Jessica R., and Charles H. Blake. 2001. *Comparing Public Policies: Issues and Choices in Six Industrialized Countries*. Washington, DC: CQ Press.

Alber, Jens, and Neil Gilbert, eds. 2010. *United in Diversity? Comparing Social Models in Europe and America*. Oxford, UK: Oxford University Press.

Alesina, Alberto, and Edward L. Glaeser. 2004. *Fighting Poverty in the U.S. and Europe: A World of Difference*. Oxford, UK: Oxford University Press.

Baer, Paul, Glenn Fieldman, Tom Athanasiou, and Sivan Kartha. 2009. "Greenhouse Development Rights: Towards an Equitable Framework for Global Climate Policy." In *The Politics of Climate Change: Environmental Dynamics in International Affairs*, edited by Paul Harris, 192–212. New York: Routledge.

Benney, Tabitha M. 2015. *Making Environmental Markets Work: The Varieties of Capitalism in the Emerging Economies*. New York: Routledge.

Bonoli, Giuliano, Vic George, and Peter Taylor-Gooby. 2000. *European Welfare Futures: Towards a Theory of Retrenchment*. Cambridge, UK, and Malden, MA: Polity Press and Blackwell.

Brooks, Sarah M. 2015. "Social Protection for the Poorest: The Adoption of Antipoverty Cash Transfer Programs in the Global South." *Politics & Society* 43 (December): 551–582. doi:10.1177/0032329215602894.

Cappelen, Cornelius. 2016. "Inta-EU Migration and the Moral Sustainability of the Welfare State." In *Democratic Transformations in Europe: Challenges and opportunities*, edited by Yvette Peters and Michael Tatham, 143–162. New York: Routledge.

CBO (Congressional Budget Office). 2007. *The State Children's Health Insurance Program*. Washington, DC: Government Printing Office.

CDC (Centers for Disease Control). 2016. *Early Release of Selected Estimates Based on Data From the 2015 National Health Interview Survey*. May 24, 2016. http://www.cdc.gov/nchs/nhis/releases/released201605.htm#1.

Commonwealth Fund. 2008. *Commonwealth Fund International Health Policy Survey of Sicker Adults.* http://www.commonwealthfund.org/Content/Surveys/2008/2008-Commonwealth-Fund-Inter national-Health-Policy-Survey-of-Sicker-Adults.aspx.

Dunlap, Riley E., and Richard York. 2012. "The Globalization of Environmental Concern." In *Comparative Environmental Politics: Theory, Practice, and Prospects,* edited by Paul F. Steinberg and Stacy D. VanDeveer, 89–112. Cambridge, MA: MIT Press.

Economy, Elizabeth C. 2010. *The River Runs Black: The Environmental Challenge to China's Future.* 2nd ed. Ithaca, NY: Cornell University Press.

Edin, Kathryn, and H. Luke Shaefer. 2016. "20 Years Since Welfare 'Reform.'" *The Atlantic.* August 22, 2016. http://www.theatlantic.com/business/archive/2016/08/20-years-welfare-reform/496730/.

Ellerman, A. Denny, Frank J. Convery, and Christian de Perthius. 2010. *Pricing Carbon: The European Union Emissions Trading Scheme.* Cambridge, UK: Cambridge University Press.

Esping-Andersen, Gøsta. 1990. *The Three Worlds of Welfare Capitalism.* Princeton, NJ: Princeton University Press.

Ferreira, Francisco H. G., and David A. Robalino. 2011. "Social Protection in Latin America: Achievements and Limitations." In *The Oxford Handbook of Latin American Economics,* edited by José Antonio Ocampo and Jaime Ros, 836–862. Oxford, UK: Oxford University Press.

Gao, George. 2015. *As Smog Hangs over Beijing, Chinese Cite Air Pollution as Major Concern.* Pew Research Center. December 10, 2015. http://www.pewresearch.org/fact-tank/2015/12/10/as-smog-hangs-over-beijing-chinese-cite-air-pollution-as-major-concern/.

Garfinkel, Irwin, Lee Rainwater, and Timothy Smeeding. 2010. *Wealth and Welfare States: Is America a Laggard or Leader?* Oxford, UK: Oxford University Press.

Gingrich, Jane, and Ben W. Ansell. 2015. "The Dynamics of Social Investment: Human Capital, Activation, and Care." In *The Politics of Advanced Capitalism,* edited by Pablo Beramendi, Silva Häusermann, Herbert Kitschelt, and Hanspeter Kriesi, 282–304. Cambridge, UK: Cambridge University Press.

Global Development Rights. 2013. www.gdrights.org/calculator.

Gough, Ian. 2014. "Mapping Social Welfare Regimes Beyond the OECD." In *The Politics of Non-state Social Welfare,* edited by Melani Cammett and Lauren M. MacLean, 17–30. Ithaca, NY: Cornell University Press.

Grassler, Bernd. 2014. "The Labor Reforms That Set off a Boom." DW.com. December 31, 2014. https://www.dw.com/en/the-labor-reforms-that-set-off-a-boom/a-18164351.

Green, David G., and Benedict Irvine. 2001. *Health Care in France and Germany: Lessons for the UK.* London: Institute for the Study of Civil Society.

Greenstein, Robert. 2016. *Welfare Reform and the Safety Net: Evidence Contradicts Likely Assumptions Behind Forthcoming GOP Poverty Plan.* Washington, DC: Center on Budget and Policy Priorities. June 6, 2016. http://www.cbpp.org/research/family-income-support/welfare-reform-and-the-safety-net.

Halpern-Meekin, Sarah, Kathryn Edin, Laura Tach, and Jennifer Sykes. 2015. *It's Not Like I'm Poor: How Working Families Make Ends Meet in a Post-Welfare World.* Berkeley: University of California Press.

Hausermann, Silja. 2018. "Social Democracy and the Welfare State in Context: The Conditioning Effect of Institutional Legacies and Party Competition." In *Welfare Democracies and Party Politics: Explaining Electoral Dynamics in Times of Changing Welfare Capitalism,* edited by Philip Manow, Bruno Palier, and Hanna Schwander, 150–170. Oxford, UK: Oxford University Press.

Ho, Peter, and Eduard B. Vermeer. 2006. "China's Limits to Growth? The Difference Between Absolute, Relative, and Precautionary Limits." *Development and Change* 37 (1): 255–271. doi:10.1111/j.0012-155X.2006.00477.x.

Huber, Evelyne, and Sara Niedzwiecki. 2015. "Emerging Welfare States in Latin America and East Asia." In *The Oxford Handbook of Transformations of the State*, edited by Stephan Leibfried, Evelyne Huber, Matthew Lange, Jonah D. Levy, Frank Nullmeier, and John D. Stephens, 796–812. Oxford, UK: Oxford University Press.

Huber, Evelyne, and John D. Stephens. 2001. *Development and Crisis of the Welfare State: Parties and Policies in Global Markets*. Chicago: University of Chicago Press.

———. 2015. "Postindustrial Social Policy." In *The Politics of Advanced Capitalism*, edited by Pablo Beramendi, Silva Häusermann, Herbert Kitschelt, and Hanspeter Kriesi, 259–281. Cambridge, UK: Cambridge University Press.

IPCC (Intergovernmental Panel on Climate Change). 2018. *Special Report: Global Warming of 1.5 Degrees C.* https://www.ipcc.ch/sr15/.

Jensen, Carsten. 2014. *The Right and the Welfare State.* Oxford, UK: Oxford University Press.

Marshall, T. H. 1963. *Class, Citizenship, and Social Development: Essays.* Chicago: University of Chicago Press.

McAdams, Doug. 2017. "Social Movement Theory and the Prospects of Climate Change Action in the United States." *Annual Review of Political Science* 20 (1): 189–208. doi: 10.1146/annurev-polisci-052615-025801.

McGahey, Richard. 2018. "Universal Basic Income and the Welfare State." In *The Welfare State Revisited*, edited by José Antonio Ocampo and Joseph E. Stiglitz, 316–336. New York: Columbia University Press.

Morton, Katherine. 2006. "Surviving an Environmental Crisis: Can China Adapt?" *Brown Journal of World Affairs* 13 (1): 63–75.

Obinger, Herbert, and Peter Starke. 2015. "Welfare State Transformation: Convergence and the Rise of the Supply-Side Model." In *The Oxford Handbook of Transformations of the State*, edited by Stephan Leibfried, Evelyne Huber, Matthew Lange, Jonah D. Levy, Frank Nullmeier, and John D. Stephens, 465–481. Oxford, UK: Oxford University Press.

Ocampo, José Antonio, and Natalie Gomez-Arteaga. 2018. "Social Protection Systems in Latin America: Toward Universalism and Redistribution." In *The Welfare State Revisited*, edited by José Antonio Ocampo and Joseph E. Stiglitz, 230–257. New York: Columbia University Press.

OECD (Organisation for Economic Co-operation and Development). 2015. "Health Care at a Glance." http://www.health.gov.il/publicationsfiles/healthataglance2015.pdf.

Olsen, Gregg M. 2007. "Toward Global Welfare State Convergence? Family Policy and Health Care in Sweden, Canada, and the United States." *Journal of Sociology and Social Welfare* 34 (2): 143–164.

Parks, Bradley C., and J. Timmons Roberts. 2009. "Inequality and the Global Climate Regime: Breaking the North–South Impasse." In *The Politics of Climate Change: Environmental Dynamics in International Affairs*, edited by Paul Harris, 164–191. New York: Routledge.

Pierson, Paul. 1996. "The New Politics of the Welfare State." *World Politics* 48 (2): 143–179. doi:10.1353/wp.1996.0004.

Rueda, David. 2015. "The State of the Welfare State: Unemployment, Labor Market Policy, and Inequality in the Age of Workfare." *Comparative Politics* 47 (3): 296–314.

Rudel, Thomas K. 2019. *Shocks, States, and Sustainability: The Origins of Radical Environmental Reforms.* Oxford, UK: Oxford University Press.

Sainsbury, Diane. 2013. "Gender, Care, and Welfare." In *The Oxford Handbook of Gender and Politics*, edited by Georgina Waylen, Karen Celis, Johanna Kantola, and S. Laurel Weldon, 313–336. Oxford, UK: Oxford University Press.

Sherman, Arloc, and Danilo Trisi. 2015. *Safety Net More Effective Against Poverty Than Previously Thought: Correcting for Underreporting of Benefits Reveals Stronger Reductions in Poverty and Deep Poverty in All States.* Washington, DC: Center on Budget and Policy Priorities. May 6, 2015. http://www.cbpp.org/sites/default/files/atoms/files/5-6-15pov.pdf.

Spies, Dennis C. 2018. *Immigration and Welfare State Retrenchment: Why the US Experience is not Reflected in Western Europe.* Oxford, UK: Oxford University Press.

Spilker, Gabriele. 2013. *Globalization, Political Institutions and the Environment in Developing Countries.* New York: Routledge.

Stetter, Ernst. 2018. "The EU Welfare State: Past, Present, and Future." In *The Welfare State Revisited*, edited by José Antonio Ocampo and Joseph E. Stiglitz, 191–212. New York: Columbia University Press.

Van Parijs, Philippe, and Yannick Vanderborght. 2017. *Basic Income: A Radical Proposal for a Free Society and a Sane Economy.* Cambridge, MA: Harvard University Press.

RESOURCES FOR FURTHER STUDY

Brady, David. 2009. *Rich Democracies, Poor People: How Politics Explain Poverty*. Oxford, UK: Oxford University Press.

Donaldson, Cam, and Karen Gerard. 2005. *Economics of Health Care Financing: The Visible Hand*. New York: Palgrave Macmillan.

Goodin, Robert E., Bruce Headey, Ruud Muffels, and Henk-Jan Dirven. 1999. *The Real Worlds of Welfare Capitalism*. Cambridge, UK: Cambridge University Press.

Huber, Evelyne. 2012. *Democracy and the Left: Social Policy and Inequality in Latin America.* Chicago: University of Chicago Press.

Jacobs, Lawrence R., and Theda Skocpol. 2010. *Health Care Reform and American Politics: What Everyone Needs to Know*. Oxford, UK: Oxford University Press.

——. 2011. "Society at a Glance 2011—OECD Social Indicators." http://www.oecd.org/document/40/0,3746,en_2649_37419_47507368_1_1_1_37419,00.html.

Rehm, Philipp. 2016. *Risk Inequality and Welfare States: Social Policy Preferences, Development, and Dynamics.* Cambridge, UK: Cambridge University Press.

Schreuder, Yda. 2009. *The Corporate Greenhouse: Climate Change Policy in a Globalizing World.* New York: Zed Books.

Sen, Amartya. 1999. *Development as Freedom.* New York: Knopf.

WEB RESOURCES

Council on Environmental Quality, U.S. Department of Energy

(http://energy.gov/nepa/council-environmental-quality)

Measure of America of the Social Science Research Council

(http://www.measureofamerica.org/tools/)

Organisation for Economic Co-operation and Development (OECD)

(http://www.oecd.org)

United Nations Statistics Division, Environment

(http://unstats.un.org/unsd/environment/default.htm)

U.S. Census Bureau, International Database

(https://www.census.gov/population/international/data/idb/informationGateway.php)

World Health Organization, Global Health Observatory

(http://www.who.int/gho/en)

GLOSSARY

absolutism: Rule by a single monarch who claims complete, exclusive power and sovereignty over a territory and its people (Ch 2)

alternative-vote (AV) system: Single-member district electoral system in which voters rank all candidates rather than voting for just one (Ch 6)

assimilation: A belief that immigrants or other members of minority cultural communities ought to adopt the culture of the majority population (Ch 4)

asymmetrical federal system: A federal system in which different subnational governments (states or provinces) have distinct relationships with and rights in relation to the national government (Ch 5)

authoritarianization: The creation of an authoritarian regime via the undermining of democratic institutions by elected incumbents; has become more common (Ch 9)

autonomy: The ability and right of a group to partially govern itself within a larger state (Ch 4)

bourgeoisie: The class that owns capital; according to Marxism, the ruling elite in all capitalist societies (Ch 1)

bureaucracy: A large set of appointed officials whose function is to implement the laws of the state, as directed by the executive (Ch 2)

cap and trade system: Market-based pollution control system in which the government sets an overall limit on how much of a pollutant is acceptable and issues vouchers to pollute to each company, which companies are then free to trade (Ch 12)

capitalism: The combination of a market economy with private property rights (Ch 10)

centripetal approach: A means used by democracies to resolve ethnic conflict by giving political leaders and parties incentives to moderate their demands (Ch 4)

charismatic legitimacy: The right to rule based on personal virtue, heroism, sanctity, or other extraordinary characteristics (Ch 2)

Christian democratic welfare states: States whose social policies are based on the nuclear family with a male breadwinner, designed primarily to achieve income stabilization to mitigate the effects of market-induced income insecurity; Germany is a key example (Ch 12)

citizen: A member of a political community or state with certain rights and duties (Ch 3)

civic culture: A political culture in which citizens hold values and beliefs that support democracy, including active participation in politics but also enough deference to the leadership to let it govern effectively (Ch 1)

civic nationalism: A sense of national unity and purpose based on a set of commonly held political beliefs (Ch 4)

civil rights: Those rights that guarantee individual freedom as well as equal, just, and fair treatment by the state (Ch 3)

civil society: The sphere of organized, nongovernmental, nonviolent activity by groups larger than individual families or firms (Ch 3)

civil war: Two or more armed groups, at least one of which is tied to the most recent regime in power, fight for control of the state (Ch 7)

closed-list proportional representation: Electoral system in which each party presents a ranked list of candidates, voters vote for the party rather than for individual candidates, and each party awards the seats it wins to the candidates on its list in rank order (Ch 6)

coalition government: Government in a parliamentary system in which at least two parties negotiate an agreement to rule together (Ch 5)

coalitional presidentialism: A presidential system with many parties in the legislature, requiring the president to form an informal coalition of parties to pass legislation (Ch 5)

code law: Legal system originating in ancient Roman law and modified by Napoleon Bonaparte in France, in which judges may only follow the law as written and must ignore past decisions; in contrast to common law (Ch 5)

cohabitation: Sharing of power between a president and prime minister from different parties in a semipresidential system (Ch 5)

collective action problem: Individuals being unwilling to engage in a particular activity because of their rational belief that their individual actions will have little or no effect yet collectively suffering adverse consequences when all fail to act (Ch 6)

command and control policies: Pollution control system in which a government directly regulates the specific amount of pollution each polluting entity is allowed (Ch 12)

common law: Legal system originating in Britain in which judges base decisions not only on their understanding of the written law but also on their understanding of past court cases; in contrast to code law (Ch 5)

comparative advantage: Theory of trade that argues that economic efficiency and well-being will be maximized if each country uses its resources to produce whatever it produces relatively well compared with other countries and then trades its own products with other countries for goods it does not produce (Ch 11)

comparative institutional advantage: Idea in the varieties of capitalism school of thought that different kinds of capitalist systems have different institutional advantages that they usually will try to maintain, resulting in different responses to external economic pressures (Ch 10)

comparative method: The means by which scholars try to mimic laboratory conditions by careful selection of cases (Ch 1)

comparative politics: One of the major subfields of political science, in which the primary focus is on comparing power and decision making across countries (Ch 1)

conditional cash transfer (CCT): Programs that provide cash grants to the poor and in exchange require particular beneficial behavior from the poor, such as children's attendance at school and visits to health clinics (Ch 12)

consensus democracy: A democratic system with multiparty executives in a coalition government, executive–legislative balance, bicameral legislatures, and rigid constitutions that are not easily amended (Ch 5)

consociationalism: A democratic system designed to ease ethnic tensions via recognizing the existence of specific groups and granting some share of power in the central government to each, usually codified in specific legal or constitutional guarantees to each group (Ch 4)

constructivism: A theory of identity group formation that argues that identities are created through a complex process usually referred to as social construction (Ch 4)

contentious politics: Political activity that is at least in part beyond institutional bounds, involving extra-institutional activity such as petitions, protests, riots, violence, civil war, and revolution (Ch 7)

convergence: Argument that globalization will force similar neoliberal policies across all countries (Ch 10)

coordinated market economies (CMEs): In the varieties of capitalism approach, capitalist economies in which firms, financiers, unions, and government consciously coordinate their actions via interlocking ownership and participation; Germany and Japan are key examples (Ch 10)

corporatism: System of representation in which one organization represents each important sector of society; two subtypes are societal and state corporatism (Ch 3)

coup d'état: When the military forcibly removes an existing regime and establishes a new one (Ch 9)

cultural nationalism: National unity based on a common cultural characteristic wherein only those people who share that characteristic can be included in the nation (Ch 4)

deficit spending: Government spending that is more than what is collected in revenue (Ch 10)

democratic backsliding: A decline in the quality of democracy, including the extent of participation, the rule of law, and vertical and horizontal accountability (Ch 9)

democratic consolidation: The widespread acceptance of democracy as the permanent form of political activity; all significant political elites and their followers accept democratic rules and are confident everyone else does as well (Ch 9)

developmental state: A state that seeks to create national strength by taking an active and conscious role in the development of specific sectors of the economy (Ch 10)

devolution: Partial decentralization of power from central government to subunits, such as states or provinces, with subunits' power being dependent on central government and reversible (Ch 5)

dictator's dilemma: An authoritarian ruler's repression creates fear, which then breeds uncertainty about how much support the ruler has; in response, the ruler spends more resources than is rational to co-opt the opposition (Ch 8)

dictatorship of the proletariat: In the first stage of communism in Marxist thought, characterized by absolute rule by workers as a class over all other classes (Ch 3)

dominant-party system: Party system in which multiple parties exist but the same one wins every election and governs continuously (Ch 6)

Duverger's Law: Institutionalist argument by French political scientist Maurice Duverger that SMD electoral systems will produce two major parties, eliminating smaller parties (Ch 6)

electoral authoritarian regime: Type of hybrid regime in which formal opposition and some open political debate exist and elections are held; these processes are so flawed, however, that the regime cannot be considered truly democratic (Ch 3)

electoral systems: Formal, legal mechanisms that translate votes into control over political offices and shares of political power (Ch 6)

elite theories: Theories arguing that societies are ruled by an economic, gender, racial, or other small group that has effective control over virtually all power; contrast to pluralist theory (Ch 1)

empirical theory: An argument explaining what actually occurs; empirical theorists first notice and describe a pattern and then attempt to explain what causes it (Ch 1)

ethnic group: A group of people who see themselves as united by one or more cultural attributes or a sense of common history but do not see themselves as a nation seeking its own state (Ch 4)

executive: The chief political power and branch of government that must exist in all modern states; responsible for implementing all laws (Ch 5)

export-oriented growth (EOG): Development policy based on encouraging economic growth via exports of goods and services, usually starting with light manufacturing such as textiles (Ch 11)

external sovereignty: Sovereignty relative to outside powers that is legally recognized in international law (Ch 2)

externality: A cost or benefit of the production process that is not fully included in the price of the final market transaction when the product is sold (Ch 10)

failed state: A state that is so weak that it loses effective sovereignty over part or all of its territory (Ch 2)

federal systems: Political systems in which a state's power is legally and constitutionally divided among more than one level of government; in contrast to a unitary system (Ch 5)

feudal states: Premodern states in Europe in which power in a territory was divided among multiple and overlapping lords claiming sovereignty (Ch 2)

first dimension of power: The ability of one person or group to get another person or group to do something it otherwise would not do (Ch 1)

"first-past-the-post" (FPTP): An SMD system in which the candidate with a plurality of votes wins (Ch 6)

fiscal policy: Government budgetary policy (Ch 10)

foreign direct investment (FDI): Investment from abroad in productive activity in another country (Ch 11)

globalization: A rapid increase in the flow of economic activity, technology, and communications around the globe, and the increased sharing of cultural symbols, political ideas, and movements across countries (Ch 10)

head of government: The key executive power in a state; usually a president or prime minister (Ch 5)

head of state: The official, symbolic representative of a country, authorized to speak on its behalf and represent it, particularly in world affairs; usually a president or monarch (Ch 5)

historical institutionalists: Theorists who believe that institutions explain political behavior and shape individuals' political preferences and their perceptions of their self-interests and that institutions evolve historically in particular countries and change relatively slowly (Ch 1)

historical materialism: The assumption that material forces are the prime movers of history and politics; a key philosophical tenet of Marxism (Ch 3)

horizontal accountability: The ability of state institutions to hold one another accountable (Ch 5)

ideal type: A model of what the purest version of something might be (Ch 2)

import-substitution industrialization (ISI): Development policy popular in the 1950s–1970s that uses trade policy, monetary policy, and currency rates to encourage the creation of new industries to produce goods domestically that the country imported in the past (Ch 11)

institutionalism: An approach to explaining politics that argues that political institutions are crucial to understanding political behavior (Ch 1)

institutionalization: The degree to which government processes and procedures are established, predictable, and routinized (Ch 5)

interest-group pluralism: Interest-group system in which many groups exist to represent particular interests and the government remains officially neutral among them; the United States is a key example (Ch 6)

internal sovereignty: The sole authority within a territory capable of making and enforcing laws and policies (Ch 2)

international capital flows: Movements of capital in the form of money across international borders (Ch 11)

Islamism: The belief that Islamic law, as revealed by God to the Prophet Mohammed, can and should provide the basis for government in Muslim communities, with little equivocation or compromise (Ch 3)

jihad: Derived from an Arabic word for "struggle" and an important concept in Islam; the Quran identifies three kinds of jihad (Ch 3)

judicial independence: The belief and ability of judges to decide cases as they think appropriate, regardless of what other people, and especially politically powerful officials or institutions, desire (Ch 5)

judicial review: The authority of the judiciary to decide whether a specific law contradicts a country's constitution (Ch 5)

judiciary: Branch of government that interprets the law and applies it to individual cases (Ch 5)

jus sanguinis: Citizenship based on "blood" ties; for example, in Germany (Ch 4)

jus soli: Citizenship dependent on "soil," or residence within the national territory; for example, in France (Ch 4)

Keynesian theory: Named for British economist John Maynard Keynes, who argued that governments can manage the business cycles of capitalism via active fiscal policy and monetary policy, including deficit spending when necessary (Ch 10)

***laïcité*:** A model of secularism advocating that religion should play no part in the public realm (Ch 4)

legislative oversight: Occurs when members of the legislature, usually in committees, oversee the bureaucracy (Ch 5)

legislature: Branch of government that makes the law in a democracy (Ch 5)

legitimacy: The recognized right to rule (Ch 2)

liberal democracy: A system of government that provides eight key guarantees, including freedoms to enable citizen participation in the political process and institutions that make government policies depend on votes and other forms of citizen preferences (Ch 3)

liberal market economies (LMEs): In the varieties of capitalism approach, countries that rely heavily on market relationships to govern economic activity; the United States and United Kingdom are key examples (Ch 10)

liberal welfare states: States whose social policies focus on ensuring that all who can do so gain their income in the market; more concerned about preserving individual autonomy than reducing poverty or inequality; the United States is a key example (Ch 12)

liberationist: Member of the LGBTQ movement who seeks to transform sexual and gender norms so that all may gain social acceptance and respect regardless of their conformity to preexisting norms or institutions (Ch 4)

majoritarian democracy: A type of democratic system that concentrates power more tightly in a single-party executive with executive dominance over the legislature, a single legislative branch, and constitutions that can be easily amended (Ch 5)

market economy: An economic system in which individuals and firms exchange goods and services in a largely unfettered manner (Ch 10)

market failure: Phenomenon that occurs when markets fail to perform efficiently or fail to perform according to other widely held social values (Ch 10)

market-based private insurance system: Health care system that relies on private insurance for the bulk of the population (Ch 12)

Marxism: Structuralist argument that says that economic structures largely determine political behavior; the philosophical underpinning of communism (Ch 1)

means-tested public assistance: Social programs that provide benefits to individuals who fall below a specific income level; TANF is an example in the United States (Ch 12)

member of parliament (MP): An elected member of the legislature in a parliamentary system (Ch 5)

military regime: System of government in which military officers control power (Ch 3)

Millennium Development Goals (MDGs): Targets established by the United Nations to reduce poverty and hunger, improve education and health, improve the status of women, and achieve environmental sustainability (Ch 11)

mixed, or semiproportional: An electoral system that combines single-member district representation with overall proportionality in allocation of legislative seats to parties; Germany is a key example (Ch 6)

mode of production: In Marxist theory, the economic system in any given historical era; feudalism and capitalism in the last millennium in Europe (Ch 3)

modernists: Theorists of political culture who believe that clear sets of attitudes, values, and beliefs can be identified in each country that change very rarely and explain much about politics there (Ch 1)

modernization theory: Theory of development that argues that postcolonial societies need to go through the same process that the West underwent in order to develop (Ch 3)

modernizing authoritarianism: A claim to legitimacy based on the need to "develop" the country via the rule of a modernizing elite (Ch 3)

monetary policy: The amount of money a government prints and puts into circulation and the basic interest rates the government sets (Ch 10)

monopoly: The control of the entire supply of a valued good or service by one economic actor (Ch 10)

moral hazard: Occurs when parties to a transaction behave in a particular way because they believe they will not have to pay the full costs of their actions (Ch 12)

multicultural integration: Accepts that ethnocultural identities matter to citizens, will endure over time, and must be recognized and accommodated within political institutions; in contrast to assimilation (Ch 4)

multiparty systems: Party systems in which more than two parties could potentially win a national election and govern (Ch 6)

nation: A group that proclaims itself a nation and has or seeks control of a state (Ch 4)

national health insurance (NHI): A health care system in which the government mandates that virtually all citizens must have insurance (Ch 12)

national health system (NHS)/single-payer system: A government-financed and managed health care system into which all citizens pay, either through a separate insurance payment or via general taxation, and through which they gain medical care (Ch 12)

nationalism: The desire to be a nation and thus to control a national state (Ch 4)

natural monopoly: The control of the entire supply of valued goods or services by one economic actor in a sector of the economy in which competition would raise costs and reduce efficiency (Ch 10)

neocorporatism: Also called societal corporatism; corporatism that evolves historically and voluntarily rather than being mandated by the state; Germany is a key example (Ch 6)

neofascist: Description given to parties or political movements that espouse a virulent nationalism, often defined on a cultural, racial, or religious basis and opposed to immigrants as threats to national identity (Ch 3)

neoliberalism: An economic theory that argues government should balance its budget and minimize its role in the economy to allow the market to allocate resources to maximize efficiency and thereby economic growth (Ch 10)

neopatrimonial authority: Power based on a combination of the trappings of modern, bureaucratic states with underlying informal institutions of clientelism that work behind the scenes; most common in Africa (Ch 3)

neutral state model: A model of secularism wherein the state is neutral about but not opposed to religion (Ch 4)

New Public Management (NPM): Theory of reform of bureaucracies that argues for the privatizing of many government services, creating competition among agencies to stimulate a market, focusing on customer satisfaction, and flattening administrative hierarchies (Ch 5)

normative theory: An argument explaining what ought to occur rather than what does occur; contrast with empirical theory (Ch 1)

one-party regime: A system of government in which a single party gains power, usually after independence in postcolonial states, and systematically eliminates all opposition (Ch 3)

open-list proportional representation: Electoral system in which multiple candidates run in each district, voters vote for the individual candidate of their choice, and the candidates with the most votes in the party get the seats the party wins (Ch 6)

pact: In a transition to democracy, a conscious agreement among the most important political actors in the authoritarian regime and those in civil society to establish a new form of government (Ch 9)

parliamentarism: A term denoting a parliamentary system of democracy in which the executive and legislative branches are fused via parliament's election of the chief executive (Ch 5)

participatory democracy: A form of democracy that encourages citizens to participate actively, in many ways beyond voting; usually focused at the local level (Ch 3)

party system: The number of parties and their relative institutional strength (Ch 6)

patriarchy: Rule by men (Ch 1)

patronage-based mobilization: Appealing to citizens via provision of material resources in exchange for political support (Ch 6)

peak associations: Organizations that bring together all interest groups in a particular sector to influence and negotiate agreements with the state; in the United States, an example is the AFL-CIO (Ch 6)

personalist regime: System of government in which a central leader comes to dominate a state, typically not only eliminating all opposition but also weakening the state's institutions to centralize power in his own hands (Ch 3)

pluralist theories: Explanations of who has power that argue that society is divided into various political groups and that power is dispersed among these groups so that no group has complete or permanent power; contrast to elite theory (Ch 1)

plurality: The receipt of the most votes, but not necessarily a majority (Ch 6)

political accountability: The ability of the citizenry, directly or indirectly, to control political leaders and institutions (Ch 5)

political actor: Any person or group engaged in political behavior (Ch 1)

political appointees: Officials who serve at the pleasure of the president or prime minister and are assigned the task of overseeing their respective segments of the bureaucracy (Ch 5)

political culture: A set of widely held attitudes, values, beliefs, and symbols about politics (Ch 1)

political discourse: The ways in which people speak and write about politics; postmodern theorists argue that political discourse influences political attitudes, identity, and actions (Ch 1)

political ideology: A systematic set of beliefs about how a political system ought to be structured (Ch 1)

political institution: A set of rules, norms, or standard operating procedures that is widely recognized and accepted by the society, structures and constrains political actions, and often serves as the basis for key political organizations (Ch 1)

political opportunity structure: The extent to which a regime is open to influence from social movements and other extra-institutional groups (Ch 7)

political revolution: The fundamental transformation of an existing regime, instigated and primarily carried out by a social movement or armed group (Ch 7)

political rights: Those rights associated with active political participation—for example, to free association, voting, and running for office (Ch 3)

political saliency: The degree to which something is of political importance (Ch 4)

political science: The systematic study of politics and power (Ch 1)

political socialization: The process through which people, especially young people, learn about politics and are taught a society's common political values and beliefs (Ch 1)

political violence: The use of physical force by nonstate actors for political ends (Ch 7)

politics: The process by which human communities make collective decisions (Ch 1)

populist mobilization: Appealing to citizens directly, often threatening established institutions, parties and elites; emphasizing a united and morally superior "people" battling corrupt elites; engaging in "bad manners"; and focusing rhetoric around a sense of "crisis" that threatens "the people" (Ch 6)

positive accommodation: A model of secularism wherein the state is neutral among but willing to support religions that it recognizes as important elements in civil society (Ch 4)

postmaterialist: A set of values in a society in which most citizens are economically secure enough to move beyond immediate economic (materialist) concerns to "quality of life" issues like human rights, civil rights, women's rights, environmentalism, and moral values (Ch 1)

postmodernist: An approach that sees cultures not as sets of fixed and clearly defined values but rather as sets of symbols subject to interpretation (Ch 1)

precautionary principle: A policy that emphasizes risk avoidance even when the science predicting a risk is uncertain (Ch 12)

presidentialism: A term denoting a presidential system of democracy in which the executive and legislature are elected independently and have separate and independent powers (Ch 5)

prime minister (PM): The head of government in parliamentary and semipresidential systems (Ch 5)

primordialism: A theory of identity that sees identity groups as being in some sense "natural" or God given, as having existed since "time immemorial," and as defined unambiguously by such clear criteria as kinship, language, culture, or phenotype (Ch 4)

principal–agent problem: A problem in which a principal hires an agent to perform a task but the agent's self-interest does not necessarily align with the principal's, so the agent may not carry out the task as assigned (Ch 5)

programmatic mobilization: Appealing to citizens on the bases of ideas, typically economic or cultural (Ch 6)

proletariat: A term in Marxist theory for the class of free-wage laborers who own no capital and must sell their labor to survive; communist parties claim to work on the proletariat's behalf (Ch 1)

proportional representation (PR): Electoral system in which seats in a legislature are apportioned on a purely proportional basis, giving each party the share of seats that matches its share of the total vote (Ch 6)

psychological theories: Explanations for political behavior based on psychological analysis of political actors' motives (Ch 1)

public goods: Goods or services that cannot or will not be provided via the market because their costs are too high or their benefits are too diffuse (Ch 10)

quantitative statistical techniques: Research method used for large-scale studies that reduces evidence to sets of numbers so that statistical analysis can systematically compare a huge number of cases (Ch 1)

quasi-states: States that have legal sovereignty and international recognition but lack almost all the domestic attributes of a functioning state (Ch 2)

race: A group of people socially defined primarily on the basis of one or more perceived common physical characteristics (Ch 4)

rational choice institutionalists: Institutionalist theorists who follow the assumptions of rational choice theory and argue that institutions are the products of the interaction and bargaining of rational actors (Ch 1)

rational choice theory: An explanation for political behavior that assumes that individuals are rational beings who bring to the political arena a set of self-defined preferences and adequate knowledge and ability to pursue those preferences (Ch 1)

rational-legal legitimacy: The right of leaders to rule based on their selection according to an accepted set of laws, standards, or procedures (Ch 2)

regime: A set of formal and informal political institutions that defines a type of government (Ch 3)

regime change: The process through which one regime is transformed into another (Ch 9)

relative deprivation: A group's or individual's belief that they are not getting their share of something of value relative to their own expectations or to what others have (Ch 7)

rent seeking: Gaining an advantage in a market without engaging in equally productive activity; usually involves using government regulations for one's own benefit (Ch 5)

research methods: Systematic processes used to ensure that the study of some phenomena is as objective and unbiased as possible (Ch 1)

resource curse: Occurs when a state relies on a key resource for almost all of its revenue, allowing it to ignore its citizens and resulting in a weak state (Ch 2)

risk assessment: Analysis of what the risks of damaging outcomes are in a particular situation (Ch 12)

risk management: Policy used to keep risks to acceptable levels (Ch 12)

ruling class: An elite who possess adequate resources to control a regime; in Marxist theory, the class that controls key sources of wealth in a given epoch (Ch 1)

second dimension of power: The ability not only to make people do something but to keep them from doing something (Ch 1)

security dilemma: A situation in which two or more groups do not trust and may even fear one another, and do not believe that institutional constraints will protect them, increasing the likelihood that violence will break out between them (Ch 7)

semipresidentialism: A term denoting a semipresidential system of democracy in which executive power is divided between a directly elected president and a prime minister elected by a parliament (Ch 5)

separation of powers: Constitutionally explicit division of power among the major branches of government (Ch 5)

sharia: Muslim law (Ch 3)

single-case study: Research method that examines a particular political phenomenon in just one country or community and can generate ideas for theories or test theories developed from different cases (Ch 1)

single-member district (SMD): Electoral system in which each geographic district elects a single representative to a legislature (Ch 6)

social capital: Social networks and norms of reciprocity that are important for a strong civil society (Ch 6)

social class: A group of people who share or perceive themselves to share a social status based on some combination of a common level of wealth, income, type of work, or education (Ch 4)

social construction: Part of constructivist approach to identity, the process through which societies collectively "construct" identities as a wide array of actors continually discuss the question of who "we" are (Ch 4)

social contract theory: Philosophical approach underlying liberalism that begins from the premise that legitimate governments are formed when free and independent individuals join in a contract to permit representatives to govern over them in their common interests (Ch 3)

social democracy: Combines liberal democracy with much greater provision of social rights of citizenship and typically greater public control of the economy (Ch 3)

social democratic welfare states: States whose social policies strongly emphasize universal entitlements to achieve greater social equality and promote equal citizenship; Sweden is a key example (Ch 12)

social insurance: Provides benefits to categories of people who have contributed to a (usually mandatory) public insurance fund; typically used to provide retirement pensions (Ch 12)

social movements: Part of civil society; they have a loosely defined organizational structure and represent people who perceive themselves to be outside formal institutions, seek major socioeconomic or political changes, or employ sustained noninstitutional forms of collective action (Ch 7)

social policy: Policy focused on reducing poverty and income inequality and stabilizing individual or family income (Ch 12)

social insurance: Provides benefits to categories of people who have contributed to a (usually mandatory) public insurance fund; typically used to provide retirement pensions (Ch 12)

social revolution: A fundamental transformation of a regime and social structure, instigated and primarily carried out by a social movement or armed group of citizens (Ch 7)

social rights: Those rights related to basic well-being and socioeconomic equality (Ch 3)

sovereignty: Quality of a state in which it is legally recognized by the family of states as the sole legitimate governing authority within its territory and as the legal equal of other states (Ch 2)

state: An ongoing administrative apparatus that develops and administers laws and generates and implements public policies in a specific territory (Ch 2)

state corporatism: Corporatism mandated by the state; common in fascist regimes (Ch 6)

strong state: A state that is generally capable of providing political goods to its citizens (Ch 2)

structural adjustment programs (SAPs): Development programs created in the 1980s; based on neoliberal principles of reduced government protection of industries, fiscal austerity, and privatization (Ch 11)

structuralism: Approach to explaining politics that argues that political behavior is at least influenced and limited, and perhaps even determined, by broader structures in a society such as class divisions or enduring institutions (Ch 1)

subcultures: Groups that hold partially different beliefs and values from the main political culture of a country (Ch 1)

supreme leader: Individual who wields executive power with few formal limits in an authoritarian regime; in the Islamic Republic of Iran, the formal title of the top ruling cleric (Ch 8)

symmetrical federal system: A federal system in which all subnational governments (states or provinces) have the same relationship with and rights in relation to the national government (Ch 5)

tax expenditures: Targeted tax breaks for specific groups of citizens or activities designed to achieve social policy goals

technocratic legitimacy: A claim to rule based on knowledge or expertise (Ch 3)

territory: An area with clearly defined borders to which a state lays claim (Ch 2)

terrorism: Political violence or the threat of violence by groups or individuals who deliberately target civilians or noncombatants in order to influence the behavior and actions of targeted publics and governments (Ch 7)

theocracy: Rule by religious authorities (Ch 3)

theory: An abstract argument that provides a systematic explanation of some phenomenon (Ch 1)

third dimension of power: The ability to shape or determine individual or group political demands by causing people to think about political issues in ways that are contrary to their own interests (Ch 1)

totalitarian state: A state that controls virtually all aspects of society and eliminates all vestiges of civil society; Germany under Hitler and the Soviet Union under Stalin are key examples (Ch 3)

trade: The flow of goods and services across national borders (Ch 11)

traditional legitimacy: The right to rule based on a society's long-standing patterns and practices (Ch 2)

tragedy of the commons: No individual has the incentive or ability to preserve a common, shared good that is free, so without collective effort, it is likely to be overused and perhaps ultimately destroyed (Ch 12)

transition to democracy: A regime change typically involving a negotiated process that removes an authoritarian regime and concludes with a founding election of a new, democratic regime (Ch 9)

two-party system: Party system in which only two parties are able to garner enough votes to win an election, though more may compete; the United Kingdom and United States are key examples (Ch 6)

universal basic income: A universal entitlement that would provide a guaranteed income to each individual citizen from birth to death (Ch 12)

universal entitlements: Benefits that governments provide to all citizens more or less equally, usually funded through general taxation; in the United States, public education is an example (Ch 12)

unitary systems: Political systems in which the central government has sole constitutional sovereignty and power; in contrast to a federal system (Ch 5)

vanguard party: Vladimir Lenin's concept of a small party that claims legitimacy to rule based on its understanding of Marxist theory and its ability to represent the interests of the proletariat before they are a majority of the populace (Ch 3)

varieties of capitalism (VOC): School of thought analyzing wealthy market economies that focuses primarily on business firms and how they are governed; divides such economies into liberal market economies and coordinated market economies (Ch 10)

vertical accountability: The ability of individuals and groups in a society to hold state institutions accountable (Ch 5)

veto player: An individual or collective actor whose agreement is essential for any policy change (Ch 5)

virtual representation: When voters' views are represented indirectly in the legislature by their chosen party's candidates who have been elected in districts other than their own (Ch 6)

vote of no confidence: In parliamentary systems, a vote by parliament to remove a government (the prime minister and cabinet) from power (Ch 5)

weak state: A state that only partially provides political goods to its citizens (Ch 2)

welfare states: Distinct systems of social policies that arose after World War II in wealthy market economies, including social democratic welfare states, Christian democratic welfare states, and liberal welfare states (Ch 12)

INDEX